D0781396

WHY ETHICS?

Why Ethics?

SIGNS OF RESPONSIBILITIES

Robert Gibbs

PRINCETON UNIVERSITY PRESS

PRINCETON, NEW JERSEY

BJ1451
.G52
2000

Copyright © 2000 by Princeton University Press
Published by Princeton University Press, 41 William Street, Princeton, New Jersey 08540
In the United Kingdom: Princeton University Press, 3 Market Place,
Woodstock, Oxfordshire OX20 1SY

All Rights Reserved

Library of Congress Cataloging-in-Publication Data

Gibbs, Robert, 1958–
Why ethics? : signs of responsibilities / Robert Gibbs.
p.   cm.
Includes bibliographical references and index.
ISBN 0-691-02686-6 (hardcover : alk. paper). — ISBN 0-691-00963-5 (pbk. : alk. paper)
1. Responsibility.   2. Interpersonal relations—Moral and ethical aspects.
3. Ethics, Jewish.   I. Title.
BJ1451.G52   2000
170—dc21   99-37482

This book has been composed in Sabon

The paper used in this publication meets the minimum requirements of
ANSI/NISO Z39.48-1992 (R1997) (*Permanence of Paper*)

http://pup.princeton.edu

Printed in the United States of America

10 9 8 7 6 5 4 3 2 1

10 9 8 7 6 5 4 3 2 1
(Pbk.)

To my teachers of American Sign Language (ASL),

*Karen DeNaples, John Tunison, Lynn Ballard Weiner, and
Glenda McCary-Moos,*

*who enabled me to respond to my deaf daughter, Ariel,
in her first language.*

NOV 1 4 2000

CONTENTS

ACKNOWLEDGMENTS

A BOOK interrupts one's life. For better and worse, this text arises in academic culture. The research began at St. Louis University, where my work was supported by the Mellon Humanities Development Fund. Princeton University supported me with generous leave time as the Richard Stockton Bicentennial Preceptor. The book has been completed in the context of the Philosophy Department at the University of Toronto, where my work has received a warm reception. This book has benefited from all those institutions.

Many people have helped me at conferences and meetings where I have offered pieces of this book. The New Haven Theology Group, the Group on Pragmatism and Empiricism in American Religious Thought of the American Academy of Religion, The Academy for Jewish Philosophy, Pluralt at MacMaster University, The Conference on Ethics after the Holocaust at the University of Oregon, The Conference on the Gift: Theory and Practice at Trent University, The Joyful Wisdom Conferences at Brock University, and the University of California Conference on Cultural Studies and Jewish Studies—all have listened and responded to earlier versions of material included here.

A few close companions have read much or all of the manuscript, and this text is much improved through their efforts, although none is responsible for its faults. These readers, moreover, are colleagues whose work has inspired me. Hugh Miller, Susan Shapiro, Daniel Hardy, David Ford, Doranne Demontigny, Eduardo Cadava, Elliot Wolfson, Peter Ochs, Edith Wyschogrod, James Bohman, Roger Simon, Cheryl Misak, and Robert Bernasconi have each made an important impact on this text. In addition, Barry Walfish, Barbara Galli, and Bettina Bergo have vetted many of my translations, for which I am greatly thankful, despite my ornery predilections to stand with my awkward choices. Moreover, my gratitude extends to my editor, Ann Wald, who cajoled and nurtured this book by steady care, and to a whole team of people at Princeton University Press, through whose enormous technical efforts the book takes its unique shape.

Finally, a brief word about company. Writing is solitary, and so I sought in this book to overcome that isolation by attending to these wise and difficult texts. But respite from that isolation was also to be found in conversation. I have enjoyed occasional discussion with Jacques Derrida. I was the beneficiary of great hospitality and encouragement in a handful of meetings with Emmanuel Levinas, z"l. And for over three years, I met with generous and stimulating shared study with Steven S. Schwarzschild, z"l. Here in Toronto I enjoy ongoing conversation with David Novak. In my several years at Princeton, I had the challenge and the pleasure of regular Talmud study with Peter Ochs, whose studies of Peirce contributed greatly to renewing my interest in semiotics. Though not the cause of this book, he has been the goal for much of my task of translating European thinkers into my strange sort of pragmatics. Shared study of traditional religious texts and philosophy represents the world-to-come in our world for Postmodern Jewish Thinkers. Beyond the familiarity that arises in that study stands only the constant company of my family. In the cares and joys of everyday life I have only gratitude to Robin, Ariel, and Deirdre, for the challenges and the comforts of a life that has been my saving interruption from this book.

I QUOTE lengthy passages from my primary authors and break them up for the purposes of commenting. The passages are numbered, and the pieces are lettered (1a, 1b, 1c . . .). In all cases I have retranslated the passages from foreign languages, and cite them *first to the original text*, and then to the standard translation.

For traditional Jewish texts, I cite standard form (Chapter:verse) for the Bible, (Chapter.Mishnah) for the Mishnah, Vilna Edition for the Babylonian Talmud, and the traditional Ashkenazi *Mahzor* (High Holiday Prayerbook). I have consulted both Soncino and Neusner for translations of the rabbinic texts, and the New JPS and other translations for the Bible.

The texts being cited are listed here (in alphabetical order, by author):

Benjamin: B "Über einige Motive bei Baudelaire," in *Gesammelte Schriften*, vol. I, 2. Ed. Rolf Tiedemann and Hermann Schweppenhäuser. Frankfurt: Suhrkamp, 1974. Trans. Harry Zohn as "On Some Motifs in Baudelaire," in *Illuminations*, 155–200 New York: Schocken, 1969.

Benjamin: L "Aufsätze, Essays, Vorträge," in *Gesammelte Schriften*, vol. II, 3. Ed. Rolf Tiedemann and Hermann Schweppenhäuser. Frankfurt: Suhrkamp, 1974.

Benjamin: OGT "Ursprung des deutschen Trauerspiels," in *Gesammelte Schriften*, vol. I, 1. Ed. Rolf Tiedemann and Hermann Schweppenhäuser. Frankfurt: Suhrkamp, 1974. Trans. John Osborne as *The Origin of German Tragic Drama*. New York: Verso, 1977.

Benjamin: P *Das Passagen Werk*, in *Gesammelte Schriften*, vol. V, 2. Ed. Rolf Tiedemann. Frankfurt: Suhrkamp, 1982. Trans. Howard Eiland and Kevin McLaughlin as *The Arcades Project*. Cambridge, Mass.: Harvard University Press, 1999.

Benjamin: Th "Über den Begriff der Geschichte," in *Gesammelte Schriften*, vol. I, 2. Ed. Rolf Tiedemann and Hermann Schweppenhäuser. Frankfurt: Suhrkamp, 1974. Trans. Harry Zohn as "Theses on the Philosophy of History," in *Illuminations*, 253–64. New York: Schocken, 1969.

Benjamin: TR "Die Aufgabe des Übersetzers," in *Gesammelte Schriften*, vol. IV, 1, 9–21. Ed. Rolf Tiedemann and Hermann Schweppenhäuser. Frankfurt: Suhrkamp, 1982. Trans. Harry Zohn as "The Task of the Translator," in *Selected Writings, Volume 1, 1913–1926*, 253–63. Ed. Marcus Bullock and Michael W. Jennings. Cambridge, Mass.: Harvard University Press, 1996.

Cohen: RR *Religion der Vernunft aus den Quellen des Judentums*. Reprint of 2nd ed., 1928. Wiesbaden: Fourier Verlag, 1988. Trans. Simon Kaplan as *Religion of Reason Out of the Sources of Judaism*. Atlanta: Scholars, 1995.

Derrida: ATM "En ce moment même dans cet ouvrage me voici," in *Textes pour Emmanuel Levinas*, 21–60. Paris: Jean-Michel Place, 1980. Trans. Ruben Berezdivin as "At this very moment in this work Here I am," in *Re-Reading*

Levinas, 11–48. Ed. Robert Bernasconi and Simon Critchley. Bloomington: Indiana University Press, 1991.

Derrida: DS   *La Dissémination*. Paris: Editions du Seuil, 1972. Trans. Barbara Johnson as *Dissemination*. Chicago: University of Chicago Press, 1981.

Derrida: G   *De la Grammatologie*. Paris: Les Éditions de Minuit, 1967. Trans. Gayatri Chakravorty Spivak as *Of Grammatology*. Baltimore: Johns Hopkins University Press, 1974.

Derrida: GL   *Glas*. Paris: Éditions Galilée, 1974. Trans. John P. Leavey Jr. and Richard Rand as *Glas*. Lincoln: University of Nebraska Press, 1986.

Derrida: M   *Marges de la Philosophie*. Paris: Les Éditions de Minuit, 1972. Trans. Alan Bass as *Margins of Philosophy*. Chicago: University of Chicago Press, 1982.

Derrida: P   *Positions*. Paris: Les Éditions de Minuit, 1972. Trans. Alan Bass as *Positions*. Chicago: University of Chicago Press, 1981.

Derrida: PC   *La Carte Postale: De Socrate à Freud et au-delà*. Paris: Flammarion, 1980. Trans. Alan Bass as *The Postcard: From Socrates to Freud and Beyond*. Chicago: University of Chicago Press, 1987.

Derrida: WD   *L'écriture et la Différence*. Paris: Éditions du Seuil, 1967. Trans. Alan Bass as *Writing and Difference*. Chicago: University of Chicago Press, 1978.

Habermas: C–C.2   *Theorie des kommunikativen Handelns*. 2 vols. Frankfurt: Suhrkamp, 1981. Trans. Thomas McCarthy as *The Theory of Communicative Action*. 2 vols. Boston: Beacon, 1984.

Habermas: JA   *Erläuterungen zur Diskursethik*. Frankfurt: Suhrkamp, 1991. Trans. Ciaran P. Cronin as *Justification and Application*. Cambridge, Mass.: MIT Press, 1993.

Habermas: MC   *Moralbewusstsein und kommunikatives Handeln*. Frankfurt: Suhrkamp, 1983. Trans. Christian Lenhardt and Shierry Weber Nicholsen as *Moral Consciousness and Communicative Action*. Cambridge, Mass.: MIT Press, 1990.

Habermas: P&C   "Peirce über Kommunikation," in *Texte und Kontexte*, 9–33. Frankfurt: Suhrkamp, 1991. Trans. William Mark Hohengarten as "Peirce and Communication," in *Postmetaphysical Thinking: Philosophical Essays*, 88–112. Cambridge, Mass.: MIT Press, 1992.

Hegel: PR   *Grundlinien der Philosophie des Rechts*. Vol. 7 in *Werke*. Frankfurt: Suhrkamp, 1970. Trans. H. S. Nisbet as *Elements of the Philosophy of Right*. Ed. Allen W. Wood. Cambridge: Cambridge University Press, 1991.

James: MT   *The Meaning of Truth*. Cambridge, Mass.: Harvard University Press, 1975.

James: P   *Pragmatism*. Cambridge, Mass.: Harvard University Press, 1975.

James: Psychol.   *The Principles of Psychology*. 2 vols. New York: Henry Holt, 1890.

Levinas: 9T   *Quatre Lectures Talmudique*. Paris: Les Éditions de Minuit, 1968. Trans. Annette Aronowicz in *Nine Talmudic Readings*. Bloomington: Indiana University Press, 1990.

Levinas: BV   *L'Au-delà du Verset*. Paris: Les Éditions de Minuit, 1982. Trans. Gary D. Mole as *Beyond the Verse*. Bloomington: Indiana University Press, 1994.

Levinas: DF   *Difficile Liberté.* 3rd ed. Paris: Le Livre de Poche, 1984 (minor corrections of 2nd ed., Paris: Editions Albin Michel, 1976). Trans. Seán Hand as *Difficult Freedom: Essays on Judaism.* Baltimore: Johns Hopkins University Press, 1990.

Levinas: EN   *Entre Nous: Essais sur le penser-à-l-autre.* Paris: Bernard Grasset, 1991. Trans. Michael B. Smith and Barbara Harshav as *Entre Nous: On Thinking-of-the-Other.* New York: Columbia University Press, 1998.

Levinas: OB   *Autrement qu'être ou au-delà de l'Essence.* Dordrecht: Martinus Nijhoff, 1974. Trans. Alphonso Lingis as *Otherwise Than Being or Beyond Essence.* The Hague: Martinus Nijhoff, 1981.

Levinas: TI   *Totalité et Infini.* 4th ed. The Hague: Martinus Nijhoff, 1971 (1st ed., 1961). Trans. Alphonso Lingis as *Totality and Infinity.* Pittsburgh: Duquesne University Press, 1969.

Levinas: TN   *A L'Heure des Nations.* Paris: Les Éditions de Minuit, 1988. Trans. Michael B. Smith as *In the Time of the Nations.* Bloomington: Indiana University Press, 1994.

Luhmann: RD   "Religiöse Dogmatik und gesellschaftliche Evolution," in *Funktion der Religion*, 72–181. Frankfurt: Suhrkamp, 1977. Trans. Peter Beyer as *Religious Dogmatics and the Evolution of Societies.* New York: Edwin Mellen, 1984.

Luhmann: SS   *Soziale Systeme.* Frankfurt: Suhrkamp, 1984. Trans. John Bednarz Jr. with Dirk Baecker as *Social Systems.* Stanford: Stanford University Press, 1995.

Luhmann: T   *Vertrauen; Ein Mechanismus der Reduktion socialer Komplexität.* 3rd. ed. Stuttgart: Ferdinand Enke, 1989. Trans. Howard Davis, John Raffan, and Kathryn Rooney as *Power and Trust.* Ed. Tom Burns and Gianfranco Poggi. New York: John Wiley and Sons, 1979.

Maimonides: LR   *Laws of Repentance*, in *Mishneh Torah: The Book of Knowledge.* Ed. Moses Hyamson. Jerusalem: Feldheim, 1981.

Marcel: MJ   *Journal Métaphysique.* Paris: Gallimard, 1927. Trans. Bernard Wall as *Metaphysical Journal.* Chicago: Henry Regnery, 1952.

Marcel: RM   *Royce's Metaphysics.* Trans. Virginia and Gordon Ringer. Chicago: Henry Regnery, 1956.

Marx: Capital I   *Das Kapital, I* (vol. 23 in *Marx-Engels Werke*). Berlin: Dietz Verlag, 1989. Trans. Samuel Moore and Edward Aveling as *Capital.* New York: International Publishers, 1967.

Mead: MSS   *Mind, Self, and Society.* Ed. Charles W. Morris. Chicago: University of Chicago Press, 1934.

Mead: SW   *Selected Writings.* Ed. Andrew J. Reck. Chicago: University of Chicago Press, 1964.

Peirce: CP   *Collected Papers.* Ed. Charles Hartshorne and Paul Weiss. Cambridge, Mass.: Belknap Press of Harvard University Press, 1960. Citations are to volume # and paragraph.

Rosenzweig: IV, 1   Vol. 4, 1.Band: *Hymen und Gedichte des Jehuda Halevi*, in *Franz Rosenzweig: Der Mensch und sein Werk: Gesammelte Schriften.* The Hague: Martinus Nijhoff, 1983. Trans. Barbara Ellen Galli as *Franz Rosenzweig and Jehuda Halevi: Translating, Translations, and Translators.* Montreal: McGill-Queens University Press, 1995.

Rosenzweig: NT "Das Neue Denken," in *Zweistromland*, vol. III of *Franz Rosenzweig: Der Mensch und sein Werk: Gesammelte Schriften*. The Hague: Martinus Nijhoff. Trans. Alan Udoff and Barbara E. Galli in *Franz Rosenzweig's "The New Thinking,"* 67–102. Syracuse: Syracuse University Press, 1999.

Rosenzweig: S *Der Stern der Erlösung*, in *Franz Rosenzweig: Der Mensch und sein Werk: Gesammelte Schriften*. The Hague: Martinus Nijhoff, 1976. Trans. William W. Hallo as *The Star of Redemption*. Boston: Beacon, 1971.

Rosenzweig: S&T III "Scripture und Luther," in *Zweistromland*, vol. III of *Franz Rosenzweig: Der Mensch und sein Werk: Gesammelte Schriften*. The Hague: Martinus Nijhoff, 1984. Trans. Lawrence Rosenwald with Everett Fox as "Scripture and Luther," in *Scripture and Translation*. Bloomington: Indiana University Press, 1994.

Royce: Ch *The Problem of Christianity*. Chicago: University of Chicago Press, 1968.

Soloveitchik: TS *On Repentance, From the oral discourses of Rabbi Joseph B. Soloveitchik* [Hebrew]. Written and edited by Pinchas H. Peli. Jerusalem: World Zionist Organization, 1974. Trans. in *Soloveitchik on Repentance*. Ed. Pinchas Peli. New York: Paulist, 1984.

WHY ETHICS?

Why Questions?

A. The Response in Responsibility

It is a commonplace that philosophy is defined by the questions it asks. Usually, the question is What: What is this? What is? What is the cause? What can we know? Often the question is How: How do we know? How do things occur? How does language refer? For others, the question is Who: Who acts? Who knows? Who has a place at the table? For us, the question is Why.

Questioning, like being questioned, occurs between people. If philosophy is a practice of questioning, then its social setting is not merely a backdrop for the thinking of thinking, but philosophy is a practice of responding to other people's questions, even if only answering a question with a question. Too often, philosophy has been conceived as the self-sufficiency of a solitary thinker. Too often, it has asserted its role as interrogator: the specialist in questions, challenging all others and answering to none. But what if a philosopher were first of all one who feels the weight of another person's question? What if a philosopher thinks not to be free of all others nor only to befuddle them, but thinks in order to respond to questions that others ask? To be master of the question is to be called to respond, to attend to others' questions. Then philosophy would begin in self-criticism, in fear before another, in hope to heed the question.

The question Why? opens up a realm of ethics: an ethics of responsibility, of an ability to respond arising in the exigency to attend to another's questioning. This book will offer an ethics of responsibility, arising out of the need not merely to speak and to act responsively, but more out of the need to think: to give an account to others of why we should respond for other people. Having found itself in question, philosophy requires an ethical justification, and we will seek such justification through an ethics—an extreme ethics for a thinking that has so much to answer for today.

This book offers an ethics whose center is responsibility and not principles of autonomy or rational deliberation or optimal benefits. I distinguish here between the ethical exigence of bearing a *responsibility* and the corresponding *responsive* performance in the following manner: I can be responsible for doing something, even when I fail to act responsively. Responsiveness is thus the fulfillment of a responsibility, but my bearing of that responsibility is independent of whether I act ethically or not. Hence responsibilities can be necessary—binding me indissolubly to the ethical exigency—while the responsiveness is inherently contingent.

Responsibility in this ethics is asymmetric: I am responsible for others in a way that they are not responsible for me. Indeed, this ethics requires me to respond for actions of others, actions I could neither cause nor control. The origin of this claim arises in being questioned: I am responsible to respond independent of the responsiveness of the other person. I am responsible to my interlocutor, responsible for what she will make of what I say, responsible to keep answering as she keeps questioning, responsible because I cannot define the situation and cannot ethically close off the questioning. The primary responsibility is for a future I cannot control or even foresee: a responsibility that arises for me in attending to other people.

We also are responsible for each other in a mutual way when justice requires us to become present, one-to-another. But even in the present, where equality and fairness have their place, the instability of ethical responsibilities arises. For first we are bound asymmetrically to each other, and ethical mutuality is possible only because of that excess of responsibility. Indeed, the logic of relations of particulars to generals itself will appear as different modes of responding, of producing responsible individuals—individuals who can respond to others. But a community, despite its hope or pretension, is never alone. It stands over against other communities, and in judging the others is itself judged. This ethics will place extreme responsibility on each community for its others, discerning ways for the "we" to be responsible for its "you."

Responsibility extends asymmetrically into the past, too. Here the gap between responsibility and blame accentuates the lack of control in responding. For some things we are to blame, but for much more we are responsible—called to respond for the sake of the future. For if we are responsible for the actions of others in the past, it means primarily that ours are the tasks of remembering and mending the damage wrought in the past. The responsibilities for the past I have collected around the responsibility for repenting. The tarrying with the past, the concern with its violence and its own failures in relation to earlier pasts, is a responsibility to reopen the past for the ones who will be able to redeem it. Just as I attend my interlocutor in the future, whose authority to question me I struggle to maintain, so the past is made into an interrogation of me, of us—an interrogation at the end of this bloody and terrifying century, to which we must respond. Responsibility claims us asymmetrically in various modes, calling for our response in extreme ways.

This ethics also requires a change in its organon, from consciousness and its thoughts to semiotics: to practices performed with signs. Indeed, I will argue for an interpretation of pragmatics as the key for semiotics. Pragmatics here will be the dimension of meaning that occurs in the relation between the sign-user and the signs. The traditional media of ethics are the will, conscious intentions, deliberate choices, or the perfection of an individual rational life. When ethics was construed around the self-consistency of a rational being or the self-rule of spontaneous wills, it struggled to reach a concept of who the ethical self was. Ethics became primarily the identification and perfection of that who. Only in the circumstances where that self was bound with others did the goodness of relations with others require discussion. A theory of deliberate action focuses on the way that means are fit to my end, making me sovereign over my action. Reason appears there to be a way of maintaining my self in my action, conserving or even expanding my being. Responsibility could never appear in its own light but was derivative from will or reason, from the activities that preserve a being in its being. Semiotics—the study of signs—replaces an ontology of presence and self-presence, where reason appears as self-rule and self-sufficiency.

This book is organized around sets of practices with signs: listening, speaking, writing, reading, commenting in the first part. Interpreting these practices, a position can be determined through the practice. Thus in addition to a speaker-position ("I, however . . ."), there will be a listener-position (a "me" in question), and others. The responsibility of the practice defines the position and is not the choice of a being who first has independent substantial existence. Each practice is called forth to respond to other people, and indeed, each position has the responsibility of heeding the authority of other people to interpret their own words and mine.

The practices that concern the responsibilities for justice and that require a presence are reasoning, mediating, judging, and making law. These practices are more recognizably philosophical, but in this book they will appear as social responsibilities and not in the first instance as cognitive functions. Justice requires us to reason and judge, to mediate individual and general terms—the need for justice produces a need for semantics and syntax. And indeed, we will give an argument based on pragmatics for these other aspects of semiotics.

The set of practices in responsibility for the past are repentance, confession, forgiveness, and remembrance. Each will appear here in terms of signs and not merely states of mind or will. The repair of the past occurs in using words and signs to repair the relations between signs in the past. Historiography appears here, then, as a way of responding for the past by interpreting texts, commodities, and even our own existence as signs of past suffering.

This book, moreover, presents an ethics of responsibility in a distinctive format: by way of commentary. The performance of the text is a juxtaposition of shorter passages from various authors with a commentary written by me. This has required unusual practices in the writing, in the composition by the printer, and in the reading. In several places within the book there are reflections on the responsibilities in reading and writing commentary. But at one level the point is quite simple: responsive writing bears responsibility for what others have written. I wrote this in response to the questions raised by other texts, striving to hold open the vulnerability of responsibility for the readers to come. I am at the service of (responding for) both the authors I cite and comment upon and my readers—although these responsibilities are not identical. Page by page, this text will juxtapose texts from Levinas, Derrida, Rosenzweig, Habermas, Benjamin, the Bible, the Talmud, Maimonides, and others with my commentary. The reader then can see my practice of reading, and so will have the authority to read otherwise.

This book then advances the claims that ethics should be reoriented by the theme of responsibility; that the organon for ethics becomes pragmatics; and that the form of composition becomes commentary and depends on the pragmatics of paratactic composition. Such claims, precisely as advanced through commentary, are not my invention. My readings have assembled texts that have themselves already performed a sea change in ethical thinking. I have attempted to collect texts here that will facilitate further thinking in this new direction of ethics and responsibility. Such an undertaking is largely introductory, forsaking the more recognizable tasks (1) of providing basic readings of these major thinkers and their works, or (2) of exploring the most difficult and complex issues that specialists debate, or (3) of offering an extended comparison and debate between the various thinkers here examined. I believe that this book will be valuable for those specialists in part because of the intersections of diverse intellectual traditions here. My hope for those seeking an introduction to Levinas, or Habermas, or the Talmud is that if the book throws you into relatively deep water it also will indicate some basic strokes. But this book is primarily an introduction for those who are seeking a new orientation for ethics, those who seek help interpreting what it means to be responsible, indeed, who find themselves responsible as intellectuals for what others have thought and written. The assembling of texts and of why questions, of practices with signs, seeks to explore a way of writing an ethics that can hold open the responsibility and the vulnerability that calls us into question and so into action.

B. SIGNS

To give a response to a question is to give something to someone, to relate with other people. This ethics examines responsibility in the medium of signs because a sign is something that refers to something for someone. When we look to signs, we are already in the midst of relations *for* another (and not only *to* another). Responsibility appears as the key to an ethics of signs—because a sign requires other people and implicates me in response to them. Just as the meaning of a sign is a something usually outside the sign, so this ethics finds its center outside the self. The inability of a sign to measure itself for itself and in itself is the opening of the proper medium for the study of ethics: referring to another for another, a sign is a doubled relation to the world and to another person. But to understand signs in play, at work, is to complete a linguistic turn in philosophy. For as long as we see signs only as a way of knowing, and so measure the frustrations in knowing that accompany the use of signs, we do not recognize the more profound contribution that the linguistic turn makes. That contribution to ethics is found in pragmatics, as the examination of the relations between signs and their users. I claim that pragmatics is originally ethical. It always addresses relations between people, indeed, relations of responsibility. The incapacities of language as a tool for knowing are to be grasped rather as its appropriateness for the activities of responding. Once we dare elevate the concerns of ethics, we can then accommodate the cognitive functions of signs as well—and indeed view them as more intrinsic to signification than the interactive and responsive functions of signs could be for epistemologists. Throughout this book, therefore, we retain a priority of ethics, and in a theory of signs, the priority of pragmatics.

The study of signs, semiotics, is a diffuse and complex set of disciplines. For the most part, it has been a descriptive discipline, exploring how signs signify and what they mean. The question Why? looks along a specific axis of view: looking at the range of activities that people perform with signs. I choose to term what I am doing here pragmatics, although the definition of pragmatics is almost unmanageable.[1] I will take recourse to definitions from Morris, where semiotics is divided into three aspects: the relations of signs with other signs (syntactics), the relations of signs with their referents (semantics), and the relations of signs and their users (pragmatics).[2] My claim, however, is that pragmatic meaning is the leading meaning of a sign. The claim of ethics always occurs in the dimension of ought that governs signifying practices, but ethics is not an account of the motives of the author or speaker. Indeed, to examine our motives in using signs would be to take recourse in the medium of consciousness. Why we should listen, for instance, is the reason within the practice and may often be ignored or transgressed in our intentions. Pragmatic meaning is not the intended meaning of the speaker, but the meaning that pervades the practice. Relations are struck in performances that exceed our intentions. Semantic meaning, at first glance, is the conventionally ascribed meaning: the meaning that stipulates a relation to a referent. Syntactical meaning is the interdependent meaning a sign has in relation to other signs. As we turn from a general theory of action to one of semiotic action, we can see the relations of signs meaning something for someone are different from a general account of enacting means toward an end, for instance.

This shift to semiotics will catch some scholars of semiotics and some philosophers of language unawares. In the process of the argument of this book I have dared to reconstitute semiotics, viewing even the relation of

[1] See Stephen C. Levinson, *Pragmatics* (Cambridge: Cambridge University Press, 1983), 1–35; and Jacob L. Mey, *Pragmatics: An Introduction* (Oxford: Blackwell, 1993), 35–52.
[2] Charles Morris, *Writings on the General Theory of Signs* (The Hague: Mouton, 1971), 43ff.

signs to their referents through the relation of users and signs. Thus what I call semantics here (in Part II) will be about the social relations that require stable definitions and coordination of meanings between people—and will displace the ethical importance of what for others was a "self-evident" need to know and to name the world with signs. We do use words and other signs to know the world, but the reason why, I will argue, has to do with the social relations for the sake of justice and responsibility for each other. Operations like thinking, mediating, and judging will appear in relation to ethical responsibilities for justice. The reason why we use codes, stabilize definitions, and the like will occupy us.

In an even more dramatic shift, I will look at syntactics not in terms of ideal logical relations, but as forms of judgment of the relation of particulars to generals performed in social relations. That is, I am more interested in the sort of universality that is performed in a society as a relation of the responsibility of members for the general community than in the abstract relations of syllogisms and deductions. The concrete logic I explore is therefore referred again back to pragmatic relations, to relations between the particular as a sign and the community as a sign-user. The difference between judging an individual as representative of a community or as a cooperative participant with others produces different kinds of relations.

At the risk of confusing or frustrating those skilled in semiotics, I will try a simplified terminology of the sign. My focus is on the act of *signifying*. I will call the sign-bearer, the specific word on the page or articulated in utterance, the *sign*. The person who utters, inscribes, gesticulates, or otherwise addresses the sign I will call the speaker, the addressor, the utterer, or the writer. The person who receives a sign, who interprets it, will be variously the listener, the reader, the respondent. The central claim of the book is that the responsibilities in attending to a sign orient all of the pragmatic responsibilities, especially the utterer's.

A sign, however, also relates to something, refers to either a perceptible object or a conceptual object. Signs refer to a world, investing it with meaning (as in Husserl's semiotic), but the key activity is not the nomination of the sign, but the *donation* to another person. Our focus will not be, therefore, on the ontological status of the meaning of signs, but rather on the giving and receiving of meanings from and to other people. Similarly, the *indexical* function of a sign, to point to something, to refer in a direct perceptual way, will not be separated from the act of signifying. The core of indexicality will be reference to myself—will be the donation of myself to another person ("at your service"). Indeed, the most extreme claim that will guide the theory of ethics here is that the "I" who uses signs is assigned, made into a sign.

In this book, I use personal pronouns extensively. In the first instance, there is an I that is the writer's voice, conducting the text on its way. But there also is a concept of the "I," an indexical position transformed into a theme. In addition, there is also an I, or often a me, who is the locus of responsibility. These different uses overlap, too. And for this book the question of the "me" is even more important, as responsibility begins not in a subject making its own choices, but with a me who is called to answer. Last, I have disrupted the exclusive masculine usage of most of my authors for describing the third person. Thus often I will write that "she is responsible," even though my authors tended to limit their discourse only to males. Rather than neuter all third persons or use the clumsy "she or he," I have opted for interweaving the masculine and feminine pronouns, and I hope that it helps disturb our readings of the pretexts.

The choice of semiotics, moreover, involves not just a theory of language but one of signs and signifying. While much of the philosophical interest in meaning and language has confined itself to our audible languages, the pragmatics of using language rests in large measure on modes of signifying that move beyond language. Late in the book I will argue that goods (commodities) can also serve as signs. They serve in a system of signification (an economy) but they bear the marks of things that do not belong to the system: the labor of the people who made the stuff. Our belongings (and our trash) are signs of a suffering that we cannot represent adequately.

But it is not only what was made that signifies, for the critical point in each part of this book is when the performance of signifying revolves and we discover that the performer has become a sign. I hesitate to do so, but I will call this form of signification *existential signifying* when the pragmatic relation does not so much collapse as become raised to a second power. I am not merely the one who has to respond to the sign, I have to respond for the sign that I am become. Such assignment of me, the one who has to respond, is not a reflexive action. I do not choose to become a sign and then choose to respond for myself. Rather, another assigns me, or rather still more passively I am assigned, and respond for that assignment. We will see this in Chapter 2, when in my skin I am assigned for the other person, again in Chapter 8, when we are judged in the form of general judgment that defines the particular social logics, and in Chapter 17, when memory and repentance single us out as a surviving remnant, responding for the suffering of those who are dead. The pragmatics of existential signs depends on insight into gesture and motion, liturgy and perception, and at many points breaks beyond the semiosis possible with language alone. The inversion of autonomy as the norm for ethics could not be more radical, because here the responsibility for myself is precisely for myself as assigned by others, responsible to others and not to myself. As a sign, my being is not separable from the complex relations of signs and users. The social dimension of signification pervades this responsibility for myself, this need to account for my existence, and is far and away opposed to any model of authenticity and self-legislation. I am given to signify and now must respond for the sign I am become. Hence the fulcrum of the pragmatics of this ethics is in Chapter 12, Why Me?, because the existential signifying of the addressee position is the key asymmetry of responsibility. Because we can be signs, can be for others, language can be used responsively. But ethics, then, is possible here only in these relations of signification. There are no responsibilities of beings per se, but only of signs and their users.

C. COMMENTARIES

The body of the book is close readings of extended passages by various authors. I write responsively, citing a text by one of the authors on the left side of the page and letting my commentary flow around it. Each page presents at least two voices: or rather two bodies of text. I call the cited texts PRETEXTS. They are usually a paragraph or two long, and I have parceled them out into chunks of one or more sentences, numbering the passages consecutively in a chapter, and labeling the chunks with letters (1a, 1b, 1c, 2a, 2b, etc.). My commentary, on the other hand, is relatively continuous, leading from one topic to the next and coordinating the various pretexts while producing a close-reading of the given pretext.

I proceeded in my writing by first forming a general interpretation of each author's work. I then chose passages for the sake of the argument in my commentary, but I found myself interrupted, challenged, and educated by the discipline the pretexts exerted. My authors just wouldn't say what I knew they should, leading me to revise the argument, from slight matters of terminology, to larger matters of the general structures of a chapter's argument, even to restructuring a whole part. The tension between my own thought and the others' texts is performed on every page. As I learned from and reread these authors, my own structuring of the sequence of texts changed.

My commentaries are postmodern. A premodern commentary would follow a whole text, line by line, presenting a new reading while serving the integrity of the text. A modern writer would choose to stand independent of previous texts, assembling a system or an essay in his own voice, asserting in composition the principle of autonomy. This text, however, performs the switch to responsibility that characterizes the ethical concepts it claims. But unlike a medieval commentary, this commentary reconstructs arguments from the various authors. Its juxtaposition of various authors (from diverse traditions) and its manner of citation (paragraphs, not chapters or whole books) force texts to meet each other. It is not so much a collision or a battle that is staged, but a peaceable conversation. The commentary 'unifies' the disparate texts, depending on the texts, and responding both to them and for them. Ultimately, the commentary is a way of eliciting from the texts a set of teachings about responsibility. The page is a way of watching my practices of reading, allowing the reader to distance herself from the commentary, and in that repetition of pretext and commentary, even from the thematic itself.

The text composition, however, is yet more complicated often by a third and sometimes fourth text block. At the bottom of the page are parallel passages usually from the author of the pretext but often from other authors, too. These texts continue the argument of the chapter, sometimes deepening the resources in a given author, other times showing the affinities with the other authors. They usually originated as texts I had chosen to write commentaries upon, but which I relegated to the bottom of the page because of redundancies they would have brought into my commentary. Again, the commentary governs the page. Nonetheless, the parallel passages do provide a third text body that offers corroboration and occasional correction to the pretexts and commentaries. It is not hard to imagine generating a parallel commentary by replacing the pretexts with these parallel texts. This hypertext compensates in a vital way to the selectivity that I was bound to in choosing my 140+ pretexts. Thus the parallel passages represent another order of disruption of my text, but not an absolute or rigorously exhaustive realm of possibility. My concern was to make available to the reader such relevent texts that would lead to a reasonable range of parallel readings.

The fourth body of texts, moreover, are texts cited and commented upon by the pretexts. These commented-upon texts are on the right side of the page, with the cited words <u>underlined</u>. There are chapters with almost none of this intertextual element, and others where the chapter is devoted to this examination of how a text comments upon another text, for instance, Chapter 4 devoted to the question Why Read? Like a play within a play, the commented-upon text serves as a challenge to the pretext, illuminating the practices of the pretext. Thus, even the responsibility I perform in commenting is itself a commentary on the performances found already within the pretexts. And at times, the commented-upon texts themselves will open up to still earlier strata of texts. I thus perform a kind of stratification of interpretations, composing the page to allow both myself and my reader to discover both the reopening of the earlier texts and the recovery of openings that later interpretations have covered over.

The result is a page that translates Talmudic form into philosophical ethics. The Talmudic page, particularly in the printed format such as the edition of Vilna, is composed of a text and its commentary (Mishnah and Gemara) surrounded by commentaries, including some supercommentaries on earlier commentaries. Moreover, there is a compendium of citations to parallel passages in the Talmud. Earlier manuscript versions do not show this format, and many Christian texts were also typeset in this fashion. But beyond the recognizably Talmudic composition, there is a further mark of translation. The Talmud cites texts with a certain apparent disregard for their contexts. When the question is an argument of the Talmudic sages themselves, it is often oblivious to the context. When the pretexts are Biblical or Mishnaic, the context has been suspended; although even a cursory re-reading of the context shows that its problem has been brought to the Talmudic text through the citation of the abbreviated text. Indeed, much of the Talmud is concerned with retroactively justifying the Mishnah's readings of Biblical texts (and the Mishnah's lack of textual relation to the Bible). I am not claiming to make a Talmud out of texts by a group of contemporary philosophers, but the relations of citation and of commentary, of juxtaposition and of representation of the intertextual relations within a wide-ranging discussion—all these are translated into a philosophical idiom: with a risk of losing what is particular to the form, and with the hope of disrupting the philosophical page.

This book requires a double-reading, and sometimes a triple. The pretext is relatively intact, but detached from its economy within its own book. The commentary both serves and organizes the texts. This form of writing is exacting and slow-paced, as I provide exercise in reading some very hard texts. My hope is that my commentaries will make those hard texts more accessible, at least for those who are willing to read them through my questions about using signs. But that exercise is also about the responsibilities in reading and writing, in judging and remembering. The texts are not just dumped together, and the thematics of the book are not merely expounded but in large measure performed.

The path through this book was set by the agenda of responsibilities and semiotic performances. I have tried to write with a certain responsibility to the texts of these authors, but I have tried to stick to most familiar texts, and so have not been attempting to master current scholarship. Rather, the goal has been to make almost obvious points about the various texts, but through recontextualization and juxtaposition to raise significant questions. I was unable to give a thorough interpretation of even one work by one author, much less of all of any author's published work. The parallel passages only accentuate the emphasis and limitations of my readings: they cannot stand for a full commentary on a given writer. You will not find here an authoritative interpretation of Benjamin or Habermas, or even Rosenzweig or Levinas. As limited as my readings of each philosopher are, all the more so limited are my readings within traditional Jewish texts. I could not, at the same time, engage the secondary scholarship with great rigor and extensive treatment. This will not be a book that instructs specialists in their own authors—but it will place their favorites into a context with often unusual others. Not a text of intellectual history, this one is historically informed but governed by the ethical responsibilities that set its task. I have provided a set of suggested readings, located at the end of each chapter. These citations are keyed to the pretext numbers and direct my readers to several of the best readings of the pretexts I comment upon. In general, my task with these suggestions is to introduce the readers unfamiliar with a given author to helpful companions for the work in this book.

The compiling of pretexts and parallel passages excluded several authors that could well have occupied me in this book. I think immediately of Maurice Blanchot, Ernst Troeltsch, Max Weber, Talcott Parsons, John Dewey, Theodor Adorno, Paul Ricoeur, Karl Barth, Jean-François Lyotard, Martin Buber, Judith Plaskow, and others. These authors would have bloated this text still further, but I find the impossibility of citing and exploring their relation to this work frustrating. More noticeable is the limited amount of dialogue I have allowed my authors. There are many important conversations to be had from pairs like Habermas and Derrida, or James and Royce, or Rosenzweig and Benjamin, or Rosenzweig and Peirce, or Levinas and Benjamin, and so on. With notable exceptions, I have been unable to explore the sometimes generous and sometimes polemical interactions of these thinkers. Instead, I have opted for an irenic mode of discourse, where the faults of each are overlooked and others are brought in to remedy the flow of the argument.

D. A Map

The paths through the Talmud are intricate and confusing. This text is written not for Talmudists but for philosophers, for students of ethics, literature, social theory, history, and religion. Its paths wind not in a forest, but among texts—the products of human art, commodities that explicitly signify. Even if you read this alone, you are not a solitary, but are already in relation not just with some authorial voice (me?) but with a set of voices—or perhaps better, a set of texts. This is a thinking with, or better, a walking with/walking in responsibility for others.

I offer now a map of some paths—paths that will not be as linear as they may look on this map. The map is not the land, or in this case, not the library—the place where the texts meet each other. But a map should offer the reader some sense of what to expect and where to look for specific issues or authors.

Part I: Attending the Future

The book is written in four parts, each part divided into chapters, each chapter itself written in sections. The table of contents displays this structure. The first part concerns attending, the very beginning of pragmatics. The actions I examine will include listening, speaking, writing, reading, and commenting. In each of these actions the actor must pay attention to other people; indeed, we will see that the other person has the authority to interpret the words I use. My responsibility is my ability to respond to the other person, and to respond for the other's words. Attending opens the future meaning of signs, opens it for the other person to interpret, in a future that I cannot control.

Chapter 1, Why Listen?   This ethics begins in a conversational situation where we ask why I should listen to another person. I explore listening by reading a set of texts from Levinas' *Totality and Infinity*. When I listen to another person, I listen to words. But I also listen to the other person. The other person's speech reveals an authority to speak, to interpret words, to question me (A = Section A). My being questioned is the call to respond, the beginning of responsibility. The other who has this authority in speaking is my teacher who appears to me as beyond my attempt to know her, as transcendent. My exigency to respond here becomes infinite. But my listening is not responsible on condition that the other listen to me. On the contrary, ethics depends on an irreversibility of the positions (B). Listening is not at first reciprocal. My teacher speaks about the world and signifies both the world and the speaker—my teacher—in different ways (C). For Levinas the key question is how I am conscious of the infinity of this transcendence of the other person. He coins his most important term, THE FACE, to name the way the other person expresses herself by disrupting any image I have of her (D). This produces a spiraling of consciousness as my self-consciousness is called into question and becomes a moral conscience. Listening does not annihilate me, but preserves me as separate from the other person who summons me, and I am called to respond, to answer for myself (E). My words are a kind of apology, attempting to justify myself—and so I continue listening to the other even while speaking.

Chapter 2, Why Speak?   Responsive speaking is more concerned to offer oneself to the other than to articulate something for the other to understand. We shift to Levinas' second major work, *Otherwise Than Being or Beyond Essence* (1974). The key distinction, between *the saying* and *the said*, emphasizes the pragmatic relation at the expense of the semantics (the said). The exposure of the speaker in the saying contrasts with the model of speaking as transferring information (A). I become a sign for the other person, by drawing near to another person bodily (B). The vulnerability in approaching signifies my availability for her, even to the point of suffering for her. Here is a substitution for another's sake, a kind of assignment as existential sign for the other. If then I speak to announce to another person that I am at her service, available for her, I can say the saying of nearness (C). To say "I" does not secure me as a subject who will choose responsibilities for itself, but allows me to say my saying, to expose my exposure to the other. As a result, dialogue has now been radically altered, as I no longer am present as a coordinate subject, but have become the position of being-assigned—and responsibility is announcing this being made into a sign for the other. Finally,

I can witness the infinite responsibility for the other as a witness to God (D). God is neither a presence nor an interlocutor, nor is my responsibility dependent on evidence, but the theme of my responsibility arises for the first time in my witness, announcing not my choice, but my responsibility. I speak to witness that I am responsible for others.

Chapter 3, Why Write? Like saying, writing is a withdrawal as the author leaves signs for unknown readers to interpret. Derrida offers most help to the argument of this book in the shift to the practices of writing and reading. My interpretations will focus on how Derrida reads Levinas. A text from *Of Grammatology* argues that written signs hold open the vulnerability of signifying with a particular clarity (A). Two other texts from the 1960s explore Derrida's claim that his own writing practices are ways of announcing to the reader that the reader has the authority to interpret the text. Can Levinas, too, be read as making writing a way of responding and holding open my exposure for the other (B)? Derrida's reading in "Violence and Metaphysics" is explored here as a reconstruction of Levinas' often polemical treatment of writing, showing a way to find even Levinas treating writing as a way of ethical responsiveness to the other's actions. Levinas' account of the trace in *Otherwise Than Being* offers a way for Derrida to interpret Levinas' writing as a series of crossing-outs, or traces (C). The TRACE is the way that the other person withdraws and does not crystalize into a presence, a subject, when addressing me. Just as I became less a present subject in speaking, so the other person who teaches me in our initial dialogue model is attenuated in a textual model. Derrida discusses how Levinas makes the withdrawal of the author appear as withdrawal by repeating the gesture in a series. Levinas assumes the role of author without authority, responding for the reader not by promoting a theory of responding for the reader, but by serially withdrawing as author.

Chapter 4, Why Read? How do I read responsively, if the author is withdrawn from the text? How do we now attend not to the other person (who has withdrawn), but to the text, to the responsibility that comes through reading itself? Derrida offers the greatest assistance here, again from his earlier writings. He explains how a text is not a source of information but a solicitation to read and reread, a reading that occurs across generations (A). Moreover, Derrida explores why we have to reread the philosophical tradition, either to disrupt it or to interrupt it with another tradition (in much of his work that has been literature, in Levinas' work—Jewish sources) (B). Levinas then provides a deconstruction of the philosophical tradition from *Otherwise Than Being*—arguing that philosophy cannot overcome the disruptions and interruptions from others, even when it overwhelms them in coherent discourse. He instructs us to read for the traces or breaks and also alerts us to the pragmatics of writing for others to read that pervades even the most systematic philosophical texts. This leads to the climax of Part I, Derrida's remarkable reading of Levinas in "At this moment itself . . . " How does repetition disrupt the drive toward having something to say, a drive that thwarts responsibility (C)? I comment on a text by Levinas that discusses how books themselves are not only the summation and reduction of the responsibility to attend, but are also pragmatically situated for others, indeed, calling for other books. Derrida then cites a line of this text twice in the midst of discussing repetition, allowing my commentary to develop the pragmatics at the levels of (1) reading texts to find the interruption, (2) reading Levinas' repetition as producing interruption, and (3) reading Derrida's re-citation of Levinas as producing another sort of interruption. Commentary itself, then, emerges as a way not to tell the reader what the previous author had wanted to say, but to redevelop the responsibility of opening the text for the next reader, to attend to the text and its breaks so as to await a reader.

Chapter 5, Why Comment?   The ethics we are presenting in the philosophical texts correlates with an ethics that arises in Jewish revealed texts, as we shift to Levinas' writing on Jewish texts. Revelation of this ethics of responsibility happens through written texts (A). Those texts gain meaning through the separation in time (B). The text means more than the author wants it to mean, and the fecundity of the text depends on historical distance and renewal. Levinas cites a pair of famous stories from the Talmud—a text from the fifth to seventh centuries that is itself a commentary on a third-century text (the Mishnah)—that claim only a limited role for Divine authority in determining the meaning of Scripture, and instead point to the vital role of human interpretation in determining the meaning of the text.

The Jewish texts and the realia of practical life mutually interpret each other (C). And those texts then continue to reveal through the orality of teaching and studying. The rabbinic texts do not sum up oral discourse, but interrupt it in order to instigate new conversations in new contexts. They bear the practices of responding for others and attending to others forward to new others, acting like a script requiring new performances of responsiveness in a ongoing cycling of writing and speaking, of reading and listening.

Part II: Present Judgments

Using language produces not only responsibilities for the future but also responsibilities in the present. The responsibilities here will be mutual, where we share authority with others, and equality and justice become possible. Such responsibilities occur in social contexts, where we are present with others—or, as we will see, where there is an ethical exigency to become present. We will consider reasoning, mediating, and judging as practices performed for others with signs. Knowledge will be interpreted as a response to the demands for justice—and not as self-justifying. Thus the theory of knowledge offered here is both fully social and fully ethical.

Chapter 6, Why Reason?   Our plural infinite responsibilities for each other produce the ethical need to measure and coordinate. Levinas interprets justice as arising from our multiple responsibilities for many others, represented by the entry of the third person (A). Within the context of responsibility for justice, we begin to recover the function of signs in knowing. For a fuller account of how authority to interpret should be shared equally in the process of moral argumentation, we turn to Habermas (B). Responsibility for justice arises in a communicative situation, where we are each present to the others. But the relation between the asymmetry of attending the other and the mutuality of a community engaging in a present discussion about its norms produces a tension (C). Habermas' suspicion of asymmetry in ethics is complicated by his own account of how each person must take on the roles of the other in a communicative situation, becoming substitute for the other's claims. Levinas insists that justice must not abandon the asymmetric responsibility and vulnerability to the other person—even as that responsibility to attend the other also requires the mutual responsibilities for justice.

Chapter 7, Why Mediate?   Responsibilities extend to those who are not present, and indeed even for the social systems that exceed our presence. The question of how to respond for not just one other or other others with whom we can talk, but for social institutions calls for us to mediate. We move from Habermas' theory of action to Rosenzweig's theory of blind acts of love to Luhmann's theory of communication, steadily losing the presence of the people who have mutual responsibilities (A). Luhmann distinguishes social relations and face-to-face interactions. Indeed, much as the textual model replaced the conversational one in Part I, so too in Part II mediated relations accentuate the possibilities for responsibility with attenuated personal presence.

   With the absence of interlocutors, we require media to respond for society (B). For Luhmann, media include spoken language, print and mass media, and also media of values (truth, love, money, power, etc.). Just as we need to reason for justice, so we also need to use a semantic system to share our mutual responsibilities. The semantic dimension of signs is here reconstructed in its role of mediating. Even the formation of a consensus can be achieved through semantic mediation, as in Rosenzweig's account of communities (C). His account of how doctrine formation allows the Christian community to expand and coordinate the responsibilities of the members resembles Habermas' account of consensual communication. Moreover, the need for a medium, for a semantically stable meaning for terms, guides Rosenzweig's interpretation of cooperative responsibility.

Chapter 8, Why Judge?   Responsibility must come back to present individuals, indeed, the ethical exigency to judge individuals and to be judged produces them. The process of attribution of responsibility—the responsible member is one by attribution—addresses the attenuation of physical presence in mediated societies. Responsibility is assigned, not chosen, but the ways that attribution singles an individual out are various. In tabular form, this chapter offers four types of judgment, each reflecting both different social relations and different logical relations between the individual and the general term. Luhmann explains why in order to develop itself as a communicative system a community needs to attribute its communications not to the system in general but to individuals (A). Following Luhmann's basic definition of system—the opposition of system and its environment constituting the communications within the system—we will explore the deconstruction of that opposition (B). Rosenzweig interprets the relations of a "we" and a "ye" as a judgment that rests first on another community but then deconstructs our own community as well. In different ways both Judaism and Christianity contest this fundamental opposition as each claims universality (C). Here social responsibility regains its infinite dimension. Judaism achieves this by contraction, by drawing every opposition within itself; Christianity, by expansion through cooperation, inviting everyone to join and coordinate with the others.

Judgment is needed for these universal, infinite responsibilities (D). Luhmann explores how Christianity needs a Last Judgment at the end of history to allow the inclusion of sinners within the community now. The goal of universality for cooperation is deferred to the end of history. In contrast, Judaism then brings the day of judgment into its yearly calendar, when on Yom Kippur the Jew prays as responsible for the whole world, according to Rosenzweig's interpretation of some of the most important prayers of Judaism. The Christian relation, for Rosenzweig, is responsive through cooperation; the Jewish, through representation.

In contrast, two other types of communal judgments finitize responsibilities, reducing social responsibilities and avoiding the self-critical judgment (E). Rosenzweig distinguishes between two forms of reductive social responsibilities: idealism and paganism, as totalizing and as subordinating the community over the individual. Briefly I will turn to Aristotle's description of ostracisim as a social practice of pagan judgment, and to Hegel's discussion of the immanent judgment by history ("Die Weltgeschichte ist das Weltgericht") as a totalizing judgment. The chapter then concludes with a table displaying the four different kinds of social logic—offering a rather different kind of reflection on syntax of signs by focusing on social responsibilities.

Chapter 9, Why Law?   Law can be a medium for the study of the mutual responsibilities of justice. Rosenzweig interprets how Jews understand the cultivation of the law as a way of justifying this world, indeed that the law redeems the world through its judgment upon the world (A). Law, more-over, engenders and preserves conflict within a community (B). Luhmann claims that law increases conflict for the sake of communication. The need for contradictory positions within the text then appears in a familiar Talmu-dic text. A more detailed commentary of a Talmudic text we cited in Chap-ter 5 will conclude Part II, providing an account of how taking advantage of another person with words becomes an image of the limits of Talmudic ar-gument, precisely in a process from which God has withdrawn.

Part III: Pragmatism, Pragmatics, and Method

Part III is a reflection on the method of this book, particularly exploring the responsibility to think about ethics in terms of pragmatics. This part has some of the most far-reaching links between thinkers, as I bring the Jewish philosophers into contact with American pragmatism. While the Jewish thinkers develop the key concepts of responsibility for others, the pragma-tists provide the semiotic methods for the interpretation of signs. The work of Peter Ochs has pointed Jewish thought to explore resonances and conflu-ences with Peirce's theories of signs and has refashioned American pragma-tism in the study of rabbinic hermeneutics in Talmud and Midrash.[3] My task is not to offer an account of American philosophy, or even of influences, but rather to explore the need for a pragmatics and pragmaticist method for this ethics.

Chapter 10, Why Verify?   I begin with an accessible model of my method, claiming that a theory will require verification. Rosenzweig's own reflections on his method claim that responsive thinking arises in taking time seriously in relation to others, and that future is the time for a theory to be made true or verified(A). I then pair Rosenzweig with James, as each claims to frame an empiricism that can verify relations, particularly relations between people and between people and God (B). But we must move from James' definition of pragmatism focusing on verification of truth to Peirce's redefinition of pragmatism as pragmaticism where the verification is no longer simply pro-ducing a sensible experience, but is an interplay between theoretical activity and habits (C). Thus the future making true of a theory will depend on social behavior, it will depend on others' interpretations.

Chapter 11, Why Thirds?   Any theory about responsibility involves an in-herent betrayal of the asymmetry of responsibility, but there is a justification

---

[3] Peter Ochs, *Peirce, Pragmatism and the Logic of Scripture* (Cambridge: Cambridge Univer-sity Press, 1998). See also Peter Ochs, ed., *Understanding the Rabbinic Mind: Essays on the Hermeneutic of Max Kadushin* (Atlanta: Scholars Press, 1990), especially his own essay, "Max Kadushin as Rabbinic Pragmatist," 165–96. See also his essay, "Charles Sanders Peirce," in *Founders of Constructive Postmodern Philosophy*, ed. David Ray Griffin et al. (Albany: SUNY Press, 1993), 43–88.

for just that betrayal and the risk of losing sight of the asymmetry. Levinas claims that language must invoke the third person and not just the private romance of me and the other (A). He is joined by Gabriel Marcel, who explores how the direct responsibility of I for you is compromised by speaking about it. But from Marcel we go back to Royce, who saw how interpretation is a three-term relation, an interpretation *to* someone (B). Royce, however, was adapting Peirce's account of thirdness and the way that signifying always involves a relation to a third, which he calls the *interpretant*. The tension between the specificity of the index and the generality of the symbol arises from the task of signifying. The task of theory is to frame a theory for others, a theory that must be, as theory, general.

Chapter 12, Why Me?   In parallel with Chapter 8 (Why Judge?), we require an attribution of responsibility, in this case the responsibility not only for others but also for theory. We redevelop the need for theory as my own responsibility for a theory about my responsibilities—and so move back to the indexicality of writing about responsibility. The argument mirrors Chapter 11, this time moving from America back to France, from Peirce to Levinas. In Peirce's account of vagueness, the utterer reserves the authority to interpret her signs (A). Royce then socializes vagueness by discussing how the other interprets her own signs to me—much like Levinas' face of the teacher in Chapter 1. It is Mead, however, who explores how "me" develops through learning how to respond for others (B). Social intercourse, precisely in its asymmetries, produces the self who can respond. We return to Levinas for an account of the thematic "me" and its relation to me (the person who is examining the responsibilities of the "me") (C). The indexicality of responsibility disrupts and orients the generality of the theory.

Chapter 13, Why Translate?   This book is located in a "here," for it works by presenting Jewish thinkers in an American context. It translates books from there to here: from Jewish sources to contemporary philosophy, from Europe to North America, from phenomenology to semiotics, from ethics to pragmatics. The alternatives are that one should leave sources in their proper tradition, or that one should sublate them into a pure philosophical discourse—with no "here." Jewish philosophers have justified such translation, in a line from Hermann Cohen, to Rosenzweig, and then to Levinas.

Cohen claims that while Jewish sources lack the scientific qualities of Greek philosophical sources, they have their own intrinsic share of reason and so have something to contribute to the exploration of an ethical rational religion (A). Rosenzweig claims there is need for a translation from theology to philosophy (B). Even as his *Star* is a philosophical book it also is a Jewish one because it is expressed in the living language of Jewish texts and prayers. Rosenzweig, in his later works of translation, explained why he had a responsibility to translate from Hebrew into German (C). His major claim is that all communication is translation and that translation cultivates new possibilities in the target language. Thus for the sake of enriching the "here" we must bring texts from "there."

Translation, however, runs the risk of betraying what was "there," failing to bring across just what was most important. A text by Levinas comments on a Talmudic discussion of the limitations of the Septuagint, the Greek translation of the Hebrew Bible (D). Levinas echoes the original problem by his own efforts to translate the argument of the Talmud into a contemporary intellectual context. Moreover, he finds in the earlier text the exigency to translate—even as it requires us to run the risk of misinterpretation. This book, moreover, runs that risk in various modes: juxtaposing translations from various languages with a commentary that also tries to translate the discourse into a more familiar American idiom of thought.

Part IV: Repenting History

Part IV examines the responsibilities we have in relation to the past, responsibilities for repenting and so changing the past. Through an interpretation of Jewish sources on repentance as returning, we will explore a series of practices (repentance, confessing, forgiving, and remembering) that use signs to respond for the past, repairing the relations of signs in the past. These responsibilities require a remembering, indeed, the writing of history, as well as an interpretation of ourselves as survivors. This part, in contrast to the first three parts, begins with Jewish sources, producing a kind of stratified history of reinterpretations of texts and practices.

Chapter 14, Why Repent? Hosea's call to the people to return to God is the primary text on repentance (A). The sages argued with prophetic texts by reinterpetation, struggling to accentuate the power of returning as capable of forcing God's hand in redeeming the world in an extended Talmudic essay on repentance, "Great is repentance" (B). But repentance in the relation between people and God differs from that between people (C). The Mishnah separates out sins between people and those before God by interpreting a Biblical text, and Levinas then comments on both sins. The possibility for a translation of the theological relation of repentance and forgiveness into a social-ethical one is questioned here, as the need to return in relations with others appears as a responsibility.

Chapter 15, Why Confess? In confessing, I attribute responsibility for the past to myself. Confession, moreover, produces the "I" as "confessing one." The chapter begins with the requirement that confession be made orally, as interpreted by Maimonides (A). He interprets Biblical texts, including the text from Hosea, in order to explain how repentance is not complete without an audible confession. Cohen claims that the specific individual who confesses is herself a task (and not a given) produced through the performance of confession (B). Soloveitchik claims that the specific preamble to confession achieves a radical transformation of the speaker. Rosenzweig then argues that the pragmatics of confession transform the self in relation to its own past, resulting in a confession of faith, that the soul knows itself forgiven (C).

Chapter 16, Why Forgive?   Not only is the the repenter changed in repentance, but that return alters the past as well. We do not merely attribute responsibility for a past that is gone, but through return and forgiveness we can change the past. The Talmudic text of Chapter 14 claimed that repentance can change intentional sins into either inadvertent ones or merits. Soloveitchik explores these two texts and their author (Resh Lakish) and distinguishes between erasing the sin (forgetting) and elevating it through repentance (forgiving) (A). But can an historian take a similar view in regard to past events? Horkheimer resists this possibility in a letter criticizing Benjamin, but Benjamin cites and then responds in his notebooks to that letter (B). Benjamin not only stands close to Resh Lakish, but he also articulates the need to think theologically as historian. But we can change the perspective again, looking at my dependence on the other person to change the past. A text from Levinas argues that time arises through the forgiveness of the other person, which changes my past (C). The shift from my repentance changing my past, to the other person's forgiveness changing my past also marks the limits of my capacity to remember the past, as the relation to the other is not initiated in rememberable time.

Chapter 17, Why Remember?   It is social practices of remembrance that make possible the mending of the past, precisely when the individual recognizes the inability to remember alone. We start with calendars as a social construction of time that marshals communal remembrance. The first texts are from the Mishnah and the Bible, showing how the timing of these holidays has been left to people to determine (A). Rosenzweig offers a sociological interpretation of the Sabbath and the holidays as ways of making eternity enter time. But Benjamin reinterprets Rosenzweig's claims and raises the challenging question: Do modern consumerist societies live by such calendars?

The responsibility to remember without the social prop of the calendar produces an historiography that contests the past (B). In a series of texts Benjamin criticizes historicism and proposes a juxtaposition of a past image with a present one in order to question the path of history and the current situation. We interpret this historiography as a kind of repentance for the past that can change the past. Benjamin also offers, in a commentary on a text by Marx, a way of reading commodities as signs of labor that itself has no historical presence. The realm of signs expands beyond language, as stuff also requires a response from us, a responsibility for the past.

What lies beyond memory can incite us to remember while holding open our responsibility for the past (C). Benjamin discusses the place of ruins on the baroque stage, as constructed gestures of decay and of human failure. But Rosenzweig then interprets Jewish existence as itself a sign, the Jews interpreting themselves as remnants and so as signs of those who have suffered and died. The existential sign is a self-critical one, for we are not the miserable victims, for they perished, but are rather the survivors who must take responsibility for the past and hold open the future of those we do not control. We signify ourselves as survivors to mark the loss and our responsible relation to it.

Epilogue

The relation of postmodern Jewish thought to modern philosophy is itself not a refusal or an obliteration, but a kind of repentance. The responsive relation to the past is not to negate it in order to forget it, but to respond for it. To reread, in this sense, is not to repeat but to recover possibilities otherwise lost. Perhaps the greatest failing in modern projects was the obliteration of their own past, their impossible claim to stand free from and no longer responsible for their ancestors. Postmodern thought must not repeat that failing (lest it be just another modern project). The responsive relation lies precisely in the rereading of the modern project as signs for a future that others will interpret.

The book as a whole thus reorients ethics by focusing on responsibility, the responsibility for what others do. The parts move in a sequence from future to present to past, with an interruption to consider the method for framing this theory of ethics. At another level, the parts stretch from literary theory, to social theory, to theory of knowledge, to historiography. And at the most concrete level we move from the asymmetry of interaction to the mutuality of relations in communities to the relations of remembrance and return. In each part there is a parallel motion from a more accessible everyday context, where the other person and I appear together, through an attenuation of that presence, until we discern the assignment of responsibility as singling me out again—despite the absence of a present subject. Indeed, the two central points of the ethics are the need first to listen (Chapter 1) and then the inescapability of my responsibility that singles me out (Chapter 12). But the task of writing this book and examining others' texts assigns the responsibility to return and repair the past, for philosophy, and also for modernity. An ethics of infinite responsibilities must not conclude, but hold itself open for further tasks.

E. THE AUTHORS AND TEXTS

I offer here only a brief introduction to the authors and the texts fom which my pretexts are cited. The composition of this book precludes a more traditional treatment of the various texts, and so for those reading these thinkers for the first time, my brief introduction will have to stand in for the tasks of giving a reading, or exploring the intellectual contexts, or developing an intellectual biography of the author. The authors are profiled in the sequence in which they appear.

Emmanuel Levinas (1905–95) was born in Lithuania and raised in both Russia and Lithuania in a modern Jewish family. He studied and then lived in France, where he was one of the first expositors of Husserl and Heidegger. Levinas was a leader in the Jewish intellectual community in Paris (a community including many Mediterranean Jews), and only later emerged as an important figure in the general philosophical world.

In *Totality and Infinity* (1961) Levinas presents a phenomenology of the ways I relate to the world and to other people. The main themes of that book are that justice requires a face-to-face responsibility for another person, for whom I am infinitely responsible, and that responsibility occurs in discourse, in my being questioned by the other. Levinas' phenomenology strains with the task of describing that infinite responsibility, but the work explores a broad range of social relations, including domesticity, erotics, and paternity with a phenomenological method.

Levinas' second major work is *Otherwise Than Being or Beyond Essence* (1974). It is a redevelopment of many of the themes from *Totality and Infinity*, but works within a narrower focus—offering a profound interpretation of how I am assigned for the other person, made responsible, in a moment that cannot be represented or experienced as a phenomenon. The argument is a reduction that determines discourse as an obsession with the other person. The book concludes with an account of the relation of philosophical discourse and prophetic glorification of the Infinite—engaging a more complex account of the limits of discourse in closer relation to a theological dimension.

Levinas wrote occasional pieces for the Jewish community and also offered yearly readings of Talmudic passages. These various texts were collected and segregated from his philosophical works. *Beyond the Verse* (1982) is the fourth volume in French of these writings and comprises a set of Talmudic readings and essays, including several on the question of interpretation of Scripture. The text offers an emphatically positive interpretation of reading, and indeed offers us an account of responsibility in attending others in the practices of commenting.

Jacques Derrida (b. 1930) was born in the Jewish community of Algiers. He proposes a theory of writing (*Of Grammatology*) (1967) as a reinterpretation of the phenomenological tradition. Derrida offers most help to the argument of this book in the shift to the practices of writing and reading—although he has also had much to say about ethics. The focus of my comments will be two essays by Derrida on Levinas. In "Violence and Metaphysics" (1967), he both offers a strong reading of *Totality and Infinity* and contests it by rereading Husserl and Heidegger against Levinas. He suggests that Levinas is too entangled in the philosophical tradition to achieve the radical reorientation he desires. For Levinas' festschrift, Derrida explored his later work, too, and wrote a very dense essay, "At this moment itself in this work Here I am" (1980), where he tried to give a gift, exploring the complexity of asymmetry and the way that Levinas' texts work.

Jürgen Habermas (b. 1929) is a German philosopher and descendant of the Frankfurt School. His major work, *The Theory of Communicative Action* (1981), offers a grand argument based on the history of social theory. He claims that communicative action is capable of arriving at rational norms for society, focusing on the mutuality practiced in rational argumentation. The very abilities to talk and reason with others themselves produce principles of justice. In the following years, Habermas redeveloped many of the themes from this work, naming his work *Discourse Ethics*, and so making the very practices of discourse into the medium for framing an ethics.

Niklas Luhmann (1927–98) was a German sociologist and a longtime dialogue partner with Habermas. His major work, *Social Systems* (1984), presents an interpretation of the self-defining nature of social systems. Indeed, his account of society is a more radical semiotics, focusing on the ways communications happen and not building society out of speaking individuals. As a social theorist he only described ethical norms and practices, and so is a less likely participant for this book. Yet his descriptions are relevant, because he, too, interprets society in terms of communication.

Franz Rosenzweig (1886–1929) was raised in a liberal Jewish home, but returned to a more traditional Judaism. He struggled with philosophy and theology, and composed the masterpiece of modern Jewish thought, *The Star of Redemption* (1921), in a virtual idiolect shared with his circle of relatives and friends. The work is dense and complex, and argues for a transformation of thought in the new organon of speech and gestural performance. After the *Star*, Rosenzweig founded a Jewish community education program in Frankfurt, but was stricken with ALS. Bedridden and incapable of speech, he managed to complete a translation and commentaries on medieval Jewish poetry and translate the first part of the Hebrew Bible into German with Martin Buber. Rosenzweig's loyalty to the world produced a challenging social theory in the *Star*, focusing particularly on the way that societies can be redeemed by responsive practices.

Hermann Cohen (1842–1918) was the founder of the Marburg Neo-Kantian School, a leader of Liberal Judaism, a commentator on Kant's works, and the author of his own system of philosophy that bore a distinct imprint of Jewish thought. His last works were explorations of Jewish sources as resources for a theory of rational religion, arguing that Judaism and ancient Greece each had a share in reason. His analyses of monotheism, repentance, love of the neighbor, and messianism in *Religion of Reason out of the Sources of Judaism* (1919) have dominated Jewish thought in this century.

Moses Maimonides (1135–1204) was the Jewish philosopher par excellence. He was a community leader for Mediterranean Jews. He wrote the defining book of Jewish philosophy, *Guide for the Perplexed*, and redacted one of the great codes of Jewish law, *Mishneh Torah* (1177).

Joseph Soloveitchik (1903–93) came from a distinguished family of Lithuanian rabbis. He was a leader of the Orthodox Jewish community in America, whose yearly lectures on repentance were edited by his student, Pinchas Peli. Soloveitchik studied Cohen's work and often commented directly on Maimonides' texts, and fashioned a radical intellectualist view of Judaism.

Walter Benjamin (1892–1940) was raised in a bourgeois Jewish Berlin family and maintained an unresolved relation with Judaism. He committed suicide, fleeing the Nazis in 1940. His work arose in the context of Gershom Scholem, Theodor Adorno, Ernst Bloch, and Bertolt Brecht. His works include several completed writings and a huge unmanageable project on the early shopping malls of the nineteenth century (*Die Passagenwerk*). We will cite not only his thesis *On the Origin of the German Trauerspiel* (1928), but also pieces from the later project, and an exchange of letters with Horkheimer. Benjamin's work struggles to frame a theory and a practice of historiography that will disrupt the presumption of survivors to justify their own presence.

PART I

Attending the Future

Listen Israel: THE LORD our God, THE LORD alone.

Deuteronomy 6:4

CHAPTER 1

Why Listen?

PHILOSOPHY IS the study of questioning. That questioning in philosophy, including what, how, who, and why, occurs in situations, and our primary situation is a conversation. We will begin in the situation of a simple dialogue, where someone speaks and another listens. Later that situation will be disturbed and the ontological conviction that the two people are present to each other attenuated. But we begin in a face-to-face dialogue, in part to discover several of the basic themes of this ethics in a context which is more familiar. We thus begin not from a theory of knowledge, where the task of knowing is primary, and where the relationship to another person might be necessary but would still be brought into the picture to allow me to know. Nor do we begin with an autonomous individual who confronts life and makes his own decisions, reasoning according to principles. Rather, we begin in a conversation, where two people respond to each other.

This displacement of ethics from a realm of thinking to dialogue is familiar today, but instead of examining the dialogue as an interchange of speaking, where you and I each take our turns speaking, Levinas discovers here a profound asymmetry. We will explore how the listener position is different from the speaker position. Moreover, the listening is primary. My first responsibility arises in listening to another person, not in speaking to her. Conversation, therefore, is not at first on a level field. (In Chapter 6 we will see the ethical need to create a level field, in considering how justice requires reason.) Still more important, we notice the indexicality of this asymmetry: the listener position becomes mine. That is, the difference in the conversation depends on me being in the listener position, and so breaking the dialogue into two distinct interactions. I listen to the other speak, and am called to respond to and for the other person; and I speak to the other who may or may not listen—but not in order to call her to respond. My speaking, which is the topic of the next chapter, is not the same as the other person's speaking.

This ethics begins then with an examination of why I should listen to another person. When I listen to another person, I listen to words. But I also listen to the other person. In a dialogue the other person has something to tell me. Beyond what she wants to say, she also reveals herself as speaker. Her speech reveals her authority to speak, to interpret words, to question me. I listen to the other as my teacher (Section A). My being questioned is the call to respond, the beginning of responsibility (Pretext 1). That call comes not from what she says to me, but from the way she challenges me, the way whatever I say is open to her questioning. The other who has this authority in speaking is my teacher (Pretext 2), and appears to me as above me or simply beyond my attempt to know her. The teacher's escape from any of my efforts to control her speech, her interpretation of her words, is real transcendence. Levinas explores the infinity of this transcendence.

In Section B we will focus on the asymmetry in listening. My listening is not responsible on condition that the other listen to me, that I get my turn to be teacher/speaker, too. On the contrary, in order to interpret how discourse is more than reciprocal dialogue, how it calls me into question and summons me to respond, ethics depends on an irreversibility of the positions (Pretext 3). So listening is not at first reciprocal.

Section C considers how we listen to words, as well as to the teacher. The teacher not only reveals herself, but she speaks of the world, too. The other person, for Levinas, becomes the principle of the objectivity of the world— given not so much in sensation or in thought, but given first of all from another person (Pretext 4). The sign I listen to signifies doubly, then. Once to the teacher and then in quite another way to the object.

But the most complex issue in Levinas' account of listening is the way that I am conscious of the infinite, this transcendence of the other person. He coins his most important term, THE FACE, to name the way the other person's unbridgeable elusiveness breaks beyond my efforts to know her. My idea of my interlocutor is questioned and broken by her speaking. Section D will explore how we experience that which transcends our experience—in the face of the other person. First, I present one of the many defining passages of the face as the self-expression of the other person (Pretext 5). And then we explore how I am aware of the teacher, despite the way she overflows my awareness (Pretext 6). Here the role of my own self-consciousness in my responsibility becomes clearer, precisely because the other's call to respond breaks into my domain, and the more vigorously I know myself, the greater my responsibilities for others. The spiraling of responsibilities in becoming aware of them produces the infinition of responsibility.

Because listening does not annihilate me, but preserves me as separate from the other person who addresses me, I am able to respond in the conversation. I find myself called to respond, to answer for myself to another person, allowing us to conclude the chapter with Section E (Apology). I listen to the other person to receive the world, to find myself questioned, to learn from the other person as my teacher, and in order to become able to respond, able to justify myself.

This interpretation of listening as the beginning of responsibility and as the relation to the other person as my teacher is a reading of Levinas' *Totality and Infinity*. While that text has its own intricate argument and style, we will propose this reading by examining a set of texts. (The justification of arguing through commentary awaits us in later chapters.) Levinas offers a layered phenomenology of my relations to what is other, but the pivotal relation is with a teacher who faces me in a conversation.

A. ATTENDING THE TEACHER

1a) Levinas TI 153/178–79 In discourse I expose myself to the interrogation of the Other Person and this urgency of response—the sharp point of the present—engenders me for responsibility; as responsible I find myself brought back to my ultimate reality.

Entering a conversation, I do not merely hold forth, I also listen and so EXPOSE MYSELF. Discourse, face-to-face conversation, is not the moment in which I am declaiming my thoughts to the walls. There is another person, to whom I offer these thoughts, to whom I try to make myself clear, in whatever mode of address (command, description, invocation, and so on). That other person is the point of the conversation for me. In the conversation, I am exposed to the other person. I have to listen for what she says, and so find myself in question. I find myself listening and INTERROGATED by THE OTHER PERSON. As questioned I find myself called, and called to respond quickly (THE URGENCY OF THIS RESPONSE). To listen is to need to respond to the Other Person, now. The present happens exclusively through this urgency, this need to answer. Listening, exposed and questioned, I become able to respond. The other person's question ENGENDERS ME FOR RESPONSIBILITY. For Levinas, the ability to respond constitutes MY ULTIMATE REALITY: to be me is to listen and be questioned by the other—not to hold forth.

1b) This extreme attention does not actualize what was potential, because it is inconceivable without the Other. To be attentive means a surplus of consciousness that presupposes the call of the Other. To be attentive is to recognize the mastery of the Other, to receive his commandment, or more exactly, to receive from him the commandment to command.

Responsibility cannot rest in my own relation to myself—because I cannot be my own teacher. The theme of this ethics is responsibility—a theme that is not derivable, nor even consistent with the claim of autonomy. In listening, in attending to the other person, I become changed, but listening DOES NOT ACTUALIZE WHAT WAS POTENTIAL. Exposed to the other's questions, the other instigates new possibilities for me. My listening provides A SURPLUS OF CONSCIOUSNESS, making me exceed my own capacities to think and to act. Only THE CALL OF THE OTHER can produce my ability to respond. Hence, we listen in order to gain responsibility; by making ourselves vulnerable to questioning, we become responsible. Such listening recognizes the other person's authority, and that authority is recognized in receiving HIS COMMANDMENT. Levinas hesitates here (OR MORE EXACTLY). The commandment is what the other teaches me: not what he says but rather the pragmatic "content" of revelation. Teaching is not information or even in-struction, but engenders responsibility by requiring something of me, the listener. It requires that I respond. I am not commanded merely to do an act that the teacher requires (HIS COMMANDMENT), but rather I receive the au-thority to speak, to teach, to reveal myself to others (THE COMMANDMENT TO COMMAND). In Chapter 6, I will discuss the responsibility to speak in claiming justice. As response, that speaking will never have the radical au-thority of the teacher—it will always be vulnerable to the other person's questions. But the teaching itself does not reduce me to silence. I am taught to respond.

1c) When I seek myself in my ulti-mate reality, my existence as "a thing in itself" begins with the pres-ence in me of the idea of the Infinite. But this relation consists already of serving the Other Person.

My position as responder, as listening and so able to answer, defines what I am to be, defines the beginning of ethics. The self is not constituted through self-reflec-tion, nor through the accumulation of sen-sible experience and rational abstraction. The self is first of all in relation with other people. Our concern is not to provide an account of the ontology of the self—indeed, ontological structures are displaced in this work, as in Levi-nas', with a responsive self, a speaker, writer, and otherwise issuer of signs in response to other people who also are semiotically construed. The claim in this passage, moreover, is that if one is looking for a definition of myself, of what I really am in myself, then the answer will require the inclusion of something that is not myself. That something is THE IDEA OF THE INFINITE, Levinas' term for my relation with another person who teaches me with authority, and not by power. Hence the self who welcomes and attends, the listener, is the "real self." But to listen is to have responsibilities, is to be bound to SERVE THE OTHER PERSON. Ethics then begins with a listening that brings me in relation with the Infinite, with an excess that is performed in another person speaking to me, calling me to answer.

We begin with questions. Not the questions I ask, but the question I am asked. When we listen, we hear the questioning that comes from the other person. I need to listen to be questioned in a way I cannot question myself—and in listening to the question I am shown the questioner. In the question the other appears as a teacher who questions me in ways I cannot anticipate.

2a) Levinas TI 146/171 My being put in question, coextensive with the showing of the Other Person in the face—we call this language. The height from which language comes we designate by the word teaching.[1]

When I listen I am PUT IN QUESTION be-cause attending to another is opening to the other, who challenges me. Just as dis-course was an opening that called for an urgent response from me, so LANGUAGE here is a relation and not a set of words.

---

[1] Levinas TI 181–82/206–7 Meaning is the face of the other person, and every recourse to words is placed inside the original face to face of language. Every recourse to the word presup-

The relation repeats my being put in question and links it with the way speaking is a SHOWING OF THE OTHER PERSON (who is speaking) IN THE FACE. Later we will examine Levinas' concept of THE FACE carefully, but here what is more important is the SHOWING. For language is the way that another exercises an authority to interpret words (hers and mine) and such authority places my use of words in question. The other speaks to me from above, from a HEIGHT, with an authority that instigates my need to listen and to respond. Since language is not a system of words, nor even a reciprocal network of relations, but is the pragmatic relation of showing her authority to interpret and putting me in question, the relation is from the other person (from above) to me. Levinas then terms this height TEACHING. Teaching, therefore, is first of all the newness of what the other person can say to me, the questioning that reveals how she is more than I know.

2b) Against a pedagogy which introduced ideas into a mind by violating or seducing that mind (which comes to the same thing), Socratic maieutic was right. It did not exclude the opening of the very dimension of the infinite which is height, in the face of the Teacher. That voice coming from another shore teaches transcendence itself.

In order to justify this stipulation, Levinas reflects on teaching. He contrasts Socrates' midwifery with inculcation and seduction. Socrates tried to protect the mind from violence, from the use of power to overwhelm it that undermines the learner. Respecting the integrity of each person, Socrates protected the learner, arguing that the learner must produce his own ideas for himself. SOCRATIC MAIEUTIC, however, DID NOT EXCLUDE a nonviolent introduction of novelty. A teacher who brings something new to me, not in what is said but in revealing herself in the act of speaking, teaches in a radically nonviolent way. Levinas refers to a DIMENSION OF THE INFINITE, an axis opening to transcendence. And the performance of teaching teaches TRANSCENDENCE ITSELF, not some content or theme. If maieutics preserves the integrity of the learner from the violence of a force exercised against the learner, then teaching in Levinas' sense teaches the possibility of an otherness that does not stand on the same plane with me, does not contest me, but opens me and in so doing founds me.

2c) Teaching signifies all the infinity of exteriority. And all of the infinity of exteriority is not first produced and afterward taught—

In the previous pretext we introduced the infinite as what is not myself but is present in me in the call to respond. Here the focus is on EXTERIORITY. Levinas is

---

poses understanding this first signification, an understanding, however, that before being interpreted as "consciousness of" is society and obligation. Signification—is the infinite, but the Infinite does not present itself to a transcendental thought, not even to the meaningful activity, but in the Other Person. He faces me and puts me in question and obliges me by way of his essence as infinite. This "something" that one calls signification arises in being with language, because the essence of language is the relation with the Other Person.

teaching is its very production. The first teaching teaches that height itself, what amounts to its exteriority, ethics.

exploring how something new comes to me without falling under my power. Listening, in this sense, is not like eating, where I can assimilate what is other into me. Rather, I listen in order to learn what I cannot make my own, the teacher teaching who remains exterior to me. THE INFINITY OF EXTERIORITY then exceeds what I could appropriate. The speaker remains behind the signs and their interpretation. My interlocutor retains her authority to reinterpret what she says and so eludes my grasp. But exteriority of such a radical kind that it can never become interior does not first exist in reality and then only AFTERWARD happen to be taught. Its PRODUCTION itself happens in speaking, in teaching. Only in teaching can such radical exteriority occur. This teaching, then, first of all, teaches the infinite dimension: HEIGHT ITSELF. The first teaching is this exteriority. It is ETHICS. But what does ETHICS mean here?

2d) ... It is fundamentally pacific. The Other is not opposed to me as another freedom, still similar to mine, and as a result, hostile to mine. The other person is not another freedom, as arbitrary as mine, which would at once pass through the infinite that separates me from him, to enter under the same concept.[2]

If Levinas admits he moves away from Socratic maieutics, where nothing new can be added to me as listener, then he must distinguish this other way of teaching from violence and seduction. For ethics is the question of the possibility for this PACIFIC relation to otherness, particularly to another person. Levinas is breaking the Hegelian dialectic of master and slave. The PACIFIC quality of the teaching relationship is not accidental, nor is it merely a moment that must be reintegrated in a conflictual relation. Teaching is FUNDAMENTALLY PACIFIC. While I may desire to assimilate the teacher, to dominate or even violate the other by exercising my freedom, the teacher does not act as I do. She is no reflection of me. To listen to a teacher is to discover an otherness that is not HOSTILE to me, not issuing from a freedom just like mine but opposed to mine. The teacher's authority is not due to her will or to her mode of being that is prior to her speaking. Rather, her authority is produced in speaking. In revealing herself to me, she becomes infinitely other, and not simply ag-

---

[2] Levinas TI 173/199   But he can struggle to oppose me, which is to say oppose to the force that strikes him, not a force of resistance but the *unforeseeableness* itself of his reaction. He opposes me thus not with a bigger force—an appraisable energy that as a result presents itself as if it made up part of a whole—but the very transcendence of his being in relation to that whole; not some superlative of power, but precisely the infinity of his transcendence. This infinite, stronger than murder, resists us already in his face, is his face, is the original *expression*, is the first word: "You shall not murder." The infinite paralyzes power by its infinite resistance to murder, which tough and insurmountable, shines in the face of the other person, in the total nudity of his eyes, without defense, in the nudity of the absolute openness of the Transcendent. Here, there is a relation not with a very large resistance, but with something absolutely *Other*: the resistance of that which has no resistance—ethical resistance.

onistically opposed to me. My freedom seems ARBITRARY because all of my efforts to interpret my teacher fall short. My interpretations are arbitrary. Were the teacher just like me, different only because of another agenda of goals, concepts, experiences, and so on, then we would be the same kind of interpreters, and the infinite of exteriority would collapse (AT ONCE PASSED THROUGH). I need to listen because the other person is not just like me, and her speaking to me reveals an authority that exceeds my freedom not by a counterfreedom, but in a radically other way.

2e) His alterity shows itself in a mastery that does not conquer but teaches. Teaching is not a species of a genus called domination, a hegemony that is played in the midst of a totality, but is the presence of the infinite making a break-in to the closed circle of totality.

My interlocutor's otherness displays itself in teaching. The violence of force and of seduction, on the one hand, is CONQUEST, a mode of DOMINATION. DOMINATION is a superior force exercised on a common plane, suppressing one by the other. Those relations form a Hegelian or post-Hegelian kind of totality. No one can gain without the other losing. And signs circulate without recourse to those who give them, for both the dominant term and the dominated term in the finite relation are signified the same way. For Levinas' pragmatics, the BREAK-IN TO THE CLOSED CIRCLE OF TOTALITY is the transcendence of the other speaker, the one who gives signs while retaining authority over the signs, the other person who can challenge my interpretations of her signs, the teaching of an exteriority that cannot be encompassed, an other infinitely requiring response. Listening, therefore, not only places me in question, but places my freedom in question precisely through the teacher showing herself as not a contrary freedom or power. In listening I can become responsible because the infinite breaks into the circle of meaning I can manage for myself. I listen to learn how to respond for what I cannot think and assimilate for myself.

B. ASYMMETRY

As profound as changing the scene of ethics to this conversational situation, and as disorienting as it is there to find listening (and not speaking) as the origin of responsibility, still more surprising and significant for this whole book is the discovery that the relations in the conversation are asymmetrical—that responsibility is not achieved in what pragmatics would call turn-taking, but that the listener position is simply never overcome. Rather, the indexicality of positions, the way mine is marked as mine, is not interchangeable. My responsibility to listen to the other speak is not reflected in the same kind of responsibility by the other person. The other's authority in speaking to me is not reflected in a similar authority in my speaking. In each position, I find myself more responsible than the other. In later chapters we will see a wide range of asymmetries, of responsibilities that even when shared rest more on me or on us. But here we need to begin with the asymmetry of listening to the other speak.

3a) Levinas TI 74–75/101   He who speaks to me and through the words puts himself forward, retains the fundamental foreignness of the other person who judges me; our relations are never reversible.

The relation of being spoken to, of attending the other, comes THROUGH WORDS, but also shows me a speaker. And while the words may be familiar to me, may be my own words, the other speaking RETAINS THE FUNDAMENTAL FOREIGN-NESS. He never loses his difference, his incomprehensibility. That otherness is not a mere difference, but is rather JUDGING ME. It is not that my teacher lords it over me, dominating and violating me, but rather that the relation is one in which as listener I am called into question. My effort to know this other person fails, and I fall under judgment. Listening encounters this exteriority, this difference, without being able to overcome it—indeed, listening is the performance that struggles with that otherness. And the key point: these relations ARE NEVER REVERSIBLE. As we take turns, I do not myself become the one who retains my otherness and judge the other by speaking. What I can responsibly do in speaking will concern us in the next chapter, and elsewhere. But I cannot ascend to the position of height in relation to the other person whom I face. I am always returned to this listener position.

3b)   This supremacy posits him in himself, outside my knowing, and it is by relation to this absolute that the *given* takes on a meaning. The "communication" of ideas, the reciprocity of dialogue, already hide the profound essence of language. It resides in the irreversibility of the relation between Me and the Other, in the Mastery of the Master coinciding with his position as Other and as exterior.

I discover that my responsibility arises in relation to another and cannot arise in my relation to myself, in any *in itself*; in conversation only the other IS POSITED IN HIMSELF. The extreme objectivity, that something would be what it is independent of my experience of it, even when I am not aware of it—or could not ever be aware of it—is posited for my interlocutor. In the face to face, he is not like me, not fundamentally in relation to me, because he shows his authority in speaking, an authority that allows him to absolve himself from the relation. Levinas claims that a normal interpretation of dialogue as THE "COMMUNICATION" OF IDEAS, requires that the two people be similar, even interchangeable. RECIPROCITY hides the radical exteriority of the one who speaks to me, as well as the origin of responsibility in listening. THE PROFOUND ESSENCE OF LANGUAGE lies in the extremity of the height, the ideas of the teaching and of the response of responsibility to being put in question. Language can serve to communicate reciprocally, but only because it also and more primarily exposes me to the other person's questioning, to the authority of the other person to interpret and to break with my interpretations. So Levinas claims that the essence lies IN THE IRREVERSIBILITY of the relation. The relation indexed as ME AND THE OTHER is one of him speaking and me listening.

Even when I eventually respond and speak, it will not be the river flowing uphill, but will be in response to this irreversible relation to the other person. He is not the same as me, nor assimilable to me, and he is EXTERIOR to me. This otherness and exteriority is the ontological expression of his performance as teacher, and indeed, here as MASTER. The one who questions and calls me to responsibility is not my companion, but my teacher.

3c) Language can be spoken, indeed, only if the interlocutor is the commencement of his discourse, if, consequently, he remains beyond the system, if he is not *on the same plane* as me. The interlocutor is not a Thou [*Toi*], he is a You [*Vous*]. He reveals himself in his lordship. Thus exteriority coincides with a mastery. My freedom is thus implicated by a Master who can invest it. Henceforth truth, as sovereign exercise of freedom, becomes possible.

While the other person who performs this teaching is not first other and then encountered, but in speaking produces the very transcendence both from what she says and from what I know of her; that same exteriority and mastery is not available to me. To say that language CAN BE SPOKEN ONLY on these conditions is to recognize that the dialogue or conversation performs relations that do not so much maintain transcendence as intrinsically produce it. Only when my teacher reveals her power to challenge the language that we share and the understanding her words produce in me, does she teach me. In listening to her I do not find myself on common ground, but to listen is to attend to her height, her authority over the words we use, her transcendence of my awareness. Hence, in opposition to Buber and Marcel, Levinas insists that she is NOT A THOU [*Toi*]. In the Philosophy of Dialogue, the decisive insight was that there is an intimate relation with another person who is addressed as a familiar you—a relationship that gives meaning in its direct address to and from another. Levinas here picks YOU [*Vous*] the formal form of direct address to accentuate how unequal I am with my interlocutor. She is not familiar to me, but other and exterior. And precisely because of that extreme independence from me and my efforts to know her—performed in her speaking—she is able to call me to FREEDOM. For Levinas the freedom required in ethics is not self-given, but is the freedom to respond, to be able to respond. Only a call that comes from outside my own instigation and my own reach can make me responsible. The one who questions with that transcendence of me is able to INVEST me with a responsibility that I no longer need doubt as complicit or self-serving. By questioning my freedom from beyond, the teacher calls me to the genuine freedom of responsibility. Listening, thus, sets me free, free to the infinity of exteriority, responsibility for others.

C. RECEIVING THE WORLD

Of course, we listen not only to the teacher teaching, but to the words the other person speaks. And much as the transcendence of the other person is performed in speaking to me, so the reality of the world is performed and produced in the words the other person speaks.

4a) Levinas TI 69/96   The objectivity of the object and its signification
come from language. This way for
the object to be posed as theme
which is offered envelops the act of
signifying. Not the act of referring
the thinker who fixes it to that
which is signified (which forms part
of the same system), but the act of
showing the signifier, the emitter of
the sign, an absolute alterity that,
nonetheless, speaks to him and even
thus thematizes—which is to say,
proposes a world.

While language does not create things,
it does provide for us their meaning and
the possibility of objectivity. The objectivity of the object comes from positing it as
a thing. Thus language denotes something
having a predicate: 'x' as 'y.' But Levinas
is not merely noting this almost commonplace of linguistic philosophy. Rather, he
is examining the ACT OF SIGNIFYING. For
the proposition itself about something is
OFFERED to another person. Signs do not
simply name, they name for another person. Even when the other person calls a
chair 'a chair,' this offering shows what Levinas calls THE SIGNIFIER: the
speaker, the face, the presence of transcendence. To name something, to
utter a proposition, not only displays that one who names is linked to what
is named. This reference between the namer and named is PART OF THE SAME
SYSTEM, because the namer is similar to what he names as in the thought of
it. But the face which I encounter in listening is AN ABSOLUTE ALTERITY, an
authority to contest any name or proposition. The other person speaks to
me, offering me a view of the world, making that world objective, while
retaining the authority to contest the world.

4b) Precisely that world, as proposed, as expression, has a meaning
that never is in the original, for that
very reason. For a signification to
give itself bodily (leibhaft), exhausting its being in one exhaustive appa-
rition, is an absurdity. But the non-
originality of what has a meaning is
not a lesser being, not a reference to
a reality that it imitates, that it rever-
berates, or that it symbolizes.

The world now proposed to me has
gained A MEANING THAT NEVER IS IN THE
ORIGINAL. The things do not speak, nor
do words. A speaker speaks, producing a
meaning for the world—but meaning is
neither the being of the world nor the
knowledge of the world. For Levinas, the
move to discourse, to a speaker speaking
who can reinterpret her own speech, is a
decisive break with the connection of
being and knowing. Meaning transcends
being and knowing through the speaker's authority to interpret her speech
to me. The entity cannot exhaust the meanings of a sign, for a sign is open
to meanings that exceed its original reference to some entity. The meanings
from discourse, even when referring to the world, are not LESSER BEINGS
than those mute entities of the world. Nor is the meaningful world, the spoken world, simply an IMITATION, or REVERBERATION, or even SYMBOL of the
extant world. Something new is said to me, but it is not a reflection, however
weak or clear, of the world that is.

4c) What has meaning refers to
a signifier. The sign does not signify the signifier as it signifies the

The ontological and epistemological interpretations of meaning overlook the ethical dimension: WHAT HAS MEANING RE-

signified. The signified is never completely present. Always a sign in its turn, it does not come in direct frankness.[3]

FERS TO A SIGNIFIER. The one who speaks the words is intrinsic to the meaning of those words. Signs signify the signified: words name the world, or propositions denote the state of affairs. But signs also indicate their utterer. The reference to the world, or even to other signs in that world, is a pointing which depends on the way that a signifier offers the world to another person and retains authority to interpret that offer. What is signified is itself never fully present in the sign. Indeed, Levinas now claims that a sign always indicates another sign, never simply a thing. The thing picked out by a proposition appears now as already a sign, and cannot simply appear as a thing in itself. Thus the signified is never simply there (IN DIRECT FRANKNESS).

4d) The signifier, he who emits the sign, *faces*, despite the intermediary of the sign, without proposing himself as a theme. Obviously, he may speak about himself—but then he would announce himself as signified and as a result as a sign in its turn. The other person, the signifier—showing himself in the speech in speaking of the world and not about himself, he shows himself in proposing the world, in *thematizing* it.

Beyond the double reference of the sign to the signified and to the speaker, the speaker himself FACES [*de face*]. The speaker appears across the words spoken (DESPITE THE INTERMEDIARY OF THE SIGN), but is not simply another signified (A THEME). The words say something (A THEME) about their referents, and what they speak about becomes another sign and is no longer the thing itself. But the speaker, despite a similar absence, not only is not signified in himself by the sign, but he also differs from the signifieds. Of course, HE MAY SPEAK ABOUT HIMSELF, trying to make himself a signified in need of interpretation as named or described, but he retains the authority to speak to me, and so always can withdraw the propositions he utters. On the one hand, the sign refers to a signified, itself another sign. On the other hand, it shows the speaker in the speaking, who does not become another sign or theme, but the presence that puts the sign in play. She shows herself not by speaking about herself, but by PROPOSING THE WORLD, by standing over against not only the world but also against the limitations of any particular description of it. She accompanies the sign, accentuating how language produces meaning by the interaction between two people and not first by reference to things nor even by reference to knowledge of essences. I listen to her, then to receive the world

---

[3] Levinas TI 64–65/92   To receive the given is already to receive it as taught—as an expression of the Other Person. . . . The world is offered in the language of the other person; it is borne by propositions. The other person is the principle of the phenomenon. The phenomenon is not deduced from him; one does not rediscover him by returning from the sign the thing would be to the interlocutor giving this sign, in a movement analogous to the course that would lead from the appearance to things in themselves. For the deduction is a mode of thinking that applies to objects already given. The interlocutor cannot be deduced, because the relationship between him and me is presupposed by every proof.

as gift, as given by the one who can teach me. That objective world, that world endowed with meaning becomes mine only in this context where my teacher is able to suspend it or revoke both that world and my claim to it. In the face to face, I listen to receive the words, but receive them only from the other person, not as my own possession nor from a discourse of things themselves.

D. The Face and Consciousness

When I listen, in order to learn from the other person, do I not also learn something? If I receive the world through her words, then do I not become conscious, do I not then know something new? Levinas writes from a context of phenomenological analysis, a context that prizes the analysis of how and what we are conscious of. If listening is about transcending consciousness, then how is this achieved within consciousness? How can a phenomenologist make the key 'experience' one that breaks with consciousness— except by first marking this breaking and then exploring how we become aware of the breaking—without remaining secure against this breaking again? A listening is needed that does not listen only once, but must remain attentive, still listening.

We turn now to a description of the way the teacher appears without becoming an appearance, without becoming part of my consciousness, a description not of what THE FACE is, but what it does.

5) Levinas TI 21/50–51 The way that the Other presents itself, exceeding *the idea of the Other in me,* we call it, in effect, face. This *mode* does not consist of figuring some theme under my gaze, as spreading out some collection of qualities forming an image. The face of the Other Person, overflowing the plastic image which it leaves me, destroys at any moment the idea to my measure and to the measure of its *ideatum,* the adequate idea. It does not show itself by these qualities, but kath' auto. It *expresses itself.*[4]

Levinas stipulates the definition as a WAY of presenting itself. This sounds like straightforward phenomenology, which so often was an analysis of different ways of presentation to my consciousness. But here it is a way of exceeding what I think, and its presence does not become presence in my consciousness. The other person exceeds THE IDEA OF THE OTHER IN ME. How can something both present itself and exceed my idea of it? The other person will have to offer not a better image or idea than I have heretofore held, but will have rather, to break or DESTROY any idea

[4]Levinas TI 37/65–66 *The absolute experience is not disclosure but revelation*: a coincidence of the expressed and the one who expresses, a showing, that is thereby the privileged one of the Other Person, showing a face beyond its form. Form incessantly betraying its manifestation—congealing in plastic form since it is adequate to the Same, alienates the exteriority of the Other. The face is a living presence. It is expression. The life of expression consists in undoing its form, where the entity is exposed like a theme, dissimulating itself by the same. The face speaks. The showing of the face is already discourse.

or image I have of the other. More, in facing me, the other person also must break with the image IT LEAVES ME. She will not only challenge my interpretation, but also disrupt the phenomenon she herself gives me. Hence, the face is not the removal of a mask to reveal a true face, but a way of disturbing the images, facing me and defacing the images. Indeed, the being put in question extends not only to the images I made and the ones she gave me, but even the correlation between my idea of her (TO MY MEASURE) and she as she would be presented in an idea (TO THE MEASURE OF ITS *IDEATUM*). For myself, I can judge my ideas, even when they fall short of true knowledge or adequacy. The other person contests not only my knowledge (as I might have done by myself), but even my criterion of adequacy. For my part, I could not know the depth of the inadequacy of my idea of the other person. Only the other person can teach me that, can show me my fundamental inability to know her. Hence, the face is not present and DOES NOT SHOW ITSELF BY THE QUALITIES that make it an image. Contrary to a common view, what Levinas calls the face is not the physiognomy of the other, as some image of God, or image of humanity, but rather an expression that is not present in any image, is present as the breaking with images. Thus, its expression is not in an image, but is EXPRESSION ITSELF, the expressing itself.

6a) Levinas TI 73–74/100–101 But what can it mean: the teacher who summons attention overflows consciousness? How is the teacher outside the consciousness that he teaches?

The ethics of responsibility occurs in a relation to otherness not modeled on presence in consciousness but on exceeding consciousness. The contrast of models is aided by a pun in French: for *conscience* means both consciousness and moral conscience. Moral conscience will appear as the welcoming of the speaking face. This teacher must both SUMMON ATTENTION, that is, call for my consciousness, and OVERFLOW my consciousness. The overflow means that my consciousness cannot contain the teacher: what I can think or represent to myself is inadequate for the activities of interpreting his signs. This overflow is a way for the teacher to remain OUTSIDE my consciousness—because discourse is between two separated terms. But if he calls me to think, calls me to answer, then I must also think about him. How can he teach me and remain independent from me, other than me?

6b) He is not exterior to it like the contents of thought are exterior to the thought that thinks them. The exteriority of the contents of thought, in relation with the thought that thinks them, is assumed by the thought and so does not *overflow* consciousness. Nothing which thought touches can overflow it. Everything is assumed freely. *Nothing, except the judge judging freedom of thought itself.*

Listening to a teacher contrasts to knowing something, in a way parallel to the contrast between the sign showing the speaker and referring to its signified. Our concern here is precisely the relation to consciousness in listening to the teacher. Because thought acts to ASSUME what comes to it from outside, thought can control the contents of consciousness. My experience is never passive simply, but always reflects my freedom of accepting or receiving what started out as external to me. Thought itself legitimates this quasi-exteriority. Thus, though it may in some way be unknowable, thinkable exteriority is not an OVERFLOWING of my power to think. Indeed, Levinas claims extreme reach for the power of thinking: nothing that thought touches or concerns can overwhelm it. Hence, thought is sovereign, ASSUMING FREELY its own contents and acting as a self-controlling gatekeeper of consciousness. But this freedom, THE FREEDOM OF THOUGHT ITSELF, is subject to judgment and to question when I listen to the other speaking—not from myself but from THE JUDGE JUDGING, from the other person who can judge me. Consciousness pretends to a self-authorizing freedom, governing its own thoughts and even the limits of its thoughts—but another person can ask me why, can question my authority, the authority of consciousness. For the task of this book, this incapacity of consciousness to question itself and to accede to exteriority points away from a phenomenology to a study of discourse. We can study responsibility in the pragmatics of language and of other signs, because we perform responsibility in using signs with other people. Levinas has to invoke another person who can pass judgment on my freedom of thought in order to capture the relation of responsibility—he has to move beyond a phenomenology of consciousness to a pragmatics.

6c) The presence of the Teacher who gives a meaning to phenomena and permits them to be thematized by his word does not offer himself to an objective knowledge. He is in society with me, by his presence.

Unlike the licensed exteriority of what I cannot fully think, licensed by my own thinking, the exteriority of the teacher questions my licensing—and never accedes to my efforts to think her. The teacher speaks about the world, thematizing and objectifying it through signs, but she is not accessible in the same way: the teacher's actions are not available, even in a limited and licensed way for my thought—because the teacher accompanies her word (THE PRESENCE OF THE TEACHER), and so contests and overflows my interpretations, even my thoughts about the teacher. Her speech produces A SOCIETY WITH ME, a relation not reducible to the thematics of consciousness—or even the network of signs. It is a society where pacific relations occur, where the other person retains difference from me not by power but by right.

6d) . . . If we call moral conscience a situation where my freedom is put in question, the association or the welcome of the Other Person is the moral conscience.[5]

What we have explored as listening and being put in question now is defined simply as THE MORAL CONSCIENCE [*CONSCIENCE MORALE*]. Listening now becomes this WELCOME OF THE OTHER PER-

[5] Levinas TI 56/84 Moral conscience welcomes the other person. It is the revelation of a resistance to my powers which is not placed in check as a larger force, but which puts in question the naive right of my powers, my glorious spontaneity of living. Morality begins when freedom, in place of justifying itself by itself, feels itself to be arbitrary and violent.

SON as the one who will question and call me to respond. We listen to welcome the teaching and the other person. Much as listening had been the investiture by the other of my ability to respond, now listening is the advent of moral conscience. We then have seen consciousness not only checked by the other person, but more, transformed into a mode that is moral.

6e) The originality of that situation is not only in its formal antithesis in relation to the cognitive consciousness. The putting in question of oneself is at once more severe the more rigorously the self checks itself. This receding of the goal at the rate one approaches is the life of moral conscience. The increase of exigencies that I have in relation to myself aggravates the judgment bearing upon me, increasing my responsibility.

Conscience contrasts with consciousness not simply FORMALLY, but as two kinds of knowing—a tension that governs much of Levinas' work. One assimilates what is other; the other welcomes the other person as remaining other. One exercises freedom; the other has its freedom put in question. These two are linked in one of the central features of responsibility: its spiral, indeed, its infinition. The expansion of the self's control in consciousness, the RIGOR of the autonomy of the thinker, produces greater criticism and greater responsibility when now questioned (THE SELF CHECKS ITSELF). The relation between knowing and speaking is more complex than we might suppose. It is not a matter of one or the other. The moral conscience is not a mode of nonconsciousness. A teacher directs me toward knowing, committing me to expand my consciousness—and at the same time that teacher subverts this activity, questioning me. The more I try, directed to control myself and to exercise freedom, the more I am subject to moral conscience, to a severe JUDGMENT UPON ME. To try to become more responsive is to become more questioned and to gain more responsibilities. To try to become more aware of my obligations is to become more aware of the limits of my awareness—and obliged by those further limits. This spiral is neither a simple sequence of more and more to do, nor is it the paradoxical failure of thought to catch up to its thinking. Rather, it indicts the freedom in thinking—an indictment delivered by another person. Even these familiar paradoxes require another person to gain their ethical valence: and even the morality of infinite duties is bound up with the development of thinking and my own agency. This specific spiral points in the direction of the ethical justification of ethical theory—and to its critique.

6f) It is in this very concrete sense that the judgment that bears upon me is never assumed by me. This impossibility to assume is the very life—the essence—of that moral conscience. My freedom does not have the last word. I am not alone.

The issue, moreover, is my lack of control or authority. For I can neither originate (author) nor legitimate (authorize) the judgment upon me, the judgment that calls into question my authority. To listen is not to accept what the other person says. It is to be subverted as speaker, to be denied the privilege that consciousness desires: to be author. While thinking governs itself, listening is the impossibility of controlling what the other person will say. To be put in question, to have my freedom of thought put under judgment, is something I can never do for myself, nor even allow or accept. THIS IMPOSSIBILITY TO ASSUME is the response of responsibility. Another person's action upon me which I cannot even accept or reject is required for me to be called to respond, to become accountable. To listen is to find myself bound to the other person's authority. The other person asks me, "Why?" Emerging from this call to speak, my thinking is never self-sufficient, despite its desire to be self-authenticating. My freedom cannot conclude a conversation (NOT THE LAST WORD), because the other person can always object. I, and this also means the "I" of consciousness, AM NOT ALONE—because the teacher is always questioning me. Responsibility precedes and challenges thought—and it calls for it as well.

E. APOLOGY

As the other person's call to me requires my consciousness, so it summons me to respond, indeed, to speak back. We listen not only to have our thought corrected, or even to become responsible, but finally for this chapter, to be summoned to speak. This summons calls me to justify myself. A question is raised not when no answer is tolerated, but when an answer is called for. To be put in question is also to be called to apologize, to justify myself. In the next chapters my position as writer, as judge, as speaker will each be explored, but our conclusion of the interpretation of Why Listen discovers a need to listen in order to be able to explain myself.

7a) Levinas TI 10/40 Discourse, from the very fact that it maintains the distance between me and the Other Person, the radical separation that prevents the reconstitution of the totality, and which is alleged in transcendence, cannot renounce the egoism of its existence.

Discourse is constituted by maintaining the RADICAL SEPARATION BETWEEN ME AND THE OTHER PERSON—the unbridgeable gap or spacing between me as listener and the other as speaker. The separation is ALLEGED in the transcendence of the interlocutor, and is contrasted to a collapse in THE RECONSTITUTION OF TOTALITY—the power of an I to assimilate what is not other enough. The other speaking to me, however, punctures the totality of immanence controlled by me. Discourse, however, involves not only the other person, but also my listening and responding. My efforts to think, to know, to represent, and then to speak, all involve a certain presence of my ego, indeed, an EGOISM. Listening and responding are not simply self-renunciation. Ethics requires not the disappearance of myself, or even of my interests, but rather the conversion of these under the questioning and instruction by the other person.

7b) But the very fact of finding oneself in a discourse consists in recognizing in the other person *a right* over that egoism and thus, in justifying oneself. The apology where the 'I' at once affirms itself and inclines itself before the transcendent is the essence of discourse. The goodness to which discourse leads (as we will see much further) and where it demands a meaning does not lose this apologetic moment.

But if the struggle to authorize myself as speaker is not canceled, it is disrupted and that disruption emerges from the pragmatics of listening (FROM THE VERY FACT OF FINDING ONESELF IN A DISCOURSE). To be in conversation, listening to another person, is to recognize the claim of the other person upon me, and so I respond by attempting to JUSTIFY myself. Because I am vulnerable to the other person's teaching, I respond by apology, explaining myself. The performance of apology is double: AFFIRMING myself and INCLINING myself before the other person. My response is constructed through this double gesture: I assert myself as speaker and I defer to the other person, the one who challenged me and still calls me into question. Levinas focuses not on what I say, but on the performance that is neither an assertion nor self-negation. Called to speak, I respond. I speak as I, but to another, to one who can criticize me. THE ESSENCE OF DISCOURSE is bound up with this interpersonal performance—a responsive, interpretative giving of signs to an interpreter recognized as authoritative. Discourse does not end in my first response, but rather leads into society, into social institutions and beyond (where a stable MEANING can be given to the signs)—but this APOLOGETIC MOMENT is never lost. The double-gesture of my response, the way it is inclined before the other person, remains as a vulnerability in my speaking. Listening is not a turn that is over when I speak, but pervades and solicits what I say.

Ethics begins with a listening, and even when I speak I am responsible because my speech is interrupted and structured by my listening for the other to teach me. The excess of that responsibility is distributed over the range of pragmatic actions, always calling me to answer. Ethics here is reoriented, looking toward the pragmatic meaning that binds me to the other person, recontextualizing the role of reasoning and consciousness within the ethical exigency to listen, to depend on the other's teaching. Because we become able to respond in listening, because we are given the world even as we are put in question, because our consciousness becomes conscience, our freedom questioned can now become responsible, listening is the beginning of responsibility and at the same time the beginning of ethics.

SUGGESTED READINGS

1   Handelman, Susan. "Crossing and Recrossing the Void: A Letter to Gene." In *Reviewing the Covenant*, ed. Peter Ochs, 173–200. Albany: SUNY, 2000.

2   Peperzak, Adriaan. *To the Other*, 61–65. West Lafayette, Ind.: Purdue University Press, 1993.
5   Wyschogrod, Edith. *Emmanuel Levinas: The Problem of Ethical Metaphysics*, 82–94. Hague: Martinus Nijhoff, 1974.

CHAPTER 2

Why Speak?

SINCE RESPONSIBILITY arises in paying attention to the other person, why we should speak seems obscure. Either I seem bound to keep silent in order to maintain the other as teacher, or if I speak I seem to usurp the role of teacher—and so cease to respond. What is the ethical responsibility to speak? Is there an ethical way of speaking, a way of saying something to another person wherein I remain responsive to the other? How can speaking make me open to interruption, to the other's interpretation?

Levinas deepens his account of my speaking in his second major work, *Otherwise Than Being*, moving below an account of apology as response to an account of witness and prophecy. He emphasizes the gap between signs and signifying that guided the account of conversation in *Totality and Infinity*, turning the words THE SAYING and THE SAID into technical terms. The act of speaking is interpreted in the analyses of THE SAYING; the content, particularly the semantic content, is analyzed as THE SAID. The contrast is between what we say and the pragmatic meaning of speaking. Those pragmatics gain still greater ethical and even religious dimension.

We begin in Section A (The Saying) with a deepening of listening, to the point where it turns over into a kind of saying. The attention of listening now becomes a drawing near to another person, which signifies as welcoming the other person. In Pretext 1, Levinas distinguishes the saying as exposure to another person from a story of communication that would be intrinsically a cognitive relation to the world.

In Section B (Bodily Signifying) we explore the way I am a sign for the other, bodily. Pretext 2 opens the path, examining how sensibility is not first a mode of knowing, but is an ethical relation to another person. I approach another, risking in my body, in order to give myself bodily for the other. In Pretext 3, that risk and exposure is sharpened by a reflection on pain, and the way becoming a sign for the other exposes me not just to rebuff but even to pain and violence. Finally, in Pretext 4 the responsibility climaxes in my responsibility for persecution done by the other—my bodily signifying serves as expiation for the other's interpretation (and violation) of me. Levinas here obliquely comments on both Jewish and Christian texts about being struck by the other (Pretexts 5 and 6), focusing on my passivity. My substitution for the other, performed bodily, is subjectivity itself.

Section C explores what happens when I announce this saying in speech, when the speaker position is produced through an attempt to say to the other that I am responsible, to the point of pain, for that other. Pretext 7 examines the tension between the word "I" and the speaking itself, the way that the indexical itself is unstable. Pretext 8, however, advances the possibility that responsive speaking will require a saying of the saying, an exposing of the exposure, and not a discourse (like this one) about the saying. Through these two pretexts, moreover, we see the "I" desubstantialize, even in a profound sense disappear, fundamentally altering the scene of two people talking in a room. My responsibility depends on my not being a presence, an entity who speaks, but an openness, assigned for another and not integral in myself.

Section D then concludes the chapter with a fuller account of the saying of the saying, termed here WITNESS. In a surprising move, we discover that responsibility has no evidence, no recourse to a direction that came from God or from the otherness of the other, but appears first in the speaking of my own voice—an announcement termed prophecy (Pretext 9). Levinas discerns in the sincerity of speaking the responsibility to announce that I am a sign for the other person. I speak to witness: to announce my responsibility for others to others.

A. The Saying

The listener position is redeveloped here. Responsibility now grows from that of the ethical need to respond to the other, into a need to become responsible for the other. Listening becomes attending as opening for the other person's sake. That performance of responsibility now is called THE SAYING. Still in a sequence, coming as a response, saying is an openness to the other that is not merely a condition of my responsibility, but is itself a giving of a sign: a way of signifying that I am responsible for the other.

1a) Levinas OB 61–62/48 To Say is to draw near to the neighbor [*approcher le prochain*], "to bring signifying" to him. This is not exhausted in "presenting meanings," inscribed as tales in the Said. Bringing signifying to the other, before all objectification, the Saying proper to speaking—is not handing over signs.

Levinas defines *the saying* most often as nearing the neighbor, playing on the sense of nearness, and coming into nearness. Nearness (others translate it as *proximity*) itself is a key term for his later work, but here we can limit our discussion to the ethical import of physical nearness. It is not contact itself but the limitation upon my actions exercised by the space next to a person. The pragmatic relations in my nearness to another person are complex. The responsibility found in the face of the other person now becomes located in this nearness. Hence nearness signifies—but here the BRINGING SIGNIFYING to the other person is itself the drawing near. To say, therefore, is not to utter words to the person near me. The context is a relation with another person, a neighbor. I bring before the other not some information or chosen meanings but the very vulnerability of myself performed in signifying. Saying, as the key action in semiosis, precedes signs and their meanings. But what is this precedence? To speak in this responsive way is to implicate myself in speaking, to offer signifying, the way of being for another, and not the signs themselves.

1b) This "handing over signs" would come down to a prior representation of these signs, as if speaking consisted of translating from thought into words and as a result in having been, previously, *for oneself* and *at home with oneself* like a substantial consistency. The relation to the other person thus is extended as a form of intentionality, starting from a posited subject, in itself and for itself, disposed to play, sheltered from all evil and measuring by thought the being disclosed as the field of that game.

If saying were the HANDING OVER of signs already imbued with meaning, then the signs would have had their meanings, and speaking would be a TRANSLATION from their prior meanings (my thoughts) into words. The meanings would already exist for a subject, would have a FOR ONE-SELF AND [AN] AT HOME, would belong in me. I would, like a bank, have many thoughts and meanings in me, ready to be translated outside myself. This would make me A SUBJECT—and my activity of saying would be an accident to my existence. Hence I could play the game of talking, but I need never risk myself. My speaking would be a kind of play in which I was SHELTERED FROM ALL EVIL because my thoughts would already exist, independent from what I say, independent from my activity of speaking with another person. My possession of already formed meanings (thoughts) allows me the self-possession to stand apart from what I say, and so to reside outside my speaking, able to MEASURE BY THOUGHT the other person and the other person's words. Can speaking be anything besides this mere play from a safe home?

1c) Saying is communication, of course, but as condition of all communication, as exposure. Communication cannot be reduced to the phenomenon of truth and of the manifestation of truth conceived as a combination of psychological elements: thought in an I—will or intention of making this thought pass into an other I—message by a sign designating that thought—perception of that sign by the other I—deciphering of that sign.

Communication occurs through the EX-POSURE of saying. The risk of myself in nearing the neighbor is the vulnerability of opening myself to her. To say is to make myself exposed. Saying serves as a condition of communication because the exposure to another person is needed even for the exchange of information. The alternate view, that communication is THE MANIFESTATION OF TRUTH, holds that the truth is propositional and is already known before we speak. Such a view reduces the action of saying to encoding a message—and thereby loses sight of the ethical responsibility in giving signs to another person. Levinas rehearses a PSYCHOLOGICAL account of communication as showing what we know to another person: first I have the thought, then I WILL another to have it. Then I use a sign to DESIGNATE the thought. Then the other person PERCEIVES my sign. Then he DECIPHERS it. This account ignores the way that a sign signifies from me to another. The model is of thought determining will, and of the receiver acting similarly (perception leading back into concept). For televisions, radios, even fax machines this works fine—but for human communication and the people who watch, listen, read, this model reduces the actions and their ethical weight.

1d) The elements of this mosaic are already placed in the prior exposure of me to the other, in the non-indifference to the Other, which is not a simple "intention to send a message." The ethical meaning of such exposure to Another Person, which the intention of making signs—and even of the signifying of the sign—presupposed, is now visible. The plot of nearness and of communication is not a modality of knowledge. The unbolting of communication—irreducible to the circulation of information that presupposes it—is accomplished in the Saying. It is not due to the contents inscribed in the Said and transmitted for interpretation and decoding done by the Other. It is in the risky uncovering of the self, in the sincerity, in the rupture of interiority and the abandoning of all shelter, in the exposure to the trauma, in vulnerability.

This psychological sequence, here called a MOSAIC to accentuate the mere juxtaposition of the elements, however, has as its PRIOR context, as its very condition, an exposure of me to the other. An opening to another person is PRESUPPOSED in both the INTENTION OF MAKING SIGNS and in the SIGNIFYING OF THE SIGN. Both the way signs signify and the activity of giving signs depend upon the prior exposure to ANOTHER PERSON. This relation is what Levinas will call ethical and gives an ETHICAL MEANING to speaking. In this book we have not yet seen this fully, but Levinas' claim depends on separating communication from knowing. This saying is the 'more' of communication, more than knowledge and THE CIRCULATION OF INFORMATION. Were communication only what is said, we could contain this kind of ethics. Semantics and its determinations are incomplete. But in pragmatics we see a

risk that exceeds our normal activities—even our normal interpretation of the actions included under pragmatics. To communicate requires, according to Levinas, that we ABANDON ALL SHELTER and expose ourselves TO TRAUMA. It hardly seems likely that saying hello on the street or good-bye on the phone is so risky. Levinas magnifies and isolates the dimension of risk precisely because even a merely information-exchanged kind of communication requires that risk. Exposure will have to be utter exposure, if the exposure in Hello or Good-Bye is to appear as taking any risk at all. Were we secure, underneath it all, or when all was said and done, then we would undercut the very vulnerability and openness that characterizes responsibility. The infinite nature of the liability, of the command to respond, the ineluctability of my responsibility requires a risk which is extreme.

B. BODILY SIGNIFYING

In *Totality and Infinity*, Levinas approached subjectivity as a being at home with oneself, focusing on the joie de vivre of material existence. It served as the self's prior withdrawal that was later inverted into ethics in listening and responding. Levinas does not abandon such inversions and conversions in his later thought, but he now interprets subjectivity and even sensibility as themselves modes of signifying. My body becomes a sign in my relation to another person. This requires an interpretation of corporeality that focuses on how the body itself is first not for itself but for the other person. To 'have' a human body, according to Levinas, is to be for other people's bodily needs. Nurturing, sheltering, nursing, even bearing a child all define the self's 'being in' a body. The saying of drawing near depends on a saying that is my bodily signifying for another person. These relations define not only the being of my body but also determine a pragmatic interpretation of perception, as sensations are not simply the radio reception of coded messages, but precisely an opening to another's bodily nearness, a kind of attending as already for an other.

2a) Levinas OB 97/77 Corporeality of the body proper signifies, like sensibility itself, a knot or an untying of being, but it also must contain a passage to the physio-chemical-physiological signification of the body. Sensibility as nearness, as signification, as one for the other certainly leads it toward that signification.

It is not enough to see that in drawing near to another person I become a being for another, open to this other person. Rather, Levinas also must account for the physicality of the BODY that draws near, much as he accounted for the objectivity of the object from the donation of signs. This is an ethics of bodily beings, not of pure wills or angelic beings. But how do bodies say or signify in the specific sense of responding for others? Levinas discovers that our bodies are not simply entities, even neurologically attuned entities. Rather, our corporeality involves A KNOT OR AN UNTYING OF BEING—there is something other than the realm of manifestation and intelligibility. Levinas offers a way to interpret SENSIBILITY not as simply a reception of knowledge. When sensibility itself is a kind of signifying, an opening to others, even if involuntary, then sensibility becomes a vulnerability to other people. The way for sensibility to be a saying, a one-for-the-other, is in NEARNESS. Sensibility, therefore, is modeled not on seeing an object nor on touching the impenetrable desk or wall, but is rather interpreted as a coming close to another person, close enough to touch and to be touched, even wounded. To interpret this ability to sense another person as a way of being for this other LEADS TOWARD the way that the body itself signifies.

2b)   It signifies in the *giving* when the *giving* offers not the overflowing of the overflow but the bread taken from one's mouth. A signification which signifies, as a result, in nurturing, in clothing, in housing—the maternal relations where matter shows itself only in its materiality.

My body can signify when I materially give. It must be a material relation with others, a giving from my own body, my own food, for the body of another person—my clothes, my bed, my physical reality given for the other person's material needs. This is a signifying that remains immanent, MATERIAL—using no signs other than my own body. The BREAD TAKEN FROM MY MOUTH does not signify by referring to me or to the other. In giving that bread to another I signify that my body is for the other person. Levinas calls these relations MATERNAL to accentuate the etymological play on material and mother, but also to invoke the pregnant relation of bearing, where the mother's body literally provides from itself for the fetus' body. Such giving is not the OVERFLOWING, when I have plenty. Rather, the finitude of materiality means I will now lack what I give to the other person. But this very expense of my own material needs is what makes ethics possible: because it is disinterested, even altruistic.

2c) The subject called incarnate is not the result of a materialization, of an entry into space and into relations of contact and money that a consciousness would have accomplished—which is to say, a consciousness of self, warned against any attack and previously nonspatial.

Levinas marks out the distance of this theory of self as a bodily sign from a tradition that saw the self as primarily CONSCIOUSNESS, somehow bound to the alienating limitations of matter. Were a subject to be first self-conscious and then related to others, it would also relate to its body as only an occasion for relations, including communication. But the subject would be secure as long as it could abstract from material conditions in its own working. Hence, for Levinas incarnation is not the indwelling of prior spirit or even of consciousness in a body. There is no way for a person to be NONSPATIAL. Space and materiality are not limiting conditions for signifying, but produced in the signifying of my body.

2d) This is because subjectivity is sensibility, exposure to others, vulnerability and responsibility in the nearness of others, the one-for-the-other, which is to say, signification and because matter is the very place of the for-the-other, the way that signification signifies before showing itself as a Said in the system of synchrony—in the linguistic system. That the subject is flesh and blood, a man who is hungry and who eats, entrails in a skin and, thus liable to give the bread from his mouth, or to give his skin.

It is not despite the materiality of my body that I signify and use signs, but because of it. I am not the referent of a term in A LINGUISTIC SYSTEM, not a topic to be talked about. Instead, I am a sign, vulnerable to those I come near, vulnerable in my body. The sequence of terms runs from SUBJECTIVITY (a center or nexus of consciousness and will) to SENSIBILITY (receptivity of a material body) to EXPOSURE to others (the way of signifying, to risk oneself in sensing), to VULNERABILITY (that I can be hurt bodily, in drawing near to the other person), to RESPONSIBILITY and NEARNESS (that my body draws near other people becoming liable, answerable for their conditions), which is SIGNIFICATION itself (to be for another). Subjectivity, therefore, is not a question of consciousness or the latent consciousness of sensation, but a bodily signifying of my vulnerability to another's words, or glance, or blows. A subject is material, vulnerable, and for the other—and only what is FLESH AND BLOOD, someone who knows lack and pain, someone who eats, can GIVE as response. For Levinas there is no ethics without bodies that know hunger, that need food, shelter, comfort. The giving of oneself, therefore, that characterizes the risk in communication requires a material body that can suffer in the giving. TO GIVE HIS SKIN is, like a mother nursing, to give myself for the other person's sake.

2e) Signification is thus thought from the one-for-the-other of sensibility and not from the system of terms which are simultaneous in a language for one who speaks—and in that very simultaneity is precisely only the situation of the one who speaks. . . .

Levinas conceives of signification from SENSIBILITY, from the materiality of my bodily being for another person and not from THE SYSTEM OF TERMS, of signs. Language will be derivative from sensibility. Indeed, only someone speaking, choosing words from an available pool, following rules of usage, and so on, can imagine that there is a field where signs stand available with fixed meanings. Prior to this set of fixed meanings is the giving, the saying in which I expose myself as materially vulnerable to another person's use of me. A sign cannot govern its interpretation, and to give myself in my body as a sign for the other is to not have control of how I will be treated. My choice in this book of general semiotics and not philosophy of language for organon of this ethics arises here in the signifying before systematically determined signs, and therefore before words, in the existential signifying where the I becomes a sign for the other. While my topics are usually linguistic performances and responsibilities, the more profound issue concerns how linguistic pragmatics are rooted in this existential pragmatics. My exposure as sign for the other lies behind signification and any system of signs. We will now explore this exposure ever deeper. Moving from the attention to the teacher's teaching, we came to the responsibility in drawing bodily near, but that exposure will lead here to pain itself as significant.

3a) Levinas OB 64–65/50 Saying, the most passive passivity, cannot be separated from patience and from pain; even if it finds refuge in the Said in rediscovering, starting from a wound, the caress where pain arises, and from there rediscovering contact and then the knowing of a hardness and of a softness, of a warm and of a cold, and from there, thematization.

The risk to myself in exposing myself as sign for the other person is not merely my bodily presence, but requires real bodily vulnerability: PAIN. The lack of control over my own signs, and hence over my own body as sign, occurs passively—not through a willing or a decision of my mind, but in the patience of not just being bodily but also being bodily for others. Much of *Otherwise Than Being* examines this passivity that makes the body itself responsible for others. The opposition of the saying and the said requires attention to the passivity of saying because this signifying is not a voluntary, deliberate choice but occurs rather in THE MOST PASSIVE PASSIVITY. Such bodily passivity is bound to PAIN. Levinas here produces a narrative of how pain is contained and transformed in thought. His point is not that pain can be overcome but that the originary signifying of my body animates and conditions the process of sensation and of 'having a perception.' Hence, a perception starts in the vulnerability that accompanies a WOUND, but we can recover from that vulnerability through a soothing CARESS to an interpretation of CONTACT with its secondary qualities (HARD, SOFT, WARM, COLD), culminating in a presentation of sensation. This sequence of fixing meaning in the said leads the wound into conceptual terms, but Levinas has thus shown the genesis of ideas of perceptions from the uncontrollable passivity of bodily pain.

3b) By itself, the Saying is the meaning of patience and of pain; by the Saying suffering signifies as a kind of *giving*, even if the price of signification is that the subject runs the risk of suffering without reason. For if the subject did not run that risk, the pain would lose its very painfulness.

The original wounding of pain also means or takes a MEANING not as a simple violation of my integrity, but rather as a SAYING. Saying arises in a lack of defense, indeed, in the RISK of being hurt by the other person. My bodily exposure itself is a kind of GIVING, open to suffering for the other person's sake, going hungry so the other can eat. To speak follows upon this coming near enough the other to be hurt, and indeed, risks that my approach will produce nothing. That I am sign for the other need not mean that the other person will find me significant and recognize my exposure as meaningful. A sign's possibility to be pointless or meaningless appears in the exposure of my body to pain from the other person. To give bodily is not to be sure of suffering reasonably. The other person may not interpret this gift within canons of reason or custom. Vulnerability requires the opportunity for the other to cause me to suffer WITHOUT REASON. Bodily risk is what makes pain truly pain—that it is uncontrollable, beyond any measure that I can negotiate. To risk such pain in approaching another person in order to be bodily for the other person is the saying wherein I become a sign.

3c) The signification as one-for-the-other, without the assumption of the other by the one, in *passivity* presupposes the possibility of pure meaninglessness [*non-sens*] invading and threatening signification. Without this madness at the edge of reason, the *one* would again become master and at the heart of its passion would recommence *essence*. Ambiguous adversity of pain. The *for-the-other* (or the meaning) goes to the point of being *by-the-other*, to the point of suffering by a thorn which burns in the flesh, but for *nothing*. Only thus is the *for-the-other*—passivity more passive than all passivity, the emphasis of meaning—protected from the *for-itself*.

But just as this painful vulnerability is the risk of saying, so the implications for all signification are poignant. Being for the other does not require an ASSUMPTION OF THE OTHER—my vulnerability does not stake a claim to the other person, least of all to a reciprocal need for the other to be willing to suffer for me. This is the asymmetry of saying, of giving signs in response to the other person. In this bodily sphere we can see the materiality of asymmetry more dramatically. The risk of pain, of suffering without reason, means that signifying includes THE POSSIBILITY OF PURE MEANINGLESSNESS [*NON-SENS*]. Bodily these are the wounds I cannot control;

in a linguistic sphere it means that I cannot control how someone takes up my signs—that this possibility of reducing what I say to nonsense is part of speaking. Exposure to the other is MADNESS, incoherence where reason ends—because without accepting this possibility of utter defeat (not merely disagreement, but rather denigration) I must refrain from risking the loss of control of the meanings of my words. This wish to retain control belongs to a theory of signifying modeled on encoded messages. We speak to expose ourselves, not to exchange thoughts of ESSENCES—fixed meanings burdened by sounds. Speaking requires a moment when I act not for myself, not as a being that is first constituted for itself and only thereafter communicates. That moment is a vulnerability first encountered in my bodily being for an other. Signifying—for the other—must go beyond a voluntary gift to a passivity in which the body suffers BY-THE-OTHER—without any strategic or teleological purpose—FOR NOTHING. To suffer for-the-other, by-the-other, for nothing—is to be an incarnate being, giving itself, beyond what it can measure or control, to become a sign.

This exposure, however, leads beyond pain to responsibility for the actions of the other: substitution. The responsibility for the teacher's teaching now becomes the more sinister responsibility for my persecutor—but both are responsibilities for the other's interpretation of my signs.

4a) Levinas OB 141/111 Passivity whose active source is not thematizable. Passivity of the trauma, but a trauma which prevents its own representation, of a deafening trauma, cutting the thread of consciousness which should have welcomed it in its present; passivity of persecution.

My exposure to the other person is not an act of will, but a PASSIVITY, something that happens to me—but which happens not as direct object of some agent. The paying attention in listening becomes here a more radically passive opening. Levinas makes of this 'experience' of the self exposed, of the vulnerability of the "I," something whose agent is unthinkable. The event itself is a TRAUMA, but one that is so radical as to derange consciousness. There is no recollection of the time of the trauma. And as pure passivity, it happens not merely against my will, but despite my consciousness. I am assigned for another person in a way that I cannot name at a time that is unpresentable in my mind. The 'event' never happens or occurs in my thought. Such passivity occurs in PERSECUTION.

4b) But passivity deserves the epithet integral or absolute only if the persecuted is liable to answer for the persecutor. The face of the neighbor in its persecuting hatred may, and by that wickedness itself, obsess pitiably—equivocally or enigmatically without escaping, only the persecuted deprived of all reference (deprived of all recourse and all help—

Persecution effects absolute passivity when it produces LIABILITY, responsibility for the action of the persecutor. The argument links the risk of the other person interpreting my words beyond my control, to wounding my body, beyond my control, to persecuting me to the point of derangement (beyond my control!), in order to accentuate the exigency of responsibil-

and this is his uniqueness and his unique identity) is the very one to bear it. To undergo *it by* the other person is only absolute patience if that "by the other person" is already "for the other person."[1]

ity for the other person—to be answerable for the other's misinterpretation of my words, answerable with my suffering for the sake of the other's suffering, and answerable for violence against me. The AB-SOLUTE nature of this passivity is precisely that when I am liable for what is not only contrary to my will but what destroys my will, as trauma itself, then I find the element of responsibility which is only a being for the other and cannot be for itself. Levinas recovers a meaning for the persecuted's obsession, the obsession with my persecutor. The destruction of the structure of my self, the helplessness with neither ESCAPE nor the pause to think, singles me out. But when I bear responsibility for my persecutor, when I shoulder it—not from reason (because it is outrageous) nor out of will (which is exhausted)—but passively, what is undergone by the other's act now becomes a suffering for that other person. An asymmetric transformation—because I cannot transform my persecuting actions into my victim's liability. To even think such a reversal is immoral absolutely.

4c) This transfer—other than interested, otherwise than essence—is subjectivity itself. "To offer the cheek to the one who strikes and to be satiated with shame"[1] to ask for that suffering in the suffering undergone (without making the *act* intervene that would be exposing the other cheek), is not to pull out of suffering some sort of magical virtue of atonement, but in the trauma of the persecution to pass from the outrage undergone to the responsibility for the persecutor and in that sense, from suffering to expiation for the other person.

Subjectivity simply is this suffering for the other. INTEREST is suspended, ESSENCE is inadequate. Subjectivity is for the other not by will or thought, but in passivity. The assignment of responsibility, the ethical need to respond is not chosen or assumed, but happens to me, making me into a me. Suffering is not invited by an act of will (WITHOUT MAKING THE *ACT* INTERVENE), but in undergoing it is accepted or asked for without intention. Levinas quotes in the text and then cites a passage from Lamentations in a footnote.

The text is about hoping and awaiting God's salvation. The suffering is undergone in remembrance and hope of God's

5) [1] Lam. 3:30 Let him offer his cheek to the one who strikes him and let him take his fill of shame.

compassion and love. The relation to the other person is minimal, and the hope is theological. The text is implicitly in contrast with Jesus' instruction in Matthew (5:39) and Luke:

The Gospel text demands an embrace of the one who oppresses me (it comes in

6) Luke 6:29 To him who strikes you on the cheek, offer the other also; and from him who takes away

---

[1] OB 134/105   In the exposure to wounds and outrages, in the sensing of responsibility, the oneself is provoked as irreplaceable, as devoted to the other, without being able to resign, and

the context of the teaching to love our ene-   your coat do not withhold even your
mies). The issue then is joined, whether   shirt.
the vulnerability of being persecuted is to
be pursued—and whether Levinas can escape a reading that binds him to the
Christian teaching.

Levinas makes a contrast here, by interpreting the Lamentations text as
more passive, noting that it does not require turning THE OTHER CHEEK. To
accept the shame for the sake of the other is not to goad the other, nor to
shame the other. For Levinas, the Jewish text tells us to wait for God to have
mercy, while the Christian teaching asks us to try to disrupt the other person
and effect a change through an ACT—and that act, for Levinas, diminishes
the vulnerability and the suffering.

Levinas continues distinguishing the ethics of the persecuted from that of
christological sacred atonement. The transformation in the self from OUT-
RAGE in persecution to RESPONSIBILITY for the other is not a work of ATONE-
MENT but EXPIATION. What separates these two theological terms? Atonement is called the result of MAGICAL action—expiation occurs without
divine intervention, without numinous accomplices. In terms of the two passages about offering the cheek, the questions are still more complex. For if
we take Jesus' suffering as atoning and reconciling God and the world, then
clearly Levinas is opposed and would label it as magic. But Jesus' teaching
in the Sermon on the Mount does not at this point implicate God, nor does
it work any magic. Indeed, it might seem that loving the enemy was more
fully expiation than the call to wait for God's action in Lamentations. In
relation to Levinas' thought, a Christian might choose to interpret the Gospel precisely as lacking the magical atonement or reconciliation, looking
instead at the ethics of loving the enemy and turning the cheek (and giving
your coat as well!).

Levinas' point is to interpret subjectivity as human suffering and not as a
symbol or as a means for a higher power's efficacy. But why then use such
theological terms? Levinas is claiming that subjectivity is the transformation of the suffering of persecution into the expiation for the persecutor. This
is a remarkable interpretation of subjectivity: the subject is not merely not
sovereign, nor merely subjected to another, but is so thoroughly subjected as
to become expiate. Subjectivity is the place where extreme suffering converts to absolute generosity in substitution. Saying becomes the way that
trust abides in the process of being betrayed, where a speaker answers not
for herself, nor to her critics, but for the faults of her listeners. Through
signifying, lack of control becomes expansion of liability, the encumbrance
with infinite responsibilities.

---

thus as incarnated in order "to offer itself," to suffer and to give. It is thus one and unique, *in
passivity from the start*, having nothing at its disposal that would enable it *to not yield* to the
provocation; *one*, reduced to itself as it were contracted as expelled into itself ouside of being.

C. Saying the Saying

With this extreme passivity, producing a responsibility that exceeds even the infinite dimensions of *Totality and Infinity*, we are at the heart of signifying. This passivity is the physical condition of the attending identified in the previous chapter as listening. The body itself can be saying, a sign prior to language, prior to signifying with words. The question that occupies us is how to interpret speech as retaining its bond with my substitution as responsibility for persecution. How can that risk of pain be in play when I speak to another person? Words are problematic. Is any said a betrayal of the saying—or is there no way to understand the uttering of words as performing my responsibilities and opening myself for the other person? The first word I will reintroduce is "I," and we will see that it is incapable of assuming a stable place in a system of signs. "I" is the term that best establishes the need for study called pragmatics, for "I" is indexical and has no semantic meaning. What is indicated by this word is exactly the transformation of suffering into generosity which defines subjectivity itself.

7a) Levinas OB 72–73/56 By abuse of language, one can name it Me or I. But the denomination here is only pro-nomination: there is *nothing* which is named *I*. I is said by the one who speaks. The pronoun already dissimulates the unique one who speaks, subsuming that one under a concept, but only designating the mask or the person of the unique one, the mask which lets the I evade concepts, which is to say, the I of the saying in the first person, absolutely inconvertible into a name, because a sign given of this giving of signs, exposure of the self to the other, in nearness and in sincerity.

The ability to respond for the other person can be signified by the word "I." I am responsible for my persecutor, passively bound prior to any thought or choice of my own. But how does "I" work as sign? Does it pick out a substance, an object with qualities? Since we are using I to 'refer to' the locus of saying, the I does not NAME a being. It is a pronoun in the sense of a prenoun, before there are substances that can be named with nouns. "I" is pronounced, uttered by the speaker. "I" means THE ONE WHO SPEAKS, who says, who is substitute for the other person. But as sign it converts this performance into a said, a recognizable, conceivable role. "I" allows the self to be thought as one of a class of speakers—as not unique. But "I" is not pure 'said,' pure conversion of the self into a member of a class. Rather, "I" serves as a MASK, as enigmatic. The word looks like it names the speaker, but it hides the speaker, THE I OF THE SAYING, under the sign in a system of signs (persons, cases, number, etc.). The speaking "I" is *indeclinable* because I cannot be replaced as the speaker. Levinas is interpreting the indexical nature of the word "I," a word whose semantic meaning is compromised by its use. But we recall that its pragmatic meaning for Levinas is that of A SIGN GIVEN OF THIS GIVING OF SIGNS. The "I" is the sign itself and yet, unlike a sign of a person, of an agent, "I" signifies the giving of signs, the risk of signifying. To say "I" is to call attention to the vulnerability of saying, of all signification. I stick my neck out when I say "I." This vulnerability is found IN NEARNESS, in approaching the neighbor, IN SINCERITY as the risk of the self, passively given as sign.

7b) The subject of responsibility, just like the unity of transcendental apperception, is not the one-time event of a unique exemplar, of the sort which shows itself in the *Said*, in a *story* "once upon a time . . ." Uniqueness signifies here the impossibility of escaping and of being replaced, in which the very recurrence of the *I* is knotted. Uniqueness of the elected or of the one required who is not an elector, passivity which is not convertible into spontaneity. Uniqueness not assumed, not subsumed, traumatic, election in persecution.

My responsibility defines UNIQUENESS: only I can answer for my neighbor. I am located uniquely not by time and space coordinates, but by my nearness to another person. While the self is hardly a self-contained or a self-reflexive subject, it is uniquely appointed to other people. I elude even the limited conceptuality of the term "I" not because of my qualities, virtues, intellectual perfections, but by the obligations for other people that I cannot duck. Levinas emphasizes that my uniqueness is not that of a ONE-TIME occurrence, of a being that signifies like a narrative moment (ONCE UPON A TIME)—but a

being bound and irreplaceable for others' sake. Uniqueness is ELECTION, where I am not the elector, and so it cannot be ASSUMED or taken on by me, it cannot be SUBSUMED—understood by me. My responsibilities are traumas, PERSECUTION which I not only do not seek, but which devastates my will. Our first attempt to examine speaking, even of the word "I," throws us back on a pragmatic dimension of uniqueness, in which the one who speaks is irreplaceably bound for the sake of others. But a second text can now explore a saying not naming the speaker, but about speaking itself, saying that saying.

8a) Levinas OB 182/143   This passivity of passivity and this dedication to the Other, this sincerity is the *Saying*. Not as communication of a Said which immediately would recover and extinguish or absorb the Saying, but Saying holding open its opening, without pretext, evasion, or alibi, giving itself up without saying anything of the Said.

The movement from the body's saying to language's spoken words requires a HOLDING OPEN of vulnerability. Responsive speech is not exclusively imparting information, nor is it a said in which the saying is EXTINGUISHED. It needs also to perform the responsiveness of a saying where I expose myself to the other. Such an exposure in language will not make excuses or attempt to duck my liability. That

holding oneself open is SINCERITY. There is a saying that communicates but communicates no SAID, whose content is empty—and still shows my vulnerability to the other person.

8b)   Saying saying the saying itself, without thematizing it, but exposing it again. Saying, thus, is to make

Levinas echoes the famous statement of Aristotle: that God is thought which thinks thought. Ethics is SAYING SAYING

signs of this very signifying of exposure. It is to expose the exposure instead of holding to it as in an act of
exposing. It is to exhaust itself by
exposing. It is to make a sign in
making oneself a sign without *resting* in the very figure of a sign.

THE SAYING: that is, giving myself *as* a giving of myself, not becoming a sign about
which I then speak, but a sign in performance as saying. Levinas finds here a way
for the self to offer and EXPOSE itself without becoming a subject choosing to do this
act of giving. Substitution, after all, was
not about a choice to stand in for the other, but about already standing in,
assigned my place for the other. Saying saying the saying is not a reflective
moment in which the saying for the other is a theme which I can now
grasp—but is a moment in which I say to the other that I am for the other,
a saying which signifies to the other the way that I am for that other, already
a sign. And this contrasts with the repossession of exposure in AN ACT, in
which I could HOLD the opening as such (not hold it open, but grasp it or
conceive it). This saying the saying beyond the saying has no semantic meaning: I am only giving the other person my givenness for her with no meaning
other than that givenness. I do not become simply a sign, as if the conversion
from sign-user to sign gave me some rest, some substance; rather, I am rest-
less even as sign. I remain in attendance, attending the other's interpretation
of me. I am not so much the *sign* made of signifying as the *making* of a sign
of signifying, saying unable to become said, restoring the passivity and the
lack of for-itself even in 'referring' to itself as sign.

8c) Passivity of a besieging extradition where one gives up to the
other this very extradition, before it
could *be established*; a prereflexive
iteration in the Saying of this very
Saying; a stating of the "Here I am"
which identifies itself as nothing except the very voice that states and
gives itself up, the voice that signifies. But to make signs this way, to
the point of making oneself a sign—
this is not stammering language, like
the expression of a mute or the discourse of the stranger imprisoned in
his mother tongue.

Such restlessness reiterating my basic
being for the other without being in myself
requires a desubstantialization of me. I am
defined not as the person or the subject
who performs acts of giving signs, but as
elusive and not-established. The signifying, saying the saying, is pulled out of me
(EXTRADITION), and in leaving no said it
leaves the "I" who speaks without any
content beyond this performance. There
is no identity beyond THE VERY VOICE
WHICH SIGNIFIES, beyond the giving,
or better, the GIVING ITSELF UP. The
words stated in this saying saying the say-
ing are "Here I am" (in French "*me voici*," in Hebrew "*hineni*"). The doubling of indexicality (HERE and I) leaves no semantic content. It does not so
much name saying or name the person giving signs as it performs saying.
When the voice stops, there is nothing 'left'—only the giving performed. But
such speaking is not a STAMMERING or a silence, a 'failure to communicate'
because of linguistic barriers. It is eloquent and will become loquacious
shortly. Silence is too reserved, failing to expose oneself, to 'refer to' the

process of becoming a sign, of signifying as vulnerability. Not a flirtation with no signifying, but rather an exposure of the saying in signifying, of the risk in saying, the unchosen assignment for the other person.

D. Witness to Glory

If I can say the saying without turning it into a theme and without turning myself into its cause or origin, then I witness *to* the other person. But I also am witness *of*, or even *for*, the Infinite. The reintroduction of this term at this point accentuates the relation of the Infinite and my freedom that we saw in the previous chapter. Levinas argues that the performance of witness is identical with saying. Some might object that there are other dimensions of a relation with the Infinite; others might want to insist that saying has no need of such metaphysical or religious terms. In following Levinas' discussion through, we can see that the Infinite is more elusive than either religious or secular critics believe, and that the very passivity of saying, and hence of saying the saying, of speech without a said, precipitates our language about the Infinite. The culmination of this chapter is the discovery of the commandment to say the saying not in a rational reflection upon responsibility, nor in a heavenly voice calling to me, but rather in my own speaking. Levinas generates what we could call an illocutionary responsibility. It appears in my speaking (and not in listening). As far as Levinas is from self-authenticating and self-justifying ethics, where self-reflexivity models ethical value, he arrives at a truly remarkable discovery: that the command to speak arises in my speaking.

9a) Levinas OB 191–92/150–51 The Infinite orders to me the "neighbor" as face without exposing Itself to me and does so more imperiously the more that nearness is contracted. An order that has not been the *cause* of my answer, not even a question that would have already preceded it in a dialogue; an order which I find in my answer itself, by which, as a sign made to the neighbor, as "Here I am," made me leave invisibility, from shadow where my responsibility could have been eluded. This saying belongs to the very glory of which it witnesses.[2]

The way to this much changed reinstallation of the "I" is precisely through the decentering we have seen so clearly. An order comes to me in the other person's approach. I am to make myself available as the sign already available for the other person. It comes from the Infinite, which never appears. I answer, respond, but it HAS NOT BEEN THE *CAUSE* of my answer— nor was the order A QUESTION to which I must answer in a dialogue. The priority of the order does not lie in a causal chain, nor even in a dialogic turn-taking conversation. I cannot find the order in the other

[2] OB 188–89/147–48 But Saying without a said, a sign given to Another Person, the witnessing where the subject leaves his clandestinity as a subject, by which the Infinite passes, is not another thing added—like information or like an expression or like a repercussion or like a symptom of who knows what experience of the Infinite or of its glory as if it there could be

person's address to me, but find it instead IN MY ANSWER, in my leaving the INVISIBILITY of silence. The ability to respond appears in the response, the obligation to respond, similarly, not before speaking but in speaking. Without appearing, without serving as a goal or a companion, the Infinite is glorified by a subject shown as remanded for another person. What compels me to risk speech, to say the saying, to glorify the Infinite, is found in my speech itself, and does not appear before then.

9b) This way for the order to come "from out of the blue," this coming which is not a remembering [*venir/souvenir*], which is not a return to a present modified or aged into a past, this nonphenomenality of the order which, beyond representation, affects me without my knowledge, "slipping into me like a thief"—we have called it *illeity*: a coming of an order to which I am subjected before understanding or which I understand in my own Saying, *august* commandment, but without constraint or domination that leaves me outside all correlation with its source; no "structure" is established with some sort of correlate precisely at the point when the saying that comes to me is my own word. . . .

The temporality of this order is at least confusing. Levinas responds by denying it PHENOMENALITY. It does not occur in a present, and so is not now gone having been here a moment ago. Here is a temporality BEYOND REPRESENTATION, because if it submitted to an a priori form of sensibility, it would not bind me to an other person, but would originate in me. The order, the command to which I am obliged to answer, originates "FROM OUT OF THE BLUE," and is referred to as IL-LEITY. Levinas coins the term ILLEITY to name the he-ness, the otherness that is so other as to defy the realm of presence altogether. The order obliges before it is understood—see the next paragraph. Its insinuation into my consciousness is immemorial—I perceive it as always already having been, but only perceive it thus when I answer to it. My saying, my speaking in which I entrust my vulnerability to another person, gives me my first UNDERSTANDING (or my first HEARING) of the command to answer. Obliged not by force, not by DOMINATION, but without any relation to the Infinite. I can only discover it in giving myself, in giving MY OWN WORD. I speak in order to discover that I am commanded, assigned to the other person, assigned to announce peace and to offer myself. I have always been so commanded, but I find the only evidence of the command in speaking of it.

9c) Obedience preceding the listening to the order. The anachronism of inspiration or of prophecy

To speak is hence to obey the command—but not to understand it first. This speech without understanding is for Levi-

---

experience of the Infinite and so something other than glorification, which is to say, responsibility for the neighbor. This Saying is not held from the first to the structures of the correlation of subject-object, signifier-signified, Saying-Said. A sign given to the other, it is the sincerity or the truth according to which glory is glorified. The Infinite then has glory only through subjectivity, through the human adventure of the approach of the other, through substitution for the other, through expiation for the other.

is, according to the recoverable time of reminiscence, more paradoxical than the prediction of the future by an oracle. "Before they call, I will answer"—a formula to be understood literally. In approaching the Other Person, I am already late for the time of the rendezvous. But this singular obedience to the order *to yield oneself*, without understanding the order, this obedience prior to representation, this allegiance before any oaths, this responsibility prior to commitment, is precisely the other-in-the-same, inspiration and prophecy, *the coming to pass* of the Infinite. . . .

nas INSPIRATION and PROPHECY. The anachronism of prophecy is not oracular, not the foreknowledge of a yet-to-come future, but the obedience of speaking a command that already binds me, a present acknowledgment of a past that is not gone, and was indeed never present. To speak becomes to respond before the other person addresses me, to make myself available before solicited.

Levinas cites a passage from Isaiah. God promises redemption in a PREDICTION of messianic time. But Levinas is not interpreting either messianic time nor

10) Isaiah 65:24   And it shall come to pass that <u>before they call, I will answer</u>; while they are still speaking I will listen.

the discourse by God. He finds human prophecy still MORE PARADOXICAL than this messianic promise. What in Isaiah is the promise of a God who responds before the people call becomes here a human obedience that precedes hearing. God listens WHILE THEY ARE STILL SPEAKING; we obey or listen before the other speaks.

The pragmatic dimension flies in the face of our normal interpretation— but it is really no more than the performance of the relation to the teacher we saw in the first chapter. To be ALREADY LATE is to give an account of the authority of the other person—my words stand already in doubt, unsaid, vulnerable. To speak is to make myself too late. The obedience in speaking is the performance of remanding myself as sign, as for-the-other person. Obviously, the authority of the teacher means that to so expose myself is precisely not yet to know what the other will teach me, not to understand the meaning of the sign that I am or the way that I am for the other person. To attend for the future is to be bound BEFORE UNDERSTANDING, without knowing what my service to the other will be. But so to give myself over to the other person is not to commit myself, nor is it to vow an oath, but is prior to a voluntary choice of responding. What makes an oath performative is this prior ALLEGIANCE: the way that I am already attending the other person, and am saying, signifying that signifying when I swear. Such passive speech, speech that preserves the passivity of assignment is INSPIRATION, the way that the other is in-the-same—the transformation of me in substitution from victim to sign for others. Levinas calls it PROPHECY because it is a way, in my speaking, to allow the other to speak—soliciting the otherness of my interlocutor, inviting another person to speak through me, even against me. This performance, which is not my act but holds myself open for another to act, is the way that the Infinite passes by here. The Infinite ordains finite beings to be for others, and so is itself for the finite beings and not only for itself and in itself. The assignment of me to the other person is a trace of the Infinite in the finite, for the finite. If God is glorified in my saying the saying, then God is anachronistically absent and not shown in my speech that holds my vulnerability open to another person.

9d)   This witness does not reduce to the relation that leads from an index to an indicated—that would be to become disclosure and thematization. It is the bottomless passivity of responsibility, and therefore, sincerity; the meaning of language before language scatters into words, in themes equal to the words and dissimulating in the Said; the opening exposed like a bleeding wound of the Saying without, moreover, the trace of witnessing of sincerity or of glory being effaced, even in its Said.[3]

WITNESS is the announcement to the other of my responsibility. Witness must bear the MEANING OF LANGUAGE that precedes and exceeds its semantic content. Because speaking is not merely the use of a sign to refer to a thing, or even to refer to another sign, but is rather a 'use' in relation to another person, witness cannot be merely telling about something. The vulnerability of the witness, the risk exposed, risk preceding exposure, exposure itself remaining passive, goes beyond and behind the task of presenting themes and grasping experience. Still more important, even when language is constituted, as schemes of meaning and content, dissimulated as only said, the saying remains. The vulnerability of the performance of the pragmatic dimension of speaking cannot be EFFACED. The epistemological conundrums produced in this theory by refusing to allow saying, and hence witness of the Infinite, to vanish, and at the same time to refuse to allow saying, witness, the Infinite, and so on, to become present are reserved for later discussions.

[3] Levinas OB 186/146   The I stripped of its ill-tempered and imperialistic subjectivity by the trauma of persecution is returned to the "Here I am" in the transparency without opacity, without deaf zones propitious for evasion. "Here I am" as a witness of the Infinite, but as a witness that does not thematize that to which it witnesses and whose truth is not the truth of representation, nor of evidence. There is only witnessing—unique structure, exception to the rule of being, irreducible to representation—of the Infinite. The Infinite does not appear to the one who witnesses it. It is, on the contrary, the witnessing that belongs to the glory of the Infinite. It is by the voice of the witness that the glory of the Infinite is glorified.

Luhmann RD 138/60   Belief only acts as a communications medium if one can assume that the one communicating believes. . . . It is fulfilled by a tradition of confessions and witnesses in which the believers attest to their belief, often under extreme stress and therefore all the more believably. They witness to themselves or witnesses witness that believers have witnessed to their belief. In this context, it is remarkable how much value is put upon presence and uninterrupted mediation, as if the medium presupposed communication among those present as a security base. Only in modern times is it replaced by (translated and printed!) Scripture, which has always been called testament.

The claim, however, is clear: responsibility for the other person is exposed and even witnessed in speaking. Indeed, the sincerity of speaking itself is a trace of the saying in all words used.

Suggested Readings

1   Handelman, Susan. *Fragments of Redemption*, 250–59. Bloomington: Indiana University Press, 1991.
2   Ward, Graham. *Barth, Derrida, and the Language of Theology*, 147–70. Cambridge: Cambridge University Press, 1995.
4   Gibbs, Robert. "Substitution: Marcel and Levinas." In *Correlations in Rosenzweig and Levinas*, 192–228. Princeton: Princeton University Press, 1992.
    Weber, Elizabeth. "Persecution in Levinas' *Otherwise Than Being*." In *Ethics as First Philosophy*, ed. Adriaan Peperzak, 69–76. New York: Routledge, 1995.
8   Llewelyn, John. *Emmanuel Levinas: The Genealogy of Ethics*, 155–56. London: Routledge, 1995.

CHAPTER 3

Why Write?

THE PREVIOUS CHAPTER'S interpretation of my speaking attenuates my presence as subject or as author of my discourse. If the task of speaking is to hold myself open for the sake of the other person, letting my vulnerability and availability for the other person appear without making it into my teaching or myself into the teacher, then what will happen when we consider writing? A written text is a way of signifying that leaves the authority to interpret to the other. Writing requires a disruption of the face-to-face conversation: I am not there when someone reads my text. But, if I also am not present (not 'there') when I speak responsively, then could not writing also serve as a way to hold my openness open, to attend to the other, a way to leave my witness available for the other's interpretation?

Or rather, and here the ground starts to shake in a somewhat familiar way today, is not the practice of writing itself the key for understanding witness? Is not writing where absence and vulnerability best emerge? Is responsibility in language, then, more a matter of the way that writing works than of the dynamics of oral conversation? At the outset I will leave aside the practice of reading another person's text, and focus instead on writing. Soon enough, we will see the practices of reading in the writing of commentary. But first, we need to understand the pragmatics of writing itself, in order to grasp the ethical responsibility in writing.

The pragmatics of writing is programmatology, or at least, a grammatology, and the texts most responsible for our familiarity with the question of writing are Jacques Derrida's. In this context, I will not develop many of the nuances of the relation between Derrida and Levinas, nor should the ordering of my argument produce the impression of a simple interchange of influence. Too many others are at least as important in each author's relation to ethics and writing—Maurice Blanchot, most of all for both. But we can pursue questions of responsibility and writing in the texts of Derrida and Levinas without settling the issues of their relation. Derrida is a keen reader of Levinas, and, as we will see, a writer who redevelops Levinas' thought and responsibility.

Levinas and Derrida each articulate a certain overlapping or interlacing of the pragmatics of reading and writing as attending. The texture of texts offers simultaneously a responsive mode of writing and a responsive mode of reading. The asymmetry that guides this work, however, will find writing and reading to be not simply reflected images of each other, but rather, renewals of the distinctions of conversational roles found in the first two chapters. We begin with writing as a way of saying the saying, or perhaps better, writing the writing, and then in the next chapter will look at reading as a way of tracing a trace. The discussion of reading leads directly to questions about commentary and commenting, which is the topic for the final chapter of Part I.

The displacement from conversation to reading and writing is effected through Derrida's program in *Of Grammatology*. In Section A (Writing Withdrawal), we will see first the deconstruction of the claim that a written sign is only a sign of an oral sign. Pretext 2 accentuates the relations of the writer to his reader, noting that writing is withdrawal, and that only at the risk of utter failure can communication occur. In Pretext 3, moreover, Derrida claims to want to say nothing in his writing (to have no theme, no said) and gives us our first indication of how hard it is to write the writing and not a written theme.

Section B (Saying and Writing) then engages the question of whether Levinas, too, can be read as writing about the writing. The first encounter is written in Derrida's first essay on Levinas, "Violence and Metaphysics," and in Pretext 4 we will see Derrida cite Levinas against Levinas' claims about orality's priority, in order to deepen Levinas' own claims about responsibility for the other. The task of interpreting Derrida's citations will lead us back to two texts from *Totality and Infinity* (Pretexts 5 and 6). The first sets up the superiority of speech because of the presence of the teacher; the second, however, complicates the question, arguing for a broadening of signs that can teach and warning of the risk of interpreting words as information.

Section C (The Trace and Crossing Out) will explore the trace, following through a comment by Derrida in Pretext 4. Levinas explains that the face is a trace of itself (Pretext 7). In the face the presence of the face is withdrawn, not securing my other in presence. This leads finally to a discussion by Derrida (Pretext 8) of how Levinas writes (and how to write about it), by withdrawing himself, leaving a series of traces or crossing-outs. This text comes from the second essay by Derrida on Levinas, "At this moment itself . . ." The reiteration of withdrawal becomes the primary gesture of responsive writing.

A. WRITING WITHDRAWAL

Our question is not how to pick between Derrida and Levinas, but rather, Why Write? The pragmatic dimensions of writing display the ethical dimension of language, the way responsibility pervades the use of a sign and the way that my use of signs points away from my authority over their meaning, attending a reader who will interpret the text. Derrida's own writing emerges in an epistemological battle with a theory of signs that holds each sign to be composed of a *signifier* (a word or gesture) and a *signified* (the thing or thought that the signifier refers to). This kind of theory, exemplified

for Derrida by Saussure, makes signification a process of encoding and secures meaning by recourse to the independent signifieds. To disrupt this
two-part theory of sign will open a space where signifying becomes vulnerable and the knower's authority over the sign is displaced onto a future interpretation. Indeed, the security of the signifieds (the preexisting thoughts)
had served to found communication on knowledge. Derrida's work, in this
context, then, is to disrupt the reduction of language to knowledge, opening
the pragmatics of language to responsibilities not determined by secured
knowledge, in a way truly parallel to Levinas'.

1a) Derrida G 15–16/6–7 By a
slow movement whose necessity is
barely perceptible, everything that
tended to and finally was mustered
under the name of language for at
least twenty centuries is starting to
let itself be deported or at least
summed up under the name of writing. By a necessity which is barely
perceptible, it seems as if the concept
of writing—ceasing to designate a
form that was particular, derivative,
auxiliary to language in general
(whether one understands it as communication, relation, expression,
signification, constitution of meaning or thought, etc.), ceasing to
designate an exterior film, an insubstantial double of a main signifier, *the signifier of the signifier*—the
concept of writing is beginning to
exceed the extension of language. In
all meanings of that word, writing
would contain language.[1]

In this programmatic text from *Of
Grammatology*, Derrida explores the relation of writing to language. Despite a subtle, BARELY PERCEPTIBLE motion, writing
is beginning to displace language: or
rather, the assembling of various functions and equipment (MUSTERED) under
the command of language now is being re-
assembled under the NAME OF WRITING.
This change of classification occurs when
the qualities of writing are not seen as DE-
RIVATIVE from speech, but as constitutive of signification in general. The written
text no longer must be DESIGNATED as a
PARTICULAR form of communication, as
AUXILIARY, or as SUPPLEMENTARY. And
the functions of language, consigned here
to a list in parentheses, covering the gamut
of the aims of speech, will now be DE-
PORTED to the concept of writing. The
chief interpretation of writing had been
that it only repeats the signifying action of

the spoken word. Words name things or ideas: writing only names words.
Writing was seen, therefore, as INSUBSTANTIAL DOUBLE. And in italics, Derrida asserts the phrase that deconstructs the hierarchy of writing and speech:
THE SIGNIFIER OF THE SIGNIFIER. To be derivative is to lack a direct relation
to the thing or idea, to require the further mediation of another sign (the oral
word). When writing can no longer be determined by these claims, then
writing begins TO EXCEED THE EXTENSION OF LANGUAGE—more happens in
writing than language can contain. And if WRITING *WOULD CONTAIN* LAN-
GUAGE, then it not only grasps it, but surrounds it and understands it.

---

[1] Levinas BV 7/x–xi A contraction of the Infinite in Scripture, unless—and here there
would be no impoverishment of the Cartesian idea, nor of the glory of God, nor of His religious
nearness—unless it is the prophetic dignity of language, capable of always signifying more than

1b) Not that the word "writing" ceases to designate the signifier of the signifier, but it appears in a strange light that "signifier of the signifier" ceases to define the accidental doubling and the fallen secondariness. "Signifier of the signifier" describes, on the contrary, the movement of language: in its origin, certainly, but one already senses that an origin whose structure can be spelled out in this way as signifier of the signifier is carried off and effaced in its own production. There the signified functions always already as a signifier.

WRITING itself still will designate a doubling of signifying, the way that a sign can itself be the referent of a sign, but this is no longer ACCIDENTAL or some sort of fall into SECONDARINESS. Writing names the way that language itself moves: that the SIGNIFIED FUNCTIONS ALWAYS ALREADY AS A SIGNIFIER. What a sign indicates is itself always another sign, and the very signification that names the original signified—the perception or conception—IS EFFACED IN ITS OWN PRODUCTION. The doubling of the term *signifier* shows that the relation of signifying is not so much a

regress as an unstoppable series: even using a term once points forward to further signifying. The very origin of signification disappears, leaving only a motion from sign to sign.

1c) The secondariness that one believed could be reserved for writing affects all signifieds in general, affects them always already, which is to say, *put in play*. There is no signified that escapes, only eventually to fall back into the play of referring signifiers that constitutes language.

The impossibility of stopping the motion means that what was unique about writing is now the characteristic of all signs: the sign is always sign of another sign. No SIGNIFIED can keep itself out of the PLAY of other signifiers: each at some point turns itself over into a signifier. Nothing, in the simplest sense, is complete

in itself and can stand independent of relation to others. Language itself is a play of signs without the resting point of objects or referents or established meanings. But for our analysis from the previous chapters, this only clarifies the way that a sign's signification requires being for another, unable to rest in itself.

1d) The advent of writing is the advent of play: play obeys itself today, effacing the limits from which one believed one was to be able to regulate the circulation of signs, carrying off with it all the reassuring signifieds, reducing all the strongholds, all the out-of-bounds shelters that watched over the field of language. This reverts, necessarily, to destroying the concept of "sign" and all of its logic.

Thus, for Derrida the emergence of writing means that the control over language that philosophy had tried to assert is gone. The lack of a limit is not the indulgence of simple skepticism, but rather the insight into the way that signs do CIRCULATE without rest. There is no access in language to a special term (STRONGHOLD) or special experience (OUT-OF-BOUNDS) which can govern the way that a sign relates to another sign. The play of significa-

---

it says, the miracle of inspiration where man listens amazed to what he utters, where he already *reads* the utterance and interprets it, where the human word is already writing.

tion does not stop with some pure referent (signified). The riskiness of signification, that a sign leads to further interpretations beyond the control of
the particular sign, cannot be arrested by use of some special referent or sign,
by picking out a referent that can govern the use of signs and hence of interpretation and meaning. The triumph of PLAY means that we cannot stop the
signifying, the relation to the other. But if it must also lead to DESTROYING
THE CONCEPT OF "SIGN," it is because that concept had presumed that there
was something (precept or concept) fully present and available for reference.
The upsurge of writing, the comprehension of language by writing, means
that control over meaning itself is bound—and reopens the realm where
responsibility exceeds what we can control.

We have entered Derrida's texts through this text from *Of Grammatology*, title to both book and the program of examining writing (at the expense
of THE CONCEPT OF "SIGN"). But we arrive there through substitution and
witness in Levinas' text: where language is itself reoriented away from the
cognitive and controlling functions that Derrida must battle. While we saw
speech holding open the vulnerability of my being for the other person, we
could not see how the sign itself is implicated in this relation, the sign as a
mark. In the section called "Envois" in *The Postcard*, Derrida assembles a
set of postcard messages, messages sent to another person, a "you"—"*tu.*"
The intimacy of address is exposed in the materiality of the texts because
postcards are always readable by the mail-carriers, and indeed, they have
now been published in a book. To write is to make open the vulnerability of
my word, the risk of failed communication, to eclipse the dialogic situation
in order to accentuate the responsibility beyond my control.

2a) Derrida PC 34–35/29   You understand, already on the inside of
each sign, of each mark, of each line,
there is withdrawal, the post, whatever is necessary to make it readable
by an other, an other than you or I,
and everything is screwed in advance, cards on the table. The condition for it arriving is that it come to
an end and even that it begin by not
arriving.

The "you" is a thoughtful, UNDER-
STANDING reader—someone who knows
the author (the "I," at least, and Derrida
only possibly). Any sign must include a
WITHDRAWAL, that the author is not present to the reader, and that for every sort of
sign—in EACH MARK, in EACH LINE, I absent myself, withdrawing. This Derrida
calls THE POST—because all writing is
sent, whether left on the table or mailed,
and because the post can always be unreli-

able. The chance for my signs to be intercepted and fail to reach their destination is intrinsic in the relation to an other. A sign cannot arrive unless it
can be lost both from the outset and at the point of arriving when the relation with the other is achieved. A sign requires a separation between myself
and the other between the emission of the sign and the reception of it. Derrida writes that the post, the mailing of writing, models the interceptability
of all signs. Signification is always risky. This interceptability of a sign, however, is what MAKES IT READABLE BY AN OTHER, AN OTHER THAN YOU OR I.

A written sign must be available to others, but cannot itself complete the relation to others. It attends its reader. If another person picks it up, then she may read it—but only because I am not there to govern the sign, to authorize certain readers, to legitimate certain readings. Derrida claims that all writing, indeed all signs, include this withdrawal of the author's authority by setting the signs out, beyond my intentions and my control. Everything is a mess, and in plain sight for anyone (CARDS ON THE TABLE). Privacy is impossible for signs—because the post is always already part of the way a sign works.

2b)   That is how the card of a-destination is read and written. Abject literature is on the way, it is on the lookout for you, crouching in language and as soon as you open your mouth, it strips you of everything, without even letting you enjoy setting out again on your way, totally nude, toward her whom you love, living, living, living, there, out of reach.

A postcard becomes a text of A-DESTINATION (sent on the condition of the possibility of never arriving). Signs become ABJECT LITERATURE, writing that is not so much a telegram sent to someone else, as a message in a bottle—only capable of communicating by running the risk of never surfacing, or surfacing in who knows whose hands. The twists here begin to resound with the vulnerability of exposure. If you speak (OPEN YOUR MOUTH) you still signify by ABJECT LITERATURE: postcards in the disguise of language that offers security (TAKING COVER). But to speak is to become stripped, totally NUDE, exposed in signifying, and unable to cover oneself—this is the way that signs are always sent on the condition of interceptability. The loss of control begins with the first sending of the card, as the sign is always already lost if it can ever become found, can ever arrive. The displacement from the sign strips it of its for itself—or it will never be able to be for the other. The TOWARD is an aiming at someone who cannot be assimilated, someone fully independent, someone LIVING, and who cannot be joined by communication. If the card gets there, I still won't. This interpretation of the separation we saw operating in conversation now is performed in writing: because writing involves sending. (Derrida's use of YOU in this sentence is a metaleptic you: you as author, not as reader, a you that can accommodate the writer of the card but also makes place for the reader as author of other writings.)

2c)   The condition by which I renounce nothing and have my love return to me, and be understood by me, is that you are there, over there, fully alive outside me. Out of reach. And that you will send back to me.

The only way to give a sign and not lose it (RENOUNCE NOTHING) is if the other person is separate. The intimacy of the postcards is here in play, as the question is also how love can be requited. I can only love if the other person is OUT OF REACH, separated and not under my control. The condition for attainment of any of these desires (not losing anything, being loved, understanding) is the vulnerability of sending a sign. And in the posting of a postcard, the other person (YOU) is not here, but there. Here

Derrida most clearly expresses the asymmetry of the "I" and the "you," the here and there. There is not just THERE, it is OVER THERE. To communicate, to be received, will require an action by the other person (SEND BACK). The gaps between my authorship and my reader (whom I want to love me, or at least to understand) cannot be overcome in a sign—the sign performs the risk of failure, and only on that condition can any of my hopes be met. Derrida's text does not here take the further step that we, on the basis of the earlier chapters, could, and claim that this exposure holds me responsible for the undesirable reactions, too. The post does, at least, require me to risk in every sign, even to invoke the failure, the founding possibility of not communicating—the gap between a sign and its meaning for another, between responsibility and responsiveness.

In an interview Derrida, in his own voice, explores his question and how he writes. The culmination is a reiteration of the risk in writing, and when Derrida claims that he has no thematics, his writing becomes parallel to the passivity in saying saying the saying in Levinas.

3a) Derrida P 23–24/14 I try to *write* (in) the space where the question of saying and of intending to say is posed. I try to write the question: (what is it) that intends to say?

The question is about SAYING and IN-TENDING TO SAY (*dire et vouloir-dire*). The question is, What is the INTENDING TO SAY? Or even, in the intending to say is anyone willing or intending? This question applies even to writing about the topic: intending to say. We first may compare it with Levinas' terms: *the saying* and the *said*. Can we match up Levinas' said and Derrida's intending to say? The *said* is the content of an utterance, the thematic material. *The saying* is the exposure of using a sign, an exposure that is profoundly passive, beyond my activities and even my intentions in a Husserlian sense. The INTENDING TO SAY is a dubious translation (my own) of *vouloir-dire*. The standard translation is *meaning*, and Derrida himself uses *vouloir-dire* for the German *bedeuten* when writing on Husserl. I chose *intending* in order to reconnect the important equivocation between purpose and will in *vouloir* and phenomenological intentionality in the standard views of meaning. Thus, to separate the SAYING from the INTENDING TO SAY is to oppose a performance along the lines of Levinas' saying with an activity that intends a meaning, a theme, or a resulting concept. What Saussure calls the signified is closely linked to what here is the intending to say and what Levinas calls the said. Just as Derrida contests the signified in the first quotation of this chapter, in this passage he claims the use of signs (the writing) contests the speaker's or author's intention. Derrida interposes an (IN) in the beginning of his sentence, alerting us to the double task: both that he writes about the question and that his own writing is in question. Writing about this question will itself have to be put into question by the question: How can he intend to say, how can he propose a theme or a meaning or even use words which themselves purport a meaning, if the intending to say is in question?

3b) It is thus necessary that in such a space and guided by such a question, writing literally would intend-to-say-nothing. Not that it be absurd, as by an absurdity that has always made a system with the metaphysical intending to say.[2]

Writing becomes a way to INTEND-TO-SAY-NOTHING. Unlike a thematic presentation or an argument for some position or some idea, writing becomes a kind of withdrawal or erasure of my intentions and my constitution of meaning. At first glance, this is laughable: Derrida writes books that mean nothing? Signs do not mean or convey the intentions or the understandings of their emitters—at least not without running the risk of failure. Derrida's writing is about the way that writing effaces the said, the claim upon the other person, the knowing which supplants revealing myself. As such, it must not advance a further claim about this saying—but must hold it open, disrupting the intending to say—LITERALLY. The letters themselves will work to thwart my writing. They withdraw and cross out my activity. The passivity we saw in the previous chapter becomes a writing with no intending to say, no "meaning." But if this is not laughable, neither is it ABSURD. For the absurd is here simply a mirror of the thematics of the intending to say, a negative image that helps form a metaphysical system. Whether every invocation of absurdity fits this description is not our concern; rather, we see what is excluded: a reflected image that can be folded into a system. The excess of Levinas' saying requires an excess in Derrida's stripping away of the intending to say in order to prevent my recovering the vulnerability that cannot be grasped.

3c) . . . It is in this sense that I risk intending to say nothing that can be understood simply, that would be a simple matter of understanding. To mix oneself up over hundreds of pages of such a writing at once insistent and elliptical, imprinting, as you have seen, even what it has crossed out, taking away each concept in an interminable chain of differences, surrounded or encumbered by so many precautions, references, notes, citations, collages, supplements—this "intending to say nothing" is not, you will grant me, an exercise of perfect security.

Derrida as writer must risk offering nothing that can BE UNDERSTOOD SIMPLY—because one could then avoid the very performance that is the point. To not have a theme or a concept (a slogan or a program) is to write how writing is the effacement of such intending to say, of the said. The text itself holds open a vulnerability to interception and to misinterpretation, in order to perform the fundamental vulnerability of signs, the attending for the readers' interpretations. He next describes the very texture of his writings, and how they perform this exhaustion of

---

[2] Derrida PC 209/194 What one cannot say, one must above all not keep silent, but write. Me, I am a man of speech, I never had anything to write. When I have something to say I say it or say it to myself, enough (*Basta*)! You are the only one to comprehend why it has been necessary that I write exactly the contrary, concerning those axiomatics, than what I desire, than what I know my desire to be, otherwise said, than you: living speech, presence itself, proximity, the proper, keeping watch, and so on. I have necessarily written for the reverse—and rendered myself to necessity.

intending to say. INSISTENT AND ELLIPTICAL: at once forceful and aggressive and at the same time hiding and suggestive of the intending to say. IMPRINTING and CROSSING OUT: both saying and unsaying, or better writing and unwriting, refusing to make even crossing out the 'point' of the theory of writing. SURROUNDED and at the same time ENCUMBERED by a set of PRECAUTIONS, NOTES, CITATIONS, SUPPLEMENTS, and so on: in order to put the body of his text into question, he contextualizes it with almost endless prevarications, protects himself with so many notes, and riddles the text with citations to others' texts. It is embarrassing because it seems that he won't tell you, or even that what he has to say (intending to say) is shameful. As if he were too insecure. But the precautions and the process of taking away the very themes he proposes serve to make himself less secure. The three pretexts here have come across genres: from a treatise, a set of postcards, and an interview—each offering its own disruption of authority and withdrawal. I write of and in responsibility in a complex weave of prevarications and withdrawals, so as not to expound a claim, but to hold open my own vulnerability. I write, moreover, to exhaust the cover that language offers for my vulnerability, to strip it off—on the page.

B. SAYING AND WRITING

In the first essay by Derrida on Levinas, Derrida questions Levinas on the priority of speech. Levinas had assigned to oral discourse the leading role of the face and its teaching. From the later work of Levinas himself we can see writing as comparable to this teaching. But Derrida's writing about Levinas' writing finds a possibility for responsibility in Levinas' text that exceeds the plain sense of that text. We can broaden the range of responsive signifying in Levinas through Derrida's reading, learning both about that operation (Derrida's 'deconstruction') and about the resources even in *Totality and Infinity*. We must begin with Derrida's questions, because they lead us into Levinas' text through a process of citation and interrogation.

4a) Derrida WD 150–51/101–2 Is "oral discourse" "the plenitude of discourse"? Is writing only "language again become sign"? Or, in another sense is it "speech activity" where I "absent myself and am missing from my products," which betray me more than they express me? Is the "candor" of expression for one who is not God essentially on the side of living speech? This question is doubtless meaningless for Levinas, who thinks the face in the "resemblance" of man and God.

Derrida interrogates Levinas' claims for speech, wondering if writing cannot serve to disrupt the reader. At first glance, it is not clear whether he is more concerned with an author's ability to teach or with a reader's ability to learn. Moreover, the quotation marks alert us to something we are 'missing.' In order to understand these first questions of Derrida, we must heed the quotation marks and look back to texts from *Totality and Infinity*. My standard procedure will be to introduce the cited text on the right and to <u>underline the words that have been cited</u> and commented upon in the pretext that is placed on the left. Levinas contrasts not only speech and writing, but also speech in two modes: speech as the teaching that we saw in Chapter 1 and speech as an activity, as a tool used for a purpose. As Levinas' texts continue, writing begins to admit the same distinction, raising the opening that Derrida will develop in the continuation of his passage.

PROPOSITIONS are not naked for interpretation but come with a 'built-in' interpretation. The first interpretation is the teacher's own: the other's authority to promulgate interpretation of her own speech. Thus, the sign comes with a KEY, THE TEACHING CHARACTER, the authority who can BRING AID TO HIS DISCOURSE. This authority and presence is the Other's, the one who speaks to me. Levinas claims

> 5) Levinas TI 69/96 The proposition is a sign that already interprets itself, that bears its own key. This presence of the key that interprets in the sign to be interpreted is precisely the presence of the Other in the proposition, the presence of someone who can bring aid to his discourse, the teaching character of all speech. <u>Oral discourse is the plenitude of discourse.</u>

that speaking, specifically ORAL DISCOURSE, best preserves the other person's authority. Again, this repeats the theme of authority and the asymmetry of presence we saw in Chapter 1.

The second text, however, is more complex. The complexities will dislodge the simple hierarchy of speech over writing. Here is another account of the authority of the other person to ASSIST her speech. She refers me not to the idea (SIGNIFIED) or even to the sign, but to herself, the utterer (whom Levinas usually calls the SIGNIFIER). A speaker is unknowable, and in

> 6a) Levinas TI 157/182 Speech is, in effect, a manifestation unlike any other: it does not complete the movement from the sign in order to go to the signifier and the signified. By making the signifier *assist* this showing of the signified, it unlocks what every sign closes at the very moment when it opens the passage that leads to the signified.

eluding me teaches me. Even as the sign points to a referent, the use of the sign points also to the speaker, and while the sign CLOSES the way back to the speaker, its use also UNLOCKS a way to the speaker's authority despite the absence of the speaker herself.

The old complaint against writing appears here simply: like Plato in the *Phaedrus*, Levinas recites the way the written word is orphaned. Signs by themselves offer no way back to an other interpreter. LANGUAGE WRITTEN, BECOME AGAIN SIGN means a linking of sign to sign without another's interruptions and without an unknowable teacher, without anyone calling to me. However, the complaint begins to spin, when Levinas allows ALL OF THE

> 6b) This assistance measures the surplus of spoken language over <u>language written, become again sign.</u> The sign is a silent language, an impeded language. Language does not group symbols in systems but deciphers symbols. But insofar as this original showing of the Other Person has already taken place, insofar as an entity *presented itself* and came to its own aid, all of the signs other than verbal signs can serve as language.

SIGNS OTHER THAN VERBAL SIGNS to signify like speech. An OTHER PERSON who addresses me can use anything, any sort of sign (and anything become sign), to teach me, to bind me, to call to me. Thus, writing, even gesture, can be part of the teaching, calling me to responsibility. All it takes is for someone to address me—for which speech seems required first. An object can speak if accompanied by another person. A text can address me if someone reads with me.

But if writing can teach me, speech also can become less than the address of the teacher. Because speech is not simply pure encounter, its words can themselves be interpreted as TOOLS. I can listen not for what is interruptive and new, but only to hear the stuff the other person uses and to interpret that. The other's speech then for me becomes her ACTIVITY—not an expression and certainly not a revelation. Speech cannot absolve itself from this risk, because it uses signs even if what we have called exposure is the why for the sign. But

> 6c) But speech itself does not always find the welcome that should be reserved for speech. Because speech contains nonspeech and may express in the way that tools, vestments, and gestures express. In its manner of articulating, in its style, speech signifies as activity and as product. It is to pure speech what writing offered to handwriting experts is to the written expression offered to the reader. Speech as an activity signifies like furniture or tools do.

if speech can be interpreted as an activity, fully graspable, then what distinguishes PURE SPEECH from this SPEECH AS AN ACTIVITY is not its orality (as opposed to its literality), but my listening (THE WELCOME). And as if to admit it, Levinas then compares this opposition to that between what writing is for HANDWRITING EXPERTS and what it is for READERS. Readers can be called, addressed by the writing, while the experts find themselves not addressed. If anything can become a revealing sign, then conversely, any mode of signifying, even speech, can become a straightforward referring for the sake of knowing. And reading then is like listening, an attending that is a way of being called to responsibility.

SPEECH-ACTIVITY lacks the CANDOR in listening, where all speech and all language arise. I will have more to say about RENEWAL in the last chapter of this part. The last few sentences, however, expose the reading I perform throughout this text. For this passage is one of the very few that allows to the "me" the role of teacher, assisting and present for my own speech. The asymmetry that is so vital for

> 6d) It doesn't have the total transparency of the gaze directed to the gaze, the absolute _candor_ of the face to face which lies at the bottom of all speech. From my speech-activity, I absent myself as I am missing from all of my products. But I am the inexhaustible source—of that always renewed deciphering. And that renewal is precisely presence or my assistance to myself.

this work, as it is for Levinas', is lacking here. Here he discounts my absenting myself from my speech, interpreting such speech as a productive activity. He does not allow for a responsive mode of absenting, for an effacing myself for the sake of my interlocutor. When Levinas later fashions witnessing as a third way of signifying, an absence that has not reduced signifying to mere activity and cognition, he has an alternative consonant with Derrida's critique. And the interpretation of the work as the result of the absent actor will also allow for a richer interpretation in Chapter 17. This text, moreover, serves Derrida's earlier essay well, because Levinas wants the authority of presence for both the "I" and the other person. Derrida's question concerns responsibility, exposure, and the violence of presenting a theme. The control over another that my presence affirms is obviously in question, but the question about presence is more complicated, for if I constitute my presence as an activity of my consciousness, if presence involves an intentionality toward the other, then the pure passivity of responsibility seems to be violated here, too. Hence, presence for me or the other may, in fact, not produce the ethics that Levinas is aiming for—a conclusion that Levinas himself reaches in later work.

To return now to Derrida's text, the questions themselves display a reading of Levinas, not so much "for" or "against," but raise the question of how writing and its form of absence compare to speaking.

4a) Derrida WD 150–51/101–2 Is "oral discourse" "the plenitude of discourse"? Is writing only "language become again sign"? Or, in an other sense, is it "speech activity" where I "absent myself and am missing from my products," which betray me more than they express me? Is the "candor" of expression for one who is not God essentially on the side of living speech? This question is doubtless meaningless for Levinas, who thinks the face in the "resemblance" of man and God.

Derrida doubts first the simple opposition of writing and speaking. Citing Levinas' words, he wonders whether speaking is "THE PLENITUDE OF DISCOURSE." This plenitude seems to be the generosity of responsibility, the giving of myself and the giving of the word in signs. Can Levinas be sure that speech affords such superfluity, or at least, that only speech affords it? Is writing simply the written signs, lacking all interruption by the other person? He asks whether writing can be grasped as the "SPEECH ACTIVITY" of absence and betrayal. He disrupts the opposition of speech and writing as presence and absence in reading Levinas' text. And he disputes that the absence in writing is simply a fault, leading to BETRAYAL. Derrida realizes that this latter question points to the complications of Levinas' criticism of writing—that writing does not exclusively or in every case serve as the way to use a sign without recourse to a signer's authority. In our first look at Derrida as reader, he notes a shift, dare I say it, a *deconstruction*, within Levinas' own text concerning the possibility for a kind of signifying which fails to bring its recipient near another person. Writing is neither simply a kind of speech activity, nor must it lack the teaching function of speech. As for the emphasized word CANDOR, Derrida questions whether it is reserved for speakers when the speakers/writers are not God.

4b) Aren't the height and magisteriality of the teaching on the side of writing? Can't one invert all Levinas' propositions on this point? By showing, for example, that writing can bring its own aid, because it *has the time* and the freedom, escaping empirical urgency better than speech does? That, neutralizing the requests of empirical 'economy,' is writing in essence more "metaphysical" (in Levinas' sense) than speech? That the writer better absents himself, which is to say, expresses himself better as an other, and addresses himself better to the other than the man of speech? And that, depriving himself of enjoyments and of the effects of signs, he better renounces violence? It is true that he only intends perhaps to multiply his writings to the infinite, forgetting thus—at least—the other, the infinitely other as death, thus practicing writing as *differance* and *economy of death*?

Derrida now follows through the decomposition of the opposition of writing and speaking as said and saying. He wonders if what is written is not more capable of TEACHING. According to our interpretation of teaching, the key element is the capacity to interrupt and to contest me, the listener. But Derrida proposes a subtle inversion and discovers that the otherness promised in this authority to contest my interpretations rests more in the absent author than the interlocutor. The benefit of BRINGING AID, the question derived from Plato's *Phaedrus*, now goes to writing, because it HAS THE TIME, and is not overwhelmed by the press of circumstance. Derrida suggests that a written text that can await its readers can better suspend the empirical and controllable dimension of another's speech The core question becomes the way that the signer can best EXPRESS HIMSELF AS AN OTHER:

Derrida suggests that the author absenting himself prevents me from grasping the other, from reasserting control over him as some presence in my consciousness. The highest authority is never around to confront but is absent. By withdrawing, the writer deprives himself of the enjoyment of the consequences of his writing. The writer thus BETTER RENOUNCES VIOLENCE—because he cannot control the use of his signs. Derrida points out an absenting that has been the topic of our discussion so far in this chapter. In order to renounce violence, to signify responsively, it is better to perform the lack of control over signs. Indeed, writing here is DIFFERANCE, the recognition that the meaning lies ahead, indeed, after my ultimate absence, my DEATH. Our question remains whether Derrida has separated the teacher from the learner. It may be that teaching is also nonviolent, is a command upon me that commands me without enslaving me, but when I respond to teaching—call it saying or writing—I am not taking up the same teacher's position. Derrida pushes us toward a new interpretation of teaching in terms of writing, of welcoming the teacher in terms of reading, but at this point he does not separate the pragmatics of reading and of writing.

4c) The limit between violence and nonviolence perhaps therefore does not pass between speech and writing, but within each of them.

The problem opens, however, as Derrida reads Levinas' text, from the opposition of writing and speech. Derrida does not propose that speech is violent because of the presence and the demands of time, but rather that the line separating violence and nonviolence runs WITHIN each of the modes of signifying and not BETWEEN them. Levinas made this claim possible by allowing signs other than words to become expressions of the teacher, and allowing speech to become reduced to the wielding of tools, and by admitting that a reader differs from a handwriting expert.

4d)   The thematic of the *trace* (distinguished by Levinas from the effect, the trail or the sign which does not relate itself to the other as absolute invisible) should lead to a certain rehabilitation of writing. The "He" whose transcendence and generous absence is announced without return in the trace, isn't it more easily the author of writing than that of speech?[3]

Derrida now refers to the *TRACE*. Levinas' use of the term will concern us immediately in the following passage, but clearly Derrida recognizes that it complicates his question to Levinas. According to Derrida, the trace is not itself a SIGN of the other person, a TRAIL that leads to a presence that is currently hidden. The trace, unlike a sign, indicates something that can never be manifest, be present, or show up—it is the indication of the OTHER AS ABSOLUTE INVISIBLE. Derrida proposes that this is not unlike writing, in that the full meaning which is deferred in writing is not occluded, not temporarily absent, but was never there. The one who leaves a trace in this sense TRANSCENDS the trace in such a way that one cannot get back to HIM from the trace. He is generous, giving the trace to another and not allowing any reciprocity or reapproach. Is this person best seen as a writer or a speaker? Derrida emphasizes the issue, Is this the AUTHOR of WRITING or of SPEECH?

C. The Trace and Crossing Out

The interlacing of reading and writing in Derrida centers on the trace, a hidden thread of the other person left in the text but not susceptible to presentation as evidence. The trace is not only not present but also cannot be made present, cannot be represented without ceasing to be trace. This trace is related to Levinas' trace of the other person. Levinas' trace means that the other person who speaks to me is not fully present, there for me, but is absent and present in a somewhat different way than I am present and absent, as assigned and sign for that other person.

7a)   Levinas   OB   119–20/93–94
The face is not the appearance or the sign of some reality—personal like itself—albeit dissimulated or

The other person teaches in her face. There she interrupts me, addresses me, and reveals the authority to interpret. The face itself is not a SIGN, particularly not a

---

[3] Derrida DS 193/167   The withdrawal of that face at the same time opens and limits the exercise of dialectics. It welds it irremediably to its "inferiors," the mimetic arts, play, grammar, writing, and the like. The disappearance of that face is the movement of differance which violently opens writing or, if one prefers, which opens itself to writing and which writing opens for itself.

expressed by the physiognomy, and which would be offered like an invisible theme. Nearness—this is the essence of the thesis expounded here—is precisely not some conjunction of such themes, a structure that their superimposition would form. The face does not function as a sign of a hidden God who could impose the neighbor upon me.

sign of something behind it or beyond it, some essence or reality that only hides in the face. Least of all is the face A SIGN OF A HIDDEN GOD. The face does not have the semiotic function of referring to another—allowing me to authorize the other who addresses me by binding that authority to some reality or some concept or some principle which I determine the other represents. Whatever might lie behind the face would then have served as the warrant of my obligation—and the otherness of the face as the open-endedness of its interpretations—would be bound, bound by something that I could know. The other addressing me would then become a representative of something I already know. Levinas fears the recourse to THEMES—even invisible ones—because the "I" can govern a theme in consciousness. The ESSENCE of Levinas' work is the refusal of themes—the unmaking of the said. In order to not govern and to authorize the other person, the face must be seen not to refer to something merely not now present or even invisible but to what would be incapable of presence.

7b) Trace of itself, trace in the trace of a forsaking, without ever lifting the equivocity, obsessing the subject without standing in a correlation with him, without equaling me in consciousness, ordering me before appearing, according to a glorious increase of obligation. These are the modalities of the signification that is irreducible to presents and to presences, differing from the present—modalities that articulate the *immensity itself of the infinite*. These signs would not await an ontological interpretation, nor some knowing that would be added on to its "essence."[4]

Instead, the face is a TRACE OF ITSELF. It has already left and has left only a trace, or rather A TRACE IN THE TRACE of leaving, of FORSAKING me. The other person is not present but has gone, or rather, even when near me the face of the other person is only a trace of something that could never appear and exceeds my consciousness. The otherness of the other person OBSESSES me, ORDERS me, and still is never graspable or present enough for me to set up a CORRELATION, a balance, an unambiguous sense of this other person. Hence, this is a signification which never has recourse to PRESENTS and to PRESENCES. It never

[4] Derrida P 37–38/26–27 Why traces? And by what right do we reintroduce the grammatic at the moment when we seem to have neutralized every substance, whether phonic, graphic, or other? Of course, it is not a matter of recovering the same concept of writing and of simply reversing the dyssymetry that now is in question. It is a matter of producing a new concept of writing. One may all it *gram* or *différance*. The play of differences supposes in effect the syntheses and the references that prohibit that at any moment in any sense a simple element could be *present* in itself and in referring only to itself. Whether in the order of spoken discourse or of written discourse, no element can function as a sign without referring to another element; which itself is not simply present. This linking makes the constitution of each 'element'—phoneme or grapheme—start from the trace in it of the other elements of the chain or of the system. This linking, this weave, is the *text*, which can only be produced in the transformation of another

happens now. The DIFFERING from the present, the incompleteness of meaning as what can never be completed or given determinate meaning is the *IMMENSITY ITSELF OF THE INFINITE.* The face is not a sign of another reality, but marks the excessive range of the Infinite, the way that the Infinite cannot become present. Levinas' resistance to ontology and knowledge leads to rejecting the claim that a face is a sign. For Levinas a sign (as opposed to saying a sign) establishes a correlation of the two terms, the sign and its referent (itself a sign). The stability and completion in that relation is ontology for Levinas, and ontology closes up my exposure to the other person. Like Derrida, Levinas wants signifying to be distanced from the assumption that signifying is for the sake of knowing, and that all a sign needs is an ontology of ideas or things. The face as trace signifies without any recourse to this collusion of presence and knowledge. The other person is already gone, as it were, when I come close, inaccessible to my knowing that would limit her freedom.

7c) The approach (which ultimately shows itself as substitution) is not speculatively surpassable: it is infinition or the glory of the Infinite. The face as trace—trace of itself, trace expelled within the trace—does not signify an indeterminate phenomenon; its ambiguity is not an indetermination of a noema, but an invitation to the fine risk of approaching as approaching—to the exposure of the one to the other, to the exposure of this exposure, to the expression of the exposure, to the saying. In the approach to the face, flesh becomes verb, the caress—Saying. The thematization of the face unmakes the face and unmakes the approach. The way in which the face indicates its own absence under my responsibility requires a description that develops only in ethical language.[5]

Levinas' problem, moreover, points already to the problematics of reading that will occupy us shortly. If he can grasp this Infinity, making it into a theme, then he has already SPECULATIVELY SURPASSED it. A discussion about the face is not identical with the face. Rather, it seems that to discuss it is to betray something of its non-presence. Hence, THE THEMATIZATION UNMAKES THE FACE—much like words could become tools and writing something for the handwriting expert. The approach to the other person, as we saw in the previous chapter, is glory. But the face as trace, and here Levinas adds EXPELLED WITHIN THE TRACE to name the very exile from presence which the trace 'is,' is not an incomplete concept, a halfway measure of my mind, awaiting some future information or insight. The face as trace is

---

text. Nothing, anywhere either in the elements, or in the system, is ever simply present or absent. There is only, through and through, the differences and the traces of traces.

Derrida G 102–3/70   Why of the *trace?* What led to the choice of this word?. . . Thus we relate this concept of *trace* to what is at the center of the latest writings of Emmanuel Levinas and of his critique of ontology: relationship to the illeity as to the alterity of a past that never was and can never be lived in the originary or modified form of presence.

[5] Levinas OB 115–16/91   The face is a trace of itself, commended to my responsibility and for which I am deficient, sinful, as if I were both responsible for its mortality and guilty myself

rather an invitation: the tracing is a performance, performed for me, inviting me to a RISK. Teaching occurs in a trace that gives me no new knowledge, only the opportunity, rather, *the call*, to express my exposure for the other person, only the responsibility to say the saying of saying. We have seen in the discussion of both saying and writing the way my response can hold open my vulnerability. My point here is that the face makes possible these ethical ways of signifying. The FLESH BECOMES WORD or VERB: my body now signifies to the point of pain for the sake of the other person. My CA-RESSES now express my saying, my vulnerability. Were the other person to appear in the face in a mode of presence or even in the mode of removal as absence, like a symptom, then I would not be called to risk myself for her sake. The trace turns the other person from a subject for thought into an invitation to signify for her. Thematization of the face, however, not only undermines the face, it also makes the vulnerability of the approach impossi-ble—UNMAKES THE APPROACH. Levinas claims that to discuss the trace of the face, the absence of the other as the invitation to my responsibility, requires AN ETHICAL LANGUAGE. The tension between the uses of language for de-scription and for witness will emerge most clearly at the beginning of the next chapter.

There is one more step in this exploration of Why Write and it leads us to Derrida's second essay on Levinas, "At this moment itself . . ." Much of our discussion of Why Read will focus on why and how Derrida reads in that essay, but in relation to the trace and the withdrawal of the author, Derrida also focuses on how to write about Levinas through a series of withdrawals. The repetition and sequencing of withdrawals is a proper conclusion to the examination of Why Write, parallel to Derrida's own reflections on his writ-ing to say nothing. To write of Levinas' writing, an ethics that prophesies responsibility, one has need of specific modes of withdrawal.

8a) Derrida ATM 48/36 This other "he," this "he" as wholly other, can arrive at the end of my phrase (unless my phrase never ar-rived there, indefinitely stopped on its own linguistic shore) only after a series of words which are all faulty, and which I would in passing, have crossed out regularly, one after the other, while leaving each its tracing force, the wake of their tracing, the force (without force) of a trace the other's passage will have left. I have

Derrida is trying to articulate who insti-gates my responsibility in reading Levinas' texts. To name the other person, the au-thor, is almost impossible. THIS "HE" AS WHOLLY OTHER is the one who teaches me through the text, but cannot appear in my commentary. Were he to become respon-sible as author of my commentary, I would become morally abhorrent—as de-manding another take responsibility for my mistakes, my faulty translations and

for surviving. The face is an immediate anachronism, more tense than that of an image offered in the directness of an intuitive intention. In nearness, the absolutely other, The Stranger, whom "I have neither conceived nor born," whom I already have on my arms, already carry according to the Biblical formula "in my breast as the nurse bears the nursing one" (Num. 11:11–12).

written in marking them, in letting them be marked with the other. That is why it is inexact to say that I have crossed them out, these words.

ignorant assertions. But even to recognize him as the one for whom I am responsible, because he writes so as to let me become responsible through reading his texts, re-

quires that he be not present. I might be closed within my OWN LINGUISTIC SHORE, unable to get through this pretext to any other person. I need to construct a series of words that will name the unnameable otherness of my teacher. THE WORDS WHICH ARE ALL FAULTY fail because the otherness cannot be caught in words. But by setting them in a series, where each displaces the previous one, leaving more the gesture of writing and crossing out, of calling out the TRACE of writing, the trace of the other in the trace of writing, I can point toward what lies beyond. Derrida has found one reason for the piling up of appositives in Levinas' writing (and in Derrida's). The trace cannot force, cannot compel, but there is something like a FORCE or an authority of the trace. Like Levinas' resistance of what has no resistance, the TRACING FORCE is a vulnerability to the reader that can allow another to find some other's needs and demands through reading. Writing has a certain privilege in setting up a series where each sign lets the next mark it. Derrida's words about the author are not CROSSED OUT, retracted absolutely, but are instead serially marked, remarked, displaced by a next word. The motion across (or down) the page lets the trace of the other happen. Writing writes this relation to others.

8b) In any case I should not have crossed them out, I should have let them be led into a *series* (twisted sequence of laced cross-outs) an interrupted series, a *series* of interruptions laced together, series of *hiatus* (gaping mouth, mouth opened to the speech cut short or to the gift of the other and to the bread from his mouth) which I would call henceforth in order to formalize in an economical way and to no longer dissociate what is no longer dissociable in this fabric, the criss-cross out [*seriature*].

Derrida qualifies the act of erasing, because writing must not leave a merely blank page, but a page that is a series of crossed-out words. He need not be in control, the designer or instigator, but can LET THEM BE LED. The texture is a set of crossouts that are then laced together. The interruptions and gaps are strung into a series. He now terms that series *CRISS-CROSS OUT* [*SÉRIATURE*]—combining crossing out with the series—making them NO LONGER DISSOCIABLE. But in this sentence, in the second parenthesis (itself a gap) there is a sequence from Levinas, a

sequence that starts with a MOUTH but moves from the mouth to the SPEECH, to the GIFT, to BREAD. Tying signifying to its material marks, the text is bound to an ethical responsibility, to a gaping of my need fed from the traces by others and acknowledged that I have been given through the words of others—a responsive commentary.

8c) This other "he," then, could arrive at the end of my sentence only in the interminable mobility of this

To write "he" at the end of his sentence is to place it in THE CRISS-CROSS OUT, not propounded as a thesis or even named as

criss-cross out. It is not the subject-author—signatory—proprietor of this work; it is a "he" without authority. One can also say that he is the Pro-noun which leaves its presignature under seal in the name of the author, E.L., for example, or inversely that E.L. is only a pronoun replacing the singular prenoun, the seal that comes before everything that can bear a name. E.L. from this point of view becomes the *personal* pronoun of "he."

an author, but as a giving to "me," as a calling me to responsibility with a call that does not bear *his* authority. That "me" functions unlike the YOU from the other passage, indicating the reader of Levinas, but not binding the reader of Derrida's commentary to the reader of Levinas. Indeed, the commentator seems somehow at a distance from the reader of the commentary. Derrida can call Levinas HE, totally other, only by reading HE not as the one in control of the text. HE is neither a philosophical subject, nor an author dictating a text, nor the one who signs the text, acknowledging it as his property. The text is not his in any of the normal senses of control, ownership, AUTHORITY. In writing as he does, Levinas is substituted for another—the reader. Derrida's critique of authorship is not at the expense of responsibility but rather is in the name of it, by honoring and discovering responsibility behind the usual tropes of agency and authority. Derrida reads Levinas as responsible for Levinas' writing much the same way that Levinas finds himself responsible in speaking—without in either case authority, control, and so on. And Derrida now switches to a reinterpretation of how PRONOUNS work—of how indexical signs relate to common nouns. For Derrida proposes that E.L. be read as the prenoun or pronoun—parallel to Levinas' account of "I." E.L. can serve to signify before or in place of the normal pronoun HE. The pronoun will take its meaning as placeholder from another placeholder still less full of content, the other as author, as he who lets writing occur. Levinas' name makes a "HE" possible. It is the *PERSONAL* PRONOUN, more personal than "he," and so still more other than "he" can be.

8d) Without authority, he does not *make* a work. He is not the agent or the creator of his work, but if I may say he *lets* the work work (a word that still remains to be led along). It is necessary to specify immediately that this letting is not a simple passivity, nor a letting to think with in the horizon of letting-be.

The writer is not the MAKER, the agent, the CREATOR—but someone who *LETS* THE WORK WORK, lets writing write. Derrida has now managed to find the letting work of writing that corresponds to the holding open of exposure in speaking that we examined in Levinas in Chapter 2. Because Levinas' writing offers itself and does not compel a reader to read responsively, Levinas has effaced his own authority, his own role in the text. This letting be is the complex passivity that we saw before, and more it is not A LETTING TO THINK—a reference to Heidegger. For the letting work of writing, a writing of the writing, leaves signs for others and is not a letting thoughts arise in the solitary thinker. Writing can break out of the closure made by discourse in a responsive way that thinking is not afforded. Derrida's own commentary lets Levinas' text work. But it not only writes about how Levinas' text lets writing write, but as commentary, writes the writing that writes—writing the letting and not only about the letting.

8e) This letting beyond essence, "more passive than passivity"— understand it as the most provocative thought, today. It is not provoking in the sense of a transgressive and complacently shocking exhibition. A thought also provoked, *first of all* provoked. Outside the law as the law of the other. It itself only provokes from its absolute exposure to the provocation of the other, exposure tensed with all possible force in order to not reduce the others *anterior* past and not to turn back the surface of the me who, finds itself delivered over, *in advance*, body and soul.

Levinas' letting work, a writing writing the writing, is more passive than passivity—in ways we saw in Chapter 2. It goes BEYOND ESSENCE, exceeding the thinking of Heidegger, with the responsibility for others' words, for others' texts. And so Derrida calls it THE MOST PROVOCATIVE THOUGHT—not in some adolescent rebellion or attempt to shock. Levinas' letting work provokes us to responsibility. What is provoked is not a compulsive obligation but a calling to read and to write— responsively. Nor is Levinas the provocateur, the initiator, but this thought itself is PROVOKED—demanding to be thought, to be written. It breaks the law not to demonstrate my superiority to laws, but in responding for THE LAW OF THE OTHER. The provocation follows upon the exposure which guards exposure (writing the writing, saying the saying), that resists a return to self-control and authority. It provokes because it is already DELIVERED. Levinas' writing, Derrida's commentary, and this commentary, oblige without compelling. Already responsive, bound over to other writings, to readings that find traces of others and offering others' meanings to others in commenting.

SUGGESTED READINGS

3   Critchley, Simon. *The Ethics of Deconstruction: Derrida and Levinas*, 31–44. Oxford: Blackwell, 1992.

4   Ward, *Barth, Derrida*, 178–83.

7   Bernasconi, Robert. "The Trace of Levinas in Derrida." In *Derrida and Différance*, ed. David Wood and Robert Bernasconi, 13–29. Evanston, Ill.: Northwestern University Press, 1988.

CHAPTER 4

Why Read?

DESPITE THE RESPONSIVENESS in Derrida's reading of Levinas, reading generally seems to lack the kind of responsibility required in writing. Since the first chapter ended, we have had less and less to say about how we learn from the other person's signs. How can the other criticize me, challenge me, put me in question, when only a book is in the room? The very complexity of effacing self-presence and of the intending to say, the said, seems to make reading even more distant from the task of attending to the teacher, to the other person. If writing as the exposure of using signs separates me from the signs I write, then how will I find another person in written signs when she is gone and all I have is the text? Do I read in order to find the face of the author who is gone? The attending in reading, moreover, is not an encounter with another person, but the attending to a text.

We begin with Derrida's reflection on how a text is not the disclosure of some information, but always a solicitation to a reading, a reading that looks into the text (Pretext 1). The seeking for this hidden thread, however, leads us to a strong claim about the philosophical tradition, the exigency to reread that tradition. Section B (Closure of Philosophy) will notice both Derrida and Levinas negotiating the challenge of why read when the task is to discern what has not been made thematic in the philosophic tradition. In Pretext 2, Derrida distinguishes two strategies: (1) to deconstruct the philosophical tradition from within, and (2) to import something radically other into it—only to admit the failure of each strategy. We will pursue the question of that first strategy in this chapter, and the second in Chapter 5, when we turn to Levinas' interpretation of the Jewish tradition of commentary. Here Levinas unravels the texture of the philosophical textual tradition, showing us how to read it for the very discontinuities it overcomes in Pretext 3.

The crisis of Levinas' account occurs when he has to reflect on his own writing, which leads to a remarkable task in Derrida reading Levinas. Section C (Re-citation) examines the responsibility in the practice of citing and re-citing others' texts. Pretexts 5 and 7 include a re-citation, a moment when Derrida is led to cite one passage by Levinas twice, in the midst of discussing Levinas' own reiterations. The citations come from a longer text by Levinas that we will comment upon first (Pretext 4), where Levinas discusses how books work, revealing precisely what they would conceal: that relations to others instigate and permeate even the most self-sufficient sorts of texts. Derrida will explore how Levinas' book works beyond the usual way to instigate responsibility in the reader through repetitions. Reading then is tripled here: (1) to read books to find the traces of others' disruptions of the thematics, (2) to read Levinas' repetitions about his own texts' interruptions, and (3) to read Derrida's repeated citation of Levinas as another level of traced interruptions—the traces in commentary that enjoin a different responsibility in the reader of commentary.

A. THE HIDDEN THREAD

The challenge in reading is accentuated by Derrida, a challenge that appeared under the name "deconstruction." Precisely because writing responsively depends on tracing and withdrawal, erasure and reiteration, with trying to say nothing, the responsibility to read must be to attend to the withdrawal in another's writing. Like listening, attending to the teacher's disruption of the image, to the break from the sign to the signifying, reading requires us to read for what disrupts the thematic, the image. In this first pretext Derrida offers an account of how a text is like a textile, woven but also subtle.

1a) Derrida DS 71–72/63–64 A text is a text only if it hides the law of its composition and the rule of its game from the first glance, from the first comer. A text remains, moreover, always imperceptible. The law and the rule do not take cover in the inaccessibility of a secret, they simply never deliver themselves to the present, to anything one could precisely call a perception. At the risk always and essentially of losing itself definitively. Who will ever know such a disappearance?

Derrida defines a text through its HIDING. A text does not display itself, but rather remains IMPERCEPTIBLE. What is it hiding? The way it works, the rules for reading it. A text is enigmatic—as Levinas says of the other person's face. A text, as Derrida says about his own writing, will not provide something to be understood easily. It does not, however, hold A SECRET or esoteric wisdom that can be uncovered by an initiate. Rather, how a text works never becomes present, never is graspable in a perception—the text is a fabric of traces, itself a kind of trace. To be legible is not the same as to be visible. A text is always at risk of interception, of not arriving, of misunderstanding. Because a text is imperceptible it must always risk being lost—even should the book be kept, even transmitted. But should the book be lost along with the text: WHO WILL EVER KNOW? A sign cannot guarantee its delivery—and service for the other (signifying) cannot count on reception, fulfillment. The suspension of perceptibility is like the teacher's face: we never know or grasp the other person, and so cannot comprehend the text.

1b) In any case the dissimulation of the texture can take centuries to unmake its cloth. The cloth envelops the cloth. Centuries to unmake the cloth. Reconstituting it thus as an

Whether lost or maintained, the texture hiding a text can produce centuries of reading in THE UNMAKING OF THE CLOTH. The history of reading a text is the unraveling of its texture, the continued seeking

organism. Indefinitely regenerating its own weave behind the cutting trace, the decision of each new reading. Always reserving a surprise for the anatomy and the physiology of a critique that believed in mastering its game, which oversaw at once all of its threads, also deceiving itself to intend to look at the text without touching it, without laying hands on the 'object,' without risking to add something, a unique chance to enter into the play in catching the fingers, of some new thread.[1]

beneath its surface for the law and the rule which define it—a seeking never consummated. The cloth or weave itself ENVELOPS THE CLOTH: the text as a kind of saying, as an opening without a theme, only opens in the text itself. The search for its structure cannot occur in a present moment but takes time, a great deal of time, generations of readers. The frayed, unwoven cloth forms again as though alive, AN ORGANISM, grafting new insights onto the old body of the text. Because the text cannot be made present, but is always

stretched out through these various readings, it in fact REGENERATES itself, its weave restored despite the cuts of analysis that a reader makes. A reading is a DECISION, a cut into the text, picking certain aspects, following a disruptive line—and that is the proper task of reading. The reader who looks for some mastery of the rules of the game or an overview of the text, a place outside it that controls it, learns nothing from the text. To attend to the text, a complex or tissue of signs is to be burned by the text, or mangled by its weave. But it also is to discover a NEW THREAD in the text, a new perspective. Hence, the unmaking of the cloth is the process of analyzing, untying, unweaving—which succeeds not in unraveling the text (in which case there is no text left), but in a new thread in the text that regenerates itself.

1c) Adding is here nothing other than giving to read. We must set ourselves to thinking this: it is not a matter of embroidering, except if we consider that knowing how to embroider is again to understand how to follow the given thread. Which is to say, if one will follow me well,

ADDING A NEW THREAD Derrida identifies with GIVING TO READ. The reader who discovers or unravels a new thread in turn gives this reading to others, allowing others to read in the text, now altered. Reading is not private (me and the text, much less me and the author), it is giving

---

[1] Levinas TN 33/24   And is the hand just a hand and not also a certain impudence of spirit that savagely seizes a text, without preparation and without a teacher, approaching the verse as a thing or an allusion to history in the instrumental nakedness of its vocables, without care for the new possibilities of their semantics, patiently opened up by the religious life of tradition? Without precautions, without mediation, without all that has been acquired through a long tradition that is not only the dead weight of a long history strewn with contingencies, but which in the opening up of horizons through which alone the ancient wisdom of the Scriptures reveals the secrets of a renewed inspiration. Touched by the impatient, busy hand that is said to be objective and scientific, the Scriptures, cut off from the breath that lives within them, become unctuous, false, or mediocre words, matter for doxographers, for linguists and philologists. Therein lies the impurity of these inspired texts, their latent impurity. It was not absurd to warn readers of the dangers brought about by the very holiness of the Torah, and to declare it impure in advance. Hands off! Contagion, or something of the sort. The impurity returns to and strikes back at the indiscrete hand from which it came.

the hidden one. If there is a unity of reading and writing, as is easily thought today, if reading *is* writing, this unity does not designate an undifferentiated confusion nor an identity of perfect security: the *is* which couples reading to writing must become picked out.

to other people to read. Not a taking but a giving—hence still a kind of writing or signifying, a responding. The difficulty is to allow for adding a new thread without transforming reading into merely making something visible—because the text itself cannot become visible. To add is GIVING TO READ—not giving to know. Derrida refers to EMBROIDERING in order to emphasize that the reader is not adding a thread of her own, but is rather following a thread that is given, that is already in the text. Not the active imposition of a reading, but the passive tracing of a thread that no one has seen before—A HIDDEN THREAD. But if to read is to give to read, to follow a thread so as to expose it—without thematizing it—then there seems to be A UNITY OF READING AND WRITING. I read in order to prolong the writing—which is for the sake of further reading. Derrida questions this unity. The two moments are not an UNDIFFEREN-TIATED CONFUSION, nor is the discovery of their unity one that gives us SECURITY and rest. The moments are different, despite their emergence in and through a text. Indeed, the coupling of the two, the *is* which seems to make each activity into a presence, must be PICKED OUT. The relation through signs (texts) is asymmetric. I do not read as I write, even if I do write my readings. To follow the unseen thread, to renew the fabric, requires tracing the traces, traces which do not lead to the true meaning or point of the text, but rather lead to new readers who will take up my thread again. The discipline the text exercises on its readers is enigmatic, only an invitation to find a command in the fabric, not a presentation of a lesson. The reader is addressed in the text, or even through the text, but the addresser never appears. The traces left do not get us back to the addresser as an author, as a presence or a representative of some rule or principle. The invitation allows me to approach, to become responsible, but what I respond to is a trace of what was never there, but which precedes me in such an absolute sense that any thought I might have of dictating it or controlling it is impossible. Thus we have a preliminary account of reading, a responsiveness to traces in the fabric of text—a responsibility for the text itself, for its provenance before we get it, a responsibility for the writings of others.

B. Closure of Philosophy

But this last text, like almost all others of Derrida, also refers to the centuries of unmaking the cloth, to one cloth from among others. The texts of Derrida and Levinas, and of the other voices awaiting us in the following chapters, belong to a specific fabric, a philosophic fabric that had tended to prefer self-presence to signification, knowledge to service, and so on. Because one can only pretend to weave a new fabric from new threads, because signs mean only in contexts of other signs, Derrida focuses on how texts in a certain philosophical tradition have worked. He will orient us in that tradition, and Levinas will augment this orientation with an account of the specific philosophical task in terms of saying and writing. In a discussion of the alternatives in contemporary thought, Derrida discusses the ways that deconstruction can relate to otherness. This text presents a doubled way of reading (and writing) familiar to readers of Derrida from other texts as well. But our interest is to see how reading the philosophical tradition can provide a glimpse beyond its closure. The discussion of strategies recognizes the risks—risks we now see as self-reflective, inherent in reading the tradition, and in giving it to others to read.

2a) Derrida M 162–63/134–35 *The strategic wager.* A radical shake-up can only come from *outside.* The one I am speaking of does not depend more than any other on some spontaneous decision of philosophical thought following some internal maturation of its history. This shake-up is played out in the violent relation of the *whole* of the West to its other.

Derrida is pursuing a disruption of the closure, which he claims can come only from *OUTSIDE.* This outside is not some place outside the text, some transcendental origin or principle that can show up as fully present. The outside must show up inside, within the text, but in so showing up, disrupt the tradition that defines reality as showing up, as being, as presence. Derrida is remembered most for claiming that "there is no outside the text", and our treatment here of otherness and responsibility contests the moralistic critiques as well as the anti-ethical embrace that "slogan" afforded. We see that what in Levinas was the disruption of the autonomy and spontaneity of my own knowing now becomes the disruption of an historical tradition. The passivity of substitution in Levinas now becomes the refusal to see deconstruction and its invocation of the outside as merely a SPONTANEOUS DECISION, an option that comes by an act of will. The WAGER is required, it has an ethical exigency, ethical because its outcome as wager is uncertain. But the shake-up is also not another stage in the INTERNAL MATURATION of history of philosophy. The need to shake up, from the outside, is not a fruit of a long process, but is marked as the exigency of THE WHOLE of the West. The West's other is poised as what can shake up the West, precisely in the midst of their relation. The West has tried to accommodate and assimilate its other, and so the question becomes how to use its other to shake it up.

2b) ... Taking into account these systemic effects, one has nothing else from that inside where "we are" than the choice between two strategies.
[1] To attempt the exit and the deconstruction without changing ground, repeating what is implicit in the foundational concepts and the

Given the systematic capacity to restabilize, Derrida concludes that only two strategies for breaching the closure of the philosophical tradition are available. The first is to try within that tradition. Here is a rereading of the tradition in order to disrupt a received reading. The FOUNDATIONAL CONCEPTS can be made explicit

original problematic, using the instruments or the available stones in the house against the edifice, which is to say, of course, in language. The risk here is to confirm, to consolidate, or to *sublate* without ceasing, at an ever more certain depth what itself one attempts to deconstruct. The continuing explicitation in view of the opening risks being sunk into the autism of the closure.[2]

and then used against the system. Otherness has left its traces within the very terms of language that seem to solidify presence, authority, control, and so on, and we can find that the texts of the tradition already are opening to other people, inviting interpretation, deferring their own meanings, and so on. This is a counterreading of sorts, but also a responding for the tradition and its texts. THE RISK, of course, is that the tradition will appropriate our reading and swallow up the otherness we are trying to trace and attend to—making us one more phase in the march of self-consciousness, of the development of knowledge, of a progressive enlightenment from prejudices. Derrida refers to this as BEING SUNK INTO THE AUTISM OF THE CLOSURE. It would be losing the exposure to what is other, and returning into autism, a pathological failure to relate to what is other.

2c) [2] To decide to change ground, in a discontinuous and irruptive manner in brutally placing oneself outside and in affirming the absolute rupture and the absolute difference. Without speaking of all the other forms of deceptive perspective in which such a displacement can be caught, inhabiting more naively, more narrowly, the within that one claims to desert, the simple practice of language ceaselessly reinstalls the "new" ground on the oldest ground. One may show from numerous and precise examples the effects of such a reinstallation or such a blindness.

Obviously these effects do not suffice to annul the necessity for a "change of ground."

The alternative is TO CHANGE GROUND, to claim to move outside, invoking other traditions, other experiences, other ways of writing and reading. To proclaim ABSOLUTE DIFFERENCE, but not as a theme, not as a philosophical option, but from an other perspective. The risks here are what Derrida calls DECEPTIVE PERSPECTIVE, for the language used to expose this outside is, of course, the inside's language and belongs to the tradition ONE CLAIMS TO DESERT. The new territory is viewed, or rather discussed, in terms retained from the old, and novelty disappears. These bold changes of ground lead back to THE OLDEST GROUND, or at least can—and we have seen that if they *could* not, they would all the more repeat the older concepts. By securing novelty, they would

[2] Derrida M xx–xxi/xxiv–xxv   One should have at the same time, by conceptually rigorous, philosophically *uncompromising* analyses, *and* by the inscription of marks that no longer belong to the philosophical space, not even to the neighborhood of its other, shifting the centering, by philosophy of its own types. To write otherwise. To delimit the form of a closure that no longer has an analogy with what philosophy can have represented under that name, according to its line, straight or circular, encompassing a homogeneous space. To determine, entirely against any philosopheme, the uncompromising which prevents it from calculating its margin, by a *bordering* violence, imprinted according to new *types*.

foreclose risk. Indeed, Derrida claims that the risk of such reinstallations of philosophical presence cannot ANNUL THE NECESSITY for this change. NECESSITY because only from outside can the greatest shaking, the shake-up which opens thought for the responsibility for others, come.

2d) And obviously between these two forms of deconstruction the choice cannot be simple and unique. A new writing must weave and interlace the two motifs. Which comes down to saying that one must speak several languages and produce several texts at once.

The need for an outside, whether within or without, cannot be reduced to one or the other (A SIMPLE CHOICE). Rather, Derrida claims that A NEW WRITING is required, one that weaves the two motifs: deconstructing the philosophical tradition and seeking out other positions, other texts from which to address the questions of writing and reading. Writing, it seems, is always plural, producing not one proposition, but SEVERAL TEXTS. Speaking not only one technical idiom, one pure genre, one dialect, but rather ONE MUST SPEAK SEVERAL LANGUAGES. As our text proceeds, the question of how to write this text responsively will recur to this double task, of stepping outside philosophy and of deconstructing within—a move that is already interwoven in the reading of texts by Levinas and Derrida. In the next chapter, we will see further just how Levinas has had recourse to Jewish texts as an outside. But first, we must examine the way that philosophical texts in general can be reopened. The responsibility in reading requires a reconceiving of the task of philosophy.

We return to Levinas' *Otherwise Than Being*, to a passage about how philosophical writing works: that is, how it imposes a coherent thematics on its writing, but also is pragrammatological—relating to its readers in its own texture.

3a) Levinas OB 215/169 This discourse [of Western philosophy] will assert itself to be coherent and one. In relating the interruption of discourse or my transport unto discourse, I am reknotting the thread. Discourse is ready to say, in itself, every break, to consume them like their silent origins or as eschatology. If philosophical discourse breaks, withdraws from speech and mumbles, or speaks *to itself*—it nonetheless speaks and speaks of the discourse where it just spoke and to which it returns to say its provisional withdrawal.[3]

The question becomes reflexive for Levinas' philosophical writing or Derrida's or ours. Philosophical discourse has the capacity to claim to appropriate everything that interrupts it, every person who claims to oppose it. By detouring through what can be thought, or known, or narrated, philosophy gains control and authority over its others. Philosophy thus represents the epitome of the failure to respond, to attend to the other person. It ASSERTS its COHERENCE and UNITY, making every break, every moment of another's interiority accessible to me, accessible in

---

[3] Levinas OB 8/7 A methodological problem is posed here. It consists of asking if the pre-original of the saying (if the anarchic, the unoriginal as we would call it) can be brought to

the light of thought. The breaks in the thread are REKNOTTED—in fact, it happens in the telling, performed in talking even about breaks. Philosophical discourse wants to authorize every break in its own authority, to legitimate even what disputes its legitimacy. Its move is to dispatch these interruptions to an ORIGIN or a telos (ESCHATOLOGY). Thus, an interruption that resists this closure will have to break with the logics of origins, presence, and goals. And even when something does break in, and philosophy must withdraw, MUMBLING to itself, it comes back and promises to return and to tell us about its withdrawal, which is only PROVISIONAL. Its discourse serves a logic of reflection—anything can be made into an experience to be related—the imperialism of thought becomes the imperialism of talk. Nothing can really unsettle the mode of philosophical discourse.

3b) And aren't we, at this moment itself, in the process of barring the exit that our entire essay attempted, and encircling our position on all sides? The exceptional words by which the trace of the past and the extravagance of the approach were said—One, God—become terms, reenter the vocabulary and place themselves at the disposal of philologists instead of confounding the philosophical language. Their explosions themselves are told.

Including Levinas' own discourse. He asks if the whole struggle of his work, to say the saying, to find a way to welcome the other without controlling the other, if his discussions in ethical theory, do not in fact betray the other person, the interruption that starts his thinking? Levinas opted for a vocabulary that helped say the TRACE, but those words are now become TERMS. Can one say saying without making saying into a said? Of course not. But the conversion of saying into said seems to make saying the saying impossible. There are Levinas scholars and experts on deconstruction, people who *know* what this work, these texts, are really about (PHILOLOGISTS). Derrida and Levinas deliver themselves over to the scholars, to the philosophers who by knowing and telling what is going on will put a stop to the performance of it—because what is going on is precisely the exposure of something which cannot be known and is then juxtaposed with what can be known.

---

betray itself in showing itself in a theme (if an an-archaeology is possible)—and if this betrayal can be reduced; if one can at the same time know and free the *known* from the marks that the thematization imprints on it in subordinating it to ontology. Betrayal that is the price of anything showing itself, even the unsayable, and that makes possible the indiscretion in regard to the unsayable—which is probably the very task of philosophy.

Derrida G 405/286   What then exceeds this closure *isn't anything*: neither the presence of being, nor meaning, nor history, nor philosophy; but something other which hasn't a name, which is announced in the thought of this closure and guides our writing here. Writing in which philosophy is inscribed as a place in a text that it does not command. Philosophy is only, in the writing, this movement of that writing as erasing the signifier and [also] the desire for the restored presence, of the being signified in its brilliance and its glamour. The properly philosophical evolution and economy of writing go on, therefore, in the meaning of effacing the signifier, which takes the form of forgetting or of repression.

3c) But clearly, this story itself is without end and without continuity, which is to say, it goes from one to the other—it is tradition. But thereby it [the story] renews itself. The new meanings arise in its meanings, whose exegesis is the unfolding or the history before all historiography. Thus the equivocal whose stitches cannot run, which language weaves, signifies.

Ethical theory becomes not impossible but insecure and, in fact, never completed because the appropriating moves of philosophical discourse take time and cannot end. If a trace is always left, then the story about interruptions that happened to me on the way maintains those interruptions. And I myself, as philosopher (not as philosophy itself), must tell that story TO THE OTHER person because stories are not ex-

ercises in consciousness but are performed for others, in response to others, in the vulnerability of interruptions by others. That story has no CONTINU-ITY in the strong sense, nothing that guarantees that each term leads to the next. Instead, it goes from one to another, jumping from one speaker to another, from one text to another. This risky motion of resaying the saying of others RENEWS the TRADITION. Here is a concept of tradition that is not repetition, or continuity, or cognitive, or credal. The NEW MEANINGS of the others, of the next generation rereading the previous, produce HISTORY. Levinas claims that it OCCURS BEFORE ALL HISTORIOGRAPHY—that the readings are first produced and then retold, knotted up into a coherent discourse. The stretching out in time, however, is history before consciousness catches up with it. Language weaves, knots, and interlaces, an equivocal sign that cannot be resolved into either 'a' or 'b.' Like a stocking that CANNOT RUN, these signs cannot split by unraveling. Language itself signifies as this unrunnable fabric, incapable of being only told—which would be to be told to no one.

3d) But isn't it then an aberration or a distortion of being that is thematized, wrenched to identity? An impossible simultaneity of meaning, the nonassemblable but also inseparable one-for-the-other, an excluded-middle signifying as the equivocal or the enigma—and yet the possibility for this beyond itself to be a notion while unmaking itself? Language would exceed the limits of the thought in suggesting, in letting imply without ever making understood—an implication of a meaning distinct from that which comes to the sign from the simultaneity of the system or from the logical definition of a concept.[4]

The self-reflecting objection comes back, again (it cannot go away—otherwise the risk would be conquered and not opened). Levinas is doing such a good job of explaining how this works that he has produced a new IDENTITY for these effects, for saying, for philosophy. He has splayed meaning and refused it simultaneity, made signifying for the other intrinsic and still unrepresentable, ruled out the EXCLUDED MIDDLE, embraced the ENIGMA (which doubles as the EQUIVOCAL)—all in order to generate a new notion in the process of picking it apart. The discontinuous story makes a good story, too. But, indeed, lan-

[4] Derrida G 25/14 We have little need to renounce these concepts that today are indispensable for our unsettling the heritage to which they belong. Within the closure, by an oblique and always perilous movement, risking without stopping a falling back on this side of what is

guage must be able to EXCEED THE LIMITS OF THE THOUGHT—and this exceeding requires a meaning that signifying performs beyond the LOGICAL DEFINITION OF A CONCEPT and the SIMULTANEITY OF THE SYSTEM. Philosophical discourse bears a double reading: (1) as the unifying and knowing of everything, even what stands outside it and challenges it, even what it harms, and (2) as a tracing of what is open-ended and incomplete, risky and vulnerable, a sedimentation of readings that cannot be concluded, in which each reader takes responsibility for the other's writing, where the meaning occurs in the responding and not in knowing about the responding. Indeed, where the responding distances itself from the knowing, methodically and at times paradoxically, in order to invite the other to join the risk, or rather to engage her own risk of reading and writing. A responsibility of reading to give to others to read.

C. RE-CITATION

To give to read is also to read, and in reading to cite and comment on another's texts. We seek not merely a theory of the responsibility to read, but also a practice, indeed, a performance of such reading. But rather than grandstand and pronounce that I am doing such a responsive reading here, I wish to trace a responsive reading in Derrida reading Levinas. Derrida comments on this topic very closely and thoughtfully in his second essay on Levinas. Thus we have an interesting nexus: we see both how Derrida reads and how Levinas writes—and in a strange metalepsis, how Derrida comments—which will illuminate how we, too, are reading and thus commenting in this text. It is not at all clear that we can distinguish the way that Derrida claims Levinas writes from the way that Derrida himself writes as commentator. That is: Derrida's reading of Levinas bears a close resemblance to Derrida's own writing—and the goals of the two styles of writings are in closest proximity. (I am not claiming that Levinas is writing just as Derrida reads him; rather that Derrida's reading resembles his own writing—and that Derrida thus learns from his reading.) It is noteworthy, moreover, that it is Derrida who devotes care to reading philosophical texts, including Levinas', this way. Levinas is largely unwilling to comment closely on other philosophers' texts and on how they wrote. To see Levinas reading in a similar way, we must turn to his reading of Jewish traditional texts—which we will do in the next chapter.

Derrida reads to discern what techniques Levinas uses to write ethically—he reads in order to attend to the responsibility in reading. The reading in the

---

deconstructed, they must surround the critical concepts with a prudent and detailed discourse, marking the condition, the context and the limits of their efficiency, designating rigorously their belonging to the machine that permits deconstructing; and at the same stroke, the fault that lets a glimpsing, still unnameable, the glimmer of beyond the closure.

second essay, "At this moment itself . . ." is one of the richest and most obscure of Derrida's writings—which places it at the frontiers of philosophical literature. The density of his prose is punctuated by citations of Levinas' texts. Derrida focuses on one passage from *Otherwise Than Being*, in which Levinas discusses how writing works ethically, frequently punctuating his analyses by reference to *this work*, and *this moment itself*. Derrida's analysis of this passage and this particular punctuation, which is also repeated in other texts, is a model of responsive reading and a model for how to read Derrida as well. Obviously, we can no more make sense of the whole of Derrida's sustained argument (which itself then proceeds to a vigorous interrogation of Levinas on gender difference) than we can of other texts we have treated. Instead, I wish to look at Derrida's comments on one key passage in Levinas, a passage that Derrida cannot read only once but must comment upon and cite twice, hence re-citation.

I will begin with the passage from Levinas in its entirety, marking the two different citations of it in Derrida's essay by <u>underlining</u> the parts that are cited the first time and by **bold** for those in the second citation. After examining the text by Levinas, I will then read each of the two commentaries upon it by Derrida. The task is complicated by both the form and the content of the texts under consideration, because Levinas' text is about how books work while Derrida's reading is about how Levinas' book in specific works—and how it works is primarily through a certain kind of repetition of phrases. My commentary, therefore, will have to make clear what is at stake in both the general question of how books work (according to Levinas) and how repetition works (according to Derrida) in order to understand how Derrida's commentary itself depends on repetition/re-citation. The guiding question, Why read?, will focus on the responsibility in reading (and writing commentary), a responsibility to hold open the vulnerability in another's text, and in so doing to remain faithful to the responsibility performed in a responsive text.

4a) Levinas OB 216–17/170–71 Are the tears of a logical text sewn up again only by logic? It is in the association of philosophy and the state, of philosophy and medicine, that the rupture of discourse is surmounted. The interlocutor who does not submit himself to logic is threatened with prison or the asylum or endures the prestige of the master and the medication of the doctor:

A few pages after the previous pretext, Levinas questions the reknotting in the text. If PHILOSOPHY is the ability to narrate even interruptions, it also is a way for a tradition to preserve traces of the breaks. The immediate question is whether LOGIC alone resews the torn cloth. Levinas discusses the function of THE STATE, MEDICINE, and even the academy to ply the needle that mends. PHILOSOPHY seems to need the extra authority of the institutions of the state and medicine in order to overcome the breaks. Logic works because the illogical person, the one who questions reason's authority to retie the shreds of material, ends up in

PRISON or the ASYLUM, instructed by a professor or drugged by a psychiatrist. Logic cannot stop someone from crazy thoughts, excessive anxieties, obsessive concerns for others. The sanction that comes not from logic but from these other institutions makes the choice of interruption and obsession unsupportable.

4b) violence or reasons of state or an approach, assuring a universality to the rationalism of logic and to the law its subject matter. Discourse thus recuperates its meaning by repression or by medication, by just violence verging on potential injustice where repressive justice lies.

Levinas claims that LOGIC cannot provide its own UNIVERSALITY nor can LAW provide a SUBJECT MATTER without the compliance of the state, medicine, and psychiatric practice. Logic in itself is not assured of its authority, nor law its content. But logic, then, is not necessarily coercive. The use of force (prison or medication) allows reason to regain a stable meaning—but this involves a JUST VIOLENCE that verges on REPRESSIVE JUSTICE. Justice is not the opposite of violence but requires a violence—a topic we will address in the next part when pragmatics opens up into a social theory. The authority of reason or logic, however, appears here based on a violence and on the warrant of force.

4c) It is by means of the state that reason and knowledge are force and efficiency. But the state discounts incurable madness and the intervals of madness. It does not untie the knots but cuts them. The Said thematizes interrupted dialogue or dialogue delayed by silences, by failure or by delirium, but

The FORCE of reason, even of the better argument, depends on THE STATE. The state cannot dismiss INCURABLE MADNESS or excuse it but must forcefully contain it. In opposition to writing, THE STATE DOES NOT UNTIE and guard knots, BUT CUTS THEM. The craziness that is ethics, that involves me in concern for what another person does, is simply destroyed by the state. Throwing me in prison or an asylum is a breakup of my life with no retying possible. Not the other's interruption but the state's authority destroys my capacity for responsibility. Indeed, THE SAID—that is, discourse—can turn interruptions into themes, managing to make a whole story out of broken threads—threads frayed by delirium and also by failure. By cutting knots the state discharges me from discourse; the philosophical said may provide a rationalization for that discharge, but it at least reknots the thread.

4d) the intervals are not recuperated. Discourse that suppresses the interruptions of discourse in relating them—doesn't it sustain the discontinuity under the knots where the thread is reknotted?

The said does not intend to preserve the INTERVALS. Its goal is to SUPPRESS the DISCONTINUITY, to make it seem as if everything fits in. Again Levinas sees discourse as acting in collusion with the forceful discharge of outlaws and lunatics—but he does distinguish the two actions. For in discourse and in texts discontinuity leaves a trace under the knot. Discourse does not utterly efface what broke into it, no matter how well it reintegrates it. Discourse differs from the prison or asylum. The place to look for interruptions is where the knots are—and in one sense the discursive knots deconstruct or unravel themselves—maintaining the very interruptions that they try to suppress.

4e) **The interruptions of discourse, found again and related in the immanence of the said, are preserved as in the knots of a thread reknotted, the trace of a diachrony that does not enter into the present, that flees simultaneity.**

The transcendence of the other person thus is immanent in discourse, in the said, in the text. It just is not easy to repress interruptions and the demands of others because they guide all use of signs, even the uses that try to maintain a self-legitimating thinking. The importance of this RE-KNOTTED thread is that it bears the TRACE of what is NOT PRESENT, what cannot be present. Levinas calls it DIACHRONY here and emphasizes the refusal of SIMULTANEITY. The transcendence of the other person's otherness can never show up, but instead leaves marks as breaks beneath the knots where rational and logical discourse claims to make sense and to make present.

4f) **But I interrupt again the ultimate discourse where all discourse is announced, in saying it to someone who listens to it and who is placed outside the Said that is said in the discourse, outside everything that it includes. And this is true of the discourse which I am holding at this moment itself. This reference to the interlocutor permanently pierces the text that the discourse claims to weave in thematizing and in enveloping all things. In totalizing being, discourse as Discourse thus provides a retraction of the very claim of totalization.**

Levinas now reintroduces the INTER-LOCUTOR, as he did in the previous pre-text. Beyond the knots and reknottings there is the pragmatic dimension of discourse: that it is given TO SOMEONE who listens, to someone who has the authority to stand outside and judge the discourse. This pragmatic dimension of discourse refuses the closure that reason craves. This theme of the interlocutor is familiar to us since the opening of Chapter 1. Levinas now applies it to his own discourse, the discourse that is going on NOW, AT THIS MOMENT ITSELF (a moment that Derrida will rightly argue never is concurrent with the reader's time). Levinas then returns to the relation to the interlocutor in general—that PERMANENTLY PIERCES the texture. Were discourse merely thought for the mind itself and for no one else, were signs only presentations of thoughts, then discourse would not provide its own RETRACTION. But discourse deconstructs itself precisely because it must be for the other person, for a reader or listener, who even in assent cannot be totalized in the discourse itself. The saying of a theme, even one about responsibility, or even one that attempts to totalize, disrupts the integrity and completeness of what is said.

4g) A reversal that resembles the one that the refutation of skepticism makes evident. In what is written, of

The retraction of the claim to totality that occurs by making that claim to another person resembles another reversal:

course, the saying makes itself pure said, simultaneity of the saying and its conditions.

THE REFUTATION OF SKEPTICISM requires answering the skeptic. Levinas' analysis of skepticism focuses on how the skeptic's saying and what is said are not simultane-ous, and so not simply contradictory. To make them contradictory I would need to reduce the skeptic to a mere mouthpiece of a thesis and thus deny him the authority to teach me, to object to my claims. Just as my responding to the skeptic recognizes that the refutation must fail in the face of my teacher, so proclaiming a story that encompasses all breaks deconstructs itself because one is awaiting the assent or denial from the interlocutor. But in THE WRITTEN text a SIMULTANEITY does occur. The saying is presented alongside its conditions, which in turn reduces the saying to the said, even to PURE SAID. So runs the objection that texts cannot teach—because they do reduce to their content. This was our earlier hesitation about an absent inter-locutor and impossibility of a responsibility to read.

4h) Interrupted discourse catching up with its own breaks is the book. But books have their destiny. They belong to a world that they do not enclose, but which they recognize in the writing and in the printing and in the making of pre-faces and in making forewords precede them. They interrupt themselves and call to other books and are interpreted in the final analysis in a saying dis-tinct from the said.[5]

Levinas now defines books as this at-tempted simultaneity, this CATCHING UP WITH ITS OWN BREAKS. The book is the crotchet of knotted and reknotted threads—all held together by a cover. But what the book is and how the book works pragmatically are different. For books are not merely the attempt for simultaneity but are written for others. The book is not the world (whatever the text might be),

[5] Levinas OB 25/20 Unless the naiveté of the philosopher appeals, beyond reflection on oneself, to the critique exercised by *the other* philosopher, whatever the imprudences he may have committed in his turn and the gratuity of his own saying. Philosophy thus instigates a drama between philosophers and an intersubjective movement that resembles neither the dia-logue of teamworkers in science nor even the Platonic dialogue, which is reminiscence of a drama more than that drama itself. It is sketched according to a different structure. Empirically, it is arranged as history of philosophy where new interlocutors are always entering, new inter-locutors who are to resay, but where the ancients retake speech in order to answer in the interpretations which they instigate, and where nonetheless, despite this lack of the "certainty in motion"—or because of it—no one is allowed either a relaxation of attention nor a lack of rigor.

Derrida DS 229–30/202 Such writing that refers back only to itself carries us back, at the same time, [*à la fois*] indefinitely and systematically, to an other writing. At the same time: this is what one must account for. A writing which refers back only to itself and a writing which refers indefinitely to an other writing, this may appear noncontradictory: the reflecting screen only ever captures the writing, without stopping, indefinitely, and the reference confines us in the element of referring. Of course. But the difficulty holds in relation between the medium of writing and the determination of each textual unity. Each time while referring to an other text, to an other determined system, each organism must refer only to itself as determined structure; *at the same* time opened and closed.

but rather belongs to others, to readers and a world that requires introducing, printing, prefacing, and so on. This may be a reference to Derrida's essay "*Hors Texte*" in *Dissemination*, which discusses the graphics of these supposedly introductory materials. Levinas' point is that were a book a pure said, it would have no need for inserting itself into a world by prefacing. A book can totalize no more than discourse could. But the relation to the world is primarily a relation to readers and TO OTHER BOOKS, indeed, a calling for other books, for readings, for commentaries. Books INTERRUPT THEMSELVES or are interrupted. The reknottings are themselves frayed or broken. The other book, like the other person, even when that book is a comment on this book, teaches. A book cannot close in on itself, but is already intertextual, both in derivation and in destination. The text is this intertext, and the saying finds refuge in these textiles of knots and reknottings.

To summarize this complex pretext from Levinas: the question is whether discourse (and then a text) is capable of overcoming the disruption that occurs through the approach of another person. Levinas begins by distinguishing the mending that logic performs from the forceful intervention of institutions (a–c). Discourse itself, however, retains the trace of the interruptions, a break that appears beneath the knots of repair (c–d). But discourse is also addressed to someone, and the relation to an interlocutor prevents the said from obliterating the saying—because even a totalizing philosophical discourse must still be addressed to another, an addressing that deconstructs and retracts the claim to totality (e–f). Finally, Levinas turns to the book—which seems to present a pure said because it achieves utter simultaneity among its signs. And here, too, like the saying, there is a pragmatic dimension, for books are published and addressed to readers, addressed as well to other books. Despite the appearance that a book is the catching up of discourse with its interruptions, a book is published for a reader who can then write a commentary. A book, then, cannot sew it all up but must leave itself open to its interpreters (g).

Derrida focuses on how Levinas can write a text without obliging his reader—and at the same time how a reader can read that text in order to find herself obligated, responsible. Derrida's goal is to understand both how I can write responsively by withdrawing myself, my themes, my claim upon an other and how I can read such a text to discover the responsibility in that mode of writing. To read responsively is to discover how the other writes responsively. And, then, to comment responsively in response. We are thus engaged in trying to read Derrida's commenting on Levinas' mode of writing—in order to understand the way that I as writer should withdraw but as reader should discover the responsiveness of the author through the text, and as commentator should link both responsive reading and withdrawing writing.

A text, remarkably, does not present the writer to the reader—and so the writer and the reader never achieve simultaneity. Indeed, for the writer the reader is a future that cannot become present and for the reader the author is a past that was never present. The text negotiates this dual absence—and so in so far as it works, as it signifies, it is never a presence or even a presenting, much less a representation. But the text tempts us to see it making everything happen at once, through its coordination of signs. Derrida focuses on how repeating a sign in different contexts illuminates the absence of its meaning as both the futurity of its interpretation and the absence of the authority, the author. Derrida finds the phrase AT THIS MOMENT ITSELF both in *Otherwise Than Being* and in various of Levinas' Jewish commentaries. That phrase itself seems to refer to a present moment, (THIS) a time in which the text signifies now, when it does its thing. The *ITSELF* [*même*], moreover, is like a gesticulating, an effort to make THIS MOMENT more real, more self-determined. But Levinas cannot mean that it makes present or even is present, precisely because the trace in the text, the trace at work *at this moment itself*, is not present, is not in the 'now.' When Derrida finds this text repeated, he begins to trace through Levinas' text the way that the opening to the future is held open at the expense of a present meaning, or even a present signifying. This phrase, which Derrida installs as his title, deconstructs the pseudopresent of the book—a move we saw in the longer passage from Levinas. Commentary on this phrase, then, can be a faithful response to Levinas' own interpretation of how books work. Derrida's interest in the iteration of the phrase becomes clear in his own text—but our interest in Derrida's reading leads us to the reiteration in Derrida's text of a short piece of Levinas' text (4d–e). Can Derrida's iteration of a citation be read the same way that Derrida reads Levinas' iteration of a phrase? Can we read his commentary by commenting upon a parallel gesture?

The first citation of part of the Levinas text comes in a passage where Derrida produces an example of repetitions of the phrase AT THIS MOMENT ITSELF. Derrida constructs his example from three passages. I will omit the first for reasons of economy; the second passage includes part of Pretext 3; and the third is part of the central Levinas text (Pretext 4). The citations to Levinas are found in the right column, where I include complete texts of Levinas; the parts that Derrida quotes in this first citation are underlined (and what he quotes in his second citation is in **boldface**). What is neither underlined nor in bold is elided by Derrida.

5a) Derrida ATM 32–33/21–22 And a little further on, the following, where you will notice the metaphor of the *reknotted thread* around the "at this moment itself." The metaphor belongs to a very distinctive fabric, that of a relation (in the

We join Derrida after the first passage, when he introduces a second. He prepares the reader by noticing how the phrase is wound around by the image of the RE-KNOTTED THREAD. His writing tone is like a teacher (YOU WILL NOTICE) as he leads

sense of a story, this time, a relation of the same that recaptures the interruptions of the Relation to the Other in its knots) by which philosophical logos reappropriates itself, recapturing in its cloth the history of all of its breaks: us through Levinas' text. Indeed, this YOU is determined both as the reader of Levinas' text and as the reader of Derrida's commentary. The commentary directs our reading, remanding us to the other's text, directly. And we find ourselves addressed already—by reading Derrida's text. Derrida alerts us to the way that Levinas' text enacts a RELATION, that in an almost Hegelian speculative manner recaptures in THE SAME the disruption that THE OTHER brought into the same. Derrida identifies two ways of describing this relation: as STORY, in which the sequence produces an ending of RECAPTURING, and as a LOGICAL move that re-appropriates what breaks into it. The question is whether philosophical discourse is adequate to the task of articulating the relation to the other that we would call ethics, and if so, whether that adequacy does not ultimately efface the very relation to the other, the discontinuity that it heralds. Derrida then quotes a long passage, riddled by ellipses, a passage that is Pretext 3 (and now Pretext 6).

Derrida begins with two sentences that are several lines before where our pretext began. Levinas affirms the POWER of discourse to overcome its interruptions, beginning to reestablish the relation RIGHT AFTER ONE INTERRUPTS. The story line is clear enough, interruption is unsteady. This passage continues to discuss the way

LEVINAS
6a) Levinas OB 215/169 _Every contestation and interruption of this power of discourse is at once related and inverted by discourse. It begins again right after one interrupts it. . . ._

that philosophy is the master discourse. Levinas focuses first on the way that philosophy, even when broken, keeps speaking in order to encompass everything (6b/3a). But he interrupts his own text, wondering if his own exposition does not reduce what he is describing to a theme, a said (6c/3b). Yet he justifies his text by invoking the open-endedness of tradition, where new meaning is given to old stories precisely by being reinterpreted, indeed, by the proliferation of commentaries (6d/3c). Levinas goes on in the passage we interpreted before, but Derrida stops to discuss how language itself is precisely what allows for the transcendence beyond what thought can think.

I now cite the rest of Derrida's citation. I provide the full text from Levinas in order to allow us to think through what Derrida is selecting for commentary. Derrida's own commentary will follow, as he pauses to reflect on this passage after citing it. But notice the ellipses. Derrida's citation is riddled with ". . . ," but these gaps are available to us as gaps, inviting us

6b) [3a] _This discourse [of Western philosophy] will assert itself to be coherent and one. In relating the interruption of discourse or my transport unto discourse, I am re-knotting the thread. Discourse is ready to say, in itself, every break, to consume them like their silent origins or as eschatology. If philosophical discourse breaks, with-_

to reread Levinas in order to see the absent texts and to interpret the gaps. Derrida omits sentences, as any commentator does. He omits Levinas' recourse to speech and mumbling (3a), where discourse is unstoppable and is clearly the act of speaking, and he omits the further discussion of the story, of history and historiography (3c). Because Derrida focuses on textuality and how it works, Levinas' own emphasis on speech would produce a digression for Derrida. The story/history sentences, moreover, seem to lead to a story that Derrida does not want to tell: of traditions that preserve openness and indeterminacy purposefully. Instead, Derrida jumps to the concluding sentence as though equivocation were not the self-renewal of tradition.

DERRIDA

5b) In the question just asked ("And aren't we, at this moment itself, . . .") the "at this moment itself" would be an enveloping form, the cloth of a text ceaselessly taking up into itself all of its tears.

draws from speech and mumbles, or speaks *to itself*—it nonetheless speaks and speaks of the discourse where it just spoke and to which it returns to say its provisional withdrawal.

6c) [3b]   And aren't we, *at this moment itself*, [my italics, J.D.] in the process of barring the exit that our entire essay attempted, and encircling our position on all sides? The exceptional words by which the trace of the past and the extravagance of the approach were said—One, God—become terms, reenter the vocabulary and place themselves at the disposal of philologists instead of confounding the philosophical language. Their explosions themselves are told.

6d) [3c]   But clearly, this story itself is without end and without continuity, which is to say, it goes from one to the other—it is tradition. But thereby it [the story] it renews itself. The new meanings arise in its meaning, whose exegesis is the unfolding or the history before all historiography. Thus the equivocal whose stitches cannot run, which language weaves, signifies. (*Otherwise than Being* . . . , 215/[169])

Derrida's explicit interpretation looks at how the "AT THIS MOMENT ITSELF" appears here as the moment when Levinas' own text threatens to envelop its tears. He notes that it arises in a QUESTION, indicating that Levinas interrogates his own text, but that as interrogation it lacks certainty. Levinas does not indict his text, but he does doubt it. Derrida's comment (WOULD BE) retains the possibility that such a philosophical text need not envelop all of its own tears. This second passage is read, then, as the moment in which philosophy undoes ethics; where Levinas' own text fails to preserve the otherness of the other, it is a cloth that effaces its own tears.

But in Levinas' own text, the recourse to a story and a tradition that renews itself emphasized how that cloth maintains and displays the otherness, and in fact is given to another (6d/3c). As I commented above, the resaying in philosophical discourse is a risky motion that renews the tradition. The pragmatics of a text, the relation between readers and authors, answers the threat of this 'at this moment' in Levinas' text. Derrida explores only the threat and leaves the irony of the question undiscussed, and indeed its retraction uncited.

DERRIDA
5c) But two pages farther on, the same "at this moment itself" is said otherwise in the text, caught in another chaining-unchaining, comes to say something totally other, that is that "at this moment itself" the interrupting piercing has a place, an ineluctable *at the moment itself* where the discursive relation, the philosophical story, claims to re-appropriate the tear in the continuum of its texture:

Instead, he moves to the third passage, where he claims the phrase "AT THIS MOMENT ITSELF" is SAID OTHERWISE—the passage that was our longer pretext. Levinas writes, comments Derrida, in order to make known that interruption does have a place, and that discourse cannot assimilate the tears, but preserves the traces of the interruption—a tracing not found in the discussion of story/history, where the history of reading, the pragmatics of relations to readers, created the otherness that was at risk. But Derrida turns Levinas' vocabulary into his own voice: he writes of this OTHERWISE as a property of the text, as adverbial of writing and not as (meta)-ontological. TOTALLY OTHER characterizes the saying here. Moreover, he italicizes the *AT THE MOMENT ITSELF*, which is not at THIS MOMENT ITSELF, but is the moment in which discourse seems to catch up with itself completely. Derrida allows Levinas' language to become pragrammatological—a move that this commentary itself also performs.

With a colon (:), Derrida now introduces the longer pretext of this chapter, including the part that will be re-cited a few pages farther on in Derrida's text. Derrida does not pause to start a new paragraph, and indeed, it almost seems as if a kind of camouflage for the citation he will repeat. In this first citation, Derrida cites units 4d, 4e, and 4f: the heart of the passage. (**Boldface** indicates the text that will be cited the second time; underline, the materials cited this time.)

We can recall that Levinas' problem centered on the institutions of power and their ability to stop discourse. Levinas then makes the double move of finding the traces under the reknotted threads (d–e) and then turns to the pragmatic issue of giving the discourse to another (f). The full analysis of this pragrammatology comes in (h)—which Derrida will not quote yet. Instead, Derrida focuses on (f), on the way that Levinas' own writing, because it is offered to another, reopens the text.

LEVINAS
4d) the intervals are not recuperated. Discourse that suppresses the interruptions of discourse in relating them—doesn't it sustain the discontinuity under the knots where the thread is reknotted?

4e) The interruptions of discourse, found again and related in the immanence of the said, are preserved as in the knots of a thread reknotted, the trace of a diachrony that does not enter into the present, that flees simultaneity.

4f) But I interrupt again the ultimate discourse where all discourse is announced, in saying it to someone who listens to it and who is placed outside the Said that is said in the discourse, outside everything that it includes. And this is true of the discourse which I am holding at this moment itself. This reference to the interlocutor permanently pierces the text that the discourse claims to weave in thematizing and in enveloping all things. In totalizing being, discourse as Discourse thus provides a retraction of the very claim of totalization.

DERRIDA

5d) At a two-page interval, an interval which neither can nor should be reduced and which constitutes here an absolutely singular seriality, the "at this moment itself" seems to repeat itself only in order to be dislocated irreparably. The "itself" of the "itself" in "at this moment itself" has remarked its own alteration, that which will always already have opened it to the other.

Derrida's comment begins with the IN-TERVAL between the two instances of the phrase (AT THIS MOMENT ITSELF) in Levinas' text. They need space between them to do their work, to become a series and not merely a stutter or hiccup. That SERI-ALITY is a repetition that produces an IR-REPARABLE DISLOCATION. Notice that part of the vocabulary is still Levinas': *intervals, tear,* and so on—which binds the commentary into the text. Does a discourse maintain intervals or recuperate them? Levinas claims (4d) THE INTERVALS ARE NOT RECUPERATED; Derrida echoes: AN INTERVAL WHICH NEITHER CAN NOR SHOULD BE REDUCED. Levinas made the separation, but Derrida interprets the obligation to separate in order to allow the phrase to deconstruct its earlier use. In this last passage, the MOMENT ITSELF of the text is a moment of holding open, the opening attending for the reader—not the end of the story where the interruption someone lodged against my discourse is recaptured, but the moment is now a future perfect, where my reader has deferred authority. THE 'ITSELF' marks this change by serial repetition.

5e) The "first" that formed the element of reappropriation in the continuum will be already *obliged* by the "second," the other, the interrupter, even before being produced and in order to be produced itself (*même*). It will already become text and context with it, but in a series where the text composed with its own (if one can still say) tearing.

Derrida examines the relation between the two uses of the phrase. The earlier somehow becomes *OBLIGED* by the second. Again a term that Levinas would use to describe relations between people becomes a relation between words, a pragrammatological responsibility. The first use depends on the second: the opportunity for discourse to appropriate breaks and differences depends in an almost ethical way on an opening of offering discourse to another. The possibility for deferred instruction coming from another person, the commentator, creates the possibility for the text's attempt to totalize over the past breaks. Because the text awaits its reader, it can be tempted to overcome its own past, the discontinuities and challenges. This is a striking claim: rooting the capacity of a text to knit diverse things together in the responsibility of holding open the meaning for a reader yet to come. The holding open, the self-effacing in writing, turns into a TEXT AND CONTEXT, a discourse without breaks, but only when the text itself is COMPOSED of such tears. Derrida's insight is to see how the two moments (the mending and the offering to another) are bound together and that the mending requires the offering—and that the series of the two instances is inverted in order further to disrupt the mending.

DERRIDA

5f) The "at this moment itself" is itself composed by way of an immeasurable anachrony, incommensurable with itself. The singular textuality of this "series" does not enclose the Other, on the contrary, it opens itself from an irreducible difference, which is the past before any present, before every present moment, before anything we believe we understand when we say "at this moment itself."

The phrase itself, "AT THIS MOMENT ITSELF," moreover, does not say what it seems to. "At this moment" is not the simultaneity of the time of writing and the time of reading, but the complete dislocation, the discontinuity of time that allows the text to be offered to its reader and that allows the interruptions in the text to lie beneath its integrity. The discourse cannot ENCLOSE THE OTHER but leads to a trace, to THE PAST BEFORE ANY PRESENT. This nonpresence of this moment itself is produced through the seriality, because the radical future of meaning, of offering the text, structures the way that interruptions lurk beneath the text, the traces of that past. We cannot overwhelm the discontinuities because we offer the text. But Derrida as commentator calls attention to the performance of the dislocation of time. Only by repeating the phrase does Levinas' text perform the relation of obligation between the iterations of the phrase.

Five pages later Derrida will cite our long pretext from Levinas, again. Our question is, Why does Derrida require this re-citation in his commentary? Does it work as a seriality similar to Levinas'? Will the second oblige the first?

7a) Derrida ATM 38–40/26–28 The metaphors of the seam and the tear obsess his text. Does this concern only "metaphors" when they envelop and tear the very element (the text) of the metaphorical? Not important for now. These seem to organize themselves in any case in the following manner. Let us call them in a word, *interruption* (it is often used), which regularly puts an end to the authority of the Said, of thematics, of dialectics, of the same,

This second passage examines not a phrase and its reiterations but rather the question of how to make interruptions or tears appear as such in the text. Derrida returns to the metaphors of sewing and the tears. He makes use of Levinas' vocabulary, particularly the verb OBSESS. He wonders whether we can make the textile terms into mere METAPHORS when the structure of the metaphorical itself depends on the breaks and reknottings. But he proposes calling the tearing *INTERRUP-*

of the economical, and so on, that which is demarcated from this series to go beyond essence: to the Other, toward the Other, from the Other. Interruption will have come to tear the continuum of a fabric which naturally tends to envelop, to close itself up again.[6]

TION. He admits in parentheses that in Levinas' text the term IS OFTEN USED. Interruption will now be the term for disrupting the said. Interruption will be the way a text goes beyond themes, essences, and so on, to other people. Interruption is then the name of the effects within the text that seem to point to what resists location

in discourse. All of the relations TO THE OTHER and FROM THE OTHER, the attending and the responding, all need to appear within the text as interruptions, as TEARING THE CONTINUUM, resisting the assimilation of philosophical discourse.

7b) ... But only on the condition of letting itself be contaminated, retaken, sewn up again in that which it made possible. The result is that the resumption is no more logical than the interruption. *Otherwise than Being*:

I elide a discussion of an example from a "Jewish" essay by Levinas in order to move more quickly to the citation from the central pretext (4). The tear precedes the seam in a diachrony we know. But Derrida also notes that the tear must also LET ITSELF BE ... SEWN UP. To appear as

tear, an interruption must run the risk that discourse will overwhelm it, will mend it. Not only is interruption the condition for discourse, but vulnerability to discourse's denial is a condition for interruption. The claim that LOGIC cannot produce the interruption—because it interrupts logic, is now doubled with the claim that mending is also not demanded by logic itself. And this serves as a preliminary view of the pretext from Levinas. Derrida re-cites the text (**boldface** indicates the text that is cited this second time, and <u>underline</u> the materials cited the first time). What is neither underlined nor in bold is elided by Derrida.

This time Derrida's quoting begins at the beginning of the longer text we interpreted. He follows through from the threat of institutional force to enforce the rationality of discourse (a). He omits (b), with its explanation of how discourse needs those powerful institutions to achieve universality and the troubling violence of justice. But he resumes quoting in (c), where the cutting by institutions is in

LEVINAS
4a) [Levinas OB 216–17/170–71] **Are the tears of a logical text sewn up again only by logic? It is in the association of philosophy and the state, of philosophy and medicine, that the rupture of discourse is surmounted. The interlocutor who does not submit himself to logic is threatened with prison or the asylum or endures the prestige of the master and the medication of the doctor:**

[6] Derrida DS 33/26   Dissemination opens, without end, this *tear* of writing which no longer lets itself be sewn up, the place where neither meaning, however plural, nor *any form of presence* fastens up the trace. Dissemination treats—on the couch—the *point* where the movement of signification regularly came *to tie* the place of the trace, thus producing history. Leaping the security of this stopping point in the name of the law. It is—at least—for the risk of making this leap, that dissemination is broached (opened). And the detour of a writing that does not return.

tension with the reknotting by discourse. The sentence which includes (d) is structured oppositionally: the said thematizes, but the intervals remain, irrecuperable, a past that cannot be made present in the story. From (d) to (e), the passage cited in both commentaries by Derrida is a move to the immanence of the said as place where the trace of the past, and so transcendence, remains.

LEVINAS

4b) violence or reasons of state or an approach, assuring a universality to the rationalism of logic and to the law its subject matter. Discourse thus recuperates its meaning by repression or by medication, by just violence verging on potential injustice where repressive justice lies.

4c) It is by means of the state that reason and knowledge are force and efficiency. But the state discounts incurable madness and the intervals of madness. It does not untie the knots but cuts them. The Said thematizes interrupted dialogue or dialogue delayed by silences, by failure or by delirium, but

4d) the intervals are not recuperated. Discourse that suppresses the interruptions of discourse in relating them—doesn't it sustain the discontinuity under the knots where the thread is reknotted?

4e) The interruptions of discourse, found again and related in the immanence of the said, are preserved as in the knots of a thread reknotted, the trace of a diachrony that does not enter into the present, that flees simultaneity.

DERRIDA

7c) Whether it severs or whether it reknots, the discourse of philosophy, of medicine, or of the state, despite itself keeps the trace of the interruption. Despite itself. But to remark the interruption, which the writing of E.L. does, it is necessary *also* to reknot, despite oneself, in the not untouched of philosophy, of medicine, and of the logic of the state. The analogy between the book, philosophy, medicine, logic, and the state is very strong.

Derrida's comments emphasize the lack of intention—the trace of the interruption is KEPT, DESPITE ITSELF. Derrida acknowledges that discourse which either cuts or reknots cannot efface interruption absolutely. Something remains—or better, the trace is inelimnable (not really there either). Moreover, in reference back to (a) (and to the unquoted [b]), he binds together the state, medicine, philosophy, logic—and the book. But to call attention to the trace of the interruption, WHICH THE WRITING OF E.L. DOES, one again produces a reknotting. Levinas' writing (like Derrida's) is not removed from philosophy and the claim of discourse to mend the torn fabric. To claim that THE ANALOGY IS VERY STRONG is to raise the question of whether Levinas' book can resist the claim to integrity, to continuity.

Derrida then cites Levinas' text (h), without breaking and indenting it, nor noting that it is a close neighbor of the long, preceding quotation. He skips (f) and (g). The first, (f), was cited in the first citation and concerns the question of how the interlocutor pierces Levinas' own text; the second, (g), held the analogy of skepticism and denial of simultaneity. What Derrida quotes in (h) deals with the tension between the catching up and the interruption: the book. Levinas had placed books in a pragmatic relation with other people, with other books, with a reading which is a saying.

Derrida's reading of (h) focuses on the attempt to distinguish Levinas' writing from other people's: to distinguish what makes Levinas' writing more responsive, more open to its readers—less like a rationalization for cutting off interruptions.

DERRIDA

7d) But he writes books, which should not be the books of state (of philosophy, of medicine, of logic). How does he do it? In his books, as in the others, interruption leaves its marks, but otherwise. The knots form there, recovering the tears, but otherwise. They let discontinuity appear in its trace, but since the trace must not be assembled itself in its appearing, it can always resemble the trace which discontinuity leaves in the logical discourse of the state, of philosophy, of medicine. Thus the trace ought to 'present' itself there without presenting itself, *otherwise*. But how?[7]

LEVINAS

4f) But I interrupt again the ultimate discourse where all discourse is announced, in saying it to someone who listens to it and who is placed outside the Said that is said in the discourse, outside everything that it includes. And this is true of the discourse which I am holding at this moment itself. This reference to the interlocutor permanently pierces the text that the discourse claims to weave in thematizing and in enveloping all things. In totalizing being, discourse as Discourse thus provides a retraction of the very claim of totalization.

4g) A reversal that resembles the one that the refutation of skepticism makes evident. In what is written, of course, the saying makes itself pure said, simultaneity of the saying and its conditions.

4h) Interrupted discourse catching up with its own breaks is the book. But books have their destiny. They belong to a world that they do not enclose, but which they recognize in the writing and in the printing and in the making of pre-faces and in making forewords precede them. They interrupt themselves and call to other books and are interpreted in the final analysis in a saying distinct from the said.

Derrida reads the text to distinguish Levinas' books from others. Levinas' writing must, like others, have interruptions with knots. It will LET DISCONTINUITY APPEAR IN ITS TRACE: the refrain of our account of texts. But, writes Derrida, the trace in Levinas' text will ALWAYS RESEMBLE the traces left in those institutional texts, the texts that tried to cut off discussion. Because a trace is not present, not

[7] Derrida G 30–31/18   The idea of the book is the idea of a totality, finite or infinite, of the

evident, it cannot appear as something specific, something determinate and different from those violent traces of the state or the psychiatric ward. All traces are both present and absent, not presenting themselves. Levinas' should do so OTHERWISE. Traces must not appear. Derrida has read our familiar passage not to redeem the knotty traces in books and traditions, but in order to seek the absence of force in Levinas' tracing of interruption.

7e) *This* book, here, the one composed of *his*, beyond any totality, how does it deliver itself otherwise to the other? From one moment to another, the difference should have been infinitely subtle, the one which recaptures the other in its meshes must leave an other trace of interruption in its meshes, and in thematizing the trace make an other knot (left to the discretion of the other in reading). But another knot remains insufficient. There must be another chain of multiple knots that would have as their singularity that they do not knot continuous threads (as a book of state pretends to do) but re-knot the cut threads in keeping the barely apparent trace (maybe, probably), of absolute interruption, of the ab-solute as interruption.

The difference must lie in the way THIS book, which is Levinas', delivers itself to other people. All books leave their meaning to the readers—all books leave traces of interruptions of breakups, breakdowns, break-ins, in their writing. Reading is seeking these in order to learn. But, Derrida finds, repeating both Levinas' text and himself, that there are always traces left of others, captured in the MESHES, in the fabric. The trace is LEFT TO THE DISCRETION OF THE OTHER, not hidden like an esoteric message but neither evident nor irresistible. Derrida discovers that one knot cannot disrupt the knots. Levinas uses a CHAIN OF MULTIPLE KNOTS—a specific chain, a series. For the series itself will generate a way of reading, a disruption of the text's unity. The state claims to knot continuous threads: it views tradition as lines that carry directly from one to the next, institutions with continuous purposes and protocols, individuals with coherent lives, and so on. Levinas' text, on the other hand, reknots cut threads: the threads of suffering, of otherness of other texts, of ruptures in our lives. Derrida allows that the books of state do not actually work with continuous threads, but Levinas' text, because it acknowledges the discontinuity of what it draws together, serves to guard the traces, to protect them in order to leave open the possibility for someone to find there ABSOLUTE INTERRUPTIONS. Interruption itself becomes the absolute, the refusal of solution, of dissolution.

---

signifier; this totality of the signifier cannot be a totality, unless a totality constituted by the signified preexists it, supervises its inscriptions and its signs, and is independent of it in its ideality. The idea of the book, which always refers to a natural totality, is profoundly foreign to the meaning of writing. It is the encyclopedic protection of theology and of logocentrism against the disruption of writing, against its aphoristic energy, and, as I shall specify later, against difference in general. If we distinguish the text from the book, we shall say that the destruction of the book, as it is announced today in all domains, strips the surface of the text. That necessary violence responds to a violence that was no less necessary.

7f) The trace of that interruption in the knot is never simply visible, sensible, assured. It does not belong to discourse and only comes to it from the Other. That is true also of the discourse of the state, of course, but here the nonphenomenality should oblige, without compelling, to read the trace as trace, the interruption as interruption, according to an *as such* which is no longer reappropriatable as phenomena of an essence. The structure of the knot must be other, though it will resemble it a lot.

Levinas is constrained: he cannot make the trace VISIBLE. He can discuss them, but he must also allow them to work, to trace without COMPULSION, because it depends on THE OTHER. Discourse cannot contain the trace, because an other person makes the interruption; an other person will have to find it again. The state's discourse depends on obedience from its citizens—but the state's discourse tries to force obligation, tries to COMPEL, by a use of discourse which makes things appear, makes them connect. The compulsion of reason justifies the violence in justice, claiming to weave together a community and a law from integral parts. Levinas' discourse, discourse that sets out to expose the exposure in the trace of interruptions, resembles these knots of force, but works otherwise because it does not seek to obligate through essence, through presence. It does not show the trace only as a symptom of something that can be brought into the light or the interruptions as gaps to be overcome. How can discourse oblige without compelling?

7g) You are never compelled to read it, to recognize it. It comes only by means of you to whom it is delivered and yet will have, wholly otherwise, obliged one to read what one is not obligated to read. He does not simply make knots and interruptions in his text, like everyone, like the state, philosophy, medicine. I say like everyone, because if there is interruption everywhere, there are knots everywhere. But there is in his text, perhaps, a supplementary knotty complication, an other manner of reknotting without reknotting.

Levinas' text, as exposure to text, effaces not only himself but also his authority. YOU, Derrida directly addresses the reader again. It seems more like his own role as reader, a YOU that means "me" or "you" (and it is the informal *TU*). This YOU [*TU*] of Derrida's text places the reader of the commentary into the play of the pragrammatologic of Levinas' writing. Not merely enjoined as reader of commentary, we are enjoined doubly into the practice of reading Levinas, and alerted that such reading obliges its reader. Doesn't reading Derrida's commentary oblige doubly: first as a you who reads Levinas and then again as the you addressed by the commentary? Levinas cannot compel us, cannot make us RECOGNIZE. He is aware of the limitations of his signs, opening this vulnerability, effacing his authority. The state's discourse compels you, or at least tries to—although it is still not clear whether discourse compels or only threatens cutting short, and that only the cut itself compels. Derrida now shifts into a discussion that focuses on the you, on he (Levinas), and even on an "I." Levinas' writing depends on its YOU, on its recipient. He will without compulsion (WHOLLY OTHERWISE) have obliged you TO READ. But how does one read Levinas—in a way unlike reading, in a way where what is read can only obligate you if you read it for the traces, not for the content or the message? Levinas' text obligates by withdrawing the obligation of the said, by contesting its own authority, and thus disrupting a reader's obedience to its statements, in order to offer traces of others through the texts. Derrida can somewhat contrast this with all of the other knottings, knottings which are EVERYWHERE made by EVERYONE. Levinas' text can at most PERHAPS knot the broken threads in a way that leaves them not reknotted. PERHAPS because it will have to do without compulsion, without the force of evidence. But Derrida can slip into the first person (I) here, because while Levinas had already distributed the knots and interruptions throughout all texts, Derrida here is no longer saying only that all texts deconstruct their own use of force. That can go without saying here, but Levinas' text somehow is able to deconstruct its own violence more actively—through its special way of making a chain of knots.

This passage from Derrida obliges us to interrogate the repetition/re-citation in Derrida. The twice-cited text from Levinas claimed this retention of knots and interruptions, of interruptions under the knots. Why did Derrida cite it twice? The first time Derrida shows how the two instances of "AT THIS MOMENT ITSELF" create a diachronic series. In Derrida's first commentary, Levinas' text became a text that could reknot and integrate only because it was first interrupted, interrupted in a time that was never present. When Derrida cites the text the second time, he indicates the distinctiveness of Levinas' text: it obligates without compulsion, and depends on the reader to see the interruption under the knot. The two citations do not disagree, but they do rehearse what Derrida sees in Levinas' repetitions: the first citation looks more to the texture of writing, the second to its readers and the pragmatic relation to readers. We can even say, re-citing Derrida:

5e) The "first" that formed the element of reappropriation in the continuum will be already *obliged* by the "second," the other, the interrupter, even before being produced and in order to be produced itself (*même*). It will already become text and context with it, but in a series where the text composed with its own (if one can still say) tearing.

The relation to the reader, the opening that cannot compel but still does oblige, determines the structure of the series by disrupting the present moment of the text. The reader makes the text do what it does, or rather obliges the text to undo its own presence, its own authority. The reader's responsiveness produces the texture of Levinas' writing. Derrida thus cites twice in order to re-cite, to make Levinas' way of writing his own, to become obliged as commentator, to produce noncompulsive obligation in his readers. His obligation is neither free nor determined by Levinas' writing, but is rather performed in his reading. And we are allowed to see the knots and interruptions in all texts, but also to see how a series of knots disrupts the authority of each knot, of each connection.

Derrida then not merely imitates the tactics, he writes responsively for us—a somewhat more restricted YOU, who are not all readers of Levinas but are only readers of his commentary. Citation and commentary open up the non-compelling obligation in reading—without abandoning discourse (and which only the most recalcitrant of readers can doubt reflects yet again on how we are reading and commenting, reading these others and writing for still other others—here, "at this moment itself" that is also not now. I read and write commentary here to hold open for others, to call for other books to read. This text is a reading text, reading in the ethical exigency to call to other readers). Derrida finds that the seriality at work in Levinas' text requires a parallel one in his own, and that commenting becomes not so much a commentator's intention of making some text available to others, but a letting be, a passivity in signifying, allowing or even signifying signifying—in short, a writing of writing the writing, the correlate of Levinas' writing, of Levinas' writing of saying saying the saying. Reading, like listening, is already a responsibility, or perhaps the responsibility to which the saying and writing respond.

SUGGESTED READINGS

2 Bernasconi, Robert. "Levinas and Derrida: The Question of the Closure of Metaphysics." In *Face to Face with Levinas*, ed. Richard Cohen, 181–202. Albany: SUNY Press, 1986.

Critchley, *Ethics of Deconstruction*.

3 Handelman, *Fragments*, 233–50.

4 Bernasconi, Robert. "Skepticism in the Face of Philosophy." In *Re-Reading Levinas*, ed. Robert Bernasconi and Simon Critchley, 149–61. Bloomington: Indiana University Press, 1991.

De Greef, Jan. "Skepticism and Reason." In *Face to Face with Levinas*, ed. Richard Cohen, 159–80. Albany: SUNY Press, 1986.

7 Critchley, *Ethics of Deconstruction*, Chapter 3.

CHAPTER 5

Why Comment?

LEVINAS AND DERRIDA have taught us how reading and writing philosophical texts should be responsive. A second model of reading and writing will now come from the Jewish textual tradition, outside the philosophical tradition. Derrida cites Levinas' Jewish writings in the midst of some of the texts we examined in the previous chapter. Those writings represent the second alternative in the disruption of the closure of philosophy: the appeal to something radically other. The undeniable similarity between Levinas' account of the pragmatics of the Jewish textual tradition and what Levinas and Derrida have developed for the philosophical tradition will concern us as a theme in Chapter 13. Our immediate task is to understand the responsibility to comment, to read in such a way as to give others to read—or rather to *write* commentary. We can interpret that responsibility through a brief introduction to Levinas' interpretation of the textual pragmatics (the pragrammatology) within Jewish texts.

This chapter moves from a close approximation in Jewish texts, indeed in all literary texts, of what we have seen in the discussion of philosophical texts, through an account of the need for history and discontinuity in reading these texts to a discussion of the qualities of the Jewish commentary, sedimented through the historical epochs. Commentary both preserves the discontinuities among readers, previous generations, and the author, and also holds open the disagreement and tensions within a stratum. Commentary thus holds open the history of interpretation and the conflict in interpretation.

We begin in Section A (The Written Command) with a text that transposes much of the account of writing we saw from philosophy to Jewish texts. It focuses on how the written word is a saying and a said, commanding its reader. Section B (Reading and Separation) notes the positive role that historical separation plays in the ongoing revelation in the texts. Pretext 2 argues that all writing is inspired because it offers more meaning than the writer intended, while Pretext 3 credits the Pharisees with developing a renewing reading that allowed a text to say new things in new contexts. In the context of that text, two famous Talmudic stories are recounted. Pretext 4 tells of Moses confused in the classroom of a second-century sage, Akiva. Pretext 5, however, tells the story of the argument among the sages when the majority refused the testimony of a heavenly voice—insisting that God is not a relevant interpreter in the ongoing activity of the reading community.

Section C concludes Part I with a discussion about commentary. First, in Pretext 6 we see the dialogue between practical life and the text, as commentary must move between the text and the "here." And last, in Pretext 7, we see how the Talmudic text, though written, preserves orality—indeed, Levinas argues that commentary in the tradition is a kind of oral teaching. Levinas cites another famous text about the toleration of contradiction within the rabbinic tradition (Pretext 8) in order to show that the tradition never stops.

A. The Written Command

In the foreword to the book *Beyond the Verse*, Levinas discusses how writing is a motion beyond the mere words of the verse—so that writing opens the ethical dimension of signification. He rehearses the themes of teaching and reading we have seen, but here in the context of the written text. Indeed, it seems as though the sort of responsibility we have been exploring is originally religious.

1a) Levinas BV 9/xii   My coordination with another person in language is expression of received orders; writing is always prescription and ethics, word of God which commands me and swears me to the other, holy writing before being a sacred text. A word disproportionate to political discourse, exceeding information—break, in the being that I am, of my good conscience as being-there. I understand it as my allegiance to the other person. It puts in question the "concern for self" natural to beings, essential to the *essence* of beings. Hence, subversion of that *essence*, disinterestedness in the etymological meaning of that word.

Writing, amidst the Jewish holy texts (the Hebrew Bible, Mishnah, Midrash, Talmud), COMMANDS me. Reading these texts binds me to other people, SWEARS ME to responsibilities for others. The texts are not primarily narrative and still less propositional knowledge, but are first of all ETHICS—and so these texts are first of all HOLY, and only subsequently SACRED. Their sacred power does not condition ethics, but vice versa. Hence, holy writings are not POLITICAL DISCOURSE, but are themselves a BREAK or tear in me, and most of all in MY GOOD CONSCIENCE. The prophetic essence of language in these texts disrupts me, obliges me, commands me, forges an allegiance to the other person, and so puts in question my desire for self-preservation, my essence as a NATURAL being. The disruption is ontological, the disruption of ontology. DISINTERESTEDNESS IN THE ETYMOLOGICAL MEANING OF THAT WORD is the breakup of essence, the possibility of being for the other, for what is not my own essence. The Bible and other writings bear responsibilities that will uproot my own being.

1b)   A wind of crisis or spirit, despite the knots of History which are reknotted after the breaks, where

And so in another context, in 1982, Levinas rehearses a set of terms thoroughly familiar to us from his philosoph-

the concern for self needs justification. This implication of ethical responsibility in the firm and sort of
closed saying of the verse that is
formed in language, as if in speaking
I were not the only one to speak and
were already obeying, isn't this the
original writing where God came to
mind and is named in the Said?[1]
ical writings of the 1970s. There is a
REKNOTTING after BREAKS, a reknotting
which we can call History with a capital
'H.' But despite the reknotting there is still
a wind of spirit, of CRISIS, of rupture. The
reknotting responds to a need for justification—not for the way a sign is for the
other, but for my SELF-CONCERN. The
breaks make self-concern defensive, and
we reknot the story to justify it. This play of knots, breaks, reknotting, traces
occurs in the VERSE, the verse of the Bible. The verse looks firm, even
CLOSED: complete and canonical. But the verse is also a saying, not only a
said. When I speak it, reading it aloud, I am not sure that I am the only one
speaking, that an other does not also speak and call to me to speak, to interpret, through the traces and knots of the text. Writing in general confuses the
reader, allowing others to speak through the text. And if there is an obligation to read, to listen in the verse for those others, then reading the verse is
ALREADY OBEYING. For Levinas, God CAME TO MIND through this writing
both named in the said as God, and commanding me in the saying of reading. The very closure of the verse, as the said, serves the obedience that
precedes understanding because its fixity incites me to comment, incites me
to attend to what is not present in the verse.

The practices of reading orient the semiotics of writings. The structures of
Jewish traditional texts will appear most clearly in relation to the ways they
are read. And their capacity to teach responsibility, a responsive teaching, a
teaching that takes responsibility, is realized in reading, a reading reflected
into the texts, but reflected also in the continuation of the texts—readings as
commentary, having become texts.

B. Reading and Separation

In an essay on Spinoza, the founder of the historical-critical method of Biblical study, Levinas examines alternatives in how to read texts. He argues that
there is a responsibility to read texts as inspired, as bearing more meaning

[1] Levinas TN 71/59   To claim to be a Jew thus, from the teaching of a book, is before all to
recognize oneself as reader, which is to say, student of Torah; it is to be excluded from idolatry
by true reading or study. Reading or study of a text that protects itself from the eventual idolatry of that text itself in renewing by an exegesis that cannot stop—and exegesis of that exegesis—the fixed letters and hearing there the breath of the living God. Of a God certainly not
incarnate, but somehow inscribed, living His life—or a part of His life—in the letters, in the
lines and between the lines, and in the exchange of ideas between readers who comment on
them, where these letters are animated and are reverberating by the prescription of the book—
commandment without enslaving, like truth—to respond to the neighbor in justice, which is to
say, to love the other person.

than the author intended. The openness to new commentary in the Jewish tradition is linked to a theory of the written text that requires this abundance of meaning—in stark contrast to Spinoza's own theory of reading signs, which fixes meaning in original historical intention only.

2a) Levinas BV 204/171   But this coming and going from the text to the reader and from the reader to the text and this renewal of meaning is perhaps the definition of everything written, of all literature, even when it does not claim to be Holy Writing. The meaning which arises in an authentic expression of the human exceeds the psychological contents of the writer's intention, be he prophet, philosopher, or poet.

Reading is a relation between text and reader. Levinas calls it a COMING AND GOING because the two do not merge nor is the process of signifying one-way. The text does not merely repeat itself for each reader, nor can each reader find the same thing in every text. Instead, a reader finds new sayings in the text (A RENEWAL OF MEANING). Signs do not complete their meaning in a full presence, but instead require interpreters. Levinas defines the interchange with readers as writing or LITERATURE—generalizing beyond holy texts. (The similarity to Derrida's concept of differance is unmistakable.) New meanings arise beyond what any author could have anticipated or controlled—even if the author is far-seeing or inspired or a master of logic and boundaries.

2b)   In being expressed, the intention crosses the currents of significations objectively carried by language and the experience of a people. These currents assure equilibrium, success, and resonance to the said. The saying makes something that precedes thought vibrate in the said. Interpretation brings it out. It is not only perception, it is constitution of meaning.

The INTENTIONS of the author travel through the medium of language. Levinas uses the images of CURRENTS to show the dynamic of language, that words and even ways of reading change and pull texts in changing directions. But not only do the canons of reading change. THE EXPERIENCE OF A PEOPLE, the context of practices and attitudes that interpreters draw upon to interpret text, is also in motion. The meanings of a text must be stabilized for its readers—their words, their experiences, their manner of reading will provide access to the sayings. The said bears the possibility for the saying. Bearing this possibility justifies the said. But, again, THE SAYING is what disrupts the reader, what VIBRATES against or even despite the experiences and the background meanings of things. Saying makes the said RESONATE. INTERPRETATION listens for it, BRINGING IT OUT. Hence reading is not merely PERCEPTION of what is already formed, alert to the meaning there; rather, interpretation CONSTITUTES meaning. Without the reader the text cannot say or mean anything.

2c)   From this point of view, every text is inspired; it contains more than it contains. Exegesis of all

But that means every writing is INSPIRED, containing more than an author puts into it. To hold more than it holds is

literature depends on the way the obvious meaning suggested by the letter is already situated in the unthought.[2]

the semiotic definition of the Infinite—a thought that thinks more than the mind can think. The excess of meaning refers not merely to those historical currents at the time of composition which the author could not make thematic in her writing. It refers to the manifold of readings, of meanings that only readers will elicit from the text. One cannot examine everything that goes into writing (or speaking), but all the more so, can one not know what a text will come to mean. EXEGESIS, a reading out of the text, always moves from THE OBVIOUS MEANING of a word to its possibilities, its relation to what cannot be thought in advance but arises first in reading. The doubled responsibility we saw of reading in response to traces of otherness and writing to keep me vulnerable for readers, returns here as the UNTHOUGHT, the responsibility oblique to information and knowledge. Because of that responsibility, reading becomes an attention to what exceeds the writer's intentions, an address to me, the reader.

2d) The holy Writings of course have an other secret, a supplementary essence that perhaps the purely literary texts have lost: but they are no less literary texts. And it is because all literature is inspired that religious revelation can become text and show itself to hermeneutics.[3]

As for holy writings, they are also inspired with something more than the writer intended. But they also have a SUPPLEMENT—some power of sacredness (perhaps), some authority called divine. PERHAPS THE PURELY LITERARY TEXTS HAVE LOST THIS—but only perhaps. Levi-

---

[2] Levinas BV 135/109   The processes of reading that one has just seen at work suggest, first, that the commented upon statement exceeds the intending to say whence it originates; that its ability to say goes beyond its intending to say, that it contains more than it contains; that a surplus of meaning, perhaps inexhaustible, remains enclosed in the syntactic structures of the sentence, in its groups of words, in its actual words, phonemes, and letters, in all of that materiality of the saying, always virtually significant. Exegesis would come to free, in these signs, a bewitched significance that smolders under the characters or which are coiled up in all these literatures of letters.

[3] Levinas BV 136–37/110–11   But, from this, language that is itself holding more than it contains would become the natural element of inspiration, despite or before its reduction to the tool for the transmission of thought and of information (if it ever is entirely so reduced). One may ask if man, animal endowed with speech, is not, before everything, an animal capable of inspiration, a prophetic animal. One may ask if the book, as book, before being made a document, is not the modality under which the said is exposed to exegesis and calls for it, and where meaning, immobilized in characters, already tears the texture that holds it. In the propositions which are not yet—or are already no longer—verses and which are often verse or simply literature, another voice resounding among us, a second sounding drowning out or tearing the first. The innumerable life of texts living by the life of people who understand them; primordial exegesis of texts called then national literature, on which the hermeneutics of universities and schools is grafted. Beyond the immediate meaning of their said, their saying is inspired. The fact that the meaning comes by way of the book attests its Biblical essence. The comparison between the inspiration conferred on the Bible and the inspiration toward which the interpretation of literary texts tends is not meant to compromise the dignity of Scripture: it affirms that of the "national literatures."

nas is not willing to draw a strict line between Shakespeare and the Bible, even between Mallarmé and the Talmud—the holy texts have something extra, but the literary texts may not have lost it. For Levinas the authority garnered and wielded by texts is itself not what makes the texts signify. Instead, he concludes this passage by affirming that the holy writings are inspired BECAUSE they are LITERARY, that they always have more to find in them. This holiness of inspiration precedes their sacrality, even their authority. Levinas makes holy writings the model for all writing, but at the same time he reverses the authority of the holy writings. The mode of signifying as the excess of meaning and the need for readers—coming and going—this is what makes writing inspired and what makes even Jewish texts oblige us to read and oblige us for others in reading.

But if the text exceeds the intentions of the author, then it seems as if time itself provided the renewal of meaning. Levinas criticizes Spinoza for obscuring the way that the meaning is renewed in commentary by the Jewish tradition's readings. In place of growing meanings, Spinoza prescribed reading only for the historical meaning that was completeable and informative. The reduction of reading to an activity of gathering information is comparable to the reduction of speaking to knowing. However, the temporal separation of our reading from the text's composition can become an aid to its revelation. History becomes not a mark of identity and continuity, but a condition for the burgeoning meaning of writing. Writing can teach because separation cannot be subordinated to a master narrative.

3a) Levinas BV 203–4/170–71
Those Spinoza calls Pharisees determined a model for exegesis that the religions issuing from the Bible perhaps followed. Writing as writing condones a call to posterity; exegesis would be the possibility for an epoch to have a meaning for another epoch. History thus is not what makes the truth of meaning relative. Distance which separates the text from the reader is the interval where the very growth of spirit resides. It alone allows full signifying and the renewal of meaning.

Spinoza had adopted the Christian polemical attitude toward the rabbinic sages, CALLING them PHARISEES, a term that still carries today the traces of a Christian polemic. By doing so, Spinoza cast their reading in the guise of legalism, literalism, arbitrary and fanciful—in short, not rational. But for Levinas the Pharisees are the ones who DETERMINED a particular MODE OF EXEGESIS. Following Pharisaical hermeneutics, the Jews and other Biblical religions made the Biblical text continue to teach, to have something to say even after centuries of change. Living in the time of the second destruction of the Jerusalem Temple, the Pharisees managed to allow the Bible to teach them despite its focus on Temple sacrifices and priestly holiness. The capacity to be taught by a book that Spinoza had claimed was "obsolete" was the genius of Biblical religions, of religions of the Book. The Pharisees made the model by discovering that writing CALLS TO POSTERITY, to the future. The effects that we have seen in interpretation and in differance are a Pharisaical model—what Biblical scholars now call a

Midrashic model. Levinas clearly believes that other religious traditions use a similar model, and we have already seen how Derrida and Levinas develop philosophical models that are similar (and we leave unresolved the question of whether Ancient Greeks also had this model). In contrast to Spinoza's historical method, Pharisaical reading accentuates the possibility for one epoch (that of Biblical times) to have a meaning for another epoch (rabbinic times). Levinas' formalization makes history into the very medium in which meaning develops, GROWS, and continues to signify. Of course, those commentary texts from rabbinic times are not exclusively glosses but also have new meanings for our period, perhaps most of all in the wider meaning of this very model. But the separation which started as spatial in Chapter 1, now has become historical, and historiography is not the retrieval of a past, completed meaning, but the way for the past to call to us. (A fuller discussion of historiography within this work will occur in Part IV.) Separation is vital not only in conversation but also historically where it alone allows for the renewal of meaning, the interpretation that exceeds the written.

3b) From exegesis one may thus speak of continuous Revelation, as one speaks in theology and in philosophy of continuous Creation.[4] Out of the practice of reading, Levinas now proposes the theme of CONTINUOUS REVELATION. Each generation must read for itself, finding new meanings in the Biblical text, renewing the signs. The text does not reveal at once, but continuously, through history (not despite the historical distance). This is a counterpart of CONTINUOUS CREATION, a theory that God renews the world each day, continuing creation, and did not simply do it once on a particular day in the past. But while philosophy and theology could produce a theory that regarded the contingency of each creature or each entity, requiring God's support for their existence, only rabbinic exegesis discovered that signs work differentially, that meaning is not self-causing, but requires support throughout history.

3c) According to one Talmudic saying (Menahot 29b), what is taught in the school of Rabbi Akiva would be incomprehensible to Moses but would nonetheless be the teaching itself of Moses. Levinas then cites two famous rabbinic stories: one about teaching, the other about argument. Levinas does not provide commentary on these passages, but allows himself to give one-line interpretations. In other contexts he does engage commen-

---

[4] Levinas BV 162–63/133 But this invitation to the search and to the deciphering, to *Midrash*, is already the participation of the reader in Revelation, in Writing. The reader is, in his way, scribe. This gives us a first indication of what one could call the "statute" of Revelation: at once speech coming from elsewhere, from outside and residing in the one who receives it. More than a listener, wouldn't human being be the unique "terrain" where exteriority comes to make itself appear? The personal, that is to say, the unique "of itself," isn't it necessary to the piercing and to the showing wrought from outside? The human as rupture of substantial identity, isn't it "of itself" the possibility for a message coming from outside, and not to strike a

tary seriously, and we will examine his commentary of a Talmudic passage in Chapter 14. Here, rather than examine the texts carefully, I will only cite them and provide a limited summary of them. In Chapter 9, the second text will be treated more fully.

Talmudic texts are themselves commentary on the Mishnah; the Babylonian Talmud edited around the sixth century C.E., the Mishnah edited at the beginning of the third century C.E. Levinas cites famous passages from the Talmud. First the story of Moses and Akiva.

Moses finds God dawdling over the ornamentation of letters of the Torah. Moses is impatient to receive the text, but God responds that these intricate CROWN-LETS will provide occasion for a great sage (Akiva) to renovate the Torah abundantly. Moses then wants to see the sage at work, but while he can read the text that he brings to the people, he cannot understand Akiva. Akiva is a great, or even the greatest, reader in Jewish history—a creative, responsive, even revolutionary reader. Moses is then comforted by a legal formula, A LAW OF MOSES FROM SINAI, that seems to ascribe the ruling to him (although its meaning in Talmudic literature is not an historical ascription to Moses). In the sequel, Moses also sees Akiva cruelly martyred by the Romans, his flesh flayed alive off his body, and the text questions the relation of Akiva's bold readings and

4) Menahot 29b Rav Yehudah said in the name of Rav: When Moses ascended on high he found the Holy One, blessed be He, sitting, tying crownlets on letters. Moses said to Him, "Master of the Universe, who detains your hand?"

He said to him, "There will be a man in the future, at the end of a few generations. His name is Akiva ben Joseph. And he will interpret stroke by stroke, heaps and heaps of laws."

Moses said to Him, "Master of the Universe, show him to me."

He said to him, "Turn around."

He went and sat behind eight rows. He didn't understand what they were saying and felt weak. But when they came to a matter, they said to their teacher, "Rabbi, where is this from?" He said to them, "It is a law of Moses from Sinai," he was comforted.[5]

his "reward." Levinas cites the story to emphasize how Moses' text could teach what Moses himself could not understand—the teaching by his reader, Akiva.

"free reason" but there to take the unique figure that cannot be reduced to the contingency of a "subjective impression"? Revelation in so far as it is calling to the unique in me—there is the distinctive significance of the signifying of Revelation.

[5] Menahot 29b (cont.)   He returned to the Holy One, Blessed be He, and said to Him, "Master of the Universe, You have a man like that and You give the Torah through me?"
He said to him, "Silence. Thus it came to my mind."

He said to Him, "Master of the Universe, I have seen his teaching, show me his reward."
He said to him, "Turn around."
He turned and saw them weighing his flesh at the market stalls.
He said before Him, "Master of the Universe, such Torah, and such reward?"
He said to him, "Silence. Thus it came to my mind."

3d) The Torah, according to another teaching (Baba Metsia 59b), is no longer in Heaven but in the discussions of men;

The second story is one of the most discussed in Jewish studies, surrounding an argument about whether a portable oven can become ritually unclean.

5a) Baba Metsia 59b They taught there: If he cut it into separate tiles, placing sand between each: Rabbi Eliezer declared it clean, the sages unclean. This was the oven of Akhnai.

Why Akhnai? R. Judah said that Samuel said: "They encompassed it with words like a snake and declared it unclean."

It is taught: that day Rabbi Eliezer brought all the answers in the world, but they didn't accept them. He said to them: "If the ruling is with me—this carob tree shall prove it." And the carob was uprooted 100 cubits (some say 400 cubits) from its place.

They said to him: "No evidence can be brought from a carob tree."

He retorted to them: "If the ruling is with me—this stream of water shall prove it." And the stream of water turned backwards.

They said to him: "No evidence can be brought from a stream of water."

He retorted to them: "If the ruling is with me—the walls of this house of study shall prove it." The walls of the house of study inclined to fall.

R. Joshua rebuked them [the walls] saying to them: "When scholars argue over rulings one with another—what benefit are you to provide?" They did not fall out of respect for R. Joshua, and they did not right themselves out of respect for R. Eliezer, and they are still standing inclined.

He retorted to them: "If the ruling is with me—it will be proved from heaven."

A Heavenly Voice resounded and it said: "What do you want from R. Eliezer? The rulings agree with him everywhere."

R. Joshua stood to his feet and said: "*It is not in heaven.*"

What does "It is not in heaven" mean? R. Jeremiah said: "The Torah was already given at Mount Sinai. We don't consider the Heavenly Voice. It was already written at Mount Sinai in the Torah, "Incline to the majority" (Exod. 23:2).

R. Nathan met Elijah and said to him: "What did the Holy One, Blessed be He, do in that hour?"

He said to him: "He laughed, and he said 'my children have defeated me, my children have defeated me.'"

Eliezer battles with the others about the oven, arguing with 'supernatural' evidence. He finally summons a Heavenly Voice that the other sages reject as well. But the sages argue that the Torah is given to human interpreters, and thus the 'author' has no longer any privilege in interpreting it. The story continues, with God delighted to be beaten in argument by the sages. But the story appears in the context of the topic of what is oppression with words, because Eliezer is then excommunicated and is thus oppressed. The details are worth pursuing (see Chapter 9). The responsibilities, even in winning the argument against Eliezer, are so extreme that his loss causes others' deaths.

3e) to be obstinate in seeking its original meaning—its heavenly meaning—is, paradoxically, as if one uprooted the trees and reversed

Levinas offers a relevant interpretation, claiming that Eliezer was seeking an ORIGINAL MEANING for the text. The original meaning is not merely Moses' intention in

the current of rivers. Exegesis as going beyond the letter is also going beyond the psychological intention of the writer.

receiving the Torah, but would be ITS HEAVENLY MEANING—the interruption by God, the author. The full meaning would be identified not with history but with the transcendental signified, recourse to an absolute meaning. Signs cannot work that way but must have recourse to human discussion—to the incompleteness of the ongoing human community. To go beyond THE PSYCHOLOGICAL INTENTION of the writer is to envision a method of reading that would not only legitimate readings against the author's intention, it must go so far as to banish even God from commenting, stripping authority from authors and placing it in the context of other commentators. That Levinas can refer to the heavenly meaning, the UPROOTED TREES, and RIVERS FLOWING BACKWARDS allows us to see this text as displacing both the genesis of the text and its claim to divine authority in favor of the community's role as readers, reading together and thus engaged in argument over the text.

C. COMMENTARIES

The commentaries that emerge in the historical gaps are not merely readings, not merely the reception of information, but are readings that respond to the text, making the life of the people itself an intertext with the verses in the book. In the introduction to his first collection of Talmudic readings, Levinas examines the relation between Oral and Written Torah, between Talmud and Bible. He presents a semiotic of Biblical signs, focusing on the way that the interpretation, the renewal of the signs, depends on practical knowledge. Talmud itself appears as the renewing of the Biblical signs (in a different style).

6a) Levinas 9T 20–21/7–8 It is from this plenitude—with all its possibilities, practically inexhaustible, but which the contours nonetheless defined by these object-signs opened—that the commentaries revive again and again from generation to generation. The Talmud, according to the great masters of this science, can only be understood starting from life. And this holds not only for the teaching itself, which brings and which supposes the experience of life (which is to say, a great deal of imagination); it also concerns the intelligence and the perception of the signs themselves.

The give and take of text and reader produces readings that REVIVE the text FROM GENERATION TO GENERATION. But the interpreter requires the practical knowledge OF LIFE—of people and things, ways of behaving and thinking, and reading and writing. Such knowledge (which Levinas realizes is largely IMAGINATION: the ability to judge and to envision possibilities) guides not only interpretations of THE TEACHING—the Commandments and their obliging us—but also the interpretation of THE SIGNS THEMSELVES. Responding is not possible without drawing upon the full range of our minds—and even at the level of interpreting the words on the page, this requires practical knowledge.

6b) Concrete realities, they are these or those depending on the lived context. Thus these signs—Biblical verses, objects, people, situations, rituals—will function as perfect signs: whatever the modifications that becoming introduces in their sensible texture, they preserve their privilege of revealing the same significations or new aspects of these same significations. Perfect signs, irreplaceable and, in this sense—purely hermeneutical—sacred signs, sacred letters, holy writings.

The meaning of the signs depends on the LIVED CONTEXT. The reader's own practical life will transform the meanings, but the signs will still exercise privilege over the reader. Levinas introduces the concept of a PERFECT SIGN: one that admits of a wide renewal of meaning but also preserves some sort of sameness of SIGNIFICATION, of meaning. The community makes it perfect—and finds in that fixity the opportunity to renew itself. Not only BIBLICAL VERSES can function that way, but also OBJECTS (the Mezuzah, Passover Matzah), PEOPLE (Abraham, Sarah, David, Moses, Hannah), SITUATIONS (the binding of Isaac, the dedication of the Tabernacle, crossing the Sea, the giving of Torah at Mount Sinai), and RITUALS (lighting candles, blessings over wine, fasting). These signs are fixed in Jewish practical life, but they are not present with a closed and complete meaning because they solicit ongoing interpretation and renewal.

6c) The signification of these symbols never simply dismisses the materiality of these symbols that suggest and that always preserve some power unsuspected of renewing that signification. The spirit never gives notice to the letter which reveals it. Rather, the opposite: spirit awakens in the letter new possibilities of suggestion. From Talmudic thought a light is projected on the symbols which bear and revive their symbolic power. But moreover, from the meanings that they serve to create, these symbols—which are realities and often figures and concrete people—receive an illumination bearing on their texture as objects, on the Biblical narrative in which these things and beings are tangled. In this sense, the Talmud comments on the Bible. In it there is an incessant movement of coming and going.[6]

In Talmudic texts these signs are cultivated for new meanings, but their very specificity and MATERIALITY are maintained. Only the concreteness can preserve the possibility for new meanings. Thus, Talmudic writing is not the specification of abstract concepts, but the engagement with concrete signs, drawing out new meanings from their very concreteness. The spirituality of such thought cannot afford TO DISMISS the particularity of the signs. Reading awakens new possibilities, or as we discussed above, discerns tears under the knots. Indeed, in the Bible, there is a TANGLING of things and beings, a tangling that is illuminated in retrospective fashion by Talmudic reading. The Talmud draws upon a practical life that the Biblical signs helped create, and then reflects that life back upon those signs. Again,

[6] Derrida WD 99/64   It concerns a certain Judaism as birth and passion of writing. Passion *of* writing, love and endurance *of* the letter where one could not say whether the *subject* is the Jew or the letter itself. Perhaps the common root of a people and of writing.

there is AN INCESSANT COMING AND GOING, from a Biblical sign through interpretation back to Biblical sign, shaping a communal, practical life, through the very modes of reading and writing. The oral teaching of Talmud requires the perfect signs of the Bible in order to renew meaning, meaning which is never complete or closed. It is a COMMENTARY in a discontinuous form, not telling us what the text meant, but finding new meanings in the concrete signs.

The Jewish tradition distinguishes between the Written Torah and the Oral Torah. TORAH literally means *teaching*—the very term that concerned us in the account of the face. Those same Pharisees (sometimes called rabbis, and best termed the sages) fashioned the distinction. The people who closed the canon of the Jewish Bible also developed the first strata of the Oral Torah—in a genre and system noticeably different. In the first two centuries of the Common Era, a time of Roman persecution, failed rebellions, martyrs, and exile, the sages formulated the Mishnah—a series of tractates on a range of legal, ethical, and ritual issues. They called it oral because it was not of the same textual antiquity as the materials they chose to include within the canon of the Holy Scriptures. The activities of these sages are discussed in a wide range of secondary literature today, and much of their achievement is subject to debate. The Mishnah received its ultimate form under Judah the Prince around 220 C.E., but even then it was likely promulgated orally. It was written down sometime in the subsequent three hundred years, and became the kernel for two sets of extensive commentaries: the Jerusalem and the Babylonian Talmuds. The relation from Bible to Mishnah is oblique: only a small portion of the Mishnah is easily grasped as commentary upon Biblical materials. But the Talmuds, especially the Babylonian, often reconnect the material in the Mishnah with Biblical laws or stories. Unlike the Biblical texts, both Mishnah and Talmud contain vast bodies of disputation, and both follow an order that is neither historical nor deductive. Exactly why the texts were constructed, compiled, and even written down is hard to discern.

7a) Levinas BV 167/137 We have said that the Oral Torah was written down in the Talmud. Oral Torah itself is thus written. But its coming to be written is late. It is explained by the contingent and dramatic circumstances of Jewish history, exterior to the nature and the modality proper to its message.[7]

Levinas opts for a prevalent argument that the body of teaching was being forgotten, and so the written texts helped preserve the communal memory. Whether the kind of argument that occurs in the Babylonian Talmud could be envisioned without written texts is doubtful, but Levinas wants to emphasize the orality of

---

[7] Cohen RR 32–33/28 There is another feature of the oral teaching: it is not immediately a product; it is a not closed or concluded, but an unceasing progressing one. The book is closed; the mouth remains opened; . . . This continuation seems totally natural. This is in no way a

these texts: that they could not exist without the social practices of teaching and study that were properly oral. Hence, unlike the Bible, the Oral Torah is not intrinsically a literature. I prefer to say only that it is a different kind of literature.

7b) Nonetheless, Oral Torah conserves in its style, even written, its reference to an oral teaching; the animation by a master addressing himself to disciples who hear by questioning. Written, it reproduces the expressed opinions in their variety, in the extreme concern to name him who brought them or who comments upon them. It records the multiplicity of opinions and the disagreement between the sages.[8]

The pragrammatology of the texts of the oral law is striking: there are teachers and students on the page, and the students not only listen, they QUESTION. Teachers are expected to answer questions, to reconcile behavior and rulings, to reconcile one opinion with another, to reconcile Biblical texts with each other and with later texts. The questioning occurs sometimes in the voices of the students, sometimes in the voices of a colleague, and sometimes in an anonymous voice. But it does not produce only victorious opinions, or even the history of the arguments, but examines a wide VARIETY of opinions. As important as the dispersion of opinions is, Levinas identifies AN EXTREME CONCERN TO NAME the author of the opinion, and even to name the prior commentators. Certain disputants argue regularly with each other. Their positions become almost predictable, and through literary lore, we even see their friendships, enmity, and personal struggles. While historical scholarship disputes the veracity of many of the stories as well as the authenticity of the attributions of positions, the literary devices seem to require further explanation. These texts are peopled with individuals, individuals who are bound to their unique interpretations of earlier texts. Clearly the commentators in this tradition valued the innovations of their precursors, and whether we should trust the attributions or not (a question not best resolved by simple faith or blanket suspicion) they create an environment where the plurality of voices is not to be reduced to a controlled script from one author.

And here the asymmetry of rabbinic texts is clearest because the author/editor/compiler/scribe of these Talmudic texts is anonymous. Despite the

---

presumption of the scribes—that opinion rests on historical ignorance—rather, it is much more the emanation of a critical self-consciousness in relation to the written law. The critical original feeling of Deuteronomy: "the Torah is not in heaven, rather in your heart" remains alive in this thought and in the courage and the clarity of this continuation. . . . Where the Talmud is studied, there the Torah is alive. The written Torah may not remain alone; it is in your heart and in your mouth; so it must become the oral teaching.

[8] Levinas TN 208/177   A *hakham* in the Talmud is a learned scholar, but one who remains within his personal uniqueness. When he is quoted, an effort is made to respect that uniqueness jealously. When he transmits the saying of another, one signals it meticulously, and often some lines of the text are devoted to going back to the one who said it first, mentioning all of the intermediaries.

painstaking preservation of attributions and the plurality of names, the text before us comes with the author(s) effaced, withdrawn. Hence as writers, the Talmudic authors committed their text to its readers without authority, without presence. But as readers, they maintained—even originated—a complex net of teachers, of rabbis, voices that could signify themselves, or rather that could give themselves over to the reader. The orality of the oral teaching comes from a commenting which does not convert to the orality of the presentation of a speaker.

7c) The great disagreement which crosses all of the Talmud between Beth Hillel and Beth Shammai (in the first century before Christ) is called a discussion or disagreement "for the glory of Heaven." Despite all its concern to find an agreement, the Talmud never stops applying to the disagreement of Hillel–Shammai—and to the currents of divergent ideas which proceed through the successive generations of sages—the well-known formula: "These ones and the others are the word of the living God."

The Talmud preserves a series of disputes that emerge from a pair of first-century sages, formulated in terms of their schools. Indeed, the Mishnah often addresses sets of their disputes. But the Talmud produces secondary, tertiary, and so on, disputes, often addressing just what issue was in question in a traditional argument between Beth Hillel and Beth Shammai. Whatever the conclusion, both schools' words are deemed necessary. Indeed, Levinas refers to a famous phrase in the midst of an important argument.

The two sides are stubborn and persevere, but another Heavenly Voice intervenes, this time to affirm both positions. Both can be right, but THE RULING will have to be made in one direction. The requirements of the living community require a resolution. But the text also justifies the choice of the resolution: Beth Hillel preserved and honored the opinions of their opponents. In Chapter 9, I will comment on this text more closely, examining the institutionalization of plurality, and the ethical dimension of jurisprudence. Levinas satisfies his reader with a mere citation of the first half of the resolution—ignoring the need for some sort of legal ruling. Instead, he notes the reiteration (NEVER STOPS) of the certification of a plurality of opinions.

8) Erubin 13b   R. Abba said that Samuel said: For three years Beth Shammai and Beth Hillel disputed, they [one side] said: 'The ruling is according to us' and they [the others] said: 'The ruling is according to us.'

Then a heavenly voice resounded saying: "These and these are the words of the living God, but the ruling is in accord with Beth Hillel.'

Since, however, "These and these are the words of the living God" what was it that earned Beth Hillel to have the ruling fixed according to them?—Because they were kindly and modest. They studied their own words and the words of Beth Shammai and went so far as to repeat the words of Beth Shammai before theirs.

7d) Discussion or dialectic which is left open to the readers, who aren't worthy of the name unless

Talmudic texts, written oral teachings, hold open the place for the readers, solicit readers, oblige them to become respon-

they enter into it on their own account. Consequently the Talmudic texts, even in their physiognomy which their typography takes, are accompanied by commentaries and commentaries and discussions of the commentaries. Permanent overlaying of the page where the life of this text remained "oral," whether weakened or reinforced, is prolonged. The religious act of listening to the revealed speech is identified thus with the discussion one wants to keep open in all the audacity of its problematic.[9]

sive—most of all by refusing closure and any simple informational content. But the syntax of the Talmudic PAGE itself reflects these pragrammatological concerns. The text is sedimented. The Gemara, the first layer of commentary on Mishnah, with the Mishnah, fills the center of the page. Medieval commentaries surround it, inside and outside, above and below. And later commentators often argue with the earlier ones, or even confine themselves to commenting upon the commentary. Levinas claims that this ongoing accrual of text makes the life of this text "ORAL."

The quotation marks alert us to the need for a continued augmentation of meaning. But the final sentence of this passage points us toward the ultimate issue of this part; for the hearing of revelation that became a responsive commenting now becomes a discussion which seeks openings, which refuses closure, a discussion of the text of the oral teaching. The text comes as only an interruption between the earlier disagreements of houses of study in Palestine and Babylonia and the reading going on today, in schools in Israel, New York, Paris, and so on. Revealed speech becomes Talmudic argument, not frozen on the page, but alive in a discussion. Life here does not mean a full presence, indeed, it means only the trace that marks what was never

---

[9] Levinas TN 198–99/168–69   The Jewish texts may have been always understood as this unceasing doubling of significant symbols, of parables, discovering of new versions, in short, they are always glossed by the *Midrash*. And philosophy's language does not signify in an intellectual way that detaches the reader from all literality, from all particularity, from what is imposed, becoming meaningless. What could be desired as the holiness of life in the Judaism of the Lithuania of my birth was not separated from the holiness of Scripture itself. Thus they mistrusted what remained mythological in a deciphered passage. It was demythologizing the text, but also research, even into the letter as a pretext for thought. And this is what is essential in that reading. Demythologizing also of what is already demythologized. A quest in order to renew meaning. As if the verses said, without respite: "Interpret me." You obviously know Rashi's formula: "Theses verses cry, *darshenu!*" This is not yet, of course, philosophical reading, but it is probably the acquisition of one of its virtues. Philosophical discourse would appear as a way of speaking that is addressed to the spirit that is absolutely unbiased that requires ideas be utterly explicit, where everything that goes without saying is said. Speech addressed to Greeks. It is a manner of speaking which is joined and animated this more confidential way, more closed, and more steady, still more chained to the *bearers of meaning*, which the signified would never have sent on leave. Scripture is holy in this also. Such are the verses and even the terms from their first and ancient deciphering by the Talmudic sages. Inexhaustible signifiers! But one day, one discovers that philosophy, too, is a plural and that its truth is concealed and calls for states, and deepens without stopping, that its texts contradict themselves, that the systems are wrought with internal problems. It seems essential to me, then, that the Jewish reading of Scripture was pursued in the uneasiness, but also in the expectation, of Midrash. The Pentateuch, the *humash*, does not see the light of day without Rashi.

present, and discussion comes from the responsibility that effaces authority, that leaves my words, as though I were already dead. But the ongoing riskiness of writing and reading is "oral" in Levinas' sense of the term.

Suggested Readings

3 Aronowicz, Annette. "Translator's Introduction" to *Nine Talmudic Readings*. Bloomington: Indiana University Press, 1990.

4 Kepnes, Steve, Peter Ochs, and Robert Gibbs. *Reasoning After Revelation: Dialogues in Postmodern Jewish Philosophy*. New York: Westview, 1998.

8 There is a vast amount of literature on rabbinic literature and culture, but I will mention only three authors here.

Halivni, David Weiss. *Midrash, Mishnah, and Gemara: The Jewish Predilection for Justified Law*. Cambridge, Mass.: Harvard University Press, 1986.

Halivni, David Weiss. *Peshat and Derash: Plain and Applied Meaning in Rabbinic Exegesis*. New York: Oxford University Press, 1991.

Jacobs, Louis. *Structure and Form in the Babylonian Talmud*. Cambridge: Cambridge University Press, 1991.

Neusner, Jacob. *From Politics to Piety*. New York: KTAV, 1979.

PART II

Present Judgments

Our Rabbis taught: A man should always regard himself as if he were half guilty and half meritorious. If he keeps one commandment, he is happy for weighting himself down in the scale of merit. If he commits one transgression, woe to him for weighting himself down in the scale of guilt, for it is said, *but one sinner destroys much good* (Ecc. 9:18). On account of a single sin which he commits much good is lost to him.

R. Elazar son of R. Shimon said: Because the world is judged by its majority, and an individual is judged by his majority, if he keeps one commandment, he is happy is for weighting down the scale both for himself and for the whole world on the side of merit. If he commits one transgression, woe to him for weighting down the scale for himself and for the whole world on the side of guilt, for it is said "*but one sinner, etc.*" on account of the single sin which this man commits he and the whole world lose much good.

Kiddushin 40a–b

CHAPTER 6

Why Reason?

RESPONSIBILITY ARISES in attending: listening, reading, drawing near to the other. Even speaking and writing are responsibilities that solicit the other, that make attending possible again. But there is a second dimension of responsibility: the responsibilities that are shared, responsibilities for justice and equality. The responsibilities to reason, to judge, and to mediate will appear here not as counterbalanced to the responsibilities of attending, but in a much more complex and sympathetic relation. For the asymmetric responsibilities instigate mutual responsibilities, even as they retain their potential for critique. Mutuality, instigated and required by asymmetrical responsibility, produces communities wherein a further dimension of ethics is performed.

The sequence of Part II leads from reasoning, to mediating, to judgment and concludes with law. These ways of using signs are all linked by the need for justice, that is, for making just relations and just communities. That need produces a specific kind of theory of knowledge: a fully social and ethical theory of knowledge. Knowing will be interpreted as a responsibility that ethics requires, and the ethics that requires it is precisely in my relation to other people, not as a perfection of my own nature or as a task of my rational capacities. Social practices are the new organon for cognitive functions. Thus, the three logical activities discussed here (reasoning, mediating, and judging) are all interpreted as social performances and not as states of isolated consciousness. Reasoning, for example, is interpreted as a group interaction, where each person is authorized to interpret the signs under discussion. The need for justice, moreover, leads communities to agree upon semantic meanings for signs. We have to agree on a somewhat fixed meaning for terms and principles. We have to know our social world. In addition, the logical relations of signs, usually called their syntax in contemporary philosophy, is also invoked here—again for the sake of justice. The relations of particular members to their communities will be the origin of the formal syntax. In Chapter 8, judgments will be interpreted as communal life-and-death judgments of individuals, judgments that are not only socially produced and performed, but which define the ethical relations of individuals and their communities. Finally, the asymmetry of individuals will be reiterated at the communal level. Justice will require asymmetry of responsibilities between the constitutive groups within a community, and asymmetrical responsibilities between communities. The exigency for mutuality is thus permeated by interruptive asymmetries.

This chapter begins with the ethical need for justice in Levinas (The Third and Justice). The entry of the third person in Pretext 1 requires a series of cognitive uses of signs. A Biblical text that Levinas interprets as binding me in responsibility not only in nearness but also for the far is Pretext 2. But the pragmatics of communal knowing takes us beyond Levinas to Jürgen Habermas in Section B (Mutuality and Justice). In Pretext 3, Habermas explains how moral argumentation implies the equal authority of each affected member to interpret the principles at stake. Ethics requires a pragmatic interpretation of reaching an understanding, and Pretext 4 will further develop the relation of justice and knowing, as Habermas makes each the model for the other.

The tension between asymmetry and mutuality, between the vulnerability of ethics and the reasoning of justice, will produce a complex interaction in Section C (Mutuality and Asymmetry). Pretext 5, from Habermas, will show a typical discomfort with asymmetry, even with the laudable love of the neighbor, as Habermas prefers to confine ethics to justice. Pretext 6, however, returns to Levinas to discover the priority of the asymmetric responsibility in relation to the "we" of justice. Levinas demands just the risk and the sacrifice that Habermas condemns. The tension is rewound, however, when in Pretext 7 we examine Habermas' account of the self-reflection needed to participate in moral argument as a theory of taking the others' roles. Justice requires selves that internalize the interpretative positions of others. This parallel to Levinas' account of substitution is further developed in the last pretext, Pretext 8, when Levinas examines the impossibility for justice to abandon the more asymmetric and vulnerable relation to the other. The extreme responsibility of Part I not only calls for justice, but it also calls justice into question, permeating justice and mutuality with a radical asymmetrical responsibility.

A. The Third and Justice

Since Levinas normally argues that ethical responsibility deserves priority over knowing, he must also address why knowing has been given pride of place in Western philosophy. Knowing, however, must be justified ethically—there is a responsibility to know, or, in the first instance, to reason. How can we justify philosophical reason, particularly when the argument of Part I has displaced that reason in favor of attending to another person?

1a) Levinas OB 199–200/157 It is not by chance nor by foolishness nor by usurpation that the order of truth and of essence—which the present account itself claims to maintain—is the first rank in Western philosophy.

What Levinas calls THE ORDER OF TRUTH AND OF ESSENCE is not a mere fluke, nor a simple interloper, a mistaken choice. Levinas considers his own work to be philosophical because it shares in this interest in TRUTH. While truth and essence may eclipse the vulnerability and hence the asymmetrical responsibility in using signs, they are still proper to a philosophical inquiry, which we can recognize as an interpretation of using signs.

1b) Why would nearness, pure signification of the Saying, the anarchic one-for-the other of beyond being, revert to being or fall into being, into a conjunction of entities, into *essence*, showing itself in the Said? Why are we going to seek *essence* on its Empyrean?

The question is, Why should the radical and liberating ethical alternative to knowing beings get itself hooked up with beings? Why should the pure vulnerability of nearness in a saying that offers myself to the service of another person become epistemologically and ontologically secure? Were Levinas proposing a simple opposition of contraries between a totality of beings we know and a responsibility that opens up to infinity, breaking off and breaking with beings—then these questions would be about a fall, an original sin, an originary forgetting of the difference between the otherwise and being. But the rhetoric of the question WHY, repeated five times, opens the possibility that the movement from the infinite to the finite, from saying to the said, from responsibility to knowing, from pragmatics to semantics, is not arbitrary. Rather, it is ethical. This seems paradoxical only because Levinas has had to oppose so vigorously a traditional philosophical view that holds all that matters is truth, essence, beings, knowing—and in opposing it he has struggled to hold open a glimpse of what is not first an essence, not first something said.

1c) Why know? Why problems? Why philosophy?

These questions revolve around a rehabilitation of knowing. Philosophy itself appears as an attempt to address PROBLEMS, to figure things out, to become rational, and so, to know the world through reasoning. Having shown that ethics begins in responsibilities that reason cannot produce for itself, the question WHY bears the force of an ethical suspicion. Is it ethical to know? Is it responsive to philosophize? In Chapter 4, we saw philosophical writing appear both to master beings by representing them and also fail to accomplish that control. The self-limitation appeared most of all in the relations to other texts and indeed to other readers. Here the question is, What is the ethical justification for even trying to know, to govern? Why reason? Is philosophizing responsible only because it cannot achieve its goal, or is there also something ethical about the goal?

1d) We must follow in signification or in nearness or in the *Saying*, the latent birth of knowing and of essence, of the Said; the latent birth of the *question* in responsibility.

Levinas now charts a new course for us: to follow the emergence, indeed THE BIRTH, of reasoning in the womb of responsibility. He juxtaposes three terms of his ethics (SIGNIFICATION, NEARNESS, THE SAYING) with three offspring (KNOWING, ESSENCE, AND THE SAID). No longer contradictories, the terms are now bound together in a genetic pattern. The birth is LATENT, going unrecognized—perhaps even by readers of Levinas. That knowing is not self-suffi-cient is surprising for philosophy, but that it is born of signification, of one-for-the-other, is certainly odd. Moreover, responsibility bears its child: THE QUESTION. Questions are no more self-sufficient than knowing is. They are no more self-generating but are born by responsibility, by the willingness to listen, to attend, and to answer another person. The questions philosophy raises are offspring of the responsibility that precedes knowing.

1e) Nearness becomes knowing, and would signify as an enigma, dawn of a light, that nearness changes into, but the other, the neighbor, would not be absorbed into the theme where he is shown. We must follow the latent birth of knowing in nearness. Nearness can remain the signification of the very knowing where it is shown.

The responsive nearness that signifies my vulnerability for the other person changes over into something that shows up: an appearance, a presence, and so into what is knowable. The DAWN of presence, of LIGHT in which things appear in con-sciousness, can still allow my neighbor to remain absent or hidden—NOT ABSORBED INTO THE THEME. While Levinas had ar-gued for a nonpresence of the other per-son, for something that could not be made into evidence, he now suggests that in certain manifestations the otherness of the other can remain, can leave a trace and not simply be reduced. We have seen this play in writing and reading. Now in the very act of knowing there remains a trace of near-ness and the signifying from one to another.

1f) If nearness had ordained to me simply the other, "there would have been no problem"—in any sense of the term, even the most general. The question would not have been born, nor consciousness, nor self-consciousness. Responsibility for the other is an immediacy prior to the question: nearness exactly. It is troubled and becomes a problem with the entry of the third.

The birth of knowing is not, according to Levinas, inherent in the responsibility I have for one other person. If I were re-sponsible for only one other, there would be no questioning or PROBLEMS: I would be bound utterly to and for the other per-son. The absence of thought would mean that I would not be in question—only under obligation. I would not need to be-come aware of anything, least of all of my-self. The mother (responsibility) need not bear any child (presence, knowledge)—provided that there is still a privacy for the two people. The very IMMEDIACY of nearness produces responsibility before any reflection. But problems emerge with another person, whom Le-vinas calls THE THIRD.

1g) The third is other than the neighbor but is also an other neigh-bor, but also a neighbor of the Other and not simply his like (his fellow). What then are the other and the third, the one-for-the other? What have they done, the one to the other? Which goes before the other?

With the entry of another person, the relations of signifying utterly change. A sign cannot be restricted to only one other person but intrinsically wanders and is di-rected toward other others. The third rep-resents someone OTHER THAN MY NEIGH-BOR, someone who also will interpret my signs. Were I to reach a private agreement with my neighbor, the third would then stand as interpreter of our agreement, judge of its worth. The third can interpret what I say to my neighbor (IS ALSO AN OTHER NEIGHBOR), but also can interpret and judge what the neighbor says (A NEIGHBOR OF THE OTHER). The third, therefore, is another person, an authority who commands each of us (me and my neighbor). What I can agree to with my neighbor is not necessarily what the third will accept, because the third is not simply HIS LIKE—the third is other than the neighbor. I cannot grasp the relation between these two others, both of whom are other from me, but also other than each other. Who is authorized to judge whom? Who commands and who must respond? I cannot prejudge their interactions, their authority.

1h) The other maintains a relation with the third—for which I cannot answer entirely even if I answer—before any question—for my neighbor alone. The other and the third, my neighbors, contemporaries of one another—distance me from the other, from the third. "Peace, peace to the neighbor and to the distant one" (Isa. 57:19), we comprehend now the sharpness of the apparent rhetoric.

Even when I am all alone and respond for my neighbor, I cannot entirely answer for my neighbor's relations with the third. I can answer for what my neighbor does to me, but I cannot for what he does to another. The risk of violence from one to the other is not mine to accept. When I myself am the vulnerable one, I substitute myself for my neighbor, but to substitute someone else (my neighbor) for another would be immoral. The nearness I have with my neighbor is moderated: because the others are multiple and not identical, my neighbors DISTANCE ME from my neighbor and from the third. I cannot substitute myself for only the one, and so I am unable to offer myself fully to either.

Levinas cites a verse from Isaiah. The text focuses on the new proclamation, itself revealed by God. The neighbor and the distant one (the third) are now each become the distant one—that is, the near

2) Isaiah 57:19   I will create fruit of the lips: "Peace, peace, to the far and to the near, says THE LORD, I will heal him."

becomes far because there is more than one near one (neighbor). I must establish peace not only with my neighbor, but also with the third, and so between the near and the far. The APPARENT RHETORIC refers to the apparent confusion of starting peace with the distant one, since it would seem more likely to begin near. But Levinas has now used this confusion to accentuate that there is no neighbor without a third.

1i) The third introduces a contradiction in the Saying whose signification in front of the other, up to that point, went one-way. It is of itself a limit of responsibility, a birth of the question: What have I to do with justice? A question of conscience.

Signification now turns around, or rather, becomes mutual. We, too, have previously focused on a ONE-WAY signifying, an asymmetry in which the other has the authority to interpret my signs. But I may no longer yield all authority to the other person. The others require me to defend their authority as interpreters, to protect them from violent readings by my neighbor. Responsibility was infinite, but now gains a limit because I am responsible for justice: first to the third, but then to the neighbor, and in relation to them, to myself. Before the third entered our analysis, the question was, "What have I to do with this other person, with responsibility?" The third brings a further concern—JUSTICE. While the saying was the pragmatic responsibility between me and another person, performed in announcing that I had become sign for the other, the entry of the third person introduces a further relation between me and the others, a relation that also is semiotic. For if the pragmatics focused on the bestowal of my bodily self for the singular other, then the question of justice (WHAT HAVE I TO DO WITH JUSTICE?) emerges because I cannot give myself in speaking or writing only to one other. The multiplicity of others requires a transformation of the interpretation of what I do with my uttered signs. My concern to render myself to each produces a QUESTION OF CONSCIENCE precisely because my self as a sign and my self as my saying of signs will have to become public in what for us is a new way. That publicity produces the stability of meaning, the semantic dimension of signification.

1j) There must be justice, which is to say, comparison, coexistence, contemporaneity, assembling, order, thematization, the *visibility* of faces and, through that, the intentionality and the intellect and in intentionality and intellect, the intelligibility of the system, and through that, also a co-presence on an equal footing as in a court of justice.

Levinas recognizes that ethics requires JUSTICE—a rational determination that involves all of the various facets of knowing and reasoning that responsibility evades at its outset. In terms of a semiotics we find here many of the traditional functions of signs, but we now see them in the context of an ethical need for knowing. Reasoning is justified in its role for justice; justice in its capacity to relate responsively with several other people. Following through Levinas' list of activities of thinking, we see ways of knowing as responsive interpretations of signs.

COMPARISON:[1] A third sign that juxtaposes two signs. To bind different things together and separate other things requires this linguistic activity. Different people will compare their various claims. Interpretation is always a continuing comparison of differences, but the justice of interpretation requires the adjudication of different signs.

COEXISTENCE, CONTEMPORANEITY:[2] Signs are always plural, occurring in

---

[1] Royce Ch 304   This problem, in the cases of comparison with which Peirce deals, is solved through a new act. For this act originality and sometimes even genius may be required. This new act consists in the invention or discovery of some third idea, distinct from both the ideas which are to be compared. This third idea, when once found, interprets one of the ideas which are the objects of the comparison, and interprets it to the other, or in the light of the other.

[2] Rosenzweig S 383/345   Brotherliness thus weaves its bond between people, of whom none is equal to the others. It is not at all the equality of all of those who bear a human face, rather it is the unanimity of people with the most diverse faces. Only this one thing is needful: that a person above all has a face—that they see themselves. The church is the community of all

the context of other signs. The meaning of any sign requires its coexistence with other signs. For Levinas the other person did not coexist with me, because the other person could resist my attempts to represent her. But the coexistence of multiple other people requires justice. Signs refer in a time common to the interlocutors, whereas the pragmatic meaning was deferred for the other to interpret, and reinterpret. In society, the semantic meaning required for justice must be simultaneous: the sign and its interpretation must happen together among contemporaneous interpreters. Justice is not to be deferred.

ASSEMBLING, ORDER: Signs allow for the collection of diverse terms under general ones despite their differences. For a just ruling, different meanings need to be assembled. Here law and generality seem bound most closely together, but not simply for the sake of simplicity in knowing, but rather for the coordination of claims, demands, interpretations. Signs themselves also order other signs, putting them in order and sequencing them. While original responsibility disordered me, and refused to locate the other person in some order, justice requires various forms of orders, organizing and prioritizing the various claims of different people.

THEMATIZATION, THE VISIBILITY OF FACES [*VISAGES*]: Signs can make explicit the meanings of other signs, of gestures, of experiences, of objects, and so on. Indeed, signs seem most of all to call to consciousness the determinate qualities of their referents—to deliver some content to reflection. The responsibility to attend the other fought an ongoing battle against the encroachment of thematization in order to preserve the otherness of the other person, but justice sacrifices that unthinkable otherness for the sake of a conceptual access. The coordination of differing claims requires thinking, requires this delivery into consciousness and refuses to tolerate the ineffable as a component of justice. What counts in justice must be discussible. Levinas had argued for the nonphenomenal quality of the other person's face, that the face was a trace. But a sign also can be present and can represent the person. The ambiguity of signs is extremely complex on this point: a face can be both visible (in the context of justice) and be only an enigma or a trace (in the original responsibility). In the latter case, a presence represents the face, but poorly—what can be visible is not the otherness of the other. Thus the trace is not in the representation but almost despite it. But justice requires evidence, presence, appearances—as appearances, and not only as traces. For the sake of justice I can face others—and not only be faced, not only respond. The other person's authority, which characterized the face in Part I, now gives birth to a limitation of that authority, as the face also becomes a presence, accessible to me and to the third. Justice is not possible on the basis of absence and absolute authority, but even requires that other people become present and evident.

---

those who see each other. It binds people as temporal companions, as contemporaries in the separated places of the distant spaces.

Other people now visible are accessible to my intellectual grasp. They become the goals of my INTENTIONALITY. For signs, this visibility recalls the intentionality of a sign's emitter—a sign can display my intending to say. This possibility of knowing what another means to say is not a complete internalization into my private act of knowing, as though both the sign and its meaning were now a correlation in my mind. Rather, other people structure the very coordination of sign and meaning: the ethical need for justice calls for an intended meaning. Intentionality is thus not first solipsistic, only to be later conformed to others' claims and aims, but is from the outset a need of justice. The 'author's intention' is needed for the sake of justice precisely to negotiate a balancing of different claims and different interpretations. When intentionality here returns to our analysis, INTELLECT also does—the activity of knowing, of holding both the sign and its meaning in the mind. The cause of justice justifies knowing and allows the completion of the one-for-the-other by a sign in a mind.

This recourse to knowing also provides access to a SYSTEM of signs. Order's knitting together in the intellect's assembling of a set of signs provides a system. Signs cohere, generating a simultaneity of diverse signs in a consistent system. Sign systems assure each person's interpretations an orderly place and protocols for interpreting it. That the system may be more or less fair does not deflect the origin of system in the multiple interpretations, the multiplicity of signs and interpreters—the need for justice. Systematicity, like order or assembling, is not unambiguous but is called for by the needs for justice. Signs are always part of systems whose function is to delimit the possibilities for meaning and steer possible communications and interpretations. Levinas does not have a rich interpretation of systemic relations, such as Luhmann or Habermas or even Rosenzweig can provide, but the need for semiotic systems here is drawn from the responsibility for justice.

Through that systematicity, Levinas arrives at the EQUALITY of the plaintiff and defendant IN A COURT. Because there can be justice only between equals, justice requires an equalization: each must be granted a limited authority to interpret signs—the right to clarify and to restate their claims, to interrogate the others' interpretations, to face the other and so to contest the claims and the testimony of each other. Only when the two are CO-PRESENT before a third can justice be done. The determination of the claims of each within a system, a legal system, a court system, is a requisite of justice.

By the entry of the third, Levinas has led us into a different aspect of responsibility: the exigency to reason, itself requiring the contemporaneity of sign and meaning. Here is a realm where justice needs its order, comparison, system—in short, rationality. Our interest is the way that the pragmatic relations of the speakers (and writers) shape the different aspects of signifying. The responsibility for justice emerges in a pragmatic relation of multiple speakers, multiple writers, and requires a rational, presenting semantics: signs must have recognizable and accessible meanings.

B. MUTUALITY AND JUSTICE

Levinas indicates how knowing is born of responsibility in the demand for justice, but he does not examine the way that conversation of multiple interpreters produces the needed communication. Jürgen Habermas, however, has richly examined both the role of mutuality in knowing and the way that cognition is directed to justice. Focusing on *The Theory of Communicative Action* and his subsequent reflections on discourse ethics, we can develop the pragmatic dimensions of knowing as a work of justice.

For Habermas ethics concerns the way justice is hammered out, the way that people communicate with each other and arrive at a common moral viewpoint. The comparison and negotiation that we saw emerge in Levinas becomes a formal pragmatics in Habermas. Habermas examines which kind of situations and what rules of interpretation facilitate the sort of knowing that Levinas claimed justice requires. Such knowing requires that the principles of justice themselves be justified in the community. Habermas' theory calls for multiple voices that mutually protect each other's authority to interpret principles of justice. The knowing needed for justice is social, formed in an environment of mutuality. We look first at how a principle of justice itself structures the space for argumentation about moral principles, looking to a text from the essay "Explanations for Discourse Ethics."

3a) Habermas JA 154–55/49–50 In moral arguments, they [the participants] must pragmatically presuppose that in principle all those affected can participate as free and equal in a cooperative search for truth, in which they may come to the conclusion only by the force of the better argument. Upon this universal pragmatic state of affairs rests the fundamental principle of discourse ethics: that only those moral rules may claim validity that could meet with the assent of everyone affected as participants in a practical discourse.[3]

Habermas interprets a MORAL ARGUMENT about principles and finds certain PRAGMATIC structures at work in the practice of arguing itself. The pragmatic conditions that Habermas advances help us understand the way that signs achieve simultaneous meaning. The key requirement is that ALL THOSE AFFECTED CAN PARTICIPATE. Habermas elsewhere will treat this as a transcendental pragmatic presupposition. Our participation is AS FREE AND EQUAL: justice makes a demand on the structure of the argument that no one be coerced. EQUALITY here is not in the distribution of goods or of duties, but

---

[3] Habermas MC 103/93   It follows from the aforementioned rules of discourse that a contested norm cannot meet with the consent of the participants in a practical discourse unless (U) holds, that is:

> Unless all affected can *without unconstraint* accept the consequences and the side effects that the *general* observance of a controversial norm can be expected to have for the satisfaction of the interests of *each individual*.

But once it has been shown how that (U) can be grounded upon the presuppositions of

pragmatic equality. Each should have equal access to the floor, to the authority to interpret the signs. The goal is to produce assent ONLY BY THE FORCE OF THE BETTER ARGUMENT. Habermas protects the moral dimension of justice, the responsibility to seek what is best without respect for power relations. Like the teaching face of the other, the better argument produces assent without compulsion, without violence. While facing the other involved no reasoning and no conceptualization; in order to argue about justice, we require the whole range of knowing activities. We have learned from Levinas that those activities run the risk of violence. The better argument will have to be the one that can produce assent without violence, without threats. This model of argument recurs to a COOPERATIVE SEARCH FOR TRUTH—the disinterest of knowing and the cooperation of a social endeavor serve as ideals of argument.

3b) By virtue of *idealizing* assumptions, which everyone who seriously enters into argument *as a matter of fact* must undertake, rational discourse can play the role of one of the explanatory procedures of a moral point of view.

Habermas construes this model of rational discourse as a key to understanding morality. He argues that our actual practice employs IDEALIZING activity. He highlights both AS A MATTER OF FACT and IDEALIZING, in order to claim that the idealization is not only actual in our practices, but that such idealizing itself may constitute the logic of morality. What we idealize are the prospects for consensus. And we are implicated. We must assume that other people will attend to what we say and will cooperatively engage in interpreting our words. Because this cooperative, free exchange of interpretations never happens purely, the assumption is IDEALIZING. But it is not an idealization to say that we enter the argument with this hope. We do *in fact* make these idealizing assumptions about conversations, and without them an argument over moral principles could not take place. One could say that Habermas has translated the idealizing expectations of moral obligation, that one should become better than one is, into a discursive responsibility. Without the responsibility to seek consensus we would not enter the argument. That responsibility governs and impels us in the conversation.

3c) Practical discourse may be conceived of as a process of seeking understanding, that according to its form, that is, on the basis of unavoidable universal presuppositions of argument alone, encourages all

The constraints on the practices of seeking mutual understanding are those of rational arguments. The way to meet these constraints is to ENCOURAGE all relevant parties to adopt the idealizing assumptions just announced. Habermas now ex-

---

argumentation through a transcendental pragmatic derivation, *discourse ethics itself* can be formulated in terms of the principle of discourse ethics (D), which stipulates:

> Only those norms can claim to be valid that meet (or could meet) with the approval of all affected in their capacity as participants in a practical discourse.

concerned parties to engage in ideal role taking *simultaneously.*

This explanation of the moral point of view privileges practical discourse as the form of communication that secures the impartiality of moral judgment together with universal interchangeability of participant perspectives.[4]

plicates this as an IDEAL ROLE TAKING. Each person imagines interpreting a given principle from the perspective of the other people involved. More important is the italicized *SIMULTANEOUSLY.* Agreements must happen in a present moment. The interchange of interpretations must occur in a common moment—a present produced from moral concern and constituted by multiple interpreters agreeing. Moral principles then become determined through the pragmatics of interpretation, for in so far as there is UNIVERSAL INTERCHANGEABILITY OF PARTICIPANT PERSPECTIVES, that is, each person can take each other's viewpoint, then communication can safeguard the IMPARTIALITY OF MORAL JUDGMENT. Habermas has discovered in moral discourse the pragmatic responsibility for a specific kind of sign exchange: a conversation in which everyone affected has equal access to interpret the principles of justice. He argues that precisely the ability to take any position will prevent a principle under discussion from unfairly benefiting one of the members. Each member is presumed both to perceive her own interests and to be able to attend to another's interpretation of her interests.

3d)   It also explains why a prospect persists of deriving the fundamental principle of a universalistic morality from the necessary pragmatic presuppositions of argumentation in general, without committing a naturalistic fallacy. Discourses rest on actions oriented to reaching understanding as their reflective form; in the symmetry conditions and reciprocity expectations of everyday praxis of speech oriented to reaching understanding, there already exist *in nuce* the basic notions of equal treatment and universal welfare around which all morality turns, even in premodern society.

Habermas links this fundamental moral principle with both argumentation and the pragmatics of seeking agreement in the EVERYDAY PRAXIS OF SPEECH. The pragmatic conditions include SYMMETRY and RECIPROCITY—that if I allow the other to speak, then the other will give me my chance. Each must have an equal chance to speak as the authority of interpretation is distributed among all members. These structures of conversation and of argumentation are themselves the core of the central themes of justice: EQUAL TREATMENT and UNIVERSAL WELFARE. Habermas presents a fundamentally egali-

[4] Habermas C 39/19   In everyday life, however, no one would enter into moral argumentation if he did not start intuitively from the strong presupposition that a justified consensus could in principle be achieved among those affected. In my view, this follows with conceptual necessity from the *meaning* of normative validity claims. Norms of action appear in their domains of validity with the claim to express, in relation to some matter requiring regulation, an interest *common to all* those affected, and thus to *deserve* universal recognition. For this reason valid norms must be capable, in principle, of meeting with the rationally motivated approval of everyone affected under the conditions that neutralize all motives except that of cooperatively seeking the truth. If we argue about morality, we always rest on this intuitive knowledge; the root of the "moral point of view" is in this presupposition.

tarian view of justice, or at least of access to justice. The universality of these superprinciples is easily enough linked to the pragmatics he proposes.

3e) The ideas of justice and solidarity are already *installed* in the idealizing assumptions of communicative action, above all, in the reciprocal recognition of persons who can orient their actions to validity claims.

He reasons, however, from a set of pragmatic rules of arguments toward principles of justice. And Habermas notes that JUSTICE AND SOLIDARITY underlie those pragmatic rules. Solidarity here emerges from the interchange of perspectives: if I can imaginatively take other people's perspectives, then I already am bound to the others. Such binding occurs in speaking, particularly speaking in a context freed of violence. The task of justifying moral principles among other people itself provides a formal structure for what sort of principles can be accepted. Justice is performed in our reasoning together.

This close proximity of reasoning and justice is yet clearer in a text from *The Theory of Communicative Action*, where Habermas argues that the task of speaking is not soliciting the other's authority to interpret me and my words, but rather the more familiar task: to understand each other. Reasoning is for the sake of justice and the capacity of using signs to understand, in Habermas, is still social and pragmatic, even if not asymmetric.

4a) Habermas C 387/287–88   If we could not take the model of speech, we would not be able to take even the first step to analyze what it means for two subjects to come to an understanding with one another. Reaching understanding is the inherent telos of human language.

Habermas claims that speaking has a privileged role for interpreting what knowing is, particularly the interpersonal knowing of reaching agreement. The best way to interpret two (or more) people understanding each other, or rather agreeing with one another, is with THE MODEL OF SPEECH. The pragmatics of a conversation models the practices of sharing knowledge. The TELOS of speech, moreover, is REACHING UNDERSTANDING. While we have previously interpreted speech in terms of response, as witness, as offering myself to another, we now see the more familiar purpose of knowing and sharing knowledge restored to speech—with an ethical transformation that such knowing is no longer the act of an isolated consciousness knowing an object. Knowing requires a sharing of knowledge between people. From our perspective, this goal (reaching understanding) is the goal of only one of language's dimensions, which is not the sole or primary telos. The relations of knowing, offering oneself, and repairing relations all inhere in signification.

4b) Of course, language and reaching understanding are not related to one another as means to end. But we can explain the concept of coming to understanding only

Habermas hurries to assure us that this relation between language and knowing is not a MEANS TO END—this is of course exactly the instrumentalization of communication that Habermas is trying to correct.

if we specify what it means to use sentences with a communicative intent. The concepts of speech and reaching understanding reciprocally interpret one another. Thus we can analyze the formal-pragmatic features of the attitude oriented to reaching understanding on the model of the attitude of participants in communication,

4c) one of whom—in the simplest case—carries out a speech-act, to which the other takes a yes or no position (even though utterances in the communicative practices of everyday life usually do not have an explicit linguistic form and often have no verbal form at all).

Instead, we can explain the process of reasoning only when we understand how language is used to COMMUNICATE. Here is theoretical RECIPROCITY, indeed, a correlation, because each term is needed to interpret the other: knowing gives a purpose to speech, speaking shows the process through which knowing occurs. The attitudes of people talking together can model those of people reasoning in order to know something together.

The simplest model would see one person saying something to another person who is free to TAKE A YES OR NO POSITION. To speak is implicitly to accept that the other person is free to interpret by assent or denial. For Habermas this authority to say yes or no constitutes communicative freedom. This ability to take a position is also reserved for the speaker. We will develop this model later in this chapter; here, we have a first sketch. Reason itself is performed in this freedom to respond yes or no granted to the other and to myself by the other. Habermas notes in parentheses that this model is not always met IN EVERYDAY LIFE— but the model shows how speech occurs in a situation where another person can agree or disagree. That pragmatic structure governs how social knowledge arises. The principles of justice require a procedure of people sharing meanings, indeed reaching understanding together, and one of the functions of using language (or signs in general) is to reason together, to understand each other. Habermas' ethics is focused on these pragmatic responsibilities to converse and engage in moral argumentation to determine the principles of justice.

C. MUTUALITY AND ASYMMETRY

What is the relation between these two dimensions of responsibility, the asymmetric call to attend the other, holding open my vulnerability, and the mutual exigency to determine principles of justice in equal interpretative authority? Or, how can we coordinate the dimensions of meaning in signifying: the futural openness to others' interpretations and the present agreement of shared semantics? We began this chapter with Levinas' transition from the first dimension to the second, but Habermas claimed that knowing, as a social process, is the goal of language. It is by no means controversial to emphasize that Habermas' own account of ethics is cognitivist. But his theory of knowledge is not grounded in an autonomous subject's isolated spontaneity. Habermas socializes reason even as he restores the place of reasoning in ethics. In the first part of this work responsiveness suspended the possibility for knowledge in order to find another purpose for signifying. Were the sequence in our presentation to become a simple narrative, that is, first we must respond, and then subsequently we learn to converse, to take turns and to exchange interpretations, reasoning toward a consensus; then we would misunderstand the ways signs work. All use of signs involves both functions, both asymmetrical responsibility and a goal of mutuality that can never leave behind the asymmetry. The responsibilities to attend the other arose from an awareness of the violence of reasoning because it limited the authority of the other person. But if we cannot move beyond asymmetry, can we ever find the striving for mutuality to be ethical? In general, Levinas says little enough about justice that we require Habermas' fuller treatment of the pragmatics of justice, but Habermas has even less time for asymmetry. Normally his concern is to overcome asymmetry, seeing it as a mark of the power of one person over another. His goal is an equality of authority. Occasionally he does refer to the possibility of a responsibility that exceeds equality and rational measure.

5a) Habermas JA 136–37/34–35 But autonomy *can make demands* only in social contexts that are already themselves rational in the sense that they take care that action motivated by good reasons will not have to oppose one's own interests. The validity of moral commands is subject to the condition that they are universally adhered to as the foundation for a *general* practice.

Rationality, mutuality, and the prospects for reaching understanding all require a RATIONAL SOCIAL CONTEXT. Such a context is one in which one's own interests are not structurally pitted against good reasoning. Imagine a perverse culture in which rationally motivated action regularly produced suffering, deprivation, exposure to violence, even death for the actor. Under more normal conditions, a moral command will likely produce A GENERAL PRACTICE that will not force a person following valid rational principles to undergo extreme suffering. Habermas realizes morality can make valid claims within a given community only if the society at large is not structured to punish such morality. The range of morality, therefore, is circumscribed more tightly than the range of ethics is for Levinas.

5b) Only when this condition for making demands is satisfied do the commands express what all could will. Only then are the moral commands in the common interest and—precisely because they are equally good for all—do they not make supererogatory claims. To this extent rational morality puts its seal on the abolition of sacrifice.

The commands of morality make a valid demand upon the interpreters precisely when commands express something that ALL COULD WILL together. (The reasoning that seeks a consensus may still be unfinished; but the morality of a moral command is that it COULD be proven/ agreed to by all.) The conditions for a moral command to command are not only the possibility of consensus but also a society that supports rational decisions. In that context, morality appears as that which is good for all and so expresses the common interest. But Habermas' account of morality excludes SUPEREROGATORY CLAIMS: claims that exceed what is good for all. Indeed, Habermas regards rational morality as the ABOLITION OF SACRIFICE. At first glance, Habermas may mean that societies often have immorally required some members to give themselves for others. This asymmetry was dignified and rationalized as sacrifice, but ultimately it is unjust and immoral. One might well recognize here the claim voiced by the oppressed: I should be freed from extreme and unfair claims. Rational morality emancipates me. One might, however, also be more subtle: for within the context of responsiveness, we can say that it is immoral to require others to sacrifice themselves. Morality puts an end to my oppression of others. But is it moral for me to make a sacrifice of myself? If morality is rational morality, then clearly I must also not allow myself to become a sacrifice, and must submit only to the universal commands of morality as much as anyone else.

5c) At the same time, someone who, for example, follows the Christian commandment to love and in the interest of the neighbor brings sacrifices that could not be demanded, deserves our moral admiration. Because supererogatory acts can be understood as attempts to go up against fateful unjust suffering in cases of tragic complexity or under barbarous living conditions that evoke our moral indignation.[5]

And yet we know that when we see someone making a sacrifice for another person we sometimes admire him. Indeed, Habermas recognizes that in certain circumstances sacrifice is not immoral—but rather DESERVES OUR MORAL ADMIRATION. If we require morality not to justify violence, not to support suffering, then we may find that ethics tolerates, even solicits, a vulnerability in tension with such morality. It is not accidental that Habermas refers to THE CHRISTIAN COMMANDMENT TO LOVE. Nor that he ignores that commandment is first a Jewish commandment. The religious context of an obligation to make sacrifices for another person's interests is at once unmistakable but also perplexing. Can we interpret that commandment in terms of pragmatics? Can it become an equal treatment of all under the conditions of consensus formation? For Habermas rational morality is coextensive with a rational society, which though imperfect, is one in which arguments can be entertained, conversa-

[5] Luhmann, T 47/43–44   A performance that does not arise from some duty but is deemed meritorious and attracts respect is supererogatory. In spite of recent attempts, the relationship between such a performance and duty remains logically and analytically obscure; however, what is of interest to us here is primarily its generative function. It entails somehow an overdraft on the normative that has some parallels with the overdraft on information discussed previously; it constitutes a surplus performance, which nobody can require, but which (for the selfsame reason) generates claims—as benefactions, for instance, engender a claim to gratitude. Trust relationships do not follow from previous prescriptions, but norm [prescriptions]. Thus the function of the superogative appears to be that it *transforms conditions for emergence into conditions for persistence.* And this is exactly what is required if trust is to emerge.

tion can flourish, and interests are not structured to be in opposition to morality. The alternative is either a situation of TRAGIC COMPLEXITY, where the conflicts between various interests create a rationally insoluble net of claims—a situation in which, while it would not be admirable or even tolerable to demand another person sacrifice her interest, I might morally sacrifice my own. The other case is one of BARBAROUS LIVING CONDITIONS—in wartime, in the lager or the gulag, in the midst of extreme poverty or filth, during a reign of terror, and so on. In those situations our only moral sentiment is INDIGNATION and the prospect of rational discussion seems absurdity itself. Habermas views these situations as extraordinary, a somewhat puzzling view, and yet one that coheres with rational morality's requirement of normalcy, whether the rationality be deontological, Neo-Aristotelean, or utilitarian. Moreover, Habermas does not speak in the first person or notice here the asymmetry of sacrifice. Indeed, he adopts an observer stance. Those who make a sacrifice move him, but he fails to register how the "I" who so wonders at responsiveness in other people might have a similar responsibility. Because he neglects the pragmatic importance of the first person here, he also fails to notice that a rational abolition of sacrifice could be preserved, with the restriction that I deny the validity of any claim upon another person for sacrifice. The return to a first-person perspective governs our reflections at the end of this chapter.

6a) Levinas OB 153–54/119–20 Differing from all of those who want to found the upsurge of the I's on a dialogue and an original *we*, and who refer to an original communication, behind the de facto communication (but without giving to that original communication another meaning than the empirical one, that of a dialogue where there is a *showing* of one to the other—and which presupposed the *we* that it is concerned to found) and reducing the problem of communication to the problem of its certainty—[6]

We turn back to Levinas now to engage a limited conversation between these two different aspects of ethics. In this text, written well before Habermas' *Theory of Communicative Action*, Levinas distinguishes himself and his interpretation of language from a theory similar but not identical to Habermas'. For us it represents not a criticism of Habermas as much as a warning of what we must avoid when restoring the knowing function to speech. The first error to avoid is deriving "I"s from a presupposed "WE." To begin with

---

[6] Levinas EN 49/43 To respect is not to bow down before the law, but before a being who commands a work of me. But for this command to allow no humiliation—which would take from me the very possibility of respecting—the command which I receive must also be a command to command him who commands me. It consists of commanding a being to command me. This reference from a command to a command is the fact of saying We, of forming a party. Because of this reference from a command to the other, We is not the plural of I.

Rosenzweig S 264/236 "We" is not a plural. The plural arises in the third-person singular, which does not arbitrarily indicate gender membership; it is in genders, in mythopoeic oversimplificaton, that the first conceptual order is introduced into the world of things. And thereby

mutuality would make asymmetrical responsiveness derivative from it. The second error is a reduction of communication to a reciprocal *SHOWING*—as if the only pragmatic relation was displaying what each had already thought. Finally, third is the reduction of communication to CERTAINTY—as though risk were a deficient moment in signifying. While the first error approaches Habermas somewhat, it is easy enough to show how Habermas intertwines the development of the self with that of society. As for the second and third, although they look like a caricature of him, Habermas' thought has discovered in the pragmatics of seeking agreement precisely the risk and the complex relations that exceed the function of mere showing.

6b) —we presuppose for the transcendence of language a relation that is not empirical speech, but responsibility, which is to say also resignation (before any decision, in passivity) at the risk of misunderstanding (as in love—unless one loves not from love—one must resign oneself to not being loved) at the risk of sin and the refusal to communicate—responsibility and substitution in which the Me that thematizes is itself founded.[7]

Levinas' view is familiar from Part I, and leads to the priority of asymmetrical risk. We cannot rely exclusively on EMPIRICAL SPEECH, which Levinas regards as the evidences of speaking (the said), because pragmatic dimensions (the saying) are only enigmatic. TRANSCENDENCE in language is not found in transcripts but in performance. Levinas opens the examination of language beyond the empirical recording in a parallel to Habermas' formalism. The vulnerability to the other person's interpretation of my speech is a vulnerability that is not so much chosen as assigned to me, to which I RESIGN myself. If to speak is to become implicated in a set of claims, then it also is to be resigned to MISUNDERSTANDING, to FAILURE, to THE REFUSAL TO COMMUNICATE. A conversation does not begin with a promise of consensus—it does not begin even with the promise that the other person will respond to me, much less take me seriously. These pragmatic risks define the speaker, make me who I am: substitute for the other person who is likely to misinterpret what I say. Communication begins then in an offering of myself up to this unhappy conversation—not in a rational, respectful debate in an established society. Levinas here compares this risk to LOVE: one cannot love without accepting that one may NOT BE LOVED in return. Only someone who does not love makes love

---

plurality as such is first made visible. The "we," by contrast, is the totality developed out of the dual. It can only be narrowed, not expanded, whereas the singularity of the "I" and its companion, the "you," can only be expanded.

[7] Rosenzweig S 240/215 Love of the neighbor always breaks forth anew. It is an ever-beginning again from before. It does not let itself be misled by disappointment. On the contrary, it needs the disappointments in order not to become rusty, not to congeal into schematically organized act, but to surge up as ever-fresh. It may not have a past nor in itself any will for a future, no "purpose." It must be an act of love wholly lost in the moment. Only disappointment can help it to this end by ever and again dis-appointing it of the natural expectation of a success such as it might expect on the analogy of past successes. Disappointment keeps love potent.

a reciprocal demand—dependent on being loved in return. The risks and resignations here are not symmetrical, not reciprocal, not even cooperative and mutual.

6c) ... Eidetically: communication is only possible in the sacrifice that is the approach of the one for whom one is responsible. Communication with an other person can only be transcendent as a dangerous life, as a noble risk to take. These words take their strong sense when, instead of designating only the lack of certainty, they express the gratuity of the sacrifice. In the noble risk to take, one has never sufficiently thought the word "noble." It is as antithetical to certainty and to consciousness altogether that these terms take their positive meanings and are not the expression of something makeshift.

While knowledge can even be defined as the mutual process of searching for justice, COMMUNICATION requires an approach to another person, an exposure of my vulnerability. Levinas here calls it SACRIFICE. While Habermas had seen rational morality as the final abolition of sacrifice, Levinas must disagree. In its asymmetry the approach to another person is not rational in either a Cartesian sense or Habermas' sense. Levinas argues that communication requires a risk that under 'rational conditions' would be impossible. Such reason is only possible if first there is the risk, the risk of offering myself to the other person's service. Habermas, despite the recognition that conversation entails risks and exposure, rejects sacrifice precisely because it is one-way. But Levinas finds a facet of signifying that cannot escape this one-way risk. Indeed, the question quite simply becomes: Is there risk, if risk is conditional on another person taking the same risk? In this way Levinas can see that RISK, GRATUITY, SACRIFICE all take on POSITIVE MEANINGS: the very being-for-an-other of signs. Because it is asymmetric between one and another, signifying cannot be secured. Reciprocal relations (not mutual ones) secure certainty at the expense of transcendence.

But if sacrifice has a place in the responsive function of signifying, we still have not seen the place of its vulnerability within mutuality. Mutuality is not to reduce the asymmetric risk to certainty. Habermas claims that we reach understanding particularly on principles of justice through a process of exchanging perspectives. Does the asymmetry of the "I" facing another person survive in the midst of this exchanging? Is there any remnant of the undeclinability of the accusative "me" we saw in Part I? There substitution for others became my unique responsibility, one that only I could bear, but here mutuality seems to require each to substitute for each. And yet the result is not as symmetrical as one might think.

7a) Habermas C.2 93/58–59 The process of socialization is at once one of individualization. Mead bases this on the diversity of the position-bound perspectives that the speaker and hearer accept. As a

Habermas has recourse to Mead to articulate the general principle that SOCIALIZATION and INDIVIDUALIZATION happen together. Both speaker and hearer can take on the perspectives of each other. A speaker must anticipate the challenge by

principle of individuation he adduces not the body but a *structure of perspectives* that is set with the *communicative roles* of the first, second, and third person. By introducing the expression 'me' to refer to the identity of the socialized individual, Mead is systematically connecting the role taking effective in socialization with the speech situations in which speakers and hearers enter into interpersonal relations as members of a social group.

her interlocutor and may also anticipate how to respond to the criticism. Both also anticipate an observer (THE THIRD PERSON). Ironically, that third-person perspective is also unstable—even though one usually might expect that the stability of theorizing, of thematizing and grasping a situation conceptually, would protect one. But these various roles circulate in the "ME." Identity is fashioned out of the various responsibilities that the individual incurs in each position—but the taking of various positions depends precisely on social interactions.

7b) 'Me' stands for the aspect that ego proffers to an alter in an interaction when the latter makes a speech-act offer to ego. Ego takes this view of himself by accepting alter's perspective when alter requests something of ego, that is, of *me*, promises something to *me*, expects something of *me*, fears, hates, or pleases *me*, and so forth.

The "me," according to Habermas' interpretation of Mead, is the PROFFER I make to another person in response to a speech-act. The other person makes some claim upon me—a claim that can either give or withhold, can harm or heal. But the other person performs this claim in speaking, setting me in the accusative (as "me"). I make myself available to the other or hold myself open. I am installed as me, TAKING as my own THE VIEW of the other person toward me. In a different vocabulary, this is what Levinas called substitution. We note, moreover, that the other person's attitudes toward me need not admit of reciprocity: should the other person HATE me, ACCEPTING ALTER'S PERSPECTIVE is not to say that I must hate him. I need not require the other to take my perspective to proffer myself for his claims. Mutuality is not the simple exchange of all attitudes, but mutuality is not possible without my substituting his attitudes for mine. Moreover, if I know that I must be able to justify my attitude toward the other person before that other person, then I anticipate the critique and begin to criticize myself and so mark my own vulnerability to critique. Were we to do this together, we could indeed come to a mutual relation of conversation and communicative action.

7c) But the interpersonal relation between the speaker and the one spoken to, I and You, first and second person, is set up so that in taking over the perspective of someone opposite, ego cannot steal away from his own communicative role. When ego takes the attitude of alter,

Moreover, I am not free to abandon my "me." I cannot dissolve myself into other perspectives. Rather, in any perspective I accept, I find myself obliged as me in that perspective (CANNOT STEAL AWAY). When I place myself in my interlocutor's position, I myself then gain his obligations to honor claims I could make from that

in order to make the latter's expectations his own, it does not exempt ego from the role of the first person: he *himself*, in the role of ego, has to satisfy the behavior patterns he first took over and internalized from alter.[8]

position. Even were I to take the role of hating me, I also realize that in that role I would have to provide grounds for why I, as me, am worthy of hate. I cannot shake the obligations that come with whatever role I take on. The "I" is formed by taking a variety of roles and trying on the various responsibilities that come with each role—but to be in each of those roles is to incur responsibilities. Thus the circulation of roles in a community does not free each person from cumbersome responsibilities, rather it implicates each, as far as each takes on other people's roles, implicates each in a wider variety of responsibilities. The equality achieved in a community is not primarily the power to prevent violence against me, but is the responsibility to prevent violence against other people, and to protect even myself when I view myself from the perspective of another person. Were I allowed to duck out, to steal away from my own role, I would not be taking other roles but simply refusing to take any role. Each role is defined by the implication of the claims of its perspective—implicated in the responsibility of answering criticisms. For Habermas, reasoning itself is the responding, the self-reflection in speaking and so in accepting, rejecting, and further interpreting the claims of the other. But even to advance my own interpretation requires the vulnerability of needing to respond for the other's claims. Internalization of a diversity of roles is multiplication of responsibility—and a pragmatics of interaction finds each of us bound over for each other.

Finally, we move back to Levinas in order to see the way that asymmetric responsibility interrupts within communal interactions of justice. The reasoning performed in interaction involves the responsibility of each one who reasons. A judge is not above the responsibility toward the other. For Levinas justice is born of asymmetric responsibility—and so the stability of signs is disrupted by the asymmetry of the participants in mutual relations.

---

[8] Habermas C.2 115/74–75   If one wanted to reconstruct how participants in interactions can learn to orient their actions explicitly to validity claims, and wanted to do so by means of the mechanism of taking the attitude of the other, the model of inner dialogues, which Mead used rather too unspecifically, turns out in fact to be helpful. When ego anticipates from alter a refusing answer to his own speech-act, and raises against himself an objection that alter could raise, ego grasps what it means to make a *criticizable* validity claim. As soon, then, as ego masters the orientation to validity claims, he can repeat the internalization of discursive relations once more. Now alter encounters him ready with the expectation that ego is not assuming the communicative role of the first person only in a naive manner, but will elaborate it, if necessary, in the role of a proponent in argumentation. If ego makes *this* attitude of alter his own, that is to say, if he views himself through the eyes of an arguing opponent and considers how he will answer his critique, he gains a *reflective relation to himself*. By internalizing the role of participant in argumentation, ego becomes capable of self-criticism. It is the relation-to-self established by this model of self-criticism that we shall call 'reflective.'

8a) Levinas OB 202–3/159–60
Justice is impossible without the one who renders it finding himself in nearness. His function is not limited to the "judgmental function": to the subsumption of particular cases under the general rule. The judge is not outside the conflict, but the law is in the midst of nearness.

A JUDGE is not merely applying the law, merely reasoning in order to know a particular case under the proper general law. Were he to hide himself in the role of determining the particular under the general rule, he would be under no obligation to the claimants. But he is implicated, not merely on reciprocal grounds, rather in the stronger sense of NEARNESS. He is obliged to each person, responsible for what each says. Only because he is so located AMIDST the reasoning, responsible to attend to each, can he deliver a just ruling.

8b) Justice, society, the state and its institutions—as exchanges and work understood from nearness—this means that nothing escapes the control of the responsibility of one for the other. It is important to recover all of these forms as starting from nearness where being, totality, the state, politics, techniques, work, are at every moment at the point of having their center of gravity in themselves, of weighing in for themselves.

Levinas argues that the various structures and values of community can all be referred back to RESPONSIBILITY OF ONE FOR THE OTHER. They are not only born of that responsibility, but they should not become immune or removed from the persistent vulnerability of criticism from the other person. Precisely because these institutions begin to stand on their own, maintaining themselves from their own authority and power, it is an ethical responsibility to drag them back to their origin in the one-for-the-other. In a court then, according to Levinas, a claimant should always be able to contest the court, contest the principles of the society, on the basis of her otherness—and to be judge is to attend to and respond for her, not merely to apply the law. Similarly, all of the stability of the state, of bureaucracy, of work, and of markets, all need to be rendered vulnerable to the claims of others. The systemic relations are brought back to face-to-face interactions. This motion from system to attribution is the distinctive function of judicial procedures, and we will see it in fuller ramification in the discussion of Chapter 8 (Why Judge?).

8c) In no way is justice a degradation of obsession, a degeneration of the *for the other*, a diminution, a limitation of the anarchic responsibility, a "neutralization" of the glory of the Infinite, a degeneration that would be as for empirical reasons, the initial two were becoming *three*. But the contemporaneity of the multiple is knotted around the diachrony of two: Justice only

Justice is not, for all that, a failure of responsibility. In the move to mutuality there is a fulfillment of responsibility. The order of these two moments is not temporal: all signifying serves these two different relations—witness to the glory of the Infinite and seeking justice. Levinas keeps returning here to the ineluctability of the two. At the same time he recognizes that justice equalizes THE NEAR AND THE FAR.

remains justice in a society where it is not possible to distinguish the near from the far, but where it also remains impossible to pass by the nearest; where the equality of all is borne by my inequality, by the surplus of my duties over my rights. The forgetting of self moves justice.

Justice must be both the equality of mutuality and the responsibility to the neighbor, the asymmetry of responding beyond my equal share. Hence justice depends not on a realm of autonomous reasoning, but on a FORGETTING OF SELF—on my obligation to give more than I receive, on an excess of DUTIES OVER RIGHTS. In my pragmatics terms, justice depends on a responsibility that exceeds an authority to interpret. The equalizing of authority to interpret and share in the conversation requires a continuing vulnerability to have less than my fair share.

8d) It is not at all without importance to know if the egalitarian and just state, where man is fulfilled (and which it is a matter of founding and, above all, maintaining) proceeds from a war of all against all or from the irreducible responsibility of the one for all and if it can do without friendship and faces.

Hence, Levinas does not doubt that there should be an EGALITARIAN AND JUST STATE, that morality must be rational and cooperative. But he does examine whether that state emerges in a Hobbesian competition of interests, or from a responsibility of each for everyone. Habermas, too, would reject the claim that the just state proceeds from A WAR OF ALL AGAINST ALL and would claim that the reason that emerges from such a war is instrumental or purposive, adjusting means to ends but failing to fulfill the most basic cooperative pragmatic conditions. Habermas would also agree that the just state requires FRIENDSHIP AND FACES: that is, mutual relationships between the members. Without those relationships, morality is not possible. If they were to disagree here, it would be solely on the extreme notion of each being irreducibly responsible for all. And yet, what we have called rational moral principles, resting upon communicative action as a mutuality of speakers and listeners, draw their exigency from the asymmetrical dimension of signifying. The responsibilities in how we mutually agree on principles of justice are now interlaced with the asymmetrical responsibilities of attending to the other person.

Suggested Readings

1   Cornell, Drucilla. *The Philosophy of the Limit*, 91–115. New York: Routledge, 1992.
    Gibbs, *Correlations*, Chapter 10.
4   Baynes, Kenneth. *The Normative Grounds of Social Criticism: Kant, Rawls, and Habermas*, 77–121. Albany: SUNY Press, 1992.
    McCarthy, Thomas. *Ideals and Illusions*, 181–99. Cambridge, Mass.: MIT Press, 1991.
6   Honneth, Axel. "The Other of Justice: Habermas and the Ethical Challenge of

Postmodernism." In *The Cambridge Companion to Habermas*, ed. Stephen K. White, 289–323. Cambridge: Cambridge University Press, 1995.

8   Lyotard, Jean-François. *Le Différend*. Paris: Les Éditions de Minuit, 1983. *The Differend*. Trans. Georges Van Den Abbeele. Minneapolis: University of Minnesota Press, 1988.

Why Mediate?

THE RESPONSIBILITIES for justice exceed those found in a context where we sit face to face with each other. Justice not only requires us to respond for others who are not present, it also instigates responsibilities for social systems, and indeed even directs us toward systemic relations. Perhaps the most daunting task for social theory is just this relation of responsibility and systems—how I can have responsibility in a global economy that effaces my role, or in a mass media web that ignores a writer's intentions. When we let the third person enter our ethics to stabilize the interruptions in the asymmetrical relationship with the other, we also risk the depersonalized stabilization of social institutions where the models of conversation are untenable.

But in Part I we followed a path from dialogue to written signs, from an interpretation of responsibility between two present people to the complex relation through texts and their traces. Mutuality will now, in Part II, be similarly transformed as we explore the attenuation of personal presence in the responsibilities for justice—and indeed as part of the responsibility for justice. While Levinas pointed toward the emergence of system with the entry of the third, he cannot guide us into the responsibility within systemic communication—indeed, he seems to lose sight of responsibility in the system at the moment a responsive self enters. Habermas is much more aware of the relation of responsibility and systems; although he is highly suspicious of systemic relations, precisely because they seem to be at the expense of communicative action. Without doubt it is Habermas' dialogue partner of over twenty years, Niklas Luhmann, who best interprets and illuminates the nature of social systems. And it will be his analyses of media as ways of enhancing communication within social systems that will be the climax of this chapter. The question, Why Mediate?, will be explored in terms of why we have a responsibility to use media, particularly written and symbolic media, in place of conversation. In the context of Luhmann's work, following Parsons, media is not so much the mass media of television and cinema, and the like, but rather the means of communication, including semantic codes of truth, love, trust, power, faith, and so on. Justice requires the stability of semantic meaning in order to develop the complex balancing, negotiation, and exchange that constitute our communal relations, and that semantic meaning itself means the displacement of the signer with the sign, as a way of mediating in a complex society.

We shift here, then, from the interaction of two people facing each other to a theory of systemic communication. In Section A, we will set a course from a theory of action to a theory of communication, displacing step by step the control of the interlocutors. We will begin with Habermas' contrast between purposive and communicative action, where the purposive actor picks means toward his ends and the communicative actor seeks understanding with others. The need for others and for their role in producing a shared understanding makes the actor in much less control of the side effects. Rosenzweig will enter with Pretext 2, contrasting purposive action with love of the neighbor. His contrast accentuates the effort to eliminate side effects in the former, and the inevitable abundance of them in blind love. Indeed, the actor seems to lose sight of his beloved, who now becomes just anyone representing the whole world. Pretext 3 examines this "anyone" as the beloved and discusses the relation of blind love and the world that it affects. Here is one way to begin to negotiate the relation of interpersonal interaction and the growth of the world as systems. Pretext 4 introduces Luhmann with his account of the relation of interaction and systems. This complex relation displaces the face-to-face interaction as the locus of social justice: justice requires a responsibility to mediate our relations with others through language and other semantic webs.

The second section provides Luhmann's account of the function of media, emphasizing the way that media reduce the risk of failed communication. Indeed, Luhmann goes beyond language to written media and generalized values. His account offers a view that connects the absence of interlocutors with the increased possibilities for communication. Section C (Mediating Consensus) returns to Rosenzweig, particularly to his accounts of how a community is formed by loving action. In Pretext 6, Rosenzweig shows us how in inviting each other a community can form. The pragmatics themselves produce the need for the semantics of a common song to sing. Finally, in Pretext 7, he narrows his view to an interpretation of Christianity as the eternal way. Its universal mission requires Christianity to be on the way, and that way is performed in a doctrine that each new member can affirm. Universality here is a cooperative interlacing of differences, producing a common semantic field: a doctrine that has for its topic being on the way, the very cooperative communication itself. Rosenzweig's account of doctrine mediating the differences of the members of the church is not explored here to expound ecclesiology proper, but as a model for the consensus-forming communicative community that we found also in Habermas. Mediation, however, is intrinsic to such a community's communication.

A. COMMUNICATION AND LOVE

Central to Habermas' project is the recovery of a positive role for reason. Many social theorists interpret the growing role of reason in modern society as an increased systematization of life, resulting in a profoundly amoral and irresponsible mode of interacting. To redeem reason, Habermas distin-

guishes between two different kinds of reasoning: PURPOSIVE and COMMU-
NICATIVE. He characterizes the different modes of reasoning in terms of the
ways people interact. Habermas thus recovers a mode of reasoning (communication) that offers an alternative to impersonal, amoral reasoning. The
latter is characterized by its attempt to sever the self from its social context,
while communicative action emerges as precisely a responsive sharing of
agency with others. We mark here a gap between a self whose actions exercise control and one whose actions practice mutual responsive interaction.

1a) Habermas C 384–85/285 The
model of *purposive-rational* action
begins with an actor, who first of all
is oriented toward the achieving of
an end that has been sufficiently specified by purposes, and then chooses
means that seem appropriate to him
in the given situation and calculates
other foreseeable consequences of
the action as secondary factors for
success.

Habermas begins with an actor choosing MEANS TO AN END. Reason chooses the
proper means and also calculates the relevant CONSEQUENCES of the action. In general, this looks like the basic Aristotelean
model of prudence or *phronesis*. The end
itself is determined BY PURPOSES and so
the person acts for the sake of some purpose. The purpose need not be idiosyncratic or egotistical, but the action is
fundamentally a question of choosing appropriate means and includes consideration of the consequences.

1b) Success is defined as the occurrence of a desired state in the world
which can be causally effected in a
given situation through action or
forbearance directed to an end. The
effects of action that occur are composed of the results of action (in so
far as the posited purpose was realized), the effects of the action (which
the actor had foreseen and intended
and had taken account of in the bar-
gain), and the side effects (which the
actor had not foreseen).

To succeed is to produce the desired result through one's prudent ACTION OR
FORBEARANCE. Even letting things happen
within one's power is a kind of purposive
action. Reason here follows causality: action causes A DESIRED STATE of affairs. Indeed, this model is widely assumed to be
comprehensive: all action is for the sake of
a purpose that is within one's control.
Such action produces three sorts of effects,
according to Habermas. First, the purpose
itself is achieved. Second, the actor can ac-

count for the consequences that were reasonably predictable. Finally, there
are SIDE EFFECTS, those consequences that either could not be foreseen or at
least that this actor did not foresee. These three sets of consequences are
obviously in a hierarchical relation: what is most important is the purpose,
then the intended consequences, and last, side effects.

1c) We call an action oriented to
success *instrumental*, if we regard it
in terms of following technical rules
of action and assess the efficiency of
an intervention in a combination of
circumstances and events. We call it

Habermas now distinguishes two kinds
of purposive action: INSTRUMENTAL and
STRATEGIC. In both cases, the task is to
choose a means to an end. But the instrumental action follows TECHNICAL RULES,
accepting mechanistic and reliable pat-

strategic, if we regard it in terms of following rules of rational choice and assess the efficiency of having an influence on the decisions of a rational opponent. Instrumental action can be connected with social interactions; strategic actions themselves exhibit social actions.

terns of action. It follows scientific reasoning and attempts to act upon an objective world, a world where there is no relevant social dimension. In contrast, strategic action is geared toward producing a result in a social context. It aims to have AN INFLUENCE upon others' decisions. Not so much mechanical reason, but rational choice theory, governs the reasoning. How can you get other people to do what you propose? What is the most effective means of influencing others? Habermas adds, moreover, that instrumental actions can also be linked to social interactions; that we can reason technically in a social context to produce a given purpose. Strategic action requires a social context, however, since the influence upon others is impossible without influenceable others.

1d) On the contrary, I speak of *communicative* actions if the plan of action of participating actors is coordinated not by egocentric calculations of success but by acts of reaching understanding. In communicative action the participants are not primarily oriented toward their own success. They pursue their individual ends on the condition that the plan of action can be harmonized with each other on the basis of common definitions of a situation.

COMMUNICATIVE ACTION is directed toward reaching understanding between interlocutors. Thus, reasoning is required of a communicative sort—for a communicative act to be successful several people must understand and agree upon a norm. Habermas bluntly claims that such interaction is not oriented around my OWN purposes. Even if someone objected that communication itself is merely one of my own purposes, subsuming communicative action under purposive action and so making communication itself into an egocentric activity, the difference between the reasoning of a single self, calculating its own means, and that of a self pursuing others' agreement would still stand. For communicative action requires the internalization of other people's perspectives, requires a reasoning that decenters the self and so is socially constituted. Were it possible to socialize the reasoning of phronesis fully, by socializing not merely the reception of social precepts but also the very modes of decision, then it would shift to a model of communicative action. Habermas is less interested in denying the possibility that communication can become an end, than to illuminate the way that other people's interests and claims become balanced in communicative action, shifting from obstacles that must be managed to goals that need to be coordinated. Hence, communicative action for Habermas is not selfless or altruistic (THEY PURSUE THEIR INDIVIDUAL ENDS), but the end of mutuality supervenes and conditions the pursuit of individual ends. For Habermas, communication is for the sake of acting as a community. The process of reaching an understanding, in this passage, focuses on the process of defining the situation—and here the task is to coordinate the various perspectives on what is relevant in choosing what to do.

Communicative action struggles to HARMONIZE different views of what is significant and to balance different factors. But the harmony is then in contrast with strategic action, which seeks influence upon others, securing an agreement through actions that are calculated to act upon the other as though her definition of the situation was merely something to be overwhelmed. Her voice is to be co-opted by my clever insight into her self-interest. Harmony, on the contrary, assumes as we saw in the discussion of mutuality in the previous chapter, that I take responsibility for her perspective, that there is something to be learned from each person involved. While purposive action is controlled by my interests and my judgment, communicative action depends on others joining and so decenters my own authority.

I now introduce a fourth voice: Franz Rosenzweig. Rosenzweig was a genius in Jewish thought. His major work, *The Star of Redemption*, published in 1921, remains largely unread and underdeveloped as a resource in contemporary thought. Due both to the tragic condition of German Jewry in the decades following its publication and to its cryptic and idiomatic form of expression, few theologians and fewer philosophers have confronted it. I turn at this precise moment because Rosenzweig also opposed a mode of communicative action to purposive action, examining many of the same issues Habermas has. There is, however, a vital distinction that goes to the core of the issues for this chapter. Rosenzweig discusses the communication of lovers as originary for speech and communication. Similar to Levinas, who was profoundly influenced by Rosenzweig's work, Rosenzweig claims that communication begins in imperatives, in commands from the other person to me. The primary command, the first word of our lived experience, is hearing the command to love. Rosenzweig explains that only a lover can command love, and he also explores the psychological development that responding to the command to love produces. (See Chapter 15.) Ultimately, the experience of being loved capacitates and commands me to love others. Love enables and requires me to love. But my love, according to Rosenzweig, is an action that lights upon the nearest other person, the neighbor—playing on the etymology in German. I am commanded in love to love my neighbor—and this action of loving contrasts with a purposive act which I choose in order to advance my own ends. Moreover, it contrasts with Habermas because in its asymmetry it suspends all knowledge of the other and all sense of my control in loving.

2a) Rosenzweig S 299–300/269–70
Love can do nothing but work. No act of love of the neighbor drops into the void. Just because the act was done blindly, it must show up working somewhere. Somewhere, but where is entirely unaccountable.

Love acts BLINDLY, unguided by intentions or foresight. But Rosenzweig argues that love always WORKS, that it cannot fall short. We require a distinction between selfish love and love of the neighbor, the latter directed to whomever is nearest to me. In the next pages we will see why love cannot fail. What Rosenzweig notes at the outset is that its effects are independent of any view of a goal. SOMEWHERE, but not where we could account for them, not where we could foresee the effects. Love is promised to work, but not under our control—hence it is risky in the sense that we will act and even respond for what we cannot control.

2b) If it were done seeing, like the purposive act, then of course it could vanish without a trace, because the purposive act doesn't enter the world broadly and openly, unprotected and unintended. Rather, it is pointed to a determined end that is seen, and because the way is seen as well as the end, because it is purposive, the way must be accounted in its accounting. Besides coming to pointing at its end, it seeks to guard the long, open flanks that were the results of this pointing against all deflecting or destructive influences which it must foresee along the way. It is pointed, intended, and guarded act,

THE PURPOSIVE ACT in contrast is seeing. It has a target, an END THAT IS SEEN. Seeing the end allows the act to follow a WAY, a sequence of means to that end. Ironically, this sort of act must seek cover, must GUARD itself because its success is defined exclusively by reaching its end. Hence its fullest completion would be if the act itself were never exposed or vulnerable. Here the strategic element of purposive action emerges as a traceless efficiency. Purposive action requires narrowness of choices, a careful thinking through of what is to be done and how to manage it. The means is precisely what one considers, and an accounting of every station through which the actions will pass is required in order to come to the end. Not only does one guard against falling short, one must also GUARD THE FLANKS, conserving one's own intentionality, one's own choices. Nothing is to INFLUENCE the action along the way. The connection of purpose and protection is complemented by the intentionality, the careful reflection of the whole sequence of means—all subordinated to achieving the purpose.

2c) and if it reaches its end at all, then it leads to its success. Its further fate is then dependent on the fate of the success. If that dies, then the act dies with it. For because it went on its way to the end as guarded as possible, the purer and more perfect the purposive act was, then it as act itself actually remained unseen, and the more purely purposive, all the more certain of reaching its end, without having committed any unwanted effects on the way.

The completion of a purposive act is its merging into its SUCCESS, the desired result. But because the end is all that is left of the act, purposive action depends on the SUCCESS. Habermas recognizes that success is measured by achieving the end through one's actions, but Rosenzweig adds that only if the result endures does the act in any sense endure. Purposive action is exclusively for its purpose: its success and value hang on the consequence, on THE FATE OF THE RESULT itself. A purposive act is for nought (DIES) if the goal disappears, even after the completion of the act. Rosenzweig explains that purity of action here means that only the purpose is achieved—and so the end is established, but the means are invisible. Only the result matters—and so not only are unwanted effects excluded, but even the action disappears, leaving only the result. Such an action requires precisely the protection from and exclusion of the risks that we have found again and again as characteristics of responsibility.

2d)   The act of love is utterly otherwise. It is very unlikely for it actually to reach the object toward which it was running. It was indeed blind, only a feeling of touching the nearest one had brought notice of its object. It does not know where it can best penetrate it. It doesn't know the way.

And now we return to the blind act of love. The NOTICE that started it in motion is barely available. Not knowledge, which requires sight, but only A FEELING OF TOUCHING, the nearness of the NEAREST person, the neighbor. Like responsibility in Levinas, love has no certainty, no prior knowledge of its other. It cannot tell what will work. It is ignorant of the means (THE WAY) to reach the person who is nearby. Unlike strategic action, it cannot calculate how to PENETRATE, how to influence the other person. Loving your neighbor is acting without control and without knowledge.

2e)   As it seeks it blindly in this way, without protection, without pointing: what is more likely than that it lose its way? And that it will surely arrive somewhere and, owing to its broad dispersion, at more than just one single somewhere, but never get to see its original object, for which it was intended.

Were loving action to require arriving at a specific end, it would always fail. Because it is not guided by knowledge and is left vulnerable, it gets lost. Unlike the direct line of means to an end, it spreads out like seed cast in the wind (BROAD DISPERSION), falling anywhere, but hardly arriving at any object in particular. Loving action is pointless: or it is foolish. Indeed, we might notice that to those convinced that all action is purposive, love seems truly ridiculous. To act toward others without care, without protection, without certain knowledge, is to risk never achieving one's own goals. But loving action aims anywhere—and so cannot fail to land—who knows where.

2f)   Perhaps it is not too much to say that the authentic effects of love are all side effects. And in no case is it without them, while for the purposive act this freedom from side effects may even occur and at any rate is always striven for.

Given the impossibility of arriving at the end that called for the act of love, all of the effects of love are SIDE EFFECTS. Or in the weaker claim, love always produces side effects. It is not eager to repress all effects other than the result—it barely knows what its result should be. But purposive acts, as we saw, struggle against side effects, trying to control not only the action and the results but also everything that might distract from the result. Habermas notes the problem for purposive action that side effects are, but he does not endorse the proliferation of side effects in communicative action. Because love is vulnerable and is an offering of the lover to whomever is met, the side effects are the dispersion of love—a consequence that is hardly in tension with the hope of loving the single neighbor. Love, more than communicative action, is a weakening of the agent's authority and control.

The place of love of the neighbor in Rosenzweig's thought is in the relation between individuals and the world, the relation of redemption. Like the other two relations (creation and revelation), redemption requires a two-way street: people act on the world and the world acts on them, or at least awaits them. From the human side, the action is this blind love; from the world, it is a growing alive, a becoming more autopoietic, more capable of defining and sustaining itself, transcending its mere creaturely existence. The risk of losing personal presence and autonomy in relation to my neighbor now requires a balancing of interpersonal interaction and social relations. Love in its blindness seems an odd choice, but it accentuates the gap that must be bridged between the two sides (sides Habermas will call lifeworld and system or Luhmann will call interaction and system). A pretext from the discussion of redemption will further develop the way that the neighbor marks the absence of a present, alive world.

3a) Rosenzweig S 267–68/240   For him every nearest that happens to him must be "any" one, a representative of every other one, of all others. He may not ask, not differentiate. It is for him his nearest. But from the world's viewpoint, the human act of love is exactly the reverse: unanticipated, unforeseen, the great surprise. The world bears in itself the law of its growing life.[1]

For the lover, love lands on the NEAREST, the neighbor, who serves as REPRESENTATIVE of all the other people. From the blindness of the act of love, any distinction would transform the nature of the action. The neighbor has no pre-given properties. And FROM THE WORLD'S VIEWPOINT, the act of love is pure SURPRISE. The world, as a system, has its own intrinsic life and order which does not require an individual's love to proceed. Just as the response of another person is the realm of the unforeseeable for the individual, so the lover's love is unanticipated in the world. Precisely because purposive action takes aim and depends on causality, it is predictable

[1] Rosenzweig S 247–48/222   What is this? An abundance that is enduring, an individuality that has something in it that does not perish but that, once there, persists? Is there in the world an individuality that is not simply in the differentiation against other individualities, and thus already, therefore, fundamentally perishable because it does not have the ground of its structure in itself, but outside itself, or in other words: because it does not itself delimit itself? Is there individuality which itself delimits itself, its size and structure determined from out of itself and which is only checked but cannot be determined by others? There is such individuality in the world, scattered and not everywhere and strictly separated, but there is such and its first beginnings are as old as creation itself—its name is: Life.

Organic life in nature is this somehow from of old present, in any case underivable from the mere existence, the mere—idealistically spoken—objectivity of the world. It is only the visible sign of a concept of life that extends its sphere of influence far beyond the bounds of organic nature. Not only living beings, but institutions, communities, feelings, things, works—everything, yes actually everything can be living. What then does this being alive mean in contrast to mere existence? Actually only what we have already said: this forming on one's own from inside out and thus necessarily enduring structure.

in the world, but loving action interrupts without warning and without security. Instrumental reason recognizes and follows the protocols of the system, bringing it no novelty. But love offers something unexpectable for the world—precisely because it is an abandoning of discernment and control.

3b) ... The act of love operates thus only apparently on the chaos of an "any." In truth it presupposes, without knowing it, that the world, all the world with which it has to do, is growing life. That it has creaturely existence does not satisfy it at all; it demands more from it: lawful duration, connection, organization, growth—in short, all that it appears to deny in the anarchic freedom, immediacy, momentariness of its act. Just because it consciously denies it, it unconsciously presupposes it.[2]

The act of love is thus doubled. On the one hand, it regards the world as mere CHAOS in which anyone can appear and so become loved. But WITHOUT BEING CONSCIOUS of it, the lover presupposes that the world will come alive. Redemption is the meeting of this love that acts without purpose and the growing life of the world—the richer differentiation and reproduction of autopoietic systems. Rosenzweig notes that if the world were only creaturely, merely a complex set of lifeless entities, love of the neighbor would not be satisfied. Love DEMANDS just the interconnections and self-definition that life provides—and most of all the endurance. Love works not by merely launching a bottle in an empty sea, but rather by offering up love into a world, a world that is alive, a system. Love itself seems to deny all stability, endurance, and structure, but it depends on the stability of the world as system for its reception. It ignores the world in loving the neighbor, but trusts in the world, and requires of the world the endurance of being alive.

Habermas' model of communicative action depends on the shared access to the floor, that anyone who is affected has a right to speak. We can term such models of social action 'interaction,' focusing precisely on the way that each person stands by her own words, even if her literal presence in the room is not required. But the question arises, clearly enough in the Rosenzweig texts about love, whether there is not also a world, a social world that forms a party to this interpersonal interaction. The risk in loving action accentuates the responsibility that I have for the others with whom I interact. But is there a further responsibility I have for society at large, for the relations that happen beyond interpersonal interaction? Doesn't the redemption of the world, the responsibility to make our interaction resonate in the system itself, produce a new relation to the world?

In order to approach this question, we must first clarify the difference between interaction and system, a distinction that is vital to Luhmann's social theory. We can see its origin here as a question about how the relation of the lover and her neighbor relates to the world. The risk of love of the

---

[2] Habermas C. 2 227–28/151   The fundamental problem of social theory is how to connect in a satisfactory way the two conceptual strategies indicated by the notions of "system" and "lifeworld."

neighbor must be balanced with a systemic growth that encourages those interactions. Luhmann's account of the reciprocity between interaction and system offers us a model for interpreting responsibilities in relation to the system. He insists that social systems are 'more' than the face-to-face conversations (the blind encounter in loving my neighbor).

4a) Luhmann SS 588–89/433 Interaction systems can and must continuously be abandoned and begun anew. This makes an overlapping semantics, a culture requisite, and this steers this process in the direction of the probable and verified.[3]

Luhmann interprets a variety of face-to-face relations as INTERACTION SYSTEMS. The problem, quite simply, is that people have to leave and go do something else. The interaction is broken off (ABANDONED), and when we meet again, we must start over. Every time the committee meets, it must rejoin together to begin deliberation. To facilitate our recommencing, to smooth over the breaks from last time to this time, we require a SEMANTICS. The semantics is OVERLAPPING because it covers not only this conversation, but also earlier ones, and also conversations we have had with other people. If there is a responsibility to do something or even to join together, then a semantics, or indeed a CULTURE, is ethically required. What the semantics will do is STEER the conversation, allowing it to depend on meanings that are probable, about which we have agreed in the past or are likely to agree upon, and thus reducing the chance that we simply won't become a community at all.

4b) Thus society works on what happens as interaction, without utterly excluding the contradictory and the deviant. Societal selection therefore does not determine; it entices with the free and agreeable, and can also take place as that which deviates from the officially offered model. It offers interaction if it pleases and when its model succeeds, the deviation becomes thus attractive, interesting, profitable.

Society provides this semantics, and so steers interaction toward what is probable. It is like the repository of living institutions that Rosenzweig called the world. Society SELECTS among possibilities for interaction and does not DETERMINE or force us to communicate in a given way, but it does ENTICE US, in part by offering the stability of things we know we share, in part by offering something a little unusual. In Chapter 9 we will see how

[3] Luhmann SS 224/163 The social reproduction of communication must proceed by the reproduction of themes, which organize their contributions themselves, to some extent. The themes are not created anew each time, but also are not given sufficient precision in advance through language as vocabulary (because language treats all words as equal and is not predisposed for the thematic capacity in communicative processes). Therefore, an intervening mediating exigency is given between interaction and language—a kind of supply of possible themes, which stands ready for quick and quickly understood reception in concrete communicative process. We call this supply of themes *culture*, and if it is stored expressly for communicative purposes, *semantics*. . . A serious, conservable semantic is a part of culture, namely, that which transmits to us the history of concepts and ideas. Culture does not have any necessary normative content for meanings, but rather makes it possible to distinguish which contributions are appropriate or inappropriate or even correct or incorrect in theme-related communications.

society harbors and depends upon CONTRADICTION, but here we can merely note that while open contradiction in a face-to-face situation is quite destructive for our communicating, at the level of society, institutions preserve contradictions. Society is a system, not a concatenation of individuals. The system OFFERS possibilities for interaction, limiting a set of possible conversations and widening the range of what is already happening in interactions. It produces other models, other ways to get together, but it does not command individuals to adopt them.

4c) ... Society is, however, the result of interactions. It is not a court that is established independently of that which it selects. It is no God. It is to some extent the ecosystem of interactions, which to the extent it channels chances for interactions, changes itself.[4]

But if society steers the interactions, it itself has no other elements to add to interaction. It is THE RESULT OF INTERACTIONS: what happens in society happens in the interactions between people. It is not the COURT of last resort, where authority resides, and it clearly does not rule like God. Society is not composed as the superset of interactions but steers interaction, acting upon them, making new possibilities and conserving old ones. But when this societal action is felt in interactions, society CHANGES ITSELF. At the level of society, there are cultural patterns and CHANNELS for communications. When the interrelations between people in face-to-face encounters change, so also do these societal relations.

4d) It achieves what interaction alone never could: always to make the improbable probable, but it achieves it (with the always more important exceptions, which we have sketched) only through interaction. Just as one can note: society selects the interactions, the interactions select society; and both happen in the sense of the Darwinian concept of selection: that means, without author.

Society MAKES THE IMPROBABLE PROBABLE. What is improbable? Communication, or in Rosenzweig's case, redemption. That is, the coming together of the individual and the world or the efficacy of love in the world (as well as many other sorts of communication, including the sort that decides on a norm and a course of political action) is unlikely. But society can steer the interpersonal interactions and make communication likely. The role of media in making these improbabilities probable

[4] Luhmann SS 552/406   The distinction between society and interaction contains a difference that is significant *as a difference* in all social relationships: every society has a relationship to interaction that is problematic *for it*, even when it enables action that is societal yet free from interaction, such as reading and writing. And every interaction has a relationship to society that is problematic *for it* because as interaction it cannot attain self-sufficiency in the sense of complete closure in the circuit of communication. Therefore every social system is codetermined by the nonidentity of society and interaction. That societal systems are not interaction systems and cannot be conceived simply as the sum of the interaction systems that occur is one side of this thesis; the other is that, although interaction systems always presuppose society and could not begin or end without it, they are not societal systems.

is the topic for the rest of this chapter. Here, however, we can add the decisive reciprocity: society and interaction SELECT each other. But there is no AUTHOR. While interaction seems to require balanced authority between the participants, Luhmann understands the social selections to be anonymous. No one is in control, no one has the authority to steer interactions, much less does society act. The eclipse of agency and authority points beyond the weakening we saw from purposive action to communicative action to loving action. In social systems interaction itself is selected without clear agency.

Given our general interest in the responsibilities in using signs and our specific interest in Part II in the responsibility in the semantic dimension of using signs, we find in Luhmann an analysis of how semantics functions beyond the control or agency of individual speakers. The system depends on a set of relations that are not actions directly under the control of the utterer or the listener, the reader or writer, the third, the lover, the participant in cooperative conversation.

We have now come to the end of a line of interpretation of action. While we began with a keen sense that communicative action depended on others' actions in a way removed from instrumental or purposive action, we have moved through a blindness in love of the neighbor that pointed toward a relation between interaction and system. A rich relationship awaits us in the next chapter, but at the moment we need to see how interaction produces media, that is, how the responsibilities in face-to-face relations enjoin us to mediated relations. The way from interaction to system produces a semantics, as we saw in the previous pretext. In the next chapter, we will see that the way from system to interaction will produce a logic of judgments: a social syntax.

B. Media for Communication

Our question here is why it is responsive to participate in social systems. If there is less agency in social systems, then responsibility seems to mitigate against moving beyond interaction systems. Is there a responsibility when communication happens beyond the agency of individuals? Wouldn't stronger agency be more responsive?

In Luhmann's discussion we can see the semantics of all communication in terms of mediation: language as well as symbols are media for reducing risk. The set of media will entangle both communicative action and symbolic mediation more closely in the emergence of society and its separation from interaction.

5a) Luhmann SS 220–22/160 We wish to call *media* these evolutionary achievements that attach to communication's breaking points and functionally serve to transform

Luhmann allows that he is stipulating the meaning of the term MEDIA. He departs from Parsons' set of four (money, power, influence, and generalized values) by finding a deeper functional need for

the improbable into the probable. Corresponding to the three kinds of improbability of communication one must distinguish three different media, which mutually enable, limit, and burden one another with consequent problems.[5]

media. We find a need for media at just those places where the risks of not communicating are greatest (BREAKING POINTS), and we see society, through media, doing what it does best for interaction: TRANSFORMING THE IMPROBABLE INTO THE PROBABLE. In a previous passage, Luhmann has identified three improbabilities in communication (understanding, reaching the other, and success), which are the risks that correspond somewhat to the three aspects of communication (understanding, utterance, and information). In this passage, we see the need for three kinds of media (and there will be several specific media) to meet the task of overcoming the risks. Our interest, moreover, is that the need for the semantic function in using signs, the stability of meaning in the interchange of meanings, is articulated here with attention to the different ways that meaning is stabilized.

5b)   The medium that enhances the understanding of communication far beyond the perceptible is language. Language is a medium that distinguishes itself by the use of signs. It uses acoustic or optical signs for meaning. This leads into complexity problems that are solved through rules for the use of signs, through the reduction of complexity, through settling into a limited combinatory capability.

Luhmann begins with LANGUAGE, allowing us to follow a theoretical sequence from the face-to-face interaction to societal events. We can communicate about much more than is present or PERCEPTIBLE when we can use a medium of signs. The signs need not be audible, but can be visual (the sign language of the deaf), and with language communication breaks free of perception and its narrow horizons. On the other hand, this produces great complexity in terms of reference and agreement on what the linguistic signs mean. To use signs, therefore, requires RULES FOR THE USE OF SIGNS that structure the complexity of what can be talked about, and indeed, what sorts of interaction can take place. Typical

[5] Habermas C.2 272/182–83   Everyday communicative practice is, as we have seen, embedded in a lifeworld context determined by cultural tradition, legitimate orders, and socialized individuals. Interpretive performances draw an advance upon a consensus from the lifeworld. The rationality potential of linguistically reaching understanding is actualized to the extent that motive and value generalization progress and the zones of what is unproblematic shrink. The growing pressure for rationality that a problematic lifeworld exerts upon the mechanism of reaching understanding raises the need for reaching understanding, and this increases the expenditure of interpretive energies and the risk of disagreement (with laying claims by the mounting capacities for critique). It is these demands and dangers that can be headed off by media of communication. These media function differently according to whether they gather up consensus formation in language through *specializing* in certain aspects of validity and through *hierarchizing* processes of agreement, or whether they altogether *uncouple* action coordination from *consensus formation in language*, and neutralize it with respect to the alternatives of either agreement or miscarried reaching of understanding.

of the development of a medium is a conjunction of greater possibility and more confined rules.

5c) The basic procedure still remains the regulation of the difference between utterance behavior and information. Taken as sign, this difference can be made the ground of communication from alter to ego, and both can be supported by the contemporaneous use of signs in their opinion of meaning the same thing. Thus, this concerns an utterly special technique with the function of broadening the repetoire of intelligible communication into a practical infinity and thus securing that almost any arbitrary event can appear and be adapted as information.

Understanding, for Luhmann, depends on noting the difference between the utterance and the information, but using signs helps to accentuate it, because the utterance of the sign is distinct from the signified. The way a sign refers accentuates and plays on the difference, facilitating a realm of information to be communicated that is much broader than perception's range (I point to the rock or the ground, but I can talk about the land beyond the desert). Luhmann interprets communication as communication to me (the sign grounds THE COMMUNICATION FROM ALTER TO EGO). Communication in language allows me to understand almost any arbitrary event. Not only can what is perceptible be signified, but through signs almost any event can be.

5d) The significance of this sign-technique is hard to overestimate. It rests, however, on functional specification. One must, therefore, also see its boundaries. A sign is not a meaning as such, nor does the sign technique of language explain which selection of signs will succeed in a communicative process.

Luhmann sets language apart as a medium for communication and not as constitutive of it, but he certainly accords it a vital role. The task is not to underestimate its importance, but at the same time to SEE ITS BOUNDARIES. Like much else in his systems theory, language is defined as a FUNCTIONAL SPECIFICATION—solely in terms of what it does—and in this case as mediating communication through the capacity of signs to refer to what is not present. Skill with language as this reference to the absent is not itself a guarantee of meeting the other two improbabilities of communication (reaching the other and success). MEANING, which is the governing concept for Luhmann, requires all three dimensions of communication. We might say that what Luhmann considers the sign and linguistic technique to be only a portion of what we are terming the pragmatics of using signs: that part that consists of presented meaning.

5e) On the basis of language, *media of dissemination* have been developed, namely, writing, printing, and broadcasting. They rest on an incongruous decomposition and recombination of linguistic units that cannot be further dissolved.

The second set of media are the MEDIA OF DISSEMINATION. Luhmann understands these to be based on language. The range of utterance is radically expanded because one can disseminate communication precisely where one is not. The rift between interaction and society gapes with this media.

5f) This results in an immense extension of the realms of communicative processes, which inversely affects what is verified as communicative content. The dissemination media select through their own techniques. They produce their own possibility for maintenance, comparison, and improvements, but can be used anywhere on the basis of standardization. In comparison with oral transmission, which is bound to interaction and remembrance, this greatly extends and at the same time confines which communications can serve as a basis for further communications.[6]

The REALMS of communication expand (wherever the post goes, wherever you can listen to the radio or plug into the internet), and at the same time this AFFECTS WHAT IS VERIFIED: a communication will have to be properly formatted. One must learn to write the A, B, C's, or how to use e-mail, or broadcast at the right wavelength (in the proper sound bite) in order to communicate. When we are sitting together, there are ways of confirming communication that are impossible through dissemination. But Luhmann is not making moral judgments on the loss of the oral culture—nor particularly praising the invention of the printing press. Rather, he sees the media of dissemination overcoming the risk of reaching others. The utterance arrives (or doesn't due to the post—see Chapter 3), but the media of dissemination overcome that risk.

5g) ... We wish to designate as symbolically generalized media those that apply generalizations in order to symbolize the connection of selections and motives, which means: exhibit their unity. Important examples are: truth, love, property/money, power/law, and in their beginnings also religious faith, art, and perhaps today the civilizing standardized "basic values."[7]

The third kind of media meet a distinctive need of contemporary society: securing success. Information can be communicated along with the motivation to accept it (whether acceptance be joining the song, or assenting to the principle, or sharing the respect for the music, etc.). Such media bind together MOTIVES and SELECTIONS: they steer the selection of communication in a specific motivational direction, offer-

[6] Habermas C.2 274/184 Writing, the printing press, and electronic media mark the significant innovation in this area, technologies with whose help speech-acts are freed from spatio-temporal contextual limitations and made available for multiple and future contexts. The transition to high-culture societies was accompanied by the invention of writing; it was used at first for technical administrative ends, and later for the literary formation of an educated class. This gives rise to the role of the author who can direct his utterances to an indefinite, universal public, the role of the exegete who develops a tradition through teaching and criticism, and the role of the reader who, through his choice of reading matter, decides in which transmitted communications he wants to take part.

[7] Habermas C.2 273/183 The transposition of action coordination from language over to steering media means an uncoupling of interaction from lifeworld contexts. Media such as money and power attach to empirically motivated conditions; they encode a purposive rational intercourse with calculable amounts of value and make it possible to exert a generalized, strategic influence on the decisions of other participants while *bypassing* processes of linguistic consensus building. Inasmuch as they do not merely simplify linguistic communication but *replace* it with a symbolic generalization of punishments and rewards, the lifeworld contexts in which processes of reaching understanding are always embedded are devalued in favor of

ing something like incentives. The examples show Luhmann departing creatively from both Parsons and Habermas. The set varies in other texts, but Luhmann has devoted monographs to trust, power, love, and faith as well as discussing art, money, and law in varying length. Indeed, each of these media provide steering of a different sort for the complex and improbable communications in society. Luhmann's interest in trust, love, faith, and so on, points to the way that society structures and selects these most basic attitudes and communicative experiences. Instead of seeing these as private or as merely prelinguistic attitudes, Luhmann examines how they are media that steer communication, making society probable.

5h) In very different ways and for very different constellations of interactions it happens in all of these cases that the selection of communication is thus conditioned, so that they at once work as means of motivation, and so the results of selection proposals can be sufficiently secured. The most successful and consequential communication in today's society is displayed in such media of communication and accordingly the chances of forming social systems are directed along the proper functions.

Luhmann identifies the diverse contexts in which communication is steered by these media, steered to produce motivation and understanding, and so constitute the work of society. Because of the improbability of success in complex situations, the media achieve truly impressive results. The recourse to media, therefore, is vital to FORMING SOCIAL SYSTEMS. Indeed, the responsibilities for justice require us to form social systems, and not only interactional events. Hence the responsibility to mediate is the aspect of communicating that stabilizes social interaction beyond the control over my own signs by trusting general terms beyond the specificity of the other person.

C. MEDIATING CONSENSUS

We shift back to Rosenzweig now to explore the pragmatics of making a communal agreement on semantic meaning. What was an interactive consensus in Habermas will become a mediated consensus here as my relation to my neighbor is coordinated with systemic relations in the living world. For Rosenzweig, the meeting of love of the neighbor and the world produces a community. Love of the neighbor recruits the neighbors, one by one. Rosenzweig interprets the performance of singing together as this accumulation of individuals. A group of people who invite each other to join together

media-steered interactions. The lifeworld is no longer needed for the coordination of action. Societal subsystems that are differentiated by such media can make themselves independent of the lifeworld, that is, shunted aside into the environment of the system. Hence the transposition of action over to steering media appears from the perspective of the lifeworld both as reducing the costs and risks of communication and as conditioning decisions in expanded latitude of contingency—and thus, in this sense, as *a technizing of the lifeworld.*

eventually becomes a loving community. Rosenzweig wonders how love of the neighbor can form a community, how it can bridge from the interaction with one person to the world.

6a) Rosenzweig S 258–59/231–32
They don't sing in common for the sake of a particular content, rather they seek a common content so that they can sing in common.

Rosenzweig's communal singing is parallel to Habermas' communicative conversation about moral norms. The pragmatics of coming together and participating freely overwhelms the semantic content of the sign—the song that is sung. The pragmatics of forming a loving community, a community that is not a task force to solve a problem but a free and equal group, determine the content (A COMMON CONTENT). The governing concern is forming a community and that generates the common content. The communication precedes any determination of norms.

6b) . . . What is now the first thing that is so established? It can only be the commonality of the song, and this commonality not as the completed fact, not as an indicative, but as a fact only just established. Thus the founding of the commonality must precede the content of the song, thus as an invitation to common singing, thanking, confessing, "that He is good"; or rather, as properly translated, considering that this singing, thanking, confessing itself is the main thing and that what is sung, thanked for, or confessed is only a reason for them: an invitation to sing, thank, confess, "because He is good."

What IS ESTABLISHED? What do they agree about as this CONTENT—the point of the community? More precisely, what is the song about that joins the individual with the community? Not a purpose beyond the communal singing but its very coming into existence. Thus the song is not a song about something COMPLETED, something that can be expressed in the INDICATIVE, as a matter of fact, a state of affairs, not what Habermas might call defining the situation. The commonality happens as the community sings. The community MUST PRECEDE the content, and working backward Rosenzweig now moves from the content of a formed community to AN INVITATION to join, an invitation that also must 'say' something. The invitation is TO COMMON SINGING, THANKING, CONFESSING: the singing we have seen as the activity, but we now broaden the speech-acts. The thanks will be not to the community, but to God; the confession, similarly. To thank and to confess "that" God is good—that one thanks for the command of love given in love by God. To sing about God, therefore, is to witness to the Infinite in the loving command to love, resembles the witnessing from Chapter 2. Here is a saying that affirms the positive disruption that the command produces. We will have much more to say about confession below (in Part IV), but these speech-acts express the transformations of the singer that lead singers into a community. One is interrupted, commanded to respond, and then confesses a need for an interruption that now has occurred, and so seeks others with which to respond. This account of the performed transformation of a singer is articulated in Rosenzweig's three activities. And indeed, Rosenzweig now recasts the sentence that is sung from a proclamation of God's existence, to the acknowledgment that we can sing, can confess and thank BECAUSE God is good. These activities all are loving actions, but they are different moments, different ways of acting without regard for purposes and efficiency.

6c) And this invitation cannot be an imperative in its turn. No invitation of the inviter to an invited one who would have had to comply with the invitation, but rather the invitation must itself stand under the sign of commonality. The inviter must himself be at the same time an invited one, must invite himself along.

But if the INVITATION to sing is not a statement of fact, it is also not an IMPERATIVE. Because I am not already in the community, my invitation is not asymmetrical like the command to love. I am still trying to form a community. In Rosenzweig's terms, the formation of a community redeems (or saves, heals) the world. But because the world is still unfulfilled, I do not speak for the redeemed world. The inviter is part of a world still seeking to become a community, hence THE INVITER MUST HIMSELF BE AT THE SAME TIME AN INVITED ONE. Rosenzweig offers the argument here that the invitation itself must be held in common, not transmitted from one to another. The image of communication here precisely shows the speech-act implicating the speaker and listener together—and making them relate in a common manner (STAND UNDER THE SIGN OF COMMONALITY). The definition of content through this commonality offers our best view of mutuality so far. The condition of common meaning is this mutuality of invitation.

6d) The invitation must be in the cohortative, regardless whether this distinction from the imperative is externally recognizable or not. The apparent invitation, "thank ye," may have the meaning only of a "let us thank." The inviter himself thanks along with them, and he invites only in order himself to be able to thank along with them.

Rosenzweig discriminates a grammatical mood to distinguish the asymmetry of commands from this mutual inviting (CO-HORTATIVE). Ironically, the grammatical forms are not always clearly distinguished: that is, a cohortative invitation 'sounds like' an imperative—as though the inviter were asymmetrically and imperatively relating to her audience. But were this appearance to guide the participants, then the invitation could not perform the summoning to community. It might command love, but it would not form a community. Hence, the ambiguity appears only to someone outside the forming community, someone reading a transcript, or standing apart. The invitation, which seems to be a command directed at a group, THANK YE, means LET US THANK in its performance, and the "us," the community, comes into existence through this speech-act. Moreover, the inviter requires a community: he invites because he needs TO BE ABLE TO THANK ALONG WITH—he cannot perform the communal thanking alone. The performance of the invitation is not to recruit others to his established cause, but to institute the commonality itself.

6e) The inviter, in summoning his soul and what is in him to praise, summons directly at the same time all the world, seas and rivers and all pagans and those who fear God: Praise the Lord! What is already in him counts for him, because it "is" as something outside, which must first be summoned, and in return the furthest, all the world, is not outside for him, but is in a brotherly harmony with him in praise and thanks.

Hence, the invitation calls upon both the INVITER and ALL THE WORLD. This invitation instigates redemption: the coming together of love of the neighbor with the healing of the whole world. The inviter has to summon himself just as he would a pagan, and as he would the realm of nature. Stepping back from the community established in its singing, we now arrive at the summoning of the community, a summoning that is also sung, but which must first collect the individual and the world. Precisely by interpreting the pragmatic dimensions of this grammatical mood, the cohortative, Rosenzweig argues that the speaker must regard herself as still outside and the farthest corners of the world as within reach. BROTHERLY HARMONY assures the potentiality for everyone to join. It is an open invitation.

This discussion of singing and the pragmatics of invitation show a responsibility to form a community and to produce a common semantics. Rosenzweig's account of the invitation and its harmony is shared for both Jewish and Christian communities. But in his account of the Christian community, Rosenzweig explores a further and specific need for doctrine as a fixed semantic: a creed. Christianity alone faces the challenge of forming itself from diverse individuals who do not previously share a history or a culture. In our terms, we will see the particular pragmatics that justify the semantics of a society organized through coordinating relations—where each is responsible for each. It is not insignificant that the theological dimension of this community is translated into a sociological dimension, where it resembles nothing so much as Habermas' communicative community.

Because the Christian community for Rosenzweig is a community of love, it is not formed by actors prudently connecting means to ends. It is not about its end, but about being on the way. Indeed, in the next chapter I will suggest that it is an eternal means to a messianic end. Here, Christianity represents a way for a community to invite the whole world to share in its responsibility. The model here is one of cooperation, where each has a voice to lend to the common song, and where the community opens to invite each in—to the point of universality. What they form a semantic agreement about turns out to be this way into the world. The way is for the whole world. But the world enters into relation with this way.

7a) Rosenzweig S 380/342–43 The world has a right to words. A faith that wants to gain the world must be faith in something. Even the smallest unifying of a few who unite themselves in order to win over a

This way goes into the world. Love seeks neighbors, seeks community. The expansion into the environment of the community requires a welcoming of what was outside. But the world requires content— IT HAS A RIGHT TO WORDS. The way thus

piece of the world need a common faith, a watchword, by which the united recognize each other. Each that wants to make a piece of his own way in the world must believe in something. Mere being faithful would never let him accomplish something in the world. Only he who believes in something can conquer a something, plainly that in which he believes.

is constituted by a semantic content. It is not some mystical, wordless communion, but precisely a linguistic and semiotically rich relation. For the world, according to Rosenzweig, requires words, something that can be known. In order for the way to gain the world, to bring others into the community, it must offer them an explanation. The way does not compel, nor does it magically seduce, but rather its love is wordy. The universality of the way requires linguistically accessible knowledge. Indeed, even to hold to one's own faith, to convert oneself, requires that there be a what, a something that is believed in.

7b) And that is valid for Christian faith exactly. It is in the highest sense dogmatic and it must be. It may not renounce words. On the contrary: it cannot have enough to do with words, it cannot make enough words. It actually had to have a thousand tongues. It had to speak all languages, because it must want that everything would become its own.[8]

Thus Christian faith requires DOGMA, according to Rosenzweig. Indeed, his argument would be that because it seeks universality any cooperative community will have to explain itself, will have to articulate its convictions. Only by offering witness for other people to examine and validate can a cooperative community exist. The need for words, written, spoken, read, taught, heard, discussed, is essential to such a community. To invite others to join the community requires that one speak with them—because the community is the organization of communication. If this community desires to be universal, which as eternal way it must, then it must SPEAK ALL LANGUAGES. Universality of cooperation requires speaking the language of each

[8] Luhmann RD 171–73/91 The key concept of the possibility of producing a binary decision of yes or no is of central significance for the organizability of the religious system as church. Acceptance of the aggregate of revelation appears in a way totally other than that of the acceptance of faith only in the existence of God. The former, because it can be accepted as the form of a decision, is at once the entry into a complex, organized social system. It is therefore more likely that the point of departure for formulating confessions of faith lay in revelation (e.g., in the historical occurrence of Christ) than in the affirmation of the existence of God. The Roman Church put these confessions in a more complete, unified, and ascertainable form, and thus obtained their suitability for the organization. In this way the *possibility* of membership for *everyone* could be opened universally, which means it was made dependent only on the confession and not on other qualities of belonging to a family or a people, strata, occupation, and so on, and at the same time factical membership was required *exclusively*. The concept of revelation is compatible with societal structural conditions, which allowed or even required a universal possibility of recruiting under autonomously specifiable conditions. Under these presuppositions, a missionary politics, outstretching beyond the given societal boundaries, for converting of the unfaithful is possible, because confession and membership are so specified that they no longer presuppose a change of all societal statures and roles of the individual. The Christian can be and remain Greek *or* Roman.

person, of engaging each person in her own language. Otherwise it fails to establish communication, and its efforts for universality are totalizing.

7c) And thus must the something in which it believes be no something, but must be rather everything. And just for that reason is the faith in the way. In believing in the way, it makes a way into the world. Thus the witness bearing of Christian faith is first of all the generator of the eternal way in the world. . . .

But the content of the faith, the something about which it must speak, must be an EVERYTHING. Because it must believe in the whole way, and not just one neighbor at a time, it must believe in everything. This belief in everything is the conviction that is willing to perform, as witness, bearing responsibility for the invitation for everyone and everything to enter the community. Thus the Christians generate the eternal way by BEARING WITNESS: that is, each offers himself for everyone, as sign of a community of cooperation that would include everyone. We see here cooperation unbound, reaching toward universality, producing a community that is organized exclusively for the sake of cooperation.

More striking, for us, however, is that the social form of relation requires an ongoing activity of consensus formation concerning specific doctrines. The emphasis on the role of cognition and cooperation in defining both the situation and the goals marks the deep similarity to what Habermas calls communicative action. But Rosenzweig is clearer that the community is defined by its need for communication (as they search for a common song in order to sing), and not that communication is needed for the sake of action. Like Luhmann, he interprets the exigency for a shared semantic from the perspective of forming society, itself a system of communications. For Luhmann and Habermas, Christianity is the primary case of a religious community, although they interpret the prospects for Christianity quite differently. For Rosenzweig, Christianity is important but less so than Judaism, as we will see. But for us, the extremity of Rosenzweig's argument about the need for dogma helps concretize the pragmatic need for a mediating way. Mediating, more than the media itself, is the focus of his account of the responsibility to form dogma. Were Christianity not universalizing, were it not a way for the world, it would have a much confined need to mediate, but if we perceive an ethical exigency to bind our interaction with the world, that is, the whole world, then, like the Christian way, we will also have a responsibility to mediate.

Although each of the three thinkers we have drawn together would recognize that social relations are communicative relations, they would not themselves form a consensus about mediation. While Habermas tolerates mediated systemic relations in order to reduce the risk of communicative interaction, he claims that norms can only be justified at the level of interaction. Moreover, in opposition to Rosenzweig, Habermas would consign religious communities to the status of traditional communities, lacking the rational processes of communally validating their norms. Luhmann, for his part, would argue that even those norms validated in Habermas' communicative communities require mediation, precisely to coordinate the speakers. Indeed, the need for a semantics is particularly related to the use of media. The need to mediate, even the responsibility to mediate, comes from a responsibility to communicate for the sake of justice. The tension between the individual's action and the living system is shared by Rosenzweig and Luhmann. That tension points in the direction of mediation because the coordination of a particular with a general in logic is mediation, binding particulars through a general. The overall transformation of cognition into performance of social relations is furthered by Luhmann's insights into media, but the question here is the way of interpreting these social pragmatics for the sake of responsibilities. Just as the need to reason arose from justice, so does that of mediation. But even as redemption depends on binding the individual to society, mediation runs its own risks of barring the way back to attribution, the way back to individual responsibilities.

SUGGESTED READINGS

1   McCarthy, Thomas. *The Critical Theory of Jürgen Habermas*, 16–30. Cambridge, Mass.: MIT Press, 1978.
4   Cornell, *Philosophy of the Limit*, 116–33.
5   Ingram, David. *Habermas and the Dialectic of Reason*, 115–34. New Haven, Conn.: Yale University Press, 1987.
    Parsons, Talcott. "On the Concept of Influence." In *Politics and Social Structure*. 405–38. New York: The Free Press, 1969.
6   Gibbs, *Correlations*, Chapters 3 and 4.

CHAPTER 8

Why Judge?

OUR FOCUS in the discussion of social theory now shifts to the complex matter of attribution, for while the use of signs coordinates society even without the face-to-face presence of interlocutors, the interpretation of responsibility requires not so much a theory of action as a theory of judgments. We will transform a logical theory or syntax of signs here by looking at the kinds of judgments that define a society—the judgments that determine the relation of particulars and generals (the responsible person and her society). While the more familiar kind of presence, agency and control over an action (call it 'autonomy'), is neither possible nor desirable in interpreting responsibility, responsibility does require the attribution of an action to me or to us. Again, we are looking at asymmetries, as the need to judge others will produce a more severe responsibility to place ourselves under judgment.

In this part we are examining the uses of signs to know the world, and the ultimate point of these responsibilities is the judgment of people, in the attribution of responsibility. We discover that social relations occur precisely around two different kinds of boundary judgments: the judgment of what lies within and without a community, and the judgment of life and death. These two judgments, in fact, overlap and engage each other. Moreover, the course of this chapter will lead us not only to these existential and constitutional dimensions of judgment, but also to a logical sense of relations of members and classes. The point of orientation, however, is a question of the responsibility to judge, an ethical need to draw boundaries and to form logical classes. The question of syntax, of how signs are related to each other in different formal relations, is now given recourse to existential signifying: logical operations here are the performances that form societies. And so the responsibilities in relation to the larger set or community become the way to interpret the pragmatic dimension of syntactical relations.

The chapter opens with Luhmann's account of the relation between a theory of action and a theory of communication (Attribution). Society is made of communications that go beyond individuals' actions, but communication itself is not observable. As a result, there is a need to interpret social communications as actions, to attribute responsibility for the uses of signs that occur at the social level.

The second section (We and Ye) examines the relation of social systems and their environments. Pretext 2, by Luhmann, sets up the basic function of the opposition of system and environment, arguing that the reflection about the boundary constitutes all communication within society. Rosenzweig will present a performance of this opposition in a discussion of the dialogue of we and ye—the dialogue between communities in Pretext 3. The responsibility to judge the ye produces a deconstructive judgment on us—as we are not the "we" we wish to be. Rosenzweig comments on a psalm (Pretext 4) where the terror of judgment turns against us. The asymmetry of indexicality helps give a pragmatics interpretation of Luhmann's theory.

Rosenzweig explores how Judaism and Christianity, however, overcome this basic account of boundaries and regain the infinite dimension of responsibility (Section C). Our interest will not be historical, or even dogmatic-theological, but rather sociological. Judaism is interpreted as universalizing by contraction, where everything in the environment is imported into the system (Pretext 5). Christianity is interpreted as an expansion into the environment—an incomplete way into the world (Pretext 6).

In Section D (Judgment Day) the relations of logical judgments are performances of the relations between individuals and communities. Luhmann, in Pretext 7, argues that Christianity needs a Last Judgment to account for the sinners within the community, to recognize that the boundary does not separate the good from the evil. The goal and norm for Christian coordination as expansion is temporally located as a Last Judgment. A contrast with Judaism, in Pretext 8 by Rosenzweig, examines a Day of Judgment within the yearly calendar and not merely at the end of days. Pretexts 9 and 10 come from the liturgy of the Days of Awe, and are cited by Rosenzweig to indicate the nature of the judgment and the way that Jews pray to atone for the sins of the whole world. The logical form of the Jewish judgment is a representative relation; of the Christian, a coordinating relation.

Two other models of communities betray our infinite responsibilities for others, making justice finite (Section E: Unjust Judgments). Rosenzweig distinguishes between idealism and paganism, arguing in Pretext 11 that idealism totalized over each individual and made ethics into a surrender of the particularity of the self. In Pretext 12, paganism appears as a part–whole relation, which also absorbs the individual in the general. But whereas idealism had an all-encompassing march through the world, paganism was content to rest within its own borders and abandon the outside. Pretext 13, from Aristotle, exemplifies the day of judgment that characterizes the pagan subordinating relation of part–whole: Athenian ostracism. In the final Pretext 14, from Hegel, *Die Weltgeschichte ist das Weltgericht* represents a totalizing judgment.

The chapter begins with a brief table about social logics, and ends with a summarizing longer table. The tables divide social logics in two ways: by the motions of expansion and contraction and by the interpretation of responsibility as either infinite or finite. The infinite logics require a responsibility for the whole world, either by cooperation whose fulfillment is deferred or by representation that makes us bear responsibility for everyone. The finite logics permit the immanent social relations to satisfy social responsibility, either by subordinating part to whole or by totalizing with an immanence that lacks self-critique. The chapter concludes with four theses that draw important conclusions about the implications for social theory and for the responsibility to judge.

TABLE 1. Four Social Logics

	Expansion	*Contraction*
Infinite	Cooperation **Christianity**	Representation **Judaism**
Finite	Totalization **Idealism**	Subordination **Paganism**

A. ATTRIBUTION

Communication, for Luhmann, construes social systems without focalized authority. But this raises the familiar question of how responsibility is possible without autonomous agents. From the perspective of communication, we will see a responsibility to ascribe authority, to produce the presence of the responsible person.

1a) Luhmann SS 225–28/164–66 A point of departure to note: communication cannot be conceived as action and the communicative process is not a chain of actions. Communication implicates more selective events in its unity than the act of utterance alone. One cannot therefore fully grasp the communicative process if one see nothing more than the utterances, from which one draws out another.

Luhmann claims that a theory of communication appears as a theory of action when it identifies the UTTERANCE as communication. Were communication merely the uttering or the script of interchanging utterances, then it would be appropriate to interpret communication as an action. But communication is not limited to the choice of utterance, the act of speaking, of gesturing, of inscribing, and so on. Indeed, this reduction to uttering alone mistakes communication as a kind of trans-

mission of my word. (A theory of signs would also be deficient if it added only the difference between the sign and the signified.) To understand communication we need more than the act of the utterer. For this book we can simply remember how listening preceded speaking.

1b) . . . *Communication cannot be directly observed, rather it can only be deduced.* To be observed or in order to be able to observe itself, a communicative system must be flagged as an action system. . . .

But in a characteristic move, Luhmann admits that communication and action are entwined (not unlike interaction and society). This time the entanglement is almost surprising: communication is invisible (*CANNOT BE DIRECTLY OBSERVED*). Because of the complexity beyond the sign and the signified, it is only interpretable in terms of the actions of the participants. The nexus of the relations in a conversation, for instance, where someone else addresses me and I interpret and offer my opinion, which then elicits a further clarification, and so on, makes the communication itself inaccessible, unless I script it and represent each of us acting in a series of actions. The truth is, however, that communication is the nexus and requires more than appears in the script.

1c)   If one has not already read action into communication, it is a symmetrical relation of multiple selections. That would be concealed by the metaphor of transmission. Communication is symmetrical in so far as every selection can lead to other selections and the directional relations can continuously be reversed. At one point the bottleneck and the sticking point lies in what can be understood; and then again new information is urgently needed; and soon after the need for utterance as such struggles through. There is, therefore, no once and for all settled direction for concentrating selection. The relations are reversible and thus highly adaptive.

Communication in contrast to action is SYMMETRICAL, indeed REVERSIBLE. Of course if we think of communication as TRANSMISSION of my word given to you, then the two parties are clearly asymmetrically related, and what results is fundamentally different from the start, and irreversibly so. But Luhmann interprets the communicative system as CONTINUOUSLY reversible—every selection leads to others, but one can just as well turn them around in the opposite direction. His example indicates how the shift from selecting utterance to selecting understanding to selecting information can go in any order. There is no clear direction through these three dimensions. While the sequence of actions in listening, interpreting, and responding is more or less rigidly fixed, the sequence of selections in communication roams through the three dimensions without presupposed selections guiding the way. The temporality of communication will turn out to be particularly complex, bloating the present with reversible relations, while that of actions is straightforwardly sequenced.

1d)   *Only through the construction of an understanding of action in the communicative happening is communication made asymmetrical.* Only through that can it maintain a direction from utterer to the receiver of utterance, and only thus can it be reversed and the receiver for his part utter something, and thus begin to act.

The ASYMMETRY of using signs, of uttering and receiving (listening and speaking), is first apparent when the communication is turned into a set of actions. While the properly communicative view of communication does not fix the roles of agents—the very roles we have constructed this ethics out of—a theory of action does transform the symmetry into asymmetry, allowing the roles to emerge.

The utterer's action is directed to the receiver, with the expectation that he can respond. The very internalization of roles and of the other's perspectives that we interpreted in Chapter 6, depend on the directionality and the

action-based analysis. The respondent position (the listener position) appears in this asymmetrization.

1e) ... A social system is constituted on the basis of the fundamental events of communication and with its operative means as a system of action. It prepares in itself a description of itself, in order to steer the progress of the process, the reproduction of the system. For the goals of self-observation and self-description, the symmetry of communication is made asymmetrical, its open stimulability is reduced by becoming responsible for consequences. And in this shortened, simplified, and thereby more easily grasped self-description, action and not communication serves as the ultimate element.

Actions are constituted through processes of attribution.

Luhmann thus defines the social system as a doubled system: (1) there are communicative events (events that are not at root actions, authored by agents) and (2) there is an action system. But, and this is vital for Luhmann, the social system itself *needs* this interpretation as action system because that interpretation helps STEER communication. Once translated into an action system, the events can be channeled and lead to the self-production of the system. The life of society requires a SELF-DESCRIPTION as a system of actions. The events are more than this description captures, but the possibility of fostering communication is greater under this simplified self-description. In place of an OPEN STIMULABILITY, in which communication seeks unusual choices because individuals do not control communication, RESPONSIBILITY arises. This self-description of the system is itself a move that animates the system by assuming responsibility, or perhaps, better, by ATTRIBUTING responsibility. But the attribution of responsibility, therefore, is the purpose of using an action-based theory. While social systems are not adequately grasped as action systems, and communication should not be seen as a sequence or script of utterances, the emergence of such interpretation is not only constituted as an assignment of responsibility for communication, it also is internally valuable for the system as self-defining and self-perpetuating. Assignments of responsibility help the system live.

B. WE AND YE

In Luhmann's work the relation of a society and its environment constitutes society as system. Indeed, Luhmann redevelops the importance of the pair system/environment in fashioning a theory of the social system as self-producing (autopoietic). Our interest is how the system requires judgments upon what lies outside it (in the environment) in order to function as a system. As this section develops, we will see that the relation is performed through the utterances of the term "Ye," whose pragmatics is constitutive for the utterance of "We." Social systems require a specific sort of relation to the environment because for Luhmann social systems are constituted in terms of meaning (or, we might say, interpretation). The question then becomes:

2a) Luhmann SS 266/195 But what are boundaries of meaning and how do they come about?

The radicalization of system theory with a view to the environmental relation and self-reference makes it possible to give a plausible answer to this question.

For Luhmann the question is how a boundary instigates MEANING within the system by separating system and environment. Social systems are constituted in terms of meaning. Biological images, although not merely mechanical because they involve the life we saw in the previous chapter, are not adequate because of the questions of communication. The question is not ontological (who is in and who is out), but rather, how limits of meaning, horizons of interpretation, occur. Because systems theory can focus on the self-creation of the system and its relations, it also interprets the very distinction of a system from its environment as self-created by the system.

2b) Boundaries of meaning are not only an external skin, which like one organ among others fulfills certain functions. They rather relate the elements from which the system is constituted and which the system reproduces to that system. Thus seen, every element makes an association with it and thereby a boundary decision. Every communication in the social system, not only the communications that cross the boundaries with the outside, lays claim to the difference from the environment and thus sustains the determination or the alteration of the system's boundaries.[1]

Luhmann contrasts boundaries of meaning with AN EXTERNAL SKIN. The biological organ has its own function. The skin is localizable and a part of a whole organism. But BOUNDARIES OF MEANING are not located in one place, negotiating only osmotic exchange across a permeable membrane. Rather, these boundaries forge a set of relations, from the elements of the system to the system. (Although the elements themselves not only constitute the system, for THE SYSTEM REPRODUCES them as well.) Thus every element is ASSOCIATED with the system's boundaries. To be in the system is to negotiate the relation to the environment, indeed, to make A BOUNDARY DECISION: to be inside of outside. But the boundary is therefore distributed over every element; each bears within it the relations of belonging and of excluding the environment. COMMUNICATIONS are the processes that produce and interrelate the elements of a social system, and so every use of signs makes a CLAIM about the boundary, claiming to lie within the

[1] Luhmann SS 25/9 The theory of self-referential systems maintains that a differentiation by systems can only come about through self-reference, which means that only through referring to itself can the system constitute its elements and the operations of its elements (be this to elements of the same system, or to operations of the same system, or to the unity of the same system). In order to make this possible, systems must generate and use a description of themselves: they must at least be able to apply the difference between system and environment within the system as an orientation and as a principle for generation of information. Self-referential closure is therefore only in an environment, is possible only under ecological conditions. The environment is a necessary correlate of self-referential operations, because just these operations cannot operate under the premise of a solipsism (one could also say, because everything that plays a role in it, including the self itself, must be introduced by distinctions).

system, to have meaning within a society. Yet precisely because a community is alive, creating itself, the boundaries are renegotiated with each act of communication. The boundary can be changed or maintained, but only through a boundary is it possible for the use of signs to have meaning for others.

2c) Conversely, representations of the boundaries have an ordering function for the constitution of the elements; they make it possible to assess which elements can be formed into the system and which communications can be risked.

But just as each use of a sign will negotiate the boundaries of meaning, so REPRESENTATION OF THE BOUNDARIES helps order the possibilities for belonging to the society. Part of negotiating boundaries is a reflexive shaping of the society: which sorts of signs can be used in which ways and still bear meaning. And, directly relevant to our discussion of media, WHICH COMMUNICATIONS CAN BE RISKED—because the representation of the boundaries alerts us to risks that should be run within a system of responsibilities. Luhmann's analysis alerts us to the functions of judging boundaries in an interpretation of society as communicatively constituted. Moreover, he shows how each individual element of the community (a specific use of a sign) is bound with a judgment of separation.

We will now switch back to Rosenzweig in order to accentuate the judgmental aspect of the boundaries of meaning. Despite marked gaps in theoretical vocabularies and in literary qualities between the two texts, Rosenzweig's *Star* recognizes a constitutive judgment of exclusion in forming a community. Moreover, he accentuates that the elements are not individual words, but words in use, speaking words (communications in Luhmann's vocabulary).

In a passage that follows upon the discussion of the cohortative that invites others to join with me, Rosenzweig discovers the limitations of saying "we." For the single word "we" seems to represent the sign that, when used communally, constitutes a community.

3a) Rosenzweig S 264/237 But it can be the last word no more than any word can. The word is never last, it is never simply spoken; rather, it is always also a speaking. This is the authentic secret of language, this is its own life: the word speaks.

The "we" cannot be THE LAST WORD—it cannot conclude human speaking, because words are always pragmatically situated, always directed toward another person, or people. Words, as signs, cannot conclude interpretation. When Rosenzweig contrasts SPOKEN with SPEAKING, he opposes the ongoing relation with others, the differential meaning of a sign with the possibility for a sign to be pure "said," to be exclusively a fixed meaning. In an uncanny presage of Heidegger's "language speaks," Rosenzweig focuses on the way that a word opens up to new interpretation, is directed toward others. Even this great word of community—"we"—is located in relation to others and to a future where it requires further interpretation. Communication continues.

3b)   And thus spoken word speaks out of the sung 'we', saying: Ye. The 'we' encompasses everything that it can grasp and reach, even what it can sight. But what it no longer reaches and what it no longer sights it must, for the sake of its own closure and unity, shove out of its bright, resounding circle into the cold terror of nothing, by speaking to it: Ye.

And indeed, even for a community to say "we" requires that the community address another—another community. In contrast to a seemingly automatic focus on how "we" is in contrast to a "they," Rosenzweig opposes it to "YE," to what we normally call a plural "you"—to you all, or y'all. With that word, we break decisive ground in the view of mutuality. We might even note the eclipse of ye in English as an indication of a limitation in our culture's awareness of this relation to other communities. If the "we" is not simply a plural, but develops out of the dual, and as such means "we all"—then must not the "ye" also develop out of the dual? Must it, as "you all," express not a plurality of you's, of other individuals, but a recognition that another community has been formed, another group has arisen through communication, indeed, through loving relations?

But what characterizes the relation from the "we" to the "ye"? The "we" expands as far as it can REACH, as it can GRASP and SEE, expanding not violently but through love, but even so it then encounters another group, a community it cannot grasp, cannot know. It turns to that other community and does not objectify it, as the use of the word "they" would. *They* are simply out there—insignificant for us. But *you all* are of intimate concern for *us*, like the simple *you*, precisely because we cannot understand you, because we close you all out. What Luhmann saw as the environment gains a structure as a community we can address—a development that Luhmann also develops in recognizing that other systems are formed in the environment of one system. But we need to close ourselves, to remain a "we," and SO FOR THE SAKE OF ITS OWN CLOSURE AND UNITY we speak to you all. The boundary of meaning is needed, and it is performed. The "we" is never said without its "you all"—its communal other, an other that is formed like it, not as a simple collection of individuals, but, rather, as communicating society, and which as "you all" can speak back to us. "They" cannot teach us, cannot speak with authority, but "you all" can—indeed, to be "we" is to be bound to other communities that can instruct us.

3c)   Yes, the 'ye' is terrible. It is the judgment. The 'we' cannot avoid making this judgment; for only in this judgment is there determinate content of the totality of its 'we,' which is not yet a particular content, taking nothing from its totality; because the judgment separates no particular content in opposition to it—no content other than the

And yet our address to the other community is TERRIBLE. We stand in JUDGMENT upon them. For, since the "we" tends to expand, to call any other group "you all" is to accept that our "we" will not be able to include everyone. This becomes a double-edged sword soon enough, but for now it indicates the "we" produces exclusion: we men excludes you

nothing; so that the 'we' achieves as content everything that is not nothing, everything actual, everything—factual. Thus the 'we' must say 'ye,' and the stronger its crescendo, the stronger the 'ye' also booms out of its mouth. The 'we' must say it, even though it can say it only in anticipation and must await the last confirmation from another mouth, the last one.

women, we Americans excludes you Asians, and so on. This exclusion is in conflict with the faith that animates saying "we"—because, as Rosenzweig explains, the "we" doesn't have A PARTICULAR CONTENT. The boundaries of meaning reduce the environment to meaninglessness, to NOTHING. The "we" cannot properly exclude anyone. "We" is bound with its other communities, its "you all"s, because

it is not yet the final "we." Instead, it only ANTICIPATES a moment when all the world will belong to its "we"—in that moment "we" will be justifiable. In the meantime, it is locked into a conversation with other communities—marking exclusions.

3d) This is the decisive anticipation, this separating judgment in which the coming kingdom is actually coming and through which eternity is factual. The saint of the Lord must anticipate the judgment of God; he must recognize his enemies as the enemies of God. It is dreadful for him; because in doing it, he places himself under the judgment of God; Lord, judge me, look at me—you examine me and know me, so prove me and know how I think, and see if there be any falsity in my soul.

But this exclusion ironically both expresses the hope for a justifiable "we"—a universal community that Rosenzweig refers to as the kingdom—and places the current "we" itself UNDER JUDGMENT. To speak a "you all" is to indict the "we"—it has not yet become "we." On the one hand, we run the risk of ANTICIPATING THE JUDGMENT OF GOD—attempting to cast the "you all" in the role of those who, by remaining outside the "we," oppose God and will be so judged. But in this attempt to recognize our others as enemies of God, we fall under judgment—because

through the redemption of the world all people can be brought together. Rosenzweig is here commenting on the end of Psalm 139, a psalm that accentuates the inescapability of my responsibility.

This psalm begins with the depth of God's knowledge of the speaker. The speaker emphasizes various ways that God knows him (EXAMINED, KNOW, UNDERSTAND, OBSERVE, FAMILIAR). Moreover, he asserts that there is not a part of his life that remains hidden. God knows him, but he does not assert a similar grasp of God. Indeed, even his speech is known before he speaks it. Here is a model of an asymmetry: the speaker is utterly exposed to the addressee.

4a] Psalm 139.1   To the chief musician. A Psalm of David. O LORD, you have examined me and know me. 2) You know my sitting down and my standing up. You understand my thoughts from afar. 3) You observe me on my path and lying down, and You are familiar with all my ways. 4) There is not a word on my tongue but that You, O LORD, know it well.

But the text that interests Rosenzweig here is the end of the psalm (underlined in the psalm text). Rosenzweig is discussing how the judgment is DREADFUL FOR HIM. The dread appeared in the almost paranoiac anxiety that exposes the psalmist to God's knowledge. But now even the seeming buoying of reckoning HIS ENEMIES to be God's offers no respite. Under judg-

4b] 21) Do I not hate, O LORD, those who hate you? And do I not loath Your adversaries? 22) I hate them with perfect hatred: I count them my enemies. 23) Examine me, O God, and know my heart; prove me, and know my thoughts; 24) and see if I pursue a damaging way and lead me in the everlasting way.

ment, known but incapable of knowing, bound asymmetrically, the gesture of despising God's enemies appears to be an unsuccessful gesture of self-justification. It fails, because the psalmist reverts to the vocabulary of the beginning: EXAMINING and KNOWING. Perhaps the insertion of PROVE ME points to the very gesture of performing judgment upon others, but the speaker seems as dependent and asymmetrically bound at the end as at the outset. Rosenzweig's own interpretation accentuates the impossibility of saying a "ye" of judgment without falling under judgment.

If judgment upon other communities is needed, is indeed responsible, its performance will be fraught with great vulnerability. For our purposes, the issue of saying "you all" illuminates a second measure of asymmetry in mutuality. In Chapter 6 we saw how each member must regard herself as sharing in the responsibilities of the others in the community. Now we see how the community is in conversation with other communities. Indeed, given the importance of the second-person form of address, we can see how to say "we" is to address another group as "you all"—and so to place our community under judgment. Because "we" are not yet properly "we," "we" is always to some extent illegitimate. "We" is properly only an anticipation. Its meaning is every bit as much in the future as the responsive speaking in Part I. Indeed, now in the context of social relations, we see that the time for true "we" saying is messianic, with the coming of the kingdom. The ethical justification of boundary judgments depends on a temporality that exceeds the continuing time of social systems. For Rosenzweig, redemption occurs through an eternalization of the communication in societies. Shortly, we will see the ways communities perform boundary judgments with respect to time, but those judgments themselves will be clearer following a further typology of social systems, of loving communities.

C. UNIVERSALITY AND THE OUTSIDE

The third part of Rosenzweig's *Star* is devoted to a sociological account of two distinct and related communities: Judaism and Christianity. Each community strives for eternalization as a means of redeeming the world. Each has its own forms of social relations, which we will examine shortly. But in relation to the boundary of meaning, each must claim to encompass all meaning, or at least to potentially overreach boundaries. Rosenzweig is not presenting an historical or a straightforward empirical account of these two communities (nor of the other two sorts), but he does claim to see redemptive norms in his accounts and to offer forms which we might well call ideal-types. Our interest, moreover, is not in assessing extant Judaism and Christianity, but rather in examining the different kinds of boundary judgments these societies practice in order to understand why we have responsibilities to make such judgments.

5a) Rosenzweig S 339/305 What does it mean, that here an individual, a people, seeks a guarantee of its persistence in nothing external and only within, precisely in its relationlessness, wants to be eternal? It means nothing more and nothing less than the claim as individual nevertheless to be everything.

Rosenzweig's account of Judaism is as the eternal life (in contrast to Christianity as the eternal way). He wonders how a particular people, by focusing inwardly, can possibly claim universality. It must claim, says Rosenzweig, AS INDIVIDUAL TO BE EVERYTHING. It seeks to annul the need for a boundary, for any relation to an environment. That desire arises from a goal in relation to time: TO PERSIST—to live without end. Rosenzweig interprets Judaism as eternally alive, secure in its self-reproduction. Later we will see pagan (and neo-pagan) society as its finite counterpart because paganism also turns inward but accepts its fated passing out of existence, and so ignores the world outside its boundaries. Judaism must claim to redeem the world, and so to be an individual that represents everything, an individual infinitely responsible.

5b) For the individual in itself as such is not eternal, because it has the whole outside of it, and in its individuality can only affirm itself, in joining somehow the whole as part. An individual thus, that nevertheless wanted to be eternal, would have to have had the all wholly in itself. And thus it happens that the Jewish people collect the elements God, world, and human, from which the all is composed in its own interior.

But qua individual, the INDIVIDUAL cannot be everything. The individual is dialectically bound to the WHOLE—to be an individual is to have an environment, and to not be that environment. Luhmann, for instance, realizes that psychic systems also have environments and also then serve as part of the environments for societies. To affirm itself, the individual must affirm the whole which exceeds it. Only if everything were within the individual could it claim universality and in that way, eternality. I will call the claim that the individual stands as representative for everyone *representative universality*. This first form of judgment holds one individual representative for all. In the concrete performance of responsibility, I hold myself responsible for everyone, or socially, we hold ourselves responsible for all other groups. This requires, however, that the "ye" be brought within, and similarly the "they." In Rosenzweig's system, God, the world, and the human are the elements that the deconstruction of monistic totality produced. Hence his claim is that the Jewish people COLLECT these elements into itself, bringing the differences inside its society.

5c) The God, the human, and the world of a people are a people's God, human, and world only by means of what distinguishes and cuts them away from the other Gods, humans, and worlds in the same way as the people itself. In just this self-exclusion of the individual people from other individual peoples consists the connection with them. All boundaries have two sides. In marking itself off, something adjoins something else. If a people is an individual people, it is a people among peoples. Its secluding itself means, then, its attaching itself.

While it is clear that there is a Jewish God, a Jewish world, a Jewish human being, it is not clear with what logical operation these Jewish elements are distinguished from other kinds of gods, worlds, ways of being human. Indeed, if other peoples are distinguished from each other on just these grounds, surely the Jews will be only one people in opposition to others. Each people, as a social system, is both produced through SELF-EXCLUSION and CONNECTED to its environment. Rosenzweig, perhaps in a Hegelian mood, explains just how 'ecological' any people has to be: it attaches itself to others precisely by secluding itself. The pagan accepts this relation of boundaries and constitution of a society. Rosenzweig realizes that the seclusion of excluding is dialectical. Thus the pagan choice is a choice to be only one among others, not to be singular. For Rosenzweig the plurality purchased by choosing to be merely an individual community denies eternity, denies the responsibility one has for the larger world.

5d) But it isn't so if the people refuse to be an individual people and want to be "the one people." Then it may not enclose itself in boundaries, through which in their two-sidedness would make it an individual people among the other peoples. Rather, it must enclose the boundaries within itself. And exactly also its God, its human, its world. It also may not distinguish against others, rather, it must drag these in their distinction within its own boundaries.

And thus the Jewish people, desiring to be "THE ONE PEOPLE," cannot be formed by exclusion or enclosing itself. To gain eternity, IT MUST ENCLOSE THE BOUNDARIES WITHIN ITSELF—must bring the various oppositions and distinctions between various individuals within it. The Jewish community must bear every sort of opposition within it, must be crisscrossed like a network of factions. Even its God, its world, its people will drag within them all of the others, containing opposing poles within them. Unlike the consensus formation of a cooperative community, the social organization must be the harboring, even the cultivation of disagreements and opposing tendencies. To represent all the world, the Jewish society must give voice to the differences of the world within itself. This internalizing of conflict will lead to an extreme view of law, as we will see in the next chapter. At this point, we have only this strange organizational move of importing every fundamental opposition within the system in order to bear responsibility for everything.

But while Judaism is interpreted as an internalizing representative for everything, Christianity is represented as a noncoercive expansion into the whole world. We will return to the Jewish representative judgment later in this chapter, but we now will have to examine the Christian judgment, which performs what I will call *a cooperative universality*, where each is led to cooperate with each other. It, too, struggles to overcome the system/environment distinction.

6a) Rosenzweig S 386/348–49 Extension into the outside, and not as far as possible, rather whether possible or impossible, extension into everything, at least everything outside, which thus then also in the momentary present can be at most a still-outside—if the extension is meant as so undetermined, so boundless, then clearly what held for the Jewish rooting into its own innermost holds for it: that nothing may any longer remain standing outside as opposed.

Christianity, in opposition to the Jewish rooting everything within, is an EXTENSION INTO THE OUTSIDE. The environment/system distinction is always produced by the system, but if the principle of the system is extending the system into the environment, then we have an unusual social system. Luhmann would quickly note that separating off the environment creates new ranges of possibilities within the system, and thus a system organized around extending will compromise something of the system's function. Rosenzweig explores a social system that is a way and not a structure. Hence, what is possible and impossible is not relevant, because the goal represents whatever is outside as AT MOST A STILL-OUTSIDE. All oppositions will be brought inside, not by discovering them within but by welcoming and coordinating the once outside into the inside.

6b) Rather also here all oppositions must somehow be dragged within its own boundaries. But even the boundaries, which the self rooted in itself had, these are utterly foreign, indeed unthinkable, to this extension into the outside—are the boundless, all boundaries are supposed to have always again bursting boundaries. The extension itself clearly doesn't have boundaries; but that outside, into which the extension takes place, may have: the boundaries of the all.

The nature of the boundaries here are not only different from the 'usual' system, where the boundary has two sides, but also are different from the all-inclusive boundaries that are drawn within the Jewish community (an all-inclusive set of subsystems, Luhmann might say). Rather, here a boundary is temporalized more radically: it is always BURSTING BOUNDARIES. Every distinction of the outside is not merely dynamic, but is rather made to be broken. There is no limit to the motion outward, to the way. Only in the outside, in the environment, are there systems with boundaries. Those boundaries are burst open as the Christian community expands, until only a universal boundary is left: THE BOUNDARIES OF THE ALL. While the Jewish community was interpreted as bringing all boundaries within it, the Christian community expands to break all boundaries, except the ultimate boundary of the all—which it fills up.

6c) This boundary, however, is not reached in the present nor even in any future present—because eternity can break into today and tomorrow but not the day after tomorrow, and the future is always merely the day after tomorrow.

Rosenzweig illumines what it means to call this way of expansion an eternal way. Eternity is not present today, nor is it an infinite progress. The overcoming of the system/environment distinction requires a time which is not a present. For Rosenzweig, the future is merely THE DAY AFTER TOMORROW—a continuation of the present, stretched out in a sort of predictable and continuous way. Eternity, on the other hand, is an interruption that can happen at any time (and not only after a long chain of tomorrows). Christianity will be on the way eternally, throughout all time of the present and the future, until a messianic BREAK INTO time occurs. That break can be today, following a long tradition of messianic interpretation, which means that the expansion never achieves in time its goal. It is always on the way, until . . .

6d) . . . Because Christianity wants to be actually all-encompassing it must shelter within itself the oppositions with which other associations have fixed the limits of each against all the others already in their names and goals; only through this may it characterize itself as the all-encompassing and thus in itself unique association. God, world, human can only thereby become the Christian God, the Christian world, and the Christian human, only if it spins out of itself and passes through each for itself the oppositions in which life moves. Otherwise Christianity would be only a club, entitled only to its specific goal and in its specific domain, but without the claim to the extension to the ends of the world.

The expansion must also not merely burst the boundaries other communities have established, rather it must also SHELTER those distinctions. An ALL-ENCOMPASSING society is not the eradication of all others but must coordinate them, welcoming them within, responsible without limits. While the other ASSOCIATIONS define themselves by excluding each other, limiting each other, the Christian goal of expanding through them all must SPIN OUT OF ITSELF the oppositions that the other systems produce and live. The expansion is not a colonizing of the conquered, but rather a process of altering the expanding society, learning how to live through the oppositions that divide others without falling prey to the judgments against others. Were the society that expanded merely imperialistic, it would be ONLY A CLUB: organized around its own specific goals and domain. Christianity advances a CLAIM to be responsible in extending to the whole world, a claim to be universalizing in its way. Only when it PASSES THROUGH the oppositions of the systems through which it breaks, only when it shelters the differences that otherwise are the life of other societies, can it be more than just another special interest, another, however successful, limited society. And its universality would become merely a pretense, an ideology to justify conquest and homogenization. But this second kind of universality, of expansion, of an eternal way, which I will call a coordinating relation, must defer its universality not to some distant historical moment, but to a never-present future: a future that will never be present, a today of messianic time.

D. JUDGMENT DAY

In opposing ways these two societies deconstruct the relation of system and environment, struggling to universalize judgment by means of eternity in order to to bear infinite responsibility for the world. The judgments upon other communities as "ye" are translated into judgments upon themselves, following the path that Rosenzweig marked out. A community that was satisfied to have only a partial "we," or one that pretended to achieve universality already or in a present moment, might not discover the turn from judgment upon others to judgment upon ourselves. As this chapter proceeds, we will accumulate a full set of four kinds of societies, each with its own distinctive judgment, and indeed with its own sense of the day of judgment. The specifically theological dimension of judgment day will guide our analysis of the social pragmatics of these kinds of life-and-death judgments. While Habermas regards religion and its problems almost exclusively in terms of an earlier stage of the lifeworld and unreflective tradition, Luhmann has devoted careful study to various issues in the sociology of religion, including just the shift we are now conducting: from boundary decisions to a judgment day for the members of the society.

Despite Luhmann's vigorous claim that systems are capable of greater complexity than interaction, his understanding of the relation of media and interaction is subtle. Media depend on interaction, in fact, on the possibility of the attributing processes that liturgically frame the idea of judgment. Luhmann recognizes that the excessive responsibilities of certain kinds of social systems lead to both surprising forms of universality and a need for a deferred but Last Judgment. The linking of excessive responsibility and universality is our primary concern, but the ethical need for Christian judgment is our interest here.

7a) Luhmann RD 146–47/68–69 Environment is to be understood as that section of the world not included in the system; world as the entirety of the possible in the system and its environment. Differentiated religious systems of this type must meet the experience that their *own members* do not satisfy the expectations of their religion. The chosen people of God do not live according to the commands of God. This

Luhmann examines how religious societies can place idealizing normative claims on their members, and how this will transform the relations of environment [*Umwelt*], world [*Welt*], and system. He notes that what we would call the extreme responsibility of these two social forms which we have been examining will disrupt the usual relation of system and environment. The crisis comes because the members of the society do not SATISFY

experience becomes stronger and requires an answer, if such expectations are formulated not merely "meritoriously" with possible profit and possible sanctification, but rather normatively as in the Hebrew tradition.

THE EXPECTATIONS. They do not live responsively. Responsiveness is commanded but is not the condition for membership in the community; rather, the infinite responsibility defines membership. This EXPERIENCE requires an interpretation because the responsibilities are NORMATIVE. Luhmann understands that one can view God's commands as merely a checklist for achievement. But already IN THE HEBREW TRADITION the commands exceed our behavior and are structured to increase. Hence the question of how to interpret a norm that requires excessive responsibility is socially played out with an interpretation of the failure by those who accept the norm.

7b)   One can no longer react to this syndrome of religious normativity and sin in the chosen people with the differentiations of friend/enemy or near/far. Later prophecy, as discussed above, treats the form of the generalization of the people's God into a God of the world and the solution of the contingency problem through an *eschatology*—which means a solution, which is postponed into the temporal and thus no longer only accepts characteristics of the people but is also already of the world. This is symptomatic and can be reconstructed by systems theory.

In the next paragraph Luhmann will RECONSTRUCT the answer through systems theory. Here he presents it first in the breakdown of polarities from political theory: FRIEND/ENEMY and NEAR/FAR. In the first we have a recourse to the we/ye distinction in Rosenzweig, but the second is still more familiar from Levinas' reiterations of the text from Isaiah. If peace is to both the near and the far, it is because both need it. The sinner is in our midst and cannot be cast out as the other to our righteousness. For Luhmann, following traditional Protestant history of Ancient Israel, the God of the Hebrews goes from a people's God to a GOD OF THE WORLD—but that move is just the move we saw in Judaism (and differently in Christianity) of making the particular God bear within it the universal God. The very intensification that Rosenzweig analyzed, as well as the expansion in the eternal way, appears in Luhmann's account of the infinite responsibilities in these religious societies. Moreover, we also have a recourse to judgment as both TEMPORAL and POSTPONED, but in just such a way as to leave room for the contingency of how the members of the community do behave. The solution is not immanent, but it also is not static and indifferent to time. Rather, because sin requires room for repentance and forgiveness, the judgment upon the sinner cannot be concluded now, neither in present time nor in some ecstatic immutable event. The *ESCHATOLOGY* which Luhmann emphasizes I would prefer to call messianic—in relation to a Jewish interpretation and a doctrine of the Second Coming. It requires a judgment upon the whole world and not merely on the members of the society. Indeed, Luhmann comes close to suggesting that the temporality of a

Last Judgment is a decisive aspect for framing a universal society, and indeed that the problem of judgment upon the sinner within the community forces a responsibility for judgment into a universality that exceeds normal social systems.

7c) In this case religious dogmatics can no longer get away with the plain differentiation of positive/negative of system and environment. It can no longer retreat to the position that the members are good and the nonmembers, in opposition, are bad. It can, therefore, no longer reconstruct the world as the totality of this opposition.

Luhmann then recasts these developments into the terms of a systems theory. While for most social systems the system/environment difference can be simply mapped as POSITIVE/NEGATIVE, that is, the members of our society are GOOD and the others are BAD, this basic relation of system and environment no longer works. Indeed, the concept of the world for this society will no longer be a simple TOTALITY which is formed through the opposition of inside and outside. Were the normative expectations not so high, were responsibilities merely practical and average, were society constituted merely through a reasonable set of roles and expectations, were ethics not about infinite responsibilities, then the judgments by we upon ye would not precipitate a crisis for the "we." A world composed of us and them fails to submit the "us" to judgment. But these religious societies, or rather these kinds of societies, are created through excessive responsibilities and cannot recognize the world as simply us and them.

7d) A defensive attitude or an indifference toward a hostile environment gives no adequate indication of how to understand the laxity and the susceptibility of one's own members to sin. Christians even have to bear the commonality of the sacraments with the wicked, hoping for a sorting out at the Last Judgment. The early Christian indifference to the environment and readiness to submit could not endure for these reasons; they had to be transformed into a relation to the world. . . .

The other whom one might regard with DEFENSIVE ATTITUDE as "ye," or with INDIFFERENCE as "they," does not deconstruct the "we" that seems remarkably susceptible to sin. The negotiation with the others, either placing them under judgment or as a matter of indifference, does not solve the problem within. The sorting out of the members of the community is not performed in our present, but is postponed to the LAST JUDGMENT. Here is the Christian form of judgment day: a temporally deferred but vigorous judgment upon the whole world, including the members of our own society. It serves not only to preserve contingency, but also to make a communal life with the sinners possible. Even the sacraments are shared WITH THE WICKED—a scandalous thought, but made possible by the messianic judgment awaiting the whole world. The very cooperation that characterizes Christian social relations forces the deferral of judgment. The cooperation is unbound even from excluding sinners. But this also meant that early on Christianity discovered that it could neither ignore nor submit to the world, but had instead to hold out a belief in a judgment that would come for the world. Yet, again in a logic we discovered in Rosenzweig, such a judgment does not only judge the others ("ye") but also rests upon the members of the society. The universality of the community is born in the Last Judgment, precisely as suspension of a present of exclusion and judgment against both members and others.

While the Last Judgment functions to allow members to worship with their sinning companions, the sacraments themselves represent a certain distance from the judgment we have been examining. Rosenzweig in the third part of *The Star* examines the liturgical calendars of both Judaism and Christianity, and indeed, argues that the study of the ritual gestures will display the way these communities verify the meaning of their theological experience. The importance of bodily interactions (even more than face-to-face conversation) matches Rosenzweig and Luhmann again (and sets Habermas apart). [Indeed, Habermas suspects the recourse to gesture is prior to linguistic discourse, and so is again much closer to the Christian consensus community, precisely because of its need for words.] Beyond that important recognition of the way that liturgy can provide pragmatic backing to semantic media, the immediate concern in this chapter with judgment leads to the more decisive linking of the judgment to the bodily individual, as well as to the bodily community. While the displacement of boundary judgments into a Last Judgment produces a judgment upon the world, including a judgment upon each member within the society, it still does not reveal the full performance of judgment. For that we turn from Christianity to Judaism.

8a) Rosenzweig S 360–61/324–25 The Days of Awe (New Year's Day and the Day of Atonement) place eternal salvation in the midst of time. The horn that blows on New Year's Day at the height of the festival makes it the 'Day of Judgment.' The judgment, that otherwise is placed in the end of time, is here set directly in the present moment.

Rosenzweig reflects upon a series of liturgical practices that are the zenith of Jewish liturgical life. For Rosenzweig these practices bear a theological interpretation: eternity enters into time. But Rosenzweig offers a sociological interpretation of these theologoumena in his own work, and we will struggle to continue along his line of interpretation. This particular passage will be a resource throughout this chapter and in later parts of this book. The Last Judgment is reserved for the END OF TIME, and must be so, according to both Luhmann and Rosenzweig because it opens up a universality that welcomes all by suspending the condemnation on others and on sinners within the community. But according to Rosenzweig, Judaism and Christianity force eternity into time. That is, they are not ecstasies through which some elect are lifted out of the realm of temporal change; rather, they are ways for eternity to enter into the temporal process. Key to that eternalizing of time is the institution of fixed hours, days, and calendars. The structuring of our time counts time, producing public time, and is a way for a community to bodily share a cycling repetition of common activities. Liturgical cycles are the backing that Luhmann recognizes as requisite for the symbolic media of religion to bear meaning. These temporal but returning communal activities eternalize our common life: what we do still takes time, but it cannot simply pass away because it will come back again.

In the Jewish calendar there are different beginnings to the year, and the key one is the one at which human beings and indeed the world as such is judged. The shofar, a ram's horn, is blown in services and the day is proclaimed a day of judgment. The dating of the day depends on a process of human calendrification, left to human reasoning (THE MOMENT MADE PRESENT) and allows the judgment upon the community to be fixed through the communal processes—already a sign of the sociological construction of the meaning of the judgment (see Chapter 17).

8b) It cannot be the world that is judged, therefore—where would it already be in this present! Rather the judgment judges the individual. The fate of each individual will be determined according to his deed. On New Year's Day the sentence for the past and for the coming year is written, and on the Day of Atonement, when the last respite of these "ten days of repentance" expires, it is sealed.

But this day is marked as a day of judging individual people. Rosenzweig comments that the WORLD is not yet ready, not yet collected to stand in court. The "we" is incomplete. There is no completed world to arraign—and just so the Last Judgment seemed to require deferral until the messianic break into time. But to make the claim that the individual is ready to stand under judgment Rosenzweig has recourse to a famous part of the New Year's Day liturgy, a prayer about God's judgment.

The prayer produces the terror of judgment. Even the angels are to be judged. And in a powerful conceit, God becomes a SHEPHERD examining each sheep as it passes under the STAFF. Not a judgment passed upon each other, nor one that is passed on the whole world, as was the case with the flood. Rather, here is an accounting, and a legal signing of a writ of judgment. Rosenzweig's references are underlined. They focus on the individuality of judgment. But the image of the shepherd's staff remains ignored. The importance of the decree, however, should not escape us. Judgment is inscription, inscribed by an author, marking a permanent sign.

9a) Mahzor "U-Netaneh Tokef" The great shofar is sounded. A still, small voice is heard. The angels are alarmed, seized with fear and trembling as they say: "behold the day of judgment." Even the hosts of heaven are judged. No one is justified in Your eyes of judgment, and everything that walks in this world passes before You like a flock of sheep. And like a shepherd who gathers his flock, bringing them under his staff, the souls of all that lives pass under Your review, as You account and sign and appoint to every creature, and write their decrees of judgment.

The prayer continues with a sentence that will become a refrain, punctuating a sober list of deaths and fates. Yom Kip-

9b) On Rosh Hashanah they are written, on Yom Kippur they are sealed.

pur, the Day of Atonement, is the tenth day, and so the judgment period, the Days of Awe, last from the time of writing to the time of sealing. Rosenzweig chooses to splice into this sentence a clause EVEN AS THE LAST RESPITE OF THESE "TEN DAYS OF REPENTANCE" EXPIRES. By adding this clause, he accentuates the interval. A judgment takes time and is played out in a social context. Even eternity enters into time by taking time, not all at once. And the differential in WRITING and SEALING, in originating the message and making it permanent, allows for human activity. I am interpreted, as sign, by a text I can only imagine, I cannot control. Arraigned, indicted, even sentenced.

What is written is not sealed, so that the decree can be suspended or even annulled. The means will occupy us in Part IV when we consider repentance, but the proce-

> 9c) But repentance, prayer, and righteous deeds annul the severe decree.

dural image governs the recitation. Between sentencing and sealing the verdict, a person has the chance to change the text. Clearly this hope for annulment is the affective goal. We announce the threat upon us in order to be propelled toward responsiveness.

> 8c) The year becomes entirely the fully valid representative of eternity. In the yearly return of this, of the 'Last' Judgment, eternity is freed from all other-worldly remoteness. It is now actually there, to be grasped and held for the individual and grasping and holding the individual with a strong hand. It is no longer in the eternal history of the eternal people, no longer in the eternally changing history of the world. It bears no waiting, no bowing down before history. The individual will be judged immediately.

This singling out before God's judgment transforms time. My vulnerability to death is not a merely ultimate issue, not something to worry about when I am older, later. To submit myself to this process of judgment each year, in the temporal sequence of my life and my work, is to make each year a REPRESENTATIVE OF ETERNITY. THE 'LAST' JUDGMENT recurs each year. But it is still 'LAST' because it is the question of my life and death, the question of how I will live or how I will die. Rosenzweig claims that not only does this yearly cycle represent [*vertreten*] eter-

nity, but that it is fully valid [*vollgültig*]—it is capable of satisfying the claim of representation completely: not because it merely recycles, and remains the same, but because the sense of judgment is central to eternity. For what is the individual being judged? The responsibilities for others who call me to join an all-inclusive community. Eternity's judgment is the assessment of a person's responsiveness and role in a mutual community, but eternity's judgment does not dwell beyond life. The praying community brings the judgment into time, FREED FROM ALL OTHERWORLDLY REMOTENESS. Not only is judgment not a way of asserting power over other communities, it is also not deferred beyond any pragmatic impact on our community. Instead, it both comes within our GRASP, and we find ourselves within its grasp. Not postponed until history delivers us all up to an accounting, not even were that an

eternal history, a history that didn't allow for the changes of empires and paradigms. Judgment is not to wait eternally for an eternal history to reach its end; still less to wait for world history to progress or degenerate to its end. Eternity interrupts history today, in a moment of communal prayer. The judgment happens now—each year, eternally repeated, and each time determining the very fate of every individual.

8d) He stands in the congregation. He says 'we.' But the 'we' in these days is not the 'we' of the historical people. The transgression of the laws that separate this people from the peoples of the globe is not the sin for whose forgiveness the 'we' cries.

The liturgical calendar requires the individuals to stand with others, to pray with others—IN THE CONGREGATION. Here each says "we"—and Rosenzweig proceeds to examine just what the range of this "we" is. First of all, the "we" is not the HISTORICAL PEOPLE—not the Jews of a particular time and place. This "we" is not the community of Torah, the community distinguished from other peoples by the law. It is not in separation from the non-Jews, from the environment, that the Jews pray for FORGIVENESS. Indeed, the "we" CRIES out, cries out for the salvation of this broken world. Cries for forgiveness, but not just of those assembled, nor even only for those who bear the yoke of the law.

8e) Rather on these days the individual stands in his naked individuality directly before God, simply in human sin; only this human sin is named in the trembling enumeration of the sin 'which we have sinned'— an enumeration that means more than an enumeration: an illuminating enticing out all of the hiding places of the breast the confessions of the one sin of the ever-same human heart.

The individual, according to Rosenzweig, stands to confess for HUMAN SIN. Indeed, for the sin that is generic, and at the same time specific, a listing that reflects a wide range of social, linguistic, interactive, emotional, and deliberative failures. Rosenzweig refers to one of the traditional confessions, the *al het*, of which each verse begins: "For the sin WHICH WE HAVE SINNED against thee." The ENUMERATION consists of two verses for each letter of the alphabet, arranged by two's in order. We will return to the topic of confession in discussions in Part IV. Here we note that this iteration is accompanied by a gesture of beating the breast with each verse. Hence the speech and the striking seem to bring sin to light together. More important, however, is the communal nature of the sin: WHICH *WE* HAVE SINNED AGAINST THEE. Each confesses each sin as one's own, but also as our collective sin. Indeed, this sin is HUMAN, not uniquely Jewish or determined by Jewish law. Hence, each confesses the sin of all humanity.

8f) And so the 'we,' in whose community the individual in his naked and mere humanity before God thus beating his breast and in whose confessing 'we' each feels his sinning 'I'

The community in which one prays, BEATING HIS BREAST, is a CONFESSING "WE" but it serves to lead the "I" to respond for all sins. Indeed, if the "we" cannot be simply the NARROWER CONGRE-

to be unlike any time in his life, this 'we' cannot be a narrower congregation than the one of humanity itself. As the year on these days directly represents eternity, so Israel on these days directly represents humanity. Israel is aware of praying 'with the sinners.' And that means, whatever the origin of the obscure saying: as the whole of humanity, 'with' everyone. Because everyone is a sinner. GATION but must now become HUMANITY ITSELF, then in the intensification of the "I," in this practice, the widest range of the "we" is grounded. The coming of eternity into time is that the "I" praying as "we" responds for all humanity. Here a social practice produces the keenest awareness of my own fate bound to that of humanity as a whole. Hence, there is double representation: the year represents eternity, Israel represents humanity. Judgment serves not to coordinate a community that stands in judgment over another, but to transform this community to a representative, vulnerable for the sins of other communities. Once again we are in the midst of a profoundly asymmetric relation. Judgment, instead of establishing a superiority over others, places our community as representative for others, representatives in confessing and asking for forgiveness. Israel becomes through this particular performance, repeated yearly, hostage for humanity.

Rosenzweig cites the most important prayer of the Day of Atonement—*kol nidre*, which means all vows. It is prayed at the outset, directly before the Day of Atonement begins, and is truly an obscure prayer. A communal court is formed in which each prays for the annulment of vows to God that will be forgotten. It begins:

The prayer pairs the court of the congregation with a divine court—asserting some cooperation or at least complicity between both courts. And "we" permit others to join, sinners and perhaps even scoffers, people who normally would avoid our congregation, and whom we might therefore exclude. The "we" that 10) Mahzor "Kol nidre" By the authority of the court on high and by the authority of this court below, with divine consent and with the consent of this congregation, we hereby declare that it is permitted to pray with <u>those who have transgressed.</u>[2]

prays together, therefore, as Rosenzweig explained, is not defined by the law; the sins in question are not solely transgressions of the law. Instead, "we" pray for the whole of humanity, for each one who has sinned. And, is there one without sin? BECAUSE EVERYONE IS A SINNER. For sin, in Rosenzweig, is the failure to offer oneself as sign before being called to offer oneself. In an unredeemed world, we each participate in innumerable failures of responsibility. The 'vanity' of praying for others, when they themselves

---

[2] Soloveitchik TS 143/225–26 The first proclamation declares that everyone, without exception, is fit to stand before God and petition Him not only for atonement and renewal of the covenant as well: By the authority of the court on high and by the authority of this court below, with divine consent and with the consent of this congregation, we hereby declare that it is permitted to pray with those who have transgressed. Everyone is fit to turn in returning and to enter the renewed covenant.

might refuse to join, refuse this God, refuse indeed to admit that they need to confess—that vanity is suspended by the simple insight that even the most virtuous individual lives in this imperfect world. Moreover, like responsibility in general, this representative performance does not subordinate the one outside the community, but rather, expresses a universal solidarity, an extreme responsibility that rests on "we" who pray, and need not be performed by others.

The sinners are welcome because of judgment. Indeed, judgment is the performance that universalizes the Jewish community, in just the way that its deferment to the messianic moment universalized the Christian community. For Rosenzweig, these two kinds of societies are both needed and are complementary if antagonistic. Judgments relate individuals to the classes, and here both classes are universal. But while Christianity forms its universal by infinitely coordinating and welcoming each within an expanding class, Judaism allows one individual to represent all the others in infinite responsibility. Intensive and extensive universalities; different logics; different days of judgment.

E. Unjust Judgment

But the story in Rosenzweig is not only of these universalities that bring redemption into the world by bearing infinite responsibilities; for there are also two other sorts of logics, two other sorts of societies, and so two other sorts of judgment days. The other two both make responsibility finite and destroy the individual in relation to the class. These other two are self-righteous, judging others but not falling under the staff of judgment themselves. These others, thus, are ways of avoiding the responsibilities of judgment. In Rosenzweig's system the worst society is one formed through an idealist project, a totalizing one. Rosenzweig had devoted himself to writing a book called *Hegel and the State* and had a deep familiarity with the logic of such a society. But just as a total society expands, so a pagan society contracts, or at least rests secure within its own borders. Rosenzweig examines paganism and the postidealist, post-Christian, neo-paganism with some care and even some sympathy. While a certain failure to strive for the responsibilities in relation to the world mar such society, it is freed of the all-encompassing violence of totalitarian society. This section, therefore, must turn to these other two kinds of societies, to understand their forms of judgment and their judgment days.

For Rosenzweig, idealism represents a way to understand the world by refusing to accept the risk of language, insisting on a synoptic view that can guarantee the future in the present. His most extensive treatment of idealism occurs in the context of his treatment of creation, which for Rosenzweig is a profoundly contingent action, preserving God's freedom and the world's intrinsic structure. The world is not created out of God, but it also is not the cause of its own existence. The contingency of created existence is emblematic for the contingency of social responsibilities, particularly love. But idealism refuses to recognize the contingency of the world and substitutes for creation a necessary generation of the world, a supposedly pure idealistic generation of the structure and specificity of the world. That generation is later reversed in an idealist theory of action, for its ethics produces necessary and unconditional universality.

11a) Rosenzweig S 158/142 ... the self surrenders to a universal. In the concept of surrender we have the counterpart to the concept of generation. The latter governs the way from universal to particular, the way down; the former governs the way from particular to universal, the way up. The two together, generation and surrender, close the idealistic world as a whole.

The third social logic is the totalitarian society's, produced in an idealist mode. The idealist relation of particular to universal is SURRENDER. But the relation is not simple, not a one-time subordination. Rather, idealism has a passion for totalizing, for absorbing everything that stands between the individual and the universal. But unlike cooperation, in which an individual must coordinate her interests and claims with other individuals, joining with other individuals and preserving her own individual authority to judge, surrender is a giving up of particularity, and so of my opening for the other's interpretation. GENERATION from universal to particular, the idealist ersatz for creation, was dominated by a necessary production of ever-more particular entities. As necessary, it could be grasped at once and did not require time for its unfolding. Responsible action in this context is surrender, not truly a response but a giving up of aspects of oneself, a renouncing of speech. The world is thus determined in one blow in its generation and in human surrender as a whole, completed in a process that partakes of reason but abandons the interaction of conversation, the differential of signifying, and the responsibility for a particular other person in substitution.

11b) The way up begins with that original surrender of the 'maxim' of one's own will—and what else is that than B = B!—to the principle of a universal legislation—and what else is that than B = A! This now goes on and on, because as soon as the final principle of a universal legislation is reached, and is admitted again into the 'maxim of one's own will,' the power of the idealistic surrender must again prove itself by again becoming the principle of a universal legislation. In this way the surrender to ever higher communities, ever more inclusive universality of life renders itself the universal. . . .

Rosenzweig now draws on an algebraic notation he developed for the early part of his book. A human being was defined as B = B to emphasize the relation of particularity to particularity: a person is an individual being with an individual will. Surrender requires one give up precisely that individuality of will, surrendering the authentic will in order to embrace what appears as a universal will. Rosenzweig symbolizes that as B = A, the particular human being willing what is universal [*besondere, allgemeine*]. But this is an incomplete process, in need of ever greater surrender, of ever greater effacement of the particularity of the individual. The act of surrender, of conforming to a universal, must PROVE ITSELF again, showing how the new maxim can still be made more universal. Thus one ascends TO EVER HIGHER COMMUNITIES through one other person, to family, to village, to people, to state, and so on. At each stage, the next level up is PRESUPPOSED, guiding the individual in dropping more and more of her particularity. The universality is not a goal or norm that grows in time, but is already given before I surrender the least shred of my particularity. Universalizing is abstracting, or rather, surrendering the particularity of my own claims. (In distinction from the cooperative expanding, which requires each person to bring her own voice, her own claims into the negotiated principles of the community, and to alter the community in its expansion, in ways that must be unforeseeable, infinite.)

11c) For this highest universality of law, this ultimate form, is where the way up finally leads. Surrender which always happens only in order to find again what was 'surrendered' in the surrender, at the goal of surrender—for it should be 'a gain', to give up oneself—this surrender rediscovers, therefore, again and again personality in each universality. Always rediscovers that the A, to which it surrenders, itself is again only the assertion about a B, and therefore itself must consider it a gain to be given up to a higher A.

This way up culminates in an ultimately UNIVERSAL LAW. Everything has been gathered into what Hegel calls the concept. But we can see Hegel's concept lingering in this text: because surrender is a negation that preserves what is negated. One carries the distinction of having a PERSONALITY that has surrendered some particularity onto the next step. One is someone who has jettisoned appetites for food, but then one will have to give up that characteristic of having given up those appetites. One rediscovers oneself as the agent of giving things up, preserving a trace in personality of what has been surrendered. But then must also surrender that quality. The motion up leads one away from the last battle to the next one. This incessant, necessary escalation of surrender is the counterpart of the necessary generation of particularity. Hence a universal (A: *allgemeine*) becomes a new particular (B: *besondere*), even in the dialectic where the universal bears the characteristic of the previous round of surrender.

The key contrast between the social logic of idealism and Christianity is the direction of the way. Christianity is an eternal way outward: reaching toward others in their particularity, preserving everyone. The eternalization of the way makes the incompleteness of the universal intrinsic to its structure, but that, in turn, makes the way a way through time, where the next step is not already given. Idealism is a nontemporal way up, a process in which the particularity of each individual is stepwise given up in the process upward to become God. Its universality is always secured in advance, just as its way down was secured against surprise. This sort of society is governed by a conviction that it marches with history, and so is always on time. Both Christianity and the Total Society move through the world, but cooperation moves by inviting difference and preserves it, while totalization absorbs it in a concept, denying to each the authority to speak for itself. Because the Last Judgment is not-yet, the Christian must listen and cooperate with the others, and because the universal is presupposed, for the idealist there is nothing to be learned beyond the immanent process of history.

Rosenzweig distinguishes the imperialism of idealism with the finitude of pagan society that reasons by exclusion. Rosenzweig analyzes pagan society as a model of subordination: each individual is absorbed as a part in whole—but the whole does not aim for a broader universality. Thus unlike the concept, there is not an inherent escalation, requiring ever greater self-surrender. Rosenzweig discusses the pagan world in a presentation of the crisis of the idealist form of the modern state. He recognizes that what we might call postmodern moment is dawning in European history, with a much deeper sense of the limits of our knowledge and a suspicion of the totalizing universality of idealism. Thus the neo-paganism of Heidegger and those who will follow him in some ways can be modeled by a reinterpretation of the pagan world, and especially its logic of wholeness without expansion. In contrasting the modern state (idealism's product) and the ancient state, Rosenzweig introduces us to the fourth kind of social form.

12a) Rosenzweig S 59–60/54–55
It seems ancient humanity solved theoretically and practically, in the metalogical sense, the problem of the relation of individual to genus. People, state, and whatever else the ancient communities might be, are lions' dens, in which the individual may see tracks going in but none leading out. Law properly juxtaposes the community as a whole to the person; he knows he is only a part. These wholes, to which he is opposed as only a part, these genera, to which he is opposed as mere representative, are absolute powers over his moral life, even though they are in themselves in no way absolute, rather themselves are again examples of the genus state, or people in general. For the individual his community is the community.

Judgment, as the relation of individual to class, emerges in what Rosenzweig calls a METALOGICAL context. This is a somewhat idiosyncratic use of the term and refers to the discovery that while the world can be known through logic, logic is not intrinsic in the structure of the world. The contingency of our particular scientific understanding of the world prompts Rosenzweig to investigate what the world's structure would be like if it was opaque to our logic. Rosenzweig can thus preserve contingency and intelligibility. But here, the ancient polis is taken to offer a way for individuals to become intelligible: by disappearing into A WHOLE. This fourth relation needs to be distinguished from idealism: it too eventually absorbs the individual. But we begin with the TRACKS GOING IN—the trace of individuality now absorbed in a whole [*Ganzes*]. The idealist absorption of the individual is into the totality. Ancient law opposes the individual to the state—and the individual recognizes himself as A PART. The individual belongs to the whole, which exercises ABSOLUTE POWER OVER HIS MORAL LIFE. Rosenzweig's pagan is bound by a rigid, traditional morality here, dictated by the whole to the particular. He is a mere example of the genus, deriving his identity and his action from his generic qualities. Indeed, even his genus is only exemplary, only an instance of a larger genus—but he relates to the one over him, not to the class of states or peoples. Indeed, only my community is a community—the others are irrelevant to me. Here is perhaps the logic of external parts: in the world there is no integrity, no universality, only the conflict of independent and indifferent wholes. The system's relation to its environment is left barely interpreted. This option, the metalogical world, appeals in our time precisely because of the collapse of the assumption that the world is necessarily known through human logic and science. In opposition to the violence of imperialism and totalizing thought, this pagan indifference seems appealing.

12b) Through this closure vis-à-vis the outside and the unconditionality vis-à-vis the interior, they become those thoroughly formed individuals. On its own this evokes a profound reflection of the comparison with an artwork. The secret of the ancient state is not organization.

This community forms by closing itself off from all others, but within it is absolute and unconditional, using its individuals as material or as mere parts to be subordinated in the whole. The almost brutal distinction of system and outside forces the inside to form fully along that opposition. The result is something with so much form (the whole forming the parts) that it is readily COMPARED WITH AN ARTWORK. For the artwork unifies the various elements or parts within one frame, but thus stands closed off from other paintings. Luhmann interprets such social systems as segmented in contrast with organizations. The pagan integrity and closure, however, is not ORGANIZATION, not formed by each contributing a distinctive function to the whole. A living body is organized, as organs themselves are functionally specific within a whole.

12c) Organization is a thoroughly idealistic formation of the state. In a highly organized state, the state and individual are not in the relation of whole to its part; rather, the state is the All, from which one centralized current of power goes through the members. Each has his own determinate place and belongs to the All of the state, by filling his place.

Rosenzweig then contrasts the organized state with the ancient state. He identifies the organized state as the idealistic state—the totalizing organization according to the concept that we saw just now. The highly organized modern state is a totality, an ALL, that distributes power to each of its members and organs from the center. The totality of the state is not the whole of which each member and each group is a part. Rather, it is an organization where power flows from a center. Individuals relate through intermediaries to the state. The problem emerges because the individual is also merely INDIVIDUAL, that is, he cannot be a sign of other peoples. Thus he either stands for himself or dissolves within a community—that still stands only for itself. The social action of subordination fails to extend responsibility beyond the limits of the agents: agents whose authority to interpret, to speak, and to know dissolves into the integrity, the wholeness, of the society itself.

The contrasts between the pagan and the Jewish and between the total-izing and the Christian social forms are determined as contrasts between kinds of judgments. While both the Christian and the total society expand, the cooperative society requires an opening universality where each contrib-utes and transforms the other, where each is responsible for each other. The total society, on the other hand, subordinates individuals to larger and larger collectives. Its judgment is a concept with no residue of individuality. Everything is absorbed in its negation. While both the representative society as an idealization of Judaism and the subordinating society of paganism abandon the expansion into the world, representative judgment allows one to represent infinitely all the others, while in the subordinating judgment the whole dissolves and replaces its individuals, which are seen as parts. Thus the sorts of logical judgments of individuals in general classes are actually forms of social relations.

But to complete this section, we need further to see that each requires a kind of judgment day. While the tension between the Christian Last Judg-ment and the Jewish Day of Judgment is clear, what are the equivalent pagan and totalitarian judgments? I will suggest that the practice of ostracism in the ancient world, first in Athens and then elsewhere, and the conviction that history itself is the ultimate judgment display just the performance of social relations that correspond.

The traditional source of information about ostracism is Aristotle. In two passages, in *The Athenian Constitution* and in a discussion in the *Politics*, where he justifies the needs of democracies and oligarchies to be rid of ex-ceptional men, Aristotle discusses its historical source.

13) Aristotle Politics 1284a18 And for this reason democratic states have instituted ostracism; equality is above all things their aim, and therefore those who seemed to predominate too much through their wealth, or the number of their friends, or through any other politi-cal influence were ostracized and banished from the city for a time.

Aristotle is discussing the problem of exceptional individuals in society. Indeed, he has admitted that the truly great do not fit into society. Not all states of antiquity ostracized, but all depended on the meld-ing of individuals into a whole. Democ-racy requires EQUALITY—at the most basic level of power. Thus some were ostracized because of extreme power. The state in-vented a means of removing the excep-tionally powerful, and the means was a vote. The oistrake was a ballot upon which a citizen wrote the name of one who should be banished. The exclu-sion from society was for the sake of the whole: one part was severed for a limited time. The community sat in judgment upon an individual, in order to restore not the safety of the community, as against traitors or murderers, but in order to restore the equality and the social relations between the numer-ous parts. Were one individual to become too powerful, he would no longer be merely one part in the whole. BANISHMENT, moreover, meant exclusion from society and as such was dismissal into nothing, into a world that barely had any meaning. Athens used this new invention regularly, and exported the institution to other cities as well.

The fourth form of judgment day is found in Hegel's account of world history, best represented by a passage from *The Philosophy of Right*. The passage serves as a transition from international law to world history, and will only receive a brief commentary here.

14a) Hegel PR, 503–4/371–72 The principles of the spirits of the nations are generally limited for the sake of their particularity in which they have their objective actuality and their self-consciousness as *existing* individuals. And their fates and their deeds in relation to each other are the manifest dialectic of the finitude of these spirits, from which the *universal* spirit, the *spirit of the world*, produces itself as unlimited, as it is, that exercises its right—and its right is preeminent—over others in which the *world's history* is as the *world's judgment*.

For Hegel, the various peoples each have their own nations, and each have their own spirits. These nations are bound to conflict with each other. We are very far up on the way from particularity to universality, as these various national individuals are now surrendered into the UNIVERSAL SPIRIT: THE *SPIRIT OF THE WORLD*. Each nation has only limited right and spirit, but beyond their struggle is a preeminent right, which is not a United Nations, or a promised Last Judgment, but is realized within the WORLD'S HISTORY. Each nation has its moment on the world historical stage. And the decision on who shall live and who shall die is made in history, by history. The world's history is the world's judgment (the judgment upon the world).

(This is, in fact, a quotation of a poem by Schiller, *Resignation*, which indeed is about resignation to the way of the world, to the ultimate loss we experience in this life. Although it is quite possible that Hegel is challenging Schiller's romanticism, and revaluing this immanent judgment upon the world.)

14b) The *element* of the existence of the *universal spirit*, which is intuition and image in art, feeling and representation in religion, the pure free thought in philosophy, in *world history* the spiritual actuality has its entire extent of inwardness and externality. It is a judgment, because in its in and for itself existing *universality* the *particular* (the penates, the civil society, and the spirits of the peoples in their colorful actuality), is only as *ideals* and the movement of spirit in these elements is to demonstrate this.

While each sphere of spirit has its own aspect of spirit, world history has the fullest range of spirit, both inward and outward. Hegel argues that history IS A JUDGMENT because the particular appears before it, as merely ideal. The UNIVERSAL sits in judgment upon the PARTICULAR, which has lost its reality to an idealization of it. History does not know the particularities in their reality, but only in reflection upon them, and in reflection upon their movement. The later ages sit in judgment upon the earlier ones not in their reality, but only in the idealization of them framed by history itself. The reality has been surrendered in order to retain a place in world history.

14c) The world's history, further, is not the mere judgment of its *power*, that is, the abstract and reasonless necessity of a blind fate, rather, because it is in and for itself *reason* and its for itself in spirit is to know, it is the necessary development of the *moments* of reason out of the *concept* of its freedom alone and thus its self-consciousness and its freedom—the exposition and *actualization of the universal spirit.*[3]

But for Hegel this judgment is not the exercise of arbitrary power because the development of history is itself rational, indeed spiritual. History is not the result of tyranny and arbitrary violence, but the internal development of reason. These themes are surely familiar, but what we can notice here is the way judgment is rendered rational and immanent. Hegel connects it with the absolute values (SELF-CONSCIOUSNESS AND FREEDOM) as he claims that spirit produces history and so sits as judge upon itself. In the last part of this book I will return to the question of history, and discuss what it means to sit in judgment upon history, and so represent historical events responsively. Here the point is simply to see how the assertion that history is the judgment on nations, and hence on the individuals, displays just the sort of surrender of the individual to ever larger and more universal social levels.

I wish to briefly summarize the four judgments of universality and four kinds of social organization and four modes of social integration. What should be clear is that these logics are formal, but that they are themselves linked to idealizations of historical communities. True enough, the Jews as a group often refuse responsibility for others, failing to live up to the representative responsibility for the world, and the Greeks produced not only the polis but also Alexander and world empire. The goal, therefore, is to disrupt both the extreme abstraction of the four forms of judgment by recourse to real judgmental practices and liturgies, while at the same time formalizing the positivist empirical record in order to discern a range of normative possibilities. The representative community and its logic is not limited to historical Jews, nor is the totalitarian logic of Hegel's philosophy limited to those who acknowledge him, nor, alas, to that time and place. The tension between social practices of historical communities and formal logic is admitted here as a responsibility in the witness for justice that social theory requires. The normative claims, moreover, are made precisely within the context of our interpretation of the responsibility for justice.

---

[3] Levinas TI 219–20/242 The objective judgment is pronounced by the existence itself of reasonable institutions where the will is secured against death and against its own betrayal. It consists of the submission of the subjective will to the universal laws that reduce the will to its objective signification. . . . There is a tyranny of the universal and the impersonal, an inhumane order, although it is distinct from the brutal. Against it, man affirms himself as an irreducible singularity, outside the totality that he enters, and aspiring to the religious order where recognition of the individual concerns him in his singularity, an order of the joy that is neither cessation nor antithesis of pain, nor flight before it (as the Heideggerian theory of *Befindlichkeit* would have us think). The judgment of history is always pronounced in absentia.

The following table (Table 2) will offer a glance at the four relations. In one sense cooperation and totalizing seem similar: each expands beyond any given bound. Similarly, subordination and representation seem content to rest within their bounds. But only cooperation and representation allow for responsibility to open for the world, infinite responsibility. Eternity becomes a pragmatic concept here, a social performance of my being under judgment for the whole world—not only for myself. The moral dimension of judgment here is accentuated—in contrast to the judgments that dissolve the particularity and hence the responsibility of the individual: the judgments of subordination and totality.

TABLE 2. Pragmatic Social Logics

Relation	Subordination	Totalization	Cooperation	Representation
Community	Pagan	Idealism	Christianity	Judaism
Individual/ Class	part–whole	organ–totality	member– chorus	speaker– interlocutor
Individual's Action	dissolve	surrender	communicate	represent
Responsibilities	finite	finite	infinite	infinite
Means/Ends	end determines means	means included in end	eternal means	eternal ends
Relation to Other Communities	one among others	rational encompassing	invitation and expanding	responsible for others
Judgment Day	Ostracism	History	Last Judgment	New Year's Day

We also can claim four conclusions as theses.

I. Universality, judgment, and reason are not necessarily totalizing. Much of the postmodern despair with reason has been provoked by envisioning all reason as imperialist in the idealistic model.

II. The acceptance of boundaries need not produce a paganism that forsakes any hope for the world. The community as representative for the responsibilities of others does not attempt to expand beyond itself.

III. Not all expansion is totalizing. The cooperative community does not compel membership but invites it, using the much heralded nonforced invitation of better arguments.

IV. Tension between a cooperative community and a representative one is inevitable. The one will look like a totalizing empire, the other like an abandonment of the world. These logics are complementary (cooperation and representation)—and opposed.

The ultimate contribution of Rosenzweig's discussion of the judgment between we and ye is to shatter not only the univocal interpretation of judgment and universalization, but even to splinter the responsive modes of judgment. From the perspective of cooperation this seems a bitter pill to swallow—it so desires one world—but it, too, must engage in dialogue with a community that performs responsively *in a different way.* This discovery of a plurality of ethical logics, of social relation and social judgment is the major product of this part.

SUGGESTED READINGS

6   Cornell, *Philosophy of the Limit*, 128–33.
9   Agnon, S.Y. *Days of Awe.* New York: Schocken Books, 1948.
13 Thomsen, Rudi. *The Origin of Ostracism.* Copenhagen: Glydendal, 1972.

CHAPTER 9

Why Law?

THE QUESTION REMAINS of how Judaism or any other community interpreted as a representative society can maintain opposition within itself, a
question that seems particularly confusing from a cooperative perspective. If
being a community means pursuing consensus, how can a community form
around disagreements? The answer takes us into the heart of the Jewish
textual tradition, for as we saw previously, the Talmudic tradition preserves,
even cultivates, disagreement. Indeed, much of the tradition is built out of
love of disagreement and a struggle with the need for agreement in society.
Given the infinite responsibilities that characterize both the social interaction in the representative and cooperative forms of social relations, it is
not surprising that these responsibilities produce a discourse that addresses
judgment directly: law. Precisely in legal texts, in their documented and discontinuous expression, we find the window onto the logics of different societies. The methodological privilege of law and jurisprudence arises through
specific modes of signifying, modes of interpretation, of judgment, of witness, of shared or concentrated authority, and so on. This, too, serves as a
mere gesture toward a series of issues that exceed the immediate reach of this
book—but occupy Rosenzweig somewhat and are addressed by Luhmann
and Habermas extensively in their recent work.

The chapter begins with a pretext by Rosenzweig that explores how the
Jewish law brings the messianic world into this world. He claims that the
law judges this world and justifies this world through the imposition of a
utopian view of the world. In the process, we will comment on a text that
portrays God studying the law in order to judge the world. Section B depicts
the way that law cultivates and preserves conflict. First, Luhmann, in Pretext 3, will discuss the way law encourages the complexity of conflict as a
means for better social communication. Then a Talmudic text presents a
tradition about the need for two contradictory positions, and for the study
of each side (Pretext 4). Finally, another pretext we cited in Chapter 5, on
Rabbi Eliezer and the argument about the oven, explores the question of
oppression and judgment. That text now will be contextualized in the question of oppression or cheating others with words, displaying the complex
relation between divine withdrawal and a community's authority to interpret law.

A. Justifying the World

As a mark of the tension that the law preserves, we will begin with Rosenzweig's account of how the law brings the next world into this one: that is, judges and then justifies life in this world through the imposition of what he will call a utopian view of the world. Here is law understood as ordering the world, itself already judged.

1a) Rosenzweig S 451–52/405–6 That the world, this world, is created and nonetheless in need of future redemption, the unrest of this double thought is calmed in the unity of the law. The law—for viewed as world it is law and not what it is as content of the revelation and demand to the individual: command—the law, therefore, in its comprehended multiplicity and power, ordering everything—the whole "exterior," namely, everything of this life, everything, that only a worldly law might somehow comprehend—makes this world and the future one indistinguishable. God Himself "learns" the law, according to the rabbinic legend.

The problem is that the world appears as both complete and incomplete: the CREATION of it is completed, but the REDEMPTION is still in the future and not reducible to a continuation of the current state of affairs. Recall that redemption was precisely the coming to life of the world joined with love of the neighbor. The doubleness of the world is calmed in the UNITY OF THE LAW. The law has a unity that can bridge this tension of the judgment. Rosenzweig distinguishes between LAW and COMMAND [*GESETZ UND GEBOT*], a distinction he had made earlier, as one between the revelation to the individual in opposition to the ordering of the world for the future. Temporality is key here: law addresses the future of the imperative, bridging its radical urgency with a transformation of the world. Hence, while commands were disconnected and disconnecting from the world, laws are complex, and reach out to everything WORLDLY, everything that can be grasped by any sort of law. The command could transform the self, giving it its soul; the law can transform the world, ensouling not the individual but the exterior realm. Thus the command performed the first real present: the present to which one must respond. Law makes the future of redemption enter this world. The gap between this world and the next is closed. Rosenzweig then cites a passage from the Talmud so famous that he calls it A LEGEND, indicating the creativity of the rabbinic framing of the law. The text itself is from the tractate on idolatry.

The day is divided into twelve hours, which in turn are grouped into four groups of three. The sequence is remarkable, even more for us than for Rosenzweig. First, God studies the Torah. Then God judges the world. Third, God feeds the world. And in the fourth God plays with the sea-monster. The context into

2) Avodah Zarah 3b   And R. Judah said in the name of Rav: "There are twelve hours in the day. The first three the Holy One, blessed be He, sits and occupies Himself with the <u>Torah</u>. The second He sits in judgment over the entire world, and when He sees that it all is guilty and deserves to be destroyed, He rises

which this saying is inserted is a question about whether God ever laughs or plays. But we can clearly enough see a logic to the sequence. In order to judge, God requires knowledge of the law, a matter not of simply looking up the law, but an ongoing engagement: like the sages. And while after judgment, there is both sustaining the world and re-creation—and a certain sort of toleration of the ugly and dangerous, indeed, of animals people might consider evil, the focus for us is the judgment. Without judgment, there would be little point in the study. But the result is quite depressing: ALL IS GUILTY AND DESERVES TO BE DESTROYED. Seen under divine judgment, the world comes off quite poorly, but then God ascends to THE THRONE OF MERCY. Mercy softens judgment, so much that God then feeds all and plays with the horrifying Leviathan. In Part IV of this book, I will return to the place of forgiveness in the relations of judgment. Here, we find that while Rosenzweig only attends to the enchanting image of God studying (*lernen* in Yiddish, more than in the German sense of the term), we can see that even God's studying is related intimately to judgment itself.

from the throne of judgment and sits on the throne of mercy. The third He sits and feeds the entire the world, from the horned buffalo to the brood of lice. In the fourth, He sits and plays with the Leviathan, as it says: "Leviathan, the one you formed to play with" (Ps. 104:26).

1b) In the law everything of this world that is affected within it, every created existence, is already immediately enlivened and ensouled as the content of the future world. That the law is only Jewish law, that this prepared and redeemed world is only a Jewish world and that the God who sits in authority over the world has more to do than merely study the law—this the Jewish feeling forgets, in just the same way if the law is meant in its traditional sense or if the old concepts have been filled with new life. For even in that case it takes only this world as incomplete, but the law that it is prepared to impose upon the world, that it might proceed from this into the future one, it takes as complete and unchangeable.

Rosenzweig discovers a certain FORGETFULNESS of the Jews, in their intimacy and faithful relation to the law. They forget that law is particular (ONLY THE JEWISH LAW), and that the world of practices is similarly particular, that God has more to do. Indeed, Rosenzweig seems himself to have forgotten (for God also judges, forgives, and of course feeds and plays with the world). The Jewish confidence in the law is the best representation of the drawing of the oppositions within, as the eternal life. But Rosenzweig erases the distinction that one would presuppose: between traditional and liberal Jews. Whether one is TRADITIONAL, accepting and observing the law in a rigorous and orthodox way, or even if as a modern or liberal Jew, one struggles to fill the OLD CONCEPTS with NEW LIFE, the law works to forget these particularities. The liberal, like the traditional Jew, takes the law as COMPLETE AND UNCHANGEABLE, and is only seeking to make the world ready for them. The life of the law is not in the law itself, but rather in the work of the law in the world. The law enlivens the world: making the world to come enter into this world.

1c) The law stands, then, even if it appears in the most modern dress as some contemporary utopia, in a deep opposition to that Christian lawlessness of the ability and will to be surprised, which still distinguishes the Christian turned politician from the Jew become utopian, which grants the latter the greater power to arouse and the former the greater readiness to achieve results. The Jew intends always that what counts is only to turn his legal doctrines around and around. . . .

The function of law in the Jewish community, even for that most liberal Jew, the UTOPIAN, is in deep opposition to the place of the law in the Christian community. Christianity depends on AN ABILITY AND WILL TO BE SURPRISED. This surprise comes from the new members, from new realms of cooperation, for its truth lies in a future beyond expectation. Christianity is, in this way, LAWLESS. Rosenzweig contrasts the two kinds of social activists: the Christian become politician has great efficacy and can get results; while the Jew become utopian is a more powerful revolutionary, AROUSING THE WORLD. Jewish law is more one-sided, and more disruptive of this world.

1d) The thought of the transition out of this world into the future one, the messianic time, which is suspended over life as an eternal, to-be-expected today—here is consolidated and made everyday into the law, in whose observance, the more perfected, the seriousness of that transition withdraws. For just the how of the transition is already firmly set. As God according to the legend, so may now also the life of the pious exhaust itself in ever more perfected "learning" of the law. His feeling gathers the whole world, which was created into existence like himself to be ensouled and which grows toward redemption, into one, and he pours it into the intimately familiar space between the law and his people, the people of the law.

The focus in our second part has been how using signs creates a present of shared meaning. The task in understanding judgment is to see how the responsibility to judge can become present: how the transcendence of a messianic future can be inserted into a today. Rosenzweig sees the Jewish law serving to make that future of judgment EVERYDAY. The issue in the responsibility for the present is not to justify what is current, the immanent situation, but to make the transcendence of responsibility disrupt the current situation, engendering a present of social meanings. Those meanings, as messianic, as bringing the world to come nearer, produce a utopian reality, or at least the CONSOLIDATION of the tension of responsibility. But Rosenzweig also discovers that Jewish law is more than observance. Rather, the relation to law is not defined as a code, but as a relation of study. The cognition that we saw emerge in Habermas' account of communicative action is reiterated here. God studies the law in order to judge; the pious EXHAUSTS his life in an infinite responsibility to study. This study doubles the asymmetry of the reading of Part I with the mutuality of social relations of Part II. The redemption of the world is just this enlivening of the whole world: the system of social relations requires the insertion of that judgment for the sake of the next world. Why study the law? To pursue judgment in this world in order to make the messianic future present. For Rosenzweig this responsibility characterizes Jewish society.

B. Preserving Contradictions

Law as more than mere code must be interpreted as a social practice or even as a system of communications. Although Luhmann is not particularly familiar with Jewish legal texts or practices, he understands law not as a means of achieving consensus, but as a way for society to hold great conflict and oppositions within it. While Rosenzweig focused on the tension between this world and the next, Luhmann offers a social translation of that into the conflictual relations within society.

3a) Luhmann SS 511–12/374 Establishing the schematism of legal/illegal or permitted/forbidden does not lead to a better understanding of the essence of action (as the theory of natural law would maintain). Instead, it sets up a way of processing information that more precisely functions when conflicts arise. Law does not serve to avoid conflicts. It leads, in comparison with the repression of conflicts in society controlled almost as interaction, to an immense multiplication of opportunities for conflicts. It seeks to avoid only the violent resolution of conflicts and to provide suitable forms of communication for each conflict.[1]

Luhmann understands law's institution of oppositions as a WAY OF PROCESSING INFORMATION—a complexification of the ways communication can happen in society. An alternate view understands law as offering insight into THE ESSENCE OF ACTION. In that theory, which is one of natural law, legal schema articulate the structure of action: that to act is to require some things be socially permitted and other acts prohibited. But Luhmann's theory prefers communications theory to action theory. His theory then focuses on CONFLICTS where shared meaning is incomplete. Law has the function of MULTIPLYING chances for conflict. It creates the space in which people can disagree and still communicate, still converse. Unlike a consensus theory, law is not about forging consensus or AVOIDING CONFLICTS—where each would agree with each. Rather, law provides new opportunities for conflicts to arise. Both specific and global issues can remain unresolved. Law, unlike REPRESSION, does not demand consensus. While many would think that all law is repressive, Luhmann distinguishes the two. Indeed, law rejects VIOLENT RESOLU-

[1] Luhmann SS 498/364–65 Even in the most intense communication, no one is transparent to another, yet communication creates a transparency adequate for connecting action. The social system constitutes the contradictions that hold for it with the help of this unity of communication. Communication's synthesis makes it apparent that two things cannot exist together. Only communication's expectation of unity constitutes a contradiction, by choosing what communication brings together. Contradiction emerges by being communicated.

TION OF CONFLICTS. Society uses law to tolerate and foster disagreement without the rule of force and the demand for agreement. The ramification of the legal system, therefore, opens up new kinds of communication and more room within society for dissent and for the oppositions that Rosenzweig discussed.

3b) As soon as someone appeals to the law, the material for communication is sorted. Texts become relevant, other cases are consulted, interpretations of particular courts become important; one can extend back over centuries, even millennia—and all of this from the viewpoint that the facts can be made information relevant to and consistent with the conflict at hand. Law serves the continuation of communication by other means. It is adequate for society only when it grasps the arising conflicts, or more authentically when it sufficiently generates many conflicts and supplies for their treatment sufficient complexity of its own to dispose of them.

Luhmann's theory focuses on what sort of communications law makes possible. Law, not as a mere code, but as a way of organizing interpretations and communications, SORTS materials. Law is a process of making past texts relevant to the present: it directs the communications to a wide range of materials, stretching back EVEN MILLENNIA. But unlike historical discourse, law makes explicit the need for the materials to be RELEVANT in the present. While Rosenzweig accentuated how law brings the judgment of the world to come into the present, Luhmann accentuates how legal reasoning negotiates with precedence, making the legal tradition alive in the present case. Luhmann quips that LAW SERVES THE CONTINUATION OF COMMUNICATION BY OTHER MEANS, parodying the axiom of war as the continuation of politics by other means. Law directs us to reexamine the previous record, to discover disagreements in the past that can be interpreted in our present. But the value of law for society is precisely its ability to GENERATE MANY CONFLICTS: to formalize and communicate just what we disagree about. Law not only produces the conflicts, but also the complexity with which to treat the conflicts. The promise of legal judgment provides the space in which dissent flourishes, in which factions can be tolerated. We judge through law in order to allow conflict to become more complex, outside the realm of force. But law marshals the complexities of the past into this present.

I would like to conclude this chapter, moreover, with two of the Talmudic texts that Levinas mentioned. They concern the nature of legal argument, both the reasoning and the pragmatics of interaction. In the inclusion of dispute, of oppositional poles, we can see a concern to represent, to stand responsible for others. In the writing of such disputes, we see the perpetuation of the argument in the attempt to make the community persist in representing, in finding new meanings in the conflicting opinions. At this point, we resume the programmatology of the conclusion of Part I, but explore it with the pragramatics of social judgment. The texts are altogether famous, and I will offer only limited readings.

4a) Erubin 13b   R. Abba said that Samuel said: For three years Beth Shammai and Beth Hillel disputed: they [one side] said, 'The ruling is according to us' and they [the others] said: 'The ruling is according to us.'[2]

We begin with a dispute, or rather with a tradition about a dispute. R. Abba, a later sage in Babylon, said that Samuel (one of his teachers, also in Babylon) said X. Already in the ascriptions we see that the dispute persists, leading later generations to reflect upon the earlier disputes.

Not only once, but doubled, in the repetition by the student. What was the story? That each side of two schools claimed they were right. The THREE YEARS is the most noteworthy aspect, because usually through argument or voting a dispute can be resolved, if only for a time (see the continuation of the Talmudic text). We learn that the community could tolerate this argument for a long time. Moreover, neither was persuaded, neither was coerced, neither was compelled to abandon its own stubborn perspective. The telling of the story is unwilling to even refer to the specific matter in question. The arguments between Beth Shammai and Beth Hillel, moreover, do tend to center on specific questions. Hence this story has a certain abstract quality about it, as though framed in this way specifically in the context of Samuel's world. Because there is a wealth of disputes between the two schools, it is imaginable in the Talmudic world for them to have a dispute for three years.

4b) Then a Heavenly Voice resounded saying: "These and these are the words of the living God, but the ruling is in accord with Beth Hillel."

But then there is drama. A Heavenly Voice proclaims two things: THESE AND THESE ARE THE WORDS OF THE LIVING GOD. And Beth Hillel is right! We have two paradoxes in performance. First, each faction is held to be correct—even though they are contraries. But the second of these two is chosen as correct. The pragmatic logic illumines the two stages. First, each position articulates the WORDS OF THE LIVING GOD. Divine signs admit of more than one correct interpretation. They are incompletable, requiring interpretation by each person, and as a result yielding a wide range of possible interpretations. God speaks through different mouths. Which is not to say that 'anything goes,' for the disputants are authorized, doubly, once by leading scholars of the age, but again by representing not only individual interpreters but schools (*Beth* here means school). And it is even possible for the authorized interpreters to be wrong, as each school occasionally retracts its position in argument with the other. Nonetheless, the story wants to insist that contrary

[2] Erubin 13b   The sages taught: for two and a half-years Beth Shammai and Beth Hillel disputed. These said th... "It would have been better for humanity not to be have been created than to have been created." And the others said, "It would be better for humanity to be created than to have not been created." They took a vote and concluded "It would have been better for humanity not to be have been created than to have been created. Now that it has been created, let humanity watch what it has done." Others say, "Let it watch out for what it is going to do."

opinions can both be valid interpretations of the law—that the opposition lies within the reading of the law, and not from an inside/outside view.

The second paradox, however, is that a ruling is made! The same divine authority that validates both schools then picks Beth Hillel. The perennial problem in retaining opposites is that something must be done practically. To pick one ruling is to yield to the needs of the present moment of the community, to authorize one interpretation, one rule, one set of practices, and so on. Both are valid; one will be followed. This seems to undermine the authority of the loser—the community will continue to practice the winner's view, the loser will have been right, but, so what? How can the opposition be maintained if practice must be singular?

4c) Since, however, "These and these are the words of the living God" what was it that earned Beth Hillel to have the ruling fixed according to them?—Because they were kindly and modest. They studied their own words and the words of Beth Shammai and went so far as to repeat the words of Beth Shammai before theirs.

Indeed, the story continues. It is not clear whether the voice now shifts to an anonymous interlocutor of Abba's, to Abba himself interrogating Samuel, or is merely Samuel's addressing himself in a rhetorical question. Clearly enough, the question raises the conflict between the two stages. The question is phrased, however, WHAT WAS IT THAT EARNED, implying that since there was not a cognitive reason for preferring one over the other (both were right), there had to be some other way of deciding, some practice or action that was deemed more worthy. The answer is in terms of moral virtues (KINDLY AND MODEST) but the practice of those virtues reveals the pragmatics of responsibility in legal dispute. THEY STUDIED THEIR OWN WORDS AND THOSE OF BETH SHAMMAI. In interpreting law we have responsibilities to study, to repeat, the words of our opponent. Indeed, the preservation of dispute requires a mode of repetition of the loser's rulings, precisely because the ruling practices will preserve only the winner's. To study the opponent's views is to assume that one can learn from them, indeed, it is to become responsible for them. It is not surprising that they went so far as to REPEAT THE WORDS OF BETH SHAMMAI BEFORE THEIR OWN. Lest one say that the study was strategic only to know the enemy, the study is interpreted as honoring their opponent.

This telling of the story, therefore, instructs us not only to notice whose ruling is accepted, but to repeat and to interpret and to learn from the rulings that are rejected. The very composition of the Talmudic text reflects this, by maintaining minority opinions, but the composing of the text, the reason for a legal text at all, reflects the need to situate ongoing practices in an oppositional context. The proponents of the normal practice must bear responsibility for retaining and teaching the arguments for practices they oppose. The mode of reasoning in Jewish law, therefore, is obliged to preserve opposition, and the study of the texts performs the representative responsibility for each person's varying claims, and even practices. Study of the law produces greater possibility for conflict than observance of the law itself, but law itself is the connecting up of past disagreements with the present case. The conflict in the past illumines the present judgment.

C. JUDGMENT AND THE OPPRESSED

The final text of this part is a complex and often cited text on the limits of legal argument in Jewish law. Levinas cited only a short phrase of it, but we will return to its context as commentary on a Mishnaic text.

5) Mishnah Baba Metsia 4:10 Just as there is oppression in buying and selling, there is oppression with words. . . .

The chapter in the Mishnah addresses the topic of fraudulent and oppressive business practices, focusing at great length on the way that currency works (see Chapter 17). But this text, late in the chapter, is surprising, because it compares linguistic dialogue to the exchange of goods and money. The semiotics of offending people, or taking advantage of them, generalizes linguistic pragmatics and monetary pragmatics. The text goes on to give examples of oppressive language, starting with commerce and ending with casting aspersions on another's ancestors. The task of interpreting the legal delimitation of linguistic interaction is the context for the commentary, which includes one of the most famous incidents, concerning a dispute over whether a portable oven could be rendered ritually impure. Our concern, as the text's, is not with the details of the oven, but rather with the modes of argumentation.

6a) Baba Metsia 59b They taught there: If he cut it into separate tiles, placing sand between each: Rabbi Eliezer declared it clean, the sages unclean. This was the oven of Akhnai.
Why Akhnai? R. Judah said that Samuel said: "They encompassed it with words like a snake and declared it unclean."

The text begins with a citation to other Mishnaic texts. First, it is a verbatim citation from the tractate Kelim (5:10), which deals with utensils. And there is a further citation of this argument in Eduyoth (7:7), but the problem here is not about the oven (which has its context most of all in Kelim), but the argument over it and its comedic-tragic ending. Again we are facing a text with R. Judah advancing a saying in Samuel's name, and again it concerns argument itself. There is a play on the word *aknah*, meaning snake. The arguments were like a snake, but one also sees the word *snake* itself snaking around. The connection to oppression with words will have recourse to this image of suspicion and cunning.

6b) It is taught: that day Rabbi Eliezer brought all the answers in the world, but they didn't accept them. He said to them: "If the ruling

There then follows a battle of arguments. It begins with Eliezer bringing ALL THE ANSWERS IN THE WORLD. Eliezer is portrayed as beginning with an encyclope-

is with me—this carob tree shall prove it." And the carob was uprooted 100 cubits (some say 400 cubits) from its place.

They said to him: "No evidence can be brought from a carob tree."

He retorted to them: "If the ruling is with me—this stream of water shall prove it." And the stream of water turned backwards.

They said to him: "No evidence can be brought from a stream of water."

He retorted to them: "If the ruling is with me—the walls of this house of study shall prove it." The walls of the house of study inclined to fall.

R. Joshua rebuked them [the walls] saying to them: "When scholars argue over rulings one with an other—what benefit are you to provide?" They did not fall out of respect for R. Joshua, and they did not right themselves out of respect for R. Eliezer, and they are still standing inclined.

dic marshalling of logic and precedent. But the other sages are resistant. The problem for this text might simply be that the text from Kelim does not explain how the opposition between the sages and Eliezer occurred, nor its outcome. In any case, Eliezer inflates the argument from reason to miraculous events. He, in fact, seems to work magic: uprooting a tree, making a stream flow backward, even calling the walls of the house of study to fall. In the first two cases, the sages simply discount the events: they do not constitute EVIDENCE. Legal disputation requires just the sorting of material into relevant and not, and miraculous workings of a disputant do not count. One is tempted to see the images as symbolic: the tree is the Torah itself, uprooted from the world; the river is time made to go backward; the house of study is the very institution of legal argument. In any case, another sage, Joshua, rebukes the walls: the institution itself cannot resolve the argument, but rather must house the people who are engaged in legal discourse. The walls remain INCLINED: they have an interest in the limits of evidence.

6c) He retorted to them: "If the ruling is with me—it will be proved from heaven."

A Heavenly Voice resounded and it said: "What do you want from R. Eliezer? The rulings agree with him everywhere."

R. Joshua stood to his feet and said: "It is not in heaven."

The climax of Eliezer's argument is a call to heaven to prove him right: and the same sort of voice that resolved the previous dispute announces that Eliezer is always right: Why do the sages argue? After all, Eliezer had provided reasons, miracles, and now the Voice of Heaven. But the decisive moment occurs when Joshua stands again and affirms that the law is NOT IN HEAVEN.

Joshua is clearly citing a text, indeed refuting the Heavenly Voice by citing the Biblical text. But what does that text say? Moses is addressing the community at the end of his life. His final address asserts that the commandments will preserve the community even without his leadership. The rule of law requires an access to that

7] Deuteronomy 30:11) For this commandment which I command you today is not hidden from you, and it is not far off. 12) It is not in heaven, that you must say "who will go up to heaven for us and bring it to us so that we may hear it and do it." 13) Nor it is across the sea that you must say "who will cross over

law, in a merely human place. The COM-
MANDMENT is available to the community.
It requires neither an ascent nor a crossing
of the sea because it is placed not far but
near. Indeed, when the text asserts that the

the sea for us to bring it to us that we
may hear it and do it." 14) Because
the word is very near you, in your
mouth and in your heart so that you
may do it.[3]

word is IN YOUR MOUTH, we cannot but think both of the performance of
readers and declaimers, who find this word in their mouth, and also of Levinas' text where he claimed that the commandment came out of the mouth of
the one commanded. The speech itself serves as a transition of authority
from the leader to the community, who readily can speak the commandments. Joshua cites it, in the simplest sense, to say that the rulings have to be
made within the community and not by a heavenly voice. But the deeper
issue is precisely the insistence that the text which he quotes is a text about
citation and re-citation: a text that was constructed to transfer authority for
legal reasoning to the community. The greatest revelation from heaven is the
injunction to cite and interpret the law.

6d) What does "It is not in
heaven" mean? R. Jeremiah said:
"The Torah was already given at
Mount Sinai. We don't consider the
Heavenly Voice. It was already writ-
ten at Mount Sinai in the Torah,
"Incline to the majority" (Exod.
23:2).

The text itself interrogates the point of
Joshua's citation. Jeremiah then explains
the text. His explanation itself has two
steps. First, he argues that since the Torah
was given in the past, there is no secondary addition tolerated from heaven. The
closure of the canon represents the limitation of divine interference in law. Divine

authority is confined because the text is now given to humanity. But Jeremiah supports this with a text, which he repeats was WRITTEN AT MOUNT
SINAI, inscribed and now free from divine interpretation. Jeremiah reads the
text as: Follow the majority. The text however, reads:

The text is concerned with perversions
of justice, and the second verse is particularly obscure. The sages elsewhere interpret it in terms of legal procedures for ac-

8] Exodus 23:1) You shall not
bear a false report nor shall you join
your hands with the wicked to be an
unjust witness. 2) You shall not fol-

---

[3] Royce Ch 291   Interpretation seeks an object which is essentially spiritual. The abyss of
abstract conception says of this object: It is not in me. The heaven of glittering immediacies
which perception furnishes answers the quest by saying: It is not in me. Interpretation says: It
is nigh thee—even in thy heart; but shows us, through manifesting the very nature of the object
to be sought, what general conditions must be met if any one is to interpret a genuine Sign to an
understanding mind.

Cohen RR 94/81   Thus the teaching is no longer in heaven, and it has not come from heaven,
but apparently its arrival is made wholly subjective: in your heart and in your mouth. In the
heart of a human being and in rational speech "the word" is contained, as the commandment
is called here. Is it not far from the spirit of people, but near to it. Revelation is here grounded
in the hearts in the ownmost power of human being, the power that speech presents.

quittal and conviction, concerned for questions about the size of the majority. But the verse warns us not to FOLLOW THE MANY, particularly in an evil matter, and not to assume that the many are correct in

low the many to do evil, and you shall not testify in a dispute to in-cline to the many in order to pervert justice. 3) And you shall not favor the poor man in his dispute.

a dispute. Indeed, the matter seems to have to do with pandering either to the majority, or to the poor. Justice must be fair to all. While the tradition of focusing on how to determine a proper majority is valuable, Jeremiah's use here must utterly recontextualize the verse. For him, the verse proves that majority rules, ignoring the beginning of the clause, which is a prohibition. The sages depend on the sense of a majority precisely because they do not insist on consensus. The matter has to be resolved in a way that tolerates dissent. In this particular case, Jeremiah argues that Eliezer must abide by the majority. But the very practice of interpretation coheres with this interpretation. The text, inscribed at Sinai, is made to justify an interpretative practice by that same practice: not what it seems to say in its context, but by a recontextualization it becomes the authority for dissenting interpretation and majority rule. If the text were not given to people, if it were still in heaven, then one could not read this text this way, nor could one use it to justify the authority of the community of interpreters against the Heavenly Voice.

6e)   R. Nathan met Elijah and said to him: "What did the Holy One, Blessed be He, do in that hour?"

He said to him: "He laughed, and he said 'my children have defeated me, my children have defeated me.'"

The text continues, with the story itself receiving an interpretation ascribed to a prophet—this interpretation of the argument is authorized, despite the rejection of the direct evidence of the heavenly voice, again showing the complexity of closing the boundaries of what can count as a legal text. Nathan's report does not have the force of law, but it is worth re-citing in the midst of an argument that rejects similar prophetic discourse. ELIJAH is understood by the sages to be an immortal prophet, who can thus deliver information from God's court. Nathan inquires through Elijah about God's response at the time when Joshua stood up to Eliezer. In an interesting overlap with the text that Rosenzweig cited about God studying the law, we find God laughing again. Laughing with the sages, who have DEFEATED ME because they have argued against the Heavenly Voice and the miraculous "evidence" of Eliezer. To give the law, even God's own law, is to give it over for interpretation by the recipients. The system of legal interpretation excludes interference by recourse to author's intention, or addenda from the author. Indeed, the system of legal interpretation of divine law excludes divine intervention: the divine author remains only environmental with relation to the communications that constitute the system. And the sages can imagine this exclusion as pleasing the author: because the author wishes to be replaced by the deliberation of the children. The children, thus, imagine that they cannot only exclude divine intervention, but that God will be amused and pleased by this exclusion.

6f) They said: "On that day they brought all the objects that R. Eliezer had declared ritually pure and burned them in fire. And they took a vote about him and excommunicated him."

The text continues with another tradition about the day, not simply resuming the story but rather linking the fateful day of excommunication with the contest between Eliezer and Joshua. The excommunication occurred only after a legal performance: all of his rulings on doubtful objects were not merely overturned, but a sentence was carried out on them. BURNED IN FIRE is what an irremediably impure object requires. Thus they may have preserved his arguments but the objects were interpreted as unpurifiable. This was a legal enactment, the appropriate interpretation following the question of whether the legal system could tolerate heavenly intervention. However, the sages went a further step: they democratically decided (VOTED), and then sentenced the man and not only his rulings and the objects upon which they ruled. EXCOMMUNICATION itself appears as a euphemism in the text (BLESSED HIM), but just which level of relations between the man and the rest of the community became prohibited is unclear. While the first portion of the story, up to Elijah's report, is a triumph for the legal system and the sages' defense of it, this latter part expresses criticism. It may, indeed, be that even the burning of objects was a too exclusionary move. But the rejection of the human voice that defends extrasystemic reasons will turn out to be an unjust action. Like so much else in this story, the relation of Eliezer and the limits of the legal system is more complex.

6g) . . . Imma Shalom was R. Eliezer's wife and Rabban Gamliel's sister. After these events she did not let R. Eliezer fall on his face [in prayer]. One day, it was the New Moon, and she mistook a full month for a defective one. Others say that a poor person came and stood at her door, and she brought out a piece of bread to him. She found him fallen on his face and she said to him: "Arise, you have killed my brother." Meanwhile the sound of a horn came from Rabban Gamliel's house that he had died.

The story continues to discuss how the world was blighted, and indeed, how a huge sea storm almost drowned Rabban Gamliel, the leader of the sages and the political authority in the community. Divine judgment is, indeed, destined to fall upon him for this act of excommunication. The story revolves around the family relations: Rabban Gamliel's sister is Eliezer's wife, Imma Shalom. She recognizes that Eliezer has now earned God's ear for his prayers of revenge, and that her brother is at risk. She protects her brother by guarding against Eliezer's supplicating prayer (FALL ON HIS FACE). But one day, it has to happen that she fails to guard and at once Eliezer does so pray, and Rabban Gamliel falls dead. The details are interesting, in that there are two interpretations of why she failed. The first focuses on determining when the new moon has come. Because the

Jewish calendar is lunar it varies in length. On the eve of the new moon supplication is particularly possible. Mistaking A FULL MONTH FOR A DEFECTIVE ONE means that she thought it was the first of the month when it was the last—a calculation depending on observation of whether the new moon has come on the thirtieth or the thirty-first day (see also Chapter 17, for a similar problem with Rabban Gamliel). The failure thus centers on her calendrical misunderstandings. The second reason is that she offers food to a POOR PERSON, clearly a meritorious action. In any case, she knows once she sees Eliezer prostrate that her brother has been killed by God in response to the prayer. She reproaches her husband, and the news arrives of Rabban Gamliel's death.

6h) He said to her: "How did you know?"

She said to him: "I have this tradition from the house of my father's father—"All gates are locked, except for the gates of oppression."

But the finale of the story arises because Eliezer does not understand how she could know. Indeed, he asks in proper Talmudic form, What is the source of her assertion? She answers, referring back to a tradition from her father's father's house (the medieval commentator, Rashi, helpfully explains that this is the family's tradition, that goes back through the political dynasty to David's family—because this ruling seems to depend on the destruction of the Temple, which occurred after the death of her specific grandfather, Rabban Gamliel, the Elder). THE GATES ARE LOCKED. At a first level, it means the gates of the Temple, the gates through which one gains nearness with God. At a second level, these are the gates to heaven: just as the law is not in heaven, so, too, there is no access to the divine court. God is neither legislator now nor judge. Human judgment is alone. EXCEPT FOR THE GATES OF OPPRESSION. The only cases God will hear are those who have been wronged—in business and also with words. Why should those gates still be open? Because God is merciful. But in the context of this argument over the closure of the system, the theology requires a more careful explanation. Those who have been wronged, who are oppressed, require redress beyond the human system. Eliezer receives a hearing (and Rabban Gamliel conviction and sentencing) because he was excluded from any access to the legal system. God can be addressed and intervene only for the sake of those who have been excluded. The cheated and the poor are also excluded from the legal system and require God's court.

For our purposes we see the severity of judgment and the risks inherent in the communications in the legal system. The relation to theology is more complex than we might have chosen. On the one hand Eliezer is rebutted when he tries to draw extra support from divine intervention. The legal system must be closed to God's actions. No privileged information is allowed. On the other hand, the judgment of excommunication is itself a violence against Eliezer, which is satisfied by recourse to divine judgment, executed in this world. Academic politics in the world of the sages was harsh. But beyond the complex negotiation of the closure of the legal system, and the need to enclose all human opposition and not only the majority's opinions, there is a further level that is expressly important for us.

This text itself is a constructed retelling of these events. Various pieces are clearly marked as assembled from different sources and throughout the text interrupt the story to highlight the performance of telling the story. How does such a text function within a legal body of texts? Surely what Luhmann calls the autopoietic aspect of the system is shining through the text here. The text is edited long after the oven of Akhnai, as well as all of the principal players, are gone. Even the commenting sages (Jeremiah, Nathan) are preserved in these texts. Within the legal texts, the anonymous editors are exploring the limits of legal debate, the limits of theological argumentation, and indeed, the limits of their power to exclude others. The same tradition that can prefer Beth Hillel for citing the opponents first invokes divine judgment against those who excommunicated Eliezer. The tale of that judgment not only raises the stakes, accentuating the responsibilities in legal disagreement, but it also institutes through the compilation, repetition, and then inscription of this very text the complexities of judgment into the very heart of the community.

Not only are the questions of jurisprudence and responsibility a pervasive topic in Talmudic texts, they also occupy several of the authors in this work. The topic can only be signaled here, but the responsibility to judge leads directly to the need for law, particularly when law is understood as a system of ongoing communication. The need to place the "we" under judgment in order to strive for justice for all, yields an intense relation with law. The pragmatics of judgment display how the responsibility to know requires the responsiveness of laws, and the need to study law in responding for those who oppose the majority and those who have no other voice in the law.

SUGGESTED READINGS

5   Boyarin, Daniel. *Intertextuality and the Reading of Midrash*, 34–37. Bloomington: Indiana University Press, 1990.
7   Urbach, Ephraim E. *The Sages*, 118ff. Cambridge, Mass.: Harvard University Press, 1987.

PART III

Pragmatism, Pragmatics, and Method

Rabbi Tarfon and the elders were reclining in the upper storey of Nitzah's house in Lod when this question was raised before them: is study greater or is practice greater? Rabbi Tarfon answered, saying practice is greater. Rabbi Akiva answered, saying study is greater. Then they all answered, saying that study is greater because study leads to practice.

Kiddushin 40b

CHAPTER 10

Why Verify?

WHEN ETHICS is based on a moral agent's free will, moral responsibility is interpreted as being accountable for one's own deliberate decisions. Reasoning concludes in a rational act for which one was responsible. But the ethics developed here focuses on the relations between people in the performances of signifying. The responsible one has switched from a rational being to a speaker and listener, that is, to a person signifying for other people. This shift produces radical ethical responsibilities, but it also requires a thoroughgoing change in method. In Part III, we must reflect on that change, not only in order to elucidate what has happened in the first two parts, but also in order to understand the intimate connection between a pragmatics and an ethics of responsibilities for others.

In a pattern that is becoming familiar, we will start with a more accessible model, that of verification of a theory. Particularly in the matter of ethics, the truth of a theory is neither a deduction nor a simple perception of what is, but requires a performance that could fail. The contingency of my response, the gap between responsibility and responsiveness, leads to an epistemology that recognizes the need for a future verification. The theory of verification will lead us from Rosenzweig to William James, and his pragmatism will lead us still further to C. S. Peirce. In Chapter 11, however, we will see that precisely for asymmetric responsibilities, the theorizing about responsibilities dissolves the very specificity of the asymmetry in responsibility. Theory occurs in the realm of a third person, or in an earlier vocabulary, thirdness as generality. While the thirdness of the theory seems to compromise the specificity of my responsibility (parallel to the disappearance of the "responsible subject"), the ethical need to reason, to produce this theory of ethics, reiterates the shift from Part I to Part II, the emergence of the need for justice. Here, moreover, is an interesting sequence from Levinas, through Marcel, to Royce, and finally to Peirce—as we see semiotic triads become personalized and ethically radicalized.

Chapter 12, moreover, will move from the semiotics of vagueness to the ineluctability of the first person, of the "me." The originary fixing of me in the position of responsibility is as vital to this theory of ethics as the need to present it in a general theory for others. Thus the zigzag away from asymmetry and back to it in attribution rehearses the motion to mediation and then to attribution from Part II. The sources here move from Peirce to Royce, to Mead and Levinas. The interlacing of American pragmatists and the European thinkers itself reflects the method at work here, a cable across the Atlantic.

But that leads to the last question of this part, Why Translate? For different traditions are in complex proximity here. Indeed, beyond the task of bringing European thinkers into an American semiotic method, there is a more challenging translation occurring here: from Jewish sources into philosophy. The ethical exigency to transport from there to here is fraught with just the risks that responsibility requires: a risk in altering the here, and a risk in altering what comes from there. The here, it seems, is less stable, less substantial than we are inclined to think. Philosophy is changed. American philosophy can be changed—and so the responsibility to run those risks, to make our home not a place of assimilation of new ideas, but hospitable precisely by undergoing renovation. The Jewish thinkers who have best negotiated the translation into philosophy will concern us, from Hermann Cohen to Rosenzweig to Levinas, teaching us why their translation is ethically needed, and in general why we have responsibilities to translate.

What does it mean to take speaking seriously? Rosenzweig wrote an essay, "The New Thinking," that was to serve as an introduction to *The Star of Redemption,* and reflected on the change of method, changing from thinking in its own domain to thinking about using signs with other people. The first pretext will notice how the new thinking takes time, that one cannot respond before the other speaks, and that a conversation depends on the future responses in order to mean. Pretext 2 then makes the methodological observation that the study of method comes after the practice. Thus we must first know something in order to produce a theory of knowledge. Section B will link Rosenzweig and James in an account of empiricism that allows for the future verification of theory. In Pretext 3 Rosenzweig calls it absolute empiricism, broadening experience to include the relations between God and people and the world, but not withdrawing into transcendental experience. In Pretext 4, James calls it radical empiricism, emphasizing that there is experience of relations.

Section C offers a brief account of pragmatism. James' discussion of it in Pretext 5 focuses on the verification of truth. But we return to two late texts by Peirce where he reclaims pragmatism under the name of pragmaticism. Pretext 6 shows Peirce reinterpreting his own pragmatic maxim, emphasizing the role of thought in pragmatism, while Pretext 7 will link the practical dimension of pragmatism with the intellectual. The chapter concludes, then, with a sense that we verify not simply to make a theory true by having recourse to a sensible experience, but because verification is an interplay between experience more broadly construed and theoretical thinking, and we also verify in order to engage in a reflection that can but does not always lead directly to practical action.

A. PERFORMATIVE METHOD

Franz Rosenzweig's essay, "The New Thinking," written several years after *The Star of Redemption*, was intended to introduce readers to his opaque system. Because of its complex construction and idiosyncratic vocabulary, *The Star* had gone unread by and large, as it has to this day. "The New Thinking" provided instructions on how to read *The Star* and reflections on methodology. While we have not offered here a comprehensive reading of *The Star*, we can still benefit from the concluding discussions of the essay, because Rosenzweig's New Thinking bears close resemblance to the manner of thinking in this book. For both, thinking must change its medium to the practices of speaking and listening (using signs or pragmatics).

1a) Rosenzweig NT 151/86–87
The method of speech appears in place of the method of thought, which all previous philosophy had cultivated. Thought is timeless and wants to be; it wants to strike a thousand associations with one stroke; the last, the goal, is first for it. Speech is time-bound, time-nourished; it cannot and does not want to forsake this nourishing soil; it does not know in advance where it will come out; it lets its key-words be given by another.

Rosenzweig claims to displace ALL PREVIOUS PHILOSOPHY, because it all focused on thought (not speech). Almost a manifesto of this linguistic turn, this claim may not be accurate about previous philosophy. THOUGHT falls suspect because of its desire for timelessness, for eternality divorced from time. It wants to achieve the end before it starts, or perhaps more accurately, at its beginning. By the THOUSAND ASSOCIATIONS, it achieves its end at the beginning. Thought can avoid time synoptically, binding together disparate things WITH ONE STROKE. On the other hand, SPEECH is bound to time and even benefits from the time that separates what I say from what the other person will say in response.

1b) It actually lives from the life of another, whether he is now the listener to a story or an answerer in a dialogue or the co-speaker of a chorus; but thinking is always alone, even when it happens between several 'philosophizers' in common. Even then, the other only makes the objections that I must authentically make myself—whence the boredom of most philosophical dialogue, even the predominant part of Plato's.

The very life of speech is the need for other speakers, and it LIVES off them. The process of speaking, its extension through interchange, takes time and is nourished by time and by the other person. Rosenzweig's own pragmatics includes these three models of speech: storytelling, dialogue, and communal singing. In each speaking activity, the other person plays a vital role for my own speaking by governing how I fashion my tale, or by making an objection, or by inviting each of us to join in. Each activity, moreover, contrasts with thinking pursued in solitude for self-sufficiency (ALWAYS ALONE). Rosenzweig rejects the counterexample that philosophers do talk together, by pointing out that even then the goal is to appropriate and AUTHENTICATE the other person's objections. I should be able to imagine his complaints myself, and so I need to engage him only to develop my own thought. Thought is solitary, in part because it pursues this self-sufficiency. THE BOREDOM OF MOST PHILOSOPHICAL DIALOGUES arises from my unwillingness to let another person surprise me. I am cast as teacher, the other as pupil, and I am not to be tricked or surprised.

1c) In actual conversation something really happens; I don't know in advance what the other will say to me, because I don't even know yet what I myself will say; nor even yet perhaps that I will say anything at all. It can indeed be that the other begins. Indeed in genuine conversation it usually is so; as one can easily persuade oneself by a comparative glance at the Gospels and the Socratic dialogues. Socrates sets most of the conversations in motion, in the motion, that is, of a philosophical discussion. The thinker really knows his thoughts in advance; he 'expresses' them only as a concession to the defectiveness of our means of reaching understanding, as he labels it; the concession is not that we need language but that we need time.

Unlike philosophical dialogues, ACTUAL CONVERSATIONS require time because the future is unknown, indeed, unknowable. Rosenzweig claims that not only do I not know WHAT THE OTHER PERSON WILL SAY, but I don't even know WHAT I MYSELF WILL SAY. I don't KNOW YET, and this YET focuses our attention on pragmatics as an issue of time. The philosopher knows IN ADVANCE. To admit that he does not himself know what he thinks is to fail as philosopher. The need to improvise is responsiveness as the possibility of changing my mind, of struggling for a new phrase, or even for a new idea. Uncertainty is displayed even more clearly by my uncertainty of my own thought and words than by my limited knowledge of what someone else will say. I might even be quiet. But the key is that THE OTHER

BEGINS. My words then are a response, and I don't make the first move. Rosenzweig notices that Jesus is usually confronted by someone else, and first must answer, living in the conversation; while Socrates seems to be in charge, anticipating the other's moves, and is rarely surprised or needs to respond to something unforeseen. The thinker does EXPRESS his thoughts, but Rosenzweig uses quotation marks to indicate how tenuous the action of speech (or writing) is. He is MAKING A CONCESSION, never really altering or responding to another. The problem is only the *VERSTÄNDIGUNGSMITTEL*, MEANS OF REACHING AN UNDERSTANDING—overlapping with Habermas' vocabulary. Our minds are a bit slow, and to reach agreement on timeless truths impinges on our instantaneous understanding. The processes of reaching understanding require concessions, but they are distractions from thought. Language, in this vision, is not the problem—because it is pure semantics, pure thought without any relation to activity of communicating thought to others.

1d) To need time means: not to be able to anticipate anything, to have to wait for everything, to be de-

Rosenzweig focuses on this NEED for time. The distention, the deferring, means that thought itself must wait. Authentic-

pendent for our own upon what is others'. All of this is utterly unthinkable for the thinking thinker, while it is uniquely suited to the speech-thinker.

ity, that OUR OWN would be solely our proper being, is replaced by dependence on WHAT IS OTHERS'. Suspending time, thought had cultivated authenticity and so abandoned the practices of signifying. And indeed, Rosenzweig

Time was the victim of the desire to need no one. And indeed, Rosenzweig realizes that these very reflections are UNTHINKABLE—*FOR THE THINKING THINKER*. A thinker who focuses only on thoughts and on the activity of thinking in isolation from speaking, from pragmatic relations with others, is a thinking thinker. There is, however, another kind of thinker (THE SPEECH-THINKER) for whom these concerns about time are uniquely appropriate.

1e) Speech-thinker—because naturally the new, the speaking thinking is also a thinking, just like the old—that thinking thinking that didn't occur without internal speech. The difference between the old and the new, logical, and grammatical thinking does not lie in loud or quiet, rather in the need for another, and what is the same, in taking time seriously.

Rosenzweig does not think that we must abandon thinking. Indeed, the key for our chapter and for the activities involved in writing this book is that the turn to language, to pragmatics as the use of signs, is not a turn away from thinking but to a new kind of thinking (THE NEW, THE SPEAKING THINKING IS ALSO A THINKING). The change brings also a reassessment of the self-understanding of the earlier thinking thinker. Rosenzweig claims that the

thinking thinker also required speech, offering signs to himself, an insight that will be borne out by Royce's interpretation of thought in general. That INTERNAL SPEECH was not a side effect of thinking, but now appears to have been a key element in the temporality of thinking, even though it pretended not to need time. Hence Rosenzweig is not interested in reducing the difference to a question of whether sounds are made, but to the question of whether ANOTHER is needed. The paired oppositions old/new, logical/grammatical, thinking/speaking can all be clearly distinguished: look to whether the dynamics of dealing with another person is important, whether my future in relation with the other is uncertain. Part I more fully examined these moves, but key here is Rosenzweig's identification of this change in method—the very change we have been pursuing.

2a) Rosenzweig NT 157–59/96–99 Today one still thinks that all philosophy must begin with considerations of theory of knowledge. In truth it may at best conclude with them.

Rosenzweig also reflects this need for time in his understanding of the responsibility to make theory. To take time seriously has implications about when one should raise methodological issues. The modern era begins in Descartes or in Bacon with the insistence that one must

first determine the method, must determine the THEORY OF KNOWLEDGE, and only on that basis will knowledge be gained. This seems to be precisely the mode of not taking another person seriously that characterizes old thinking—because one will know everything in advance. Not surprisingly, Rosenzweig contrasts this still prevalent presumption (in 1925 or 1999) with a claim that such theoretical concerns must come after the practice of thinking. The post hoc quality of theory of knowledge emerges in Rosenzweig in this passage, and it is not by chance that I interrogate my own method only here, in Part III.

2b) ... All critique comes after the performance. Just as a theater critic has little to say in advance, even were he ever so clever, because the critic should not produce it from his cleverness, which he already has in advance, but rather from what the performance produces in him: so theory of knowledge also has little meaning preceding the knowing, that precedes this knowing. Because all knowledge, if something actually is known, is an individual act and has its own method. . . .[1]

Why should theory or knowledge not come first? Rosenzweig proceeds by analogy with A THEATER CRITIC. This moves the meta-theory itself into bold relief. Because knowing itself becomes a performance, and so takes time. Knowing is not a timeless atunement to timeless truths, but a temporal process—in the manner a speech-thinker should recognize. Hence the obvious claim (ALL CRITIQUE COMES AFTER THE PERFORMANCE) is used to understand the time for theory and the time an act of knowing takes. Critics don't write their reviews before the performance because they are responding to what they see and hear. Even very CLEVER critics are called upon to respond to the performance, and not only to what they know IN ADVANCE. Similarly, theory of knowledge has little to say before dealing with a specific act of knowing. Rosenzweig claims that knowing is THIS KNOWING, the THIS indicating the nongenerality, the individuality of knowing, indeed, the reality of AN INDIVIDUAL ACT—and so particular knowing is like the very indexicality of performance that characterizes pragmatics in general. Any knowing, as particular, will be individual and follow ITS OWN METHOD. Even pragmatic theory must be subjected to a pragmatics. To stipulate general, a priori, conditions for pragmatic knowledge would be to fail to recognize that even a theory of pragmatics is situated pragmatically—most of all by the knowledge already achieved. If speech-thinking is for someone and directed to someone, it is also about SOMETHING—and not merely concerning any object in general.

2c) ... This last [truth] must be other than the philosophers' truth

Rosenzweig's account of how knowing comes after implies that even the ulti-

---

[1] Rosenzweig NT 149/83–84 The New Thinking knows exactly what the age-old healthy common sense does, that it cannot know independently from time—what was nonetheless the highest claim to fame which philosophy previously has assumed. Just as one cannot start a conversation from the end, or a war with the peace treaty (which in any case the pacifists would like), nor life with death, one must for better or worse learn actively and passively to wait, even if it is far, and may not jump over any moments, so also is knowledge bound in each moment to that moment and cannot make its past not passed nor its future not futural. This is valid for everyday things, and everyone concedes it. Everyone knows that for a physician the treatment is the present, the getting sick is past, and the death certificate future. . . .

that may know only itself. This must be for someone. And if it must still be one, it can be so only for the One. And therefore necessarily our truth becomes manifold and 'the' truth changes into our truth. Truth thus ceases to be what 'is' true, and becomes what as true wants to be verified.[2]

mate truth (THIS LAST TRUTH) is truth FOR SOMEONE—that knowledge is always in relation to people and not merely in relation to thought. Ultimacy cannot overcome this relation of knowing and performance. Even the unity of truth, which Rosenzweig retains as a goal for knowledge, is not the simple unity of authenticity, or self-sufficiency. Truth still works as a sign. Its unity must be deferred to God alone (THE ONE), while for us, the plurality of interpreters cannot cease, and so truth BECOMES MANIFOLD. Indeed, Rosenzweig focuses on the relation of the truth and us. OUR TRUTH is a relation coordinated by the AND. It is not a simple appropriation of the truth but a relation of two terms. The result is that truth itself requires a relation in order to be our truth. It 'IS' not simply true in isolation from all people. Rather truth needs the *and*: it WANTS TO BE VERIFIED. Verification, as we will see, is a relation. The *and* will become the conjunction that will verify what is true beyond knowing.

2d)   The concept of the verification of truth becomes the basic concept of this new theory of knowledge, which displaces the old theories of noncontradiction and objects, and introduces a dynamic concept of objectivity in place of the static. Those hopeless static truths, like those of mathematics, which were made the point of departure for the old theories of knowledge, without actually getting out beyond those points of departure—[those truths] from here are grasped as the *lower* bound, just as rest is the limit of motion, because only from here can the higher and highest truths be grasped as truths without having to be labeled as fictions, postulates, or needs.

Rosenzweig now advances the central claim: that VERIFICATION IS THE BASIC CONCEPT for the theory of knowledge. The older theories depended on NONCONTRADICTION and static objectivity. To know was to ascertain the coherence of a system of thought, and the OBJECTS did not change. But knowledge now becomes a temporal relation, an act that requires an independence of two terms producing new knowledge in time. Just as speech is DYNAMIC and I do not know what I will say next, so the truth which I know is DYNAMIC and is not predetermined before I begin to know it. Of course there are static truths that retain their place even in this new theory of knowledge. Static concepts and static truths serve as a *LOWER* BOUND of what is true: the barest kind of truth. The old theories preferred static truths because they could not change and required no change in the knower. They were HOPELESS, because they did not allow for hope. If their static quality is made constitutive of knowledge, then no other types of knowing are possible. The result was that the

---

[2] Rosenzweig S 437/393   The truth must thus be veri-fied and exactly in the way, one commonly denied: namely, to leave alone the "whole" truth and still know the part which one has oneself as the eternal truth. It must happen because here it becomes something eternal. In eternity it will triumph over death.

higher and highest truths were seen as not really truths, but as merely FIC-TIONS, POSTULATES, NEEDS of reason, and so on. They were CANCELED in advance like a debt or coin, and were not knowledge but only accessories that could not measure up to truth as hopeless and timeless. In one sentence, Rosenzweig thus retains the static truths and opens the horizon for higher truths.

2e) From those unimportant truths of the stamp "two times two is four," to which it is easy for a person to assent, without any expense other than a little brain grease—for small (times tables) less, for relativity theory some more—the way leads to those truths, for which a person pays something, to those, that he cannot verify otherwise than with the sacrifice of his life, and finally to those whose truth can only be verified at the risk of life of all generations.

What makes them higher is not what is known but the manner of verification, that is, the pragmatic requirements in knowing. Not their content (the sublime truths) nor their origin (revealed by spiritual sources) but the relation to that truth, the cost to the thinker, the RISK. Theory of knowledge itself becomes pragmatics, or even becomes a pragmatism (see below). The scale Rosenzweig sets up begins with mathematics and its static truth, extending as far as RELATIVITY THEORY, all of which share only the requirement of mental effort—all of which cost only the time of thinking and do not expose the knower to any risk. Next are those that cost something, cost perhaps money, or physical effort, or public exposure, or . . . These are verified by investing oneself. Next are those for which one would have to SACRIFICE HIS LIFE. A truth one would die for compels in a way far beyond the truths one can verify in an armchair of a library. But Rosenzweig takes the scale one more step: to those truths which the whole human race could verify and verify precisely by risking its life again and again. Something so high that the judgment of its verification cannot come in time. Or perhaps Rosenzweig is thinking not of the truths of humanity but those of Judaism. Generation after generation has risked its life for truths to which a people bears testimony in repeated exposure to death and humiliation. Such a verification exceeds the range a 'normal' theory of knowledge can entertain. How can one person justify a truth claim of that sort? Only a community, a people, or the whole of humanity can bear witness to it. And when can it be proven?

B. EMPIRICISMS: ABSOLUTE AND RADICAL

The need for a future for thinking pragmatically has become the need for a messianic future for verifying the highest truths. But all talk of verification is bound to some theory of experience. Clearly, experience itself will not be mere reception of sense-data. Rather, experience is the interpretation of the pragmatic relations, experience as social experience and even redemptive experience. But a theory of knowledge also requires a label as theory. Why should we label Rosenzweig an empiricist?

3a) Rosenzweig NT 160–61/101–2
Truly this work, where I sought to
explain the New Thinking, turned
against some slogans with an especially excessive opposition (beyond
the special aversion against all isms);
should I nonetheless let this book be
tied down to the usual counterpart
of those isms? Can I do it?

At the end of his essay Rosenzweig has
still not offered a slogan for the interment
of his method—a postmortem would not
elicit further thinking but would allow us
to not think further, to already know
what *The Star* is about and so make future
reading of it riskless. Moreover, Rosenzweig has railed against 'isms' throughout
the essay for reasons connected to the

need for verifying truth. He admits an excess and now fears that his book
will be labeled anyway, labeled AS THE USUAL COUNTERPART OF THOSE ISMS.
The ism of greatest opposition was idealism—because in idealism the ideas
can develop themselves at once, and they brook no interruption from other
people, from the particularity of experience. Rosenzweig fears that he will be
simply labeled an empiricist—and in this he might even relish the argument
of Derrida, who labels Levinas an empiricist for opposing totality. Rosenzweig hesitates to label his own thought, but he also realizes that it will be
labeled, willy-nilly, and so his choice is to let it be labeled by another or label
it himself. CAN he DO IT?

3b) Most nearly I would have to
allow the designation absolute empiricism; at least it would cover the
peculiar approach of New Thinking
in all three regions—the preworld of
the concept, the world of actuality,
and the hyperworld of truth.[3]

His choice is ABSOLUTE EMPIRICISM, not
simply empiricist (which was the default
label for an idealism's opposite), but an
absolute variety. This ABSOLUTE provides
a conjunction of several varieties of experience. It provides for logic and concepts

---

[3] Levinas TI 170/196   An articulation analogous to the ontological argument is produced
here: an exteriority of a being is inscribed in its essence. Except that here it not articulated as a
reasoning, but the epiphany that occurs as a face. The metaphysical desire of the absolutely
other which animates intellectualism (or the radical empiricism that confides in the teaching
of exteriority) deploys its *en-ergy* in the vision of the face, or in the idea the infinite. The idea
of infinite exceeds my powers (not quantitatively, but, we will see later, by putting them
into question.) It does not come from our a priori depths—it is consequently experience par
excellence.

Levinas DF 262–63/188   Rosenzweig denounces this totality and this way of seeking to
achieve totality through reduction. Totality in fact gives no meaning to death, which each dies
for himself. Death is irreducible. We must therefore turn back from philosophy which reduces
what is irreducible to experience. An empiricism which is in no way positivist.

Derrida WD 225/152   Despite the Husserlian and Heideggerian stages of his thought, Levinas
does not even draw back from the word *empiricism*. On two occasions at least he appeals to
"the radical empiricism that confides in the teaching of exteriority" (TI). The experience of the
other (of the infinite) is irreducible, and is therefore, "experience par excellence" (ibid.). And
concerning death which is indeed its irreducible resource, Levinas speaks of an "empiricism
which is in no way positivist."

Derrida DS 39–40/33   The breakthrough toward radical otherness (with respect to the philo-

in a world without language, without relations; for relations performed in language, and for a verification that steps beyond language. What is experienced is not only sensual, but also logical experience and social experience. The method concerns the concepts, the performance of the using signs, and the verification of the knowledge afforded by the conjunction of signs and concepts (truth). This is, if you will, a thick concept of experience. And were Rosenzweig to be labeled a mere empiricist, at least two-thirds of his thought about experience would make little sense.

3c) This approach, that also knows to know nothing about heavenly things, except what it has experienced—this, however, also is actual, even if philosophy already slandered it as knowledge 'beyond' all 'possible' experience—and also to know nothing about the earthly things, which it has not experienced—this, however, is not at all what philosophy praised as the knowledge 'before' all 'possible' experience.

But Rosenzweig now seems to take up a battle again with philosophy, particularly German idealism, and to echo Socrates' own apology. For Socrates claims not to know, or indeed KNOWS TO KNOW NOTHING—particularly about HEAVENLY THINGS. Yet Rosenzweig qualifies Socrates, by permitting WHAT IT HAS EXPERIENCED—that God can reveal himself in language to people. Not speculation about God's nature, but what is experienced. And philosophy had dismissed as 'BEYOND' ALL 'POSSIBLE' EXPERIENCE just this mode of experience—experiences that arise in using signs. Rosenzweig also restricts claims about earthly things to what has been experienced, objecting that philosophy had contented itself with the 'in advance,' with the conditions for possible ex-

---

sophical concept—to the concept) always takes, *within philosophy*, the *form* of an a posteriority or an empiricism. But this concerns there an effect of the specular reflection of the philosophy that cannot inscribe (comprehend) what is outside it except by assimilating the negative image of it, and the dissemination is written on the back—the *tain*—of that mirror. Not on its inverted specter. Nor in the triadic symbolic order of its sublimation. The question is to find out what it is that, written under the mask of empiricism, turning speculation upside down, *also does something else* and renders a Hegelian sublimation of the preface impracticable. This question calls for prudent, differentiated, slow, stratified readings.

Derrida GL 232/162   Within the closure, one can only judge its style as a function of the accepted oppositions. It may be said that this style is empiricist and in a certain way that would be correct. The *departure* is radically empiricist. It proceeds like a wandering thought on the possibility of itinerary and of method. It is affected by nonknowledge as by its future and it *ventures out* deliberately. We ourselves have defined the form and the vulnerability of this empiricism. But here the very concept of empiricism destroys itself. To *exceed* the metaphysical orb is an attempt to escape the orbit (*orbita*), to think the entirety of the classical conceptual oppositions, particularly the one within which the value of empiricism is held: the opposition of philosophy and nonphilosophy, another name for empiricism, for this inability to sustain on one's own and to the limit on the coherence of one's own discourse, for being produced as truth at the moment when the value of truth is shattered, for escaping the internal contradictions of skepticism, and so on.

perience, THE KNOWLEDGE 'BEFORE' ALL 'POSSIBLE' EXPERIENCE. In both cases Rosenzweig accentuates the false claim to catalogue 'possible' experience—not that there can be no proper discussion of what is possible, but that philosophy had contented itself with a much too limited account of this 'POSSIBLE.' It excluded the access to God through revelation in language, and it failed to distinguish between the conditions of knowing the possible world and knowing the existent world, the created world. Rosenzweig is not opening the gates of heaven for an inundation of mystical and numinous veridical experiences, but rather looking to the use of signs, to speech-thinking, to break through from an empty transcendental possibility into existence. The relations struck in using language, in speech, are the central topic of experience, a topic that philosophy (and much empiricism) had neglected.

3d) Such trust in experience would be really what is teachable and transmittable of the New Thinking, if it is not, as in any case I fear, already itself a sign of a renewed thinking—and if the same given slogan is not itself one of the notes, which precisely because they come from the author himself, appear to the reader, like certainly many others from the previous pages, in part not simply easy, but all too easy and also in part harder than the book itself.

And so the key insight of speech-thinking, of Rosenzweig's pragmatics, is a TRUST IN EXPERIENCE, but an experience permeated by signs and interpretation, by traces and experience of logic, and culminating in the experience of verifying knowledge through social action. Yet, he fears, again, that formulating the theory of knowledge will allow for a RENEWAL of old thinking—and not its replacement by new thinking. To interpret his own book by his authority reduces the need to think in response to either the essay or the book. An act of pragmatic thinking calls for further pragmatic thinking—by others. If the author retains his authority, he circumvents the reader's, tempting the reader to know too much in advance. The author ignores the range of readers' readings. The author's interpretation is both TOO EASY and too HARD—simplifying the pragmatics of reading but also leading the reader to think that only reproducing that authorized interpretation is adequate. This theory of theorizing, the pragmatics of pragmatics, may collapse the range of the pragmatics of interpretation, or at least complicate it beyond its original shape. A problem that we cannot circumvent in this book either.

I now turn to radical empiricism, an empiricism that resembles the absolute kind. There is only one reference to James in Rosenzweig's writings, and it indicates only familiarity with James' image in general European culture—as expected in psychology and 'religious experience.' My turning to James is motivated, then, by the striking affinity of the two empiricisms. It is an affinity that also will help us connect speech-thinking with pragmatism and with pragmatics itself. Our concern, therefore, is not to engage in a tendentious search for influences—rather, we will try to connect up the method of

Rosenzweig with the way of thinking that was developed, over twenty years earlier, in America.

I begin with one of several passages that define radical empiricism.

4a) James MT 6–7   I am interested in another doctrine in philosophy to which I give the name of radical empiricism, and it seems to me that the establishment of the pragmatist theory of truth is a step of first-rate importance in making radical empiricism prevail. Radical empiricism consists first of a postulate, next of a statement of fact, and finally of a generalized conclusion.

In *The Meaning of Truth*, James sets out to defend pragmatism and particularly the concept of truth it requires. James immediately announces that he is now defending a larger theory, of which pragmatism is only one representative. That larger theory needs a new name, so he calls it RADICAL EMPIRICISM. James hopes that the PRAGMATIST THEORY OF TRUTH will contribute to justifying the larger theory—and in this we see a parallel with Rosenzweig's need for a theory of truth as verification in order to make his absolute empiricism work. But before we look at James' theory of truth, we need a definition of this empiricism.

4b)   The postulate is that the only things that shall be debatable among philosophers shall be things definable in terms drawn from experience.

James starts with a POSTULATE. He will not deduce or prove this, but he does show its value in philosophy. More to the point, it does not stipulate what is real or good, but is only a methodological rule, determining what SHALL BE DEBATABLE. Moreover, it does not say that only experience is real, but rather looks to what is DEFINABLE IN TERMS DRAWN FROM EXPERIENCE. Thus, the postulate limits debate to things for which we can provide an experiential definition—the question is how to define, not what is. James will soon open this range of what experience can define beyond what most empiricists can tolerate.

4c)   The statement of fact is that the relations between things, conjunctive as well as disjunctive, are just as much matters of direct particular experience, neither more so nor less so, than the things themselves.[4]

Unlike the postulate, THE STATEMENT OF FACT concerns experience itself and not just our debate about it. The fact is: RELATIONS are given to DIRECT EXPERIENCE. These relations are between distinct things, and they are both relations of CONJUNCTION AND DISJUNCTION. Conjunction Rosenzweig called the little word: *and*. Disjunctive relations, on the other hand, are the ones that set the two things apart: the distance between two things. James requires that we can experience relations that obtain between separate beings—and indeed, we can experience the relations just as

---

[4] Levinas TI 9/39   But I who have no common concept with the Stranger, I, like him, lack a genus. We are the Same and the Other. The conjunction *and* indicates neither addition nor the power of one term over the other. We shall try to show the *relation* of the Same and the Other—upon which we seem to impose such extraordinary conditions—is language.

much as we might experience the things. Radical empiricism, therefore, takes relations seriously—as given in experience, and not as merely constructed by thought.

4d) The generalized conclusion is that therefore the parts of experience hold together from next to next by relations that are themselves parts of experience. The directly apprehended universe needs, in short, no extraneous transempirical connective support, but possesses in its own right a concatenated or continuous structure.

THE GENERALIZED CONCLUSION is the combination of the rule for discussion with the fact of the experience of relations. In short, we are given a practical syllogism here. The conclusion is in the form of veiled imperative: do not look beyond experience for some TRANSEMPIRICAL CONNECTION—look in the world given in experience. While Rosenzweig found the relations of one thing to the next to be language, indeed language speaking, James here does not opt for such a turn to language. Rather, he settles for a more 'basic' claim: relations are THEMSELVES PARTS OF EXPERIENCE. The result is that experience already involves connections. It is CONCATENATED, that is, linked together—and we experience the links. Indeed, perhaps one point to note here is that we can experience the links, as *links*. Experience seems to come in two flavors for James: things and relations—but maybe there is still a third flavor: a three-part relation (for our interest this will occur more clearly in Royce and Peirce).

Rosenzweig's construction of elements in Part I of *The Star* provided to each element (God, world, human) its own intrinsic unity—without requiring the intervention of another. Thus the world hung together without God's action and without human cognition. Experience itself provides the connections—and in Rosenzweig's case, the key relation between human beings and the world occurs in speech. That these relations between things are themselves a mode of signifying is not clear in James. But that relations are experienced, and that we find relations without transcending experience, are the thrusts of both radical and absolute empiricism. Moreover, for both accounts of relations the concept of truth is transformed.

C. PRAGMATISM AND PRAGMATICISM

James was hardly the inventor of pragmatism—that occurred in a circle in Cambridge, Massachusetts, in the 1870s, and indeed it was early essays of Peirce that established a pragmatist maxim. But James reinvigorated pragmatism at the turn of the century, and while Peirce tried to reclaim his progeny, James' popularization retained the copyright. James wrote a book entitled *Pragmatism* in 1907, and there championed both the method and particularly the theory of truth. He moved the focus from an objectivist notion of truth in itself to verification of truth. In this passage, we can easily enough see the similarity with Rosenzweig's interpretation of truth.

5a) James P 97   Pragmatism, on the other hand, asks its usual question. "Grant an idea or belief to be true," it says, "what concrete difference will its being true make in anyone's actual life? How will the truth be realized? What experiences will be different from those which would obtain if the belief were false? What, in short, is the truth's cash-value in experiential terms?"

James discusses what makes an idea true. His opponents presuppose "an inert static relation" (P 96). Truth is a question of knowing what is—and it does not change me, the knower. But the USUAL QUESTION of pragmatism, that is, the way of proceeding, is to ask WHAT DIFFERENCE WILL IT MAKE IN ANYONE'S ACTUAL LIFE? (This, to be sure, is James' way of proceeding, and Peirce might well qualify it—but the point is familiar: truth is something that makes a difference in my life, not only in my head.) The concept of truth will produce some DIFFERENT EXPERIENCES. An idea that merely resolves a theoretical conundrum, which doesn't make any difference to someone who 'knows' it or 'adheres' to it, simply is empty. The economic term CASH-VALUE reminds one of the cost analysis we have seen in Rosenzweig. James' account requires 'profits,' not investments, but it follows a similar line. For the question HOW WILL THE TRUTH BE REALIZED? points to the task of realizing it, of making a difference in our lives.

5b)   The moment pragmatism asks this question, it sees the answer: *True ideas are those that we can assimilate, validate, corroborate, and verify. False ideas are those that we cannot.* This is the practical difference it makes to us to have true ideas; that, therefore, is the meaning of truth, for it is all that truth is known-as.

Hence, there is an immediate answer for pragmatism: truth is verifiability. James himself explains this in emphatic italics with a sequence of activities that constitute the truth of an idea. *ASSIMILATE*: to make the truth mine—not anyone's truth, not true for others but not for me, but rather, something which I can make my own. *VALIDATE*: my activities, in a laboratory, for instance, or in my social life, must redeem the validity claims. The truth is dependent on my ability to prove the claims implicit and explicit in the idea. *CORROBORATE*: the knower must bring evidence, must be able to offer his or her own experience of the idea. And finally, *VERIFY*, which in some ways seems to subsume the other activities. If there is no way to bring the idea into experience, it is not true, indeed, James claims here that it is FALSE. Hence, THE MEANING OF TRUTH, the value of this concept, lies in what practical difference it makes to us—practicality not being merely what chores it performs, but how our life changes under its impact. Because radical empiricism is about the relations between things, the truth itself is a particular kind of relation requiring activity by the knower.

5c)   This thesis is what I have to defend. The truth of an idea is not a stagnant property inherent in it. Truth *happens* to an idea. It *be-*

Ideas *are not* in a state of truth. They *BECOME* true. The relation of truth is achieved, and can be *MADE*. This theory calls for activities by which ideas are made

comes true, is *made* true by events. Its verity *is* in fact an event, a process: the process, namely, of its veri-fying itself, its veri-*fication*. Its validity is the process of valid-*ation*.

true. Here, too, James does not represent a linguistic turn, and yet he grasps the temporality of truth, that it is not A STAGNANT PROPERTY INHERENT IN an idea. Pragmatism requires not merely a dynamic concept, but also one which is not necessary, not some lockstep dialectic producing the next truth by strict causal connection. Rather, the relation between an idea and a knower opens into an undetermined future, and so requires a process of testing, of trying it on, of checking up on the inferences drawn from an idea, in order to make the idea true. James accentuates the processive activity by hyphenating and italicizing the fication in VERI-*FICATION*. For our purposes, moreover, the truth of an ethical theory will not be in the ideas of the theory, but in the processes of making the theory true—processes that are bound to a range of experiences. For our theory, indeed, it is the processes of using signs that must corroborate the theory, if the theory is to become true. The theory is not true without such recourse to experiences of how signs are used: experiences like the four social judgments that perform the four modes of the logic of generals.

Peirce is the 'originator' of pragmatism. He first proposed a pragmatic maxim in 1878, but felt compelled to restate it as *pragmaticism* in 1905. The gap centers around the real possibility that is not actualized. Verification is not reducible to what happens but to what would reasonably happen. We need to clarify the need for possibility in pragmaticism, for Peirce's critique of James feared a nominalism that denied reality (not existence itself) to whatever was not experienced. This emphasis on possibility is the space for ethics—but for Peirce its role is also vital for science and for all intellectual endeavor. His suspension of a rigorous immanentism, that only what occurs is valid, is a requirement also for ethics: where what ought to be often does not occur. An ethics must still be verifiable as the would-be's of the future, but not simply verified in the present.

Real possibility arises in the characteristic of signs that Peirce calls generality. Moreover, contingency and transcendence are in play in the use of signs: again, pragmatics offers a privileged insight into how responsibility is an exigency that lacks compulsion. To open up a space for real possibility is to open the authority of an interpreter to improvise a new meaning for a sign: this improvisation appears both when I give and when I receive signs. Peirce's later essays on pragmaticism are in constant recourse to the earlier ones (which so influenced Royce, James, and others). Indeed, the reinterpretation of his own words, even through rephrasing, is characteristic of Peirce's semiotic. We look to "Issues in Pragmaticism," one of a set of articles published in 1905, that marks his own shift to the new term.

6a) Peirce CP 5:438 Pragmatism was originally enounced in the form

Peirce begins this article by stating, and then restating, the pragmatic maxim. We should note that he cites the earlier text,

of a maxim as follows: consider what effects that might *conceivably* have practical bearings you *conceive* the objects of your *conception* to have. Then your *conception* of those effects is the whole of your *conception* of the object.

precisely through repetition to distance himself from the earlier formulation. The original essay is called "How to Make Our Ideas Clear" and was published in 1878. But at the same time he resorts to accenting with italics five times, marking what he claims as the key to the earlier statement. The maxim concerns CONCEPTION, focusing on what one conceives, on what is conceivable, and on the conceptions one makes. Pragmatism is a rule for thinking, first of all. The rule claims that the content of what is thought is limited to the EFFECTS of a PRACTICAL BEARING that *would* result from the thought. The meaning of a thought is identified only with the practical consequences that flow from thinking some thought of an object. One is to think about (CONSIDER) the practical effects of some object of thought. Only what can be thought of as a practical effect can be thought of properly.

6b) I will restate this in other words, since oft times one can thus eliminate some unsuspected source of perplexity to the reader. This time it shall be in the indicative mood, as follows: The entire intellectual purport of any symbol consists in the total of all general modes of rational conduct which, conditionally upon all the possible different circumstances and desires, would ensue upon the acceptance of the symbol.[5]

But Peirce RESTATES the maxim. Variation seems to help clarify an idea: repetition in itself is inadequate, especially in the case of a maxim that has been taken as a slogan. The rephrasing, however, sets the maxim not as a practical maxim (in the imperative), but now as a definition (IN THE INDICATIVE MOOD). It no longer is a command to think, but concerns more clearly the way one would act if one accepted a thought. The relation of thinking and practice is subtly shifted here, as

[5] Peirce CP 5:453   . . . Classification is true or false, and the generals to which it refers are either reals in the one case, or figments in the other. For if the reader will turn to the original maxim of pragmaticism at the beginning of this article, he will see that the question is, not what *did* happen, but whether it would have been well to engage in any line of conduct whose successful issue depended upon whether the diamond *would* resist an attempt to scratch it, or whether all other logical means of determining how it ought to be classed *would* lead to the conclusion which, to quote the very words of that article, would be "the belief which alone could be the result of investigation carried '*sufficiently far*.'" Pragmaticism makes the ultimate intellectual purport of what you please to consist in conceived conditional resolutions, or their substance; and therefore, the conditional proposition, with their hypothetical antecedents, in which such resolutions consist, being of the ultimate nature of meaning, must be capable of being true, that is, of expressing whatever there be which is such as the proposition expresses, independently of being thought to be so in any judgment, or being represented to be so in any other symbol of any man or men. But that amounts to saying that possibility is sometimes of a real kind.

James MT 111   Intellectualist truth is then only pragmatist truth *in posse*. That on innumerable occasions men do substitute truth *in posse* or verifiability, for verification, or truth in act,

thought itself seems to be for the sake of RATIONAL CONDUCT. At the same time Peirce understands that there is an INTELLECTUAL PURPORT, that thought is not merely analyzable for its practical effects, but it has its own sort of purpose: the development of GENERAL MODES OF RATIONAL CONDUCT. Instead of the contents of a thought, Peirce now considers the intent of the thought, and the sense of practice is now reconfigured in terms of habits or dispositions that are not mechanical but general and open to disturbance. Peirce is saying that the answer to Why Think? is in order to give a general direction to my rational conduct, to transform my conduct, or at least my general habits. Peirce is clarifying the relation of thought and practice: thought is to guide practice, but thought's content is the consequent practices. This seems, precisely because of its subjunctive mood, to take us beyond the empiricism of what now is or what was into a realm where thoughts are verified in practice. Peirce is concerned with the logic of experience: binding logic to the range of practical modes that follow from accepting an idea. The SYMBOL, therefore, requires interpretation in order to gain its meaning. And interpretation takes us beyond the bounds of simple cogitation, into kinds of rational conduct. Thinking itself is one mode of rational conduct, but it is not isolated from all other possible modes. Clearly the meaning of a thought has a certain range of possible CIRCUMSTANCES AND DESIRES, meanings that would appear in the future. Interpretation is, in this context, the reflection about what sorts of conduct would follow, not merely what the material consequences of an idea are. Peirce emphasizes the possibilities of action, not the achieved results, precisely because he is discussing the range of the meaning of the thought. The possibilities here are the possibilities in interpreting the real symbol—the range of interpretants that each symbol admits. But the pragmatic range of interpretants is a range of real possibles, not limited to extant objects, nor open to a limitless arbitrary play of signs.

Peirce's choice of mood (subjunctive versus indicative, indicative versus imperative) is also complicated by a statement made in 1903 in a series of lectures on pragmatism. Here we find the clearest relation of indicative to imperative, the relation of practical truth.

7) Peirce CP 5:18 Pragmatism is the principle that every theoretical judgment expressible in a sentence in the indicative mood is a confused

Again, we cannot miss the point that pragmatism concerns THEORETICAL JUDGMENTS. The claim, however, is that A SENTENCE IN THE INDICATIVE MOOD has its

is a fact to which no one attributes more importance than the pragmatist: he emphasizes the practical utility of such a habit. But he does not on that account consider truth *in posse*—truth not alive enough ever to have been asserted or questioned or contradicted—to be the metaphysically prior thing, to which truths in act are tributary and subsidiary. When intellectualists do this, pragmatism charges them with inverting the real relation. Truth in posse *means* only truths in act; and he insists that these latter take precedence in the order of logic as well as in that of being.

form of thought whose only mean- | only meaning as a maxim IN THE IMPERA-
ing, if it has any, lies in its tendency TIVE MOOD. Now, the maxim itself is
to enforce a corresponding practical duplex: it is a conditional sentence whose
maxim expressible as a conditional conclusion is a command. The meaning of
sentence having its apodosis in the a theoretical statement is a translation of
imperative mood. the sort: if that is the case, then you must

do this. Peirce claims that indicative statements are confused: one may or
may not have meaning, because we may not be able to figure out a proper
command for it. Theory, therefore, is meaningful when it can issue conditional commands—just the sort of imperatives that Kant called pragmatic
and not categorical. Lacking any practical expression, a theoretical concept
is meaningless. The discussion of logic in Part II displays precisely how logic
of particulars and generals might produce such conditional commands. A
coordinating universal requires social actions of coordination to be meaningful. But for the question about theory, there is still more here. Theory
itself does not transpire in the imperative, even ethical theory. Theoretical
judgments are indicatives. The question one asks of a theory, as a pragmatist
or a pragmaticist, is how we could translate that into practice: but the practice at stake is itself not categorical, only conditional. Pragmatism is the
translator, the interpreter of theory, teaching us how to recast theory into
practical maxims. But if we are engaged in an ethical theory, then we are
seeking to find the practices that verify the theory—the ethics that we are
discussing in the indicative.

We verify to make an ethical theory ethical, to return our theories from
the plane of theory (in the indicative) to the level of practice. The responsibility to verify pertains to theory as theory, accentuating the ethical dimension
of theory. A theory of theory recurs here, and it bears with it the claim that
all theory is ethical, or has an ethical responsibility to become ethical—but
at the same time it does not refuse theory, or even a meta-theory about how
to determine the meaning of a theory. Pragmatism, in the interpretation
given here of James and Peirce, is not only *not* antitheoretical, it is positively
theoretical: a meta-theory that examines how theories become practical, or
if you prefer, an interpretation of how general signs are verified. That signs
are at once cognitive and practical is key to the development in the first two
parts of this book. That an indicative requires a translation into a conditional imperative, a joining of indicative and imperative, is perhaps the core
of our interpretation of signs. But that pragmatism is the theoretical vantage
point from which best to interpret the pragmatics of these issues in interpreting signs is the central achievement of this chapter.

Suggested Readings

3   Casper, Bernhard. "Responsibility Rescued." In *The Philosophy of Franz Ro-senzweig*, 89–105. Ed. Paul Mendes-Flohr. Hanover and London: University Press of New England for Brandeis University Press, 1988.

6   Apel, Karl-Otto. *Charles S. Peirce: From Pragmatism to Pragmaticism*. Trans. John Michael Krois. Amherst: University of Massachusetts Press, 1981.

Bernstein, Richard J. "Action, Conduct, and Self-Control." In *Perspectives on Peirce*, 66–90. Ed. Richard J. Bernstein. New Haven, Conn.: Yale University Press, 1965.

Misak, C.J. *Verificationism: Its History and Prospects*, 97–127. New York: Routledge, 1995.

Ochs, Peter. *Peirce, Pragmatism and the Logic of Scripture*. Cambridge: Cambridge University Press, 1998.

CHAPTER 11

Why Thirds?

EXPERIENCE seems to promise verification by an achievable present event, where something happens, so that we can know our theory is true. But responsibility, alas, does not occur in a realm of certainty—neither in relation to one other person, nor in communities, nor should it surprise us, in the theorizing about responsibility. Already in Peirce's demand to recognize the generality of the meaning of a concept or symbol, we saw the reduction to immanence (either achieved or securable) contested. The space of would-be's disrupts the certainty that we might associate with empiricism. The question, Why Thirds?, is one of the places where many roads through this book converge: for the third is not only a property of Peirce's semiotics and phenomenology, it also conducted us from the responsible situation attending one other person to the social need for justice in Levinas. And for both thinkers the third is characteristic of theory and its exigency. One of the challenging tasks here is to connect Levinas to Peirce, through the intermediaries of Royce and Marcel. The guiding question concerns the way that thirds are required for knowing, or more precisely, for verifying. The departure from the concreteness of an asymmetrical index to the generality of a symbol is the repetition of the move we saw in Part II in mediating—not merely inescapable but in its own way part of the responsibilities of justice. To compromise the asymmetry by framing a theory of asymmetry is one of the singular characteristics of pragmatics.

The chapter starts with Levinas and the impossibility for language to signify only in private. Equality and the demand for justice are linked to the thirdness of language itself. Pretext 2 introduces Gabriel Marcel, whose work had profound influence on Levinas. Marcel explores how the direct responsibility between I and you is effaced in reflecting upon it, making the dialogue into a third something. Section B (Interpretation and Thirds) traces this thirdness back through Royce to Peirce. The stakes will be a fundamental insight into how signs work: by relating indexicality and iconicity for a third. Royce interprets a translator who not only grasps the meaning of a text but offers it to another (a third). Then we consider two definitions of thirdness in signifying in Pretexts 6–7 by Peirce. The absence of a third is the absence of interpretable meaning for another; thus the practice of framing theories depends on the invocation of thirds.

A. The Third Person

Levinas' account of the relation between the other person and me was a point of departure for this work. We noticed there the asymmetry of the face, and in Part II, we discussed how the entry of a third person was the cradle for knowledge and reason. But the two moments separated between Parts I and II interweave in the address of the face, in language.

1a) Levinas TI 187–88/213 Language, as presence of the face, does not invite us to a complicity with a preferred being, to the "I-thou" which is self-sufficient and forgets the universe. In its frankness, language refuses the secrecy of love where it loses its frankness and its meaning and transforms itself into laughter and cooing.

Perhaps the point by now is not as surprising: language has two roles at once: to maintain the asymmetry of the two-term relation, and to depart from that relation. In Part IV, moreover, we will see yet a third role for language in repairing signs. But in this text Levinas examines the tension of these two roles. Were the function of signs reduced only to that two-term relation, it would FORGET THE UNIVERSE. Speaking is not exclusive, is not a private matter. And perhaps this is why Levinas is so circumspect about both the "I-THOU" and dialogue in general. Such 'honeymoon' language in LAUGHTER AND COOING undermines the FRANKNESS of language, making the facing in speaking into a mere play, undermining the responsibility in response to another.

1b) The third looks at me in the eyes of the other person—language is justice. It is not that first there would be the face, and then the being that it shows or expresses, who is concerned with justice.

Pragmatics requires a third person, and LANGUAGE IS JUSTICE. Not only the one to whom I must respond, the one whose authority appears in speaking to me, but also others (THE THIRD) exercise authority over me (LOOKS AT ME), in the person of my interlocutor. I am addressed on behalf of not only one who can contest my interpretations, but for all who may. Moreover, there is no temporal sequence here. There is not FIRST a face, AND THEN someone who represents others. Of course, we presented these two aspects sequentially in Part I and Part II, but they are not sequential in using language. In use, language is both two-term and three-term relations.

1c) The epiphany of the face as face opens up humanity. The face, in its nudity of the face, presents to me the destitution of the poor and of the stranger; but this poverty and this exile, that call to my capacities, sight me, and do not deliver themselves to my capacities like givens, but remain the expression of a face.

Hence the general (HUMANITY) confronts me in the one interlocutor. DESTITUTION is not uniquely the other person's property, but invokes the social dimension of poverty, of exile. All of the hungry confront me, not only this one—the open-ended iterability of signs is retained (REMAIN THE EXPRESSION OF A FACE). I cannot take the signs that confront me in the face and keep them out of social conversation—and so other calls from the destitute accost me in the particular one that now addresses me.

1d) The poor one, the stranger, presents himself as an equal. His equality in this essential poverty consists in referring himself to the *third*, thus present at the encounter and whom, in the midst of its destitution, the Other Person already serves. He *joins* with me. But he joins me to him in order to serve.

Paradoxically, the height and the humility of the other person also is equality—the instigation of social relations. Such equality CONSISTS IN REFERRING HIMSELF TO THE *THIRD*. My interlocutor also requires me to answer to another person, another hungry one, another who has authority over my interlocutor. For though destitute and higher than me, my teacher ALREADY SERVES AN OTHER PERSON. These relations with a third, each serving an other, produce cooperation, an equality of authority (or of lack of authority). HE *JOINS* HIMSELF TO ME. His joining is the possibility for each to share with the other—but IN ORDER TO SERVE—the responsibility for others. In order to listen to others, we are granted limited authority to speak. In each word I speak, I exercise that authority precisely because of the public and open-ended process of interpreting. Signs are not private, and the authority that allows for social cooperation is generated in a context of asymmetrical relations. Without that asymmetry, the three-term relation would only be an oppressive one-term relation: everything would simply fall under the sway of a genus and only exist or have authority insofar as it instantiated that one. Signs are themselves not insistent on the one, but are for the other. And they are not only for the other but among others.

While Levinas does not develop the relation of the third as one of his primary themes, we have done so, particularly in Part II. Here, however, we are examining not the third person as much as the methodological importance of the third. In Levinas the origin of knowledge and justice lies there, but the concern applies also to the very reflection about the two-term relation from another to me. As reflection, that reflection about using signs seems to invoke a third and to disrupt the asymmetry of the relation to another. That is, the theory seems to undo the exigency in experience. If Rosenzweig made theory risky in order to preserve the futurity of meaning, then here we have a parallel problem: how to use signs to indicate what is properly pragmatic: the qualities of the signifying and not of the sign.

Levinas did not invent his interpretation of the asymmetry of ethics, but adapted and transformed various previous interpretations. Gabriel Marcel's interpretation was prominent in Levinas' milieu. Elsewhere I began the task of examining their relationship, a task that is conceptually extremely rich, for Marcel carefully develops many of the phenomenological studies that Levinas uses for his own thought: hospitality, donation of meaning, unverifiability, witness, and the third. For Marcel, the third enters disrupting the I-you relationship. Levinas distances himself from the I-you, in part because of the intimacy in Marcel's treatment, in part because of the reciprocity in

Buber's treatment. Thus, I do not turn here to Marcel in order to understand the I-you—we have seen Levinas' suspicion of defining ethics through that relation. But in Marcel we can see how the entry of the third disrupts the two-term relation. Moreover, we can see how thought transforms the relation in its use of language, looking at it from outside.

Such escape is bound to the knowable world. In a journal passage from 1918 that Marcel himself cites again in later works, he considers the third at the very moment when he makes the discovery of the I-you. Unlike Buber, however, there is no analysis of the I-you without the "he," without the third. Both thinkers would claim that the moments of I-you are short-lived, and that the other relation intrudes. But Marcel goes much further than Buber. (In passing I might mention that this is the very week Rosenzweig began writing *The Star* at the Eastern front.) We can begin with the *I* and the *you*: to say "I" is to say it to some "you," and here Marcel makes the relation symmetric—a symmetry he later qualifies. But here we see the I-you in its symmetry, in order to observe the intricate relation to thirds.

2a) Marcel MJ 145/146   23 August 1918. But this *I* appears to be posited always facing a you, for whom I am myself a *you*; and it is as a function of this dialogue and in relation to it that a *him* can be defined, which is to say, an independent world or at least treated as such (fictively no doubt).[1]

THIS *I* is the "I" of assertion, of utterance. Such speaking is POSITED FACING A YOU. Marcel understands the pragmatics of the speech situation as an address to another person, not as pure activity of the "I." Moreover, to address another person is also to be addressable, to be A YOU for this other. Just as I must speak to someone, I perceive that someone can also speak to me, making me into a 'you.' Our hesitation, from Levinas' work, is that to be addressed is not merely the inverse of addressing someone. In any case the third, A HIM, is both a FUNCTION of the speaking and CAN BE DEFINED IN RELATION TO IT. The function seems to mean that in its working, a dialogue produces a third. The definition implies that what the third means, what it does, can be recognized in relation to the two-term relation. The third functions as an outside, as a context, for the dialogue: AN INDEPENDENT WORLD. Or at least the implication of one as the presupposition for an I-you dialogue. Thus the intimacy of the I-you produces and seems to require the assumption of others, of a stable context that does not immediately depend on the speakers.

[1] Marcel MJ 293–94/303   5 March 1923. Following a conversation with B. I must recognize that it is absurd to speak of *the* 'you' and thus to take substantively that which is fundamentally the very negation of all substantiality. In reality, when I objectify, after having isolated, a certain aspect of the experience of intimacy; I detach from the *we* the element of the 'non-I' and call it the 'you.' This element automatically tends to take the figure of *him*; and it is only to the extent that I succeed in reviving that experience after the fact that I am able to resist this temptation. But can I examine myself concerning the immutability of that 'you' without converting it into a 'him'? "It's always the same!"

2b) This is the profound scope of Royce's triadism that seems to me not to have been sufficiently explicated. All independent reality, I would say in a more intelligible language, may and must be treated as a *third*.[2]

Marcel's thought arose in relation to Royce. Marcel studied Royce thoroughly and wrote studies that became a book (*Royce's Metaphysics*). He engages Royce many times in the journal and seems even later in his citation of this passage to honor Royce with decisive influence on his discovery of the I-you. In just a minute we will look at Royce's triadism in its own voice. Here, Marcel gives himself some credit for explicating THE PROFOUND SCOPE that had not been (by Royce himself, or James, or . . .) SUFFICIENTLY EXPLICATED. Marcel realizes that the American thinker as pragmatist did not arrive at the I-you, even though his triadism was the cradle of its genesis. The I-you here seems necessarily bound up with insight about the *THIRD*. For Marcel the third is a principle of INDEPENDENT REALITY, and elsewhere he will argue that all verification occurs in the third person. Indeed, in place of the somewhat obscure discussion of a HIM, Marcel calls the term A *THIRD* A MORE INTELLIGIBLE LANGUAGE. For Marcel the recourse to Royce is a clearer way of speaking. And I may hope that the switch to a semiotic vocabulary is more intelligible, because it is one of the distinctive switches that we have been pursuing throughout this book.

2c) And if a third presupposes a dialogue, it is no less true to say that all dialogue is given to itself as a third.[3]

The conclusion of Marcel's paragraph suggests the sequence of thought we most emphasize. A THIRD PRESUPPOSES A DIALOGUE: using language to know by sharing meaning in a community of possible interpreters requires the asymmetrical relation of the face-to-face. The three-term relation presupposes the two-term relation. Moreover, ALL DIALOGUE IS GIVEN TO ITSELF AS A THIRD. In the self-reflection of a speaker on the pragmatics of speech, speaking appears as a third, as a said, as something to be known: not as an asymmetric signifying. Theory of signs depends on the ethics of giving signs, but at the same time renders that giving of signs itself

---

[2] Marcel MJ 316/326   Let us notice at the outset that the object cannot not be conceived by me as "something with which I am in communication." The relation between subject and object is presented in the first case as a relation of two terms. Only, as Royce saw in his later philosophy with an admirable clearness, this is only an appearance—and that relation is in reality triadic. The *object* is characteristically *that which I am discussing with a real or ideal interlocutor:* it is as third in relation to a certain discourse which I pursue with X and which bears on it. It is in this sense interposed between me and myself, and thus the use of the somewhat surprising term *insularity* is found to be justified.

[3] Marcel MJ 154n/154n   12 December 1918. It is essential to note that all this links up with what I said about the unverifiable. All that is of the order of the *he* or *it* is verifiable; that which allows only for a dyadic relation is unverifiable (that is, it transcends verification). (It must be added that verification supposes the possibility of an indefinite number of substitutions, substitutions that on the contrary are inconceivable when I am in the presence of a *thou*. This is an essential point.)

now a sign (no longer a giving). The third is not a reiteration of secondness, but is in permanent and ineluctable tension with it. We have recouped the semiotic meaning of the third person—the generality of knowing that has compromised the indexicality of the relation to one other.

B. INTERPRETATION AND THIRDS

The relation to thirdness pervades interpretation itself, or perhaps we should say constitutes it. Indeed, the indexicality of my relation to another is not abandoned in offering a general sign. In this section we can trace the triad in Royce back through Royce to Peirce's semiotics.

What Marcel called ROYCE'S TRIADISM will help clarify the task of interpreting. In his later works Royce redeveloped his idealistic system as sign interpretation—focusing on the specific exigencies of using signs and of the ways that signs mean. In *The Problem of Christianity*, Royce argues that the Christian community is a community of interpreters—a phrase that echoes in Apel and Habermas. The community's commonality is its activity of interpreting the Christian story. In the chapter entitled "Perception, Conception, and Interpretation" he argues for the distinctive properties of the cognitive activity of interpretation. Here the triadism is most clear.

3a) Royce Ch 286–87 Interpretation always involves a relation of three terms. In the technical phrase, interpretation *is* a triadic relation. That is, you cannot express any complete process of interpreting by merely naming two terms—persons, or other objects—and by then telling what dyadic relation exists between one of these two and the other.

A THREE-TERM RELATION is surely the one we have been examining for many pages. The TECHNICAL PHRASE (TRIADIC) is clearly from Peirce. The three terms are not reducible to two terms. For when we see interpretation as a PERSON standing over against an OBJECT, we may think that to interpret is more or less like sensing the object, or thinking the concept. It is something I do to it. But, Royce objects that INTERPRETATION is a different kind of relationship.

3b) Let me illustrate: Suppose that an Egyptologist translates an inscription. So far two beings are indeed in question: the translator and his text. But a genuine translation cannot be merely a translation in the abstract. There must be some language into which the inscription is translated.

He proceeds to an illustration—itself an attempt to clarify for us, his readers, the third activity: interpretation. He posits an EGYPTOLOGIST, that is, someone with arcane knowledge, working with AN INSCRIPTION. Here is an expert using his own knowledge. But Royce posits him TRANSLATING: that is, bringing the inscription into a modern language. Translating serves as a model for interpreting. In Chapter 13 we will more fully develop a theory of translation. Translating is not done IN THE ABSTRACT. We translate into SOME LANGUAGE. Like Rosenzweig's claim that to think of speech is TO SPEAK TO SOMEONE (see above), so to translate is to translate into someone's language. The interpretation requires a consideration of its audience, its reader—its pragmatics in its being directed to someone.

3c) Let this translation be, in a given instance, an English translation. Then the translator interprets something; but he interprets it only to one who can read English. And if a reader knows no English, the translation is for such a reader no interpretation at all. That is, a triad of beings—the Egyptian text, the Egyptologist who translates, and the possible English reader—are equally necessary in order that such an English interpretation of an Egyptian writing should exist.

And almost yielding to his own audience, Royce picks ENGLISH as the target language: the very language of his listeners to these lectures. (Again, the hope to translate the arcane knowledge of Levinas, Rosenzweig, Habermas, and Derrida into a more accessible English is the very key to my project, an interpretative project not reducible to code switching.) Only a reader of English will be able to decipher the translation by the Egyptologist. Indeed, for A READER WHO KNOWS NO ENGLISH, who is perhaps fluent in modern Egyptian, or modern Chinese, and so on, this interpretation will simply not be an interpretation, *for her*. Hence the triad: the text, the interpreter, and the reader. To make an interpretation we need all three. The relation to the reader, the *for her*, is not ancillary or after the fact, but governs the whole process of translating. What is translated is obviously required, and the one who makes the interpretation, the utterer or sign-user, is clear enough in the work that we have done. The example, ironically, works by recourse to our 'native' English, by making us the recipients of both the Egyptologist's translation and the theory of it.

3d) Whenever anybody translates a text, the situation remains, however you vary texts of languages or translators, essentially the same. There must exist some one, or some class of beings, to whose use this translation is adapted; in the English text while the translator is somebody who expresses himself by mediating between two expressions of meanings, or between two languages, or between two speakers or two writers. The mediator or translator, or interpreter, must in cases of this sort himself know both languages, and thus be intelligible to both the persons whom his translation serves.

In an almost blithe manner, Royce now generalizes from this illustration: whatever the language, text, or interpreter, we always need the three things. Royce emphasizes, in an almost telltale Hegelian way, not the target language, but the translator. He EXPRESSES HIMSELF BY MEDIATING: what he has to say is bound *to* the text in question *for* the desired language. He may mediate between two people, or two meanings, or two languages— but his self is this mediation, this bridge building. Moreover, were he to translate between two speaking people, he must KNOW BOTH LANGUAGES. On the surface this seems reasonable enough, but in reality the relation to the original language is different than that to the target language. (Much as we saw a difference between listening and speaking.) But Royce could note that when going between two people, one must be able to treat each language as both target and origin—a facility that would obscure precisely how asymmetric the relation of translation is.

3e) The triadic relation in question is, in its essence, nonsymmetrical—that is, unevenly arranged with respect to all three terms. Thus somebody (let us say A)—the translator or interpreter—interprets somebody (let us say B) to somebody (let us say C). If you transpose the order of the terms—A, B, C—an account of the happening which constitutes an interpretation must be altered, or otherwise may become either false or meaningless. Thus an interpretation is a relation which not only involves three terms, but brings them into a determinate order. One of the three terms is the interpreter; a second term is the object—the person or the meaning of the text—which is interpreted; the third is the person to whom the interpretation is addressed.

So he notes. For a triadic relation IS, IN ITS ESSENCE, NONSYMMETRICAL. The third does not generalize the first two, but co-ordinates them as unequal. The trace of discrepancy is not altogether removed in the completed interpretation. He writes of this as UNEVENLY ARRANGED. Interpretation requires three terms that are not interchangeable, but are specific to the task. He now proposes a generalization of the three-term relation. A person (A) is the INTERPRETER. That person interprets something (B), which Royce claims is another person, retaining the notion that a human utterance is interpreted. And finally it is interpreted to somebody (C). (Of course A, B, and C could overlap, explaining to you what I just said, or to you what you just said, and so on, but they need not.)

Royce's sensitivity is capable of inspiring Marcel and Levinas, for the ORDER OF THE TERMS cannot be transposed without changing the very content of the activity of interpretation: indeed, it risks becoming simply FALSE OR MEANINGLESS. Royce is noting that if the text were to interpret the interpreter to the recipient, we would not have interpretation. Or if the recipient became the agent of interpretation, and not the one to whom it is given, and so on . . . The three roles are different and distinct—even though an interpretation requires all three roles. Not that we might not change roles, even midsentence, but the three roles must remain. The indexicality of the interpreter, the iconicity (what) of the utterance to be interpreted, and the symbolic openness to interpretation in the translation—these are all needed. We might notice that the *what* of interpretation is dependent on the one to whom it is interpreted—that the *for the other* is the context of the sign's referential meaning, but we cannot collapse that latter meaning into the former.

Royce's theory of interpretation is a self-conscious appropriation of Peirce's semiotic. While one might be able to follow thirds back through Hegel, and especially Kant, all the way back to the third-man argument in Plato, the pragmatic relation in the use of signs properly stops with Peirce. Throughout his works, Peirce develops the idea of triads, and particularly focuses on thirdness as a phenomenological and as a semiotic quality. Peirce's theory of signs evolved, as did the place of thirdness and meaning, but we can start with a relatively simple definition and then proceed to a more complex exposition of the three aspects of signifying.

4) Peirce CP 2:303 Anything which determines something else (its *interpretant*) to refer to an object to which itself refers (its *object*) in the same way, the interpretant becoming in turn a sign, and so on *ad infinitum*.[4]

Peirce is providing a dictionary definition of sign. Signifying requires a sign, an OBJECT, and an INTERPRETANT. The sign REFERS to its object and it produces a third something that will also REFER to that object. Thus the third (the interpretant) replicates the relation of the first two (the sign referring to its object). An interpretant is not simply an interpretation: it is an interpretation that works, that BECOMES IN TURN A SIGN. Signifying spawns signs, which to be signs must signify to further interpretants, and so on. Here is the reaching forward of interpretation beyond a particular sign, indeed beyond a particular act of signifying.

5a) Peirce CP 2:274 A *Sign*, or *Representamen*, is a First which stands in a genuine triadic relation to a Second, called its *object*, as to be capable of determining a Third, called its *Interpretant*, to assume the same triadic relation to its Object in which it stands itself to the same Object.[5]

We now shift to a more technical version of this definition, in order to see just how complex the triadic replication is. Peirce suggests a larger class in which signs occur, THE REPRESENTAMEN, and at the end of this passage suggests just what defines signs as a subclass. The larger class will include signifying relations in nature as part of Peirce's project to make nature signify and to reduce the anthropocentrism of a philosophy of consciousness. Peirce now labels the three aspects with his distinctive first, second, and third. The *INTERPRETANT* is called a third. Signifying reproduces its RELA-

---

[4] Peirce CP 1:340 The easiest of those [ideas in which Thirdness is predominant] which are of philosophical interest is the idea of a sign, or representation. A sign stands *for* something *to* the idea which it produces, or modifies. Or, it is a vehicle conveying into the mind something from without. That for which it stands is called its *object*; that which it conveys, its *meaning*; and the idea to which it gives rise, its *interpretant*.

Derrida G 72/49–50 The *representamen* functions only by giving rise to an *interpretant* that itself becomes a sign and so on to infinity. The self-identity of the signified conceals itself and moves on ceaselessly. The property [*propre*] of the *representamen* is to be itself and another, produce itself as a structure of reference, separate itself from itself. The property of the *representamen* is not to be *proper*, that is to say, absolutely *near* to itself (*prope, propius*). But the *represented* is always already a *representamen*. Definition of the sign: [the commented-on text by Peirce].

[5] Peirce CP 2:228 A sign, or *representamen*, is something which stands to somebody for something in some respect or capacity. It addresses somebody, that is, creates in the mind of that person an equivalent sign, or perhaps a more developed sign. That sign which it creates I call the *interpretant* of the first sign. The sign stands for something, its *object*. It stands for that object, not in all respects, but in reference to a sort of idea which I have sometimes called the *ground* of the representamen. "Idea" is here to be understood in a sort of Platonic sense, very familiar in everyday talk; I mean in that sense in which we say that one man catches another man's idea. . . .

TION TO ITS OBJECT in the interpretant. If we could exemplify signification by language or gesture, then the reproduction here is not that A names object B, and can make C also name object B. Rather, A gives B to C, and in so doing makes C also give B to D. Signifying is the opening of reinterpretation, of what Levinas called fecundity. The relation to the third is not merely assimilating the third to the relation a sign has to its object, but is the possibility for a new triadic relation between the third and the object—a relation that will produce another third.

5b) The triadic relation is *genuine*, that is, its three members are bound together by it in a way that does not consist in any complexus or dyadic relations. That is the reason the Interpretant, or Third, cannot stand in a mere dyadic relation to the Object, but must stand in such a relation to it as the Representamen itself does. Nor can the triadic relation in which the Third stands be merely similar to that in which the First stands, for this would make the relation of the Third to the First a degenerate Secondness merely.

That the relation is GENUINE means for Peirce that it cannot be assembled from DYADIC RELATIONS—no combination of two-term relations can produce this third. To be triadic means that the interpretant itself must reproduce the relation of sign to object, leading through the object to another interpretant. We might say that interpretation calls for further interpretation. Nor can it relate only to the FIRST, the sign, and omit the object to which the sign refers. If an interpretant lacked all relation to a referent, merely invoking further play of signs, then the interpretant would merely relate to the sign (A DEGENERATE SECONDNESS). In Peirce, secondness is the brute fact of otherness, of what cannot be simply encompassed in an idea, in a sign. The two-term relation of sign and referent is irresolvable and asymmetrical. And were the interpretant itself not to refer to the object, the interpretant would lapse into the role normally played by the object. In Royce's example of the translation, the English reader now relates to the text and can discuss it with a friend. Hence, signification requires the sign and the object and the interpretant—opening for another interpretant a relation from signifying itself to the object.

5c) The Third must indeed stand in such a relation, and thus must be capable of determining a Third of its own; but besides that, it must have a second triadic relation in which the Representamen, or rather the relation thereof to its Object, shall be its own (the Third's) object, and must be capable of determining a Third to this relation. All this must equally be true of the Third's Thirds and so on endlessly;[6]

The third has a relation to the object that requires another third. It interprets the sign, BUT BESIDES THAT, it also has a relation to the sign's relation to its object. At first, Peirce hesitates, indicating only a relation to the sign (as object), but then (OR RATHER) realizes that the sign as the interpretant's object is not mere object, but is itself a signifying, a relation of sign to object. Thus an interpretant continues interpreting the object, but it also intro-

[6] Royce Ch 290–91   Thus both perception and conception are, so to speak, self-limiting processes. The wealth of their facts comes to them from without, arbitrarily. But interpretation

duces a meta-reflection about the way that the sign signifies its object. That listener in Royce's example also thinks about how the Egyptologist interpreted the text. To understand a word is not only to understand what it is talking about, but also *the way* the word talks about it. In both cases these pairs of 'objects' are given over to another interpretant. But much as Marcel saw that the third's reflection upon the dialogue grasped the dialogue as an it, so Peirce sees that the third produces not only a new interpretation of the object, but also a methodological reflection on the way that the sign signifies the object. Moreover, this reiterates, ENDLESSLY. The infinity of signification is implicit in any act of signifying: signs are always going to spawn new interpretants, and are going themselves to become objects as the relations to their referents.

5d)   and this, and more, is involved in the familiar idea of a Sign; and as the term Representamen is here used, nothing more is implied. A *Sign* is a Representamen with a mental Interpretant.

Peirce claims that this is THE FAMILIAR IDEA OF A SIGN. The relation to a third, and then its intrinsic reproduction, and in addition its reflection upon the way that it arises for a sign relating to its object—these for Peirce are not discoveries of esoteric knowledge. Rather, these realizations are only the explication of the familiar, everyday understanding of how signs work. Hence he introduces the term REPRESENTAMEN, only to imagine a superclass, in which signs would belong. And the discriminant of the sign would be that it requires A MENTAL INTERPRETANT, but Peirce can imagine natural events, of plants and water and rocks, which also fall in this superclass. Our interest in the objects of signs is directly related to the questions of justice and communal practices and relations. In another context, we might well investigate the signs that are not themselves words, but how we would discuss natural signs is beyond the scope of this chapter.

To signify is to instigate a three-term relation, a relation that incites signifying through the third. But just because it opens to further signifying, thirdness exceeds the certainty of a single empirical event. If we consider the account in Marcel of Levinas, we see that the use of a sign can produce the theory of the specificity of my relation to another, and as theory, produce it for indefinite others. Like prophecy, this is a theory for others—not just for my interlocutor. The privacy of interaction is compromised for the sake of justice: and semiotics and ethics meet in the third.

---

both requires as its basis the sign or mental expression which is to interpreted, and calls for a further interpretation of its own act, just because it addresses itself to some third being. Thus interpretation is not only an essentially social process, but also a process which when once initiated, can be terminated only by an external and arbitrary interruption, such as death or social separation. By itself, the process of interpretation calls, in ideal, for an infinite sequence of interpretations. For every interpretation, being addressed to somebody, demands interpretation for the one to whom it is addressed.

Suggested Readings

3 Apel, Karl-Otto. *Towards a Transformation of Philosophy*, 110–27. Trans. Glyn Adey and David Frisby. London: Routledge & Kegan Paul, 1980.
   Smith, John E. *Royce's Social Infinite: The Community of Interpretation*, 2nd. ed., Chapter 3. New York: Archon Books, 1969.

4–5 Ochs, *Peirce, Pragmatism*.

CHAPTER 12

Why Me?

DESPITE THE RISK of losing the asymmetry of responsibility in formulating a theory of asymmetry, the need for justice forced us to think in general terms about the specific responsibilities that rest on me. But just as there was a motion back to attribution and judgment after the responsibility to mediate, so there is a need to see that even the responsibility to theorize and to generalize singles me out, indeed the task of thinking about ethics rests asymmetrically on me, even as my responsibility for other people produces the "me" who must respond. Responsibility invokes, even constitutes, me, the one who has to respond. While we are not propping up our ethics with a rational, autonomous subject—an "I"—to ground ethics here, indeed, we have seen, again and again, how insubstantial I am; at the very heart of this ethics is the discovery that responsibility creates a respondent position, the one who is ethically required to be responsive. The "me" is produced in responding to the demands of responsibility. The theory of indexical responsibility is not only a *theory* through thirds, but is also a theory of *indexical responsibility*—about my responsibility. The need to produce an ethics is part of *my* responsibility, and not a general responsibility that is first a universal human task and mine only deductively by individuation. Why Me? is, thus, not only about the way that I am singled out for responsibilities for others, it is also the way I am singled out to produce a theory of responsibility.

The path of this chapter mirrors the previous one, moving from semiotics to ethics, from America to France, from older to more recent in pursuit of the indexicality that installs me in a responsible position. We begin with Peirce and the distinction between *vagueness* and *generality*, claiming that vague signs reserve the right to further interpretation—like the teacher in Levinas. Pretext 2 considers Royce's account of the other's role in interpreting his own signs, making vagueness take on a social relation to the other. Section B (Me and I) will then consider George Herbert Mead's discussion of how the self becomes a "me." Role taking allows signs to signify, as I produce in myself the same response I produce in an other, and so I become myself by being the other (Pretext 3). In Pretext 4, the self emerges as the internalization of the expectations of a network of others, using the example of baseball. Here the "me" precedes the "I" as the bearer of responsibility. Finally, in Section C, a longer text from Levinas explores how the *theory* of "me" rests upon me. The choice of theorizing with "me" is rooted not merely in a good account of signification, but more important, in the responsibilities that are my own. The index breaks through the generality of the theoretical discourse.

A. INTERPRETERS AND SIGNS

The need for interpretation lies in signs themselves. Signs are never fully determinate in use: they require their interpreters or interpretants. But indeterminacy can be classified, and in so doing the question of authority can be linked to qualities of utterances—and not only to contexts. Peirce contributes an important distinction by isolating the quality of vagueness, even though he readily acknowledges that all signs are somewhat vague.

1a) Peirce CP 5:505   Logicians have too much neglected the study of *vagueness*, not suspecting the important part it plays in mathematical thought. It is the antithetical analogue of generality. A sign is objectively *general*, in so far as, leaving its effective interpretation indeterminate, it surrenders to the interpreter the right of completing the determination for himself. "Man is mortal." "What man?" "Any man you like."

In a manuscript from 1905, Peirce fashioned a dialogue between a pragmaticist and other philosophers. In this excerpt from a speech by the pragmaticist, Peirce is discussing the nature of indubitable beliefs. The logic of these beliefs requires attention to indeterminacy: the utterance of a given belief does not in itself pick out a specific, fully determinate state of affairs. Peirce begins here, however, by noting that indeterminacy is not limited to metaphysical or ethical beliefs: rather, VAGUE-

NESS is a key topic for understanding MATHEMATICAL THOUGHT. Peirce himself was a mathematician and logician and focuses on the failure to grasp how different kinds of indeterminacy (with correspondingly different needs for interpretation) are central to the most precise and rigorous thought. Our recourse to this distinction, therefore, will 'apply' it in only the one sphere of language.

The key distinction is between GENERALITY and VAGUENESS. The two are antithetical, for in the first the authority to interpret is given to the listener; in the latter, to the utterer. Peirce now defines the two terms. Given that a sign will remain indeterminate (need some interpretation in order to have a meaning), a general sign SURRENDERS TO THE INTERPRETER THE RIGHT OF COMPLETING THE DETERMINATION FOR HIMSELF. An utterer relinquishes control over the sign, giving it to the other person, and giving THE RIGHT to interpret it. Its meaning will depend on the authority of the other person, the listener. Peirce illustrates with a universal claim: "ANY MAN YOU LIKE." The interlocutor (YOU) is authorized by the utterance to interpret. Peirce's example here points to the nature of general (or even universal) claims: the claim does not interpret a specific case until the listener interprets them further.

1b) A sign is objectively *vague*, in so far as, leaving its interpretation more or less indeterminate, it reserves for some other possible sign or experience the function of completing the determination. "This month," says the almanac-oracle, "a great event is to happen." "What event?" "Oh, we shall see. The almanac doesn't tell that."[1]*

Now Peirce can define VAGUENESS: it does not surrender rights to the listener or reader, but hoards them (RESERVES) in order to require either a sign or experience to allow for a complete interpretation. In other contexts, Peirce emphasizes that this is saved for the utterer, but in any case, the listener is not authorized to complete the determination. Notice in the example from the almanac that the answer is not of the sort "You pick" but rather "WE SHALL SEE." The WE shows how the determination is reserved for the utterer. Vagueness, then, is opposed to generality precisely because it reserves to the utterer the authority to determine the sign, to provide the interpretation. It leaves the listener unable to complete an interpretation.

Peirce appends a footnote that accentuates the authority retained by the utterer. The question is about a vague phrase "A CERTAIN MAN," in particular, about OUR USE of it. In using it, we (as utterers) leave UNCERTAIN to our listeners (or readers) just who we have in mind. Either the utterer or some other person knew who it was—but the listener or reader is left in the dark. The authority resides on the side, even if behind, the utterer, limiting the ability of the receiver to interpret.

* This is illustrated in our use of the phrase "a *certain* man" which means that the determination which is left *uncertain* to the reader or auditor is, nevertheless, or once was, *certain* either to the utterer or to some other person.

1c) The *general* might be defined as that to which the principle of excluded middle does not apply. A triangle in general is not isosceles nor equilateral, nor is a triangle in general scalene.

Peirce then rephrases the definitions in terms of logical principles that require some level of determinacy. One cannot apply THE PRINCIPLE OF EXCLUDED MIDDLE to general signs. The excluded middle means that we could pin down any sign to either affirm or deny a given predicate. While any triangle must be either isosceles or equilateral or scalene (its angles must all be different, or two of them equal, or all three equal), the phrase A TRIANGLE does not pick out any particular triangle, and without further determination cannot be claimed as one or the others. Peirce has switched

---

[1] Peirce CP 5:447 A sign that is objectively indeterminate in any respect is objectively *vague* in so far as it reserves further determination to be made in some other conceivable sign, or at least does not appoint the interpreter as its deputy in this office. *Example:* "A man whom I could mention seems to be a little conceited." The *suggestion* here is that the man in view is the person addressed, but the utterer does not authorize such an interpretation or *any* other application of what she says. She can still say, if she likes, that she does *not* mean the person addressed. Every utterance naturally leaves the right of further exposition in the utterer; and therefore, in so far as a sign is indeterminate, it is vague, unless it is expressly or by a well-understood convention rendered general.

here from a question about utterers and listeners to one of applicability of logic. The switch accentuates how indeterminacy eludes basic logical rules. And the point here is that until a particular is picked out of the general class named by a sign, the sign itself stands free of the excluded middle.

1d) The *vague* might be defined as that to which the principle of contradiction does not apply. For it is false neither that an animal (in a vague sense) is male, nor that an animal is female.

But the logical claim about vague signs is that THE PRINCIPLE OF CONTRADICTION DOES NOT APPLY. The principle of contradiction provides that nothing can have both a predicate and its contradictory. But a vague sign (like animal) is not merely not either male or female (using the law of excluded middle again), but rather the stronger claim can be advanced: the sign admits of contradictories—until determined. Animal is both male and female, until the vagueness is resolved by interpretation. Then any specific animal cannot be both of the contradictories.

We can see that these two kinds of indeterminacy reflect, in abstraction, the two sides of signifying from Parts I and II of this book. On the one hand, a sign is vague when it requires further interpretation by the utterer— a way of describing the quality we found in the teacher's address, and in the reader's attempt responsively to interpret a text. On the other hand, we have the generality of a sign when the utterer gives to the listener the authority to interpret; or the author yields authority to the reader. The ethical dimensions require, in short, that I receive signs by attending to their vagueness, and give signs by accentuating their generality. Peirce avoids this kind of normative claim. There may be some ethics of responsibility woven into this description of using signs as vagues and generals, but his focus here is much more on the way that signs and indeterminacy relate to logic—in a positive way. We might say, however, that in the discussion of the ongoing interpretation of texts and especially of law that we see how legislation depends on both vagueness and generality. "These and these are the words of the living God"—the law of noncontradiction held in suspense precisely because the law itself must be interpreted as vague, with more to teach us. And the need for majority rule depends on generality to suspend the law of excluded middle, until the assembly decides. The very problems of logics of social decisions are enriched by attention to modes of indeterminacy.

Here, however, we have a further interest in seeing how the third-person discussion of auditors and utterers can become indexically bound to me— and hence to my responsibilities. If I wish to claim that I should interpret the other person's signs as vague, in need of the other's continuing elucidation, and that I should on the other hand deliver the authority to interpret my signs (making them general) with the sign, then I first need to clarify how Peirce's asymmetric accounts of indeterminacy can become socially fixed in a way that requires responsiveness from me.

The first step beyond Peirce is forward to Royce's *Problem of Christianity*. The context is the appropriation of Peirce's semiotics, but the problem is one we have not shared: postulating other minds. (At the conclusion of this passage, I will discuss why this is not our problem.) Royce focuses on interpreting ideas that another person gives me. Indeed, the authority to interpret is precisely what is at stake. In Peirce's terms, we will find that Royce invokes an exigency to see the other's signs as vague signs.

2a) Royce Ch 360–61   When you address me, by word or by gesture, you arouse in me ideas which, by virtue of their contrast with my ideas, and by virtue of their novelty, and their unexpectedness, I know to be not any ideas of my own.

Royce begins with ME addressed by YOU. I am attending, to either WORD or GESTURE, in short to a sign, and find that I am surprised by what you signify for me. I do not receive ideas, but the signs AROUSE IDEAS, and those ideas I contrast with my own, and find them new and un-expected. Indeed, the UNEXPECTEDNESS captures precisely the interruptive quality we found in Levinas' account of the address. And also like that account, the "I" can inventory its mind and note that something new has come in.

2b)   Hereupon I first try, however I can, to interpret those ideas which are not mine. In case you are in fact the sources of these new ideas of mine, I fail to find any success in my efforts to interpret these ideas as past ideas of my own which I had forgotten, or as inventions of my own, or as otherwise belonging to the internal realm which I have already learned to interpret as the realm of the self.

My response is TO INTERPRET. Assuming that "you," the other person, have taught me something, I find that I cannot simply make the ideas into some of my old ones. Again, we see the profoundly anti-Socratic thrust of listening to the teacher. The ideas are neither old ones, nor even INVENTIONS OF MY OWN, recombinations or transformations of what I already knew. My self has come in contact with something that exceeds it—because I cannot interpret these ideas as my own. My initial attempt to assimilate the new ideas fails.

2c)   Hereupon I make one hypothesis. It is, in its substance, the fundamental hypothesis of all our social life. It is that these new ideas which your words and deeds have suggested to me actually possess an interpretation. They have an interpreter. They are interpreted.

That failure to interpret them for myself as my own is what throws me upon a question whether the new ideas are simply absurd—irremediably obscure or indeterminate. Royce invokes an HYPOTHESIS. The principle is that someone can interpret the other's signs. Royce calls it an hypothesis in order to indicate its contingency—but it plays a fundamental role: facilitating ALL OF OUR SOCIAL LIFE. Royce claims this hypothesis is a necessary condition for social interaction because only if signs are interpretable, and indeed, if there is someone who can act as interpreter of signs, can we communicate, share, teach, judge, and so on. Royce makes a kind of pragmatic claim: signs can mean only if interpretation is a real possibility and not a merely logical or formal possibility. Social interaction requires that new ideas can be interpreted to me—to an "I" that learns. Royce insists that this possibility requires a person who can interpret the signs—AN INTERPRETER. Royce is exploring how the interpreter position is constitutive of the signifying of a sign. While the case of the Egyptologist may have been a complex reappropriation of Peirce's triads, here we have a simple and forceful personification of the interpretant. And we may even bring Peirce with us here, for the qualification is a context of social interaction, of someone giving a sign to another person—and Royce is only claiming that here there must be an interpretant who is a person, an interpreter. Here is vagueness made social.

2d) This hypothesis simply means that there exists some idea or train of ideas, which, if it were present within my own train of consciousness, would interpret what I now cannot interpret. This interpreter would mediate between the new ideas which your deeds suggested to me, and the trains of ideas which I already call my own. That is, this interpreter, if he fully did his work, would compare all these ideas, and would both observe and express where lay their contrast and its meaning. My hypothesis is that such an interpreter of novel ideas which your expressive acts have aroused in me, actually exists.

What the hypothesis provides is an interpreter interpreting. That interpretation consists of other ideas that could mediate and provide a comparison between what I used to think and what I am trying to learn, and so could teach me ITS MEANING—the meaning of the new ideas. Such an interpreter WOULD INTERPRET WHAT I NOW CANNOT (emphasis mine) The modality is key: at this moment I CANNOT, and indeed my incapacity to interpret is temporally bound. The newness may yield to understanding as the conversation continues. But even more striking, the WOULD, in the subjunctive or perhaps as a kind of optative, indicates a real possibility but not the indicative certainty

(what someone *will* interpret to me). Interpretation, for Royce, consists precisely in this kind of comparison, between diverse things. But the key to the hypothesis is the actuality not of interpretation, but of the interpreter. The interpreter, the teacher, makes real interpretation possible.

2e) Now such an interpreter, mediating between two contrasting ideas or sets of ideas, and making clear their contrasts, their meaning, and their mutual relations, would be by hypothesis, a mind. It would not be my own present mind; for by myself alone I actually fail to interpret the ideas which your deeds

Royce now defines such an interpreter as A MIND. Mind is not so much a substance as a capacity to perform the key function of interpreting. Like Peirce that function transpires in a realm of ideas, of cogitations. And mind seems to come in only two forms here: mine and another's. Obviously I cannot introduce into myself the ideas I cannot understand and at the

have aroused in me. And these ideas
which your doings have aroused in
me are simply not my own.[2]

same time interpret them. I began with the
discovery that I can have ideas occur to me
which are not my own, not interpretable
by me. Ideas that are vague and require
interpretation beyond my mind. Perhaps most striking to Royce's readers,
however, is that Royce does not invoke the mind of God here. The interpreter could be named God or the Holy Spirit. And perhaps just because
Royce hesitates to identify whose mind is interpreting, and because Royce
has a strong idealist bent to his thought, a reader waits for just that sort of
theological deus ex machina.

2f) Now this hypothetical interpreter is what I mean by your self,
precisely in so far as I suppose you
to be now communicating your own
ideas to me. You are the real interpreter of the ideas which your deed
suggests to me.

But instead, Royce identifies his interlocutor—YOU—as the interpreter. The utterer who addresses me, whom I presume
TO BE NOW COMMUNICATING to me,
teaching me, is the REAL INTERPRETER.
Reality is giving signs and then interpreting them to me, or perhaps giving signs
and retaining the capacity to interpret the
signs to me. The real interpreter might not actually complete the determination of the signs, might not interpret them adequately, but that interpreter
could so interpret them. Another person is real, then, when giving signs to
me and teaching, in just the sense that we defined it when examining Levinas. This text, from 1913, parallels my reading of teaching in texts by Levinas from almost fifty years later. The authority to interpret a sign, to teach

---

[2] Peirce CP 4:551   Admitting that connected Signs must have a Quasi-mind, it may further
be declared that there can be no isolated sign. Moreover, signs require at least two Quasi-minds;
a *Quasi-utterer* and a *Quasi-interpreter*; and although these two are at one (i.e., *are* one mind)
in the sign itself, they must nevertheless be distinct. In the Sign they are, so to say, *welded*.
Accordingly, it is not merely a fact of human Psychology, but a necessity of Logic, that every
logical evolution of thought should be dialogic.

Royce Ch 345   In its most abstract definition, therefore, a Sign, according to Peirce, is something that determines an interpretation. A sign may also be called an expression of a mind; and,
in our ordinary social intercourse, it actually is such an expression. Or again, one may say that
a sign is, in its essence, either a mind or a quasi-mind—an object that fulfills the functions of a
mind.

Habermas, P&C 9/88   The discourse is not about the relation between a speaker who uses an
expression and an addressee who understands the expression. Rather, only that every sign
requires two quasi-consciousnesses (quasi-minds)—"a *Quasi-utterer* and a *Quasi-interpreter*;
and although these two are one (i.e., *are* one mind) in the sign itself, they must nevertheless be
distinct. In the Sign they are, so to say, *welded*." Peirce speaks of quasi-consciousnesses here
because he wants to seize the interpretation of signs abstractly, detached from a model of linguistic communication between a speaker and a hearer, detached even from the basis of the
human brain.

me what you mean; the authority to determine vague signs supposed to rest upon the one who speaks to me, the one to whom I attend, is the key to social life. Royce argues here that a semiotic provides an insight into the foundation of society. And that insight is that I must suppose the authority of my interlocutor. The asymmetry here is unmistakable (even if it will later be reintegrated in a social mutuality). And the indexicality of me—that I must assume this in order to learn from "you," and indeed, that social life depends upon this first responsibility are all in play here.

What is interesting, moreover, is that Levinas, unlike Royce, is not at all interested in seeing this authority to interpret as a way of proving that the other person has a mind. Royce has appropriated semiotics, but still is trying to promote an agenda that was determined by a philosophy of consciousness. Not the authority of the other to interpret her own signs, but the chance to call that a mind governs Royce's discourse. But this shows all the more clearly that despite the prevalence of Husserl's phenomenology in Levinas' work, and indeed, in the extensive inventories and analyses of consciousness, Levinas is more pragmatic, more semiotical. His reluctance to reflect on what kind of consciousness the other person has, indeed, his insistence that we not subordinate the speaking authority to any ontology or phenomenology, displays how apt a reading of him that turns away from consciousness can be. And in just this way, Peirce was interested in the functions of the interpreter and utterer more than in their being. Even Royce, who of these various authors has the most interest in a conscious subject, must constitute the mind of the other through the functions of interpreting signs to me. Moreover, in a direct and simple way, the other utters the sign and interprets it to me—a teacher for me, a use of vague signs.

B. ME AND I

While Royce transformed Peirce's semiotic by exploring the context of human language, it fell to Mead to examine the social dimension of pragmatics: the way that responding to other people constitutes my own ability to speak, as well as the functions of my consciousness. We turn to him not only because of his influence on Habermas, but also to see how the development of the "me" is precisely the integration of a complex of responsibilities—and not simply a one-to-one interaction. Mead studied with Royce, and there is a profound relation between the two. But the point of departure in Mead is not idealism, and not really semiotics. Rather, semiotics appears in the guise of psychology, and Mead's psychology is a social behaviorism, interpreting the development of the self through its social interaction. From that perspective, however, we see the primacy not of an independent "I," but of a responsive self. The ability to respond, moreover, arises through taking the role of the other, what Levinas called substitution. In this first text, we can see Mead linking the possibility for a sign to mean with the emergence of the self.

In a series of essays and lectures from 1905–13, Mead discovered the significant symbol, a social interpretation not only of behavior and the self, but of semiotics and of pragmatics in particular. A passage from a later essay ("A Behavioristic Account of the Significant Symbol," 1922) offers a clear account of how an utterer responds to the sign in the same way that the interlocutor does. Much as the Royce passage illumined how we read Levinas, so this account in Mead will also help identify the method of reading not only in Part I but also in Part II. In the discussion of Habermas there, we saw how role playing and anticipation of the other's criticism became internalized in communication. At that point we promised a treatment of Mead—here our interest is precisely the way that a behaviorism can capture what happens with signs, that a phenomenological theory of consciousness is not itself intrinsic to pragmatics. Human language use involves mechanisms of self-reference, or rather, of self-response. Mead raises the question of the importance of significance, and in a complex sequence he layers the set of responses and pragmatic effects of that gesture which is a significant symbol.

3a) Mead SW 244   The gesture not only actually brings the stimulus-object into the range of the reaction of other forms, but that the nature of the object is also indicated; especially do we imply in the term significance that the individual who points out indicates the nature to *himself.*

Mead proposes at first a simple answer: that a symbol not only has meaning to others but that it also indicates an object. The basic relation of a sign to others (people or animals) is that it allows the others to respond (REACTION) to the thing (STIMULUS-OBJECT). But the sign also indicates the thing, and indeed says something about it (THE NATURE). This closely parallels a minimal side of the giving of the world in giving signs that we found in Chapter 1. But even more important is a self-relation: the sign also signifies for the one who uses it. The sign INDICATES THE NATURE of the thing to the utterer (*HIMSELF*). Even before we gain the key social account of signification, we can already find that a sign is not exclusively from one to the other, but also is to the one as well.

3b)   But it is not enough that he should indicate this meaning— whatever meaning is—as it exists for himself alone, but that he should indicate that meaning as it exists for the other to whom he is pointing it out. The widest use of the term implies that he indicates the meaning to any other individual to whom it might be pointed out in the same situation.

Mead now circles back again to the first moment: calling the others to notice something. He is both circling back and also guarding against an individualistic account of meaning. For if the sign must indicate to the user, then one might think that it first indicates to the user and need not indicate for anyone else—I express what I think. Hence: BUT IT IS NOT ENOUGH. The BUT cautions us, as the sentence itself argues. Signs do not have meaning for only the user, BUT (repeated) must also have meaning FOR THE OTHER. Mead then examines claims that this meaning must in principle be for ANY OTHER. Mead claims a universality that is not for everyone, but only for anyone, and this is supported by the optative MIGHT BE POINTED OUT. That is, a sign must be capable of bearing its meaning for anyone who comes along, for any other. Not only is a meaning not significant exclusively to the utterer and thus open to the current interlocutor, but it must also be open to thirds, to other others. Such generality is not a rigid, totalizing universality because it recognizes the potential for meaning and it accepts that meaning occurs in contexts (IN THE SAME SITUATION), but Mead moves more quickly to this semantic side of using signs than we did.

3c) Insofar, then as the individual takes the attitude of another toward himself, and in some sense arouses in himself the tendency to the action, which his conduct calls out in the other individual, he will have indicated to himself the meaning of the gesture. This implies a definition of meaning—that it is an indicated reaction which the object may call out.

By accounting for how a sign can have a meaning for both the user and the interlocutor, Mead determines the way that a sign means. The user must TAKE THE ATTITUDE OF ANOTHER TOWARD HIMSELF. The utterer does not simply take the other person's attitude toward the object, the referent, but must also take that attitude toward himself, imagining how the other person will respond to his utterance. But TAKING THE ATTITUDE is not a merely imaginative act, it rather produces within the utterer a response or the tendency to respond. Taking the attitude of the other AROUSES IN HIMSELF the readiness to act, to respond as the other would. A sign CALLS OUT a response, and the utterer is also called—by the same uttering, the same gesturing. When the user produces the response in himself that the other would have, HE INDICATES TO HIMSELF THE MEANING of the sign. From a signification by the other, a symbol comes to signify to the utterer as self-response. Mead can now define meaning as a reintegration of the original split between the reference for the other and the reference for the utterer. The OBJECT, which is the referent of the sign, calls out a REACTION from others, a response to a sign that indicates it. To have the meaning of the sign is to be able to arouse in myself the response that another will have to my use of the sign to indicate its object. The meaning is the other's response to the sign.

3d) When we find that we have adjusted ourselves to a comprehensive set of reactions toward an object we feel that the meaning of the object is ours. But that the meaning may be ours, it is necessary that we should be able to regard ourselves as taking this attitude of adjustment to response.

But meaning is not only one person's response to the signified object, it also requires a relation to other people's responses as well. Mead regards society as a complex of responses. And so to FEEL THAT THE MEANING OF THE OBJECT IS OURS, to be confident that we understand the meaning, we need to be able to adapt

A COMPREHENSIVE SET OF REACTIONS. The dialogic mechanism requires a broadening, to include many modes of response, modes that are interconnected. It requires a web of meanings, or a syntax of responses, composed through different people's coordinating and connecting responses. The jump to this syntax and complexity is exactly the socialization of the self. For Mead recognizes that in order to adjust ourselves to the set, we must also look at ourselves TAKING THE ATTITUDE OF ADJUSTMENT TO RESPONSE. This is a double change. First, the emphasis on adjustment implies the alternating and ongoing responsive relations to others. It is not just a two-move game, but an ongoing process of learning how the other responds, of learning how to call out the same response in ourselves. But second, there is also the awareness here that we must regard ourselves as performing this adjustment.

3e) We must indicate to ourselves not only the object, but also the readiness to respond in certain ways to the object, and this indication must be made in the attitude or role of the other individual to whom it is pointed out or to whom it may be pointed out. If this is not the case it has not that common property which is involved in significance.[3]

And so Mead reiterates. Not only the object but also the set of responses to the object, not only for one other, but also for anyone TO WHOM IT MAY BE POINTED OUT. Again, Mead claims that the potential generality is intrinsic to signification. Here we see the set of responses as potential interlocutors. The set of roles we take constitutes the COMMON aspect of significance. Were I able to play only one role, that of my lover or of my enemy, I could not signify. The signs 'work' because I am a synthesis of various responses, and so find a common meaning for my words in the internalized attitudes of others to those words.

[3] Habermas C.2 26–27/13   Taking the attitude of the other is a mechanism that bears first on the behavioral reaction of the other to one's own gesture, but it gets extended to additional components of interaction. Once the first organism has learned to interpret its own gesture in the same way as the other organism, it cannot avoid making the gesture *in the expectation* that it will have a determinate meaning for the second organism. This consciousness means a change in the attitude of the one organism toward the other. The first organism encounters the second as a *social object* that no longer merely reacts adaptively to the first's gesture; with its behavioral reaction it expresses a meaning of its own gesture. The second organism encounters the first as an interpreter of the first's own behavior; this means in terms of a changed concept. The attitude of the latter to the former as well is also changed. The first organism behaves toward the second as toward an addressee who interprets the coming gesture in a certain way, but this means that the first produces its gesture with communicative intent. If we further assume that this holds for the second organism as well, we have a situation in which the mechanism of internalization can be applied once again: to the attitude in which the two organisms no longer simply express their gestures straightaway as adaptive behavior, but *address them to one another*. When they can take this *attitude of addressing the other* toward themselves as well, they learn the communication roles of hearer and speaker; each behaves toward the other as an ego that gives an alter ego something to understand.

3f) It is through the ability to be the other at the same time that he is himself that the symbol becomes significant.

Mead then switches back to the singular utterer (HE). Symbols become significant in this social sense when the utterer is able TO BE THE OTHER. This seems as close as we could come to Levinas' thoughts about substitution. What is still more striking is that the utterer does not cease to be HIMSELF. A speaker must be both a responsive self and the other to whom he would be responding. It is not simply imagining what my debating opponent will say next, but rather taking his role, and so adjusting what I must say in response to his response. Meaning is shared when the utterer takes on the roles of the set of others, internalizing what Mead will also call the generalized other. As we noted in discussing Habermas' use of this idea, the asymmetry of responsiveness is multiplied here in the one who speaks and is not simply equalized through reciprocity. To be other and himself is to be for the other and to be responsible as himself for the response of the other.

Mead, moreover, links this emergence of the self with the pronouns "I" and "me," emphasizing the responsiveness of the "me." We turn to Mead's lectures, edited posthumously as *Mind, Self, and Society*. Mead explains how the "I" does not appear, but leaves its mark as always past.

4a) Mead MSS 175–76   The "I" is the response of the organism to the attitudes of the others, the "me" is the organized set of attitudes of others which one himself assumes. The attitudes of the others constitute the organized "me," and then one reacts toward that as an "I."[4]

At the final stage of defining signification, Mead introduced the adjustment of the self to the COMPREHENSIVE SET OF REACTIONS. Here that set, now organized within the self, is termed THE "ME." Mead's "me" is built by ASSUMING THE ATTITUDES OF OTHERS. The responsive-

---

[4] Mead SW 140–41   The "I" lies beyond the range of immediate experience. In terms of social conduct this is tantamount to saying that we can perceive our responses only as they appear as images from past experience, merging with the sensuous stimulation. We cannot present the response while we are responding. We cannot use our responses to others as the materials for construction of the self—this imagery goes to make up other selves. We must socially stimulate ourselves to place at our own disposal the material out of which our own selves as well as those of others must be made. The "I" therefore never can exist as an object in consciousness, but the very conversational character of our inner experience, the very process of replying to one's own talk, implies an "I" behind the scenes who answers to the gestures, the symbols, that arise in consciousness.

James Psychol. I 378–79   The consciousness of Self involves a stream of thought, each part of which as 'I' can 1) remember those which went before, and know the things they knew; and 2) emphasize and care paramountly for certain ones among them as '*me*' and *appropriate to these* the rest. The nucleus of the '*me*' is always the bodily existence felt to be present at the time. Whatever remembered-past-feelings *resemble* this present feeling are deemed to belong to the same *me* with it. Whatever other things are perceived to be *associated* with this feeling are deemed to form part of that me's *experience*; and of them certain ones (which fluctuate more or less) are reckoned to be themselves *constituents* of the me in a larger sense—such are the clothes,

ness in this assumption is characteristic of the self. Moreover, there is also the RESPONSE to this organized set within oneself. Mead now calls this THE "I." A self is the set of assumed attitudes, but a self then reacts to that set, responding to the attitudes that it has already made its own and responded for. This opposition between what the self is made of and what the self does goes back as far at least as far as Kant, but Mead's terms reflect responsiveness to other people and for other people.

4b) . . . Now, in so far as the individual arouses in himself the attitudes of the others, there arises an organized group of responses. And it is due to the individual's ability to take the attitudes of these others in so far as they can be organized that he gets self-consciousness. The taking of all of those organized sets of attitudes give him his "me"; that is the self he is aware of.

Mead now expands on these definitions. Because the dialogue is not restricted to only one other person, and because the world confronts us as already organized (people come in networks of relations), the process of taking others' attitudes produces AN ORGANIZED GROUP OF RESPONSES within the self. If they can be coordinated, then the individual becomes aware of himself *as* that very coordination of groups of responses corresponding to the groups of people encountered. The "me" is the internalized community of responses. The syntax of relations among people becomes the syntax of relations of attitudes within the self. The self as "me" appears to the self as nothing more than this syntactical network of responses—which originate in other people and in the INDIVIDUAL'S ABILITY TO TAKE THE ATTITUDES OF THESE OTHERS. The social relations between others complicate substituting the others' attitudes for my own as those responsive relations also become who I am. One might say that only because I become substitute for others, can I become a self, and then argue that the why of substitution is in order to become a "me." But that would be to mistake the constitution of the self for its purpose.

4c) He can throw the ball to some other member because of the demand made upon him from the other members of the team. That is the self that immediately exists for him in his consciousness. He has their attitudes, knows what they want and what the consequence

Instead, we can define who the "me" is by showing how his responses are shaped by the expectations of the others as a social group. Mead uses the ball game image to show how responsiveness reflects a social network. But in the process, the individual organism becomes personified—

the material possessions, the friends, the honors and esteem which the person receives or may receive. This me is an empirical aggregate of things objectively known. The *I* which knows them cannot itself be an aggregate; neither for psychological purposes need it be considered to be an unchanging metaphysical entity like the Soul, or a principle like the pure Ego, viewed as 'out of time.' It is a *Thought*, at each moment different from that of the last moment, but appropriative of the latter, together with the all that the latter called its own.

of any act of his will be, and he has assumed responsibility for the situation. although in the third person. The player throws the ball to someone else. He doesn't do it because he feels like it, or because the other person called for it.

Rather, he does it because everyone on the team expects him to make the right play. He is aware not only of his friend to whom he throws it, but of how each team member interprets the play. If he is going to play with them, play his position and fulfill his role, he has to know that the others expect him to make plays in specific situations. Knowing that they expect this of him, HE HAS ASSUMED RESPONSIBILITY FOR THE SITUATION. Their attitudes have made him who he is IN THE SITUATION. But to have become that person is to have become the set of responses, and so to have become the organization of the team members' attitudes. Responsibility here is the assuming of these other responses.

4d) Now, it is the presence of those organized sets of attitudes that constitutes that "me" to which he as an "I" is responding. But what that response will be he does not know and nobody else knows. Perhaps he will make a brilliant play or an error. The response to that situation as it appears in his immediate experience is uncertain, and it is that which constitutes the "I." The "I" is his action over against that social situation within his own conduct, and it gets into his experience only after he has carried out the act. Then he is aware of it.

The "me" is then the set of responses that the self brings to each play. The responsibility for the others is the "me," to which the "I" then responds. That response is free and therefore unknowable for both the others and even for the self who is acting (HE DOES NOT KNOW). While the responsibilities for the others' attitudes constitute the self passively, the response itself, at any given moment, is free. The limits of knowing here closely follow the accounts in both Rosenzweig and Levinas. The response is known only in the past (ONLY AFTER HE HAS CARRIED OUT THE ACT). And when it is known it is known only as part of the "me." The "I" is not present and not knowable.

4e) He had to do such a thing and he did it. He fulfills his duty and he may look with pride at the throw which he made. The "me" arises to do that duty—that is the way in which it arises in his experience. He had in him all the attitudes of others, calling for a certain response; that was the "me" of that situation, and his response is the "I."

The awareness in the "me" of what "I" have done integrates the social expectations and responsibilities with the 'new' event—my play. The network of internalized responsibilities now includes another piece, the narrative of my developing virtues at third base is continued. While the "I" might flub the throw, the "me" will see a good play as FULFILLING HIS DUTY.

The DUTY was the synthesis of ALL THE ATTITUDES OF OTHERS; fulfilling these attitudes was the proper response. The duty occurs in the "me," before he responds as an "I." Mead here is developing themes familiar to us. That the saying is not determined by the said; that the saying appears only in the context of a said; that first I am addressed, and then I can respond; that the limitations of knowledge become a way to interpret the need for responsiveness. Most important, for this chapter, Mead is helping us understand the mechanism by which the importance of being addressed, of being called to respond, singles me out. Responsibility is social but it is not derived from a general attribute of a group, but is rather vested in me first, and becomes general only through the particularity of the "me."

C. The Indeclinable Accusative (Me)

The final text of this chapter is from Levinas' *Otherwise Than Being*, and deals with the indexicality of "me" yet again. Not unlike Mead, Levinas argues that the "me" becomes me through its relations with others. And that relation in Levinas is the radical relation of substitution—as we saw in Chapter 2. By reintroducing Levinas, I am not claiming a line of influence on the topic of the "me" from Peirce through Royce, James, and Mead to Levinas. Rather, I am examining my own earlier exclusive use of a semiotic vocabulary for exploring the ethical issues in Levinas and the others. The anchoring of asymmetric responsibility on the "me" position, the respondent and not the initiator or autonomous self, is the fulcrum for the reorientation of ethics here. Moreover, we see here the ethical responsibility for this theory, resting on not the "me," but me.

We have advanced two requirements: a decentering of the self in its relation to others and an accentuation of the responsibilities of that self. Not only is the "me" before the "I," but to be "me" is to be responsible. Whether the "I" will be responsive, fulfilling its responsibility is the real contingency that ethics must honor. Mead explains how the study of signs requires an account of social responsibility, that pragmatics is itself intrinsically ethics. Levinas, for his part, argues that the study of responsibility occurs in the medium that I call pragmatics (use/mention, indexicality, utterer and listener positions), although pragmatics terms are employed in modes of interpretation that are generally unfamiliar to pragmatics. The question of the "me" offers the deepest connection of these two claims. Not only does ethics require pragmatics as its organon, but pragmatics itself needs to be intrinsically ethically oriented.

We now turn to a passage at the end of Levinas' discussion of substitution that examines the uniqueness of the "me" who is responsible for others. Levinas not only insists that I am substitute for others, but he also examines the way that studying this radical index is in tension with the index itself.

5a) Levinas OB 161–63/126–27
My substitution. It is as *mine* that substitution for the neighbor is pro-

The themes are familiar to us from Part I and also from Mead. Levinas is focusing on the "me"—italicizing it four

duced. Mind is the multiplicity of individuals. Communication opens in
me—in me and not in another, in me
and not as an individuation of the
concept *Me*.

times in four sentences. The first word of
the paragraph is MY [MA], in italics—Levinas inquires how this relation of responding to and for others can be possessed, can
belong to me. He claims that I become me
only by becoming the other. It happens IN ME—the locus for the response,
following the summons and fulfilling the need to respond is "here." The
meaning of this "me" is not found through a deduction or specification of a
concept of the "me"—but in the approach to the neighbor. Signs do receive
their pragmatic meaning not from deduction but from responding to the
other person. And so reason (again in close proximity to Mead) IS THE MUL-
TIPLICITY OF INDIVIDUALS. I think only through taking a variety of roles—
thought is the internalization of the complex of responsibilities.

5b)   It is me who is integrally or absolutely Me and the absolute is my
affair. No one may be substituted
for me who is substitute for everyone.

But Levinas is trying to find the ethical
resonance of responsibility. His concern is
not only how the "me" arises or how I
learn to respond and thence to think.
Rather, why does it matter to me? Why
me? Why is it MY AFFAIR? In order to re-
spond I depend upon the indexicality of speaking and of being addressed.
And really me—not someone else. Sometimes when a postmodern ethics is
discussed, people object that without autonomous subjects we cannot be
responsible. The attack on rational, self-controlled authority seems to leave
a vacuum in which no one ought to do anything. Levinas locates an inescapable responsibility that rests on me first. I have purposefully toyed with the
standard philosophical translation of the French *Moi*, rendering it continuously *Me* (even though usually it is translated as *the "I," or the ego*)—in
order to clarify Levinas' own play with the accusative case. He is recalling
that the philosophical concepts of the "I," and even the "Me," arises from
me—from my own being addressed and called to respond. I am first me,
substitute for others, and then the concept of the "Me" can be formed. But
as me, NO ONE MAY BE SUBSTITUTED FOR ME. The asymmetry of substitution
is that I am responsible in a way that no one else is, or in a way that even if
everyone were, still would not relieve me of my responsibility. Unlike a dissolution of responsibility that critics fear, the discovery of a "me" that precedes the "I" secures an inalienable responsibility in me.

5c)   ... Philosophy which is consigned to the *Said*, converts the disinterest and its meaning into essence, and—by an abuse of language, of course—in order to reduce
its pretensions into a new *said* says
that of which it is only the servant
of, but makes itself the master of it
in the saying. I universalize myself—

Levinas addresses the role of thinking
about this pragmatic, indexical relation.
For philosophy thematizes, and so RE-
DUCES every saying to a said. Thus the responsibility in substitution becomes a
NEW SAID, and as theme becomes SERVANT
of reason and logic—even though substitution is at first MASTER. Again, we have

me—the posited subject is deposed. And there also lies my truth—my truth as a mortal, belonging to generation and corruption that the negativity of universalization presupposes.

followed this transformation more closely in Part I and in the discussions about theorizing the I-thou in the previous chapter, but here we may note the parallel difficulty according to Mead's account of the "I." Levinas articulates the loss of the indexicality of the "me" in the process of universalizing. I UNIVERSALIZE MYSELF: I frame the concept of the "me," and locate myself within a general class of people who are summoned and addressed. But this is still MY TRUTH, because it is I who perform this loss of my uniqueness under a concept. Levinas connects this loss with death and corruption. Indeed, THE NEGATIVITY OF UNIVERSALIZATION is dependent on the very vulnerability of me—because I am mortal, I can absorb my assignment for others into a general rule, and in the process lose myself, dying into a concept.

5d) But the concept of the Me would only correspond to me to the extent that it can signify the responsibility that is assigned to me irreplaceably, which is to say, in my flight outside the concept which is neither naiveté nor the blindness of the nonthought because positively it is the responsibility for my neighbor. (It is time to denounce the abusive confusion between foolishness and morality.)

Levinas now turns from the universality to the loss of me in THE CONCEPT OF THE ME. In order to grasp me, the concept would have to signify the unique responsibility assigned to me. While every concept involves some sacrifice of concrete content over the particular, in the case of the "me," the cost is precisely THE RESPONSIBILITY FOR MY NEIGHBOR. And that responsibility is what makes me FLEE CONCEPTS, or stand above the hierarchy of subordinating logic. My particularity is my signifying for others and contests the grasp of concepts directly. Parallel to arguments in contemporary pragmatics, Levinas struggles to isolate the indexical aspect of the sign *me* from the semantic interpretation of that sign. But while that parallel is strong, Levinas differs by identifying indexicality precisely with the relation of responsibility for others, with the social responsiveness that lies within the act of speaking. Levinas' parenthetical comment about foolishness and morality claims that responsibility refuses conceptuality, not from naiveté or nonthought. Just as in pragmatics one might insist that the claim for a nonsemantic meaning of an indexical is not irrational nor non-sense, Levinas finds this ethical relation not to be ignorant.

5e) Thus there is a vying between the conceptuality of the Me and the patience of refusing the concept, between universality and individuation, between mortality and responsibility. The very diachrony of truth is in this alternation. It is an ambigu-

Levinas now interprets two moments VYING with each other. In Mead they would be the "me" and the "I." But here they are CONCEPTUALITY OF THE ME AND THE PATIENCE OF REFUSING THE CONCEPT. Mead's "I" is this patience, the unknown and unpredictable response. And Mead's

ity that puts the concept in question to the extent that it shakes the very idea of truth as result, of truth holding in the present, of one meaning, as though somehow monosyllabic.

"me" now appears as the concept of the "me." Levinas continues juxtaposing the logical opposition of UNIVERSALITY AND INDIVIDUATION. But the third pair is most striking: MORTALITY AND RESPONSIBILITY. Responsibility is unique and rests upon me (Mead's "I"), but conceptuality represents me in my being toward death. The temporality of truth (DIACHRONY) appears in the alteration of the pairs. Truth now becomes not a RESULT but an ALTERNATION between said and saying, between concepts and responses to others. Levinas does not think that truth is only responsibility. Rather, it is an alternation, even a competition, between saying and said, between "I" and "me."

5f) The Me of responsibility is me and not an other, me with whom one would like to pair a sister soul, from whom one could exact substitution and sacrifice. But, to say that an Other Person ought to sacrifice herself to others would be to preach human sacrifice!

Levinas then reexamines the way that responsibility singles me out to bear responsibility for others. He emphasizes the impossibility of framing a bare theory, and so returns to the notion of prophecy we saw above. A conceptual theory of the "me" would provide that others also ought to sacrifice themselves under that concept. Were I to allow the generality of theory to dissolve the position of the theoretician (me, who is responsible for proposing this theory), I would then have company bearing extreme responsibility, someone else FROM WHOM ONE COULD EXACT SUBSTITUTION AND SACRIFICE. Levinas precisely forbids anyone TO SAY that. At the level of saying, of responsive address, to make claims upon others TO SACRIFICE themselves is TO PREACH HUMAN SACRIFICE. Levinas uses an exclamation mark (!) to show how vigorously he opposes that interpretation. Hence, to read Levinas as proposing a general theory of ethics is to miss his witness to his own assignment. As a general theory or bare concept, substitution would become abominable. The indexicality of my assignment marks my vulnerability to this horrifying misinterpretation of my theoretical discussion of ethics. The move to generality must, therefore, be disrupted recurrently by reference to me in a particularity that cannot be captured in any concept. The rhythm of existential signification with its extreme indexicality that governs this book foils the theoretical generality itself.

5g) ... But it is me—me and not an other—who am hostage for the others. It is my own being and not that of another that comes apart in substitution. And it is by that substitution that I am not "an other," but me. The *self* in being is exactly this

Levinas returns to ME. Not my sister, not my reader, not others. I am hostage for the others. And when MY BEING COMES APART IN SUBSTITUTION, when my integrity or self-authority is disrupted, when I become a sign for another, it happens to me, and it is only me who is de-

"not being able to hide" from an assignment that does not aim for any generality. There is no common ipseity between me and the others, me is the exclusion of that possibility of comparison, as soon as comparison is set down.

centered. But what makes me me, is that it happens to me, that I become substitute for the other. Here the parallel to Mead is so striking, because the birth of self-consciousness as well as the birth of speech is precisely this becoming the other. I cannot be myself without substituting myself for another. Being assigned and being unable to duck or avoid the assignment is the self. (Which is not to say that I will necessarily fulfill the assignment, but that I am assigned.) And more to our interest, the assignment is not itself a general task but is a unique one, bearing upon me alone. As assignment, as a sign for others, I am not a member of a class. How I will respond and how I will be interpreted by others are not assured. Levinas denies any COMMON IPSEITY with others in order to accentuate that I find myself assigned independent of any common essence or common ground with others. The assignment is, instead, that on the basis of which I can make comparisons, indeed, it is the origin of my thinking. Again, we see the parallel with Mead and with Royce where comparison originates in the need for the other's interpretation of new signs.

5h)   As a result ipseity is a privilege or an unjustifiable election that chooses me and not the Me. I, unique and chosen. Election by subjection.

Finally, Levinas concludes that the ipseity is not a property of THE ME, but only of ME. He hesitates to call it A PRIVILEGE. For becoming unique and capable of meaning is a privilege, but to so be elevated requires an arbitrary ELECTION. I experience this choice as utterly passive. I do not chose, but am CHOSEN. And so to be chosen, to become me, is also to be subjected and now responsible for another person. Levinas identifies the uniqueness of me with a nonconceptual way of being—responsible for another before any choice or reason. Not a specification of a common genus, but rather an ethically oriented, asymmetrical indexicality of my position. Myself begins with being addressed, with being chosen.

The question, Why Me?, is now answered in various ways. In a genetic account of my ability to respond, I first am addressed, and then respond. My experience that forms who I am accumulates around me, a "me" that is the story of past relations. To become myself, I must internalize the responses of others, indeed, the network of expectations and behaviors of many others. But finally and decisively for this part's treatment of method, to reflect on the indexicality of the sign "me" is to discover that the lack of generality, of semantic content, itself singles me out as assigned to respond. The tension between our particularity in responsibilities and the generality of a theory about those particularities is fastened to my responsibility, that is mine as the author of this book, as the commentator, as theorist, and as responsible in all these complex ways. A theory about the nonrefractoriness of signs to conceptual and logical analysis, even while construed in concepts and with rigorous logic, preserves that pragmatic meaning precisely by accentuating its own indexicality: it is me, called to respond for these thoughts of such extreme responsibility.

SUGGESTED READINGS

1   Ochs, *Peirce, Pragmatism*, Chapter 7.
    Raposa, Michael L. *Peirce's Philosophy of Religion*, 56ff. Bloomington: Indiana University Press, 1989.
2   Colapietro, Vincent M. *Peirce's Approach to the Self*, 1–25. Albany: SUNY Press, 1989.
3   Joas, Hans. *G. H. Mead. A Contemporary Re-Examination of His Thought.* Trans. Raymond Meyer. Cambridge, Mass.: MIT Press, 1985.
4   Lewis, J. David. "A Social Behaviorist Interpretation of the Meadian 'I.' " In *Philosophy, Social Theory, and the Thought of George Herbert Mead*, 109–33. Ed. Mitchell Aboulafia. Albany: SUNY Press, 1991.
5   Levinson, *Pragmatics*, Chapter 2.

CHAPTER 13

Why Translate?

THE PRETEXTS for this book have largely been by Jewish philosophers. In addition, I have commented upon several Biblical and rabbinic texts. Nonetheless, the interpretations offered have not been presented as an account of Jewish beliefs and practices, much less has it been a Jewish version of dogmatic theology. Yet if the account of responsibilities has been successfully rendered as philosophy, it has also pushed at the normal boundaries of what philosophy is—not only by the texts read, but also through use of some theological concepts. What sort of philosophical book this is must have puzzled almost any reader. Is it simply Jewish theology? Or is it simply philosophy? If it is some sort of Jewish thought, then why should Jewish thought become philosophy?

In this part, I have addressed the ethical exigency for the method of this book. The index of "me" situates the work in an indexed "here." Though theoretical and often abstract, this book is not written in a no-place of pure universality. The "here" is in North America, in a university culture that stands in a complex relation to a diverse Jewish community. The book serves to bring texts from there to here, to translate. It translates from Europe to North America, from Jewish tradition to contemporary philosophy, from semiotics to ethics. The transportation from there to here itself requires reflection. Shouldn't I argue for an interpretation of Levinas that situates him in his own context: in terms of French phenomenology? Shouldn't I leave Talmudic texts in the context of Jewish Studies? Is it appropriate to take Luhmann and interpret him without exploring the relation to Parsons and social systems theory? Or consider the stronger claim: that even if philosophy must start from somewhere, shouldn't its goal be to frame a universal discourse that transcends that specificity by advancing arguments that are valid for every rational being?

The responsibility to bring texts from there to here, to translate, exceeds the intellectual task of interpreting texts within their own contexts. The relation between Jewish thought and philosophy is here viewed as that between two specificities, and not from a particular into a universal. As such, the argument recognizes not only that the two realms of textuality are different and specific, but also finds me called not merely to *tolerate* difference but to *translate*, to attempt to say from one context into another, into here. The specific relation of Judaism and philosophy offers rich insight into a way that distinct communities can responsively enter into relations with what may be taken to represent the modern, hegemonic Western world. If translation were impossible, then the dominant discourse would either exclude or subsume any distinctive community. (The Jews either would have to be excluded as Jews, or would have to be assimilated into the modern world.) Translation models ways to learn from others, to attend to the saying or the writing without subsuming or simply merging. In the process, the here is changed. In this way the translation of Jewish thought in philosophy may serve as a model for other others of the dominant discourse, for African Americans, for women, for gays and lesbians, for Native Americans, for Catholics, and so on. In each case, the white, male, straight, Protestant (or post-Protestant secular) dominant community has something to learn from these others—and what these others have to say will take on new meanings when translated for that dominant community. There are risks to be taken, but there is also a responsibility to attempt the translation.

This chapter explores a sequence, almost a tradition, of three Jewish philosophers: Hermann Cohen, Rosenzweig, and Levinas. Different images of the relation of Jewish thought and philosophy occur, starting with Cohen's complex negotiation of how Jewish literary sources are a resource for a rational religion in Section A. The first pretext distinguishes Jewish sources from Greek philosophy, acknowledging the absence of science, logic, and ethics in the Jewish sources. Pretext 2 then justifies the recourse to those sources in a philosophical endeavor to interpret religion, indeed arguing that they have their own intrinsic portion of reason.

Section B (Jewish New Thinking) returns to Rosenzweig's reflections on the method of *The Star*. Pretext 3 discusses the relation of theology and philosophy, arguing for a translation project from theology to philosophy. Pretext 4, moreover, addresses the question of the Jewishness of Rosenzweig's work. He recognizes its Jewishness as the language in which he speaks, emphasizing that the words still can renew the world (in the way that historical studies of Ancient Israel cannot). He cites the frontispiece of *The Star*, which quotes a verse of Psalm 45, in the service of truth (Pretext 5). This then leads to Section C (Contemporary Translation), where Rosenzweig explores his own translation projects. Pretext 6 addresses the theoretical impossibility of translating faithfully, but then proposes that all semiosis requires translations, and that we are always translating. The text has a pointed citation of Jesus' teaching about serving two masters (Pretext 7). Pretext 8 shifts to the relation of languages and translation, arguing that translations cultivate new possibilities in the target language.

In Section D (A Necessary Trial) Levinas comments on a Talmudic text about translation of the Bible into Greek—a practice that Levinas links with his own philosophical work. Pretext 9 argues for the exigency of that translation into Greek, into the discourse of philosophy. In the process a Talmudic pun is explored, developing a line of commentary from Genesis 9 to Mishnah and Gemara (Pretexts 10–12). Levinas' own work develops translation from the earlier task of translating Biblical wisdom into Greek, into the process of bringing rabbinic textuality into the philosophical realm. Our concern is why we ought to do so, and hence what makes a translation responsive. In the case of these thinkers, we will see that they argue that Judaism intrinsically is called to address others, to run the risk of being misinterpreted.

A. Reason and Jewish Sources

The first texts come from Hermann Cohen's *Religion of Reason out of the Sources of Judaism*. Cohen was the intellectual leader of German Jews in the first part of this century. While some (including Rosenzweig) claimed that he underwent a return to his Judaism in his later years, I have argued that his major philosophical system itself was profoundly Jewish. In any case, during the years of the First World War, Cohen wrote a book that explored rational religion but used Jewish literary sources as resources.

Just how the theological and philosophical interrelate in Cohen lies beyond our interest here. We have a specific question for Cohen: How do Jewish sources and Greek philosophy relate? The depth of and interest in this question in Cohen arises from a recognition of a difference between the two rational traditions. Cohen argues that Judaism is intrinsically interested in knowing. But this interest, even in ethical knowledge, is different in kind from that found in philosophy, especially in Greek and Hellenistic sources.

1a) Cohen RR 105–6/90 Monotheism arose in a spiritual culture that lacked a creative share in scientific culture. Nonetheless, the spirituality of monotheism requires its share of reason, its share of knowledge, especially if indeed monotheism is also to produce ethics.

At the risk of appearing quaint today, we must rehearse distinctions between cultures that are unfashionable. It is, however, hard to find anything like modern science or even ancient Greek science in the Biblical texts. While someone might attempt to show a parallel at some conceptual level, at the level of modes of discourse, styles of text, and reasoning, it seems clear that Judaism arose IN A SPIRITUAL CULTURE THAT LACKED A CREATIVE SHARE IN SCIENTIFIC CULTURE. Of course, others might say either that the Greek scientific culture was not as scientific as it tried to look, or even that it has no connection with contemporary scientific culture. There are connections for Cohen—particularly in his study of mathematics and physics. The Greeks not only founded important scientific concepts, but they also fashioned the ideal of scientific culture. Cohen also wants to claim that monotheism can strive for knowledge, its SHARE OF REASON. Monotheism, at least in its earliest sources, is found in Biblical Judaism. Though the earliest Judaism emerged in a nonscientific culture, it still required an ethics. Because monotheism will not settle for only speculating about God as Being or origin of creation, knowledge of God requires a rigorous, rational ethics.

1b) Ethics, however, is in the Greek, the scientific, sense determined through logic. And logic is again determined through the progressive connection with science. Prophetism has no science, and thus also no scientific, no philosophical logic, and thus also no scientific, no philosophical ethics; and, nonetheless, it must acquire its portion in knowledge.

But it was Greek philosophy and not Biblical sources that defined ethics as a science. And a SCIENTIFIC ETHICS requires a LOGIC. And logic requires a relation to natural SCIENCE. Cohen characterizes Greek thought as three phases bound by rigorous connection (DETERMINED). The phases are ethics, logic, and science. Levinas, for instance, will characterize what is Greek or 'philosophical' quite differently.

But Cohen, the founder of Neo-Kantianism with its profound respect for modern science, ultimately ties the rationality of philosophical ethics to progresses in the logic of scientific inquiry. Unfortunately for Judaism, PROPHETISM (another name for ancient Judaism, or monotheism) lacks that specific way of knowing the natural world. The Bible contains wonderful descriptions of mountains, the heavens, the seas, and animals, but it has no organized, rigorous rational examination of them for the sake of knowledge itself. It also lacks anything like Aristotle's *Analytics* or *Categories*. The prophets are not illogical, but they are unwilling or unable to abstract and analyze the logic of inference, or definition, and so on. However much this unfashionable opposition can be confounded in exploration of Hellenistic civilization or medieval philosophy and mathematics, at the historical origin of both traditions, it is undeniable that the literary sources reveal different kinds of traditions. The Jewish sources lack both science and logic. But the punchline, perhaps as striking as anything Cohen could write about Judaism, is that it also has NO SCIENTIFIC, NO PHILOSOPHICAL ETHICS. In his own philosophical ethics, Cohen argued that Judaism had important conceptual contributions to make to ethics, and indeed, the *Religion* is in some ways an elucidation of the distinctive ethical importance of religious concepts that arise through prophetism. Ideas like compassion for the poor, messianism, self-creation through repentance, and in general the discovery of the uniqueness of both God and the "I"—these all are Jewish contributions to ethics. But those sources do not themselves elucidate these ideas in a rigorous, philosophical ethics. If Judaism contributes ethical insights, they will not be in philosophical form. But in order to achieve its correlation with God, these Jewish sources MUST ACQUIRE their portion. The way to become rational without developing science remains to be determined, but Cohen is noting that for internal reasons, Jewish sources also needed rationality—in a different way.

But if Judaism needed philosophical reason, is the inverse true? Cohen addresses the suspicion that using Jewish sources will compromise the rationality of the concept of religion that he develops.

2a) Cohen RR 9–10/8–10 It would be, therefore, an irreparable

The primary objection Cohen addresses holds that using Jewish sources CONTRA-

mistake in our formulation if we were to circumscribe and restrict the religion of reason to the Jewish religion because of its literary sources. This constriction would be an unresolvable contradiction to the signpost of reason.

DICTS reason. Particular sources seem to compromise the claim to universality and to deny equality of access to reason. The religion of reason cannot be limited by any parochialism. But the universality that Cohen requires is not an empirical one. Cohen is an idealist, and so the religion of reason is not shared by every religious group—it is not even practiced as such by Jews. But the Jewish ideal, which is to be found in its LITERARY SOURCES, must not be exclusive. If Jewish religion (as an ideal) were accessible only to Jews, then it would not be rational. And this objection is perhaps the most constant one against Jewish philosophy: if it remains identifiably Jewish it contradicts the requirements of philosophical reason.

2b)   But if in Judaism the concept of the *source* for the religion of reason holds a specific meaning and a peculiar method, things are otherwise. Then this source does not form a cordon against other religious monuments, rather it becomes an *originary source* for other sources, which for their part always keep an unweakened recognition as also sources for the religion of reason.

Cohen then develops an alternative understanding of how Jewish sources function. Here it is an hypothesis—to be proven through the course of his book (Cohen as a critical epistemologist must put his methodology before his performance). He italicizes SOURCE in order to show that he is changing the way we think about a literary source. Both as term (MEANING) and in relation to what is to be done with that term (METHOD), Cohen develops a different way of understanding its relation to reason. He claims not to weaken the recognition that other religions also can serve as SOURCES FOR THE RELIGION OF REASON. Various religions, therefore, can contribute something to the rational religion. Judaism does not exclude other religions, nor does it alone function as rational. Cohen proposes a different relation: not exclusion, but ORIGIN. Through the literary sources of Judaism we can grasp how other religions also contribute to the religion of reason. Not everything to be found in other religions will be included within Judaism: the origin does not, as origin, contain all of its later developments. But studying the originary source will guide us toward the goal of a rational religion as we study other resources.

2c)   Then there would be less to fear from an isolation of the Jewish people and their religious productions, rather that would keep the Jewish sources in a fresh and vital fruitfulness for all the other sources that have gushed forth from them. Only in so far as the originary source, as such, has an unmistakable spiritual and psychological lead

Cohen now addresses the FEAR that motivates the objection. I sense a broader objection beyond the methodological concern. Not only is Cohen arguing that the emphasis on Jewish literary sources for his study of religion will not distort his study, he is also saying that the persistence and ISOLATION of the Jewish people is not a failure to join the self-proclaimed univer-

must this supremacy of reason in the originality of the sources of Judaism remain uncontestable.

sal, rational religion: Christianity. Indeed, it is remarkable that Cohen has so little to say about the Christian polemic against Judaism—that the stubborn Jews fail to make the rational and spiritual progress of joining the Christian world. He pairs Judaism and philosophy, while his intellectual world paired Christianity and philosophy. Cohen thus has as one of his tasks the justification of formulating a non-Christian concept of philosophy, a concept that somehow will fit more closely with Judaism than with Christianity. By focusing on Jewish sources as originary, he also argues that Christianity must acknowledge Judaism as its origin. Jewish isolation has allowed its sources to remain origins FOR ALL THE OTHER SOURCES: that is, Christianity and Islam. Were Judaism to have assimilated into another religion (Christianity), it would have lost its FRUITFULNESS. The originary source is still flowing. But to claim originality is not simply historical: it also must prove itself to have a SUPREMACY OF REASON. Judaism must be, if not universally followed, at least universal in ideal. Moreover, the literary sources will have to display exceptional modes of rationality—both SPIRITUAL AND PSYCHOLOGICAL. The originality of Jewish sources will depend on their novel insights into the spirit of religion and the development of the soul along rational lines.

2d) ... Their [The Greeks'] philosophy brought forth their science, and one may also say in a certain sense: their science brought forth their philosophy. This science and especially this philosophy became the common property of cultured peoples.

The claim for supremacy in reason must also confront that absence of all science from the Jewish sources. Cohen defines Greek PHILOSOPHY in relation to natural SCIENCE. It is not clear which is the origin and which the resultant actuality. If philosophy is supposedly universal but excludes the Jewish religious sources, then it,

too, is not universal enough. Cohen realizes that science only reached its fullest expression when permeated by a philosophy that in some ways was derivative from it. In a kind of shorthand, we could say that the Platonic and Aristotelean philosophic science was drawn from the sources of pre-Socratic physical speculations. But clearly the originary sources required a further rational, philosophical development to bring forth their distinctive cultural contribution. Once so developed, that philosophy (and its science) became empirically universal: that is, it spread to ALL CULTURED PEOPLES. Its universal reception depended most of all on the philosophy (ESPECIALLY) but its origin was specific in the Greek world.

2e) Even though the Jews opposed their science, they could not carry off any opposition to their philosophy. They made the religion of reason, and to the extent that the share of religion in itself always co-

And for the Jews the philosophy was irresistible. The science, which was utterly foreign to the Jews, did not contribute to the task of rational religion, to the correlations of social ethics and theology. But the philosophy proved to be an ally. Cohen

produces positively the essence of reason, so this homogeneity requires, even if not a connection with science, at least unavoidably one with philosophy.

reasons that the CONNECTION is through reason itself. Since Jewish sources produced the religion of *reason*, then there must be a connection, a cooperation of some sort, with the reason of philosophy.

Reason may have different sources, even different origins, but the rivers of reason flow together. If Greek science overcame its particularity in philosophy, then Jewish prophetism will also have to overcome its particularity in reason—in order to produce the religion of reason. Cohen does not try to find Greek science in Jewish sources, but the relation to philosophy's reason will be more complex.

2f) We may not conceal that the concept of philosophy will be changed and distorted if it is not attended to as scientific philosophy. But the universal character of reason nonetheless connects religion and philosophy, even if science is excluded.[1]

That relation is, indeed, just the sort we are exploring. If we make philosophy accommodate a rational source that is not bound to science and its logic we will CHANGE AND DISTORT what we mean by philosophy. Again, the specificity of this lack of science needs to be carefully determined: it does not mean that following the

impact of Judaism, philosophy will cease to be universal, rational, and the like. It rather refers to a central place for natural sciences—as the measure of rationality and truth. The distortion here may be simply the elevation of practical reason over theoretical; or it may be the priority for the individual's responsibility over the classification of a particular under a general. Indeed, Cohen himself refuses to allow any contradictions within reason—and so would not opt for a notion that fragmented knowledge in which rational religion could make claims that would contradict science. While Cohen seems slightly uneasy with this alteration of philosophy, he also insists that even when science is excluded, RELIGION AND PHILOSOPHY SHARE one reason. For our purposes, however, we see that Jewish sources, in order to produce rational religion, open up to philosophy and also produce a change in philosophy. "Prophetism" offers something that changes the concept of philosophy, displacing the importance on knowing found in natural science. Such a correlation is not only possible but needed.

[1] Levinas TN 204/173–74   And one might also ask whether, despite the bedazzlement of Western science engendered by philosophy, philosophy's primordial curiosity for the *hidden presuppositions* of knowledge was not a transposition of the cult of the sacred into which the nearness of the *absolutely other* pitched thought before revealing itself in the face of the neighbor. But the remark in question has a less banal and less approximate meaning. Religion's recourse to philosophy need indicate no servility on the part of philosophy, nor any lack of understanding proper to religion. It rather concerns two distinct but linked moments in this unique spiritual process that is the *approach* to transcendence: an approach, but not an objectification, which would deny transcendence on the one hand. And on the other hand, an objectification which is necessary for that approach without substituting itself for it.

2g) Therefore, the sources of Judaism must be researched also for original philosophical motives, in which and by the strength of which the religion of reason succeeds. And we will have to note that this originary power of reason begins to make itself felt not for the first time in the later history of Judaism, when Greek influences had already become factual, but rather such connection with philosophical reason already emerges in the original thoughts, whose traces therefore attest to themselves as the oldest monuments, and must in no way be thought to be later insertions, following an historical template.

In order to respect the originary quality of the Jewish sources, we must look FOR ORIGINAL PHILOSOPHICAL MOTIVES. These motives are prephilosophical in terms of Greek philosophy, not only conceptually, but also historically. We can find a nonscientific but almost philosophical reasoning emerging in Jewish sources (for example, that emphasis on knowledge in relation with God). The Jewish sources are an origin for a 'kind' of philosophy. Without that original motive, Judaism could never have helped produce the ideal that a religion of reason is. Judaism, therefore, has a purchase on reason, even on a role as an origin of philosophy, which is independent of Greek historical influence. Cohen argues against assuming that Judaism became rational only in the Hellenistic period when GREEK INFLUENCES HAD ALREADY BECOME FACTUAL. The real origins in Jewish sources leave TRACES. In contrast to much of Protestant Old Testament studies, Cohen argues that these traces are not LATER INSERTIONS, but instead are texts of great antiquity (from at least the time of the Babylonian captivity). If one is attentive to the originary role of these sources in developing rational religion, then one can reject the presupposition of a Christian HISTORICAL TEMPLATE that viewed all potentially rational or philosophical texts as due to interpretation and interpolations from Greek influence. Changing the concept of source and origin, we can now recognize not a scientific philosophy in early Jewish sources, but rather THE OLDEST MONUMENTS of a reason that itself is an origin for philosophy.

Cohen thus argues that the recourse to Jewish sources is a recourse to an other source of reason, indeed of philosophy. Cultivating and examining that source will alter philosophy, offering a social ethics and a psychological potential that Greek, scientific philosophy lacked. Moreover, because those Jewish sources function as an origin for the religion of reason, they have as their goal the development of that philosophical religion. Cohen does help us see that the difference between Judaism and philosophy is best seen as a difference between two particular communities, and not between one stubborn particularity in contradiction to the universal human truth. Each community desires universalization. Cohen argues, for instance, that the human universal (humanity) is itself an idea that springs from Jewish sources, discounting the Stoic 'invention' as not bound together by social responsibility. The process of connecting Jewish sources and philosophical ones involves an intricate correlation, with two-way transformations.

B. Jewish New Thinking

Rosenzweig's own reflection on his method within *The Star* explores the relation of Jewish sources and philosophy. He has a deep sense of the particularity of the Jewish tradition and its production of particularity in his work. But he also understands that the relation of theology and philosophy in general also demands a negotiation of the particularity of the disciplines. Neither can know the whole truth alone—even as general disciplines, each requires the other. We will first see the model of translation in the general relation—called New Thinking—and then in Pretext 4 we will return to the question in relation to Jewish thinking.

Within *The Star*, Rosenzweig seemed to shift from philosophy to theology and yet still need philosophy to be a kind of transcendental condition for the experiences of speaking and listening. When he redescribes his New Thinking, he is clearer on a reciprocal relation between theology and philosophy—but claims that *The Star* "is simply a system of philosophy" (NT, 140/69). In that context he claims it is not "a Jewish book" or a philosophy of religion. But as he proceeds, the terms (philosophy, theology, Jewish) all are carefully reconstructed. Rosenzweig amalgamates theology and philosophy in what he considers a new way—a way much like Cohen's method of correlation. Because he is anxious about the traditional interpretations of their relation, he pauses to identify a new relation (New Thinking) for the task of relating the two particularities.

3a) Rosenzweig NT 153/89 Theology may not humiliate philosophy as handmaiden, and just as degrading is the role of cleaning lady, which philosophy has gotten used to expecting of theology in more modern and the most modern times. The true relation of the two renewed sciences, as the mentioned introduction developed it, is sibling, and, indeed, it must lead to personal union among their representatives.[2]

In the introduction to Part II of *The Star*, Rosenzweig had discussed the sorry fate of miracles in modern theology. He had proposed a cooperation between two renewed disciplines, and he showed how historicism had driven both modern disciplines onto the rocks. Here, Rosenzweig begins with a medieval image of philosophy as HANDMAIDEN for theology. He then shifts in modern and even contemporary thought to the reversal, where theol-

[2] Rosenzweig S 119/107 Thus philosophy today is called in by theology, in order theologically speaking, to strike a bridge from creation to revelation, a bridge on which the centrally important connection for today's theology of revelation and redemption might take place. From theology's point of view, philosophy thus is to perform, not some reconstruction of theological content, but its anticipation, or rather more correctly, its foundation, showing the preconditions upon which it rests. And since theology itself understands its contents as events and not as ingredients—that is, not as life but as lived experience, similarly, these preconditions are not conceptual elements, but rather extant actuality; the concept of creation is inserted in place of philosophical concepts of truth. Philosophy contains therefore the complete content of revelation, but has this content not as revelation, but rather as preconditions for revelation, as prior to revelation, and therefore not as revealed, rather as created content. All of the content of

ogy is delegated the role of CLEANING LADY. Both degradations are unacceptable. If philosophy serves to make theology pretty, accompanying it and serving to make it comfortable, or if theology is regarded as relegated to cleaning up the mess, then each discipline will collapse in the radical historicism of the turn of the century. Instead, the two must become SIBLINGS, and the people who study them will have to study both and talk with each other. The refusal to subordinate one to the other, particularly in the latter role of cleaning lady, asserts the value of each. This sibling relationship allows for postmodern theology and postmodern philosophy. While it may be clear that for theology this possibility is more real; in philosophy, particularly in postmodern philosophy, it is less clear that theology has any role. Yet if one examines many of the thinkers here, one can see the place for theology, especially in Jewish postmodern philosophy. And a parallel argument can be made for some Christian philosophers today. Moreover, Rosenzweig might well interrogate the postmodern philosophy that spurns theology, asking whether it has freed itself from the hold of radical historicism. Is Nietzsche patron saint of a thought that still cannot find a social or ethical vision worthy of human existence? Such polemics stand beyond both the range of this book and the commentary tasks here—but for some, at least, the renewal of philosophy and theology has begun in this postmodern context.

3b) The theological problems want to be translated into human ones and the human propelled into theological. The problem of the name of God is only a part of the logical problem of names in general; and an esthetic, which has no

Between siblings the problems are exchanged, correlated. But looking more precisely at Rosenzweig: theology's will be TRANSLATED. Instead of dwelling beyond the social realm, theology must address its problems in a human context, with

---

revelation, but has this content not as revelation, but rather as preconditions for revelation, as prior to revelation, and therefore not as revealed, rather as created content. All of the content of revelation, which includes redemption, according to the concepts of faith of the current epoch, is "foreseen" in creation. Philosophy, as the theologian practices it, becomes prediction of revelation, an "Old Testament" so to speak of theology. Thus revelation achieves for our surprised eyes its genuine miraculous character—genuine for it becomes utterly fulfillment of the promise that occurred in creation. And philosophy is the oracle of the Sibyl, which by foretelling the miracle made it into the "sign," into the sign of divine providence.

Benjamin Th I (693/253)   There is a well-known story about an automaton constructed in such a way that it is supposed to win a game of chess, answering each move of an opponent with a countermove. A puppet in Turkish attire and with a hookah in its mouth sat before a chessboard placed on a large table. A system of mirrors created the illusion that this table was transparent from all sides. Actually, a little hunchback who was a master chess player sat inside and guided the puppet's hand by means of strings. One can imagine a philosophical counterpart to this apparatus. The puppet called "historical materialism" is supposed to win all the time. It can easily be a match for anyone if it enlists the services of theology, which today, as is well known, is small and ugly and has to keep out of sight.

thoughts concerning whether an artist can be saved, is really a courteous but also an incomplete science.[3]

human problems. Human problems on the other hand are not countertranslated: they are PROPELLED [*VORGETRIEBEN*]. From the human side, the merely human must be pushed to break beyond into a realm of theology. Human questions can be driven to a transcendent dimension. But theological problems are translated into human issues. The correlation of these two motions (propelled/translated) arises directly from Cohen's project. The difficulties of translation as a model will occupy us for the rest of this chapter. Here Rosenzweig gives two examples of the correlation: first is the essence of semantics. THE NAME OF GOD, which is a complex problem of reference, is a key question within the problem of names. How do proper names refer? Rosenzweig claims that we need to address the logical question in order to address the 'theological' problem. As a complement, an aesthetics that ignored the issues of the artist in relation to God, that refuses to inquire about the role of theological creativity in artistic creativity, would be only COURTEOUS—an aesthetics for courts and decoration—but profoundly incomplete.

But if Rosenzweig has qualified the way his book is simply a philosophical book—by instigating a new relation between a new philosophy and a new theology—then it is also worth considering how he reclaims the book as a Jewish book. For the "Jewishness" of his book, and indeed, of the work undertaken in this book, lies in his way of using specific words. In the next passage we can begin to see the words used, and in the following passages we will see the pragmatic dimension of this way of using those words.

4a) Rosenzweig NT 154–55/92 But the "Jewish book"? Doesn't it announce itself as that on the title page?

The question is whether Rosenzweig can deny that *The Star* is a Jewish book. Rosenzweig puts JEWISH BOOK in quotation marks, to indicate that the idea Jewish book needs renewal. He asks himself whether he can deny what is proclaimed on the title page. On the title page is a Jewish star, a star of David. There is even a quotation in Hebrew, lest one get confused that this is Not-Jewish.

The citation is to Psalm 45, a psalm in praise of a king. Rosenzweig selects the portion of verse 5 that calls for a verifying of words, for action for the sake of truth. The psalm, however, depicts this as polemical, figuring the king as warrior for truth (and for meekness). Rosenzweig's citation invokes the image of battling for

5] Psalm 45:2) My heart overflows with a good word. I say my song to the king. My tongue is the pen of a ready writer. 3) You are fairer than men. Grace is poured into your lips, and thus has God blessed you forever. 4) Gird your sword on your thigh, O warrior, your glory and your majesty. 5) And in majesty ride

---

[3] Levinas, OB 199/156   Revelation of the beyond being is of course maybe only a word; but this "maybe" belongs to an ambiguity where the anarchy of the Infinite resists the univocity of an origin or of a principle; belongs to an ambiguity where an ambivalence and an inversion is stated precisely in the word God—the hapax legomenon of vocabulary.

truth and righteousness, ignoring the way that language (words, writers, pens, lips) is the subject matter of this psalm. His point here is that if he puts this quotation

successfully for the true word, and meekness and righteousness, and let your right hand teach you terrible things.

and a star of David on the title page, how can the book not be Jewish? Several pages into the essay, Rosenzweig is willing to refine what that Jewishness means.

4b) I would like to speak as softly as the poet when he concluded his mighty, extensive fugue on the theme of cosmic beauty with the unforgettable usage: it appeared to me in the form of a youth, in the form of a woman—in order to be able to say completely truthfully what I now have to say.

In a somewhat opaque sentence, Rosenzweig begs the chance to speak very quietly IN ORDER TO BE ABLE TO SAY what he has to say. To speak quietly, lest someone overhear, lest someone mistake the claim he wants to make for quite another. But notice also that the issue in speaking so quietly is SAYING, in a way that is very close to Levinas' use of the term. Rosenzweig is worried that he will be unable to say what he needs to say—that what is said will fall short. And indeed, Rosenzweig now distinguishes between saying truly and saying. To say truly will be to say so that another hears, to say and in saying to make the words true.

4c) I received the New Thinking in these old words, and so have I given it back and given it on. I know that instead of my words a Christian would have words from the New Testament come to his lips; a pagan, I think, would use not words from his holy books—because their ascent leads away from the original speech of humanity, unlike the earthly ways of revelation leading to it—but perhaps wholly his own words.

Rosenzweig explains that he is a transmitter in a relay. OLD WORDS are handed to him, words which he hands on. The words are theological, even if now they will become translated into a philosophical use. Rosenzweig is loyal to the words, and he implies it has to do with having received the New Thinking IN them: that to interpret we must have a specific language, and that one cannot jump out of it. And so he contrasts three sets of words: his Jewish ones, Christian ones, and pagan ones. These alternatives involve two sets of texts (Jewish and Christian ones), and a pagan set of contemporary words. A Christian wants to hear this New Thinking in New Testament phrases. A pagan, however, opts for HIS OWN WORDS because his HOLY BOOKS lead off into the gods' speech, away from an access to human (EARTHLY) speaking. Revelation, by which Rosenzweig means both Judaism and Christianity, reveals its truth in human words, leading us toward THE ORIGINAL SPEECH OF HUMANITY. This original speech is not an historic claim about an adamic speech but rather a reference to the experience of social conversation, to the pragmatics with which this book began. Rosenzweig recognizes that each of these three traditions can provide access to the New Thinking, to the experiences and responsibilities of speaking and listening, but the textual traditions of both

Judaism and Christianity themselves solicit it. The pagan texts, be they Homer, Ovid, Sophocles, or Plato, do not achieve the same result, but the current pagan thinkers and writers (from Hölderlin and also Goethe to Nietzsche, and we would add Heidegger and his followers) also approach that original speech, the pragmatics required by this linguistic turn in thought. Rosenzweig realizes that most readers would prefer Christian or pagan words because the Jewish words are not their own and seem too alien.

4d) For me, however, these words. And this is really a Jewish book; not one that deals with "Jewish things," because then the books of Protestant Old Testament scholars would be Jewish books; rather it is a Jewish book because the old Jewish words come for what the book has to say, and specifically for what it has to say that is new. Jewish things are like things in general, past; Jewish words have, however, even if old, part of the eternal youth of the word. And when the world is opened to them, they will renew the world.

But Rosenzweig says simply THESE WORDS. He will transmit the Jewish words—and that is what, for Rosenzweig after all, makes this A JEWISH BOOK. Unlike the question of which words to use, there is now a clearer distinction: between WORDS and THINGS. What makes a Jewish book Jewish is not the things—because the PROTESTANT OLD TESTAMENT SCHOLARS write about Jewish things, about Ancient Israel, and the society and its cultic artifacts. But Rosenzweig knows that things are generally PAST. To study Jewish things is to study the Jewish past. To study

them, but not because they could say something to us, but only in order to know what they once were for others in the past. Rosenzweig says, however, that his book has something to say, something NEW, something not about the past, but for the future. In order to say that, THE OLD JEWISH WORDS offer an opportunity to say something because they have a share in the power of words to renew meanings: THE ETERNAL YOUTH OF THE WORD. What makes their youth eternal is that in every generation the words are still capable of saying something new, something young. If *things* are past, then *words* are the way to be young, even if the words themselves are old. And so Rosenzweig concludes with the real possibility of the signs, the possibility TO RENEW THE WORLD. The words have that possibility, and one might even say that the place where the real possibility occurs is in words, maybe especially old words. Realizing that possibility requires that THE WORLD IS OPENED TO THEM: that people will listen, and listen not only for what is said, but also for what the words say. Here the recognition that Jewish thought and tradition has something to offer is bound precisely to semiotics.

C. CONTEMPORARY TRANSLATION

To use the old words to say something new, to say it to a new generation of people, is not to repeat the words. It becomes Rosenzweig's work to translate the old Jewish words into German—where they become both Jewish and German, or perhaps Jewish German words. In *The Star*, Rosenzweig

wrote about concepts that were to be found in Jewish sources. He wrote
words about creation, revelation, and redemption, about confession and
atonement, and so on. He wrote of them in German. Hence the old words
were already renewed. Their Jewishness was not found in Hebrew language,
much less Hebrew script. Rosenzweig wrote Jewish words in German, and
it is clear that New Testament words would also have been in German,
and pagan words would also be in German. But shortly after writing *The
Star*, Rosenzweig began in earnest to translate Jewish texts from Hebrew
into German. The sense that an old Jewish word could renew the world required a more intimate examination both of Hebrew Jewish words and of
the very task of finding a way to bring the old text into the German present.
The translation projects were twofold: a translation of medieval Jewish liturgical poems by Judah Halevi, and a collaborative translation of the Bible
with Martin Buber. Each project also spawned theoretical writings about
what translation does, and indeed about why we translate. The next passage
below comes from an essay called "Scripture and Luther," which addresses
the issues in Bible translation. It was written late in 1925. Rosenzweig addresses the impossibility of translation, as well as necessity of translation,
even at the level of speaking and hearing.

The passage I cite is the opening passage of the essay.

6a) Rosenzweig S&T III, 749/47
To translate means to serve two
masters. Thus no one can do it. Thus
it is like everything that looked at
theoretically no one can do; practically it is everyone's task. Everyone
must translate, and everyone does it.

Rosenzweig begins with a Biblical allusion. It is to Jesus' Sermon on the Mount:

7) Matthew 6:24 "No one can
serve two masters, for either he will
hate the one and love the other, or
he will be devoted to one and despise the other. You cannot serve
God and Mammon."

The text claims that serving God and
money is impossible. To cite this saying of
Jesus in an essay on Luther and translation is more than ironic. In fact, it quickly
becomes polemical. For what Jesus denied, Rosenzweig asserts—that one
cannot serve two masters IN THEORY, but PRACTICALLY everyone does it.
Perhaps Rosenzweig also means to claim that Jesus was wrong about money
and God—that practically everyone is responsible for both the material conditions and the theological dimension of existence. In any case, Jesus seems
to be a sorry theoretician, if only indirectly. It is less clear whether Luther—
the translator—eventually appears as a disciple of Jesus' impossible theory,
or in fact, as someone who understood well that he was serving two masters.

In any case, for Rosenzweig translation is not simply to control two languages, but TO SERVE them. The theoretical problem is that if one loves the
original language, the translation into the other (the target language) will be
inadequate. And similarly the reverse. Rosenzweig goads us: what theory
prohibits, our life sets for us as A TASK. We have an ought that seems to go

against our can, and maybe the nature of responsive tasks is just this—they require us to do what we know (or at least think) we cannot. Translation is therefore, one of a group of practices—they look impossible and still we MUST do them. As Rosenzweig proceeds, we will see that translation becomes the paradigm for semiosis, for using signs. The shocking thing, of course, is that EVERYONE DOES IT. Jesus aside, we go on and do what responsibility requires. Translation is a practice that makes pragmatists of us all. We manage to serve both the original language and the target language.

6b) Whoever speaks translates from his meaning into his expectation of the other's understanding, and not of a nonpresent universal other, rather of this utterly determinate one whom he sees before him and whose eyes open or close accordingly.

Rosenzweig then makes translation the model for speech. Speaking translates from what I MEAN into what I think the other person CAN UNDERSTAND. Parallel to Mead's account of speech and response, Rosenzweig claims that to speak is not just to say my mind: it is always to another person, and specifically to my EX-PECTATION OF THE OTHER'S UNDERSTANDING. Of course, I might mistake my interlocutor. Another person will challenge me, and I will try to learn what she thinks. But I frame my words for this other person, for my image of the other's comprehension. Speaking involves this other person as the addressee. Rosenzweig is clear that the reason speech is like translation is that there is a specific target. I do not speak to a UNIVERSAL OTHER, to an absent everyone. Rosenzweig accentuates that the other person to whom I speak has eyes that see me. Those eyes will OPEN OR CLOSE, will allow my words in or not. My translation effort is checked and accepted or qualified at the very moment that I speak. Indeed, this eye contact seems to be a challenge or response to my words. Rosenzweig had written in *The Star* that my own words are drawn out of me by the other person's eyes. Through the eyes the need to translate, and indeed the possibility of it arises. (Although, following the discussions in Part I, it is not clear that the trust in the other's authority to validate my translation is greater in person, as opposed to a written sign.)

6c) Whoever listens translates words which sound in his ears into his understanding, concretely said: into the language of his mouth. Each has his own language. Or rather: everyone would have his own language, if there were in truth a monological speaking (as the logicians, these would-be monologians, claim for themselves), and if all speaking were not already dialogical speaking and thus—translation.

Just as speaking is translating in relation to the expectation of the target language, so listening is also translating. A listener translates the audible sounds into words he understands. Rosenzweig hesitates to opt for a simply cognitive target (HIS UNDERSTANDING), and substitutes a language, THE LANGUAGE OF HIS MOUTH. The language of responding is the target language of listening. To listen is not to decode the other's speech so as to share an idea: rather, it is to translate what I hear into a language that I can speak, to prepare me to respond. But so far is conversation from sharing some cognitive content that Rosenzweig can identify each speaker's responsive language as one's OWN. In the next passage, I will consider the possibility of common language. But here Rosenzweig cannot quite rest content with this notion of idiolects. Indeed, it quickly degenerates into a subjunctive false possibility: if one only spoke to oneself, then each would have a private, authentic language. MONOLOGICAL speaking requires just these idiolects—and communication seems all but impossible on this assumption. But only one group of people would ever claim a self-enclosed sign system: LOGICIANS. Even they cannot succeed, but they wish they could. (It is hard in this context not to think of Wittgenstein writing about the impossibility of private languages.) The reason we cannot use this model is that using language engages us pragmatically with others. Rosenzweig broadly claims that ALL SPEAKING is dialogical, involving responding to others and speaking to others. But the result is that all speaking is TRANSLATION—precisely in the sense we have in mind here. Translation is a paradigm for the responsiveness that pragmatics requires: the taking account of and responsibility for what others do and say.

But if we return from the issue of speech as translation to literary issues, then we can see that a translator works on both the text in the original language and the target language that receives the translation. Rosenzweig's task was to transform the Hebrew words into German words, to create a new way of speaking German Jewish words. This task occurred not only in the Biblical translation, but also in his translations of medieval poems by Judah Halevi. That work also had a concluding essay about translation. While the passage I present speaks in general about translation, and so helps us in our general inquiry (Why Translate?), it is in constant reference to the translations from Jewish sources into modern German—a translation project that, again, models the specific issues of contemporary Jewish philosophy. Rosenzweig claims that the target language is changed by the translation, and indeed, that translation cultivates the possibilities of language more than literature created in that language.

We begin when Rosenzweig has been discussing the sort of translation a businessperson needs—accurate and convenient.

8a) Rosenzweig IV, 1:3–4/171 They translate, as a person speaks who—has nothing to say. Since he has nothing to say, he also doesn't need to demand anything of language. And the language upon which the speaker does not make demands grows torpid into a means for reaching an understanding, from which any Esperanto can justify its existence.

Again the discrimination between having something TO SAY and not having anything to say. The business service has, we hope, nothing to say of its own. They translate not needing TO DEMAND ANYTHING OF LANGUAGE. Again, translation is not only the poetic task of coining words. Rather, to have something to say is always to require language to communicate something new, and so to stretch the understanding of one's reader. Language maintained as a transparent medium of businesslike transactions will grow TORPID. Indeed, speaking becomes an inconvenience in transferring information. Again, we see the opening theme of this book—and also a striking critique of the interpretation of communicative action as a mere MEANS OF REACHING AN UNDERSTANDING. Rosenzweig recognizes that this instrumental use of language is possible, and that the fantasy of an artificial language (ESPERANTO) arises here. While the logicians imagine a purely monological private language, the social theorists who ignore the way that we say something to someone imagine a pure language as means for communication.

8b)   Whoever has something to say will say it in a new way. He becomes the creator of language. After he has spoken, the language has another face. The translator makes himself the mouthpiece for the foreign voice, which he makes audible across the abyss in space or in time.

But to have something to say is to need to say old words IN A NEW WAY. To say something is to become THE CREATOR OF LANGUAGE. It is not so much coining new words as combining them in new ways, turning the language in such a way that something new appears. If language grows torpid from businesslike use, then it becomes young through those who have something to say. It must change, gaining a new FACE after the creator HAS SPOKEN. (If we pause and imagine the translation from one person to another, we see also how the one who listens will hear new things, even if in old words.) But it is almost as if once Rosenzweig mentions the face, he cannot pull back from the physicality of the face: VOICE, MOUTH. The listener appears again: listening for the strange voice—or perhaps more simply translating not only the foreign words, but more important the foreign voice. Rosenzweig is thinking about Halevi's voice and how to make it sound in German. The translator has to make the voice re-sound or maybe simply echo ACROSS AN ABYSS. One cannot make the separation disappear, but the translator still brings language across. Rosenzweig is concerned mostly with a temporal gap, but between German and French and English we might have simply a spatial gap.

8c)   If the foreign voice has something to say, then the language afterward must appear other from what it was before. This result is the criterion for the conscientiously realized success of the translator. It is utterly impossible that a language which Shakespeare or Isaiah or Dante has actually spoken into would have thereby remained untouched.

Rosenzweig now distributes having something to say over this FOREIGN VOICE. Just as someone who has something to say must remake her own language, so a translator who attends to the foreign voice will also make the target language change. Rosenzweig goes so far as to demand this as THE CRITERION for successful translation. Precisely because a translator has heard something that now she wants to say, the translator must renew the target language, revealing possibilities that had previously not been available in that language. Rosenzweig flatly asserts that translating great literature (SHAKESPEARE OR

ISAIAH OR DANTE) would have to change the target language: if they HAVE
ACTUALLY SPOKEN into it.

8d) It will experience a renewal, exactly as if a new speaker were to arise within it. Even more so. Because the foreign poet calls into the new language not simply what he himself has to say; rather he brings along the inheritance of the universal linguistic spirit of his language to the new one, so that what happens is not only a renewal of language through the foreigner people, but also through the foreign linguistic spirit.

Rosenzweig then makes explicit the comparison with an indigenous author. But Rosenzweig claims that a translator changes a language EVEN MORE SO, more than an indigenous author. A translator brings in what the foreign poet wants to say, but also brings in the INHERITANCE that lives in the foreign language. In the final part of this book, I will examine the complex relations of signs that are our inheritance and how the inheritance is in play whenever someone tries to say something. Rosenzweig realizes, however, that the renewal of a language renews not simply by what one wants to say, but also by how one can say it. Indeed, the why of translation contributes a distinctive renewal through this how. Each language has its own specific inheritance, much as each person has her own linguistic patterns and habits and history. Rosenzweig then surprises us by affirming a UNIVERSAL LINGUISTIC SPIRIT. The role borne by universality emerges in the next sentences, but Rosenzweig clearly here does not see the inheritance as merely the grammar or vocabulary of a language. There is also a spirit which is performed and dwells within the language, particularly of a language in use.

8e) That such a renewal of language through a foreign one is possible at all obviously presupposes that just as the language has already itself given birth to each of its speakers, so also all human speaking, all foreign languages that are spoken and that will be spoken, are at least in germ, contained in it. And that really is the case. There is only one language. There is no linguistic particularity of one language even in regional dialects, the nursery prattle, or class slang, that does not lie at least in the germ of every other.[4]

Rosenzweig resorts to a simple transcendental argument: the condition for the possibility of translation, or more precisely the possibility of RENEWAL through translation, implies that a target language has the resources, even if only in germ, to receive what other languages say—indeed, to receive their inherited linguistic spirit. Perhaps it is ironic that in this passage, Rosenzweig argues for the *theoretical* possibility that previously we saw dismissed as impossible (serving two masters). Or maybe, rather, we see here an *abduction*

---

[4] Benjamin TR 12/255 Translation thus ultimately serves the purpose of expressing the innermost relationship of languages to each other. It cannot possibly reveal or establish this hidden relationship itself; but it can represent it by actualizing it embryonically or intensively. This representation of a significance through an attempt at making the embryo visible is so characteristic a way of representing that it is rarely met with in the sphere of nonlinguistic life. This, in its analogies and signs, can draw on other types of suggesting meaning than intensive—that is, anticipative, intimating—actualization. As for the posited innermost relation of

from the reality of the practice of translation: a theory that is not so much a priori, but is helping to interpret what already can happen—real possibilities. The resources of a particular language are first evident in the production of the diverse speakers of the language. A language gives birth to EACH OF ITS SPEAKERS—indicating the fecundity of a language, its capacity to engender diversity. Thus, Rosenzweig argues, it also must be presupposed to be able to receive all of the diversity of various languages: indeed, of all that ever WILL BE SPOKEN. Rosenzweig advances: THERE IS ONLY ONE LANGUAGE. This claim is not the claim about adamic language—that once we all spoke the same language. Instead, it serves as a future ideal. But it also recognizes that mutual translatability of each language into each other—an image of possibility that will require great efforts but at least is not, in theory, impossible. Moreover, Rosenzweig addresses the rich registers of any language: suggesting the range of usage by providing three of the many axes of differentiation. By broadening the concept of a language beyond the literary bookshelf, including the special usage of different groups, we already begin to see just how rich and varied are the possibilities of any language.

Again, we are at a methodological junction: what seems impossible from a monological concept of language becomes not only a necessary condition, but also an ideal that governs the responsibility to translate when viewed from the dialogical reorientation. Hence, Rosenzweig can argue in one place that the compromises of serving two masters are practical proof that the theoretical prohibition on translation lies rebutted. But, in a different context, as an afterword to his own translations, he can write of the condition for translation and generate a theory of language that requires each to harbor the possibility of each other within it. The performance that precedes his essay makes translation real—and so the theory is required to explain how it was possible, and he is permitted to abduct more general conditions that make the performance possible. Perhaps just this junction for theory defines the possibility not only for a chapter like this one, but also indeed for a project like the one that guides this book: a theoretical account of responsibilities that generalizes on the basis of what it itself performs, and in so performing finds others performing these responsibilities as well.

8f) The task of the translating, its can, may, and should, is grounded on this essential unity of all languages and on it also rests the command for reaching universal human understanding. One can translate because every language contains within it the possibilities of every other.

Rosenzweig returns to the language of TASK—the why of translation. Translation requires the almost transcendental condition (THE UNITY OF ALL LANGUAGES) not as achieved, but as a real possibility. The command to translate, therefore, also rests on this unity and is directed toward a

languages, is the one characteristic convergence. It consists of this: languages are not strangers to one another, but are, a priori and apart from all historical relationships, related in what they want to say.

One may translate, if one can actualize this possibility through cultivation of such linguistic fallow fields. And one should translate, so that the day of that concord of languages will come, a day that can grow only in each individual language and not in the empty space "between."

universal understanding. Again, we find the universality that first appeared in Part II, and indeed it is linked to that activity that Habermas most explored: REACHING UNDERSTANDING [*VERSTÄNDIGUNG*]. What is missing, however, is a community that speaks that unity of all languages— that is, there is no spoken language that is itself this universal language. One only has to remember Rosenzweig's protestations against Esperanto. The command binds us to move from one language to another but not to abandon the languages people speak for a neutral medium. The unity of all languages is not neutral but is colored, multiplex. Rosenzweig now moves through three modalities: CAN, MAY, AND SHOULD. The theory of the unity of all languages provides the CAN. But the MAY depends upon the active capacity of the translator, who is defined as the one who may CULTIVATE THE FALLOW FIELDS. A translator who renews the target language will find possibilities in that language that have not been actualized, ways of speaking that have not yet been used. Finally, the SHOULD is in order to hurry the day when all people will be able to speak to each other. That day comes through the negotiation in individual languages, not in a sign system that no one lives in. The Esperantist aims to cultivate a language IN THE EMPTY SPACE "BETWEEN" languages. Rosenzweig recognizes that universal human understanding can only be built from one to another: from one person to another, from one language to another, from one community to another. Not a subordinating relation, much less a totalizing one, but ultimately a cooperative relation.

Or perhaps it is not so much the networking languages, of each to each, that Rosenzweig has in mind. For ultimately, he hopes to cultivate the possibilities of all languages in one. That all-in-one points back to representative logic, to the logic we saw exemplified for Rosenzweig by Judaism. The cooperative web of interaction only requires that each have its own say, a hope for mutual tolerance and even understanding. The representative move, on the other hand, requires a more active translation project. Rosenzweig is theorizing with a model that he produced by generalizing from a uniquely Jewish way of judging. He has been trying within German to cultivate the saying from Hebrew. He has not been engaged in bringing various European literature and languages into the Hebrew language, or even into Jewish culture. If Judaism represents the model of a way for everything to be possible within a single community, then Rosenzweig's translation projects show how the model can be applied in another context. If Rosenzweig can try both to allow German new possibilities to say what the Hebrew texts have to say, and to cultivate within German the possibilities that the inheritance of Hebrew carries, then he can form a general theory of how each language can be like the Jewish model: each language can be representative of humanity.

D. A Necessary Trial

This interpretation of translation overlooks the other aspect of the passage we considered before: the need for practical, life-giving compromises. The translation is not simply a bestowal of the riches from one community upon an other community. The cultivation of fallow fields also requires changes. And it is not merely the target language that changes; the original saying is altered. The saying cannot be protected from a risk in translating, in communicating (to refer back to translation as the basic semiotic event, speaking or writing from one person to another). Thus for the process of bringing Jewish sayings into philosophical discourse, there are changes within both philosophy and the Jewish sayings. Compromises. The question is not whether compromise coincides with translation, but whether the risk of compromise is to be taken. Why translate, if there is a risk that what one tradition says will be unclear in another tradition?

The final text for this chapter and this part is from Levinas. He is giving a reading in French of a Talmudic text (in Hebrew and Aramaic). And that text concerns the tale of the translation of the Hebrew Scriptures into Greek, the Septuagint. For Levinas, his own activity is closely parallel to this translation into Greek—and Greek is a topic of great interest in his fourth volume of Jewish essays, dating from 1981 to 1986. While Levinas had been extremely hostile to the tradition of Western philosophy earlier in his writings, in this latter stage he begins tacitly to refer to his own project as this kind of translation of a Jewish saying into Greek language. Ironically, it all takes place in the French language. Even the Talmudic passages are presented not in Hebrew characters, but in French language. Thus the interpretation of the Talmudic text brings it into a second language, bringing both the saying and some sense of the linguistic heritage. Our passage, moreover, is a theoretical reflection on the reading that is going on in the Talmud.

Levinas has been discussing a list of phrases that were held to be untranslatable from Hebrew into Greek. He argues for two vocations in reading the Hebrew texts: (1) an ongoing Hebrew interpretation—the Oral Torah as discussed in Chapter 5, and (2) the translation into Greek. The Jewish tradition is not an historical contingency but essential to the revelation of the Bible. But in addition, there is a spiritual exigency to try to present the Bible to others.

9a) Levinas TN 62/51 To present this Scripture to the Greek reader, for whom philosophy, that is, for whom its speaking brings us beyond its vocabulary and its grammar, is another spiritual miracle: the language of an intelligence and an intelligibility open to the unbiased spirit is a necessary trial for the Torah. It

Levinas claims that translation into Greek, too, is a spiritual vocation, indeed a vocation that is a SPIRITUAL ADVENTURE. Here Levinas offers one of his characteristic definitions of Greek: it is AN INTELLIGENCE AND AN INTELLIGIBILITY OPENED TO THE UNBIASED SPIRIT. Greek is a way of knowing (INTELLIGENCE), and

belongs to the very spiritual adventure that could not lose any of its essential vocations.[5]

it pursues what is knowable with an opening to the unbiased, an opening to go
wherever the knowledge takes the knower.

Levinas is not claiming that Greek is un-
biased, only that it is AN OPENING to the unbiased spirit (or mind). Just as the
Jewish sources are not transcendent, but offer an opening to a trace of transcendence, so the Greeks open the way for an unbiased thought. The translation, Levinas makes clear, goes beyond Greek language because to speak
Greek is to identify the intelligibility of what is said: to ask *what* it is and
how can we know it. The Greek interrogation, the demand first to know, is
A NECESSARY TRIAL FOR THE TORAH. Our concern is with this necessity, and
it echoes the argument from Cohen that Judaism needs to claim its share of
reason. If reading of Scripture with the Oral Torah opens up the possibility
for the text to reveal, then the translation into Greek opens up the possibility to become known. Both readings are, according to Levinas, essential to
the Torah.

9b)   The verse commented upon in
the very last part of the Talmudic
text offered for our reflection (and
to which we are going to return) will
thus bear witness to this: "God en-
large Japheth. May he dwell in the
tents of Shem" (Gen. 9:27). According to the interpretation by Shimon
ben Gamliel, according to R. Johan-
nan, this would signify precisely
"May the speech of Japheth dwell in
the tents of Shem."

The argument that this is an essential task
for Torah is now bolstered by a citation of
a Biblical verse in a Talmudic text. The
Biblical verse is from the end of the Noah
story and is a kind of original racial
theory.

10) Genesis 9:27 "God expand
Japheth. May he dwell in the tents
of Shem, and Canaan shall be his
servant."

---

[5] Derrida WD 124–25/84 In the final analysis it never is authorized by Hebraic theses
or texts. It wants to be understood in a *recourse to experience itself*. The experience itself,
and what is most irreducible in experience: the passage and leaving toward the other: that,
in the other itself, than which nothing is more irreducibly other: the other person. Recourse
which is not to be confused with what one has always called philosophical bearing, but which
reaches a point where the exceeded philosophy cannot not be concerned. Truthfully, messianic eschatology was never literally uttered; he concerns himself only with designating in
naked experience a space or a hollow where it may be understood and where it must resonate.
This hollow is not one opening among others. It is opening itself, the opening of opening, that
which does not allow for enclosure in any category or totality, which is to say, that something of experience cannot be described in the traditional conceptuality and itself resists every
philosopheme.

What does this explication and reciprocal surpassing of the two origins and the two historical speeches, Hebraism and Hellenism, signify? A new impetus, some strange community which
is announced that would not be the spiral return of Alexandrine promiscuity? If one remembers
that Heidegger also wanted to open the passage to an ancient speech which takes support in
philosophy, carrying beyond or to this side of philosophy, what does this other passage and this
other speech signify? And above all, what does this support required of philosophy signify,
philosophy where he still continues the dialogue?

The Biblical text is Noah's blessing and curse, expressing his fury at his son's illicit sexual behavior. He asserts the priority of Shem and Japheth against Canaan. The Israelites will descend from Shem (Semites), while the to-be-conquered Canaanites will be from Canaan, who is the son of Ham (the brother of Shem and Japheth). The Biblical text, therefore, asserts the welcome of Japheth within the Israelites, and the exclusion of the Canaanites. While the Mishnah cites a ruling of Gamliel's son, Simeon, it does not explain his ruling at all. Instead, he seems to have a certain preference for the Greek language. (It should be remembered that he lived under the political and cultural domain of Hellenistic culture.) But the commentary seeks a REASON for this ruling and finds it in the Biblical verse. The Talmudic text only cites the first part, as Japheth is identified with the Greeks, because of a play on the words (*Yevanit* is Greek, *yafet* means beauty and Greek is associated with beauty). Levinas' translation of this text omits the reference to GOMER AND MAGOG, the children of Japheth, who seem to have a claim like the Greeks. But that omission distracts from

11) Mishnah. Megillah 1:8
. . . R. Simeon ben Gamliel says that books also were permitted to be written in Greek.

12) Gemara 9b   R. Abbahu said that R. Yohanan said: The ruling agrees with Simeon ben Gamliel. R. Yohanan said what is Simeon ben Gamliel's reason? Scripture says, "God expand Japheth. May he dwell in the tents of Shem." The words of Japheth shall be in the tents of Shem. And what about Gomer and Magog? R. Hiyya b. Aba said: Here is the reason it wrote "God expand Japheth," that the real beauty of Japheth shall reside in the tents of Shem.

the question at hand. (I would also add that Levinas on his next page gives a more complex and thoughtful commentary on this text. I cite it here only to provide the background for the current paragraph of Levinas' text and not in order to read it thoroughly.)

9c)   For us others Jews, certainly this is a way to claim our modernity alongside our antiquity more ancient than all antiquity: the possibility and the necessity of knowing how to speak—or of trying to speak—the Torah in Greek also.[6]

Levinas now jumps forward to US OTHER JEWS. To the modern Jews the accommodation of Greek means something quite different, if no less political. We can lay claim to the older Biblical tradition, older than that of the Ancient Greeks (in resonance with Cohen's historiography).

But we also need to learn how to speak THE TORAH IN GREEK. We can claim the tradition that opens to revelation, and we can respond to a necessity of

[6] Levinas BV 94–95/75   This passage from the Hebrew to the universality that I call Greek is thus very remarkable. It is the formula *ba'er hetev*, "very distinctly," recommending the clarity and the distinctness of Scripture, that sets to signifying complete translatability. The freeing and universalizing must be, therefore, continued. We have not yet finished translating the Bible. The Septuagint is incomplete. More, we have not finished translating the Talmud. We have barely begun. And for the Talmud, we must say that the task is delicate. A heritage that until now has been reserved for oral teaching passes, perhaps too quickly, into foreign languages and loses in the new forms its unusual bearing.

translating into the language of knowing. Levinas hesitates here in a critical moment with his dashes: not that we must KNOW HOW TO SPEAK, but only that we must TRY TO SPEAK. The complexity of translation is precisely what is exposed by these dashes. Because we may not actually be able to succeed in making the Greeks understand what the Torah says.

9d) ... For the tradition of Shem the spiritual trial consists of accepting Japheth's speaking while exalting—in contrast to the nineteenth century, which renounced it—the Oral Torah's peculiar genius in its infinite creativity of meaning through the rabbinic reading of Scripture. It is to bring that creative thought and life into Greek expression of the universal civilization— for joining or judging.

We Semites (from Shem), who translate the Torah into Greek, need to bring the tradition of the Oral Torah also. Scripture is undetachable for us from the tradition of interpretation. Nineteenth-century Jewish thinkers often tried to bring the Jewish Scriptures into their world, but they RENOUNCED the tradition of the Oral Law. The CREATIVITY in interpretation, a creativity that produces not only new words and thoughts but also a renewing way of life for the community—that creativity was abandoned as an embarrassment before the contemporary rationality. In some ways this century offers a novel opportunity to speak Greek and to translate not only the concepts from Jewish sources but also the linguistic spiritual inheritance of which Rosenzweig wrote. Levinas here still regards Greek as THE UNIVERSAL CIVILIZATION—but dashes again alert us to a questioning of that claim to universality. Again, Cohen has alerted us to a limitation of the Greeks—for whom Hebrew seems too foreign. And so Levinas uses his dashes to indicate that speaking Greek may either allow the Jewish saying to join the Greek civilization, or it also may allow a new judgment of that civilization to be heard in its own language. In Levinas' philosophical work, the Jewish saying clearly challenges and judges the modern Western philosophical tradition. But in order to make even that judgment intelligible, it is necessary to translate into that Western language. What Levinas is also cautioning in the earlier set of dashes is that the translation project must preserve its sensitivity to the original language, to the peculiarity of rabbinic hermeneutics precisely because they spawn the riches of interpretations that open the way for revelation.

9e) Into Greek expression, which is to say, according to the mode of our Western university language; even if its unbiased intelligence risks sometimes remaining naive and from which something maybe lacking in its "clear and distinct ideas!"[7]

Now Levinas is explicit about what Greek means in our world: THE MODE OF OUR WESTERN UNIVERSITY LANGUAGE. That language is OURS: as philosophers we speak it. Levinas' own writings are in French, but they are in the mode of the university (not the Jewish Yeshivah).

---

[7] Levinas TN 156–57/134–35 I call Greek, beyond the vocabulary and the grammar and the wisdom which was founded in Hellas, the manner of expressing or of trying to express itself, the universality of the West, overcoming local particularities of the quaint, folkloric, poetic, or

Levinas makes his task, therefore, the translation of what the Jewish texts say into the idiom of the university. But here he explicitly indicates the limitations of that idiom. Its very absence of bias makes it sometimes NAIVE, and more important, the absence of bias leaves it LACKING SOMETHING. Its naiveté is that it cannot see the indirection of rabbinic interpretation, the indirection necessary to say what can never become a said. And what it lacks, by pursuing Descartes' "CLEAR AND DISTINCT IDEAS," are precisely those enigmatic ideas that characterize the pragmatics interactions that open to transcendence. It lacks the tools for interpreting this responsive ethics—because it wants to pin down the conceptuality in univocal signs, and even when it looks to pragmatics it expects pragmatics to continue its task, and even when writing of ethics it cannot accept vagueness and asymmetry. In Levinas' own work, he takes the risk of presenting a saying in a language that honors only what is said. And so the most one can do is TRY to speak the Greek language because exactly what manages to become said in Greek necessarily will not be what the Torah says. The open question is to what extent it is possible for Greek to harbor a saying. Levinas must hesitate, because even to answer that question definitively is to betray the risk of translating, while not to take that risk is to yield too readily to the Greek self-understanding as being concerned only with knowing, and in such a way that no tradition can be honored.

9f) A spiritual trial for the tradition of opening Shem's tents to Japheth; tents where the Torah is studied, according to the Midrash. It is the measure of the tradition, even if the pure translation of the verse is infringed upon sometimes by a "correction," and if in a written expression—separated in Greek from its oral perspective—it must prefer a modified meaning to a dangerous misunderstanding from the literal meaning; even if, despite all the glamour—or because of all the glamour—of unbiased judgment, the translation reveals the dissonances in the text that one day will

The risk Levinas takes is to invite the university into the tent: into the Jewish study-houses where the Torah is studied. He tries not only to translate the Bible but also to bring the processes of rabbinic interpretation into our intellectual world. Just this attempt to translate Talmudic discourse into a philosophic idiom is what Levinas is performing in the text from which this passage comes. While Rosenzweig and Buber translated the Bible, Levinas (along with some others) also translates rabbinic texts, the Oral Torah—in order to offer it to the university discourse both to join and to judge. But this transla-

religious. A language without bias, a speaking that bites reality without leaving a trace and is capable of saying the truth, of erasing the traces it leaves, of unsaying, of resaying. A language that is already meta-language, concerned and able to protect the said from the structures themselves of its tongue which would pretend to be the categories of meaning. A language which means to translate—and ever to translate anew—the Bible itself and which, in the justice that it allows to found, could not forever offend the uniqueness of the other person, nor the mercy that it appeals for—at the heart of the subject—nor the responsibility for the other person that alone opens the lips in response to the word of God in the face of the other person.

be examined by philosophy and that through the Midrash have already been fecund in another dimension of meaning.

tion is a great risk, and so Levinas praises THE MEASURE OF THE TRADITION. Considering the logics of Part II again, one option for a tradition is the pagan option of ignoring all that lies beyond its borders. Such a tradition avoids translation (even as a totalizing tradition only translates into itself), but a representative tradition must pursue this risk. Levinas constructs three exceptions. First, sometimes it must allow for "CORRECTIONS" in the translations, accepting the untranslatability of a given phrase from there to here. The second is the problem of a written text in Greek that will be separated from the Oral Torah and so will be mute, not crying out for interpretation. This care to avoid A DANGEROUS MISUNDERSTANDING, a possibility for a false literalism by the university study of the text, produces, however, a MODIFIED MEANING. Again, we see just how the Jewish saying will be changed in the translation, just as the Greek language will be changed. Finally, third, there is the quality of Greek language: its unbiased judgment which has a certain glamour or brilliance. To achieve the translation into that light will produce DISSONANCES IN THE TEXT—just the sort of textuality that will solicit interpretation. Once exposed in Greek, those dissonances someday will draw philosophy into their exploration. But for the third exception, and the conclusion of the chapter in Levinas' reading, is that within the Jewish reading those texts HAVE ALREADY BEEN FECUND. Even though the oral tradition has already explored the conflicts within the written texts, it still binds itself to offer a translation into a philosophical language, where those conflicts will be reopened for a different kind of reading. Levinas does not say that this reopening bears no risk for the Jewish texts—just the opposite! Translation is as risky as any semiotic event, maybe more so. Levinas, even while assessing those risks for the Jewish sources, argues that the effort of translation lies as an essential task for us.

In the next part, I will interpret layers of traditional Jewish sources—beginning with ancient religious texts and concluding with contemporary philosophical ones. That reversal of order (in Parts I–III, I began with general contemporary texts and ended with Talmudic discourse) will be justified in the performance. But before I leave the thematic discussion of methodology, I wish to indicate that the responsibility of translation is infinite. While Cohen, Rosenzweig, and Levinas all sought to bring Jewish sources to bear on the philosophical discourse of their time, each had to retranslate the saying and the texts into a different philosophical idiom. My task here is to retranslate that saying again. My idiom is semiotics, specifically, a kind of overtaxed pragmatics, but my argument is not that the Jewish sources always say the same thing in these different contexts. Quite the opposite: the translations reveal new meanings, and also take new risks of distorting the Jewish sources. My own problem is accentuated by the coordinate problem of literally translating the various texts into English. This I must do twice:

once on a too literal level, sentence by sentence in the pretexts. But a second time, perhaps on too interpretative level, as I struggle to represent the sayings of various philosophers in an American idiom that will speak to my readers. The literal translation allows a reader to hear some kind of echo of the authors' unusual and exacting voices; the interpretative one, I hope, allows a reader to hear better what the authors have to say. The very juxtaposition of *pshat* and *drash* on one page is my way of bringing the peculiar genius of rabbinic texts into a philosophic conversation.

SUGGESTED READINGS

1   Gibbs, *Correlations*, Chapter 4.
3   Kepnes, Ochs, and Gibbs, *Reasoning After Revelation*.
8   Galli, Barbara Ellen. *Franz Rosenzweig and Jehuda Halevi: Translating, Translations, and Translators*. Montreal: McGill-Queens University Press, 1995.
9   Gibbs, *Correlations*, Chapter 7.
    Robbins, Jill. *Prodigal Son/Elder Brother: Interpretation and Alterity in Augustine, Petrarch, Kafka, Levinas*, 100–32. Chicago: University of Chicago Press, 1991.

PART IV

Repenting History

Rabbi Eliezer used to say: ". . . Repent one day before your death."

Rabbi Eliezer was asked by his disciples: "Does, then, a man know on what day he will die, that he should know when to repent?"

He said to them: "All the more, let him repent today lest he die tomorrow; let him repent tomorrow, lest he die the day after; and as a result all his days will be spent in repentance."

Avot de Rabbi-Natan, Chapter 15

CHAPTER 14

Why Repent?

WHILE THE OTHER PARTS of this book raised the unexpected question of why in recognizably philosophical contexts (Why Listen?, Why Verify?, Why Judge?), this part examines a context that itself is unexpected. For repenting is obviously a theological activity. For some readers the question, Why Repent?, may defy any reasonable answer. But the pragmatics of repentance is directly relevant for an inquiry into ethics, particularly an ethics oriented by responsibility. Repentance is one of a set of practices that repair damaged or broken relations. That set includes repentance, confession, restitution, reconciliation, and forgiveness. The question could be simple: Why repair harm done to another person?—and the answer would focus on the responsibility to mend what I have broken. Even at this level we readily see that the relations are not reciprocal—the role for the repenting person is quite different from the forgiver's. Indeed, the asymmetries indicate that another person's actions structure my responsibilities. But the question will be made more complex because of the way that I relate to my past and to the past before my birth. Indeed, in the final chapter of this book, we will be drawn to consider the social or communal dimensions of these responsibilities for the past. Several dimensions of repentance are at stake here: the relations with God and the relations with other people, the relations to my own past, the relations of the past in the present, the social dimension of the responsibility for the past.

To gain access to these responsibilities we will have recourse to pragmatics again, to a set of semiotic practices that not only perform these relations, but indeed constitute new roles for speakers and signers. The task of repair will become, first of all, a repair of faulty signs and faulty sign use. The need to reinterpret past uses will guide us for an understanding of the need to respond for our past. Practices such as repentance, confession, and forgiveness preserve earlier signs and earlier interpretations in the midst of reinterpretation. This repair is not simply a substitution of a new interpretation of a sign for the older, inadequate one. Rather, it is a motion between the two interpretations, a motion that adjusts each by the other, often by means of yet a third, still earlier interpretation. The play between these interpretations is not, therefore, a progressive sequence, but a careful adjudication of the relations between signs. By exploring these relations as social, moreover, ethical issues point forward to the new range of interpretations that can be opened for another.

This motion into the past is for the future's sake, for the opening of interpretation for my other. The Hebrew concept of repentance is linked to the root *sh u v*, which means *turn* and, most often, *return*. The mending of words and of signs and their meanings is a kind of returning. *Teshuvah* is translated as repentance or penitence, but it is not identical to the more familiar Christian concept. Most of all, *teshuvah* signifies a way of return in relationship with God. A *baal teshuvah* is a Jew who returns from sinful ways to a righteous relation with God, and in contemporary usage it refers to someone who returns to traditional observance from a modern, secular way of life. This Part is not, however, an apology for Jewish observance, nor is it an attempt to construct a dogmatic theology of *teshuvah*, nor even an attempt to provide a comprehensive history of *teshuvah*. Instead, the return explored here will become one of social ethics in the use of words.

Hosea's call to the people to return to God and to make a promise of improvement is the originary Jewish text on repentance (Section A). Section B shifts the scene to a rabbinic development of repentance, reinterpreting the Biblical account of the relations with God. The Mishnah elevated repentance in the economy of divine forgiveness in a time when Temple sacrifices were impossible (Pretext 2). Pretext 3 is an extended Talmudic text, transforming the prophetic message by constantly enhancing repentance, shifting the responsibility to the human repenters and allowing them to force God's hand. This text requires readings of Biblical texts (Pretexts 4–5, and the Hosea text again). The sages' 'historical' freedom allows them to push the texts against their plain sense.

Finally, in Section C we will turn from the need to return to God to the need to return to my human other whom I have harmed. The transition itself between the theological and the ethical occurs within these theological texts—in a way we discerned in the previous chapter. Jewish theological reflection translates itself into ethics. The dynamics are more complex, but not obvious, as the possibility of appeasing a person is different from the possibilities of appeasing God. In Pretext 6 a Mishnaic text defines a realm of social sin. It produces that realm by reading a verse from Leviticus (Pretext 7) that stipulates the establishment of the Day of Atonement. Levinas comments on that text in Pretext 8—a commentary that pushes beyond the realm of individual ability to respond to identify the need for a social cooperation. This is the first step of translation from theology to social ethics, making the social practices themselves part of the returning to the relation with God and requiring an appeal in a theological dimension to commission me to return to my companion I have harmed.

A. RETURN

1a) Hosea 14:2 Return, Israel, to THE LORD, your God, for you have stumbled in your guilt.

Hosea was a prophet at the time of the destruction of Israel, the Northern Kingdom (Eighth Century B.C.E.). In the final chapter of his book, repentance (return) is preached. The overall tone has been bleak, promising destruction. In the last part a small hope is opened that if Israel repents, then God will forgive. This text is regarded by historical Biblical critics as the primary early text on returning—and we will see that both its obscurities and what it has to say govern traditional rabbinic interpretation of returning as well. It begins with an unambiguous command: RETURN. The relation is both spatial and moral. The people have moved away, distancing themselves, and they have sinned and are GUILTY. But either the guilt has a subsequent effect of making them STUMBLE, or the sinning itself is a falling. The prophet calls them to return to a way of righteousness, a way that one can walk. The people must take the next step in response to the command: they themselves will have to return. Able to respond to the command, the people have not been prevented from returning by their stumbling.

1b] 3) Take words with you and return to THE LORD. Say to him: "Take away all guilt, accept what is good. We will offer our words for bulls. 4) Assyria will not save us; we will not ride on horses, nor will we say 'Our God' to the work of our hands, for in you the orphan finds mercy."

To return to God requires TAKING WORDS. Indeed, the spiritual or psychological dimension is quickly replaced by the directions about how to speak. Like a script, Hosea instructs the people to prepare a speech, then return to God, and then speak. Perhaps the return is only the preparation for delivering the speech, or perhaps the return is the whole act concluding with delivering the speech. In either case, Hosea dictates to the people a specific sequence of requests and promises. Unfortunately, our text is extremely obscure. What is said in verse 3 is hard to understand. It begins with a double request: TAKE AWAY GUILT/ACCEPT GOOD. What tripped the people up (GUILT) should now be removed. This may have disturbed the relationship between God and the people, but it also may be something that disturbs the people alone. Clearly, however, ACCEPT WHAT IS GOOD is relational. Indeed, the next line—the most obscure—points to a contested issue in the relation. This text originated in a time when animal sacrifices were required. The word BULLS is contested, but I adopt the traditional Jewish reading that the people are to bring WORDS instead of animals. The relationship will now be mended by these words. Hence the term ACCEPT asks God to accept as sacrifice what is good. The relationship, whether with animals or with words, is symbolic: the performance of offering and accepting constitutes the relationship, a relationship of loyalty and love. (Hosea's prophecy extensively develops marriage imagery as the relationship between God and Israel.) In verse 4, the people continue to make promises. The first step is the recognition that a political alliance with Assyria will not protect them from destruction. Nor will their own military might (RIDE ON HORSES) protect them. Finally, they will no longer regard their own work as their god. This sequence promises to accept an exclusive dependence on God—neither a foreign political alliance nor a military alliance nor their own productivity will be their vital trust. Instead, they will trust God and depend on God. They can depend on God because God is merciful to those without power, to the ORPHAN. Within this speech is a further performance: the speech they will not say by calling their work their god. To offer the words of return it becomes important to cancel previous speech, to refer to it, in order to exclude it. At its most simple this is an apology: a request to restore a relationship coupled to a promise to trust the other and not to trust only in oneself. Returning needs such words in order to exclude the words that represent the break of the relation.

1c] 5) I will heal their turnings. I will love them freely; because my anger has turned away from him.

Hosea now speaks in the voice of God, providing what in some sense is a precondition for returning and speaking. Israel can expect this response. But one could read it as the next interchange in the dialogue. It seems that the promise of forgiveness makes the command to return possible. What God promises is HEALING, but just which object is less clear. The root of the word I translate TURNING is related to the root of return, but is usually translated as apostasy or backsliding. The meaning is clear: God will heal or mend the break initiated by the people. The promise arises because God loves freely; we might say unconditionally. The hesitation from Israel is, however, justified: only now is God's anger TURNED AWAY FROM HIM. When Israel sinned, God could not be addressed. Indeed, the destruction of the Northern Kingdom is interpreted throughout Hosea as justified and violent anger from God. The hope—that one could actually return, and after apologizing and promising, be healed by the other—appears in these verses in some contrast to the rest of Hosea. We can see two different roles in a complex narrative. A relationship has been broken, leaving the one party angry and the other stumbling and open to suffering. With the promise of love and healing, the one party commands the other to return, to come back and to promise to do well. The theology clearly creates a disparity in the roles, but the roles are connected, each dependent on the other and each responsible only in relation to the other. And each performs its role in speaking—or so the prophet instructs us. God has fashioned a role for the people: the returner.

B. Great Is Repentance

The asymmetries in the Biblical relationship are transformed in the time of the sages, the "Pharisees," or founders of the Judaism that leads to modern Judaism. Repentance is not merely a needed move in the divine plan, a role for the people to fulfill in a context of punishment and eventual forgiveness. No, repentance itself becomes a power to force God's hand, to repair the world, indeed, even to change the past. This blossoming of *teshuvah* is achieved in two textual stages. First, we can jump ahead a thousand years, to the time of the Tannaim, the earlier sages. The Second Temple has been destroyed, and the sacrifices have ceased—as they have until today. In a period of relatively peaceful relations with the Roman Empire, Judah the Patriarch promulgated the Mishnah—a text that stood largely independent of the textuality of the Scriptural canon. In that text much care is devoted to describing the sacrifices, now obsolete, that had been offered in the Temple. Moreover, the whole economy of relations of offerings, priests, tithes, holidays, and so on are discussed continually. Thus in the division of the Mishnah devoted to fixed times (we would say, holidays), one of the longest tractates concerns the order of events on Yom Kippur, the Day of Atonement. We discussed the holiday, particularly in contemporary observance in Rosenzweig earlier, but in the times of the Temple, the ritual included the scapegoat, the audible proclamation of the name of God, and the high priest entering the Holy of Holies. These events were unique in the year, and by the time of the Mishnah they were impossible. Only after several chapters of discussion of the series of the washing, sacrificing, offering, and praying of the high priest, in the last long chapter of the tractate, do the sages turn to the observances and spirituality of the rest of the people. The last two texts from this chapter will concern us: the last one later, the earlier one now.

2) Mishnah Yoma 8:8 The sin offering and the guilt offering atone. Death and the Day of Atonement atone with repentance. Repentance atones for light transgressions—both against positive and against negative commandments—but against heavy ones it suspends until the Day of Atonement, which atones.

The issue here is what ATONES? The question is both what is the human side in restoring the relation with God, and also what discharges the guilt. The Mishnah begins with a technical pair of sacrifices that were offered according to requirements in Leviticus. Each is the responsibility of someone who has sinned, and the text claims that sacrifice alone was enough. But the second sentence speaks more directly to the time when there are no longer sacrifices. It begins deceptively and shockingly: DEATH AND THE DAY OF ATONEMENT ATONE. The shock comes from DEATH. When the Temple stood, bringing a sacrifice atoned. God allowed for a restoration of the sinner through the offering of an animal. But now the sinner himself will have to die to be atoned. Or alternatively THE DAY OF ATONEMENT can repair the relation: the Day, however, without the sacrifices, the scapegoat, the proclamation of the name. Or perhaps only the combination of death and this day, a day much changed but still observed—only a combination will atone. Indeed, the text complicates the process by insisting with its last two words upon REPENTANCE. Even the ultimate sacrifice, death, even the communal observances will not atone without a return. If the first sentence made atonement seem straightforward and external, asking only for a sacrifice of an animal, the second sentence now makes atonement seem to risk the sinner's life and to require a return. And thus the third sentence moves still further toward the requirements upon the sinner. Transgressions come in two kinds: LIGHT AND HEAVY. This is an uncharacteristic distinction (in contrast to the POSITIVE/ NEGATIVE one), but what surprises here is that REPENTANCE ATONES FOR LIGHT TRANSGRESSIONS. Repentance has moved from being a concomitant condition with death and the Day, to replacing all of the other means. Not sacrifice, not death, not the Day, but repentance on its own now atones for many sins. Moreover, in the case of severe transgressions, repentance is capable of suspending until the Day comes, which then atones. The Day is fixed in the calendar. But what is suspended? Punishment, of course, and that easily enough could mean death. The three sentences then show a set of different frames of reference: (1) sacrifices in the Temple, (2) death and the Day, with repentance, (3) repentance for part, repentance and the Day for part.

I would not choose to claim that this text is unambiguous, nor that it represents the sole position from this strata of the tradition. But what is clear here is that both repentance and the Day are elevated through this Mishnah. Indeed, while the Biblical sources call for turning and returning, it is with rabbinic sources of this period that *teshuvah*, the returning (repentance), becomes a noun. I comment on this text, therefore, because it shows *teshuvah* emerging as a category of its own, in some key way replacing sacrifice as the center of the human role in mending the broken relations. Moreover, like the Hosea text, this is an originary source, and as we proceed we will have recourse to this text.

The next step is to the Babylonian Talmud. Taking as its pretext the Mishnah, the later sages (Amoraim) continued a process of interpretation and argumentation. After four hundred years, schools in Babylonia edited and constructed a new literary form in a kind of commentary upon the Mishnah. Much of the interpretation developed intertextual connections between sayings that were canonized in the Mishnah and sayings that were collected outside the Mishnah, between Mishnaic rulings and Biblical texts, between apparently conflicting Biblical texts, and so on. In the lengthy discussion about our Mishnah, there is a unit (*sugya*) that stands as one of the rabbinic traditions' great accounts of *teshuvah*, of returning. It is structured around a refrain: Great is repentance.

3a) Yoma 86a–b   R. Hama bar Hanina said: "Great is repentance: it brings healing to the world, as it is said: 'I will heal their turnings. I will love them freely'" [Hos. 14:5].

The Talmudic text begins with an attribution to a sage who lived two generations after the editing of the Mishnah. It reports that he praised repentance because IT BRINGS HEALING TO THE WORLD. He cites God's promise in the fifth verse from our text from Hosea.

This is not simply a proof-text, as though citing Hosea authorized his point. Rather, he interprets Hosea: repentance BRINGS

1c] Hosea 14:5) I will heal their turnings. I will love them freely; because my anger has turned away from him.

healing. God's healing of the Israelites' separation and brokenness is consequent to their repentance. If they did not repent, there could be no healing here. Hosea could have meant this, but Hosea made God's love the source of healing—R. Hama argues that repentance, which lies within human hands, is responsible for creating healing.

3b) R. Hama bar Hanina raised contradictory verses: "It is written: 'Return, turning children' [Jer. 3:22], that is, you began as turned, and it is written 'I will heal you from your turning' [Jer. 3:22.]."

The text now elucidates the relation of healing to repentance, citing another saying of R. Hama. It examines a tension between two phrases in Jeremiah (although there is a textual variant that cites a different verse from Jeremiah). We first consider the text of Jeremiah, and then interpret R. Hama's interpretation.

Jeremiah was a prophet at the time of the fall of the Southern Kingdom, Judah (587 B.C.E.). The historical scholars hold that the passages cited here are self-consciously imitative of Hosea, a claim that is easy to see in the play on the root turn/return. This text comes at the end of a difficult passage and culminates in a dialogue where God calls to the people to

4] Jeremiah 3:21) A voice is heard on the high hills, weeping and supplications of the children of Israel, for they have perverted their ways, and forgotten THE LORD their God. 22) "Return, turning children, and I will heal you from your turning." "Here we are, we have come to you: for you are THE LORD our God . . ."

turn, and they respond, returning and confessing God. The first verse here is somewhat obscure. It may mean that THE VOICE is God's voice, weeping for the people, weeping like Rachel in a similar verse, who weeps for her children. This text suggests that God calls to the people to return, to remember God. God promises healing from their turning away, and as a result of that promise the people return.

Just what R. Hama has in mind is obscure. The first phrase recognizes that the people were already turned away, and calls for them to return. The second, however, sees God as healing them from being turned away. R. Hama splits the two, interpreting that in the first healing is brought into the world by repentance, but in the latter case, healing is in God's hands and does not depend on repentance. The Jeremiah verse seems to make the people both turned away (and so the initiators in the healing) and returned by God from being turned away (and so not responsible).

3c) This is not a problem: there—from love, and there—from fear.

The text explains the contradiction by offering a further determination of the term *return*. In one case return is out of LOVE, in the other case out of FEAR. This interpretation of a vague sign into two contradictories is often used in the Talmud. But what does it mean here? When those who had turned away turn themselves back, returning to God freely: that is out of love. When the turned away are healed by God while still turned away, they may indeed return, but it happens out of fear, for God reminds them that they were turned away. Thus when God tells them,

"I WILL HEAL YOUR TURNING," they return, but are made to recall their sinfulness. R. Hama's position is qualified, for it is only as a return from love that repentance initiates healing—when God's healing happens first, it produces the fearful return. The greatness of repentance, the power in human hands, comes from love and is backed by God's punishing judgment, which is reserved for producing fearful repentance. But the plain sense of the prophetic text showed a greatness in God's desire for the people, and allowed for repentance only within a script that was dominated by God. The Talmudic text reinvests the Biblical text with a complexity at most hinted at in itself. It makes the historical text more complex—precisely in relation to the question of whether God is manipulating the people to return or the people are responding freely, and so responsively healing the world.

The Talmudic text then proposes several other ways that *teshuvah* is great, including suspending prohibitions of the Torah and bringing redemption, in each case reinterpreting Biblical prophetic texts. It leads, however, to a pair of rulings about the power to change the past, a pair by one sage, Resh Lakish.

3d) ... Resh Lakish said: "Great is repentance: by it intentional sins are made like unintentional errors, as it is said: 'Return, Israel, to THE LORD your God, for you have stumbled in your guilt' [Hos. 14:2]. Guilt is intentional, but it calls it stumbling. Is this so!?"

With Resh Lakish, the text brings forward a twist within the spiritual economy of sin and righteousness. Indeed, he is cited twice, once interpreting Hosea; once interpreting Ezekiel. These two moves will expand and be reinterpreted as the heart of our semiotic interpretation of repentance. Here repentance is capable of transforming INTENTIONAL SINS into unintentional ones (ERRORS). In a legal framework unintentional errors are more readily redressed than intentional sins. This follows common sense: if someone chooses to harm another person, or willfully breaks off relations, it seems almost impossible to repair the relations. Someone who inadvertently harms another, no matter how grievously, seems more capable of mending the relation. But Resh Lakish now claims that repentance can transform the willful into the inadvertent. Even if I chose to harm another, when I repent I realize that I did not know what I was doing. The effort to return and to readdress the other transforms my past action from a cruel deed into one whose effects I did not understand. This is truly a remarkable effect. Resh Lakish's text is the first verse of the Hosea passage.

He interprets the command (RETURN) as governing the latter clause. The textual question is whether STUMBLING and GUILT belong together. For us the question about this juxtaposition was whether the stumbling happened with sinning or was an action that followed after the guilt had been committed. Resh Lakish now interprets the problem by noting that STUMBLING is not an intentional act, but an error. The guilt, moreover, is clearly the result of intentional sin. Thus

1a) Hosea 14:2 Return, Israel, to THE LORD, your God, for you have stumbled in your guilt.

in the space of the verse, we see the intentional sin becoming error, through the power of repentance.

3e) But Resh Lakish said: "Great is repentance: by it intentional sins are made like merits, as it is said: 'When the wicked man turns from his wickedness and does what is just and right, then because of them he shall live'" [Ezek. 33:19].

The Talmud now brings a different text from Resh Lakish, a text that seems to challenge the interpretation of repentance just advanced. For here Resh Lakish claims repentance is able to transform intentional sins INTO MERITS. The idea of merits is complex in rabbinic tradition, but the most basic sense requires that my sins become something held in my favor, something good, perhaps even beyond the average or supererogatory. This claim is paradoxical, but it perhaps reflects that a mended relation can be stronger and better, precisely because each party has had to transform the relation. The repentant one has had to recognize his fault, and has struggled to reapproach the other; the offended one has had to forgive and accept the apology. This paradoxical claim, that by repenting I will gain credit for what I had originally intended with malice, is the claim that will open up other semiotic transformations in Chapter 16.

Resh Lakish uses a text from Ezekiel. This text comes from a chapter in which Ezekiel is invested with responsibility for the fate of others, and is charged to warn them. God instructs Ezekiel to say this

5) Ezekiel 33:19 'When the wicked man turns from his wickedness and does what is just and right, then because of them he shall live.'

promise as well as several threats. TURNING is again the point, and it is a turning from WICKEDNESS to what is RIGHT. The text seems to say that because of his newfound righteousness, he will live. But Resh Lakish raises a problem with the Hebrew word translated BECAUSE OF THEM. Are we sure which deeds are referred to as THEM? Resh Lakish wants to argue that the emphatic claim about living must refer not to the righteous deeds, but to the wickedness. The text is stretched, again, in order to make repentance itself transform the wicked deeds. Ezekiel might have been happy to have a person live from moral improvement; Resh Lakish requires that life come as reward for having sinned and repented.

3f) It is not a problem: there— from love, there—from fear.

The Talmudic text has thus created a conflict between two positions of Resh Lakish. Does he see repentance turning intentional sins into ignorant mistakes or into merits? Again, the vagueness is resolved by the familiar determination, from LOVE or FEAR. We have to pursue the distinction. When a person FEARS punishment, the returning only manages to make the sins into simple mistakes; when someone returns out of LOVE for the other, her past sin now becomes a credit to her. For a loving return has the power to change the past radically, making what was ill-intended into a loving desire. The tension between these two kinds of return, and the way they change the past, will occupy us in Chapter 16.

3g)   R. Isaac said (or they say in the west in the name of Rabbah b. Mari): "Come and see that the character of the Holy One, Blessed be He, is unlike the character of flesh and blood. When someone of flesh and blood angers his companion with words—he may be able to appease him, or he may not be able to appease him, and if you say that he appeases him, words may be enough to appease him, or words may not be enough to appease him. But with the Holy One, Blessed be He, if a man transgresses a transgression in secret—He is appeased by him with words as it is said: 'Take words with you and return to THE LORD' [Hos. 14:3]. Furthermore he accounts it to him as good, as it is said: 'accept what is good' [ib]. Furthermore Scripture accounts it to him as if he had offered up bullocks, as it is said: 'We will offer our words for bulls'" [ib].

The difficulty of making these theological relations and the need for repentance into an ethics is made clear in the next piece. It neither cites contradictory verses nor recites the refrain (great is repentance). Instead, a parable is introduced. It offers the traditional parabolic contrast between God and someone of FLESH AND BLOOD. The text begins with the human, and then contrasts the way God acts. A person ANGERS HIS COMPANION WITH WORDS. The break in the interpersonal relations begins in a semiotic performance. An insult causes a break. The parable allows that APPEASING someone who was insulted is touchy. Just because I return and offer something does not force my companion to be satisfied. And even if I can make good the relation, it is not clear that WORDS can be used. It may take deeds, money, even silence. An insult seems to degrade words most of all. Returning is far from guaranteed, even if it is most needed, and the linguistic mending is the most unsure.

The Talmud now claims that God responds differently. First, while the insult is public, there are many private ways to offend God. Hence, God is insulted and offended many times over, and yet God can be APPEASED. Not only can God be satisfied, but WORDS alone are enough. The parable teaches that in relation to God words can be used to mend the offense. But our interest is only piqued here, precisely because the text now justifies this claim by reinterpreting the most obscure verse in the Hosea passage:

In interpreting the passage, we already saw that Hosea was proposing that returning with words would be acceptable. This text, however, interprets the sequence—TAKE WORDS, and then RE-TURN—as indicating that the bringing of

1b] Hosea 14:3)   Take words with you and return to THE LORD. Say to him: "Take away all guilt, accept what is good. We will offer our words for bulls."

words makes the return possible, and the return here is seen as appeasing God. But the talmudic text moves on (skipping the phrase TAKE AWAY ALL GUILT) to the phrase ACCEPT WHAT IS GOOD. What is good? The words that are brought to appease God. Indeed, here words of apology are not merely seen as acceptable, rather bringing words is ACCOUNTED AS GOOD. Here we see Resh Lakish's sense of sin become merit, as insult becomes a good in the return to God. Finally, the last phrase is interpreted along the lines we proposed above: WORDS FOR BULLS. The bulls that would have represented the appeasing offering are now replaced by words—with a subtle emphasis: SCRIPTURE ACCOUNTS IT. There is a recording of the shift of insult to merit, of apologies in lieu of animals. The text that was obscure on its own terms has been rendered clear: returning with words can appease God, indeed can transform insult into merit. The Scriptural requirement for sacrificial animals is itself recorded as met by the returning, apologetic words.

3h) You might say that it is obligatory bulls—but it says 'I will heal their turning. I will love them freely' [Hos. 14:5].

There is one more objection: to be accounted as credit, the offering of words must be free—not OBLIGATORY. If the people were merely offering words in place of required sacrifice, then their offering is not fully to their credit. The offering of words itself displays responsibility best if the responders are not compelled.

The text continues, by interpreting the last verse of the passage from Hosea, insisting on the word FREELY. This interpretation applies the word describing God to the returning people. The return is from

1c] Hosea 14:5) I will heal their turnings. I will love them freely; because my anger has turned away from him.

love, replacing sins with merit, and so offers words freely in place of free-will offering of bulls. The returning to appease God is thus fully within the power of the returners, and in their power as they speak, as they perform this apology and promise.

3i) ... It was taught by a tanna: R. Meir used to say: "Great is repentance: because of a single person who makes repentance, the whole world is forgiven as a whole, as it is said: 'I will heal their turning. I will love them freely; because my anger has turned away from him' [Hos. 14:5]. It does not say 'from them,' but rather 'from him.' "

The final refrain is cited as a teaching of an earlier sage, R. Meir. Repentance is great because A SINGLE PERSON can save the whole world, representing and repenting for all through his singular action. Here is a classic statement of representation in the sense of our discussion of Rosenzweig in Chapter 8. R. Meir proposes not that each saves only himself, nor that those who fail to repent are lost. One person returns, and not only the Jewish people, but THE WHOLE WORLD is forgiven by God.

The text of course is Hosea—the last verse. The text begins with THEIR TURNINGS, a plural community, but it ends with God's anger turned FROM HIM. One could

1c] Hosea 14:5) I will heal their turnings. I will love them freely; because my anger has turned away from him.

easily enough see the play of singular and plural subordinated to changing reference to the community as one. (One might even suspect a scribal variant.) R. Meir, however, changes the meaning radically by reading it backward. Because it says HIM, then it means that when God turns His anger away from even one person, God heals everyone's turning away. God's healing is coerced by one returner. And so the opening comment of R. Hama is shown now in its richest extension: repentance brings healing into the world—one repentant sinner brings healing for the whole world.

I wish to make a few notes on this passage and commentary. First, its form: we have a rondo of sorts, with a set of voices each presenting its own variation on a general theme. While there is a sequencing of the various opinions, including a circular motion beginning and ending with the verse that refers to healing, there is neither a deductive structure, nor is there a narrative that links the sequence. Moreover, key to the form is a motion back and forth from Biblical texts. One of the central tasks is to relate a wide range of opinions to earlier texts, most of which are themselves problematic. But this leads to my second point: the sages are not primarily interested in producing an historical reading of the Biblical texts. Their interest is double: to advance a set of theological innovations, and to negotiate that set with Biblical pretexts. The rabbinic reading both transforms the contextual meaning of the verses cited and at the same time is rooted deeply in the language of the verses. These are far from obvious readings, but they are not oblivious of the effort in the reading. The theological innovation is itself critical of alternative theological views: the importance of *teshuvah* seems to overwhelm a theology that centers on God's authority. Each of the praises of repentance challenges an absolute theological position, championing human agency. *Teshuvah*, by humans, can replace attributes traditionally reserved for God. The negotiation of the relation with Biblical texts makes this novel importance of the human role of returning plausible. The task of return is now granted excessive capacity; the responsibility to return is made excessive in turn.

Finally, third, return is accomplished as a pragmatic intervention. Beyond the way that the sages transform the role of human return and the interpretative strategies they take up with the Bible, there is a further interest for us: offering words becomes substitute for offering animals. After the destruction of the Temple, atonement can no longer rest on sacrifices (and death). But the justification for the elevation of the act of bringing words has two relevant dimensions for us. (1) The sages interpret the prophets as already making the shift. The sages may be innovating, but in some way, they are returning to the insights from the times of the fall of the Davidic Kingdoms. We see, then, in their action a rereading of the past, an attempt to return to the prophetic texts and to refigure those texts in relation to their own times. The sages' interest in interpretation is precisely a kind of return to a past. (2) The sages are most interested in the pragmatics, in the parallel between *offering* animals and *offering* words. The performances are made parallel, and we might well see that for a rabbinic interpretation of sacrifice, the animals are themselves symbolic. Of course, only appropriate animals and appropriate words are to be offered, but it is through offering the words that the sins become merits. Which leads to the final note here: the sins themselves are in this text seen as signs. In their account of appeasing, the sin is committed with words, but in general, the transformation of the sin into a merit is the transformation of a sign, a reinterpretation, a discovery of a new meaning for a past event. The pragmatics of offering words is linked to the pragmatics of sinning, and return itself becomes semiotic—through this remarkable effort of rabbinic interpretation.

C. Social Repentance

To bring this discussion back to ethics, we need to be more exacting about the difference between interhuman relations and the theological relations between a person and God. I have selected theological texts with the hope that the pragmatics in the theological relation might translate into a social context. We must now face the question that the Talmud raised with its parable: God is readily forgiving, but people can be less so. How can returning function when the one to whom I return is only human? What may I hope? Should I bother?

In the discussion of the first Mishnah, I promised a second Mishnaic text. It is one of the most familiar of all rabbinic texts and occurs at the end of the tractate Yoma.

6) Mishnah. Yoma. 8:9 . . . Transgressions between a human and God—the Day of Atonement atones. Transgressions between a human and his companion—the Day of Atonement does not atone until he has satisfied his companion. Rabbi Elazar ben Azariah interpreted: "From all your sins before THE LORD, you will be cleansed" [Lev. 16:30]: transgressions between a human and God—the Day of Atonement atones; transgressions between a human and his companion—the Day of Atonement does not atone until he has satisfied his companion.

The Mishnah asserts a fundamental division: transgressions against God and transgressions against other people. It understands transgressions as relational (BETWEEN), and so is concerned with repairing the relations. The term translated COMPANION extends as if it were neighbor, friend, buddy, pal, or possibly 'other.' But the point of the term *companion* is to make the idea of SATISFACTION reasonable. Someone with whom a person has had a relationship is the paradigmatic choice for making the point that the other person must be satisfied. As for the sins against God, we are again in the context where THE DAY itself atones. A traditional interpretation of atonement for those sins against a companion requires a two-stage response: (1) satisfy the other person, and then (2) return to God to complete the atonement. The Mishnah supports such an interpretation, by claiming that the Day DOES NOT ATONE UNTIL. Even after satisfying the other person, the Day is still needed for atonement. What is still more interesting, however, is that the Mishnah advances a specific sage who makes an exegetical remark. Until this point in this chapter of the Mishnah there have been no citations of Biblical texts. The process of interpreting Scripture occurred in the Talmudic commentary upon the earlier Mishnaic text. R. Elazar's interpretation indeed opens the door to two remarkable interpretations by R. Akiva about cleansing water, and indeed, about the availability of forgiveness. Our task is to examine what R. Elazar found, and why he needed to look to Scripture.

The Leviticus text is one of the most basic about Yom Kippur. The first verse establishes the key elements of the law: a fixed calendrical assignment, the practices of rest and affliction, and the inclusion of all who live among the people. We have already discussed the last, in the context of Rosenzweig's interpretation and in general with the issue of translation. We might find in the concept of the resident

7] Leviticus 16:29) And this shall be a law for you forever: In the seventh month, on the tenth day of the month, you shall afflict your souls and do no work at all, neither the citizen nor the resident alien in your midst. 30) Because on that day atonement will be made for you to cleanse you from all your sins; before THE LORD you will be clean.

alien (pilgrim) some light on the reconciliation between people. And in our last chapter the importance of the calendrification will become clear. But R. Elazar is looking at the next verse. The verb CLEANSE is used twice, and the grammar causes some confusion. I would suggest that the plain sense is to insert a break between SINS and BEFORE. The second clause, then, is the resulting cleanliness before God that the atonement and the cleansing of the Day brings. The problem in the verse is that if in the first part the Day does cleanse the people, then the second part is redundant: of course they are clean before God—before whom else could they be clean? R. Elazar, however, pushes against this break, and interprets FROM ALL OUR SINS BEFORE GOD, YOU WILL BE CLEANSED. R. Elazar, therefore, argues that the first time the root TO CLEAN appears, it concludes the phrase by stating that the purpose of the Day is to cleanse. The second half then explains not that the cleansing is before God, but that the relevant sins are those committed before God. Hence, R. Elazar restricts the SINS to only those BEFORE GOD, and so claims that the interhuman ones are not cleansed by the Day. The first half refers to the appeasement of the companion, the second to atonement before God.

Why does the Mishnah need R. Elazar's interpretation? What is novel is not that the Day atones, but that the Day cannot atone for the sins between people. The Mishnah is substantializing a category of interhuman relations (we might call it *ethics*), and separating it from the category of sins against God. If we are right, however, to say that the ethical infractions also partake of sin against God, we still have the production of a category that would be characterized as social sins, and the remedy includes working things out with someone who has been harmed. The other person is clearly in control: he must be satisfied. The point is not that before the Mishnah was edited, Judaism did not know that when another person has been hurt, I must first satisfy her. Rather, the formalizing of this concept helps to focus my attention on the social repair. The recourse to the Biblical interpretation both authorizes the new category and allows us to see its novelty.

In 1963, Levinas presented a reading of this Talmudic text to the annual conference in Paris of French Speaking Jewish Intellectuals. That year the topic was Forgiveness. Levinas commented on the Mishnah we have just discussed and on the Gemara that itself comments on this Mishnah. Levinas accentuates the limits of the repenter's authority, not so much diminishing its responsibility but rather interweaving it with the other's authority to forgive.

8a) Levinas 9T 36–39/16–17 My sins in relation to God are forgiven without my depending on his good will! God is in one sense *the Other* par excellence, the other as other, the absolutely other—and nonetheless my disposition with this God depends only on me. The instrument of forgiveness is in my hands.

Levinas claims that the contrast between the sins against God and against the other person allows me to control the dispensation of forgiveness in relation to God. God is so OTHER that forgiveness is not a question of satisfying the other, but only of repenting—or of repenting and the Day. The general question about the dynamics between the two people in repentance and forgiveness gets exactly the twist that has concerned us. God can be counted on to forgive, but the other person must not be presumed to forgive.

8b) In contrast, the neighbor, my brother, a human, infinitely less other than the absolutely other is, in a certain sense, more other than God: to obtain his forgiveness on the Day of Atonement, I must as a precondition appease him. And if he refuses? As soon as there are two, everything is in danger. The other may refuse to forgive and leave me forever unforgiven. . . .[1]

The CONTRAST, however, accentuates just how much harder it is to be forgiven by another person. I am in her hands. I must respond to her freedom to forgive or not. The other person becomes more free, MORE OTHER THAN GOD! Levinas notes this paradox and that the structure of asymmetry with another person is in some ways more rigorous than the relationship with God—because of the profound

---

[1] Cohen RR 249/213 Therefore, just as self-sanctification constitutes the concept of human, insofar as he becomes the individual-I through it, so God also must exclude any collaboration in the forgiveness of sin. It is the essence of God to forgive human sins. This is the most important content of the correlation God and human. Through goodness the yield of this correlation becomes clarified and distinguished. God's goodness, connected with holiness, secures the morality of the human as the I. The success of self-sanctification is secured in God's goodness.

Therefore no special *arrangements* in God's essence are necessary for the forgiveness of sin. Creation and revelation are the sufficient preconditions; they both create the human holy spirit. And this holy spirit, whose self-preservation is accomplished by self-sanctification, is entirely secured against relapse into sin through God's goodness whose particular task is forgiveness.

unpredictability of the other's response. While Levinas does emphasize how vulnerable we are in relation to others, especially to those others we have harmed, he also integrates the unexpectable fact that others do forgive, do allow us to return. If the dependence and responsiveness to another is dramatically clear in relation to another person, is the sense in which forgiveness is in my own hands in relation to God simply liberating?

8c) ... The ritual transgression—and that which is the offense to God in the offense to the neighbor—would destroy me more profoundly than the offense against the other person, but taken in itself and separated from the impiety which it conceals, it is the origin of my cruelty, of my harmfulness and of my complacency with myself. That an evil requires repairing of the self by the self is the measure of the depth of the wound. The effort that moral conscience makes to reestablish itself as moral conscience, the *Teshuvah*, the Return, is at the same time the relation with God and an absolutely interior event.

Turning against God causes profound harm to my moral conscience. Unlike a broken relationship with someone, which might be replaced by a relationship with another, the break here breaks me in breaking the relationship with God. This breaking is an ORIGIN for CRUELTY toward others and for COMPLACENCY. My own lack of concern, indeed, my own violence against others arises through my turning away from God and the commands to be righteous. Levinas interprets these sins as internalized in a way resemblant of Kant's account of the radical evil. Moreover, only autonomous action, action by the self in order to repair itself, will fix what is wrong with the self. Here Levinas interprets repentance in a strikingly nonsemiotic and autonomous way. AN ABSOLUTELY INTERIOR EVENT—the relation with God is precisely nonsocial and seems here almost atemporal.

8d) There would not be a more profound interiorization of the concept of God than that which one finds in the Mishnah: stating that my sins, in relation to the Eternal, are forgiven by the Day of Atonement. In my most rigorous isolation, I receive forgiveness. But we therefore understand why Yom Kippur is necessary to obtain this forgiveness: How would you have a moral conscience affected to its marrow find in itself the necessary support for beginning this advance toward its own interiority and toward solitude?

Levinas, indeed, is advancing to a paradoxical height. No one who has followed my interpretation (or any other) of Levinas thus far can help but be surprised that interiorization and self-relation are now extolled. He concludes with a shocking comment: IN MY MOST RIGOROUS ISOLATION, I RECEIVE FORGIVENESS. But in the sentence before he sets himself up for the unmasking of this highly modernistic interpretation of forgiveness. For the Mishnah stated that the Day of Atonement atones. Levinas switches languages in his troubling question, referring to the Day as

YOM KIPPUR, and accentuating thereby that the Day is not a generic day in which atonement occurs, but is the Jewish Day, set in the specific language as in the specific calendar. This efficacy of the Day, of Yom Kippur, has become altogether troubling. If the moral conscience is rotten to the core (TO

ITS MARROW), how can it pull itself out of the morass? The Münchhausen/ Autonomy model of repentance seems inconceivable. A lonely man, even with faith, cannot return.

8e) It needs recourse to the objective order of the community to obtain this intimacy of deliverance. There must be a day fixed on the calendar and all of the solemn ceremony of Atonement in order that the "damaged" moral conscience might attain its intimacy and reconquer the integrity that no one can reconquer for it. A work that is equivalent to God's forgiveness. To us this dialectic of the collectivity and of the intimacy seems very important. . . .[2]

Levinas argues that the social CALENDAR, the human CEREMONY, the COLLECTIVITY of the people—these provide the context in which the individual can attain forgiveness. The isolated person cannot confess, cannot achieve the return. Our last chapter will deal with calendars and ritual performance in greater detail, but here I want to examine, briefly, how Levinas has resocialized the forgiveness for the sins against God. For those sins that are against another person, one must appease the other person. The vulnerability and the responsive role left to the sinner is unmistakable. But in relation to God the rabbinic texts had contended that repentance is potent because one can count on God's forgiveness. But Levinas redevelops the logic of self-renewal, accentuating the isolation and extremity of the sin. Levinas then interprets the rabbinic account of the Day as providing the social context in which an individual can return. That context is not a result but is the very condition for what otherwise would be impossible. While we may be in the other's hands for the offenses against her, we are also still beholden to the others, to the others become a community, for the return to responsibility that makes us able to receive forgiveness from God. Thus Levinas can argue, quite traditionally, that the ritual as social performance both accentuates a theological relation of the individual and a social relation within the community.

From Levinas, we see how difficult the process of repentance itself is. In relation to another person, there is a gulf between my repentance and the other's acceptance and forgiveness. In relation to God, the gulf centers on

---

[2] Soloveitchik TS 91/119 The difference between individual confession and communal confession is tremendous, for the Assembly of Israel confesses one way, the individual confesses another. The individual confesses from a state of insecurity, depression, and despair in the wake of sin. What assurance does he have that there is atonement for him? And who can say to him that his transgression will be wiped out and will not haunt him till the end of his days? The confession of the Assembly of Israel—and each and every Jewish community is a microcosm of the whole of the Assembly of Israel—is not like this. The confession is said out of a state of security and even a state of rejoicing. For it is said before a loyal ally, before its most beloved one. In fact, in certain Jewish communities (I myself heard this in Germany) it is customary when the leader chants the al-het confession for the whole congregation to sing it together in heartwarming melodies.

The individual does not sing al-het; the individual weeps the al-het. Not so the community, because it does not come to plead for atonement; the community claims that atonement comes as its right.

my inability to return, an inability that makes me depend all the more on other people. While being a forgiver may be 'easier,' return is all the more hard, and the only strengthening of my ability to respond comes from the social responsibilities with others. Levinas accentuates how we need others for both kinds of sins, and indeed, shifts the dynamics in repentance from its greatness to its dependence on other people. The responsibility to repent is structured in relation to other people. The social relations that enable me to return are themselves performed by social return, in the form of a social remembrance. The atonement for sins against my companion will require both appeasing her and then the Day, the practice of my community. We repent in order to return, to repair our social relations in a responsibility that is first an interaction with the other person and then a communal performance.

Suggested Readings

1   Wolff, Hans Walter. *Hosea: A Commentary on the Book of the Prophet Hosea*, 231–35. Trans. Gary Stansell; ed. Paul D. Hanson. Minneapolis: Fortress, 1974.

4   Holladay, William L. *Jeremiah 1, 2: A commentary on the Book of the Prophet Jeremiah*, V. I, 123–24. Ed. Paul D. Hanson. Minneapolis: Fortress, 1986.

5   Zimmerli, Walter. *Ezekiel 2: A Commentary on the Book of the Prophet Ezekiel, Ch. 25–48*, 182–98. Trans. James D. Martin; ed. Paul D. Hanson with Leonard Jay Greenspoon. Minneapolis: Fortress, 1983.

CHAPTER 15

Why Confess?

WHILE THEOLOGICAL ETHICS may make significant distinctions among repentance, restitution, contrition, and confession, our task here is to explore distinctive contributions that focusing on repair and return can make to this ethics of responsibility. This chapter examines the performance of confession by considering four Jewish thinkers. The past here is my personal past, indeed, confessing is the performance where I discover that I am responsible for my past, responsible and also forgivable. We shift here back to theology, as confession to another person is not a focus for this tradition. For this ethics, however, the responsibility to confess is the responsibility to readdress my past, making myself as a relation to my past for the future of an other's forgiveness. Confession is parallel to the indexicality of "me" examined in Chapter 11, and also to the problems of attribution and judgment (Chapter 8) and of substitution (Chapter 2). Through a linguistic performance, I become responsible, announcing my responsibility—but this time for past events.

This short chapter begins with the requirement for verbal performance, for saying the confession. Six hundred years after the editing of the Talmud, Maimonides in the *Mishneh Torah* (1177 C.E.) defined repentance as a set of actions culminating in oral confession (Pretext 1). He builds his interpretation by interpreting Biblical texts (Pretexts 2–3), including the text from Hosea. The self arises through the performance of confession, as an ethical self responds for its past and fashions its freedom in confessing and suffering for that past (Section B). Pretext 4 by Hermann Cohen, another seven hundred years later, accentuates the juristic situation, claiming that the "I" first appears when it confesses its sin in the past. Following upon both Cohen and Maimonides, Soloveitchik in Pretext 5 focuses on the procedure that begins the act of confessing. He notices that the preparatory phrase, "I beseech you, O LORD," achieves the return of the sinner to nearness. He also cites Maimonides and a Biblical text to explore the repairing of the past distance (Pretexts 6, 7).

Finally, Rosenzweig shows how the confessing soul transforms itself before the other (Section C, Confession of Love). My confession of responsibility for the past makes me responsible for the present, and indeed, produces the "I" that can overcome its own past, offering itself to the other (Pretext 8). In a striking presage of Levinas' account of the commandment coming out of my own mouth (Chapter 2), Rosenzweig presents

confession as the confession of faith, of the conviction of being loved—
the faith which establishes the relation with God by transforming my
own past.

A. Confessing Orally

In composing his code, the *Mishneh Torah*, Maimonides drew heavily on
the very texts we have considered, but his text is structured in a more systematic and deductive manner. In the tractate called the Laws of Repentance,
Maimonides presents his own codification and interpretation of not only
the Talmudic texts but also the tradition that intervenes between it and his
own text.

1a) Maimonides, LR 2:2 What is repentance? The sinner forsakes his sin and removes it from his thoughts and resolves in his heart not to do it again, as it is said: "let the wicked forsake his way and the sinner his thoughts" [Isa. 55:7].

Maimonides begins this paragraph
with a general question that resembles the
question with which his preceding paragraph began ("Which repentance is perfect?"). He sets out a sequence of actions
that move from past to future, from
thought to language. Maimonides does
not ignore the complexities, but he pro-
ceeds without recourse here to the polyphony of the voices of the sages. The
first phase has three steps: (1) FORSAKING SIN, (2) stopping THINKING (or
planning) for it, and (3) resolving NOT TO DO IT AGAIN. The moral reforma-
tion indicated here is clear enough. First, one must stop sinning, stop the
action. And then one must stop making plans and deliberating how to do the
sinful action. To abandon the deliberation while still doing the sinful actions
is not likely. The third part, however, is more subtle: there is a need to steel
the heart against the sin, and so the resolution in this first part is IN HIS
HEART. This first phase breaks the pattern of action, of thoughts and of
will—but does not itself turn outward. While Maimonides does not make
use of the rabbinic texts, he does cite the Bible.

The text from Isaiah is an extremely hope-
ful call to repent. The call is for a person to
depend on God, and indeed to return to
God. The text juxtaposes SEEKING and
CALLING to God with the actions in the
second verse. In verse 7, the sequence is
first to give up the wicked ways, then to
give up the thoughts, and then to return.

2] Isaiah 55:6) Seek THE LORD while he can be found. Call to him while he is near. 7) Let the wicked forsake his way, the sinner his thoughts [plans], and return to THE LORD, and He will have mercy upon him, to our God because He forgives abundantly.

This whole set of actions depends on the hope that God WILL HAVE MERCY
and FORGIVES. The hope of acceptance and of forgiveness structures the acts
of return. Maimonides interprets the verse as identifying the return with the
first two actions (giving up wicked ways and giving up planning). What is

missing in this verse, however, is the resolution in the heart. Maimonides has inserted the change of heart, the determining of the will.

1b)   And that he regret his past, as it is said: "For after I turned away, I was sorry. And after I was made to know, I struck my thigh" [Jer. 31:19].

The second phase in repentance is a relation to the past, the relation of REGRET or remorse. Moral reform itself is not returning. The past recollected is painful, indeed, may make one sorrowful. This relation has a remarkably different pathos than the first phase, where I resolve to avoid sin, and I stop deliberating how to achieve sinful goals. Now I engage myself with my faults and produce regret within myself.

The text Maimonides turns to is from Jeremiah. The context shows us that this verse is provided as God's ascription of the people's repentance. Notice the prevalence of the turn/return words. God proclaims the hopefulness of the people's situation: it rests upon their regret for their past and their eagerness to return. The proclamation claims to HEAR the people's LAMENT. That lament recognizes the decisive role of PUNISHMENT or suffering. Suffering leads to the desire for returning. That desire is connected, then, with the

3] Jeremiah 31:17)   "There is hope for your future," declares THE LORD. "Your children shall return to their boundaries. 18) I can hear Ephraim lamenting: 'You punished me and I suffered punishment like an untrained calf. Turn me back and I will return because You, LORD, are my God. 19) For after I turned away, I was sorry. And after I was made to know, I struck my thigh. I was ashamed, even humiliated, because I bore the disgrace of my youth.' "

SORRY, SHAME, STRIKING THE THIGH, HUMILIATION. This lament encourages God. Maimonides' interpretation focuses on verse 19, where the first words AFTER I TURNED AWAY, I WAS SORRY, may admit of another meaning: after I returned, I was sorry. Maimonides' reading suggests that returning brings sorrow or regret. While the prophetic text seems to view the human response (regret) as the result of divine action, Maimonides makes that response a product of the human returning.

1c)   That he calls the Knower of secrets to witness, that he will never return to that sin, as it is said: "nor will we say 'Our God' to the work of our hands, for in you the orphan finds mercy" [Hos. 14:4].

The third phase of repentance is a confession. While neither the first nor second phase reached beyond the self, the third phase begins with the need for a WITNESS. Maimonides identifies God here as the one KNOWER OF SECRETS—who thus is privy to all of the sinner's sins, even the ones that he is reluctant to admit to himself. God, therefore, is already witness to the sin, but cannot witness the return until the returner calls for God to witness. Maimonides does not prescribe here what one says, but reports indirectly: THAT HE WILL NEVER RETURN TO THAT SIN. Maimonides plays on the word RETURN, using it to show how a relapse into sin would also be a kind of return. One promises, before God, to never turn away again. This relation to the future is highlighted by the play on the word: one returns to God in order to never return to sin. Speaking itself seals the future, testifies against myself—binding me to not return to sin. The asymmetries of the past turning from God, returning to God in the present, and never turning again to sin are performed by speaking.

Maimonides justifies this general claim with a specific interpretation of Hosea 14:4. We noticed before that this verse was richly semiotic. "Returning needs the words, in order to exclude the words

> Chap. 14.1b] Hosea 14:4 "Assyria will not save us; we will not ride on horses, nor will we say 'Our God' to the work of our hands, for in you the orphan finds mercy."

that represent the break of the relation" (p. 310). Maimonides neglects the issue of trusting foreign powers or military might, but his interpretation of the verse suggests a deepening of the temporality of the words. The excluded words, 'OUR GOD' TO THE WORK OF OUR HANDS, indicate a specific kind of sin: that of a self-enclosed relation. Hosea is willing to use direct speech in order to disqualify certain speeches, speeches that have an explicit pragmatic dimension, for it is not the words 'OUR GOD' that are themselves to be excluded, but the addressee: to speak them *to* the work of our hands. Maimonides pushes further by calling this a kind of return. We might say that this citation serves to thwart repetition. The impossibility of saying this again can only be promised. Of course, words cannot be banished per se, but we can cite them, in order to bind ourselves to not repeat them.

> 1d) It is necessary to confess orally, and to say the resolutions he made in his heart.

Maimonides then adds the decisive addition: this speech must be CONFESSED ORALLY. For the first time, we encounter the technical term CONFESS. Of course, the apologies for past sins and the promises to not repeat sins are confessions, but we see here that confession is not simply admitting regret. It is also binding oneself before another for the future. Such a binding must be oral. The words to be brought according to Hosea 14:3 are themselves ORAL, or as the Hebrew indicates, from the lips. One might think that speaking to God, who sees into the hearts of people, would not require words, or at least not audible words or visible signs. The issue seems to resolve around the performance, that it must involve a saying in the world, and not only IN HIS HEART. While Maimonides seems to regard speech to be merely expressing resolutions made in the heart, we might turn this claim around: the resolution is only sealed when it is offered to another. The pragmatics of confession is inherent in the whole process—guiding the thoughts in the first phase and the regret in the second. It is in this last sentence that Maimonides uses the word NECESSARY, and so here the legal obligation applies its force. Repentance, as much as it is developed here as a sequence of the returner's actions, is not a self-relation, but is a binding of the self from the past for the future—before another. Without another, there is no return.

B. PERFORMANCE OF THE "I"

We will now jump another seven hundred years to the scene of twentieth-century Jewish philosophy. Through a novel interpretation of Ezekiel, Hermann Cohen argues that the individual, the unique "I," is produced in repenting. According to Cohen, this "I" is one of the distinctive contributions that religion can offer philosophy and ethics, hence his interpretation of repentance in correlation with God's forgiveness is one of the climaxes of his *Religion*. He calls this self-transformation a self-sanctification, but we are looking first at the place of confession in the transformation, where he introduces the practice of confession as the heart of repentance. Cohen explores repentance, distinguishing the penance of German religious thought from the returning in confession.

4a) Cohen RR 227–28/194 For the self-confession of guilt, the way of legal procedure shows us the right way. If the individual must *re*-cognize [*e r kennen*] himself as the originator of his guilt, then he must also confess [*b e kennen*] himself as such. In this confession the I comes on the scene for the first time. *The confession of sin is the penance that the sinner must take on himself.*[1]

Cohen identifies the way that guilt can be lifted: through SELF-CONFESSION. While Maimonides required confession in order to testify for the future (I will no longer sin), Cohen clearly requires the confession for the sake of lifting off the weight of the past (I have sinned). Cohen, characteristically, interprets confession in terms of theory of knowledge. The sinner must RE-COGNIZE [*E R KENNEN*] that he is the maker of his own GUILT. Cohen italicizes the prefix of *kennen*, to accentuate the parallel with confession [*b e kennen*], for in both cases there is a kind of knowing. Returning is learning to know yourself again, to find your own agency in the actions that you have committed. In what I propose to do in the future, I know my role; but my role in past deeds requires a recovery by recognition. Cohen holds that all sin is inadvertent, hence the ignorance of my own role in sinning is intrinsic to sinning. Only by re-cognizing my deed as my own can I hope to know

[1] Cohen RR 225–26/193 In this way the individual becomes the I so that the new person is born. The sins cannot prescribe the course of life. It can become possible to return from the way of sin. The person can become a new person. *This possibility of self-transformation makes the Individual into the I.* A person first becomes an individual through his or her own sins. But the sinning individual becomes the free I through the possibility of turning away from sin. And the correlation with God can first become true with this reborn person. God does not want the sinner and his death, but rather is pleased with the return of the person from his straying and in that measure from his life to his new life.

Soloveitchik TS 252/182–83 Judaism has always believed that it lies within man's power to renew himself, to be reborn and to redirect the course of his life. In this task, there is none besides himself who can help him. A man himself and ony himself is able to do this. He makes himself and is his innovator. He is his own redeemer; he is his own messiah who has come to redeem himself from the darkness of his exile to the light of his redemption.

myself as author of my misdeeds. Why then must this be confessed? Knowing myself is an act of transforming myself; confessing makes me know myself. The transformation of the self from ignorance of its own agency to knowing its past agency is a making itself known—first to itself, but then before others. Cohen does not think that one can return without God to return to. Moreover by publicizing the failure in the past, the making known of confession becomes a punishment. To become anew, the old must not be jettisoned but rather recalled as now abandoned—not only re-cognized, but made known as now decisively past. The returner confesses that he is no longer what he was. He makes the past known in order to know himself as changed.

But most important for Cohen, this act of confession is the first appearance of the "I." (We might note that the idiom that Cohen uses, KOMMEN AN DEN TAGE, literally come into the day, may mean not only the light of day, but may be a reference to Yom Kippur, the Day of Atonement, which is called simply THE DAY in rabbinic tradition. For what day is the Day of "I," of confession? The Day—of Atonement.) Since one central task of the *Religion* is to account for the "I," it is noteworthy that this most intimately cognitive speech-act, CONFESSION [*BEKENNTNIS*], is how "I" enters. "I" is an indexical performance before another of confessing that I am no longer what I was. "I" is not simply present, nor a futural promise, but is this precise return to the past for the sake of the future. To be "I" is to be this complex position of returning to my past to mark my emergence against that past. I must confess my past, and in so doing become new and free from that past and so take upon myself a punishment for my past. The "I" that so speaks is transformed in the speaking from that past person. The "I" is, in Cohen, always new, and in some ways this corresponds to the imprevisibility of the "I" in Mead. But, far more interesting in relation to idealism generally, the "I" appears in confessing. It speaks, making its past known. Not the simple re-cognition of itself, but rather a re-citation of a past that is not itself, but is what it was, when it was ignorant, indeed when it was not. The confessing I is not a recursion of the self with itself (a simple recognition), but a radical return of the self to what it did not know as itself, through the speaking of "I," through the making known of its own relation to its past.

4b) . . . This confession, with all of its pain and misery, in all its remorse and its doubt bordering on self-condemnation, is the beginning of the execution of sentence, which the sinner must impose upon himself, if God is to free him. This self-punishment is the first step in his freely given return.

Cohen focuses on the affect of confession: PAIN, MISERY, REMORSE, DOUBT. All are measures of representations of my past self. What I am is the feeling of pain caused by who I was—and taking on this pain by confessing is a BEGINNING OF THE EXECUTION OF SENTENCE. Unlike ransom, I myself suffer, suffer to become an "I," and so the transformation itself is the punishment. To be "I" is to accept the pain of becoming "I" and to impose upon myself my own sentence by speaking. Unlike a move to moral reform, the return dwells on the past; but unlike a judgment delivered by others, return is a judgment upon myself. This process FREES me to become I. I do it, but God serves as the one who commands it and before whom I confess, making known my sinfulness. God gives me the opportunity and indeed the ability to respond, which now is my responsibility. To become "I" is to become responsible, able before the other to speak of my own turning, of my returning.

Repentance was a central topic for the Jewish thinkers who followed Cohen in this century, including Rosenzweig, Buber, Levinas, and others. Before commenting on Rosenzweig's interpretation of confession, however, I wish to introduce another contemporary philosopher: Joseph Soloveitchik. One of the leaders of the Orthodox Jewish community, Soloveitchik also studied Cohen's philosophy, as well as contemporary philosophy in general. His student and friend Pinchas Peli edited in Hebrew and then translated into English a series of lectures that Soloveitchik gave on repentance. Those lectures display not only a relation to Cohen's interpretation, but also involve a most complex interrogation of the text of Maimonides' *Laws of Repentance*. At this point I turn to Soloveitchik because Cohen has begun to explore the pragmatics of confession, and with both Soloveitchik and Rosenzweig we can benefit from a more rigorous interrogation of the specific words and their relevant performative dimensions.

5a) Soloveitchik TS 129/211 What then does he request in "I beseech you, O LORD?" It seems that with these words he requests only that he be allowed to approach God.

Soloveitchik pauses over the first phrase of the traditional confession: "I beseech you, O LORD." Confession is not a petitionary prayer but is a making known of past sins and a promise to abandon them. But why then does it begin with BESEECH? After briefly discussing a Talmudic text, Soloveitchik offers his own interpretation of the performance. What does a repentant person ask for in this petition? It is too soon to ask for forgiveness much less for personal goods. Soloveitchik suggests that he requests TO BE ALLOWED TO APPROACH GOD. The words make a preliminary request. We can easily recall the issue of drawing near in Levinas or alternatively in the parable from the Talmud. After one has broken off relations and turned away from a person, approaching near to the other person may no longer be possible. How can I appease someone I have angered? How do I get close enough to her so that I can speak and she will listen? While drawing near may be the first responsibility, at this point, nearness is just what rests within the other's power, absolutely.

5b) Confession is a conversation between the Holy One, blessed be He, and the sinner. The sinner

Repentance requires confession, A CONVERSATION, because the two parties interact as in a script. The first step is for the

begins by requesting from God the authority to start the conversation. Sin places the human at a distance, separates one from the Holy One, blessed be He, as Maimonides puts it: "Last night this one was separated from the Lord God of Israel . . . as it is said, " 'Your iniquities made a separation between you and your God [Isa. 59:2]' " (Laws of Repentance Ch. 7, sec. 7).

SINNER to request the ear of the other, the authority to start talking. In a broken relationship, this first authorization to speak again is the hardest to acquire. Soloveitchik shows us through an interpretation of Maimonides just why it is hard to receive the authority to speak: sin is a DISTANCING. Returning, in this sense, is drawing near physically, but it requires permission from the other. Like night and day, the sinner stands separated from God. The initial approach is past, and now my distancing has separated me from the other, and I cannot simply reapproach, but must first ask permission.

Consider, if briefly, the citation of Maimonides. He asked how high repentance ranks on the spiritual ladder. His answer develops a contrast between last night and today in which isolation and distance is contrasted with a nearness to God following repentance. Part of the 'last night' are

6) Maimonides LR 7:7 How exalted is the degree of repentance? Last night this one was separated from the Lord God of Israel as it is said, "Your iniquities made a separation between you and your God [Isa. 59:2]" . . .

prayers that God does not hear, and he cites five prophetic texts to accentuate the separation; he can then cite several texts in the continuation of this paragraph where today the repenter is near God.

The passage that Maimonides cites and Soloveitchik re-cites takes us back to a clearer text in Isaiah. Isaiah is explaining why prayers go unanswered, and rejects the claim that God is somehow impotent (HAND TOO SHORT) or ignorant (EAR TOO DULL). Rather, the people are separated

7] Isaiah 59:1) Behold, the hand of THE LORD is not too short to save, nor His ear too dull to hear. 2) But your iniquities made a separation between you and your God. And your sins have hidden His face from you, and He does not hear you.

from God by their guilt. Indeed, this is like the guilt that Hosea wanted removed, or the sins that cause stumbling. Isaiah, defending God, makes clear that the obstacles are man-made, that God is open to the people, but the people are separated and have prevented their own approach to God. Maimonides builds upon this separation, but contrasts it with the next morning: that repentance on its own can bring the people back to God. Isaiah, in verse 20 of this chapter, does promise redemption for those who have repented, but as we saw above, the center of the prophet's account is God's agency to redeem. Maimonides, however, follows the rabbinic exaltation of repentance.

5c) An iron curtain separates the sinner from God. The sinner has neither merit nor capacity to stand

And Soloveitchik? He cites this doubled text not to emphasize the power of repentance but the reality of the separation

before God; how, then, can he confess? For confession requires him to summon the Holy One, blessed be He, and designate Him as witness to the saying of his confession, and it is impossible to designate witnesses in their absence.

(MADE A SEPARATION). Indeed, that separation is AN IRON CURTAIN. Cohen's account makes confession start too quickly, too easily. How does one even get near enough? The obstacle that I have made has a moral dimension: I lack the agency and indeed the moral right, the MERIT, to stand before the other. (Jewish prayer is generally said standing—one has to stand up to address God.) But the moral poverty leaves me too weak to stand. Soloveitchik, like Cohen and much of the tradition, is most interested in the legal problem. Maimonides instructed us that God becomes a WITNESS in confession. There is no confession without a witness: confession is a making known. Soloveitchik himself shifts into a more specifically pragmatic and legal term, THE SAYING OF HIS CONFESSION—the uttering must be witnessed. But God must then be SUMMONED to be witness—called in to hear the saying. And were God to be only assumed, or worse still absent, then there would be no witness, and the saying would not be a confession, and the return would be incomplete. A witness must appear face to face, and so the request to approach must precede whatever is to be witnessed. Just as the judgment is the moment when the speaker becomes sign, indexed beyond all mediation, so the confession begins with a summons that enables the speaker to confess.

5d) Therefore, the petition comes at the beginning of the confession with the plea, "I beseech Thee, O LORD!"—please allow me to drop the curtain in order to come before You so that I may be able to repent and say confession. Immediately after this he says, "I have sinned."

Soloveitchik thus interprets the opening request as the summons of God to witness: a plea to allow the returner to be disencumbered of the separation—thereafter to be disencumbered of the sins themselves. Permission to speak is actually construed as permission to DROP THE CURTAIN, to approach. While in the next passage, we will see how returning and atonement occur in the performance of confession, here we see what may indeed be the hardest step: the permission to speak at all. That permission, also, is obtained by speaking. God's willingness to listen is what allows the sinner IMMEDIATELY to go on to say, "I HAVE SINNED." In returning to another, it would be a mistake to presume that the other will listen. Permission to speak, a faith in the other's promise to attend, is in fact obstructed by the consequences of the broken relation. What Soloveitchik discovers is that that permission is acquired by another performative utterance. One does not first remove the obstacle, mending the way to the relationship, and thereafter speak to the other. Rather, even the access to nearness in which confession occurs is won through speaking. What is broken will be mended with words, and the approach to the other that precedes the mending is gained with words as well.

C. Confession of Love

Following Cohen, we have seen the emergence of an "I" who in speaking becomes responsive for her past. While Soloveitchik further developed the growth in my ability to respond through my request to draw near, Rosenzweig will accentuate the way that speaking cleanses the soul, the steps in confession that lead to the recognition of being loved. Like the steps in Maimonides' account of repentance, there is a sequence, but here it is all performed with words. For Rosenzweig confession is a response to God's command to love. In love, God commands the human to love God, and revelation is completed when a human soul achieves faith that that divine love is steady: that the soul is enduringly beloved.

8a) Rosenzweig S 200–201/180 The soul speaks, I have sinned, and does away with shame. In so speaking purely back into the past, it cleanses the present from the weakness of the past. I have sinned means: I was a sinner.

"I have sinned"—this is the core of confession. These are the first human words of response to the command "Love me." The lover commands love, but the beloved does not simply answer, "Yes." Instead, it responds in SHAME. Rosenzweig claims that the soul was ashamed because prior to hearing God's command to love the self had been oblivious to the absence of love, its lack of relation with another. How this utterance about my past does away with shame will be clearer shortly. More important for us is Rosenzweig's account of the temporality of the utterance. Such a speech is in the perfect tense and as such is about a completed past. It separates the present from the past, making the present CLEAN and free of the past. To confess is therefore to mark the past as past and gone—a past that when it was present did not appear to be sinful. A past, in this specific way, that was never a present. Hence, my relation to my past in saying "I have sinned" is distanced. It means that the "I" that speaks is not the sinning one. Rather it means: "I WAS A SINNER."

8b) With this confession of the having sinned, however, the soul clears the way for the confession: I am a sinner. This second, however, is already the full admission of love. It throws the compulsion of shame far away and gives itself wholly to love. That the person was a sinner is done away with in confession; to make this confession he had to overcome shame, but it remained standing near him, as long as he confessed.

Rosenzweig notes, however, that to be speaking of my past, what I used to do, is also to speak about the "I" who now speaks. To confess to my own past is to free the path to the second confession: I AM A SINNER. As speaker I now announce my own sin, the sin that is present and accompanies me now in opposition to the sins I once committed. Rosenzweig argues that the ability to say those words requires that I speak to someone whose love for me I ADMIT FULLY. To confess depends on an ability to respond. To be able to say that in my speaking now that I am a sinner is to make myself utterly vulnerable and bespeaks my surety of being accepted by the other. But it also is no longer to feel ashamed of myself. Rosenzweig subtly argues that one OVERCOMES SHAME by the confession in the past, but one is not done with it. It hovers as the way I felt until I confessed, as part of the past that threatens to return as a hesitation over my own sinfulness.

8c) Only now when he, although it has to do with past weakness, precisely confesses to still being a sinner, does the shame retreat from him. That his admission ventures into the present is the mark that it has overcome shame. So long as it lingered in the past, it did not yet have the courage to speak out fully and trustingly. It still could doubt the answer that was coming to it.

The contrast is clear: to speak only of the past sin is to lack trust in the other, trust that the other will still love me as sinner. As reformed I am lovable, but as still sinning? Thus when the soul admits its sin as still present, it realizes that it is beloved not due to worth, but from freely given love. And so in shifting to "I am a sinner," I become free of shame. This admission itself works as a sign, THE MARK, that I have overcome shame. To confess here is TO SPEAK OUT, to make myself known as sinner who trusts my interlocutor.

8d) ... Thus the soul that wanted to confess, still doubted whether its confession will find admission. Only when it moves out of the confession of the past into the confession of the present does the doubt fall away from it. In that it confesses his sinfulness as still present sinfulness and not as "sins" that happened, it is certain of the answer, so certain that it no longer needs to hear this answer aloud. It perceives it within itself.

Rosenzweig harps on this moment of DOUBT that is resolved by confessing in the present. I am worried about how I will be interpreted, whether my sinfulness will make me unlovable or even rejected. My certainty comes, moreover, in the performance of saying. The relation to the past is complex, however. I must see the identification of sin move from my past to my present, belonging to me still, in order to be sure that I will be accepted. The confession of the past changes not only my past but also my present, activating a self-transformation of my present abilities to respond. The faith in the other's love is not first felt and then expressed; rather, I become CERTAIN of it by confessing. And that certainty no longer hangs on the other's affirmation of me—now I know in myself—that the other accepts me. The performance not only changes my relation to my past, it also offers the surest knowledge, thereby circumventing the deferral to the other for the future. I do not need to wait to hear if I will still be loved: I know it now.

8e) ... rather, the soul speaks: "I also love now, but still in this most present of moments, not as much as I—know myself beloved."

The confession of sin becomes a confession of God's love, an affirmation of the forgiveness within the command to love, the forgiveness that loves me despite my sin. In that perspective, Rosenzweig now allows us to see that the relation to the past is all for the sake of the affirmation of being loved. My confession is a response to love, in love. Indeed, I speak of the past only in order to speak of the present, and of the present sins only to speak of being loved. The performance of confessing sins (past and present) has led to confessing being BELOVED, and in order to make that motion, my own performance has been fueled and governed by my love—a love that I lacked in the past. But, and this is perhaps most spiritual, that response is less loving than the command to love which initiated the repair of the relation and to which I respond. I can perform wondrous things by confessing, by returning, but returning is a responsibility, a response that I must make but cannot initiate. Hence in responding, I know myself beloved more than I can love.

8f) This confession, however, is already the highest blessedness for it because it encloses the certainty that God loves it. Not from God's mouth, but rather from its own mouth comes this certainty.[2]

Finally, in an astonishing moment—for a dialogic thinker—the speaker himself provides the certainty of being loved by confessing God's love. A presage of Levinas' account of the command coming from HIS OWN MOUTH, Rosenzweig's discovery that my own speech can attest to the other's love is the ultimate realization that dialogic thought can interpret listening to oneself as well as listening to another.

Inheriting a tradition that shifted the balance of agency in relation to God to the returning human, the twentieth-century Jewish philosophers accentuated the place of confession within returning. In part because of philosophical scruples about the theology that the prophetic texts depicted, and in part because of insight into the rabbinic preference for human responsibility in response to divine absence, these philosophers concentrated on the human role and the power of repentance. Even when they recognized the responsive role for the repenter, they interpreted that role as self-transforming and as a kind of monologic performance. The forgiver, in particular, seemed to have a dwindling role, as in Rosenzweig's claim that forgiveness is extended in the command to love and need not be further expressed. The appropriateness of a performative interpretation of confession is clear, and if repentance has power to produce this self-transformation, then in Rosenzweig we see the uttering itself produce a reinterpretation of the past, a repair of the relation between my past utterance and my present. The responsibility to confess connects the responsibilities of becoming me with my past, allowing me to emerge as the speaker who responds for my past in the present for the sake

[2] Cohen RR 436/375   One recognizes ever more clearly the origin of prayer in the psalm, and in it the dialogue which repentance conducts between the I and God. This dialogic monologue could not be aroused by prophetic rhetoric; it could be created only by lyric poetry, which is the original form of love in longing. The psalm, however, idealizes this longing, in analogy to eros, by means of the highest human life goal; it forms the redemption from sin into that freedom of confidence in God, thanks to which the love for God is, at the same time, the foundation for the continuous renewal of the I.

of opening for another's interpretation of me in the future. The relations to the past, however, are more complex, precisely because of the challenge of the social horizon for responsibility.

SUGGESTED READINGS

2   Westermann, Claus. *Isaiah 40–66*, 287–88. Philadelphia: Westminster, 1969.
3   Holladay, *Jeremiah* 1, 2, 153, 189–91.
8   Gibbs, *Correlations*, Chapter 3.

CHAPTER 16

Why Forgive?

IF WE NOW FOCUS not on the repenter or the confessing person, but on the past that is made into my past, that I respond for, we can also see that repentance has an unusual effect upon the past. It does not merely produce new attributions of responsibility (what was her deed becoming mine). Rather, the past itself is changed as past. It is also not merely the re-presentation of the past, making the past event now become part of the present. No, the past is changed as Resh Lakish indicated in the Talmudic text in Chapter 14. This susceptibility of the past to my resignification is a startling but important aspect of this ethics. As we explore it in this chapter, we will see first that repentance is capable of opening the past for reinterpretation. But that repair of past signs will then ultimately depend on the other person's forgiving me.

The chapter begins with an extensive reflection by Soloveitchik on Resh Lakish's two statements. In Pretext 1 (which requires re-citation of the Talmudic texts from Chapter 14) Soloveitchik argues that the highest repentance is from love, where sins are elevated and not blotted out. The tension between forgiving and forgetting offers insight into the kind of repentance that can repair the past. Section B (Historiography) raises the question whether an historian must treat the past as similarly open. We consider an exchange of letters between Max Horkheimer and Walter Benjamin, in response to the latter's efforts to produce a new methodology for studying history—with the intention of redeeming the past (or at least holding it open for our responsibility). Horkheimer's letter (Pretext 3) defends a common-sense moral judgment on the past, but Benjamin's interpretation of that letter and his own response (Pretext 2) resonates closely with Resh Lakish, and also articulates the responsibility to think theologically about history (without doing dogmatic theology).

Levinas, however, proposes his characteristic transformation in Section C (Being Forgiven): the other changes my past in forgiving me. Repentance might prepare me and my past for this action, but I can do no more than hold open my past. The other will have to change it, to mend it. In the diachrony of assignment for the other person my power to represent the past is limited (Pretext 4). What I must respond to is never present; it occurs in a past that was never present. Levinas cites the Song of Songs (Pretext 5) to evoke the missed encounter. An other's forgiveness can mend time, restoring my past by repeating it (Pretext 6). While there is some tension between these authors, the juxtaposition of their reflections points us toward the responsibility not only to confess my past for the future, but to reinterpret and so to alter the past for the future.

A. FORGIVE OR FORGET

Returning cannot ignore the past, it must readdress it. Can repenting not only dismiss the past but rather preserve a past changed in the ongoing performance of return? The two passages from Resh Lakish in the Talmudic text will help frame this discussion: either sins become inadvertent errors, or they become merits. Cohen opted unambiguously for the first choice, regarding all sin as ignorance and repentance as a way of producing a new man. Repentance was a great boon for moral reform, for progress, for the future. Even Rosenzweig in the passage with which we ended the previous chapter seems to favor a repentance that does away with the past by dealing with it. In the next chapter Rosenzweig's interest in the past will go beyond this lyrical moment to a concern to understand the historian as a survivor. If we consider another text from Soloveitchik's lectures, however, we will see that he recognizes that both models are accessible in the tradition, but that the view of sins become merits deserves greater praise and yields new insights.

1a) Soloveitchik TS 177/256 In light of this, Resh Lakish's comments which were cited earlier can now be understood: "Great is repentance: by it intentional sins are made like unintentional errors." He was speaking here of repentance by means of which sin is annihilated. Such repentance erases sin, but it has no creative power and does not give life to anything new. Intended sins are made like errors, as if they never were. They are erased.[1]

Soloveitchik has been discussing the ways that sin either becomes blotted out or becomes an instigation for great creativity precisely by being remembered. At this point he cites the sayings of Resh Lakish.

Chap. 14.3d Yoma 86b ... Resh Lakish said: "Great is repentance: by it intentional sins are made like unintentional errors, as it is said: 'Return, Israel, to THE LORD your God, for you have stumbled in your guilt' [Hos. 14:2]. Guilt is intentional, but it calls it stumbling. Is this so!?"

Soloveitchik cites neither the verse from Hosea nor the central claim that STUMBLING, unlike GUILT, is not intentional. Instead, Soloveitchik interprets the claim

---

[1] Cohen RR 260/223 Error, even as man's lot is to err, but *shegagah* [unintentional sin] is the limit of human error. When this boundary is transgressed, there God may know what is happening to the person. Human wisdom is perplexed before the possibility of evil in humans. The Day of Atonement upholds the fiction of the unshakable moral uprightness of everything human: all human sin is *shegagah*. Thus can God forgive, without renouncing His righteousness.

that they were unintentional errors to make the claim that no sin happened (only a mistake). The willfulness of sin is removed, and with it the events seem to disappear. Clearly the event *as sin* is ANNIHILATED. The image here is not a crossing out but a text ERASED, a board wiped clean. Signs simply gone, without a trace. My past is now more past than before repenting: repentance has recalled the past in order to destroy it completely. Forgiveness is a more radical kind of forgetting that first remembers in order to delete.

1b) But in his second comment Resh Lakish said that "great is repentance: by it intentional sins are made like merits": and here he intended repentance by means of which evil is elevated. This repentance causes a person to do the commandments with more strength and vigor then he did before he sinned. And it causes him to study Torah in another way than he studied it before he sinned.

Soloveitchik now shifts to the more radical relation to the past. The past becomes an opportunity for CREATIVITY, the return brings one closer than before. And so he cites Resh Lakish's second saying.

Chap. 14.3e Yoma 86b But Resh Lakish said: "Great is repentance: by it intentional sins are made like merits, as it is said: 'When the wicked man turns from his wickedness and does what is just and right, then because of them he shall live' [Ezek. 33:19].

Again he omits the Biblical text and its problems. He interprets by claiming that the evil is raised up (ELEVATED). This raising transforms what was sin into merit, making the past, as retold in the present, a source of righteousness. Soloveitchik then interprets the change biographically. Returning will change the way a person lives and studies: he will apply himself more VIGOROUSLY. Soloveitchik is not merely claiming that he will do better than he did when he sinned, but also better than he did BEFORE HE SINNED. Soloveitchik makes this claim twice, once in terms of fulfilling the COMMANDMENTS, once in relation to STUDYING TORAH. One struggles more eagerly both to understand and to do what is needed for the relationship after having lost it.

1c) What caused Resh Lakish to be made the closest companion of Rabbi Yohanan, the most esteemed sage of the land of Israel? The repentance he did and by means of which he had elevated and exalted the evil used for thievery and turned it into the goodness in studying Torah.

Soloveitchik now refers Resh Lakish's second comment to Resh Lakish's own life. In the Talmud, the story is told that Resh Lakish had been a brigand and was converted to the study of Torah by R. Yohanan's beauty. Soloveitchik has cited a story in one of the commentaries that Resh Lakish had first been a scholar and then became a brigand, and then repented. The biographical issues are fascinating, even though dependent on unverifiable stories—including a cruel jest that causes the death of both men, a jest about Resh Lakish's intimate knowledge of the tools of the thief. But Soloveitchik's interest is to call attention to the authority that Resh Lakish gained—authority present in the ascription of these two opinions to him. How did he get such authority? By repenting. Repentance allowed him to become a greater scholar; it was itself a testimony in his life to the value of his past. Leaving aside the professional knowledge that could be useful, there is the more basic translation: from evil into good.

1d) Repentance in which evil is elevated is repentance from love, and because of it, intentional sins become like merits; while repentance in which evil is blotted out is repentance from fear, and because of it, intentional sins are erased and made like unintentional errors. In repentance from love, love rises with the repentance and burns brightly in the fires fanned by sin; it draws a person in bands of love up to great and exalted heights.

Soloveitchik can now map his basic opposition of blotting out versus elevation onto the two texts of Resh Lakish and at the same time onto the opposition of repentance from LOVE and repentance from FEAR. Fear of punishment prompts one to erase the past, but love leads one to bring the past back into a source for new growth. In place of this organic image, Soloveitchik now chooses an image of fire. Sin FANS THE FIRES, providing the excitation of the flame of love. Such fire now blazes upward. And the person rises; the returner is EXALTED. Higher than the person who has not sinned and repented stands the returner. The past can be redeemed, altered into a source for an elevation of the repenter. Forgetting is possible, but being forgiven is still better.

B. CHANGING THE PAST

The spiritual struggle with the past seems to be at some distance from the task of the historian, particularly if one assumes that the historian is a positivist who tries to determine the brute facts of past events. In the next chapter we will explore Benjamin's account of the responsibility to study history, a responsibility that implicates me, as historian, in the past I study. But here we can see that the question of changing the past is of vital interest to Benjamin in response to Horkheimer. The historical past is not secured by its pastness from reinterpretation—and indeed, the ethical dimension of historiography emerges here in relation to theological questions about our retroactive abilities to respond.

For Benjamin theology still has a role to play in what he calls historical materialism. Benjamin is a rigorist in making translations from a theological context to an historical and nontheological context. The immediate context is a comment that Benjamin filed in the section of his *Arcades Project* entitled "Theory of Knowledge, Theory of Progress" (N). Benjamin collected materials for the project for over a decade, and sorted them in complex and overlapping ways. But one particular comment that speaks directly to us is a comment on a letter from Max Horkheimer.

2a) Benjamin P (N 8,1) 588–89/471 On the question of the lack of closure of history, a letter from Horkheimer from 16 March 1937:

In response to an essay by Benjamin, Horkheimer had written him a strongly supportive letter. But he had raised a question ON THE LACK OF CLOSURE OF HISTORY. This presents a form of the question about whether repentance can change the past. Benjamin then quotes from the letter, starting not at the beginning and carefully editing sentences. It is not clear that the sheaf called Konvolut N was intended for publication, and so it is not clear whether this editing served only Benjamin's purposes in rethinking the objections, or whether he had meant to edit it for others. In any case, in a parallel to the treatment of Levinas by Derrida, I will first interpret the letter (on the right side), and then focus on the editing and commentary of Benjamin (on the left side). (The quoted material is underlined).

Horkheimer admits that the question of how to effect the past, indeed, whether it is possible, has long concerned him. Benjamin had addressed the question in a draft of an essay called "Edward Fuchs: The Collector and Historian," but we are more interested in the later response. What is relevant in Horkheimer's letter is the RESERVATION. The PERSONALLY seems to make the question itself subjective in an

3a) Benjamin L 1332. Horkheimer to Benjamin, 16.3.37 I have been pondering the question of how far the work of the past is closed for a long time. Your formulation may still stand simply as it is. Personally, I would make the reservation, that here also it concerns a relation that is only to be laid hold of dialectically.

almost arbitrary way. The objection takes the general form of many objections from both Horkheimer and Adorno: that the historian's task must be construed DIALECTICALLY. Just what dialectical relation to the past as open or vulnerable to change will appear in what follows. Benjamin omits this whole opening in his quotation.

Horkheimer's dialectic involves regarding the past as both closed and not-closed. What he fears is that INJUSTICE can be reviewed and dressed up as justice, even as mercy. His point is that the victims (THE SLAIN) cannot be resurrected by rewriting history. Indeed, the task of changing the past will run the risk of denying their suffering once we open the past. The charge of IDEALISM cautions against a

3b) The stipulation of the lack of closure is idealistic, if closure is not also admitted in it. Past injustice has happened and is closed. The slain are actually slain. Ultimately your assertion is theological. To take the lack of closure fully seriously, one would have to believe in the Last Judgment. My thought is too materialistically contaminated for that.

theodical willingness to fold in the suffering of the victims into a possibly triumphal account of the past, leading to the Hegelian justification of whatever happens in world history. To secure the other's suffering from such 'happy endings' seems to be an essential task of historiography. But Horkheimer then suggests that Benjamin's own position is not so much idealistic as THEOLOGICAL, depending on A BELIEF IN THE LAST JUDGMENT.

Horkheimer thinks that this power to judge history and to redress the wrongs of the past requires the kind of judgment that only God can provide and cannot be produced in history itself. Levinas often speaks of ethics judging history—but Horkheimer thinks that such a judgment cannot be maintained in a rigorously imminent and materialistic perspective. Horkheimer does not foreclose the possibility of the kind of historiography that depends on the conviction that justice can be determined from a demand that exceeds what is actualized in history. He phrases his objections to it in terms of his own CONTAMINATION—a material condition itself. (My interpretation of Benjamin's ellipses will follow below.)

Horkheimer now proposes an asymmetrical distinction: the NEGATIVE past is closed, but the POSITIVE is not. Horkheimer's division of events into two categories links the mode of historiography to the event to be remembered. When others suffer, our memory of them cannot undo the injustice and pain. And yet, if we recall some state of JOY, even of JUSTICE, we will be able to transform it through re-presenting it. Horkheimer borrows a certain kind of realism about events: that the warrant

3c)   Perhaps in relation to the lack of closure there is a difference between the positive and the negative, so that the unjust, the horror, the pain of the past is irreparable. The exercise of justice, joy, works themselves behave otherwise toward time, because their positive character is extensively negated through their transience. This holds most of all for the individual existent, in which not the happiness, but rather the unhappiness is sealed by death.

for changing the past through memory of it lies in the objective transformations that greet positive events. On their own, independent of memory, they become negative THROUGH THEIR TRANSIENCE. Because good things don't last, the process of remembering them can aid in this process of decay. Politically, this means that positive accomplishments in the past are subject to critique by historiography—and that suffering in the past is not to be redeemed into a happy story. Horkheimer's argument recognizes this asymmetry most fully in biography: a person's unhappiness IS SEALED BY DEATH. We cannot make out others' suffering as a good way of life after the fact. But we may discover that their own sense of happiness was either illusion, or even dependent on events after death that reverse the positive achievements during life.

Horkheimer discerns the limitations of a certain kind of logic—one that regards the opposition of good and bad as INDIFFERENT for the concept. His claim is ever more realist: he is not discussing how we think or remember good and bad events,

3d)   The good and the bad do not behave in the same way to time. The discursive logic, in which the content of opposing concepts is indifferent, is also insufficient for these categories.

but the way that good and bad behave themselves. The bad sticks and cannot change; the good passes away. Logic seems insufficient, unless it can be made to reflect differences that depend on objective moral character. (This claim, which Benjamin omits to cite, takes us far from the asymmetry of pragmatics, allowing an almost wooden realism to obliterate the question of the one who remembers and the others to whom the remembrance is given.)

2b) The stipulation of the lack of closure is idealistic, if closure is not also admitted in it. Past injustice has happened and is closed. The slain are actually slain. Ultimately your assertion is theological. To take the lack of closure fully seriously, one would have to believe in the Last Judgment. My thought is too materialistically contaminated for that. Perhaps in relation to the lack of closure there is a difference between the positive and the negative, so that {only} the unjust, the horror, the pain of the past is irreparable. The exercise of justice, joy, works themselves behave otherwise toward time, because their positive character is extensively negated through their transience. This holds most of all for the individual existent, in which not the happiness, but rather the unhappiness is sealed by death.

Benjamin's citation of Horkheimer's letter reveals a few key thoughts, even before reading his commentary and response. What is quoted is underlined; what is omitted is unmarked; what is added is in *italics*. First, he omits the opening (and the similar closing) comments that situate the question as a somehow personal objection (3a and 3d). The issue for Benjamin is not how to interpret someone (Horkheimer) who thinks this way, but rather the thought itself. More interesting is the omission of the sentence about theology—precisely because Benjamin will directly claim to be doing theology here. But the third change is the insertion of a word (ONLY, [NUR]) into the sentence that describes what is irreparable (indicated by *italics* and {}). This insertion serves to make Horkheimer seem to be merely restricting the past which is still open, and not to be largely denying the very openness that Benjamin requires.

2c) The corrective to this way of thinking lies in the consideration, that history is not only a science, but is nothing less than a form of remembrance [*Eingedenkens*]. What science has "established," remembrance can modify. Remembrance can make the unclosed (happiness) into a closed and the closed (suffering) into something unclosed.

Benjamin then proceeds to respond. (See also the letter L, 1338, which is more personal.) He is interested in how to reconceive of historiography, and so turns from the question of objective events to the way that they are present to us. The terms he opposes are SCIENCE and REMEMBRANCE—and perhaps the issue with Horkheimer is that he had assumed that the realist basis of events would require simply a scientific historiography, a kind of mirroring re-presentation. In the act of remembering, the events that seem determined by scientific historiography are changed. Benjamin takes the asymmetry of bad and good quite differently than Horkheimer: he accepts Horkheimer's distinction as indeed the scientific position: that the happiness will decay and so seems unclosed, and that suffering is closed. But just so, remembrance can change the status of these events: the good things can be remembered into a stable goodness and joy (CLOSED); suffering can become something that still can be remedied and worked on (UNCLOSED). Indeed, Benjamin's historiography does not fold in the worst past events as part of an idealistic progress, but finds a way to make them linger into our present and continue to require redress. Injustice cannot be finished—rather, the remembrance of injustice is part of the responsibility of righting our unjust relationship with the past.

2d) That is theology; but in remembrance we make an experience that forbids us to conceive of history as fundamentally atheological, as little as we try to write it in immediate theological concepts.

Horkheimer has opted for a past that cannot be changed because he does not see the theological dimension of responsibility in relation to the past. Benjamin admits, without reserve, that THIS IS THEOLOGY. Indeed, he claims that the pragmatics of remembrance FORBIDS an ATHEOLOGICAL interpretation of historiography. If remembrance does reopen the suffering and assign us a continuing task in relation to it, then the Last Judgment does inform our own activity of judging the past. But, and perhaps most resonant with this book: such an activity is not conducted IN IMMEDIATE THEOLOGICAL CONCEPTS. Benjamin least of all the Jewish authors here is willing to perform dogmatic theology. His work represents a profound translation of the concept of repentance and judgment into historiography. And despite Horkheimer's claims to be more of a materialist, it is not clear that Benjamin's translation does not provide a richer materialism than one bound, as Horkheimer's is, to an objectivist realism, where memory only mirrors a dead past. Throughout the final stage of Benjamin's work, he devoted himself both to the task of remembrance as reopening the past, and to the complex task of theorizing this reopening. His extensive archival cultural studies of the Arcades of Paris, of the junk left over from an earlier commercial era, perform the very reopening that he calls for. The term *repentance* is not prominent here, but precisely the remembrance that reopens and awaits a Last Judgment displays the present responsibility for the past.

C. Being Forgiven

We quite rightly fear the revisionists, the historians who will delete the record of suffering, whitewashing the past for the glory of their patrons. We even may fear that repentance in its historiographic guise, or otherwise, has become bridled in the service of that most obnoxious self-righteousness that parades about proclaiming its wicked past and its newfound righteousness. We even must be honest and fear that if I am given the power to change my past, I will lose my bearings and my past—seeking neurotically for failures or narcissistically for excellence. Despite the suspicion of theology as self-justification, we must rather see this changeable past in relation to other people and as part of the social relations we interpret.

If we turn then to Levinas, we will again see him struggling with the social ethics of repentance, and just because the other person is involved, the need for forgiveness. But my power to repent encounters in the other person a limit—and indeed a limit in my power to change the past. The re-presentation of the past, be it through remembrance, recollection, or reconfiguring, meets in the relation to the other person an impasse. I can remember what I said, and even what the other person said, but the call to which I respond precedes any said of my neighbor. Levinas, like many others, opens up a past that was never present, an immemorial past. That past gapes beyond any repentant return, any dialectical historiography, any power of re-presenting—and it opens in my relation with another person.

To resignify my past is to regain my own speaker position (or author position), but to remember the past that others have made is to become responsible for their works, and for the transmission of their works. Reading displays much of the pragmatics of responsibility and the limits of access to the author. In Levinas' later work, the idea of a past that was never present, a diachrony that cannot be retold, becomes the central concept in exploring the passivity in responsibility. The result is an immemoriality that pervades all experience, or in our own idiom, a signifying that can never become part of the systematic weave of signs—and the responsibility in relation to that deep past is not to quell the work of memory, but to incite it precisely in responsively accepting the impossibility of remembering.

4a) Levinas OB 112/88–89 The neighbor's face signifies to me an unrefusable responsibility, preceding all free consent, all agreements, all contracts. It escapes representation; it is the very defection from phenomenality. Not because it is too brutal to appear, but because, in a sense, it is too frail, a nonphenomenon because "less" than a phenomenon. The unveiling of the face is nudity—a nonform—self-abandon, aging, dying; more naked than nudity: poverty, wrinkled skin; wrinkled skin: a trace of oneself.[2]

Levinas locates this deep past in the assignment of RESPONSIBILITY in the face. Nearness and the face as themes intersect, producing my responding position: that to be responding and to have responsibilities is to be assigned and not to CONSENT, AGREE, OR CONTRACT. The term PRECEDING here is under consideration. Levinas is not interested in a diagrammable sequence, but in the precedence of the call to my ability to respond. He seeks to free the face from my own powers of memory. Levinas notes that this moment of assignment of calling is not only not represent-

[2] Benjamin B 613/161 In Freud's view consciousness as such receives no memory traces whatever, but has another important function; it is to act as protection against stimuli. "For a living organism, protection against stimuli is an almost more important task than the reception of stimuli; the protective shield is equipped with its own store of energy and must above all strive to protect the special forms of conversion of energy operating in it against the effects of the excessive energies at work in the external world, effects which tend toward an equalization of potential and hence toward destruction." The threat from these energies is one of shocks. The more readily consciousness registers these shocks, the less likely are they to have to reckon with a traumatic effect of these shocks. Psychoanalytic theory strives to understand the nature of these traumatic shocks "on the basis of their breaking through the protective shield against stimuli."

able; it also is the VERY DEFECTION FROM PHENOMENALITY. Levinas seems almost to confess his own defection or betrayal from the phenomenological method: reflecting on a moment when something not only does not appear, but where the tracing itself cannot lead back to an appearance. What follows, however, is a strange negotiation of this defection: for Levinas is at his most "phenomenological" examining the "experiences" of AGING, of the self decaying, THE SKIN WRINKLING, the way that the self is unable to represent itself, unable to maintain its own phenomena. But these failures are not converted into phenomena of failure, but the failure of appearing, of making present. Thus Levinas rejects the claim that the trace is TOO BRUTAL TO APPEAR, as though the wound or the interruption overwhelms the organs of reception (as would be the case in certain theories of trauma). Rather, the signs are TOO FRAIL, too subtle and evanescent to be stabilized in consciousness. My consciousness cannot catch sight of the vulnerability of the face without securing that vulnerability in an image that is too reliable for me, too present to call upon me without a chance to refuse.

4b) My reaction misses a presence that is already the past of itself. Past in no way *in* the present, but like a phase retained; past *of* this present, a lapse already lost of the aging escaping all retention, changing my contemporaneity with the other. It lay claim to me before I could come. Irrecoverably late. "I opened . . . he had disappeared" [Song of Songs 5:6].

By the time I react, I have missed the moment of assignment, the moment of being called. That moment was ALREADY THE PAST OF ITSELF. Such a pastness is not merely a lingering of the previous notes in the final chord, not A RETAINED PHASE, but A LAPSE, a past *OF THIS PRESENT*. Levinas uses the juxtaposition of italicized *IN* and *OF* to show that the past has escaped my memory already, and so was never stabilized in any present, never available to my thinking. I cannot re-present what was not present, cannot return to it as a present in the past. The moment of being called claimed me BEFORE I CAME. I am always too late for that meeting. And Levinas then cites a verse from the Song of Songs (identified in the footnote—with a miscitation in both French and English of 4:6—the verse is 5:6).

This verse is part of a night-scene in the woman's bedroom. She is wakened (or dreams wakefulness) by the call of her lover. But when she arises or is aroused she is too late. His call is finished and her longing for him unquenchable. Were it a dream, then he was never there; were it reality, that past is clothed in desire and she still cannot find him. The dialogue is impossible; only her response is present, and it is too late. Levinas cites but elides the love and the erotic desire, avoids the ambiguity of the night—but, like the rabbinic authors, cites it for those of us who recall the text, or even those who will look it up despite the typo in the citation. What

5) Song of Songs 5:6 <u>I opened</u> to my beloved and my beloved <u>had turned away</u>. My soul departed when he spoke. I sought him and I did not find him. I called him and he did not answer.

we notice, moreover, is that the "I" is the woman, and that the dynamics of love here are bound not only to human erotics but also to the mystical erotics of the soul responding to God. I am too late for revelation, too late for my assignation. Too late for my lover and so my desire is woken too early—as the refrain of the women's chorus warns.

4c) My presence does not respond to the extreme urgency of the assignation. I am accused of having tarried. The common hour marked by the clock is the hour when the neighbor unveils himself and delivers himself in his image; but it is precisely in his image that he is no longer near; already he permits me an "as for me," distance, a commensurable remains, on the scale of my power and of my present where I am "apt to do . . ." [à même de . . .]: capable of giving account of everything by my identity.

The lapse has moved from my own aging to my lapse in catching my lover. The moment in which we would meet, in which I would be able to choose, is gone—in a lapse in the present moment, a lapse where the past was never present. Clocks enter the discussion. Levinas claims that the CLOCK allows for common time, but at the expense of nearness and the immemorial aspect of relations with the other person. The clock coordinates the other with me: allowing me to see him IN HIS IMAGE, and that image is available for consciousness, for my intentionality, for my role as interpreter, as authorized to compare and to act. Levinas does not despise this image and its common time, but he warns us that the appearance of an image is the other's choice: a REVEALING, a PERMITTING—which empowers me, makes me ready to tell the story, to know, to act. The vulnerability in the meeting is contained. In place of the immemoriality of the assignment, I now have an image before me, an image that only represents the other person. The image of the other person, in its presence, its phenomenality, cannot adequately lead me back to the face, to the nearness. The responsibility to repent seems hobbled, as the moment of assignment and the encounter with the otherness of the other remains always beyond memory.

The gap that I cannot recover, that binds me to responsibility and that challenges my responsibility to return, can be bridged from the other. In a move parallel to the end of Chapter 14, this chapter again looks to the other and to my responsibility in relation to the other's action—this time the action of repair, of forgiving me. The text we now cite comes from a chapter called "The Infinity of Time," from the last section of *Totality and Infinity*. Beyond the asymmetry of my responsibility to approach the face is a further responsibility for another's responsibility for others. Levinas calls this reproduction of responsibility *fecundity*—the responsibility for others' responsibilities. In this relation of fecundity the "I" experiences being forgiven. Levinas is particularly phenomenological in this passage—but we will see shortly that the moves he identifies as transpiring in consciousness in fact break beyond a study of consciousness, and are indeed performed semiotically.

6a) Levinas TI 259–60/282–83
The irreparable does not depend on the fact that we conserve a remembrance of each moment; the remembrance, to the contrary, is founded on this incorruptibility of the past, or the return of the me to itself.

The problem is the obduracy of the past. If we want to argue that repentance changes the nature of the past, then must we not first be clear whether the past is changeable at all? Indeed, after harming another, I may not be able ever to displace that record, even if I can make good the damage. Levinas suggests that this unchangeableness does not come from our remembering it. Instead, our memories themselves arise in relation to THIS INCORRUPTIBILITY. Here is a straightforward Husserlian analysis of the intentionality of the remembrance: it intends and so depends on this quality of pastness of the past. What is a little less obvious, however, is that such pastness is also THE RETURN OF THE ME TO ITSELF—which I take, here, to be the integration of the memories into the "me," in Mead's or James' sense, of connecting up the previous cognitions with the current ones.

6b) But doesn't the memory that arises in each new instant already give to the past a new meaning? In this meaning, better than in joining itself to the past, doesn't memory already repair the past? In this return from the new instant to the old instant, resides in effect the salutary character of succession. But that return weighs on the present instant, "heavy with all of the past," even if it is big with all of the future. Its old age limits its power and opens it to the imminence of death.

Levinas asks, Doesn't the new memory of the old past change the MEANING of the past? Like a rereading of an old text, the act of remembering finds NEW MEANINGS in the past, and so the self does not merely join one thing to another, merely JOINING itself to a 'dead' past, but rather it REPAIRS THE PAST. Levinas here sees the SALUTARY CHARACTER of narrative. I keep retelling my past, finding new meaning for all of those events I cannot change. My remembering repairs the lost past, making it live again. (This interpretation closely resembles Scheler and Augustine.) The present gets rather bloated: it now bears within it the meanings of the whole past, but it also is pregnant with the whole future (BIG WITH ALL OF THE FUTURE). This internal time consciousness of the "I," representing the past for the future, repairs the past—without recourse to others. But it encounters its finitude: it only has power over the past years of its own life (ITS OLD AGE LIMITS ITS POWER), and the future it can plan for and reach toward extends only to its death. This "I" can repair only so much of the past, and indeed, may produce a huge present, but it is utterly finite, closed off from ethical temporality: ultimately it is not responsive to other people.

6c) The discontinuous time of fecundity makes possible an absolute youth and a recommencement, all the while leaving to the recommencement a relation with the re-

In place of this more familiar account of temporality, Levinas proposes a temporality that is DISCONTINUOUS, in which forgiveness bestows a radical new beginning and freedom is not the freedom of

commenced past, in a free return—free with another freedom than that of memory—to the past and in free interpretation and free choice, in an existence as completely forgiven. This recommencement of the instant, this triumph of the time of fecundity over the mortal and aging being's becoming, is a forgiveness, the very work of time.

re-presentation. We will see this reconnect with Resh Lakish and Soloveitchik in the next sentences, but the term FECUNDITY must detain us briefly. Levinas is interested in the way that responsiveness can reproduce itself in others. His privileged image is of parent and child, that a parent is responsible for the child, and indeed, for the responsibilities of the child, and that the hope of parenting is to produce a responsive child. (Levinas uses images of fathers and sons exclusively, with some extremely limiting gender claims.) A parent achieves a new beginning in the child, AN ABSOLUTE YOUTH, for the child is the hope of starting again, a beginning without the experiences, including the sins, of the parent. Levinas uses intergenerational imagery because the forward relationality in generations typifies the hope and the need for discontinuity. But he does not restrict fecundity to procreation in a bodily sense: rather, his point is to explore the fecundity in relations where I hope that the other, too, will become responsive, and where I see my responsibilities as one-way, including those for what the other person does. Because that hope exceeds the range of my intentional time-consciousness by including the temporality of the other's intentionality, which I cannot represent but must only hope for, fecundity opens up a way of moving beyond my own consciousness. The other person can forgive me, and if she does, then I begin again from her eyes. My responsibility exceeds my reach but then continues beyond myself. Time opens out, here, in what Levinas will call THE VERY WORK OF TIME—because time opens up through discontinuity, beyond the realm of the bloated present.

6d) Forgiveness in its immediate meaning is connected to the moral phenomenon of sin: the paradox of forgiveness depends on its retroaction. And, from the vulgar point of view of time, it represents an inversion in the natural order of things, the reversibility of time.[3]

Levinas locates forgiveness in the economy of SIN. The question about the past, therefore, is not merely a cognitive one but is MORAL. Levinas translates the moral and theological dimensions to the very heart of the question of knowing the past. Forgiveness is PARADOXICAL: it changes the past or acts upon the past. It is AN INVERSION IN THE NATURAL ORDER—the present acts only for the future but not on the past. One should note that memory itself was capable of mending the re-presented past, but it is not clear that it could make time REVERSIBLE. Indeed, the whole bloated-present model was that one could bring the past

---

[3] Rosenzweig S 442/397   Thus instead of the past being made present, the present is conducted back into the past. Everyone shall know that the Eternal brought him personally out of Egypt. The present "here" dissolves in the great "now" of the remembered experience. The Christian way becomes expression and expropriation and irradiation of the outermost, while the Jewish life becomes memory and internalization and burning through of the innermost.

forward, but one could not go back to the past and change it! Thus THE VULGAR POINT OF VIEW, that the past is past, may not agree with a phenomenology of time-consciousness, but neither the vulgar nor the phenomenological point of view adopts a thematics of forgiveness.

6e) It contains several aspects. Forgiveness refers to the elapsed instant. It permits the subject who had compromised himself in an elapsed instant to be as if that instant had not elapsed, to be as if the subject had not compromised himself.

The key element is the way that forgiveness permits the doer of the intentional deed (THE SUBJECT WHO HAD COMPROMISED HIMSELF) to become as if it he had not acted (AS IF THE SUBJECT HAD NOT COMPROMISED HIMSELF). Resh Lakish, clearly, but still unclear whether for Levinas the sin has become error or merit. Notice, however, that it is FORGIVENESS that changes the past, *not* repentance. The forgiving person does not change her own misdeeds into merits or errors, but rather allows a change in the other person's deeds. Of course, we can easily enough make this coherent with the previous texts: God's forgiveness is the context and condition for human repentance. But Levinas is willing here to shift the focus to the other person, a double shift. First to the other person who concerns him in the concept of forgiveness. Second, it is the other human. Levinas is not speaking theologically here, or certainly not primarily theologically.

6f) Active in a stronger sense than forgetting, which does not concern the reality of the forgotten event, forgiveness acts on the past, in cleansing the event, repeats it in some manner. Moreover, forgetting annuls the relations with the past, whereas forgiveness conserves the forgiven past in the cleansed present. The forgiven being is not the innocent being.

Levinas now contrasts FORGETTING and FORGIVING. Forgetting abandons the past, blots it out. In Soloveitchik's interpretation, the return from fear would culminate in forgetting, for the goal is to eradicate the past event. But clearly Levinas' account of forgiveness matches up with the return from love which elevates the sin. Here is language of CLEANSING (again), and importantly, the notion of repetition. The past has to happen again, but differently. Not re-presented in the present, but repeated in the past. Forgetting is opposed to memory, to the construction of a heavy present; forgiveness achieves a freedom in relation to the past, by REPEATING it and CLEANSING it. To forgive is not merely to remember, not merely to give a new meaning to an old event, but is to change the past event, and to conserve the change (THE FORGIVEN PAST) in the present. The repetition appears as repetition, as a doubled past, both the sinful one and the cleansed one. Hence, like Soloveitchik, Levinas can be clear that forgiveness does not restore INNOCENCE.

6g) The difference does not allow us to place the innocence above forgiveness. It allows us to distinguish in forgiveness a surplus of happi-

Indeed, like Resh Lakish, we now see that forgiveness is greater than innocence. A forgiven sin is a merit. In parallel to the strange economy of Rosenzweig, where to

ness, the strange happiness of recon- | accept all the weight was to be freed of it,
ciliation, the *felix culpa*, given in here Levinas can write of a SURPLUS OF
a common experience which no HAPPINESS. Levinas does not stint: he calls
longer shocks us. | it a *FELIX CULPA*, the happy guilt of Chris-
tian theology. While at this point we are not shocked by this strange economy, which NO LONGER SHOCKS US, the Latin Christian term does shock us.
What can we make of Levinas' rhetoric? Is he using a Christian term to
appeal to a Christian audience? Or has the idea itself become Christian?
There is a certain discontinuity between Levinas and the rabbinic tradition.
Levinas need not be doing anything other than translating for an audience
that is more familiar with Christian theology. At the same time he is exploring the interpersonal relations, the asymmetrical roles in forgiveness and
repentance (which is not even mentioned in this passage).

6h) The paradox of forgiveness of sin refers to forgiveness as constitut-ing time itself. The moments do not join indifferently the ones with the others—but spread out from the Other Person to Me. The future does not come to me from a swarming of indiscernible possibles that would flow toward my present and that I would seize. It comes to me across an absolute interval for which the Other Person as absolutely other—though he were my son—alone is ca-pable of staking out the other shore and of reknotting with the past. But by the same capability of retaining from that past the ancient Desire that animated it and that the oth-erness of each face increases and deepens still more profoundly.

Levinas now proposes the strongest claim: that time itself is CONSTITUTED by forgiveness, by the other person's cleans-ing of my past. While the phenomenologi-cal tradition tried to secure temporality by recourse to the activity of my conscious-ness, for Levinas time occurs in relation to the other person. There is not a set of pos-sibles from which I happen to select or build or SEIZE the ones that become my past. The accretion of the "me" occurs through the other person, who is sepa-rated from me by AN ABSOLUTE INTERVAL. Time itself is socially given, but most strik-ingly, the other gives me my past, retells my story, REKNOTS the present with the past. This generosity of the other is not her dictation or her invention of a past for me,

but is a forgiving of my past, and so reconnects me to the past, in such a way
as to illumine the ANCIENT DESIRE THAT ANIMATED IT—the desire for goodness itself. Forgiveness discovers the responsiveness in another's past, and in
so doing reconnects it with a present responsiveness. Levinas himself links
this discovery with the image of fecundity: the way that the desire for the
other's good is increased and deepened with each new face, with each new
other. The redemption of the past requires a recovery of the past that finds
in it an ethical responsiveness and not merely a memorable event. But Levinas has now moved the structure of this past beyond what any one person
can achieve: it is dialogic in the stronger sense. If repentance and confession
were only before the other, forgiveness is given by the other. We become
dependent or perhaps better, responsible, for the other whom we cannot
control. We return to our past, bringing our present back to our past (and

not merely bloating the present with images of the past), in order to reopen it, but the repair will require the free action of the other person. As for the question of my forgiving others, Levinas has little to say. Hence this chapter offers a hope of being forgiven, but does not explore the responsibility to forgive others. We have explored the power to repair the past, and found that the past can be held open by repentance, and by historiography, but that only the other person can repair my past, can forgive me and transform my sins into merits.

SUGGESTED READINGS

1 Boyarin, Daniel. *Carnal Israel: Reading Sex in Talmudic Culture*, chapter 7. Berkeley: University of California Press, 1993.
2 Tiedemann, Rolf. "Historical Materialism or Political Messianism? An Interpretation of the Theses 'On the Concept of History.'" In *Benjamin: Philosophy, Aesthetics, History*, 175–209. Ed. Gary Smith. Chicago: University of Chicago Press, 1989.
  Wolin, Richard. "Experience and Materialism in Benjamin's *Passagenwerk*." In *Benjamin: Philosophy, Aesthetics, History*, 210–27. Ed. Gary Smith. Chicago: University of Chicago Press, 1989.
4 Weber, "Persecution," 69–76.
6 Gibbs, *Correlations*, Chapter 10.

CHAPTER 17

Why Remember?

IN THIS FINAL CHAPTER the goal will be to interpret the semiotic activities by which repentance becomes fully social, becomes a way for a community to return. Remembrance is not about recalling the past or about preserving it, but is needed to disrupt the present. The challenge in the present will exceed the image of the past, but that disruption transpires through the remembering. This chapter will explore social remembrance and the responsibility to interpret ourselves as survivors responsible for the past—not as the victims to whom the past happened, nor necessarily as blameworthy, the ones who perpetrated violence and horror. Rather, following the argument of this book, we are the ones who have an ethical need to respond for the past, interpreting our present as implicated in the suffering of others.

At the end of Chapter 14, Levinas claimed that repentance requires an objective, communal procedure as opposed to a private confession. We now turn to the social construction of time as the main way of making repentance public. That social time is constructed in calendars, calendars that structure society for repenting and remembering (Section A). Pretext 1 returns to the Mishnah for an argument about the authority in determining when the new month has begun. By recourse to a Biblical text (Pretext 2) Akiva justifies the authority of Gamliel to sanctify the astronomically wrong day. The responsibility to sanctify time rests in the community (not in God or nature). Rosenzweig interprets the innovation of the Sabbath and the cycle of the week in Pretext 3. Here the interruption is interpreted for its social release from labor and creates the self-consciousness of both labor and rest. Benjamin redevelops Rosenzweig, discussing how the festivals are modes of communal remembrance that interrupt the flow of time by inserting the present into a cycle of remembered past events (Pretext 4). But Benjamin also contests the possibility for calendrical remembrance in the contemporary world.

The responsibility for remembrance without that social performance survives in historiography (Section B). Not that the remembered past is individualist, or that the context of the rememberer (the historian) is isolated, but rather that as a society we must cultivate historiography as the work of scholars. In Pretext 5, Benjamin describes his historiography as juxtapositions of past and present. The relation of past and present becomes a moment of challenge to the present, as images from the past are yanked out of their past to address the present. In Pretext 6, Benjamin contests historicism and disrupts the narrative of transmission, showing how the past and its arrival in the present depend on injustice and violence. The task of historiography is to brush history against the grain, to make lost possibilities of the past register in disrupting our present. Finally, in Pretext 7, Benjamin reflects on the commodity as a sign of the past, and on history as reopening that sign. He cites and reflects on Marx (Pretext 8) to disrupt the eclipse of the pragmatic dimension of the commodity: that someone made it and others use it. The pragmatics of commodities will resemble that of texts, but in this discussion the responsibility to write history, to respond for the past, will be accented.

Memories can be constructed and performed in order to open the gap between what can be remembered and what cannot be represented (Section C, Ruins and Remnants). In Pretext 11, Benjamin argues that ruins were constructed in order to empty our images of the past. Pretext 12, however, interprets not things but people as ruins, as remnants or survivors. A text from Rosenzweig emphasizes how the Jewish people regularly constructs itself as a remnant, interpreting its own past critically and interpreting its existence as challenged by its past. Like the development of the "I" in confession, the "we" here is an existential sign whose position is produced in self-criticism for its past. Pretext 13, moreover, takes us back to the Biblical text in Amos that is one of the earliest uses of the term *remnant*. As survivors we bear responsibility and fashion our existence in relation to a past of suffering. To interpret our own existence as survivors is to respond for others' suffering in the past. Remembrance appears as a way of interrupting the present with the past, a past which itself is challenged and criticized. Our future, our hope for redemption, our responsibility to hold open our own meaning for the others to interpret requires a remembering of ourselves as not victims but survivors who must now respond for the past.

A. CALENDARS

I begin with another familiar story from rabbinic sources. It concerns the setting of the calendar, not in the sense of its structure, but in the application of its structure to the perceptible world. Because the Jewish calendar follows the moon there is a question each month whether the new moon comes on the thirtieth or the thirty-first day. In our times, the question is resolved by an algorithmic calculation, but in earlier times observation of the new moon was determinative. Anyone could witness the new moon, and if that witness were deemed valid by the ruling court, the new moon was proclaimed. Hence, the holidays for a whole month might shift a day, depending on whether or not the new moon had been seen. There is a series of stories about the authority of the court to resolve this question, some of which impugn the knowledge of the leaders in matters of astronomy. Our story addresses precisely questions of authority, and our interest beyond that plain meaning of the text is to see that the rabbinic sages were aware of the social dimension in determining holy time—indeed, they affirmed the value of socially ascribed authority precisely for the process of setting the calendar.

1a) Mishnah Rosh Hashanah 2:8b–9 Another two came and said: "We saw it in its time," but on the night of the extra day it was not seen. Rabban Gamliel accepted their evidence.

R. Dosa ben Hyrcanus said: "They are false witnesses. How can they testify that a woman has given birth and then the next day her belly is between her teeth?"

R. Joshua said to him: "I approve your words."

We begin in the midst of Mishnah 8, having previously encountered two sets of witnesses that others rejected but whom Rabban Gamliel, the leader familiar to us from the story of R. Eliezer's excommunication, accepted. We meet the ultimate impossibility: two saw the new moon on one night, and it could not be seen the next night. Due to their evidence, the day that was either the first of the new month or the last of the previous was made the first, but on that night it could not be seen. As is usual in this set of stories, RABBAN GAMLIEL ACCEPTED THEIR EVIDENCE. Some commentaries argue that Gamliel was only trying to encourage witnesses to come forward and that he knew (who would not?) that they were wrong. But on the other hand, the decision to accept their evidence is false to empirical reality. Hence two rabbis dissent: first Dosa ben Hyrcanus. He uses a metaphor of the pregnant woman who is still pregnant the day after having reportedly given birth. R. Joshua also from the story with Eliezer, now joins him, APPROVING YOUR WORDS. The question here begins as a simple astronomy question: When is the moon new? But the text itself moves beyond the question of astronomical events: instead the issue is accepting witnesses, declaring them false, and even approving another's words. Indeed, it just this performative set of actions that raises Gamliel's ire.

1b) Mishnah 9 Rabban Gamliel sent to him: "I decree to you that you come to me with your staff and your money on the Day of Atonement according to your reckoning."

The first act of the story concludes with a shocking DECREE. Again, a specific pragmatic act occurs: the patriarch of the community issues A DECREE. The argument has abandoned the moon and become one solely of authority: Gamliel requires Joshua to violate the Day of Atonement ACCORDING TO YOUR RECKONING. Because the Day of Atonement is a solemn fast day, one is allowed to carry neither objects nor money—one cannot do any work at all on it. But Joshua's calculation will make the "wrong" day the Day of Atonement—hence, to carry on that day will not be a violation of anything—except his own calculation. The challenge here is whether Joshua will stick to his own reasons (which are actually Dosa's), or will submit to what he knows is false. It is, moreover, not happenstance that the day in question is the Day of Atonement, the single Day that atones for sins. This is the same day that we have been discussing—the day that must be communal in order to work, in order to help an individual repent. Gamliel is requiring Joshua to join the community at the cost of his intellectual integrity.

1c) R. Akiva went and found him troubled. He said to him: "I can teach you that all that Rabban Gamliel has done is validly done, as it is said: 'These are the appointed seasons of THE LORD, even holy convocations, which you shall proclaim' [Lev. 23:4]. Whether in their time or not in their time, I have no other appointed seasons."

A fourth character opens Act II, R. Akiva. He goes to make peace between the two factions: a peace of obedience without compromising intellectual integrity. Joshua is TROUBLED. He suffers from just the dilemma we have already seen. Akiva argues that Gamliel has acted validly, that Joshua's Day of Atonement, while accurate astronomically, is not actually the Day of Atonement. Akiva argues

by use of a Biblical verse. The warrant for Gamliel's decree lies beyond political power in the very legitimation of political power. The evidence of perception in the 'real' world is displaced by recourse to a verse.

The verse is extremely repetitive. There is the repetition of the SEASONS: the season of God and IN THEIR SEASONS. In the Mishnaic text, Akiva does not repeat the second one, but it is clear that the season is

2) Leviticus 23:4   These are the appointed seasons of THE LORD, holy convocations, which you shall proclaim in their seasons.

appointed for God. The other repetition is that the word for CONVOCATIONS shares its root with PROCLAIM. A convocation is made by proclamation, or perhaps is itself for the sake of the proclamation. The plain sense of the text is that God is setting up a series of holidays that Moses is to announce to the people.

But Akiva reads the need to proclaim the seasons as proof that only *by proclamation* do the days become holidays. THERE ARE NO OTHER. Indeed, Akiva argues that the 'timeliness' of the holidays is not relevant. The holidays are appointed by YOU, the Jewish people. Again we can see Levinas' interpretation of THE DAY ATONES is linked to the authority of the community to proclaim and to convene (words with the same root in Hebrew). The convention is achieved by proclamation, or even, if we dare, they are the same activity: whenever the community proclaims a holiday, the community as proclaimer already has convened, already is celebrating. The calendar is the purpose for convening: to draw the people together is to hallow it. A community needs a calendar, needs convocations and communal time—to question that need is to destroy the community. Gamliel is not the issue, and the Mishnah records his mistake, precisely in order to illuminate how the community has need of its court.

We introduced the issue of the calendar from Levinas' discussions of the individual's need for social help in repenting and in constituting time through the other's forgiveness. We see in this Mishnaic text that the determination of the calendar involves a set of speech-acts, and that the community itself must determine its own time, the time for communal repentance, confession, and atonement.

This theme is developed at greatest length by Rosenzweig in his introduction to the third part of *The Star*. Rosenzweig's question is how to hurry the process of redemption, which is a way of asking what sort of social action undertaken by social groups is capable of developing a community as an interconnection of face-to-face interaction and systemic relations. The culmination of that discussion is an account of the social gestures that liturgically structure public time. In many ways the final third of *The Star* is a pragmatic interpretation of these gestures, at the expense of a specifically linguistic pragmatics (which is found in Part II). Our immediate interest is in Rosenzweig's account of the calendar—as a repetitive structure that allows eternity to enter time. In Chapter 8 we saw how Rosenzweig interpreted eternity in terms of social relations. Our experience of events in time is not produced individually but rather socially, and the possibility of repetition and of counting units itself is a liberation from the transience of the steady slipping away of time into the past. His discussion of the week, marked by the Sabbath as a day of rest, represents the key moment in temporality.

3a) Rosenzweig S 324–25/291–93
The week is set between the day and the year. It is based on heaven, by the orbit of the moon, even if disconnected from that long ago, even where the phases of the moon still determine the measuring of time, and thus the week became an authentic and purely human time.

The real innovation in the cycles and the repetition of time is the WEEK. The day and the year are measured by the sun and by human labor, but the week is only loosely connected to the phases of the moon. Rosenzweig admits that there is some astronomical basis (not unlike Gamliel), but he is interested in it because the moon does not produce four weeks that are stable. Instead, this is a PURELY HUMAN TIME that neither the earth nor the heavens know for themselves. As such it is AUTHENTIC, or rather, our own, our invention for the sake of producing the experience of time.

3b)   And purely human, without a basis in the created world, like the day based in the alternations between waking and sleeping, or the year in the alternations between sowing and harvesting, and for that reason in Scripture explained only as an analogy of the work of creation itself, that the week is made into a *nunc stans* for people, posited as the alternation between work and rest day, labor and contemplation.

Rosenzweig now juxtaposes the three units (day, year, week) by noting that the cycles parallel (WAKING/SLEEPING; SOWING/HARVESTING; WORK/REST). But the third pair emerges here as different in kind. The possibility of rest from labor is not 'natural' (THE CREATED WORLD), but even Scripture can only explain the week by recourse to the opposition of work and rest. The week is made solely to interrupt the sameness of labor. It is a *NUNC STANS* because of its interruptive power, a moment that stops, that stands still, that allows for a pause in the flowing away of time. It produces not only rest but also CONTEMPLATION. The Sabbath is a socially institutionalized reflection upon labor, that makes labor into labor by organizing the collective moment of rest.

3c) Thus the week with its day of rest is the proper sign of human freedom. Scripture thus explains the sign by its purpose and not its basis. The week is the true "hour" of all the times of the common human life, posited for people alone, set free from the orbit of the earth and thus altogether law for the earth and the changing times of its service.[1]

Rosenzweig interprets the week, or perhaps the Sabbath, as the PROPER SIGN OF HUMAN FREEDOM. It signifies not as a linguistic term, but more basically in the shared practice of the community, freeing them from laboring on the earth. Rosenzweig's claim that it is explained PURPOSIVELY and not in its origin recognizes that this sign's meaning lies in the performance of resting, in the performance of the interruption that a lived week is, and not in its BASIS, in the derivation of the sign. It is the most human of the units of time, and so also the one that most produces a COMMON HUMAN LIFE—because it stands independent of particular experience and rather conditions social experience itself. Through it time becomes more than just the cycling of seasons, governed by the sun and moon, and so time becomes livable through a human freedom to set the times for working the earth. But this freedom is connected by an AND to SERVICE, indeed, to service to God. Rosenzweig here begins to connect the question of liturgy and temporality. For the regulation of the week is made regular by services, prayers, and, in earlier epochs, offerings. The issue here is not to institute a dogmatic theology of liturgy, but rather to discern in the sociological structuring of time the place of a theological dimension.

3d) ... But how then does the power to force eternity to accept the invitation reside in prayer? ... Because time which is prepared for the visit of eternity is not the individual's time, not mine, yours, or his secret time: it is everyone's time. Day, week, year belong to everyone in common, are grounded in the world's orbit of the earth which patiently bears them all and in the law of labor on earth which is common to all. The clock's striking of the hour is for every ear.

Rosenzweig asks how human culture can make eternity enter time. In Chapter 6 we saw the growth of life in society was not easily linked with the redemptive power of the individual's love of the neighbor. The advance of social systems is not identical with the entry of eternity into time. Rosenzweig himself hesitates, in a series of doubting questions. The answer, however, lies at the heart of the issue for interpreting social time and social memory. Time is not private: rather, time is structured communally and so belongs to

---

[1] Cohen RR 182–83/157   The Sabbath is to be thought of not only as a sociopolitical measure but as a peak of religious inwardness. And Jeremiah again makes the social meaning clear: "You shall not bear a burden on the Sabbath day" (Jer. 17:27). God's love for human beings secures itself in the Sabbath, as God's pity for those whom he has driven out from paradise to work. In principle the Sabbath sublates again that distinction among people which developed in their modes of labor. The manual laborer, too, becomes master of himself. The weekly rest on a definite day makes the worker equal to the master.

EVERYONE. Unlike Heidegger and Bergson, Rosenzweig sees the public nature of temporality as redemptive, as inclusive, and as liberating. Not SE-CRET TIME, time restricted to rulers and priests, but a public cult and public prayer is produced through the law of the week, and through the organization of the cult. From the human side we have the ground of astronomy and THE LAW OF LABOR. Redemption itself will work upon this commonality, this foreshadowing of community. Public time is not a falling away from the authentic inward experience of time but is the stepping forward as equals in common with others.

The power of prayer, for Rosenzweig, is not merely to transform the self, but also to transform the community by transforming communal time. To hasten redemption is to make time ready and to invite eternity into time: which is not merely to speak with God, but is to make time accept eternity, to build a clock and a calendar, a *nunc stans*, in which all together can rest from labor and contemplate the interruption itself.

The Jewish calendar of festivals, of convocations of community, structures time in yearly cycles. The repetition, like the weekly cycle of the Sabbath, is a performance of social memory, performed in gesture and not merely held in the privacy of the mind. In *The Star*, Rosenzweig interprets both Jewish and Christian holiday celebrations and even examines the evolution of the secular calendar in Christian and post-Christian countries. He claims that the cycles of social time hurry redemption by interrupting time's flow, but festival remembering can also be questioned through criticism of social time—not in the name of authentic private time, but precisely in the name of the interruption of time. The stability of the calendar can become not the hurrying of the kingdom, but the way to forget the disruption in time. Memory's responsibility is to disrupt time, to prepare for a messianic today of redemption.

Benjamin was a serious reader of Rosenzweig's *Star*, and he explored the possibility of using memory to interrupt time. He engages Rosenzweig's view of calendars in a thesis on history, written toward the end of his life in the midst of his uncompleted major work, *The Arcades Project*.

4a) Benjamin Th XV 701–2/261–62 The consciousness of bursting the continuum of history is characteristic of the revolutionary classes in the moment of their action. The great revolution introduced a new calendar.

REVOLUTION is the exemplary act of hurrying redemption, of trying to change the social world today, now. But one characteristic of that change is to disrupt THE CONTINUUM OF HISTORY. That continuum implies that things must stay as they are, or even if they are changing, continue to change in the same way at the same rate. To BURST that steadiness is to disrupt the way we understand our relation to past and future. And for Benjamin the key here is CONSCIOUSNESS. Revolution does not only change material conditions or power relations, but is itself an awareness, a reflection upon the STRUCTURE of HISTORY, of the relation with the past. This recognition that the views of history must change is dramatically achieved in the French Revolution by changing the calendar. By INTRODUCING A NEW CALENDAR, the revolutionaries enacted their awareness that they were disrupting historiography or historical consciousness. They not only inserted a new date in the old calendar, but they also threw out the old system of counting and reckoning the past. The past had to be reconceived and made accessible to experience anew.

4b) The day, with which a calendar begins, functions as an historical time-lapse camera. And it is basically the same day that always returns in the form of festival days, the days of remembrance [Eingedenkens].²

Benjamin now states that a calendar works like a TIME-LAPSE CAMERA. The sequence of days and months, repeating in sequence, lead a community through their history in the shortened space of a year. Martin Luther King Jr. in January, Abraham Lincoln and George Washington in February, Civil War in May, Revolution in July, Pilgrims in November: this sequencing shows "American History" through the year. But Benjamin is actually thinking more about Rosenzweig: for he now links the calendar to THE EVER-RETURNING SAME DAY. A calendar, by cycling time, allows a day to repeat or indeed to become eternal (in Rosenzweig's terms). Indeed, Benjamin refers to THE DAYS OF REMEMBRANCE and the FESTIVALS—the days of the Jewish calendar that Rosenzweig had examined. Rosh Hashanah, the Jewish New Year, is the Day of Remembrance, and on other holidays remembering the events that happened (Exodus from Egypt, Giving of the Law, Binding of Isaac, Destruction of the Temple) is liturgically central for the Jewish holidays. Benjamin uses his choice word for memory, EIN-GEDENKEN, which means literally thinking into, but carries a strong relation to the past event—which we will explore below. Rosenzweig had defined the remembering in terms of the calendar, also, but Benjamin will help us see what is involved in this form of remembering.

4c) The calendar, therefore, does not count time like clocks. They are the monuments of an historical consciousness, and for a hundred years in Europe not even the slightest trace of them appears.

Benjamin now distinguishes CLOCKS from CALENDARS. Rosenzweig had argued that the clock was part of the calendar and that the chiming of the clock allowed the hour to start again and again. But Benjamin here seems to see clocks as not producing the repetition that builds a public time. What clocks do is less clear here. But calendars become MONUMENTS OF HISTORICAL CONSCIOUSNESS. They are the temporal monument, the

² Rosenzweig S 351–52/316 Because the feasts are only apparently feasts of remembrance [*Erinnerung*]; in truth the historical is in them wholly and thickly present and what is said to every participant at the first one goes for each of them: each must celebrate the feast as if he himself had been freed from Egypt. Beginning, middle, and end of this national history; founding, height, and eternity of the people—with each new generation, no—with each new year, the old will be born anew.

social structure that is not built of stone, but builds up consciousness and memory. Benjamin seems to have validated Rosenzweig's claims about calendars—but the sentence continues: for a hundred years there has not been THE SLIGHTEST TRACE OF THEM. Here Benjamin shocks: he claims that Europeans have stopped living according to the calendar. This is not a simple empirical claim but rather the radical claim that there is no proper remembrance in the way that brings eternity into time in the recent past of Europe. That recent past, for Benjamin, is the time of the industrial and consumerist transformation of Europe. Rosenzweig may have an accurate picture of how the Jewish liturgical calendar is supposed to function, and by extension other calendars, too, but the culture of Europe has abandoned that manner of experiencing time and remembering history. Benjamin here appears as the critique not of Rosenzweig's theory of calendars and memory, but of the world which has moved away, beyond, below such means of remembering. Benjamin is questioning Rosenzweig's (and so our) reliance on a theory of calendars when it will not address the social situation of our time. Memory cannot be entrusted to calendars in this age.

The issue that remains for us is twofold. (1) Is a calendrical memory of the sort that Rosenzweig interprets obsolete? Can we understand the task of remembering without recourse to it, even if it is obsolete? And if we wish to interrupt the flow of time, may we not still have recourse to the gestures of clock and calendar? (2) And if the ways of memory must move on, then what is the kind of remembering that is now possible, and how will it address the decay of social time and the loss of socially structured interruption? Is there a social performance that can replace society's calendar, or are we left with individuals or schools of historians?

B. HISTORIOGRAPHY

Continuing with Benjamin's work, we will see that the possibility for a remembering or returning social performance of a community is now attenuated. But the acts of remembrance can be carried further in the work of the historian—a work that is not the task of an isolated consciousness, but of a socially located interpreter. While Rosenzweig had hoped to resuscitate the Jewish community in Germany at the end of the First World War, Benjamin despairs of that community while living in Paris on the eve of the Second World War. What is more important for us, however, is how the structuring of interruption that Rosenzweig discovered can become a way, even a task, for the historian.

Benjamin collected a set of theoretical reflections in a folder entitled "Theory of Knowledge, Theory of Progress." One of the key texts tries to explore just how the past is still open—open, that is, for a specific moment. The relation depends on an account of the remembered images of the past in the present. Specifically, Benjamin is exploring the images of the Shopping Arcades, the images of nineteenth-century advertising, and so on. The topic is the status of the historical research itself, the particular kind of remembering. The question becomes, quite simply, how to coordinate the locations of both the historian and the past.

5a) Benjamin P (N3,1) 577–78/462–63 ... The historical index of the images says not only that they belong to a determinate time, it says above all, that they first come to be legible in a determinate time. And indeed this "to be legible" is reached in a determinate critical point in the motion in its interior. Every present is determined through these images, those that are synchronic with it: every now is the now of a determinate knowability.

The question of HISTORICAL INDEX refers not only to the claim about the past, that an image BELONGS TO A DETERMINATE TIME. But it also says that the image is to be interpreted at a specific time. Indeed, indexicality here is not simply double, but must focus on the index of the interpreter, on "me" who is responsible for reading the image. Benjamin writes that this indexicality of the now when the image is read is ABOVE ALL the moment of historiography that must detain us. Neither the phenomenological discourse of essences nor the positivists' treatment in categories takes the historian's own moment seriously enough. Benjamin will argue, moreover, that the moment in which the image is available for reading, my moment of interpreting the image, is A CRITICAL POINT IN THE MOTION IN ITS INTERIOR. The past imaged, the sign from the past, bears with it a history and a development in the set of readings, a set that belongs to the image and not only to the readers. But any present moment itself is a set of images, images that are ready to be read at that moment, or perhaps we should say a set of readings of images, as an image is the source of various readings. To be a NOW is to have a set of readings, a set of interpretations of the images of the past. Each moment is precisely this distinctive set of available readings of images from the past.

5b) In it the truth is loaded with time to the point of exploding. (This explosion is nothing other than the death of the intention, which coincides therefore with the birth of genuine historical time, the time of truth.)

The now is LOADED WITH TIME, because it consists of images of the past. The now is a composite of various moments in the past, borne as images that in their legibility in the now make the now an unstable moment. It is on the verge of EXPLODING, of flying off into the shards of the various pasts that have come together. Another parenthesis notes that THIS EXPLOSION, this tenuous holding together of the now, is itself THE BIRTH OF GENUINE HISTORICAL TIME. While in Mead we saw the self as composed of the set of responses that drew together in a now, in Benjamin we have a more temporalized, more historicized sense of how a now occurs. Because the images from different pasts enter into the present set of readings, those readings in the now are not a discerning of the original INTENTION of the event or the agent, but rather register the historical impact by the then on the now. Historical time is not simply a continuous effective-history, but it does measure the historical effect as the now's distinctive reading of a distinctive image from the past. Such historical time is also THE TIME OF TRUTH—precisely because the risk of doing anything, of leaving anything for another, could only be validated in a future, validated in a subsequent now in which what was left behind becomes legible. Truth is this rhythmic juxtaposition of a sign and its reading.

5c) It is not that what is past throws its light on what is present or that what is present throws its light on what is past, rather the image is that in which the past and the present meet in a lightning flash in a constellation. In other words: image is the dialectic at a standstill. While the relation of the present to the past is a purely temporal one, the relation of the gone to the now is a dialectical one: its nature is not temporal but imaged.[3]

This rhythm is structured so that the past and present are related without becoming identified. It is not that the present is assimilated to the past, a mythic repetition of what has already happened (PAST THROWS ITS LIGHT ON WHAT IS PRESENT). For the past's light would only show in the present what the past had already contained, and so the present moment would be subsumed. But similarly, the present does not merely find itself in the past (PRESENT THROWS ITS LIGHT ON WHAT IS PAST). At each now there is a new reading of a past image, but what is read is not identical or necessarily easily assimilated into the present. Thus the key is the juncture, the reality of the relation, the "and" that in the image juxtaposes THE PAST AND THE PRESENT in a meeting. The light emerges from the juxtaposition: IN A LIGHTNING FLASH. It is not a durable image of the past, nor the phenomenologically distended moment of lived time, but rather is simply a flash, like a photographic exposure. The juxtaposition is not, as in Rosenzweig, a figure [*Gestalt*], but rather a CONSTELLATION, a set of discrete stars. But the next sentence is the one that defines Benjamin's historiography: the flash prevents any dialectic that has its own necessary motor, its own ongoing, progressive zigzag through suffering and reconciliation. To interrupt the dialectic is to catch DIALECTIC AT A STANDSTILL— a relation of past and present that borrows no dynamic inherent connectivity. Which is not to say that it is merely a positing of two points in time. From the present to the past is TEMPORAL: looking back measures a time that is elapsed, a gap from here to there. But the past is related to the present through its legibility in the now. The gone is not merely directed toward a future which now occurs, but is rather itself bound up with the now of reading in so far as the past is past. Thus the past appears through the

---

[3] Benjamin P ⟨I°, 2⟩ 1014–15/846   The true method for making things present is to represent them in our space (and not us in theirs). That is why only anecdotes have the power to move us. The things, so represented before us, endure no mediating construction from "major connections."—This is also the sight of major past things—Chartres Cathedral, the temple of Paestum—in truth, they are received in our space (not empathy for their builder or priests). We are not transposed in them; they step into our life.—The same technique of nearness is to be observed, calendrically, in relation to epochs.

image, through a DIALECTICAL relation with the present, while the present looks back in a simply temporal way. Again, we have found ourselves at the heart of an asymmetry: that the past appears mediated through the legible image of the interpreter, but the present does not appear in the same way as mediated for the past—because looking forward is looking beyond intention, is waiting for another to come, another to read what I write. Here is a parallel to the translation from there to here, temporalized, as responsibility for the past constitutes the present precisely in this juxtaposition of then and now.

5d) Only dialectical images are genuinely historical, that means, not archaic images. The image read, which is to say the image in the now of knowability, bears to the highest degree the stamp of the critical, dangerous impulse that lies at the base of all reading.

Benjamin now defines the HISTORICAL precisely through these DIALECTICAL IMAGES, in contrast to the ARCHAIC IMAGES. The latter would be the images that do not measure the distance that time marks but merely repeat a nontemporal, myth—obliterating time, change, and the discontinuity that governs the signifying of the past. Indeed, Benjamin concludes with a reflection about the DANGEROUS IMPULSE for ALL READING. As dialectical image, the past images in the moment of being read destabilize not only our vision of the past as more or less identical to our present, but more significantly, destabilize our present. Implicated by the image of the past, the reader reads CRITICALLY, precisely because of the interruption of historical narrative, because of the shock that the imaged past bears upon the now of reading. Just as previously we found that the gap between the text and the reader challenges and invests the reader, now we find the temporality of that gap to lie in relation to a past that appears in an image, but differs fundamentally from the moment of reading. We remember, then, in order to be criticized, to reopen the past in a way that can reopen the present—for the sake of the future. It is that kind of juxtaposition that has occurred here in discussing Biblical and rabbinic texts in the context of Rosenzweig, Levinas, and Benjamin. The "narrative" on the topic of *teshuvah* has read traditional texts in a now, and has arrested a notion of narrative from then to now.

The risk of studying history is that one will not challenge the present, but will interpret it as justified (The world's history as the world's judgment). That challenge to the winners, moreover, is distributable over not only the past, but also the transmission of the past, the winners' stories through time. The task of juxtaposing dialectical images is not merely asymmetric with respect to time, but also bears a unique responsibility for the past—for the past as unjust. Benjamin examines the tendency of historicism to view events sympathetically, but in so doing to justify the victors in history. The historicist refuses any responsibility for the past, and experiences a depression because he occupies himself with a past that does not address him, that has nothing to say today.

6a) Benjamin Th VII 696–97/256–57 ... The nature of this depressiveness will be clearer if one raises the question, with whom then does the history writer of historicism authentically sympathize? The answer resounds irrefusably: with the victor. The masters of the moment are, however, the heirs of all of those who were victorious. The sympathy with the victors comes, therefore, always to the benefit of the masters of the moment.

Benjamin, however, is eager to display not only the pathos of historicism, but rather its moral failing, the effort to duck responsibility. For the sympathetic construction of the past must always validate the VICTOR. The historian himself has outlived the past, and in looking back on the past, seeing only himself, sees himself as not vanquished but as victorious. To be alive is to be a winner: he who plays last, wins. Benjamin argues for this with a rigorous claim: that THE MASTERS OF THE MOMENT are the HEIRS of the winners. To rule or exercise power today, in the moment of reflecting on the past, is to be the successors of those who were not slaughtered, those who were not excluded, oppressed, obliterated. To sympathize with the victors is ultimately to serve to bolster and justify the present rulers. National historiography that leads up to the glories of our nation, the greatest nation on earth, must identify with each of the winners, each of the conquerors. Benjamin argues here, however, not only that imperial history is the history of the victors, but that a historicism that neglects to relate the past dialectically to the present, and fails to respond to the address from the images of the past, will support not only the victors in history, but also help conserve the powers of the current moment.

6b)   For historical materialists, that is enough said. Whoever, even to this day, carries off the victory, marches in the triumphal parade of today's master over those who came before, who are today lying on the ground. The spoils will be brought along, as is customary, in this triumphal parade. One designates them cultural treasures.[4]

Benjamin now lodges the tacit objection: that to support the rulers by studying the past is to say ENOUGH about the historicist's activity. Historical materialists understand the complicity with a certain telling of the past, a complicity that robs the present of its responsibilities. The history of the victors is a MARCH through time over the prostrate bodies of yesterday's victors. To win is to be able to humiliate the past, to sympathize only with the last one marching. But A TRIUMPHAL PARADE also strips the most recent victors (now lying in the dirt) of their goods, of the glories of their culture. The spoils are borne forward as CULTURAL TREASURES, as the evidence of how great the loser was in order to

[4] Levinas TI 204/228   Destiny does not precede history but follows it. Destiny, that is, the history of the historiographers, narrative of the survivors who interpret, which is to say uses the works of the dead. The historical retreat which makes this historiography, this violence, this possible enslavement, is measured by the time necessary for the complete loss of the will of its work. Historiography recounts the way that the survivors appropriate the works of the dead will; it rests on the usurpation accomplished by the victors, which is to say, by the survivors; it recounts the subjection in forgetting the life that fights against slavery.

elevate the victor still higher. The famous Roman frieze of the looting of the Jerusalem Temple by the Romans carrying the menorah in triumphal procession is a relevant image. The victor thus transmits the plunder, producing a national museum, a commemorative coin or arch, a chronicle of the greatness of those vanquished.

6c) In historical materialism they are esteemed with a distanced regard. Because he cannot think of what at a glance are cultural treasures without exception, without horror at its descent. Their existence is not thanks only to the efforts of the genius, who had made it, rather also to the nameless drudgery of his contemporaries. There is no document of culture which is not at the same time one of barbarism.

Again, the historian who allows the past to address her and invest her with responsibilities must take a distance from the victor's history of sympathy and sloth. She regards the CULTURAL TREASURES from a distance. The DISTANCE marks both the limits of sympathy, that the image is different from my own perspective, but also the suspicion of the suffering that the spoils signify. Reflection upon the descent and origin of the artwork, or the column or painting, or engraving, or literary text, or . . . , awakens a HORROR. For the production of the object itself reflects not only GENIUS, but also NAMELESS DRUDGERY. The conception may bear a recognizable signature, but the manufacture bears signs of laborers who remain unidentifiable, having left their marks on the columns, their scribbles in the manuscript margins, their blood on the pyramid steps. To consider what is unrecognizable, what was coerced, and what was suffered in order to produce the cultural treasure is to begin to see the signs of those who were not victorious. Benjamin insists that every DOCUMENT, every object produced in a culture, bears the marks of suffering and oppression, and so is also a document of BARBARISM.

6d)   And as itself is not free of barbarism, neither also is the process of transmission, in that it has descended from one to another. The historical materialist removes himself as far as possible from it. He regards his task to be brushing history against the grain.

But Benjamin discerns a second dimension of violence and suffering, to be read in the object: for just as it was produced through labor that was anonymous, so also it has been transmitted through a sequence of conquests and dispossessions. The history of TRANSMISSION is not a validation of victors, for Benjamin's historian, but an augmenting indictment of each new victor. THE PROCESS OF TRANSMISSION is not neutral, much less positive, but is a sequence that can itself be read as compounding the suffering in the original manufacture. Thus to read the history of transmission as an historical materialist is to question it at each step, to read it not for the victor and successful handing down, but to BRUSH HISTORY AGAINST THE GRAIN, and so to read each handing over with a questioning of that transaction. The victor is always subject to critique, and as the historian is descended from victors, the critique of the victors is a critique of myself. The past does not appear to validate me by naturally leading up to me, but to interrogate me and my existence, as I find that the books I read and the monuments I live with are stolen from others, at the expense of still others. My world is thus stolen from nameless others, even at the moment of my mere existence. Historiography, therefore, juxtaposes the past and present, not merely to learn something new for the present, but to interrogate my present, and to address my responsibility for others' suffering from which I have directly benefited.

The task of reading the images of the past, the stuff of previous generations, is a complex task in Benjamin's latter work. We turn to it in order to develop a semiotic theory adequate to the pragmatics of remembrance. The historiographic task appears in the responsibility to interpret the documents of barbarism and the violence of transmission. In the last section of this chapter, we will see the historian's own position as a survivor, a remnant. But before turning to that, we need to explore how stuff itself serves as signs, becoming legible. How do commodities or stuff signify in systems of signification? Benjamin's historiography becomes a way to increase our responsibilities in the past. In an important parallel to the absence of the author and speaker in Part I, and the transition from interaction to society in Part II, and the importance of thirds in Part III, we see the commodity as a sign of a worker who is neither present nor was present. The responsibility for the worker through the work depends on a trace, an absence that is not to be made good through representation. Responsibility increases through the works twice: for the past in returning, and for the present in disrupting the reification of works, restoring their semiotic indeterminacy. The absent author, absent interlocutor, absent worker—all are understood within this theory as unrecoverable, but our responsibilities to interpret the signs left, the traces and tears, are exorbitant.

The obvious antecedent for the task of interpreting commodities is Karl Marx's own historiographic research—in the attention to stuff and the relations of production. Benjamin and his companions, however, stripped dialectical determinism of a necessary, continuous, progressive vision. One folder of the materials for the Arcades Project is a set of reflections and citation from Marx, and one in particular inserts us into an argument about money as a sign, and from there to stuff as signs as well.

7a) Benjamin P (X 3,6) 805/655–56
Marx opposed the view that gold and silver are only imaginary values.

Benjamin himself does little more than cite a text from Marx's *Capital I*. He introduces it with a claim that in fact could even mislead us, because it raises only the question of whether money has value, while, as we will see the text claims that not only does money as sign have value, but valuable commodities are also signs: in short, value and signification are not opposed but linked. And of course, that is of interest not only for an ethics about signs, but also for Benjamin's historiographic effort to reconstrue the signification of things.

I begin with the uncited beginning of the paragraph from Marx that Benjamin cites. The question is how money can have VALUE. Marx claims every commodity has its value from the labor required to produce it. Money as COMMODITY, obviously, is produced through mining and minting. Money then became a medium for exchange of values. In the previous paragraphs (ONE SAW) that money is a universal commodity, a way of measuring in the exchange the exchange value of all commodities. ALL THE OTHER COMMODITIES enter into a system of exchange and so could be used as currency, but money assumes this role of scale for exchanges. If one only looks at a money economy, then money has already been stripped of its own labor value, indeed, of its exchange value, and become merely a medium of exchange and in itself barren of value. This mere "medium" is the COMPLETED FORM of money. But in the earlier stages money itself is valued only in relation to other goods. When we exchange stuff, we do not produce their value, but only the SPECIFIC VALUE FORM—how much money it is worth. The monetary value, therefore, is a sign of a prior value—even in the case of money itself.

Several theorists (Marx cites John Locke and others in a footnote) concluded that there was no intrinsic value to the metals from which money is made. This confusion arises from the failure to distinguish a commodity's value outside the money economy and the specific monetary price assigned a commodity. Marx is not only helping to clarify how money functions for coordinating the exchange process, he also is developing a semiotics both

8a) Marx Capital I 105/90 One saw that the form of money is only the reflex of the relationship of all the other commodities fixed on one commodity. That money is a commodity is therefore, a discovery only for those who proceed from its completed form, so as to analyze backwards to it. The exchange process gives to the commodity, that is converted into money, not its value, but its specific value form.

8b) The confusion of both determinations mislead some to hold that the value of gold and silver was imaginary. Because money in determinate functions can be replaced by mere signs of it, the other error arose that it itself is a mere sign. On the other side lay the presentiment that the money form of the thing is itself superficial and mere form of appearance, under which human relations are hidden.[5]

[5] Mishnah Baba Metsia 4:1   Gold acquires silver, and silver does not acquire gold. Copper acquires silver, and silver does not acquire copper. Bad coins acquire good ones, and good ones do not acquire bad ones. Unminted metal acquires coin, and a coin does not acquire unminted metal. Movable property acquires coin, and coin does not acquire movable goods. This is the rule: all movable goods acquire each other.

Marcel RM 121   To use James' terminology, if the concept is a bill to which the coins of perception must always correspond, it is only too clear that your mind cannot be "conceived" by me, for no metallic reserve, no perception can ever detail it for me. There is thus a third mode of knowledge to which we must give a special name. We will choose the term "interpretation" for reasons which will clearly appear. Monetary exchange will furnish us the best illustration of

of money as representative of all exchange values, and of all stuff once it enters into economy. With the second sentence, Benjamin begins his quotation. A second error is that money has no intrinsic value but is MERE SIGN. This error arises through the use of paper bills for coin—the paper serving as a mere sign of the money, merely designating the mined and minted coins. The question of whether paper money is MERE SIGN would lead us to a questioning of Marx's account as well, but clearly the paper is a sign of the coin, which itself is not MERE sign. The question is how coin as sign points beyond its systemic function in the economy of commodities. Is it possible to read a signifying relation to the labor that produces the sign, not to an author's intention, but as a trace of human work? Clearly the questions of mediation and attribution that we examined in Part II are relevant again here. But if one adopts the view of money as mere sign, as mere medium, a question arises whether monetary value is simply a convention. In which case it is a MERE FORM OF APPEARANCE, and the real HUMAN RELATIONS ARE HIDDEN. This suspicion of exchange values in the money economy are healthy, but Marx also is suspicious of the way that this severing of the signs of value from the signified labor value will insulate and isolate the exchange values from critique. What is lacking here is the awareness that money is a commodity and only as such can it work as a medium for exchange of other commodities.

But the conclusion is not only that money has labor value, but also that EVERY COMMODITY WOULD BE A SIGN. Indeed, the description of value as a shell over the human labor seems to fit Marx's general sense of how labor value is obscured by the market. But the question is not whether the commodity is merely a sign in system of exchange values. Rather, the semiotics must have a relation to the labor value, must indicate beyond the simple coordination of signs to the way that the signs themselves are produced. Hence, the reduction of commodity to mere sign is a way of ignoring the SOCIAL CHARACTER OF THE OBJECT—that an object sig-

8c) In this sense every commodity would be a sign, because as value it is only the objective shell of the human labor expended on it. But if the social character of the objects or the objective character which socially determined labor as foundation of a particular means of production are declared to be mere signs, one explains them at once as arbitrary human thought products. This was the favorite view of the eighteenth-century Enlightenment, in order at least to strip off the appearance of strangeness from the puzzling forms of human relations whose process of establishment they were still unable to decipher.

nifies in a specific social context, bearing pragmatic relations to its users, which relations are the locus of the ethical relations. Moreover, this reduction also permits ignoring the material OBJECTIVE CHARACTER of the means of production. Thus both the circulation of signs is made less social, and the

---

this process, since it corresponds to the regulated passage from one determined system of values to another. Interpretation is essentially social, as opposed to perception. . . .

labor of producing the signs is made insignificant. What Marx is arguing, therefore, is that a semiotics of commodities will require more than a pure syntactics of the market economy in which prices are all that matter, and that "more" will be reflections upon the social character of the objects both in their use and in their production. The pragmatic dimensions in the present use of the sign and in relation to their historical production make the commodities as signs more than ARBITRARY HUMAN THOUGHT PRODUCTS. The exchange of stuff is not separable from a set of pragmatic concerns that point to responsibilities. This attempt to reduce the signification of commodities to mere convention did appeal to the eighteenth-century Enlightenment, because their economic theories were unable to see how the monetary signs related to exchange processes, and so it helped make early capitalism seem less bizarre. We might well ask, following Marx, how interconnected any semiotic theory would be with the state of economic systems of its time. If the theory of mere signs here, which is rich in syntactic dimensions but devoid of both history and social pragmatics, suits a certain kind of capitalism, then how is the semiotics I am offering, focusing on asymmetric responsibilities in pragmatic relations, interrelated to the economic crises of the late twentieth century?

7b) "Because money in determinate functions can be replaced by mere signs of it, the other error arose that it itself is a mere sign. On this other side lay the presentiment that the money form of the thing is itself superficial and mere form of appearance, under which human relations are hidden. In this sense every commodity would be a sign, because as value it is only the objective shell of the human labor expended on it. But if the social character of the objects or the objective character which socially determined labor as foundation of a particular means of production are declared to be mere signs, one explains them at once as arbitrary human thought products."

7c) To "human labor" a note: "If one considers the concept of value, the thing itself will appear as only a sign; it is not valid as a thing itself, rather only as what it is worth . . ." (Hegel, *Rechtsphilosophie*, Zusatz zu § 63)."[6]

To return to Benjamin's text, which is mostly a citation (the elided material is not underlined). We can see Benjamin not cite the previously reached conclusion: that money's ability to serve as an exchange medium is only a clear example of how all exchange values of commodities work. Nor does he identify the Enlightenment recourse to mere convention as a solution to its own incapacities that follows the quotation. Rather, he focuses on the way that money is not mere sign, and that commodities are not purely systematically determined signs. His one elision is the phrase that signals the social character of the objects, of stuff, but as an elision it is hard to interpret fully.

Benjamin does cite one piece of a long footnote by Marx that deals with various authors and quotes a one-sentence line by Hegel. Benjamin cites Marx's citation, verbatim, and includes a helpful citation to the text in the *Philosophy of Right*. The

[6] Hegel PR Zusatz zu § 63 137/93 The qualitative disappears here in the form of the

re-citation of Hegel by Marx displaces the former's claim to have only mere signs in the exchanges of goods. But Benjamin's further citation of only Hegel from the long footnote seems to either send us to reconsider Hegel, or to illumine the risk of things being ONLY SIGNS, as though signs and values were separate. Benjamin's interest, again, is to understand how stuff can signify not only in relation to exchange, but also bearing the traces of production and transmission, the suffering for which the reader/historian must take responsibility.

Like our discussion at the end of the previous chapter, a gap opens here from the sign to the worker or author. The laborer is gone, leaving no emphatic references to herself. Gone, not without a trace, but without evidence. Works, as signs, indicate a maker, but cannot yield access to their originator. This is not a new theme for this book: reading in general was the struggle to find traces that led beyond the book, through the book, but did not lead to a referent, much less a presence. But we can turn this again: if we understand that memory is not merely the confident securing of myself in my own place in the story, then memory itself must be instigated in response not only to the image of the others, but also in responsibility for what is not imaged. The mending of signs does not occur in a closed economy of signs, but rather in relation to a lapse of time that instigates the signs and cannot be made into an image or sign. The deep past never becomes part of the economy, but haunts it in every moment. The remembering that mends the past for the sake of the other, that repents and awaits forgiveness, that dialectically discovers its own complicity with violence, that memory responds for a past that it cannot remember by continuing to remember images.

C. RUINS AND REMNANTS

Such a work of remembrance must not only commemorate the image but also the loss of the face in the image. That loss, which can appear only in images, is itself witnessed in a mending of the images. Like a saying of the saying, an image of the past can accentuate the loss in the present of a past that was not present—even though it cannot render that lost itself present. In the concept of allegory Benjamin found a kind of mortification of images, performing in the image the impossibility of the image. Benjamin wrote a

---

quantitative. Namely, when I speak of need, this is the title under which the most manifold things can be brought which makes the commonality of the same, that I can measure them as such. . . . If one considers the concept of value, the thing itself will appear as only a sign; it is not valid as a thing itself, rather only as what it is worth. A bill of exchange, for example, does not represent its nature as paper; rather, it is only a sign of another universal, of value. The value of a thing can be very varied in relation to need; if one, however, wants to express not the specific, but rather the abstract of value, then that is *money*. Money represents all things, but in that it does not describe the need but only what is a sign for the same, it is itself again governed by the specific value which is expressed only as an abstraction.

failed thesis on the origin of the German *Trauerspiel*, before conceiving of the Arcades Project. His investigation of the baroque remained one of his major benchmarks, as he recalled that study extensively in his later reflections on Baudelaire and the study of dialectical images. Our interest is the way one imagines the loss of the face in the image (*faces hypocratica*), or more generally, how images can be used to remember without being able to re-present.

9a) Benjamin OGT 353–54/177–78 If history wanders into the theater with the *Trauerspiel*, it does it as script. "History" stops on the countenance of nature in the alphabet of transience. The allegorical physiognomy of natural history which is placed on the stage through the Trauerspiel, is actually present as ruin. History was distorted in the theater physically by the ruin. And history was indeed stamped, and thus formed, not as a process of an eternal life, but much more as a procedure of unarrestable decay.

Benjamin argues that the German baroque drama [*Trauerspiel*] developed history in a distinctive manner: as the history of passing away. Historical processes were staged as A PROCEDURE OF UNARRESTABLE DECAY. The norm of such decay is NATURAL HISTORY—a story that addresses loss, change, and death, not one of recovery of the past into a living present. The central entrance of such history on the stage was THE RUIN. Ruins are not themselves natural, but do bear the marks of the passing of natural time and decay upon the human objects. They are inserted into the scene as an image of the incessant toll that time takes on human art, on human achievement, naturalized in the objects. Historiography in this case is the invented story of loss, the *Trauerspiel*, the mourning plays. The historiographic task is to map the loss in human events onto the material, natural processes of decay. Stuff, artifacts, works, are made to bear the history that in disordered calamities beset the human characters. But Benjamin also uses a vocabulary of SCRIPT, ALPHABET, and the FACE and its PHYSIOGNOMY. Benjamin thus draws the notions both of a fixed iconography (the alphabet) and of the imaged face into this discussion of history. His concern is not the trace of an immemorial past but the remembrances in a system of signs—that can be used to invoke the transience that is not itself memorable.

9b) Allegory thereby confesses itself as beyond beauty. Allegories are in the realm of thoughts what ruins are in the realm of things. This is whence the baroque cult of the ruin. . . .

Benjamin thus interprets ALLEGORY through the RUINS in the stage set. If the ruin is the historiography of the baroque, then allegories in thought also map disorder and loss. This analogy of allegories in thoughts to ruins among things lies at the heart of Benjamin's own semiotics. One of the striking tasks of Benjamin's work is to restore the value of allegory—at the expense of metaphor. The arbitrary connections of two terms in an allegory reflect not a failure of thought but the conscious checking of thought. If the insertion of the ruin into the artwork served to signal the loss of meaning in the work, the eventual decay and betrayal through time, then the allegory also signals the way that an image does not capture a hidden meaning, but rather itself hides meanings, or rather cannot even make meanings appear. What Benjamin discovers here is how the historiographic placement of the ruin on the stage remembers the loss, much as an allegory marks the irrecuperable meaning that happens in discourse but does not appear. Ruins become the way of remembering what cannot be recalled—in the realm of things.

9c) The contemporary stylistic feeling succeeds here much more than the antiquarian reminiscences. What lies cast in wreckage, the highly meaningful fragments, the broken pieces, are the noblest material of baroque creation. Because in this literature it is common to pile up completely unorganized broken pieces without clear representation of a goal and in the unceasing expectation of a miracle to take stereotypes for elevation. The baroque writers had to have regarded the artwork as a miracle in this sense.

The use of ruins was not antiquarian, not an effort to recapture the once present past, but rather was much more about how the present uses images of the past to challenge itself. BAROQUE CREATION is the assembly of fragments. It is creation because the initial, autonomous creation from nothing is not possible for historically situated people. The broken stuff itself serves as *memento mori*, dialectically relating to the past that was never present, because it is created simply to appear as broken. The PILING UP of broken stuff, what we would call junk, is not directed to composing a whole, a system, or even a story with a GOAL. Rather, it is somehow hoping for an ELEVATION, some augmentation from more and more junk. This is a messianic hope performed by exhausting the world of things. This hope is for a MIRACLE: that somehow this piling up of junk will come to be full of meaning in a future that is unforeseeable. This artwork was not the construction of a tight semiotic field, but a mess of that alphabet of iconic images, juxtaposed without a plan, awaiting a miracle of redeemed meaning, of forgiveness from sin.

9d)   And if it otherwise signaled as the calculable result of heaping them up, it is in no way easier to unite both of these than it is to unite the perceptible miraculous "work" with the subtle theoretical recipe in the consciousness of the alchemist. The practic of adepts resembles the experimentation of the baroque poets. What antiquity left behind is for them piece by piece the elements out of which the new whole is mixed. Rather: built. For the perfected vision of this new was: ruins.

But at the same time, this piling up of junk also bore some relation to a calculation on the part of the artist. Benjamin compares the combination of miraculous meaning and calculation and construction of ruins to the miracle of the alchemist—who also follows a RECIPE. The issue for Benjamin is precisely the historiography: the openness to redemptive meaning when openness is staged, constructed, witnessed through a careful deconstruction. What is left behind is only a collection of pieces which the baroque artist can reconstruct, cannot so much mix but BUILD. The historian is left pieces with which to build—and the baroque historian, dramatist, built ruins. Not a new Jerusalem, not a systematic whole, but a calculated construction of junk—in order to dislodge both present and past, in order to set the present under the sign of loss, loss of origin, loss of what never really was present. A ruin of an unbuilt temple. A memory that gauges its own fault against what lies beyond the range of memory.

While the allegory is a method of juxtaposing images in order to remember and to respond for what lies beyond memory, and the ruin is the material sign, in the world of things, there is still one more semiotic field: the role of the person who signifies like a ruin, like an allegory—the survivor. The survivor can be no more than image for those who perish, but the survivor can witness to those who died. The ruins and the allegory were constructed. They dialectically displayed a responsibility performed for the past, the past others made. The survivor also can become a construct—in the role of the remnant. For a remnant is not merely what happens, but is a way of witnessing in surviving. The role of remnant is central to Jewish existence since the time of the prophets. It performs the responsibility of remembering and hoping in a way that can model the social form of remembrance. The remnant makes the one who remembers herself into sign of a loss, sign of suffering of the others who cannot be fully remembered, and a sign for others to interpret. The final existential signifying is this assignment to witness as remnant. I turn to Rosenzweig again, to a passage very late in *The Star*, where he is discussing the Jewish person—who seems so narrow, so closed within.

10a) Rosenzweig S 450/404   If the Messiah comes "today," the remnant is ready to receive him. Jewish history is, in contrast to all worldly history, history of this remnant, about which the word of the prophets always holds: that it "will remain."[7]

Rosenzweig sees the Jews as a remnant awaiting redemption, perennially guarding the post of waiting for a future. That mode of waiting, however, stands in opposition to all other history, producing a strange kind of history: THE HISTORY OF THIS REMNANT. This remnant is not the victors, nor truly the victims who have only their own suffering to witness. The remnant waits and promises to remain. Or perhaps it is promised to remain—it is assigned a post it cannot renounce: it must remain until the redemption. As a history of a remnant, history is the witness of suffering in anticipation, a witness to exposure that cannot be renounced.

---

[7] Benjamin Th B 704/264   For the soothsayers, who inquired of time what it hid in its lap, time certainly was experienced neither as homogenous nor as empty. Whoever keeps this before him comes perhaps to a concept of how past time was experienced in remembrance [*eingedenken*]: namely, just so. It is known that the Jews were prohibited from investigating the future. The Torah and the prayer instruct them, in opposition, in remembrance. This disenchanted the future for them, to which all who consult the soothsayers for information are ruined. For the Jews, however, the future was nonetheless not turned to homogenous nor empty time. Because in it every second was the narrow gate through which the Messiah could enter.

Rosenzweig cites Isaiah's promise of return. The text, clearly set in the future, offers a promise of returning of both Kingdoms (Israel and Judah) and clearly addresses a political, even world-historical situation. The diaspora Jews will be returned from each of the various enemy countries. For Isaiah, the promise is directed to a future redemption; for Rosenzweig, the intermediary situation is what interests him. He cites only the phrase

11] Isaiah 11:11) On that day it will happen that My LORD will apply His hand a second time to redeeming the remnant of his people which will remain from Assyria, and from Egypt, Pathros, Nubia, Elam, Shinar, Hamrath and the coastlands. 12) He will hold up a signal to the nations and assemble the banished of Israel and gather the dispersed of Judah from the four corners of the earth.

WILL REMAIN, because his interest is in the remnant's act of remaining. While Isaiah talks about A SIGNAL TO THE NATIONS that will be the sign of return, Rosenzweig is interested in the way that the remnant is itself a sign before returning.

10b) All worldly history deals with expansion. Power is, therefore, the grounding concept of history. Because in Christianity revelation has begun to spread over the world and so to all, even the consciously and purely worldly will to expand became the nonconscious servant of this great movement of expansion.

The other kind of history is the history of EXPANSION, of power—victors' history. For Rosenzweig, such history is not neutral but bespeaks the Christian task of universalizing community. Even the secularist and the neo-pagan are, for Rosenzweig, taking part in the worldwide mission of Christianity—a task of building brotherhood throughout the world. We will leave

aside the dangers of such historiography and Rosenzweig's willingness to take that risk, for the alternative historiography is our concern.

10c) Judaism, and nothing else in the world, maintains itself by subtraction, by narrowing, through formation of ever-new remnants. This holds externally in opposition to the regular outwards falling away. However, it also holds within Judaism itself. It is always cutting off the unjewish from itself, in order to procure in itself ever again a new remnant of originary Jewishness. It regularly assimilates to itself what is external, in order to be able to exclude again from within.

Judaism exists uniquely BY SUBTRACTION. Jewish waiting and witnessing is always in search of what is most narrowly Jewish. In each stage, it cultivates within itself the perception not merely that the Jews represent the world, but that this group of Jews are the representative of all Jews—that only they are left to witness to the purer waiting, the purer life. History is then told by an historian located within a small group, within a small group, within a small group . . . and so that at each stage the ones who are left must bear witness

to the ones who have FALLEN AWAY. The world obliges by stripping off many Jews through persecution and in our times assimilation—but the ones who are left bear witness by remaining, by becoming A NEW REMNANT. We are left to resignify ourselves, as witness to the suffering of all. The Jewish community constructs itself by struggling to narrow itself. The performance of exclusion requires precisely wholesale ASSIMILATION TO ITSELF WHAT IS EXTERNAL—in order to be able to cut off other aspects. To make a remnant, like making a ruin, requires building and materials—and so appropriation allows for the performance of refashioning the remnant.

10d) There is no group, no movement, indeed scarcely an individual in all of Judaism who does not regard his way of giving up incidentals in order to secure the remnant as the uniquely true way and himself as the true "remnant of Israel." And so he is. The Jewish person is always somehow a remnant. He is always somehow a survivor, an inner whose outer was driven away and seized by the world's current, while he himself, the survivor in him, remained on the bank. Something in him waits.[8]

The performance of giving things up, of cutting off, pervades Jewish life. Rosenzweig writes that each Jew as well as each group and movement defines itself as the TRUE remnant, and regards its particular constriction as the UNIQUELY TRUE WAY. But what is more important, Rosenzweig claims that each is the true remnant, each is ALWAYS SOMEHOW A REMNANT. The Jew is a SURVIVOR, surviving because the world has seized something of him and left him behind on the bank. He is left waiting. The Jew testifies to a counterhistory as a sign of the destruction that has left him behind, and as a promise of a future that is not present. Rosenzweig can claim that a Jew is always a survivor in 1919 because Jewish history had fashioned history from the concept of remnants—as the life of the people itself. The community can become a sign that brushes history against the grain. In order to disrupt the present and intensify their responsibilities, the Jews should remember by returning, witnessing to loss that cannot be caught in images.

If we now return to earlier prophetic texts that fashioned the concept of the remnant, we find that the birth of Jewish history is not merely a liturgy of suffering—rather, it is a mode of repentance, a mode of dialectically relating to the loss of sovereignty, and most of all, a loss of most of the community to death and destruction. The remnant signifies both that loss and the self-indicting repentance in the context of a hope, a miraculous hope for redemption. Amos' prophecy to the Northern Kingdom in the eighth century B.C.E. is a particularly gloomy one. It focuses on social injustice and the coming judgment against the people. One of the few glimmers of hope occurs in the midst of a bitter indictment.

12a] Amos 5:11) Therefore, because you tax the poor and exact from him a grain tax: you have built houses of hewn stone, but you will not live in them; you have planted

I begin this excerpt with an indictment, of which the fifth chapter is full, in order to see how the remnant is not a term of self-righteousness, but rather of repentance and hope. Verse 11 juxtaposes

[8] Rosenzweig S 455–56/409–10 Now the pride of the "remnant of Israel" arrives at its universal meaning in the representation of the Shekhinah. For the suffering of this remnant, the constant need to separate itself and separate out from itself, that all now becomes a suffering for God's sake, and the remnant is the bearer of this suffering.

delightful vineyards, but you will not drink their wine. 12) For I know your many transgressions and your countless sins: You afflict the just, you take bribes, you subvert the cause of the needy at the gate.

excessive unjust taxation of the poor with a vain future. The labor of building and planting is dispossessed—the worker will not enjoy the wine, will not be safe within the stone house. This dispossession is promised as response to the oppression of the poor, stealing not their house and joy, but their grain—their very existence. The judgment is then juxtaposed with a first-person address: the "I" knows the "you"s manifold wickedness. The general multiplicity of sins is then specified by a set of offenses: oppressing both the poor and the just, and the corruption of institutional life—bribery. Amos reproaches the community for social injustice, not for being cultically improper. The prophet witnesses to the injustice of his own community, to a past that continues into the present—a past of oppression.

12b] 13) Therefore at such a time the prudent keeps silent, for it is an evil time. 14) Seek good and not evil that you may live. So that really THE LORD the God of Hosts will be with you as you have said. 15) Hate evil and love good and establish justice in the gate. Perhaps THE LORD, the God of Hosts, will be gracious to the remnant of Joseph.

In this context, the text advises KEEPING SILENT—because words spoken will be abused and used to persecute the one who would speak the truth. But despite this prudent advice, the prophet continues with the most basic exhortation: SEEK GOOD AND NOT EVIL. God will be with them if they HATE EVIL, if they forsake their own evil and cleave to the good. While Amos does not use the word for return, the action he calls for is clearly that return. Moreover, to return will make what they HAVE SAID become true. Or rather, it will be the condition. For in verse 15, we have the interruption of PERHAPS. The hope of forgiveness is tentative, depending on the other's action. Grace cannot be promised to us, nor can we be certain of it. The remnant may be forgiven—if we repent. The survivors can be forgiven, may be allowed to be survivors—if they repent.

12c] 16) Therefore, thus says THE LORD, the God of Hosts, THE LORD: In every square there will be lamentation, in every street they will cry 'Alas, alas.' And the farmhand will be called to mourn, and those skilled in wailing to lament. 17) In every vineyard there will be lamentation, for I will pass through your midst, says THE LORD.[9]

But a remnant is not free of suffering. The remnant that may survive would be the remnant of those promised certain suffering. In the public squares, in the streets, even in the vineyards—there will be terrible wailing. The CRYING, MOURNING, LAMENTATION all are the speech of survivors, the performance that decries the loss, the death of their own community.

---

[9] Isaiah 10:20)   And on that day it shall be that the remnant of Israel and those of the house of Jacob that escaped will no longer lean upon him who smote them, but they will lean upon THE LORD, the Holy one of Israel in truth. 21) A remnant shall return, a remnant of Jacob,

To be a remnant is not to be happy, but to perform mourning in the context of repentance, in the context of return and redress of suffering visited upon others. Heirs of an unjust community, the remnant survives to witness to the brutality of their past and the misery of loss—in fragile hope of forgiveness.

In this return, we can find the multiple dimensions of responsibility. Responsibility for the past, as memory of those who are lost, responsible for having survived. Responsibility for the present, in the need of judgment and mutuality of the community that returns—for the Torah is instituted and repeated as law in the midst of return from Babylon. And responsibility for the future, in the opening of inscription and the act of witness. An adequate interpretation of the Biblical account of the remnant would exceed the limitations of this book. But for we who examine the dimensions of pragmatics in search of signs of responsibilities, the remnant signifies a demanding engagement with the past within the context of a very tenuous hope for our own future. Finally, it interprets our own existence as sign of the past, and in so doing strives to mend our past.

Suggested Readings

4   Comay, Rebecca. "Benjamin's Endgame." In *Walter Benjamin's Philosophy: Destruction and Experience*, 251–91. Ed. Andrew Benjamin and Peter Osborne. New York: Routledge, 1994.

Moses, Stéphane. "Walter Benjamin and Franz Rosenzweig." In *Benjamin: Philosophy, Aesthetics, History*, 228–46. Ed. Gary Smith. Chicago: University of Chicago Press, 1989.

5   Buck-Morss, Susan. *The Dialectics of Seeing: Walter Benjamin and the Arcades Project*, 216–52. Cambridge, Mass.: MIT Press, 1989.

9   Handelman, *Fragments*, 116–48.

10   Cohen, Richard A. *Elevations: The Height of the Good in Rosenzweig and Levinas*, 3–39. Chicago: University of Chicago Press, 1994.

12   Paul, Shalom M. *Amos: Commentary on the Book of Amos*, 171–81. Ed. Frank Moore Cross. Minneapolis: Fortress, 1991.

---

to the mighty God. 22) Even if the your people, Israel, are like the sand of the sea, a remnant will return. Annihilation is inscribed, overflowing righteousness. 23) For annihilation is strictly decided: my lord, THE LORD of hosts, will do it in the midst of all the earth.

Deuteronomy 30:1) And it shall come to pass, when all these words have come true for you, the blessing and the curse, which I set before you, and you turn your hearts amidst all those nations, where THE LORD your God has banished you. 2) You will return to THE LORD your God and you will listen to His voice, according to all that I command you today, you and your children, with all your heart and with all your soul. 3) And THE LORD your God will return your captivity and have compassion upon you, and return and gather you from all the peoples among whom THE LORD, your God has scattered you. 4) If your outcasts are at the ends of heaven, THE LORD your God will gather you from there, and he will fetch you from there. 5) And THE LORD, your God, will bring you into the land which your ancestors possessed and you shall possess it: and he will do good for you and make you more numerous than your ancestors.

Postmodern Jewish Philosophy
and Modernity

THIS BOOK AROSE in a specific moment, a moment identified often enough as the postmodern. While postmodern in many contexts is an invention to address a crisis for modernist aesthetics or Cartesian subjectivity or the dreams of progress, for Jewish thought postmodern must mean post-Holocaust, after the Nazi destruction of European Jewry, after the Shoah. For over fifty years, the Jewish community has been struggling with what it means to survive and what the Jewish witness to the world can now mean. In more recent years, intellectuals have much more vigorously explored the limitations of memory in relation to our survival. The reflections on memory and the immemorial in this book are not a comprehensive address to those problems, but they point in the direction of greatest responsibility. I do not say blame, for our relation to the atrocities of this century is not primarily a question of blame—although justice does also require assessment of blame and requires restitution where possible. But to be not to blame is not the same as not to be responsible for events, not to have to respond for them and to redress the violence and suffering that emerged in and through events. Even we Jews must respond for our survival and for the loss and violence done to our community, struggling to repair the past and the significance it bears for the future. From that perspective, the task of the book as a whole may become clearer.

I have claimed that there is an ongoing translation project among the Jewish philosophers, particularly linking Cohen to Rosenzweig to Levinas. That project is a witness to what Jewish survival is for, and its focus is some sort of address for social ethics. The task of thinking about ethics, beyond the task of acting ethically, is a vital task for our world at the end of modernity. This century bears all too much evidence of barbarism and cruelty more excessive than ethical theories can reasonably allow. If there is an ethical response to our survival, it requires an exorbitant reorientation of ethics—a view that alters radically the terrain of what constitutes an adequate interpretation of a good will or an ethical action. Jewish traditions offer resources for philosophical ethics in this mournful moment. While it is clear that some Jews have survived the end of modernity, it is less clear what sort of Judaism will survive—and it is far from clear that philosophy can survive.

The task for this book, then, has been to identify the reorientation already taking place and bring it into sharper focus as the sea change that it is. From agency to responsibility; from consciousness to semiotics; from continuities to discontinuities; from equality to asymmetry—these changes are not simply novelties in the philosopher's supermarket, but point rather to our profound losses: loss of life, loss of culture, loss of bearing, loss of meaning, and loss of hope in thought itself. The violence of total states and systems of oppression seems so unstoppable that thought now requires of us changes that displace and reorient much of the logic of our world. Extreme responsibilities have become the only ones worthy of addressing in our situation. Ethics now becomes something excessive, as life in our world has betrayed so much.

There are many motives for using signs, and there certainly are many ways of using them, but throughout this work the goal has been to identify in which ways using signs is responsive to and for others. I have identified the interpersonal implications of different ways of using signs, emphasizing not that the liability is fulfilled, but that it is engaged in certain uses of signs. We become responsible for others even if we do not live up to those responsibilities. I focus on the strongest justification of a given performance and not on the average motives. In that extreme of justification we find ethics of responsibility, for we have need of that extremity to understand the limitations we come to accept in our everyday life. In general, I would claim that we could achieve other less responsive goals without these practices, or by limiting the uses of signs. But the ethical edge I have sought resided within the practice itself as a relation with others.

Throughout the book the relation between the texts I interpret and my own commentaries has been in question. One choice that I rejected was to put forward an argument solely on my own authority, as though I held within my own thought a systematic account of responsibilities. A second alternative was to confine myself to commenting on one text, Levinas' *Otherwise Than Being*, for example. I resisted that task because I needed other voices to account adequately for the full range of responsibilities herein. But if I have orchestrated the various voices, I have also lent my own to the task at hand. The translation of Jewish thought (and a good deal of continental philosophy) into some hybrid form of pragmatics governed my interpretations. The texts in general supported this translation because the texts addressed signs and their uses. But it is also true that pragmatics as target language has not heretofore had to say what I have made it say here. Indexicality, for instance, has not had to do so much work in interpreting the excessive asymmetric responsibilities that rest upon me. Nor have the existential signs, the way that sign-users become signs, assigned for others, been a topic in pragmatics. But the commentaries have marshaled various voices, allowing for a certain paratactic cooperation, coming into a common space and still preserving differences.

There is a more important dimension to these commentaries and translational practices, however. For our postmodern moment the negotiation with the past is distinctly different from the modern philosopher's approach. Not only is the past not forced into a progressive sequence leading to this moment, but it also cannot be rejected as superseded. The importance of the last part of the book reaches to the heart of what it means to write philosophy in relation to our history. It requires not merely a repetition of what people used to write but also accepts no simple displacement of the old thoughts. For Jewish thought after the Shoah, modernity seems particularly bitter and poor, but here, too, the negotiation of the relationships with modernity as with rabbinic and Biblical tradition is more complex. This is also a moment in which not only did a great deal of philosophical writing become legible as resource for ethics, but in which also a crisis in Jewish life and thought allowed rabbinic texts to become legible for new audiences. It is not too hard to see Rosenzweig and Levinas returning to the traditional Jewish texts precisely to address the questions of our time, the question of why survive and why remain Jewish. In the last part, I engaged in a return through Jewish texts, sensitive to the different pressures exerted in interpretation, stratifying the tradition to accentuate the discontinuities that govern its way. In a somewhat similar way, some of the interconnections made between pragmatism and Rosenzweig and Levinas open the template of historical research through juxtaposition as much as through 'influences.'

But this responsibility to reread the moderns in order to return through them is not completed here. If *Why Ethics* is not be a manifesto for yet another new approach in the modern mode of thinking, then it requires not a celebration of its novelty (born of suffering and destruction as it is). Instead, it requires a more generous and indebted relation to the modern philosophical and modern Jewish traditions. It is not quite enough to offer commentaries on contemporaries' works, because the historical relation and reconfiguration with modernity can only be reworked with the modern texts. Perhaps Levinas' maddening respect for Descartes is a model of such retrieval of the modern.

It should be not in the least surprising to find this book ending with a set of responsibilities still to be performed. The return to the modern is itself, obviously, connected to the return to premodern philosophy and to traditional rabbinic texts—which texts are not themselves free of ambivalences for us. They have a different legibility today, too. Part of what lies incomplete in this book is the reading of those texts across axes unique to our time: axes of feminism, of racism, of gender, of the environment, and of economic oppression. Texts that were usually read only by Jewish men of a given class and privilege can now be read in specifically challenging ways across various differences, read by readers who bring differences to bear on their readings. Similarly, the Western metaphysical tradition is being crisscrossed by other others, other than the Jewish other, as it is reread with challenging and liberating results. The extremity of the ethics I have explored here is, I think, not at the expense of so many axes of otherness, but requires us to invite multiple vulnerabilities and responsibilities in the exorbitance of other readings.

But in another vein, the work of this book leaves glaringly incomplete the intersection of the second and fourth parts: the role of law in social responsibility and the responsibilities to remember and repair. My own work, and that of others, now turns to legal texts as guidelines to social responsibility, and not only to the logic of legal argument, but to the historical specificities of ways of legal reasoning, of discursive forms of legal texts, of modes of legal education, and kinds of legislation and legislative process. Different societies at different times produce different kinds of texts that address and perform these various activities. Neither the theory of law and conflict nor the mere sampling of old favorites from Jewish sources presented here constitutes an adequate treatment of the historical responsibilities we have for the study of our society and its resources in historical legal texts. This book could not hope to exhaust the realm of ethics, but only to initiate several intricate conversations.

The justification for engaging in ethics as a theoretical discipline lies within the book. But the justification for stopping the book, for treating of so much and leaving so much more unsaid itself, requires one more text, from the Mishnah.

Avot 2:20–21 Rabbi Tarfon used to say: The day is short, the work is great; the workers are lazy, the reward is great, and the master is insistent.

Our lives (THE DAY) are short. We do not have much time, and we will not survive forever. Our responsibility (THE WORK) is vast. We know ourselves (THE WORKERS) to be lazy, preferring to ignore or shirk our responsibilities. And just what the reward might be, I will not hazard here, but THE MASTER, the one who calls us to respond, is insistent. The responsibilities are urgent, vast, and emphatic. We who would duck our responsibilities are charged and bound to them.

He also used to say: You are not called to complete the work, nor are you free to evade it. . . .

But at the end of the day, we learn that we do not have TO COMPLETE THE WORK, for the task is not merely too vast for us, but it depends on the future and on the others who will come and interpret what we are doing now. A completion pretends to fix the meaning, when the task is how to open the meaning and invite interpretation. But neither are we FREE TO EVADE IT. Our interpretations are demanded. We are called to respond, despite our laziness and our wish to duck out. A response is called for, a response that will solicit others' responses. The text is always incomplete.

3 5282 00488 6290